THE COMPLETE WORKS OF ROBERT BROWNING

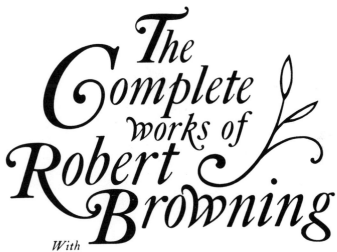

The Complete works of Robert Browning

With
Variant Readings & *Annotations*

EDITORIAL BOARD

ROMA A. KING, JR., *General Editor*

MORSE PECKHAM

PARK HONAN

GORDON PITTS

OHIO UNIVERSITY PRESS
ATHENS, OHIO 1970

Copyright © 1970 by Ohio University Press
Library of Congress Catalog Card Number: 68-18389
ISBN 8214-74-6

Printed in the United States of America

CONTENTS

I CONTENTS

This edition of the works of Robert Browning is intended to be complete. It is expected to run to thirteen volumes and will contain:

1. The full contents of the first editions of Browning's work, arranged in chronological order. The poems included in *Dramatic Lyrics, Dramatic Romances and Lyrics,* and *Men and Women* appear in the order of their first publication rather than the order in which Browning rearranged them for later publication.

2. All prefaces, dedications, and advertisements which Browning wrote for his own works or for those of Elizabeth Barrett Browning and others.

3. The two known prose essays which Browning published: the review of a book on Tasso, generally referred to as "The Essay on Chatterton," and the preface for a collection of letters supposed to have been written by Percy Bysshe Shelley, generally referred to as "The Essay on Shelley."

4. The front matter and the table of contents of each of the collected editions (1849, 1863, 1868, 1888–89a, and 1889) which Browning himself saw through the press. The table of contents will include both the pagination of the original volume and of this edition.

5. Poems by Browning published during his lifetime but not collected by him.

6. Unpublished poems by Browning which have come to light since his death.

7. John Forster's *Thomas Wentworth, Earl of Strafford* to which Browning contributed significantly, though to what precise extent cannot be determined.

II GENERAL TEXTUAL PRINCIPLES

The assumptions on which we have prepared the text are, we think, reasonably straightforward, if not entirely conventional. Our principal departure from current textual theory is that we question the conventional meanings of *text* and *author*. For a work which varies in a series of documents and editions, there is no such empirical entity as the *text*. Consequently, the problem of *the transmission of the text* is not a real one; rather, the real problem is to understand the character of the decisions which were responsible for the successive and varying states of the work. Conventionally, it is assumed that only those texts should be used for which evidence of authorial control can be demonstrated, but, as with *text,* the *author* is a constructed entity; not only is it the fact that the *author* (conceived as a static entity) no longer exists; it is equally the case that the *author* (so conceived) never did exist. Our focus, therefore, shifts from *text* and *author* conceived as static metaphysical entities to the dynamic process of creating and editing involved in the compilation of a series of documents.

Any writer's work consists of two processes: he generates an utterance and he corrects that utterance by balancing his current conception of the coherence of what he has so far written, and his grasp of the conventions applicable to the kind of discourse he is composing as they then obtain and as he understands them. Thus, instead of making a distinction between *author* and *editor,* we make a distinction between *authorial function* and *editorial function.* It appears to us that in exercising his editorial functions the author's basis for his activity is continually changing, and may continue to change throughout his life. His grasp of both the coherence of his work and of the conventions may improve or deteriorate; he may come to feel that the conventions are either more or less binding on him. *Author* refers, then, not to a stable entity but to an unstable and continuously innovating continuum.

Furthermore, a writer's attitude towards the exercise of the editorial function may vary from an insistence that he alone has the right to exercise it to an acceptance of virtually any editorial decision made by another. The explanation for this phenomenon is that the author, as every practicing author knows, is not necessarily the one best equipped to balance the two demands at work in the editorial decision-making process. If he is unusually intelligent and richly cultivated at the high cultural level, however, the probability that he is best equipped increases, especially if his cultural situation is relatively limited and stable and imposes upon him a demanding notion of the editorial function. Consequently, there is no logical difference between an author's exercise of the editorial function and an editor's, who is also an unstable and continuously innovating continuum, but whose editorial function is precisely the same as the author's.

Other individuals also exercise the editorial function: the compositor, the printer, and the copyreader. In the history of printing, each of these has been responsible for variants, and insofar as such variants reflect a grasp of the coherence of the work and of current conventions, they cannot be classified as errors. An error is a variant which self-evidently damages the coherence of the text and departs from the conventions as the textual critic himself understands both factors as they were at work in the historical situation from which the work emerged. The history of printing has moved in the direction of trying to limit the printer to errors, to train the compositor to set only what is before him, and to restrict the copyreader to the detection of errors by requiring him to refer questionable variants to the editor and author. Actual practice varies from house to house, within the history of each house, and according to the kind of discourse.

We also depart from one line of current textual theory by assuming that punctuation is not to be categorized as an accidental. An accidental, we maintain, is a variant that cannot alter the semantic function of the semiotic data. Spelling, for example, can delay the recognition of a semantic function, but if the current standard spelling can be unequivocally substituted, then it is truly an accidental, and so with word divisions and the like. But whatever the semantic function of punctuation may be—and it is a matter which is little understood—everyone feels it, though some feel it more than others, and this instability of semiotic response is also true of authors. Punctuation, under which we include paragraphing, does not merely *affect* the semantic continuum; it is part of that continuum. Thus, the study of a series of editorial decisions in a passage involving only punctuational variants can, and usually does, have both an interesting and an important effect upon the interpretation of a passage. It seems to us, therefore, that particularly in a nineteenth- or twentieth-century work, punctuational variants must be considered as substantive changes and so recorded.

The problem, then, is this. Given a work which varies in a series of documents and editions, which document exhibits evidence of the most adequate exercise of the editorial function, and on what grounds is this decision to be made? Or, given a work which so varies but apparently has never had adequate editing, to what degree should the textual editor carry out the task? The textual editor must recognize that he is not restoring or establishing a text, but is continuing the editorial function initiated by the author. When it comes to what variants to record and what emendations to make, the textual critic cannot console himself by falling back on a nonexistent metaphysical entity, the *author*.

III SPECIFIC PROBLEMS IN EDITING BROWNING'S WORKS

The works of Browning offer few problems (though some are of genuine interest) and provide a great redundance of data. Aside from a handful of uncollected poems, all short, everything but *Asolando* went through two or more editions during Browning's lifetime. Except for *Pauline, Strafford,* and *Sordello,* everything published before 1849 was republished in newly edited form in the 1849 collection. *Strafford* and *Sordello* were newly edited for the collection of 1863, as were all other works in that edition. The 1868 collection added a newly edited *Pauline* and *Dramatis Personae* to the other works, which were themselves re-edited. The 1888–89a collection in sixteen volumes included everything so far published in volumes (certain poems published only in periodicals were not included; *Asolando* was added as Volume XVII after Browning's death). The printing of this edition was completed in July, 1889, and the exhaustion of some of the early volumes led Browning to correct the first ten volumes before he left for Italy in late August. The second edition of this sixteen volume collection is dated 1889 on the title pages; the first eight volumes of the first edition are dated 1888, the rest, 1889. We have designated Volumes IX to XVI of the first edition 1889a.

We have designated the existing manuscripts and editions either as primary or secondary materials. The primary materials include:

1. The manuscript of each volume (when such exists; see table at the end of preface);

2. The proof sheets (when such exist);

3. The original edition of each volume (and subsequent separate editions when such exist);

4. The collected editions over which Browning exercised editorial control:

> 1849–*Poems by Robert Browning.* Two Volumes. London: Chapman and Hall.
>
> 1863–*The Poetical Works.* Three Volumes. London: Chapman and Hall.
>
> 1868–*The Poetical Works.* Six Volumes. London: Smith, Elder and Company.
>
> 1888–*The Poetical Works.* Volumes 1–8. London: Smith, Elder and Company.
>
> 1889a–*The Poetical Works.* Volumes 9–16. London: Smith, Elder and Company.
>
> 1889–*The Poetical Works.* Volumes 1–16. London: Smith, Elder and Company. (Vols. 1–10, a revision of 1888–1889a; Vols. 11–16, a reprint of 1889a).

All other relevant materials now known to exist or which may be discovered while this edition is being prepared will be called secondary. Examples of such materials are: the copy of the first edition of *Pauline* which contains annotations by Browning and John Stuart Mill; the copy of the first edition of *Paracelsus* which contains corrections in Browning's hand; Elizabeth Barrett's suggestions for the revision of *A Soul's Tragedy* and certain of the short poems which composed *Dramatic Romances and Lyrics* (1845); and the edition of *Strafford* by Miss Emily Hickey for which Browning made suggestions.

Given all these diverse materials, our first problem is to determine the nature of the decisions for the variants. We are concerned, of course, with all kinds of substantive variants, not only of word and line but also of punctuation. That Browning was responsible for changes of words and lines seems obvious. As far as our records indicate, no one other than Elizabeth Barrett recommended specific changes in the actual wording of Browning's poems. Of the numerous suggestions which she made for changes in the poems which composed *Dramatic Romances and Lyrics* (1845), he accepted some and rejected others. In the case of *Paracelsus,* for example, there are no differences in wording or lines between Browning's corrected manuscript and the printed first edition which suggest that an editor other than Browning was responsible for word changes in the text. Here, then, we need ask only if he were also responsible for changes in punctuation, or if these were imposed upon his poems by the publisher.

To begin with available evidence, the practice of Tennyson and of Swinburne, for example, suggests there was a strong tendency in the nineteenth century to allow a poet general control over the punctuation of his own work. Byron (not very typically) sought editorial help in punctuating; but, as a rule, English poets when their reputations had become established seem to have been able to insist that even their eccentricities in pointing be followed by compositors—both before the 1840s, when punctuation practice tended to be more anarchic, as well as after the publication of John Wilson's comprehensive, systematic, and highly influential *A Treatise on Grammatical Punctuation* (Manchester, 1844). Thus, the general practice today of publishers deferring to the editorial function of the author according to his literary status seems already to have been in existence, and the similar practice of ascribing high status to a poet, or at least higher than that granted to a novelist, seems to have obtained.

We do know that for the final 1889 edition Browning had full control over all variants, including punctuation. Indeed, the probabilities indicate that by at least 1863 Browning had principal control over the editorial function. Moreover, in writing to Chapman in the 1850s he shows concern for punctuation. ("I attach importance to the mere stops . . . ." *New Letters of Robert Browning,* eds. William Clyde DeVane and Kenneth Knickerbocker, New Haven, 1950, p. 83.)

Still earlier, the history of the *Paracelsus* texts is of the highest interest and importance. The manuscript of that poem exhibits either an ignorance of punctuation conventions or a refusal to consider them

very seriously. For whatever reason, Browning exhibits in this manu-
script a wide latitude of innovation even from a variety of conflicting
current punctuational conventions. The manuscript shows, however,
housestyling, or the exercise of the editorial function by someone
other than Browning for one leaf in Act I and all but the first and
last pages of Act III. Several other pages show editorial changes in
punctuation which may be Browning's. What precisely happened to
the styling of some of the manuscript before it was finally printed is
uncertain. Either a new manuscript was prepared, or proof was set up
from the manuscript as it stood after partial editing and was then
thoroughly revised. The manuscript shows signs of heavy use, indica-
tions for the signatures (corrected for one signature), and what are
evidently compositors' names. The second possibility, then, seems the
more likely. The results are significant. First, although the printed
punctuation of the edited portions of the manuscript does not corre-
spond with that editing, it is in the same style as that editing. Second,
the printed punctuation of the unedited portions is in the same style
as the printed versions of the edited portions, and thus of the editing
in the manuscript. Third, subsequent published works for which no
manuscript exists are in the same style as the printed 1835 *Paracelsus*.
Finally, the next available manuscript of major significance, that for
Christmas-Eve and Easter-Day, prepared for the printer by Elizabeth
and Robert, shows virtually no variation from the first edition of 1850.
Everything leads to the probability that Browning exercised final con-
trol of the punctuation from the printed 1835 *Paracelsus* through the
rest of his career. Indeed, we are aware of Mrs. Sutherland Orr's state-
ment (*Life and Letters of Robert Browning*, London, 1891, p. 265)
that Browning invariably sent proof sheets of his work to his French
friend Joseph Milsand for corrections. There is no indication, how-
ever, that, in seeking such help, Browning relinquished his own final
editorial function.

All evidence, then, indicates that from 1835 onward Browning
was responsible for all substantive variants to be found in the several
editions of his works over which he had nominal supervision. (There
were indeed during his lifetime a number of editions and selections
over which he exercised no control and which, as a result, we have
eliminated from consideration here.)

IV CHOICE OF TEXT

By 1889, Browning was the most experienced editor of his own
poetic discourse. It seems to us, therefore, that the 1889 edition of his
works provides the most satisfactory basic text, not just because it is

chronologically the last one he worked on. Rather, the probability is that in 1888 and 1889 he had a better grasp of the coherence of individual works and of this particular style of the conventions, including the conventions of punctuation, than anyone else. The text we have presented is the 1889 text for the contents of the first ten volumes, emended only to correct a few obvious compositor's or printer's errors; the 1888 text for the contents of the last six volumes, emended in the same way; and the 1889 first edition of *Asolando,* similarly emended for the contents of that volume. The text for the uncollected material is based on the original publication. Compared with the textual critic of an Elizabethan play, the textual critic of Browning has on the whole an easy decision to make about what edition to select as the basis for his own text and what further editorial functions are to be exercised.

V PRESENTATION OF VARIANTS

The presentation of the variants is not conventional. Indeed, there is no standard way to offer variants. Initially, we attempted to follow a system sometimes adhered to but, because of the nature of the materials, found it inadequate. We were forced therefore to improvise. We believe that the style we have adopted, which is explained in detail below, has the advantage of presenting the history of the variants in the order in which they appeared, from the first form through the final one, and in a way in which the full text of each line of each edition is most accurately and readily reconstructed.

In presenting the variants from the 1889 text we print at the bottom of the page variants found in the manuscripts, when available, and in the first and subsequent editions—that is, variants found in the primary materials. It seems to us that we can give a clearer, more concise notion of Browning's editorial function if we separate primary materials from secondary materials. Moreover, we must assume that additional manuscripts may become available between now and the time the last volume of this edition is published, making a supplemental volume of variants necessary. We have decided, therefore, that it would be logical to place all variants derived from secondary materials together in a final volume. This final volume will also include *Thomas Wentworth, Earl of Strafford* by John Forster, to which Browning's contribution was considerable but indeterminable.

TABLE OF SIGNS

All signs used by Browning himself have been avoided. The symbols essential to an understanding of the variant notes are set out in the following table of signs:

§ . . . §	Editor's note
< >	Words omitted
/	Line break
//,///, . .	Line break plus one or more lines without internal variants

All variants are placed at the bottom of the page of text to which they refer. A variant is generally preceded and followed by a pickup and a drop word (*a*). No note terminates with a punctuation mark unless the punctuation mark comes at the end of a line. If a variant drops or adds a punctuation mark, the next word is added (*b*). If the normal pickup word has appeared previously in the same line, the note begins with the word preceding it. If the normal drop word appears subsequently in the line, the next word is added (*c*). A single capitalized pickup word indicates the beginning of a line of poetry. When a capitalized pickup word occurs within the line, it is accompanied by the preceding word. A single variant in the capitalization of a word, however, is considered an internal change and does not require a pickup and drop word (*d*).

No pickup or drop word, however, is used for any variant consisting of an internal change, for example, a hyphen in a compounded word, an apostrophe, a tense change, or a spelling change. Nor is a drop word used when the variant comes at the end of a line (*e*). Illustrations from *Sordello*:

a   [611]| *1840:* but that appeared   *1863:* but this appeared
b 1. at end of line:
  [109]| *1840:* it, "taken < > intrigue:"   *1863:* it, taken < > intrigue.
  2. [82]| *1840:* forests like   *1863:* forests, like
c [183]| *1840:* after clue and   *1863:* after clue, and
  [77]| *1840:* Who managed < > that night by   *1863:* She managed < > that, night by night,   *1888:* by night
d 1. a single capitalized pickup word:
  [61]| *1840:* Now—nor, this   *1863:* Now—not this
  2. a single capitalized pickup word within line:
  [295]| *1840:* at Padua to repulse   *1863:* at Padua who repulsed
  3. a capitalized internal change:
  [367]| *1840:* Hell   *1863:* hell
e 1. [285]| *1840:* shall   *1863:* should
  2. at end of line:
  [86]| *1840:* sky: *1863:* sky.

Each recorded variant will be assumed to be incorporated in the next edition if there is no indication otherwise.

Genuine accidentals which occur in the plays in the presentation of the cast of characters, place locations, stage directions, and character designations are not listed. Specifically we do not record: 1 accidentals for stage directions which involve only change in manner of statement such as *Enter Hampden* instead of *Hampden enters* (Such accidentals are standardized to the 1889 text when they are used as pickup or drop words.); 2 accidentals for stage directions such as *Aside* instead of *aside*, [Aside] instead of [Aside.], [Strafford.] instead of [Strafford!]; 3 accidentals for character designations such as *Lady Carlisle* instead of *Carlisle* or *Car*. All character designations which appear in variant entries will conform to the 1889 text as it appears in this edition. In typing variants we ignore character designations unless the designation comes within a numbered line, in which case we treat it as any other word. In such cases, therefore, it is used as pickup or drop word. When it is used as a pickup word, however, the general rule regarding pickup words which begin with a capital letter does not apply.

Two kinds of variants which we regard as genuine accidentals have been emended and not recorded. For a time during Browning's career it was the practice, as every student of Victorian literature is aware, to precede every line of a quotation with a quotation mark. We have eliminated all but the first and last quotation mark, in accordance with modern practice and with the practice of some of the original Browning editions. Secondly, during most of his career, a space was left in contractions of two words; thus "it's" was printed "it 's." These we have closed up, in accordance with modern practice.

VI COLLATION

Finally, there remains the question of collation within an edition. In the first place all printings of the 1868 edition except the first have been eliminated. Those volumes were evidently sold separately, for some of them were reprinted, according to the dates on the title pages, a number of times. There is also evidence that, though the edition may have been stereotyped, there was some resetting. Since there is no indication that Browning had anything to do with the resetting and since, for the reasons given above, we have decided that his editorial decisions are to be preferred when known, we have disregarded these versions. In any case, it would be impossible to be sure that all of them had been discovered, even a representative sampling. As for the other editions, Browning was not a popular author and the editions were small. A sampling of various exemplars of several editions has not revealed a significant yield among them. However, in case of doubt about incomplete inking and dropped endline punctuation and letters, a sample collation with other exemplars of the same edition has been undertaken.

VII ANNOTATIONS

Browning scholarship is not yet fully mature. The notes we have presented, therefore, are not intended to be exhaustive or final. The format of the edition has been planned to allow for revision of the notes without disturbing the text. If the text proves satisfactory, it can be reprinted indefinitely with new sets of notes.

As a general principle, we have annotated proper names, phrases that function as proper names, and words or groups of words the full meaning of which requires factual, historical, or literary background. Thus, we have attempted to hold interpretation to a minimum, although we realize that the act of selection itself is to some extent interpretative.

Specifically, we have annotated the following: (1) proper names; (2) geographical locations; (3) allusions to Biblical and other literature; (4) words not included in *Webster's Collegiate Dictionary*, Seventh Edition (since some limits must be imposed upon our work and because this dictionary is generally accepted and readily available. We annotate words used by Browning in a sense other than that given in this dictionary. For a more accurate understanding we have relied heavily upon Samuel Johnson's dictionary); and (5) other items requiring factual information which is not of current common knowledge or easily available. All passages in a language other than English are translated into English. Occasional quotations from Browning's sources are included when such source quotations seem especially pertinent and are of difficult access.

For notes, particularly on historical figures and events, we have tended to prefer fullness and even to risk the tangential and unessential. As a result, some of the information provided may be perhaps unnecessary for the mature scholar. On the other hand, it is impossible to assume that all who use this edition—the ordinary reader and the undergraduate and graduate student, for example—will be fully equipped to assimilate unaided all of Browning's copious literary, historical, and mythological allusions. Thus we have directed our efforts toward an audience conceived as a continuum from the relatively uninformed to the trained.

TABLE OF ABBREVIATIONS AND SHORT TITLES USED IN ANNOTATIONS

B   Browning

Duff	*An Exposition of Browning's Sordello*, With Historical and Other Notes. David Duff. London, 1906.
Griffin and Minchin	*The Life of Robert Browning*. W. H. Griffin and H. C. Minchin. New York, 1910.
Holmes	"The Sources of Browning's *Sordello*," *SP* xxxiv (1937), 467–496.
Hood *Ltrs*	*Letters of Robert Browning Collected by Thomas J. Wise*. Thurman L. Hood. New Haven, 1933.
Orr *Hbk*	*Handbook to The Works of Robert Browning*. Mrs. Sutherland Orr. London, 1885.
P-C	*The Complete Works of Robert Browning*. Eds. Charlotte Porter and Helen A. Clarke. 12 Volumes. New York, 1900.
Whyte	*Sordello*. Ed. The Rev. Arthur J. Whyte. London, 1913.

VIII TABLE OF MANUSCRIPTS

The following manuscripts are known to exist in the locations indicated:

Paracelsus
Forster and Dyce Collection,
Victoria and Albert Museum, Kensington

Christmas-Eve and Easter-Day
Forster and Dyce Collection,
Victoria and Albert Museum, Kensington

Dramatis Personae
Pierpont Morgan Library, New York

The Ring and the Book
British Museum

Balaustion's Adventure
Balliol College Library, Oxford

Prince Hohenstiel-Schwangau
Balliol College Library, Oxford

Fifine at the Fair
Balliol College Library, Oxford

Red Cotton Night-Cap Country
Balliol College Library, Oxford

Aristophanes' Apology
Balliol College Library, Oxford

The Inn Album
  Balliol College Library, Oxford
Of Pacchiarotto and How He Worked in Distemper
  Balliol College Library, Oxford
The Agamemnon of Aeschylus
  Balliol College Library, Oxford
La Saisaiz and The Two Poets of Croisic
  Balliol College Library, Oxford
Dramatic Idyls First Series
  Balliol College Library, Oxford
Dramatic Idyls Second Series
  Balliol College Library, Oxford
Jocoseria
  Balliol College Library, Oxford
Ferishtah's Fancies
  Balliol College Library, Oxford
Parleyings With Certain People of Importance in Their Day
  Balliol College Library, Oxford
Asolando
  Pierpont Morgan Library, New York

Each manuscript is fully described in this edition in the section given to annotations on the corresponding text.

The following manuscripts are not known to be extant:

Pauline   *A Blot in the 'Scutcheon*
Strafford   *Colombe's Birthday*
Sordello   *Dramatic Romances and Lyrics*
Pippa Passes   *Luria*
King Victor and King Charles   *A Soul's Tragedy*
"The Essay on Chatterton"   "The Essay on Shelley"
Dramatic Lyrics   *Men and Women*
The Return of the Druses

We should like to request that anyone with information about any of the manuscripts which are presently unknown to the scholarly world communicate with the Director of the Ohio University Press, Athens, Ohio.

IX REQUEST FOR CORRECTIONS

We have tried to make this edition free from error, but we know that the history of printing proves that such an ambition is impossible of fulfillment. We urgently request that whoever discovers errors will report them to the Ohio University Press, Athens, Ohio, where a file of such errors will be kept so that any future printings can take advantage of such reports.

X ACKNOWLEDGMENTS

We express our appreciation especially to the following: the Ohio University Press, the Ohio University Library, and the Ohio University English Department for providing money and services which have made it possible for us to assemble the vast materials required for preparation of this edition; The Armstrong-Browning Library, Baylor University, Waco, Texas, and its director, Professor Jack Herring for various favors.

The frontispiece, a pencil drawing by Count Ripert Monclar in 1837, represents Robert Browning as he appeared to a very close friend at the time he was writing the contents which compose this volume. Browning became intimate with Monclar, a young French Royalist, in 1834 and in 1835 he dedicated *Paracelsus* to him. The drawing is here reproduced by the kind permission of the Armstrong-Browning Library.

The Editors
Athens, Ohio

A description of each of these may be found in Section A, pp.
1–60 of *Robert Browning: A Bibliography*, 1830–1950. Compiled by
Leslie Nathan Broughton, Clark Sutherland Northrup, and Robert
Pearsall. Cornell University Press, 1953.

STRAFFORD

Edited by Gordon Pitts

SORDELLO

Text Edited by John Berkey

Annotations by Roma A. King, Jr.

STRAFFORD

Edited by Gordon Pitts

STRAFFORD

AN HISTORICAL TRAGEDY

DEDICATED, IN ALL AFFECTIONATE ADMIRATION,

TO

WILLIAM C. MACREADY

LONDON: April 23, 1837.

1837: MACREADY, ESQ. / BY / HIS MOST GRATEFUL AND / DEVOTED FRIEND, / R.B. / April 23, 1837.

PREFACE

I had for some time been engaged in a Poem of a very different nature, when induced to make the present attempt; and am not without apprehension that my eagerness to freshen a jaded mind by diverting it to the healthy natures of a grand epoch, may have operated unfavorably on the represented play, which is one of Action in Character rather than Character in Action. To remedy this, in some degree, considerable curtailment will be necessary, and, in a few instances, the supplying details not required, I suppose, by the mere reader. While a trifling success would much gratify, failure will not wholly discourage me from another effort: experience is to come, and earnest endeavor may yet remove many disadvantages.

The portraits are, I think, faithful; and I am exceedingly fortunate in being able, in proof of this, to refer to the subtle and eloquent exposition of the characters of Eliot and Strafford, in the Lives of Eminent British Statesmen now in the course of publication in Lardner's Cyclopaedia, by a writer whom I am proud to call my friend; and whose biographies of Hampden, Pym, and Vane, will, I am sure, fitly illustrate the present year—the Second Centenary of the Trial concerning Ship-Money. My Carlisle, however, is purely imaginary: I at first sketched her singular likeness roughly in, as suggested by Matthew and the memoir-writers—but it was too artificial, and the substituted outline is exclusively from Voiture and Waller.

The Italian boat-song in the last scene is from Redi's *Bacco*, long since naturalized in the joyous and delicate version of Leigh Hunt.

---

§ Preface in 1837 only §

9

DRAMATIS PERSONÆ.

(Theatre-Royal Covent Garden, May 1, 1837.)

Charles the First	MR. DALE.
Earl of Holland	HUCKEL.
Lord Savile	TILBURY.
Sir Henry Vane	THOMPSON.
Wentworth, Viscount Wentworth, Earl of Strafford	MACREADY.
John Pym	VANDENHOFF.
John Hampden	HARRIS.
The younger Vane	J. WEBSTER.
Denzil Hollis	G. BENNET.
Benjamin Rudyard	PRITCHARD.
Nathaniel Fiennes	WORREL.
Earl of Loudon	BENDER.
Maxwell, *Usher of the Black Rod*	RANSFORD.
Balfour, *Constable of the Tower*	COLLETT.
A Puritan	WEBSTER.
Queen Henrietta	MISS VINCENT.
Lucy Percy, Countess of Carlisle	HELEN FAUCIT.

Presbyterians, Scots Commissioners, Adherents of Strafford, Secretaries, Officers of the Court &c. Two of Strafford's Children.

---

§ In 1837 only §

10

CHARLES I.

Earl of HOLLAND.

Lord SAVILE.

Sir HENRY VANE.

WENTWORTH, Viscount WENTWORTH, Earl of
STRAFFORD.

JOHN PYM.

JOHN HAMPDEN.

The younger VANE.

DENZIL HOLLIS.

BENJAMIN RUDYARD.

NATHANIEL FIENNES.

Earl of LOUDON.

MAXWELL, *Usher of the Black Rod.*

BALFOUR, *Constable of the Tower.*

A Puritan.

Queen HENRIETTA.

LUCY PERCY, Countess of Carlisle.

Presbyterians, Scots Commissioners, Aherents of Strafford, Secretaries,
Officers of the Court, &c. Two of Strafford's children.

11

STRAFFORD

1837

ACT I

SCENE I—*A House near Whitehall.* HAMPDEN, HOLLIS, *the* younger VANE, RUDYARD, FIENNES *and many of the Presbyterian Party:* LOUDON *and other Scots Commissioners.*

VANE I say, if he be here—
RUDYARD   (And he is here!)—
HOLLIS For England's sake let every man be still
Nor speak of him, so much as say his name,
Till Pym rejoin us! Rudyard! Henry Vane!
5   One rash conclusion may decide our course
And with it England's fate—think—England's fate!
Hampden, for England's sake they should be still!
VANE You say so, Hollis? Well, I must be still.
It is indeed too bitter that one man,
10   Any one man's mere presence, should suspend
England's combined endeavour: little need
To name him!
RUDYARD For you are his brother, Hollis!
HAMPDEN Shame on you, Rudyard! time to tell him that,
When he forgets the Mother of us all.
15   RUDYARD Do I forget her?
HAMPDEN   You talk idle hate
Against her foe: is that so strange a thing?
Is hating Wentworth all the help she needs?
A PURITAN The Philistine strode, cursing as he went:

---

§ Ed. 1837, 1863, 1868, 1888. No MS extant. §   § Stage Directions §   *1837:* Commissioners: some seated, some standing beside a table strewn over with papers, &c.   *1863:* Commissioners.   ¹| *1837:* here . . . ¶ RUDYARD And <> here!   *1863:* here— ¶ RUDYARD (And <> here!)—   ⁴| *1837:* us! Rudyard—Vane—remember   *1863:* us! Rudyard! Henry Vane!   ⁸| *1837:* well <> still!   *1863:* Well   *1868:* still.   *1888:* still   *1889:* still.   ⁹| *1837:* man—   *1863:* man,   ¹⁰⁻¹²| *1837:* man . . . ¶ RUDYARD You are   *1863:* man's mere presence should suspend / England's combined endeavour: little need / To name him! ¶ RUDYARD For you   *1888:* presence, should   ¹⁵| *1837:* her? . . ¶

13

But David—five smooth pebbles from the brook
20   Within his scrip . . .

RUDYARD   Be you as still as David!

FIENNES Here's Rudyard not ashamed to wag a tongue
Stiff with ten years' disuse of Parliaments;
Why, when the last sat, Wentworth sat with us!

RUDYARD Let's hope for news of them now he returns—
25   He that was safe in Ireland, as we thought!
—But I'll abide Pym's coming.

VANE   Now, by Heaven
Then may be cool who can, silent who will—
Some have a gift that way! Wentworth is here,
Here, and the King's safe closeted with him
30   Ere this. And when I think on all that's past
Since that man left us, how his single arm
Rolled the advancing good of England back
And set the woeful past up in its place,
Exalting Dagon where the Ark should be,—
35   How that man has made firm the fickle King
(Hampden, I will speak out!)—in aught he feared
To venture on before; taught tyranny
Her dismal trade, the use of all her tools,
To ply the scourge yet screw the gag so close
40   That strangled agony bleeds mute to death;
How he turns Ireland to a private stage
For training infant villanies, new ways
Of wringing treasure out of tears and blood,
Unheard oppressions nourished in the dark
45   To try how much man's nature can endure

HAMPDEN—You *1863:* her? ¶ HAMPDEN You **20|** *1837:* scrip . . . ¶ HAMPDEN—Be
1863: scrip . . . ¶ HAMPDEN Be **23|** *1837:* sate <> sate *1863:* sat <> sat
24–26| *1837:* returns: / —But <> Now by *1863:* returns— / He that was safe in Ireland, as
we thought! / <> —But <> Now, by **27|** *1837:* They may be cool that can, silent
that can, *1863:* cool who can, silent who will— *1888:* Then may **28|** *1837:* way:
Wentworth is here— *1863:* way! Wentworth is here, **29|** *1837:* Here—and *1863:*
Here, and **30|** *1837:* this! and *1863:* this. And **31|** *1837:* us—how *1863:* us,
how **32|** *1837:* Roll'd back the good of England, roll'd it back *1863:* Rolled the
advancing good of England back **33|** *1837:* Past <> place . . . *1863:* place,—
1868: past <> place, **34|** § This line given to A PURITAN in 1837 § *1837:* be! *1863:*
be— *1868:* be,— **35|** *1837:* . . . How *1863:* How **36|** *1837:* —Hampden
<> out!—in *1863:* (Hampden <> out!)—in **37|** *1837:* Tyranny *1868:*
tyranny **40|** *1837:* death: *1863:* death— *1889:* death; **41|** *1837:* —How
1863: How **43|** *1837:* and gore, *1863:* and blood, **45|** *1837:* Man's *1863:*

—If he dies under it, what harm? if not,
Why, one more trick is added to the rest
Worth a king's knowing, and what Ireland bears
England may learn to bear:—how all this while
50 That man has set himself to one dear task,
The bringing Charles to relish more and more
Power, power without law, power and blood too
—Can I be still?

HAMPDEN   For that you should be still.

VANE Oh Hampden, then and now! The year he left us,
55 The People in full Parliament could wrest
The Bill of Rights from the reluctant King;
And now, he'll find in an obscure small room
A stealthy gathering of great-hearted men
That take up England's cause: England is here!

60 HAMPDEN And who despairs of England?

RUDYARD   That do I,
If Wentworth comes to rule her. I am sick
To think her wretched masters, Hamilton,
The muckworm Cottington, the maniac Laud,
May yet be longed-for back again. I say,
65 I do despair.

VANE   And, Rudyard, I'll say this—
Which all true men say after me, not loud
But solemnly and as you'd say a prayer!
This King, who treads our England underfoot,
Has just so much . . . it may be fear or craft,
70 As bids him pause at each fresh outrage; friends,
He needs some sterner hand to grasp his own,

---

man's   46| *1837:* not . . . *1863:* not,   47–49| § In 1837 these lines are
distributed among different speakers § *1837:* FIENNES Why <> knowing RUDYARD—And
<> bear. ¶ VANE . . . How *1863:* bear: how   52–53| § In 1837 these lines are
distributed among different speakers § *1837:* Power . . . ¶ RUDYARD Power <> law . . . ¶
FIENNES Power <> too . . . / VANE . . . Can *1863:* Power, power <> law, power <> too— /
—Can *1868:* too, *1888:* too   54| *1837:* Oh, Hampden <> us *1863:* us, *1868:*
Oh Hampden   55| *1837:* The People by its Parliament *1863:* The People in full
Parliament   56| *1837:* reluctant King: *1863:* reluctant King;   57| *1837:*
now,—he'll *1863:* now, he'll   59| *1837:* is—here! *1863:* is here!   60| *1837:* do
I *1863:* do I,   61| *1837:* If Wentworth is to *1863:* If Wentworth comes to
64| *1837:* longed for <> say *1863:* longed-for <> say,   66| *1837:* And, [*turning to
the rest*] all <> me! not loud— *1863:* Which all <> me, not loud   67| *1837:*
prayer: *1863:* prayer!   68| *1837:* This Charles, who <> under foot, *1863:* This
King, who <> underfoot,   69| *1837:* much—it <> craft— *1868:* much . . . it <>

15

Some voice to ask, "Why shrink? Am I not by?"
Now, one whom England loved for serving her,
Found in his heart to say, "I know where best
75 The iron heel shall bruise her, for she leans
Upon me when you trample." Witness, you!
So Wentworth heartened Charles, so England fell.
But inasmuch as life is hard to take
From England . . .
MANY VOICES Go on, Vane! 'Tis well said, Vane!
80 VANE Who has not so forgotten Runnymead!—
VOICES 'Tis well and bravely spoken, Vane! Go on!
VANE —There are some little signs of late she knows
The ground no place for her. She glances round,
Wentworth has dropped the hand, is gone his way
85 On other service: what if she arise?
No! the King beckons, and beside him stands
The same bad man once more, with the same smile
And the same gesture. Now shall England crouch,
Or catch at us and rise?
VOICES   The Renegade!
90 Haman! Ahithophel!
HAMPDEN   Gentlemen of the North,
It was not thus the night your claims were urged,
And we pronounced the League and Covenant,
The cause of Scotland, England's cause as well:
Vane there, sat motionless the whole night through.
95 VANE Hampden!

---

craft,   72| 1837: shrink?—am   1868: shrink? Am   73| 1837: —A man that
England   1863: Now, one whom England   76-78| 1837: you! / But   1863: you! / So
Wentworth heartened Charles, so England fell. / But   80| 1837: . . . Who <>
Runnymead . . .   1863:—Who <> Runnymead!—   82| 1837: . . There   1863:
There   1868:—There   83-86| 1837: her! no place for her! / When the King
beckons—and   1863: her! She glances round, / Wentworth has dropped the hand, is gone
his way / On other service: what if she arise? / No! the King beckons, and   1868: her.
She   87| 1837: smile,   1863: smile   88-90| 1837: same savage gesture! Now let
England / Make proof of us. ¶ VOICES Strike him—the Renegade— / Haman—Ahithophel!—
¶ HAMPDEN / [To the Scots] Gentlemen   1863: same gesture. Now shall England crouch, / Or
catch at us and rise? ¶ VOICES The Renegade! / Haman! Ahithophel! ¶ HAMPDEN
Gentlemen   1868: crouch.   91| 1863: thus, the   1868: thus the   92| 1837: the
League and Covenant   1868: the League and Covenant,   93| 1837: Of Scotland to be
England's <> well!   1863: The cause of Scotland, England's   1868: well:
94| Vane, there, sate   1863: Vane there, sat   95| 1837: Hampden . . . ¶ FIENNES Stay

FIENNES   Stay, Vane!

LOUDON   Be just and patient, Vane!

VANE   Mind how you counsel patience, Loudon! you

Have still a Parliament, and this your League

To back it; you are free in Scotland still:

While we are brothers, hope's for England yet.

100 But know you wherefore Wentworth comes? to quench

This last of hopes? that he brings war with him?

Know you the man's self? what he dares?

LOUDON   We know,

All know—'tis nothing new.

VANE   And what's new, then,

In calling for his life? Why, Pym himself—

105 You must have heard—ere Wentworth dropped our cause

He would see Pym first; there were many more

Strong on the people's side and friends of his,

Eliot that's dead, Rudyard and Hampden here,

But for these Wentworth cared not; only, Pym

110 He would see—Pym and he were sworn, 'tis said,

To live and die together; so, they met

At Greenwich. Wentworth, you are sure, was long,

Specious enough, the devil's argument

Lost nothing on his lips; he'd have Pym own

115 A patriot could not play a purer part

Than follow in his track; they two combined

Might put down England. Well, Pym heard him out;

One glance—you know Pym's eye—one word was all:

Vane! ¶ <> Be patient, gallant Vane!   *1863:* Hampden! ¶ FIENNES Stay, Vane! ¶ <> Be just and patient, Vane!   97| *1837:* and a brave League   *1863:* and this your League 98| *1837:* still—   *1863:* still: 99-100| *1837:* brothers (as these hands are knit / So let our hearts be!)—hope's <> yet! / <> you why this Wentworth   *1863:* brothers, hope's <> yet. / you wherefore Wentworth   101| *1837:* This faintest hope   *1863:* This last of hopes   102| *1837:* you this Wentworth? What <> ¶ LOUDEN Dear Vane,   *1863:* you the man's self? what <> ¶ LOUDEN We know,   103| *1837:* We know <> new . . . ¶ VANE   *1863:* All know <> new. ¶ VANE   104| *1837:* life? Why Pym himself . . . *1863:* life? Why, Pym himself—   105| *1837:* ere Wentworth left our   *1863:* ere Wentworth dropped our   107| *1837:* People's <> his,—   *1863:* people's <> his,   109| *1837:* But Wentworth cared not for them; only   *1863:* But for these Wentworth cared not; only   110| *1837:* sworn, they say,   *1863:* sworn, 'tis said, 111| *1837:* together—so they   *1863:* together; so, they   112| *1837:* At Greenwich: Wentworth   *1863:* At Greenwich. Wentworth   114| *1837:* nothing in his   *1863:* nothing on his   115| *1837:* A Patriot <> not do a purer thing   *1863:* patriot <> not play a purer part   117| *1837:* Could put <> out—   *1863:* Might put <> out;

"You leave us, Wentworth! while your head is on,
120 I'll not leave you."

HAMPDEN   Has he left Wentworth, then?
Has England lost him? Will you let him speak,
Or put your crude surmises in his mouth?
Away with this! Will you have Pym or Vane?

VOICES Wait Pym's arrival! Pym shall speak.

HAMPDEN   Meanwhile
125 Let Loudon read the Parliament's report
From Edinburgh: our last hope, as Vane says,
Is in the stand it makes. Loudon!

VANE   No, no!
Silent I can be: not indifferent!

HAMPDEN Then each keep silence, praying God to spare
130 His anger, cast not England quite away
In this her visitation!

A PURITAN   Seven years long
The Midianite drove Israel into dens
And caves. Till God sent forth a mighty man,

PYM *enters.*

Even Gideon!

PYM   Wentworth's come: nor sickness, care,
135 The ravaged body nor the ruined soul,
More than the winds and waves that beat his ship,
Could keep him from the King. He has not reached
Whitehall: they've hurried up a Council there
To lose no time and find him work enough.
140 Where's Loudon? your Scots' Parliament . . .

119| *1837:* us, Wentworth: while <> on   *1863:* us, Wentworth! while <> on,
120| *1837:* Has Pym left *1863:* Has he left   123| *1837:* this! [*To the rest*] Will
1863: this! Will   124| *1837:* speak! ¶ HAMPDEN *1863:* speak. ¶ HAMPDEN
127| *1837:* VANE [*As* LOUDON *is about to read*]—No—no— *1863:* VANE No, no!
129| *1837:* praying God a space *1863:* praying God to spare   130| *1837:* That he will
not cast England *1863:* His anger, cast not England   131| *1837:* visitation! [*All
assume a posture of reverence*] ¶ A PURITAN *1863:* visitation! ¶ A PURITAN
133| *1837:* caves. ¶ Till *1863:* caves. Till   134–137| *1837:* Even Gideon! [*All start
up*] ¶ PYM Wentworth's come; he has *1863:* Even Gideon! ¶ PYM Wentworth's come: nor
sickness, care, / The ravaged body nor the ruined soul, / More than the winds and waves that
beat his ship, / Could keep him from the King. He has   140| *1837:* LOUDON Is firm:

LOUDON   Holds firm:

We were about to read reports.

PYM   The King

Has just dissolved your Parliament.

LOUDON AND OTHER SCOTS   Great God!

An oath-breaker! Stand by us, England, then!

PYM   The King's too sanguine; doubtless Wentworth's here;

145   But still some little form might be kept up.

HAMPDEN   Now speak, Vane! Rudyard, you had much to say!

HOLLIS   The rumour's false, then . . .

PYM   Ay, the Court gives out

His own concerns have brought him back: I know

'Tis the King calls him. Wentworth supersedes

150   The tribe of Cottingtons and Hamiltons

Whose part is played; there's talk enough, by this,—

Merciful talk, the King thinks: time is now

To turn the record's last and bloody leaf

Which, chronicling a nation's great despair,

155   Tells they were long rebellious, and their lord

Indulgent, till, all kind expedients tried,

He drew the sword on them and reigned in peace.

Laud's laying his religion on the Scots

Was the last gentle entry: the new page

160   Shall run, the King thinks, "Wentworth thrust it down

At the sword's point."

A PURITAN   I'll do your bidding, Pym,

England's and God's—one blow!

PYM   A goodly thing—

We all say, friends, it is a goodly thing

To right that England. Heaven grows dark above:

1863: LOUDON Holds firm: 141| *1837:* reports . . . ¶ PYM   *1863:* reports. ¶ PYM
143| *1837:* us England then!   *1863:* us, England, then!   146| § In 1837 this line is
given to Hollis §   147| § In 1837 Hollis's part of this line is given to Hampden §
149| *1837:* 'Tis Charles recalls him: he's to supersede   *1863:* 'Tis the King calls him:
Wentworth supersedes   151| *1837:* played: there's   *1863:* played; there's
154| *1837:* That, chronicling a Nation's   *1863:* nation's   *1888:* Which, chronicling
155| *1837:* Lord   *1863:* lord   157| *1837:* them, and   *1863:* them and
159| *1837:* entry:—the   *1863:* entry: the   161| *1837:* bidding, Pym,—   *1863:*
bidding, Pym,   162| *1837:* and your's . . . one <> A glorious thing—   *1863:* and
God's—one <> A goodly thing—   164| *1837:* that England! Heaven <> above,—

165 Let's snatch one moment ere the thunder fall,
   To say how well the English spirit comes out
   Beneath it! All have done their best, indeed,
   From lion Eliot, that grand Englishman,
   To the least here: and who, the least one here,
170 When she is saved (for her redemption dawns
   Dimly, most dimly, but it dawns—it dawns)
   Who'd give at any price his hope away
   Of being named along with the Great Men?
   We would not—no, we would not give that up!
175 HAMPDEN And one name shall be dearer than all names.
   When children, yet unborn, are taught that name
   After their fathers',—taught what matchless man . . .
   PYM . . . Saved England? What if Wentworth's should be still
   That name?
   RUDYARD AND OTHERS We have just said it, Pym! His death
180 Saves her! We said it—there's no way beside!
   I'll do God's bidding, Pym! They struck down Joab
   And purged the land.
   VANE   No villanous striking-down!
   RUDYARD No, a calm vengeance: let the whole land rise
   And shout for it. No Feltons!
   PYM   Rudyard, no!
185 England rejects all Feltons; most of all
   Since Wentworth . . . Hampden, say the trust again
   Of England in her servants—but I'll think
   You know me, all of you. Then, I believe,
   Spite of the past, Wentworth rejoins you, friends!
190 VANE AND OTHERS Wentworth? Apostate! Judas! Double-dyed

1863: above: *1868:* that England. Heaven   **165**| *1837:* fall   *1863:* fall,
170| *1837:* When She is saved (and her   *1863:* dawns,   *1868:* she is saved (for her <>
dawns   **171**| *1837:* dawns—it dawns)—   *1863:* dawns—it dawns)   **174**| *1837:*
One would not . . no, one would   *1863:* We would not—no, we would   **175**| *1837:*
names: *1863:* names.   **178**| *1837:* . . . Saved England? ¶ What   *1863:* Saved England?
What   **180**| *1837:* her! ¶ FIENNES We said that! There's   *1863:* her! We said
it—there's   **181**| § In 1837 this line is given to A PURITAN §   *1837:* do your bidding
1863: do God's bidding   **182**| § In 1837 And <> land. is conclusion of A PURITAN'S
lines §   **183**| *1837:* No—a   *1863:* No, a   **184**| *1837:* Rudyard, no.   *1863:*
Rudyard, no!   **186**| *1837:* Since Wentworth . . . ¶ Hampden, say the praise again
1863: Since Wentworth . . . Hampden, say the trust again   **187**| *1837:* That England
will award me . . . But   *1863:* Of England in her servants—but   **189**| *1837:* —Spite
<> past,—Wentworth   *1863:* Spite <> Past, Wentworth   *1868:* past   **190**| *1837:*

A traitor! Is it Pym, indeed . . .

PYM   . . . Who says

Vane never knew that Wentworth, loved that man,

Was used to stroll with him, arm locked in arm,

Along the streets to see the people pass,

195 And read in every island-countenance

Fresh argument for God against the King,—

Never sat down, say, in the very house

Where Eliot's brow grew broad with noble thoughts,

(You've joined us, Hampden—Hollis, you as well,)

200 And then left talking over Gracchus' death . . .

VANE To frame, we know it well, the choicest clause

In the Petition of Right: he framed such clause

One month before he took at the King's hand

His Northern Presidency, which that Bill

205 Denounced.

PYM   Too true! Never more, never more

Walked we together! Most alone I went.

I have had friends—all here are fast my friends—

But I shall never quite forget that friend.

And yet it could not but be real in him!

210 You, Vane,—you, Rudyard, have no right to trust

To Wentworth: but can no one hope with me?

Hampden, will Wentworth dare shed English blood

---

§ Speech tag reads RUDYARD AND OTHERS § Wentworth! Apostate . . . ¶ VANE Wentworth,
double-dyed . . .   *1863:* § Speech tag reads VANE AND OTHERS § Wentworth? apostate! Judas!
double-dyed   *1868:* Apostate <> Double-dyed   191| *1837:* indeed . . / PYM   *1863:*
indeed . . . / PYM   192| *1837:* that Wentworth—loved that Wentworth—   *1863:* that
Wentworth, loved that man,   193| *1837:* Felt glad to <> lock'd   *1863:* Was used to
<> locked   194| *1837:* the People pass   *1863:* people   *1888:* pass,   197| *1837:*
sate down . . . say   *1863:* sat down, say   198| *1837:* thoughts   *1863:* thoughts,
199| *1837:* us, Hampden, Hollis   *1863:* us, Hampden—Hollis   201| *1837:* . . To <>
it Pym, the   *1863:* To <> it well, the   202| *1837:* of Rights: which Wentworth
framed   *1863:* of Rights: he framed such clause   *1888:* Right   203| *1837:* A month
1863: One month   205| *1837:* Denounced . . . . . ¶ RUDYARD And infamy along with it! / A
PURITAN For whoso putteth his right-hand to the plough / And turneth back . . . ¶ PYM
Never   *1863:* Denounced. ¶ PYM Too true! Never   206| *1837:* went;   *1863:*
went.   208| *1837:* friend!   *1863:* friend.   209| § In 1837 line begins with stage
direction [*After a pause*]. §   210| *1837:* You Vane, you Rudyard   *1863:* You,
Vane,—you   *1868:* you, Rudyard   211| *1837:* That Wentworth . . . O will no   *1863:*
To Wentworth: but can no   212| *1837:*—Vane—think you Wentworth will shed
1863: Hampden, will Wentworth dare shed

Like water?

HAMPDEN   Ireland is Aceldama.

PYM Will he turn Scotland to a hunting-ground

215 To please the King, now that he knows the King?
The People or the King? and that King, Charles!

HAMPDEN Pym, all here know you: you'll not set your heart
On any baseless dream. But say one deed
Of Wentworth's since he left us . . .   [*Shouting without.*]

VANE   There! he comes,

220 And they shout for him! Wentworth's at Whitehall,
The King embracing him, now, as we speak,
And he, to be his match in courtesies,
Taking the whole war's risk upon himself,
Now, while you tell us here how changed he is!

225 Hear you?

PYM   And yet if 'tis a dream, no more,
That Wentworth chose their side, and brought the King
To love it as though Laud had loved it first,
And the Queen after;—that he led their cause
Calm to success, and kept it spotless through,

230 So that our very eyes could look upon
The travail of our souls, and close content
That violence, which something mars even right
Which sanctions it, had taken off no grace

²¹³| *1837:* water? ¶ A PURITAN Ireland is Aceldama!   *1863:* water? ¶ HAMPDEN Ireland is
Aceldama.   ²¹⁶⁻²¹⁷| *1837:* the King? The People, Hampden,/ Or the King . . . and that
King—Charles! Will no one hope? / HAMPDEN Pym, we do know   *1863:* the King? and that
King, Charles! / HAMPDEN Pym, all here know   ²¹⁸| *1837:* baseless thing: but   *1863:*
baseless dream. But   ²¹⁹| *1837:* Of Wentworth's, since <> ¶ VANE Pym, he   *1863:*
Of Wentworth's since <> ¶ VANE There! he   ²²⁰| *1837:* him!—Wentworth!—he's
with Charles—   *1863:* him! Wentworth's at Whitehall,   ²²¹| *1837:* king <> him—
now—as we speak . .   *1863:* King <> him, now, as we speak,   ²²³| *1837:*
himself!—   *1863:* himself,   ²²⁴⁻²²⁵| *1837:* Now—while <> is— / Do you hear, Pym?
The People shout for him! / FIENNES We'll not go back, now! Hollis has no brother—/
Vane has no father . . . ¶ VANE Pym should have no friend! / Stand you firm, Pym! Eliot's
gone, Wentworth's lost, / We have but you, and stand you very firm! / Truth is eternal,
come below what will, / But . . I know not . . if you should fail . . O God! / O God! ¶ PYM [*Apart
and in thought*] And   *1863:* Now, while <> is! / Hear you? ¶ PYM And
²²⁸| *1837:* after—that   *1863:* after;—that   ²²⁹| *1837:* success and   *1863:*
success, and   ²³¹| *1837:* soul   *1863:* souls and   *1888:* souls, and
²³²| *1837:* Right   *1863:* right   *1868:* rights   *1888:* right   ²³³| *1837:* That
sanctions   *1863:* Which sanctions   *1868:* sanction   *1888:* sanctions

From its serene regard. Only a dream!

235 HAMPDEN We meet here to accomplish certain good
By obvious means, and keep tradition up
Of free assemblages, else obsolete,
In this poor chamber: nor without effect
Has friend met friend to counsel and confirm,
240 As, listening to the beats of England's heart,
We spoke its wants to Scotland's prompt reply
By these her delegates. Remains alone
That word grow deed, as with God's help it shall—
But with the devil's hindrance, who doubts too?
245 Looked we or no that tyranny should turn
Her engines of oppression to their use?
Whereof, suppose the worst be Wentworth here—
Shall we break off the tactics which succeed
In drawing out our formidablest foe,
250 Let bickering and disunion take their place?
Or count his presence as our conquest's proof,
And keep the old arms at their steady play?
Proceed to England's work! Fiennes, read the list!

 FIENNES Ship-money is refused or fiercely paid
255 In every county, save the northern parts
Where Wentworth's influence . . .   [*Shouting.*]

 VANE   I, in England's name,
Declare her work, this way, at end! Till now,
Up to this moment, peaceful strife was best.
We English had free leave to think; till now,
260 We had a shadow of a Parliament
In Scotland. But all's changed: they change the first,
They try brute-force for law, they, first of all . . .

 VOICES Good! Talk enough! The old true hearts with Vane!

234–253| *1837:* dream! / Proceed <> work: who reads the list? § 1863 adds lines 235–252 §
1863: Proceed <> work! Fiennes, read the list!   **254|** § In 1837 Fiennes' speech on
lines 254–256 is given to A VOICE §   *1837:* "Ship-money   *1863:* Ship-money
255| *1837:* northern ones   *1863:* northern parts   **256|** *1837:* influence" . . . [*Renewed*
shouting] ¶ VANE [*passionately striking the table*] I, in <> name   *1863:* influence . . .
[*shouting*] ¶ VANE I, in <> name,   **257|** *1837:* till now—   *1863:* end! Till
now,   **258|** *1837:* moment—peaceful strife was well!   *1863:* moment, peaceful strife
was best.   **259|** *1837:* think! till   *1863:* think; till   **260|** *1837:* a Parliament:
1863: a Parliament   **261|** *1837:* 'Twas well: but all is changed: they threaten us:
1863: In Scotland. But all's changed: they change the first,   **262|** *1837:* They'll try <>
law—here—in our land!   *1863:* They try <> law, they, first of all . . .   **263|** § In 1837

VANE Till we crush Wentworth for her, there's no act
265 Serves England!

VOICES   Vane for England!

PYM   Pym should be
Something to England. I seek Wentworth, friends.

SCENE II—*Whitehall.*

LADY CARLISLE *and* WENTWORTH.

WENTWORTH And the King?

LADY CARLISLE   Wentworth, lean on me! Sit then!
I'll tell you all; this horrible fatigue
Will kill you.

WENTWORTH No;—or, Lucy, just your arm;
I'll not sit till I've cleared this up with him:
5   After that, rest. The King?

LADY CARLISLE   Confides in you.

WENTWORTH Why? or, why now?—They have kind throats, the knaves!
Shout for me—they!

LADY CARLISLE   You come so strangely soon:
Yet we took measures to keep off the crowd—
Did they shout for you?

WENTWORTH   Wherefore should they not?
10   Does the King take such measures for himself?
Beside, there's such a dearth of malcontents,
You say!

LADY CARLISLE I said but few dared carp at you.

WENTWORTH At me? at us, I hope! The King and I.
He's surely not disposed to let me bear
15   The fame away from him of these late deeds

---

the speech tag is MANY VOICES § *1837:* True hearts with Vane! The   *1863:* Good! Talk
enough! The   265| *1837:* PYM [*As he passes slowly before them*] Pym   *1863:* PYM
Pym   266| *1837:* to England! I <> friends!   *1863:* to England. I <> friends.
1| *1837:* LADY CARLISLE Dear Wentworth <> me; sit then;   *1863:* LADY CARLISLE
Wentworth <> me! sit then,—   *1868:* Sit then!   3| *1837:* No; or—Lucy *1868:*
No;—or, Lucy   6| *1837:* Why? why now? ¶ —They <> the people!   *1863:* Why? or,
why now?—They <> the knaves!   7| *1837:* me . . . They!—poor fellows. ¶ LADY
CARLISLE Did they shout?   *1863:* me—They! ¶ LADY CARLISLE You come so strangely
soon: 8| *1837:*—We took all measures   *1863:* Yet we took measures   12| *1837:*
say? ¶ LADY CARLISLE <> you . . .   *1863:* say! ¶ LADY CARLISLE <> you.   13| *1837:* us,
Carlisle! The   *1863:* us, I hope! The   15| *1837:* Away the fame

In Ireland? I am yet his instrument
Be it for well or ill? He trusts me, too!

LADY CARLISLE The King, dear Wentworth, purposes, I said,
To grant you, in the face of all the Court . . .

20 WENTWORTH All the Court! Evermore the Court about us!
Savile and Holland, Hamilton and Vane
About us,—then the King will grant me—what?
That he for once put these aside and say—
"Tell me your whole mind, Wentworth!"

LADY CARLISLE   You professed
25 You would be calm.

WENTWORTH   Lucy, and I am calm!
How else shall I do all I come to do,
Broken, as you may see, body and mind,
How shall I serve the King? Time wastes meanwhile,
You have not told me half. His footstep! No.

30 Quick, then, before I meet him,—I am calm—
Why does the King distrust me?

LADY CARLISLE   He does not
Distrust you.

WENTWORTH Lucy, you can help me; you
Have even seemed to care for me: one word!
Is it the Queen?

LADY CARLISLE No, not the Queen: the party
35 That poisons the Queen's ear, Savile and Holland.

WENTWORTH I know, I know: old Vane, too, he's one too?
Go on—and he's made Secretary. Well?
Or leave them out and go straight to the charge—
The charge!

---

from *1863:* The fame away from   ¹⁷| *1837:* ill? ¶ He trusts me then? *1863:* ill? He
trusts me, too!   ¹⁸| *1837:* I know *1863:* I said,   ²²| *1837:* me . . . Lady, *1863:*
me—What?   ²³| *1837:* Will the King leave these—all these—and say *1863:* That he
for once put these aside and say—   ²⁴| *1837:* LADY CARLISLE But you said *1863:* LADY
CARLISLE You professed   ²⁷| *1837:*—Broken <> mind— *1863:* Broken <>
mind,   ²⁸| *1837:* time *1868:* Time   ²⁹| *1837:* half . . . His *1863:* half.
His   ³⁰| *1837:*—But now, before <> him,—(I am calm)— *1863:* Quick, then,
before <> him,—I am calm—   ³²| *1837:* me . . you *1863:* me; you   ³³| *1837:*
me: help me! *1863:* me: one word!   ³⁴| *1837:* No—not the Queen—the *1863:* No,
not the Queen: the   ³⁵| *1837:* ear,—Savile—and Holland . . . *1863:* ear, Savile and
Holland.   ³⁶| *1837:* know—I know—and Vane *1863:* know, I know: and *1868:*
know, I know: old Vane   ³⁷| *1837:* made Secretary—Well? *1863:* made Secretary.
Well?   ³⁸| *1837:*—Or <> charge! *1863:* Or <> charge; *1868:* charge, *1888:*

LADY CARLISLE Oh, there's no charge, no precise charge;
40   Only they sneer, make light of—one may say,
      Nibble at what you do.
WENTWORTH   I know! but Lucy,
      I reckoned on you from the first!—Go on!
      —Was sure could I once see this gentle friend
      When I arrived, she'd throw an hour away
45   To help her . . . what am I?
LADY CARLISLE   You thought of me,
      Dear Wentworth?
WENTWORTH   But go on! The party here!
LADY CARLISLE They do not think your Irish government
      Of that surpassing value . . .
WENTWORTH   The one thing
      Of value! The one service that the crown
50   May count on! All that keeps these very Vanes
      In power, to vex me—not that they do vex,
      Only it might vex some to hear that service
      Decried, the sole support that's left the King!
LADY CARLISLE So the Archbishop says.
WENTWORTH   Ah? well, perhaps
55   The only hand held up in my defence
      May be old Laud's! These Hollands then, these Saviles
      Nibble? They nibble?—that's the very word!
LADY CARLISLE Your profit in the Customs, Bristol says,
      Exceeds the due proportion: while the tax . . .
60   WENTWORTH Enough! 'tis too unworthy,—I am not
      So patient as I thought. What's Pym about?
LADY CARLISLE Pym?

---

charge   *1889:* charge—   ³⁹| *1837:* LADY CARLISLE O <> charge—no <> charge—
1863: LADY CARLISLE Oh <> charge, no <> charge;   ⁴⁰| *1837:* of . . . one may say
1863: of—one may say,   ⁴¹⁻⁴²| *1837:* know: but Lucy, / Go on, dear Lucy—Oh I need
you so! / I   *1863:* know! but Lucy, / I   ⁴³| *1837:* . . Was <> gentle girl   *1863:*—Was
<> gentle friend   ⁴⁵| *1837:* her weary friend . . . ¶ LADY CARLISLE   *1863:* her . . .
What am I? ¶ LADY CARLISLE   ⁴⁶| *1837:* WENTWORTH . . But <> The People here . . .
1863: WENTWORTH But <> The party here!   ⁴⁷| *1837:* Government   *1888:*
government   ⁵⁰| *1837:* very things   *1863:* very Vanes   ⁵¹| *1837:* me . . not
<> vex me,   *1863:* me—not <> vex,   ⁵³| *1837:* Decried—the sole   *1863:* Decried,
the sole   ⁵⁵| *1837:* in its defence   *1863:* in my defence   ⁵⁶| *1837:* Old Lauds! ¶
These Hollands then   *1863:* Old Lauds! These Hollands, then   *1868:* Hollands then
⁵⁸⁻⁶⁰| *1837:* says, . . . / WENTWORTH   *1863:* says, / Exceeds the due proportion: while the tax
. . . / WENTWORTH   ⁶¹| *1837:* thought! ¶ What's   *1863:* thought! What's   *1888:*

WENTWORTH   Pym and the People.

LADY CARLISLE   Oh, the Faction!
Extinct—of no account: there'll never be
Another Parliament.

WENTWORTH   Tell Savile that!
65 You may know—(ay, you do—the creatures here
Never forget!) that in my earliest life
I was not . . . much that I am now! The King
May take my word on points concerning Pym
Before Lord Savile's, Lucy, or if not,
70 I bid them ruin their wise selves, not me,
These Vanes and Hollands! I'll not be their tool
Who might be Pym's friend yet.

                              But there's the King!
Where is he?

LADY CARLISLE Just apprised that you arrive.

WENTWORTH And why not here to meet me? I was told
75 He sent for me, nay, longed for me.

LADY CARLISLE   Because,—
He is now . . . I think a Council's sitting now
About this Scots affair.

WENTWORTH   A Council sits?
They have not taken a decided course
Without me in the matter?

LADY CARLISLE   I should say . . .

80 WENTWORTH The war? They cannot have agreed to that?
Not the Scots' war?—without consulting me—
Me, that am here to show how rash it is,
How easy to dispense with?—Ah, you too
Against me! well,—the King may take his time.

---

thought. What's   62| *1868:* Pym ¶ WENTWORTH   *1888:* Pym? ¶ WENTWORTH
63| *1837:* account—there'll   *1863:* account: there'll   67| *1837:* not . . . not what I
1863: not . . . much that I   70| *1837:* Girl, they shall ruin their vile selves   *1863:* I bid
them ruin their wise selves   71| *1837:* and Hollands—I'll <> tool—   *1863:* and
Hollands / I'll <> tool   72| *1837:* Pym would receive me yet! ¶ —But then the
King!— / I'll bear it all. The King—where is he, Girl? / LADY CARLISLE He is apprised that you
are here: be calm! / WENTWORTH And why not meet me now? Ere now? You said
75| *1837:* He sent for me . . he longed for me!   *1863:* longed for me! ¶   *1888:* me.
1837: Because . . / He   *1863:* Because,— / He   77| *1837:* affair . . . ¶ WENTWORTH
1863: affair. ¶ WENTWORTH   79| *1837:* in this matter   *1863:* in the matter
80| *1837:* War   *1863:* war   81| *1837:* War   *1863:* war   82| *1837:* Me—that
1863: Me, that   83| *1837:* with? ¶ —Ah   *1863:* with?—Ah   84| *1837:* may find

85 —Forget it, Lucy! Cares make peevish: mine
    Weigh me (but 'tis a secret) to my grave.
        LADY CARLISLE For life or death I am your own, dear friend!

                                                    [*Goes out.*]

    WENTWORTH Heartless! but all are heartless here. Go now,
    Forsake the People!
                        I did not forsake
90 The People: they shall know it, when the King
    Will trust me!—who trusts all beside at once,
    While I have not spoke Vane and Savile fair,
    And am not trusted: have but saved the throne:
    Have not picked up the Queen's glove prettily,
95 And am not trusted. But he'll see me now.
    Weston is dead: the Queen's half English now—
    More English: one decisive word will brush
    These insects from . . . the step I know so well!
    The King! But now, to tell him . . . no—to ask
100 What's in me he distrusts:—or, best begin
    By proving that this frightful Scots affair
    Is just what I foretold. So much to say,
    And the flesh fails, now, and the time is come,
    And one false step no way to be repaired.
105 You were avenged, Pym, could you look on me.

    PYM *enters.*

---

me here.   *1863:* may take his time.   85| § In 1837 this line is preceded by stage
direction [*As* CARLISLE *is going*] §   *1837:* it, Lucy: cares   *1863:* it, Lucy! cares   *1868:*
Cares   87–88| *1837:* friend! / [*Aside*] I could not tell him . . . sick too! . . And the King /
Shall love him! Wentworth here, who can withstand / His look?——And he did really think
of me? / O 'twas well done to spare him all the pain! [*Exit*] / WENTWORTH Heartless! . . . but
<> here ¶ Go   *1863:* Friend! [*Goes out*] WENTWORTH Heartless! but <> here.
Go   89| *1837:* people! ¶—I   *1863:* the People!—I   *1888:* the People! ¶ I
90| *1837:* it . . . when   *1863:* it—when   *1888:* it, when   91| *1837:* once   *1863:*
once,   92| *1837:* I . . . have   *1863:* I have   93| *1837:* Throne: *1868:*
throne: 95| *1837:* trusted! ¶ But <> now: *1863:* trusted. But <> now.
96| *1837:* And Weston's dead—and the Queen's English   *1863:* Weston is dead: the
Queen's half English   97| *1837:* More English—oh, one earnest word   *1863:* More
English: one decisive word   98| *1837:* These reptiles from . . . [*footsteps within*] ¶
The step   *1863:* These insects from . . . the step   99| *1837:* 'Tis Charles!—But
now—to tell him . . no—to ask him   *1863:* The King! But now, to tell him . . no—to
ask   100| *1837:* me to distrust   *1863:* me he distrusts   102| *1837:* foretold: I'll
say, "my liege" . . . .   *1863:* foretold. So much to say,   103| *1837:* And I feel sick, now!
and <> come—   *1863:* And the flesh fails, now <> come,   *1868:* now, and
104| *1837:* repaired. . . .   *1863:* repaired!   *1888:* repaired.   105| *1837:* were

WENTWORTH I little thought of you just then.
PYM   No? I
Think always of you, Wentworth.
WENTWORTH   The old voice!
I wait the King, sir.
PYM   True—you look so pale!
A Council sits within; when that breaks up
110 He'll see you.
WENTWORTH Sir, I thank you.
PYM   Oh, thank Laud!
You know when Laud once gets on Church affairs
The case is desperate: he'll not be long
To-day: he only means to prove, to-day,
We English all are mad to have a hand
115 In butchering the Scots for serving God
After their fathers' fashion: only that!
WENTWORTH Sir, keep your jests for those who relish them!
(Does he enjoy their confidence?) 'Tis kind
To tell me what the Council does.
PYM   You grudge
120 That I should know it had resolved on war
Before you came? no need: you shall have all
The credit, trust me!
WENTWORTH   Have the Council dared—
They have not dared . . . that is—I know you not.
Farewell, sir: times are changed.
PYM   —Since we two met
125 At Greenwich? Yes: poor patriots though we be,
You cut a figure, makes some slight return
For your exploits in Ireland! Changed indeed,
Could our friend Eliot look from out his grave!

---

revenged, Pym <> me!   *1863:* were avenged, Pym   *1868:* me.   [107|] *1837:*
WENTWORTH [*Aside*] The   *1863:* WENTWORTH The   [108|] *1837:* pale: *1863:*
pale!   [109|] *1837:* council   *1863:* Council   [113|] *1837:* He   *1863:* he
[116|] *1837:* that.   *1863:* that!   [118|] *1837:* [*Aside*] Does *he* <> confidence?
[*To* PYM] 'Tis   *1863:* (Does *he* <> confidence?) 'Tis   *1868:* he   [121|] *1837:*
need—you   *1863:* need: you   [122|] *1837:* me. ¶ WENTWORTH Have they, Pym . . . not
dared—   *1863:* Have the Council dared—   *1868:* me! ¶ WENTWORTH   [123|] *1837:* you
not—   *1863:* you not.   [124|] *1837:* Farewell—the times   *1863:* Farewell, sir:
times   [125|] *1837:* At Greenwich? Yes—poor   *1863:* At Greenwich? Yes: poor
[126|] *1837:* You shall see something here, some   *1863:* You cut a figure, makes some

29

Ah Wentworth, one thing for acquaintance' sake,
130 Just to decide a question; have you, now,
Felt your old self since you forsook us?
WENTWORTH   Sir!
PYM Spare me the gesture! you misapprehend.
Think not I mean the advantage is with me.
I was about to say that, for my part,
135 I never quite held up my head since then—
Was quite myself since then: for first, you see
I lost all credit after that event
With those who recollect how sure I was
Wentworth would outdo Eliot on our side.
140 Forgive me: Savile, old Vane, Holland here,
Eschew plain-speaking: 'tis a trick I keep.
WENTWORTH How, when, where, Savile, Vane, and Holland speak,
Plainly or otherwise, would have my scorn,
All of my scorn, sir . . .
PYM   . . . Did not my poor thoughts
145 Claim somewhat?
WENTWORTH   Keep your thoughts! believe the King
Mistrusts me for their prattle, all these Vanes
And Saviles! make your mind up, o' God's love,
That I am discontented with the King!
PYM Why, you may be: I should be, that I know,
150 Were I like you.
WENTWORTH   Like me?
PYM   I care not much
For titles: our friend Eliot died no lord,

129| *1837:* Ah, Wentworth <> acquaintance-sake; *1863:* acquaintance' sake, *1868:* Ah
Wentworth   131–132| *1837:* Really felt well since <> ¶ WENTWORTH Pym— / You're
insolent ¶ PYM Oh, you misapprehend! *1863:* Felt your old self since <> ¶ WENTWORTH Sir!
/ PYM Spare me the gesture! you missapprehend! *1888:* misapprehend.   133| Don't
think I <> me: *1863:* Think not I <> me.   135| *1837:* I've never <> then,—
1863: I never *1868:* then—   136| *1837:* Been quite <> see, *1863:* Was quite
1888: see   139–140| *1837:* side. / WENTWORTH By Heaven . . . / PYM Forgive me: Savile,
Vane, and Holland *1863:* side. / Forgive me: Savile, old Vane, Holland here,
141| *1837:* trick I have. *1863:* trick I keep.   142| *1837:* where,—Savile <>
speak,— *1863:* where, Savile, Vane and <> speak, *1868:* Vane, and   143| *1837:*
otherwise,—would *1863:* otherwise, would   144| *1837:* My perfect scorn, Sir . . . ¶
PYM . . Did *1863:* All of my scorn, sir *1888:* sir . . . ¶ PYM . . . Did
146| *1837:* their speaking, all *1863:* their prattle, all   147| up, all of you, *1863:* up,
o' God's love,   149| *1837:* may be—I *1863:* may be: I   151| *1837:* Lord, *1868:*

Hampden's no lord, and Savile is a lord;
But you care, since you sold your soul for one.
I can't think, therefore, your soul's purchaser
155 Did well to laugh you to such utter scorn
When you twice prayed so humbly for its price,
The thirty silver pieces . . . I should say,
The Earldom you expected, still expect,
And may. Your letters were the movingest!
160 Console yourself: I've borne him prayers just now
From Scotland not to be oppressed by Laud,
Words moving in their way: he'll pay, be sure,
As much attention as to those you sent.
WENTWORTH False, sir! Who showed them you? Suppose it so,
165 The King did very well . . . nay, I was glad
When it was shown me: I refused, the first!
John Pym, you were my friend—forbear me once!
PYM Oh, Wentworth, ancient brother of my soul,
That all should come to this!
WENTWORTH   Leave me!
PYM   My friend,
170 Why should I leave you?
WENTWORTH   To tell Rudyard this,
And Hampden this!
PYM   Whose faces once were bright
At my approach, now sad with doubt and fear,
Because I hope in you—yes, Wentworth, you
Who never mean to ruin England—you
175 Who shake off, with God's help, an obscene dream

_____

lord,   152| *1837:* Lord <> Lord: *1868:* lord <> lord;   154–159| *1837:*
therefore, Charles did well to laugh / When twice you prayed so humbly for an Earldom. /
WENTWORTH Pym . . . . ¶ PYM And your letters   *1863:* therefore, your soul's purchaser /
Did well to laugh you to such utter scorn / When you twice prayed so humbly for its price, / The
thirty silver pieces . . I should say, / The Earldom you expected, still expect, / And may. Your
letters   *1868:* pieces . . I   *1888:* pieces . . . I   161| *1837:* opprest <> Laud—   *1863:*
oppressed <> Laud,   162| *1837:* And moving   *1863:* Words moving
164| *1837:* False! a lie, Sir! ¶ . . Who told you, Pym? ¶ —But then   *1863:* False, sir!—Who
showed them you? suppose it so,   *1868:* sir! Who <> Suppose   165| *1837:* well . .
nay   *1888:* well . . . nay   166| *1837:* shewn me why;—I first refused it!   *1863:* shown
me: I refused, the first!   167| *1837:* . . . Pym, you were once my friend—don't speak to
me!   *1863:* John Pym, you were my friend—forbear me once!   171| *1837:* this! . . . ¶
PYM   *1863:* this! ¶ PYM   172| *1837:* approach . . now   *1863:* approach—now   *1868:*
approach, now   173| *1837:* you—Wentworth—in you   *1863:* you—yes, Wentworth,
you   175| *1837:* shake, with God's great help, this frightful dream   *1863:* shake off,

31

In this Ezekiel chamber, where it crept
Upon you first, and wake, yourself, your true
And proper self, our Leader, England's Chief,
And Hampden's friend!
                    This is the proudest day!
180 Come, Wentworth! Do not even see the King!
The rough old room will seem itself again!
We'll both go in together: you've not seen
Hampden so long: come: and there's Fiennes: you'll have
To know young Vane. This is the proudest day!
[*The* KING *enters.* WENTWORTH *lets fall* PYM's *hand.*]
185 CHARLES Arrived, my lord?—This gentleman, we know
Was your old friend.
                    The Scots shall be informed
What we determine for their happiness.

                                        [PYM *goes out.*]
You have made haste, my lord.
WENTWORTH   Sir, I am come . . .
CHARLES To see an old familiar—nay, 'tis well;
190 Aid us with his experience: this Scots' League
And Covenant spreads too far, and we have proofs
That they intrigue with France: the Faction too,
Whereof your friend there is the head and front,
Abets them,—as he boasted, very like.
195 WENTWORTH Sir, trust me! but for this once, trust me, sir!

---

with God's help, an obscene dream   **176|** *1837:* Away, now, in this Palace, where
1863: In this Ezekiel chamber, where   **177|** *1837:* and are yourself—your good   *1863:*
and wake, yourself—your true   *1868:* yourself, your   **178|** *1837:* And noble self—our
Leader—our dear Chief—   *1863:* And proper self, our Leader, England's Chief,
179| *1837:* Hampden's own friend— ¶ This   *1863:* And Hampden's friend! ¶ This
180| *1837:* Come Wentworth   *1863:* Come, Wentworth   **182|** *1837:*
together—you've   *1863:* together: you've   **183|** *1837:* long—come—and there's
Vane—I know   *1863:* long: come: and there's Fiennes: you'll have   **184|** *1837:* You'll
love young Vane! This   *1863:* To know young Vane. This   **185|** *1837:* Lord <>
Gentleman, we know,   *1863:* gentleman   *1868:* lord <> know   **186|** *1837:* friend: ¶
[*To* PYM] The   *1863:* friend. ¶ The   **187|** *1837:* happiness, [PYM   *1863:* happiness.
[PYM   **188|** *1837:* my Lord. ¶ WENTWORTH Sire . . . I   *1863:* WENTWORTH Sir, I   *1868:*
lord   **189–190|** *1837:* To aid us with your counsel: this Scots' League   *1863:* To see an
old familiar—nay, 'tis well; / Aid us with his experience: this Scots' League
192–195| *1837:* the Faction, too . . . / WENTWORTH [*Kneels*] Sire, trust me! but <> once trust
me, Sire!   *1863:* too, / Whereof your friend there is the head and front, / Abets them,—as he
boasted, very like. / WENTWORTH Sir, trust me! but <> once, trust me, sir!   *1868:* the

CHARLES What can you mean?

WENTWORTH   That you should trust me, sir!
Oh—not for my sake! but 'tis sad, so sad
That for distrusting me, you suffer—you
Whom I would die to serve: sir, do you think
200 That I would die to serve you?

CHARLES   But rise, Wentworth!

WENTWORTH What shall convince you? What does Savile do
To prove him . . . Ah, one can't tear out one's heart
And show it, how sincere a thing it is!

CHARLES Have I not trusted you?

WENTWORTH   Say aught but that!
205 There is my comfort, mark you: all will be
So different when you trust me—as you shall!
It has not been your fault,—I was away,
Mistook, maligned, how was the King to know?
I am here, now—he means to trust me, now—
210 All will go on so well!

CHARLES   Be sure I do—
I've heard that I should trust you: as you came,
Your friend, the Countess, told me . . .

WENTWORTH   No,—hear nothing—
Be told nothing about me!—you're not told
Your right-hand serves you, or your children love you!
215 CHARLES You love me, Wentworth: rise!

WENTWORTH   I can speak now.
I have no right to hide the truth. 'Tis I
Can save you: only I. Sir, what must be?

CHARLES Since Laud's assured (the minutes are within)
—Loath as I am to spill my subjects' blood . . .
220 WENTWORTH That is, he'll have a war: what's done is done!

Faction too,   196| 1837: me! now! 1863: me, sir!   199| 1837: Sire 1863:
sir   202| 1837: To . . . Ah <> heart—one's heart— 1863: To prove him . . . Ah <>
heart   205| 1837: It is 1863: There is   206| 1837: me . . as 1863:
me—as   208| 1837: Maligned—away—and how were you to 1863: Mistook,
maligned, how was the King to   209| 1837: here, now—you mean to 1863: here,
now—he means to   210| 1837: sure I will— 1863: sure I do—   211| 1837:
came 1863: came,   212| 1837: Even Carlisle was telling me . . . ¶ WENTWORTH 1863:
Your friend, the Countess, told me . . . ¶ WENTWORTH   213| 1837: me! you're 1868:
me!—you're   215| 1837: me . . only rise 1863: me, Wentworth: rise   217| 1837:
you; only I. Sire, what is done! 1863: Sir, what must be? 1868: you: only   218| 1837:
assured . . . the <> within . . 1863: assured (the <> within)   219| 1837: Loath

CHARLES They have intrigued with France; that's clear to Laud.

WENTWORTH Has Laud suggested any way to meet
The war's expense?

CHARLES He'd not decide so far
Until you joined us.

WENTWORTH Most considerate!
225 He's certain they intrigue with France, these Scots?
The People would be with us.

CHARLES Pym should know.

WENTWORTH The People for us—were the People for us!
Sir, a great thought comes to reward your trust:
Summon a Parliament! in Ireland first,
230 Then, here.

CHARLES In truth?

WENTWORTH That saves us! that puts off
The war, gives time to right their grievances—
To talk with Pym. I know the Faction,—Laud
So styles it,—tutors Scotland: all their plans
Suppose no Parliament: in calling one
235 You take them by surprise. Produce the proofs
Of Scotland's treason; then bid England help:
Even Pym will not refuse.

CHARLES You would begin
With Ireland?

WENTWORTH Take no care for that: that's sure
To prosper.

CHARLES You shall rule me. You were best
240 Return at once: but take this ere you go!
Now, do I trust you? You're an Earl: my Friend

1863:—Loath   223| 1837: expence <> decide on that   1863: expense <> decide so
far   225| 1837: You're certain   1863: He's certain   226| 1837: [Aside] The <>
us! ¶ CHARLES Very sure.   1863: The <> us. ¶ CHARLES Pym should know.   227| 1837:
(The <> us . . were <> us!)   1863: The <> us—were <> us!   228| 1837: Sire
<> trust!   1863: Sir <> trust: 229| 1837: parliament   1863: Parliament
230| 1837: And then in England. ¶ CHARLES Madness! ¶ WENTWORTH [Aside] That puts
1863: Then, here. ¶ CHARLES In truth? ¶ WENTWORTH That saves us! that puts
231| 1837: war—gives time to learn their   1863: war, gives time to right their
232| 1837: Pym—[To CHARLES] I <> faction, as   1863: Pym. I <> Faction   1888:
Faction,—Laud   233| 1837: They style it, . . ¶ CHARLES . . Tutors Scotland! ¶
WENTWORTH All   1863: Laud styles it, tutors Scotland: all   1888: So styles it,—tutors
234| 1837: parliament   1863: Parliament   236| 1837: treason; bid them help you,
then!   1863: treason; then bid England help: 237| 1837: refuse! ¶ CHARLES   1863:
refuse. ¶ CHARLES   239| 1837: me: you   1863: me. You   240| 1837: go! [Giving a

34

Of Friends: yes, while . . . You hear me not!

WENTWORTH Say it all o'er again—but once again:

The first was for the music: once again!

245 CHARLES Strafford, my friend, there may have been reports,

Vain rumours. Henceforth touching Strafford is

To touch the apple of my sight: why gaze

So earnestly?

WENTWORTH I am grown young again,

And foolish. What was it we spoke of?

CHARLES   Ireland,

250 The Parliament,—

WENTWORTH   I may go when I will?

—Now?

CHARLES Are you tired so soon of us?

WENTWORTH   My King!

But you will not so utterly abhor

A Parliament? I'd serve you any way.

CHARLES You said just now this was the only way.

255 WENTWORTH Sir, I will serve you.

CHARLES   Strafford, spare yourself:

You are so sick, they tell me.

WENTWORTH   'Tis my soul

That's well and prospers now.

                                This Parliament—

We'll summon it, the English one—I'll care

For everything. You shall not need them much.

260 CHARLES If they prove restive . . .

WENTWORTH   I shall be with you.

CHARLES Ere they assemble?

WENTWORTH   I will come, or else

---

paper] *1863:* go!   242| *1837:* yes, Strafford, while   *1863:* yes, while
243| *1837:* once again—   *1863:* once again: 244| *1837:* music—once   *1888:* music:
once   245| *1837:* my brave friend, there were wild reports—   *1863:* my friend, there
may have been reports,   246| *1837:* rumours . . Henceforth   *1863:* rumours.
Henceforth   249| *1837:* foolish! . . what   *1863:* foolish. What   251| *1837:* of me?
WENTWORTH My King. . . .   *1863:* of us? WENTWORTH My King!   252| *1837:* so very
much dislike   *1863:* so utterly abhor   253| *1837:* way!   *1863:* way.   255| *1837:*
Sire <> you! ¶ CHARLES <> yourself—   *1863:* Sir   *1888:* you. ¶ CHARLES <>
yourself: 256| *1837:* me, . . . ¶ WENTWORTH   *1863:* me. ¶ WENTWORTH
257| *1837:* and happy, now! ¶ This   *1863:* and prospers now   *1868:* now. ¶ This
259| *1837:* every thing: You <> much!   *1863:* everything. You <> much.
260| *1837:* you!   *1863:* you.   263| *1837:* dust! My § Stage direction § [*As* STRAFFORD

35

Deposit this infirm humanity
I' the dust. My whole heart stays with you, my King!

[*As* WENTWORTH *goes out, the* QUEEN *enters.*]

CHARLES That man must love me.

QUEEN   Is it over then?
265 Why, he looks yellower than ever! Well,
At least we shall not hear eternally
Of service—services: he's paid at least.

CHARLES Not done with: he engages to surpass
All yet performed in Ireland.

QUEEN   I had thought
270 Nothing beyond was ever to be done.
The war, Charles—will he raise supplies enough?

CHARLES We've hit on an expedient; he ... that is,
I have advised ... we have decided on
The calling—in Ireland—of a Parliament.

275 QUEEN O truly! You agree to that? Is that
The first fruit of his counsel? But I guessed
As much.

CHARLES This is too idle, Henriette!
I should know best. He will strain every nerve,
And once a precedent established ...

QUEEN   Notice
280 How sure he is of a long term of favour!
He'll see the next, and the next after that;
No end to Parliaments!

CHARLES   Well, it is done.
He talks it smoothly, doubtless. If, indeed,
The Commons here ...

QUEEN   Here! you will summon them
285 Here? Would I were in France again to see
A King!

CHARLES But, Henriette ...

QUEEN   Oh, the Scots see clear!

goes   *1863:* dust. My § Stage direction § [*As* WENTWORTH *goes*   264| *1837:* me!
¶ QUEEN   *1868:* me. ¶ QUEEN   265| *1837:* Why he <> well,   *1863:* Why, he   *1868:*
Well,   267| *1837:* Of his vast services   *1863:* Of service—services   271| *1837:*
War   *1863:* war   275| *1837:* that? Is this   *1863:* that? Is that   277| *1837:*
Henrietta!   *1863:* Henriette!   278| *1837:* best: He   *1863:* best. He   280| *1837:*
favours!   *1868:* favour!   282| *1837:* done: *1863:* done.   283| *1837:* doubtless:
if   *1863:* doubtless. If   286| *1837:* A <> But Henrietta ... ¶ <> O the Scots   *1863:*

Why should they bear your rule?

CHARLES   But listen, sweet!

QUEEN Let Wentworth listen—you confide in him!

CHARLES I do not, love,—I do not so confide!

290 The Parliament shall never trouble us

. . . Nay, hear me! I have schemes, such schemes: we'll buy

The leaders off: without that, Wentworth's counsel

Had ne'er prevailed on me. Perhaps I call it

To have excuse for breaking it for ever,

295 And whose will then the blame be? See you not?

Come, dearest!—look, the little fairy, now,

That cannot reach my shoulder! Dearest, come!

Henriette ¶ <> Oh, the Scots see clear! *1868:* But, Henriette   **287|** *1837:* Do well to
spurn your <> But, listen, Sweet . . . *1863:* Why should they bear your <> But listen,
Sweet! *1868:* sweet!   **288|** *1837:* Let Strafford listen   *1863:* Let Wentworth
listen   **289|** *1837:* not, Love—I <> confide . . *1863:* confide! *1868:* love,—I
291| *1837:* . . . Nay <> schemes—such schemes—we'll   *1863:* schemes, such schemes: we'll
1888: . . . Nay   **292|** *1837:* that, Strafford's counsel   *1863:* that, Wentworth's
counsel   **294|** *1837:* it—for ever—   *1863:* it for ever,   **296|** *1837:*
Dearest!—look! the *1868:* dearest!—look, the   **297|** *1837:* come! [*Exeunt*]   *1863:*
come!

ACT II

SCENE I—*(As in Act I. Scene I.)*

The same Party enters.

RUDYARD Twelve subsidies!

VANE   Oh, Rudyard, do not laugh
At least!

RUDYARD True: Strafford called the Parliament—
'Tis he should laugh!

A PURITAN   Out of the serpent's root
Comes forth a cockatrice.

FIENNES   —A stinging one,

5   If that's the Parliament: twelve subsidies!
A stinging one! but, brother, where's your word
For Strafford's other nest-egg, the Scots' war?

THE PURITAN His fruit shall be a fiery flying serpent.

FIENNES Shall be? It chips the shell, man; peeps abroad.

10   Twelve subsidies!—Why, how now, Vane?

RUDYARD   Peace, Fiennes!

FIENNES Ah?—But he was not more a dupe than I,
Or you, or any here, the day that Pym
Returned with the good news. Look up, friend Vane!
We all believed that Strafford meant us well

15   In summoning the Parliament.

HAMPDEN *enters.*

---

§ Stage Directions §   *1837: enters confusedly; among the first, the younger* VANE *and*
RUDYARD.   *1863: enters.*   1| *1837:* O   *1888:* Oh   3| *1837: A* PURITAN
[*entering*]—Out   *1863:* A PURITAN Out   4| *1837:* FIENNES [*entering*]—A
1863: FIENNES—A   7| *1837:* nest- egg—the Scots' War?   *1863:* nest-egg, the Scots'
war?   9| *1837:* abroad: *1863:* abroad.   10| *1837:* subsidies!— ¶ Why, how now
Vane? ¶ RUDYARD Hush, Fiennes!   *1863:* subsidies!—Why, how now, Vane? RUDYARD Peace,
Fiennes!   11| *1837:* Ah? . . . but   *1863:* Ah?—But   12| *1837:* here the   *1863:*
here, the   15| *1837:* the Parliament . . . ¶ (Hampden <> VANE [*Starting up*] Now

VANE   Now, Hampden,
Clear me! I would have leave to sleep again:
I'd look the People in the face again:
Clear me from having, from the first, hoped, dreamed
Better of Strafford!
HAMPDEN   You may grow one day
20 A steadfast light to England Henry Vane!
RUDYARD Meantime, by flashes I make shift to see
Strafford revived our Parliaments; before,
War was but talked of; there's an army, now:
Still, we've a Parliament! Poor Ireland bears
25 Another wrench (she dies the hardest death!)—
Why, speak of it in Parliament! and lo,
'Tis spoken, so console yourselves!
FIENNES   The jest!
We clamoured, I suppose, thus long, to win
The privilege of laying on our backs
30 A sorer burden than the King dares lay!
RUDYARD Mark now: we meet at length, complaints pour in
From every county, all the land cries out
On loans and levies, curses ship-money,
Calls vengeance on the Star Chamber; we lend
35 An ear. "Ay, lend them all the ears you have!"
Puts in the King; "my subjects, as you find,
Are fretful, and conceive great things of you.
Just listen to them, friends; you'll sanction me
The measures they most wince at, make them yours,
40 Instead of mine, I know: and, to begin,

1863: the Parliament. ¶ (Hampden <> VANE Now   ¹⁶| *1837*: again!   *1863*: again;
1868: again: ¹⁷| *1837*: again!   *1863*: again: ¹⁹| *1837*: of Strafford! Fool! ¶
HAMPDEN You'll grow   *1863*: of Strafford! ¶ HAMPDEN You may grow   *1888*: of Strafford ¶
HAMPDEN   ²⁰⁻²²| *1837*: to England, Henry Vane! ¶ RUDYARD Ay, Fiennes, / Strafford
<> Parliament: before,   *1863*: to England, Henry Vane! / RUDYARD Meantime, by flashes I
made shift to see / Strafford <> Parliaments: before,   *1888*: to England Henry
²⁴| *1837*: a Parliament.   *1863*: a Parliament!   ²⁵| *1837*: death!)   *1868*:
death!)—   ²⁶| *1837*: Why … speak <> and, lo,   *1863*: Why, speak   *1868*: and
lo,   ²⁷| *1837*: T'is spoken!—and console yourselves. ¶ FIENNES   *1863*: 'Tis spoken! so
console   *1868*: yourselves! ¶ FIENNES   ²⁹| *1837*: on ourselves   *1863*: on our
backs   ³⁰| *1837*: burthen   *1863*: burden   ³¹| *1837*: length: complaints   *1863*:
length, complaints   ³²| county: all   *1863*: county, all   ³⁴| *1837*: the
Star-chamber: we   *1863*: the Star-chamber; we   *1888*: Star Chamber   ³⁵| *1837*: ear:
"ay <> have,"   *1863*: ear. "Ay <> have!"   ³⁷| *1837*: you: *1863*: you.
³⁸| *1837*: friends: you'll   *1863*: friends; you'll   ³⁹| *1837*: yours   *1863*: yours,

They say my levies pinch them,—raise me straight
Twelve subsidies!"
FIENNES   All England cannot furnish
Twelve subsidies!
HOLLIS   But Strafford, just returned
From Ireland—what has he to do with that?
45 How could he speak his mind? He left before
The Parliament assembled. Pym, who knows
Strafford . . .
RUDYARD   Would I were sure we know ourselves!
What is for good, what, bad—who friend, who foe!
HOLLIS Do you count Parliaments no gain?
RUDYARD   A gain?
50 While the King's creatures overbalance us?
—There's going on, beside, among ourselves
A quiet, slow, but most effectual course
Of buying over, sapping, leavening
The lump till all is leaven. Glanville's gone.
55 I'll put a case; had not the Court declared
That no sum short of just twelve subsidies
Will be accepted by the King—our House,
I say, would have consented to that offer
To let us buy off ship-money!
HOLLIS   Most like,
60 If, say, six subsidies will buy it off,
The House . . .
RUDYARD   Will grant them! Hampden, do you hear?
Congratulate with me! the King's the king,
And gains his point at last—our own assent
To that detested tax? All's over, then!

42| *1837:* FIENNES *and others* All   *1863:* FIENNES All   44| *1837:* From Ireland . .
what *1863:* From Ireland—what   46–47| *1837:* assembled: Rudyard, friends, / He
could not speak his mind! and Pym, who knows / Strafford *1863:* assembled. Pym, who
knows / Strafford   53–55| *1837:* sapping, . . ¶ A PURITAN . . Leavening / The <> leaven.
¶ A VOICE Glanville's gone, / RUDYARD I'll *1863:* sapping, leavening / The <> leaven.
Glanville's gone. / I'll   57| *1837:* our House *1863:* our House,   58| *1837:*
Would <> that wretched offer *1863:* I say, would <> that offer   59| *1837:* off
Ship-money? *1863:* ship-money!   60| *1837:* If . . . say six subsidies, will *1863:* If, say,
six subsidies will   61| *1837:* RUDYARD . . Will *1863:* RUDYARD Will   62| *1837:*
Oh, I congratulate you that the King *1863:* Congratulate with me! the King's the
king,   63| *1837:* Has gained his <> last . . our *1863:* And gains his <>
last—our   64| *1837:* tax! all's over then! *1863:* over, then! *1868:* All's *1888:* tax?

65 There's no more taking refuge in this room,
Protesting, "Let the King do what he will,
We, England, are no party to our shame:
Our day will come!" Congratulate with me!

PYM *enters.*

VANE Pym, Strafford called this Parliament, you say,
70 But we'll not have our Parliaments like those
In Ireland, Pym!
RUDYARD   Let him stand forth, your friend!
One doubtful act hides far too many sins;
It can be stretched no more, and, to my mind,
Begins to drop from those it covered.
OTHER VOICES   Good!
75 Let him avow himself! No fitter time!
We wait thus long for you.
RUDYARD   Perhaps, too long!
Since nothing but the madness of the Court,
In thus unmasking its designs at once,
Has saved us from betraying England. Stay—
80 This Parliament is Strafford's: let us vote
Our list of grievances too black by far
To suffer talk of subsidies: or best,
That ship-money's disposed of long ago
By England: any vote that's broad enough:
85 And then let Strafford, for the love of it,
Support his Parliament!
VANE   And vote as well
No war to be with Scotland! Hear you, Pym?
We'll vote, no war! No part nor lot in it

All's   65| *1837:* room   *1863:* room,   66| *1837:* And saying, "Let   *1863:*
Protesting, "Let   67| *1837:* shame,—   *1863:* shame: 69| *1837:* this Parliament,
'tis like—   *1863:* this Parliament, you say,   71| *1837:* forth, that Strafford!   *1863:*
forth, your friend!   73| *1837:* more—and   *1863:* more, and   74| *1837:* covers. ¶
OTHER VOICES Pym,   *1863:* covered. ¶ OTHER VOICES Good!   76| *1837:* you! ¶
RUDYARD   *1863:* you. ¶ RUDYARD   77| *1837:* Court   *1863:* Court,   78| *1837:*
once   *1863:* once,   79| *1837:* Had saved   *1863:* Has saved   82| *1837:* best—
1863: best,   83| *1837:* Ship-money's   *1863:* ship-money's   84| *1837:* By
England; any   *1863:* By England: any   87| *1837:* war's to   *1868:* war to
88| *1837:* War   *1863:* war   89| *1837:* War   *1863:* war   90| *1837:* Bishop's

For England!

MANY VOICES Vote, no war! Stop the new levies!

90 No Bishops' war! At once! When next we meet!

PYM Much more when next we meet! Friends, which of you

Since first the course of Strafford was in doubt,

Has fallen the most away in soul from me?

VANE I sat apart, even now under God's eye,

95 Pondering the words that should denounce you, Pym,

In presence of us all, as one at league

With England's enemy.

PYM   You are a good

And gallant spirit, Henry. Take my hand

And say you pardon me for all the pain

100 Till now! Strafford is wholly ours.

MANY VOICES   Sure? sure?

PYM Most sure: for Charles dissolves the Parliament

While I speak here.

                    —And I must speak, friends, now!

Strafford is ours. The King detects the change,

Casts Strafford off for ever, and resumes

105 His ancient path: no Parliament for us,

No Strafford for the King!

                    Come, all of you,

To bid the King farewell, predict success

To his Scots' expedition, and receive

Strafford, our comrade now. The next will be

110 Indeed a Parliament!

VANE   Forgive me, Pym!

VOICES This looks like truth: Strafford can have, indeed

No choice.

PYM   Friends, follow me! He's with the King.

Come, Hampden, and come, Rudyard, and come, Vane

War *1863:* war *1868:* Bishops' ⁹¹| *1837:* meet! ¶—Friends *1863:* meet! ¶
Friends ⁹²| *1837:* doubt *1863:* doubt, ⁹⁴| *1837:* sate <> now, under
1863: sat *1888:* now under ⁹⁷| *1837:* enemy! ¶ PYM *1863:* enemy. ¶ PYM
⁹⁸| *1837:* spirit, Henry! Take *1863:* spirit, Henry. Take ¹⁰⁰| *1837:* VOICES 'Tis
sure? *1863:* VOICES Sure? sure? ¹⁰¹| *1837:* sure—for *1863:* sure: for
¹⁰²| *1837:* here! ... [*Great emotion in the assembly*] ¶..And *1863:* here. ¶—And
¹⁰³| *1837:* ours! The *1863:* ours. The ¹⁰⁵| *1837:* us— *1863:* us, ¹⁰⁶| *1837:*
the King! Come all of you *1863:* the King! Come, all of you, ¹⁰⁸| *1837:* Scots *1863:*
Scots' ¹⁰⁹| *1837:* now! The *1863:* now. The ¹¹¹| *1837:* truth—Strafford <>
indeed, *1863:* truth: Strafford *1888:* indeed ¹¹²| *1837:* choice! ¶ PYM <> he's
<> King: *1863:* choice. ¶ PYM <> He's <> King. ¹¹³| *1837:* Come Hampden,

This is no sullen day for England, sirs!
115 Strafford shall tell you!

VOICES   To Whitehall then! Come!

SCENE II—*Whitehall.*

CHARLES *and* STRAFFORD.

CHARLES Strafford!

STRAFFORD   Is it a dream? my papers, here—
Thus, as I left them, all the plans you found
So happy—(look! the track you pressed my hand
For pointing out)—and in this very room,
5   Over these very plans, you tell me, sir,
With the same face, too—tell me just one thing
That ruins them! How's this? What may this mean?
Sir, who has done this?

CHARLES   Strafford, who but I?
You bade me put the rest away: indeed
10 You are alone.

STRAFFORD   Alone, and like to be!
No fear, when some unworthy scheme grows ripe,
Of those, who hatched it, leaving me to loose
The mischief on the world! Laud hatches war,
Falls to his prayers, and leaves the rest to me,
15 And I'm alone.

CHARLES   At least, you knew as much
When first you undertook the war.

STRAFFORD   My liege,
Was this the way? I said, since Laud would lap

---

and come Rudyard, and come Vane—   *1863:* Come, Hampden, and come, Rudyard, and
come, Vane!   *1888:* Vane   ¹¹⁴| *1837:* for England, Vane!   *1863:* for England,
sirs!   ¹¹⁵| *1837:* Then! Come! [*Exeunt omnes*]   *1863:* Then! Come!
§ Stage Directions §   *1837:* CHARLES *seated,* STRAFFORD *standing beside a table covered with
maps, &c.   1863:* CHARLES *and* STRAFFORD.   ¹| *1837:* Strafford ... ¶ STRAFFORD   *1863:*
Strafford! ¶ STRAFFORD   ²| *1837:* Thus—as <> them—all   *1863:* Thus, as <> them,
all   ³| *1837:* The   *1863:* the   ⁴| *1837:* out!)—and <> room   *1863:*
out)—and <> room,   ⁵| *1837:* Sire,   *1863:* sir,   ⁶| *1837:* too,—tell   *1868:*
too—tell   ⁷| *1837:* what   *1863:* What   ⁸| *1837:* Sire <> Strafford, none but
1863: Sir <> Strafford, who but   ⁹| *1837:* away—indeed   *1863:* away: indeed
¹⁰| *1837:* alone! ¶ STRAFFORD Alone—and   *1863:* alone. ¶ STRAFFORD Alone, and
¹¹| *1837:* scheme's grown   *1868:* scheme grows   ¹²| *1837:* those who <> it leaving
you to   *1863:* those, who <> it, leaving me to   ¹⁴| *1837:* me—   *1863:* me,
¹⁵| *1837:* alone! ¶ CHARLES   *1863:* alone. ¶ CHARLES   ¹⁷| *1837:* Is this   *1863:* Was

43

A little blood, 'twere best to hurry over
The loathsome business, not to be whole months
20 At slaughter—one blow, only one, then, peace,
Save for the dreams. I said, to please you both
I'd lead an Irish army to the West,
While in the South an English . . . but you look
As though you had not told me fifty times
25 'Twas a brave plan! My army is all raised,
I am prepared to join it . . .
CHARLES   Hear me, Strafford!
STRAFFORD . . . When, for some little thing, my whole design
Is set aside—(where is the wretched paper?)
I am to lead—(ay, here it is)—to lead
30 The English army: why? Northumberland
That I appointed, chooses to be sick—
Is frightened: and, meanwhile, who answers for
The Irish Parliament? or army, either?
Is this my plan?
CHARLES   So disrespectful, sir?
35 STRAFFORD My liege, do not believe it! I am yours,
Yours ever: 'tis too late to think about:
To the death, yours. Elsewhere, this untoward step
Shall pass for mine; the world shall think it mine.
But here! But here! I am so seldom here,
40 Seldom with you, my King! I, soon to rush
Alone upon a giant in the dark!
CHARLES   My Strafford!
STRAFFORD [*examines papers awhile*]. "Seize the passes of the Tyne!"

---

this   **18|**   *1837:* o'er   *1863:* over   **19|**   *1837:* business—not   *1863:* business,
not   **20|**   *1837:* blow—only one—then, peace—   *1863:* blow, only one, then,
peace,   **21|**   *1837:* dreams! I   *1863:* dreams. I   **22|**   *1837:* Army   *1863:*
army   **23|**   *1837:* the South the English . . . . . but   *1863:* the South an English . . .
but   **25|**   *1837:* Army <> raised—   *1863:* army <> raised,   **30|**   *1837:* This
English Army   *1863:* The English army   **33|**   *1837:* Army   *1863:* army
34–35| *1837:* plan? / I say, is this my plan? / CHARLES You are disrespectful, Sir! ¶ STRAFFORD
Do not believe— / My <> yours—   *1863:* Is <> plan? ¶ CHARLES So disrespectful, sir? /
STRAFFORD My <> yours,   **36|**   *1837:* ever—'tis <> about—   *1863:* ever: 'tis <>
about: **37|**   *1837:* yours! Elsewhere   *1863:* yours. Elsewhere   **38|**   *1837:*
mine—the <> mine—   *1863:* mine; the <> mine.   **39|**   *1837:* But, here! But, here
<> here!   *1863:* seldom here,   *1888:* But here! but here! I   **40|**   *1837:* my King!
I—soon   *1863:* my King! I, soon   **41|**   *1837:* Alone—upon a Giant—in   *1863:* Alone
upon a giant in   **42|**   *1837:* STRAFFORD [*Seats himself at the table; examines papers*

But, sir, you see—see all I say is true?
My plan was sure to prosper, so, no cause
45 To ask the Parliament for help; whereas
We need them frightfully.

CHARLES   Need the Parliament?

STRAFFORD Now, for God's sake, sir, not one error more!
We can afford no error; we draw, now,
Upon our last resource: the Parliament
50 Must help us!

CHARLES   I've undone you, Strafford!

STRAFFORD   Nay—
Nay—why despond, sir, 'tis not come to that!
I have not hurt you? Sir, what have I said
To hurt you? I unsay it! Don't despond!
Sir, do you turn from me?

CHARLES   My friend of friends!

55 STRAFFORD We'll make a shift. Leave me the Parliament!
Help they us ne'er so little and I'll make
Sufficient out of it. We'll speak them fair.
They're sitting, that's one great thing; that half gives
Their sanction to us; that's much: don't despond!
60 Why, let them keep their money, at the worst!
The reputation of the People's help
Is all we want: we'll make shift yet!

CHARLES   Good Strafford!

STRAFFORD But meantime, let the sum be ne'er so small
They offer, we'll accept it: any sum—
65 For the look of it: the least grant tells the Scots

---

awhile; then, breaking off] .. "Seize <> Tyne" ...   *1863:* STRAFFORD [*examines papers*
awhile] "Seize <> Tyne"!   *1868:* Tyne!"   **43|** *1837:* But don't you   *1863:* But, sir,
you   **44|** *1837:* prosper,—so   *1863:* prosper, so   **46|** *1837:* them—frightfully ...
¶ CHARLES Need this Parliament?   *1863:* them frightfully. ¶ CHARLES Need the
Parliament?   **47|** *1837:*—Now <> sake, mind—not   *1863:* Now <> sake, sir,
not   **48|** *1837:* error—we   *1863:* error; we   **49|** *1837:* resource—this
Parliament   *1863:* resource: the Parliament   **51|** *1837:* Nay—don't
despond—Sire—'tis   *1863:* Nay—why despond, sir? 'tis   *1868:* sir, 'tis   **52|** *1837:*
you? Sire—what   *1863:* you? Sir, what   **53|** *1837:* you? I'll unsay   *1863:* you? I
unsay   **54|** *1837:* Sire   *1863:* Sir   **55|** *1837:* STRAFFORD [*after a pause*] We'll
<> shift! Leave   *1863:* STRAFFORD We'll <> shift. Leave   **56|** *1837:* They help us
<> little but I'll   *1863:* Help they us <> little and I'll   **57|** *1837:* A vast deal
out <> fair: *1863:* Sufficient out <> fair.   **58|** *1837:* sitting: that's <> thing: that
1863: sitting, that's <> thing; that   **59|** *1837:* us: that's   *1863:* us; that's
62| *1837:* CHARLES Dear Strafford!   *1863:* CHARLES Good Strafford!   **66|** *1837:* ours ...

The Parliament is ours—their staunch ally
Turned ours: that told, there's half the blow to strike!
What will the grant be? What does Glanville think?

CHARLES Alas!

STRAFFORD   My liege?

CHARLES   Strafford!

STRAFFORD   But answer me!

70 Have they . . . O surely not refused us half?
Half the twelve subsidies? We never looked
For all of them. How many do they give?

CHARLES You have not heard . . .

STRAFFORD (What has he done?)—Heard what?
But speak at once, sir, this grows terrible!

[*The* KING *continuing silent.*]

75 You have dissolved them!—I'll not leave this man.

CHARLES 'Twas old Vane's ill-judged vehemence.

STRAFFORD   Old Vane?

CHARLES He told them, just about to vote the half,
That nothing short of all twelve subsidies
Would serve our turn, or be accepted.

STRAFFORD   Vane!

80 Vane! Who, sir, promised me, that very Vane . . .
O God, to have it gone, quite gone from me,
The one last hope—I that despair, my hope—
That I should reach his heart one day, and cure
All bitterness one day, be proud again

85 And young again, care for the sunshine too,
And never think of Eliot any more,—
God, and to toil for this, go far for this,
Get nearer, and still nearer, reach this heart

their   *1863:* ours—their   67| *1837:* Is ours <> there's scarce a blow   *1863:* Turned
ours <> there's half the blow   69| *1837:* Alas . . . ¶ STRAFFORD <> Strafford . . . ¶
STRAFFORD   *1863:* Alas! ¶ STRAFFORD <> Strafford! ¶ STRAFFORD   70| *1837:* us all?
1863: us half?   71| *1837:* All the   *1863:* Half the   72| *1837:* them! How   *1868:*
them. How   74| *1837:* Sire—this   *1863:* sir, this   76| *1837:* 'Twas Vane—his
ill-judged vehemence that . . . ¶ STRAFFORD Vane?   *1863:* 'Twas old Vane's ill-judged
vehemence. ¶ STRAFFORD Old Vane?   77| *1837:* them, as they were about to vote   *1863:*
them, just about to vote the half   78| *1837:* The half, that nothing short of all the
twelve   *1863:* That nothing short of all twelve subsidies   80| *1837:* Vane! and you
promised me that   *1863:* Vane! Who, sir, promised   *1888:* me, that   81| *1837:* me
1863: me,   82| *1837: my*   *1868:* my   88| *1837:* heart—   *1863:* heart

And find Vane there!

    [*Suddenly taking up a paper, and continuing with a forced calmness.*]

                Northumberland is sick:

90 Well, then, I take the army: Wilmot leads
The horse, and he, with Conway, must secure
The passes of the Tyne: Ormond supplies
My place in Ireland. Here, we'll try the City:
If they refuse a loan—debase the coin
95 And seize the bullion! we've no other choice.
Herbert . . .

          And this while I am here! with you!
And there are hosts such, hosts like Vane! I go,
And, I once gone, they'll close around you, sir,
When the least pique, pettiest mistrust, is sure
100 To ruin me—and you along with me!
Do you see that? And you along with me!
—Sir, you'll not ever listen to these men,
And I away, fighting your battle? Sir,
If they—if She—charge me, no matter how—
105 Say you, "At any time when he returns
His head is mine!" Don't stop me there! You know
My head is yours, but never stop me there!

CHARLES Too shameful, Strafford! You advised the war,
And . . .

STRAFFORD I! I! that was never spoken with
110 Till it was entered on! That loathe the war!
That say it is the maddest, wickedest . . .
Do you know, sir, I think within my heart,
That you would say I did advise the war;
And if, through your own weakness, or what's worse,

90| *1837:* Well then <> Army   *1863:* army   *1868:* Well, then   91| *1837:* The
Horse, and he with Conway must   *1868:* The horse, and he, with Conway, must
94| *1837:* loan . . . debase   *1863:* loan—debase   96| *1837:* Herbert . . . ¶ [*Flinging
down the paper*] And   *1863:* Herbert . . . ¶ And   97| *1837:* go,—   *1863:* go,
98| *1837:* Sire,   *1863:* sir,   102| *1837:* Sire   *1863:* Sir   103| *1837:* Sire,   *1863:*
Sir,   104| *1837:* me—no matter what—   *1863:* me, no matter how—   105| *1837:*
You say, "At   *1863:* Say you, "At   106| *1837:* mine." Don't   *1863:* mine!"
Don't   107| *1837:* yours . : . only don't stop   *1863:* yours, but never stop
112| *1837:* know, Charles, I think, within   *1863:* know, sir, I   *1868:* think within
114| *1837:* thro' <> weakness, falsehood, Charles,   *1863:* through <> weakness, or what's

47

115 These Scots, with God to help them, drive me back,
You will not step between the raging People
And me, to say . . .
                    I knew it! from the first
I knew it! Never was so cold a heart!
Remember that I said it—that I never
120 Believed you for a moment!
                          —And, you loved me?
You thought your perfidy profoundly hid
Because I could not share the whisperings
With Vane, with Savile? What, the face was masked?
I had the heart to see, sir! Face of flesh,
125 But heart of stone—of smooth cold frightful stone!
Ay, call them! Shall I call for you? The Scots
Goaded to madness? Or the English—Pym—
Shall I call Pym, your subject? Oh, you think
I'll leave them in the dark about it all?
130 They shall not know you? Hampden, Pym shall not?

PYM, HAMPDEN, VANE, *etc., enter.*

    [*Dropping on his knee.*] Thus favoured with your gracious
        countenance
    What shall a rebel League avail against
    Your servant, utterly and ever yours?
    So, gentlemen, the King's not even left
135 The privilege of bidding me farewell
    Who haste to save the People—that you style
    Your People—from the mercies of the Scots
    And France their friend?
        [*To* CHARLES.]   Pym's grave grey eyes are fixed
    Upon you, sir!

---

worse,   115| *1837:* back . . .   *1863:* back,   117| *1837:* knew you! from   *1863:*
knew it! from   118| *1837:* knew you! Never   *1863:* knew it! Never   122| *1837:*
share your whisperings   *1863:* share the whisperings   123| *1837:* With Vane? With
Savile? But your hideous heart—   *1863:* With Vane? With Savile? What, the face was
masked?   *1868:* With Vane, with   124| *1837:* had your heart to see, Charles! Oh, to
have   *1863:* had the heart to see, sir! Face of flesh,   125| *1837:* A heart <> smooth,
cold, frightful   *1863:* But heart   *1868:* smooth cold frightful   130| *1837:* you?
Hampden, Pym shall not. . . .   *1863:* you? Hampden, Pym, shall not?   134| *1837:* [*To
the rest*] So, Gentlemen   *1863:* So, gentlemen   139| *1837:* you, Sire! ¶ [*To the rest*]

Your pleasure, gentlemen?

140 HAMPDEN The King dissolved us—'tis the King we seek
And not Lord Strafford.

STRAFFORD   —Strafford, guilty too
Of counselling the measure. [*To* CHARLES.] (Hush . . . you know—
You have forgotten—sir, I counselled it)
A heinous matter, truly! But the King

145 Will yet see cause to thank me for a course
Which now, perchance . . . (Sir, tell them so!)—he blames.
Well, choose some fitter time to make your charge:
I shall be with the Scots, you understand?
Then yelp at me!

                    Meanwhile, your Majesty

150 Binds me, by this fresh token of your trust . . .

[*Under the pretence of an earnest farewell,* STRAFFORD *conducts*
CHARLES *to the door, in such a manner as to hide his agita-*
tion from the rest: as the King disappears, they turn as by
one impulse to PYM, *who has not changed his original pos-*
ture of surprise.]

HAMPDEN Leave we this arrogant strong wicked man!

VANE AND OTHERS Hence, Pym! Come out of this unworthy place
To our old room again! He's gone.

[STRAFFORD, *just about to follow the* KING, *looks back.*]

PYM   Not gone!

[*To* STRAFFORD.] Keep tryst! the old appointment's made anew:

155 Forget not we shall meet again!

STRAFFORD   So be it!
And if an army follows me?

VANE   His friends

Your <> Gentlemen?   *1863:* you, sir! ¶ Your <> gentlemen?   ¹⁴¹| *1837:*
STRAFFORD . . . . Strafford   *1863:* STRAFFORD —Strafford   ¹⁴²| *1837:* measure: [*To*
CHARLES] (Hush . . you know . .   *1863:* measure. [*To* <> know—   *1868:* Hush . . .
you   ¹⁴³| *1837:* forgotten . . Sire <> it!)   *1863:* forgotten, sir <> it)
¹⁴⁴| *1837:*—[*Aloud*] A   *1863:* A   ¹⁴⁶| *1837:* perchance . . (Sire <> so!) . . he
1863: Sir <> so!)—he   *1868:* perchance . . . (Sir   ¹⁴⁷| *1837:* charge—   *1863:*
charge: ¹⁴⁸| *1837:* the Scots—you understand?—   *1863:* the Scots, you
understand?   ¹⁵⁰⁻¹⁵¹| § Stage Directions §   *1837: rest:* VANE *and others gazing at*
them: as   *1863: rest: as*   ¹⁵²| *1837:* Dear Pym   *1863:* Hence, Pym   ¹⁵³| *1837:*
again! Come, dearest Pym! ¶ [STRAFFORD   *1863:* again! He's gone. ¶ [STRAFFORD
¹⁵⁵| *1837:* STRAFFORD Be it so!   *1863:* STRAFFORD So be it!   ¹⁵⁶| *1837:* Army   *1863:*

Will entertain your army!

PYM   I'll not say
You have misreckoned, Strafford: time shows.

                                                        Perish
Body and spirit! Fool to feign a doubt,
160   Pretend the scrupulous and nice reserve
Of one whose prowess shall achieve the feat!
What share have I in it? Do I affect
To see no dismal sign above your head
When God suspends his ruinous thunder there?
165   Strafford is doomed. Touch him no one of you!

                          [PYM, HAMPDEN, *etc., go out.*]
STRAFFORD   Pym, we shall meet again!
LADY CARLISLE *enters.*

                                        You here, child?

LADY CARLISLE   Hush—
I know it all: hush, Strafford!
STRAFFORD   Ah? you know?
Well. I shall make a sorry soldier, Lucy!
All knights begin their enterprise, we read,
170   Under the best of auspices; 'tis morn,
The Lady girds his sword upon the Youth
(He's always very young)—the trumpets sound,
Cups pledge him, and, why, the King blesses him—
You need not turn a page of the romance
175   To learn the Dreadful Giant's fate. Indeed.
We've the fair Lady here; but she apart,—
A poor man, rarely having handled lance,
And rather old, weary, and far from sure

army   157| *1837:* Army   *1863:* army   158| *1837:* time will. . . . ¶ Perish
1863: time shows. Perish,   *1868:* time will. ¶ Perish   159| *1837:* doubt—   *1863:*
doubt,   161| *1837:* prowess is to do the   *1863:* prowess should achieve the   *1868:*
prowess shall achieve   162| *1837:* it? Shall I   *1868:* it? Do I   165| *1837:*
doomed!—Touch   *1863:* doomed. Touch   166| *1837:* Pym we <> here, girl? ¶ LADY
CARLISLE   *1863:* Pym, we <> here, child? ¶ LADY CARLISLE   167| *1837:* all—hush,
dearest Strafford <> Ah?   *1863:* all: hush, Strafford <> Ah? you know?   169| *1837:*
All Knights <> enterprise, you know,   *1863:* knights <> enterprise, we read,
170| *1837:* morn—   *1863:* morn,   171| Youth—   *1863:* Youth   172| *1837:*
sound—   *1863:* sound,   173| *1837:* and . . . and . . . the   *1863:* and, why, the
174| *1837:* Romance   *1868:* romance   175| *1837:* fate! Indeed   *1863:* fate.
Indeed.   177| *1837:* man, never having   *1863:* man, rarely having   179| *1837:*

His Squires are not the Giant's friends. All's one:
180 Let us go forth!

LADY CARLISLE   Go forth?

STRAFFORD   What matters it?
We shall die gloriously—as the book says.

LADY CARLISLE To Scotland? Not to Scotland?

STRAFFORD   Am I sick
Like your good brother, brave Northumberland?
Beside, these walls seem falling on me.

LADY CARLISLE   Strafford,
185 The wind that saps these walls can undermine
Your camp in Scotland, too. Whence creeps the wind?
Have you no eyes except for Pym? Look here!
A breed of silken creatures lurk and thrive
In your contempt. You'll vanquish Pym? Old Vane
190 Can vanquish you. And Vane you think to fly?
Rush on the Scots! Do nobly! Vane's slight sneer
Shall test success, adjust the praise, suggest
The faint result: Vane's sneer shall reach you there.
—You do not listen!

STRAFFORD   Oh,—I give that up!
195 There's fate in it: I give all here quite up.
Care not what old Vane does or Holland does
Against me! 'Tis so idle to withstand!
In no case tell me what they do!

LADY CARLISLE   But, Strafford . . .

STRAFFORD I want a little strife, beside; real strife;
200 This petty palace-warfare does me harm:
I shall feel better, fairly out of it.

friends: well—well—   *1863:* friends. All's one: *1868:* one.   *1888:* one: [182|]   *1837:*
not   *1888:* Not   [184|]   *1837:* Beside the walls <> me! ¶ LADY CARLISLE   *1863:* Beside,
these walls <> me. ¶ LADY CARLISLE   [186|]   *1837:* too! Whence   *1863:* too.
Whence   [189|]   *1837:* contempt; you'll <> Pym? Friend, Vane   *1863:* contempt.
You'll <> Pym? Old Vane   [190|]   *1837:* you! And <> fly?—   *1863:* fly?   *1868:* you.
And   [192|]   *1837:* success—adjust the praise—suggest   *1863:* success, adjust the praise,
suggest   [193|]   *1837:* there!   *1863:* there.   [194|]   *1837:* Oh . . I <> up—   *1863:*
Oh,—I <> up;   *1868:* up!   [195|]   *1837:* it—I   *1863:* it: I   [196|]   *1837:* what Vane
does or what Holland   *1863:* what old Vane does or Holland   [197|]   *1837:* withstand
them—   *1863:* withstand—   *1868:* withstand!   [198|]   *1837:* Strafford. . . .   *1863:*
Strafford . . .   *1868:* But, Strafford . . .   [199|]   *1837:* beside—real strife: *1863:* beside;
real strife;   [200|]   *1837:* petty, palace-warfare   *1888:* petty palace-warfare

LADY CARLISLE Why do you smile?

STRAFFORD   I got to fear them, child!

I could have torn his throat at first, old Vane's,

As he leered at me on his stealthy way

205 To the Queen's closet. Lord, one loses heart!

I often found it on my lips to say

"Do not traduce me to her!"

LADY CARLISLE   But the King . . .

STRAFFORD The King stood there, 'tis not so long ago,

—There; and the whisper, Lucy, "Be my friend

210 Of friends!"—My King! I would have . . .

LADY CARLISLE   . . . Died for him?

STRAFFORD Sworn him true, Lucy: I can die for him.

LADY CARLISLE But go not, Strafford! But you must renounce

This project on the Scots! Die, wherefore die?

Charles never loved you.

STRAFFORD   And he never will.

215 He's not of those who care the more for men

That they're unfortunate.

LADY CARLISLE   Then wherefore die

For such a master?

STRAFFORD   You that told me first

How good he was—when I must leave true friends

To find a truer friend!—that drew me here

220 From Ireland,—"I had but to show myself

And Charles would spurn Vane, Savile and the rest"—

You, child, to ask me this?

LADY CARLISLE   (If he have set

202| *1837:* them, girl! *1863:* them, child!   203| *1837:* first, that Vane, *1863:* first, old Vane's,   205| *1837:* closet, Lucy—but of late *1863:* closet. Lord, one loses heart!   206| *1837:* it in my heart to *1889:* it on my lips to   207| *1837:* "Vane—don't traduce *1863:* "Do not traduce   209| *1837:*—There, and *1863:*—There; and   211–212| *1837:* . . Sworn <> I will die <> / LADY CARLISLE [*Aside*] What can he mean? You'd say he loved him still! / [*To* STRAFFORD] But go not, Strafford! . . . But *1863:* Sworn <> I can die <> / LADY CARLISLE But go not, Strafford! But   213| *1837:* Die! wherefore *1868:* Die, wherefore   214| *1837:* you! ¶ STRAFFORD And he will not now: *1863:* you. ¶ STRAFFORD And he never will.   215| *1837:* for you *1863:* for men   216| *1837:* That you're unfortunate *1863:* That they're unfortunate   221| *1837:* spurn Vane, Savile, and *1868:* spurn Vane, Savile and   222| *1837:* You, girl, to <> that? ¶ LADY CARLISLE [*Aside*] If *1863:* You, child, to <> this? ¶ LADY

His heart abidingly on Charles!)
                                    Then, friend,
I shall not see you any more.
STRAFFORD   Yes, Lucy.
225 There's one man here I have to meet.
LADY CARLISLE   (The King!
What way to save him from the King?
                                    My soul—
That lent from its own store the charmed disguise
Which clothes the King—he shall behold my soul!)
Strafford,—I shall speak best if you'll not gaze
230 Upon me: I had never thought, indeed,
To speak, but you would perish too, so sure!
Could you but know what 'tis to bear, my friend,
One image stamped within you, turning blank
The else imperial brilliance of your mind,—
235 A weakness, but most precious,—like a flaw
I' the diamond, which should shape forth some sweet face
Yet to create, and meanwhile treasured there
Lest nature lose her gracious thought for ever!
STRAFFORD When could it be? no! Yet . . . was it the day
240 We waited in the anteroom, till Holland
Should leave the presence-chamber?
LADY CARLISLE   What?
STRAFFORD   —That I
Described to you my love for Charles?
LADY CARLISLE   (Ah, no—
One must not lure him from a love like that!

CARLISLE (If   223| 1837: Charles! ¶ [To STRAFFORD] Dear friend   1863: Charles!) ¶
Then, friend,   224| 1837: more! ¶ STRAFFORD Yes, girl—   1863: Yes, Lucy.   1868:
more. ¶ STRAFFORD   225| 1837: here that I shall meet! ¶ LADY CARLISLE [Aside] The
King!—   1863: here I have to meet. ¶ LADY CARLISLE (The King!   226| 1837: soul . .
1863: soul—   228| 1837: That clothes the King . . he <> soul!   1863: the King—he
<> soul!)   1888: Which clothes   229| 1837: [To STRAFFORD] Strafford . . . (I   1863:
Strafford,—I   230–232| 1837: me.) . . . You would perish, too! So sure! . . . / Could <>
my Strafford,   1863: me: I had never thought, indeed, / To speak, but you would perish, too!
So sure! / Could <> my friend,   1868: perish too, so   233| 1837: Image   1863:
image   236| 1837: diamond which   1863: diamond, which   238| 1837: Nature
<> ever! . . .   1863: ever!   1868: nature   239| 1837: be? . . . no! . . yet was   1863: be?
no! Yet . . was   1888: Yet . . . was   242| 1837: LADY CARLISLE [Aside] Ah   1863: LADY

Oh, let him love the King and die! 'Tis past.
245 I shall not serve him worse for that one brief
And passionate hope, silent for ever now!)
And you are really bound for Scotland then?
I wish you well: you must be very sure
Of the King's faith, for Pym and all his crew
250 Will not be idle—setting Vane aside!
STRAFFORD If Pym is busy,—you may write of Pym.
LADY CARLISLE What need, since there's your King to take your part?
He may endure Vane's counsel; but for Pym—
Think you he'll suffer Pym too . . .
STRAFFORD   Child, your hair
255 Is glossier than the Queen's!
LADY CARLISLE   Is that to ask
A curl of me?
STRAFFORD   Scotland——the weary way!
LADY CARLISLE Stay, let me fasten it.
                              —A rival's, Strafford?
STRAFFORD [*showing the George*]. He hung it there: twine yours around
    it, child!
LADY CARLISLE No—no—another time—I trifle so!
260 And there's a masque on foot. Farewell. The Court
Is dull; do something to enliven us
In Scotland: we expect it at your hands.
STRAFFORD I shall not fail in Scotland.
LADY CARLISLE   Prosper—if
You'll think of me sometimes!
STRAFFORD   How think of him
265 And not of you? of you, the lingering streak
(A golden one) in my good fortune's eve.
LADY CARLISLE Strafford . . . Well, when the eve has its last streak
The night has its first star.   [*She goes out.*]

CARLISLE (Ah   244| *1837:* past.....   *1863:* past.   246| *1837:* hope .. silent <>
now!   *1863:* hope, silent <> now!)   247| *1837:* [*To* STRAFFORD] And <> Scotland,
then?   *1863:* And   *1868:* Scotland then?   252| *1837:* need when there's your king
1863: need, since there's your King   254| *1837:* STRAFFORD Girl, your   *1863:* STRAFFORD
Child, your   258| *1837:* it, girl!   *1863:* it, child!   260| *1837:* foot: farewell:
the   *1863:* foot. Farewell. The   261| *1837:* dull: do   *1863:* dull; do   262| *1837:*
In Scotland; we   *1863:* In Scotland: we   265| *1837:* you? of you—the   *1863:* you? of
you, the   266| *1837:* eve?   *1863:* eve.   267| *1837:* Strafford....¶ Well   *1863:*
Strafford ... Well   268| *1837:* star! [*Exit*] ¶ STRAFFORD <> hers ...   *1863:* star.

STRAFFORD   That voice of hers—
You'd think she had a heart sometimes! His voice
270 Is soft too.
                 Only God can save him now.
Be Thou about his bed, about his path!
His path! Where's England's path? Diverging wide,
And not to join again the track my foot
Must follow—whither? All that forlorn way
275 Among the tombs! Far—far—till . . . What, they do
Then join again, these paths? For, huge in the dusk,
There's—Pym to face!
                 Why then, I have a foe
To close with, and a fight to fight at last
Worthy my soul! What, do they beard the King,
280 And shall the King want Strafford at his need?
Am I not here?
                 Not in the market-place,
Pressed on by the rough artisans, so proud
To catch a glance from Wentworth! They lie down
Hungry yet smile "Why, it must end some day:
285 Is he not watching for our sake?" Not there!
But in Whitehall, the whited sepulchre,
The . . .
                 Curse nothing to-night! Only one name
They'll curse in all those streets to-night. Whose fault?
Did I make kings? set up, the first, a man
290 To represent the multitude, receive

[*She goes out*] ¶ STRAFFORD <> hers—   271| *1837:* path! . . .   *1863:* path!
272| *1863:* wide   *1868:* wide,   274| *1837:* way—   *1863:* way   277| *1837:* then I
<> Foe   *1863:* then, I <> foe   279| *1837:* That's worth my soul! What—do <>
King—   *1863:* Worthy my soul! What, do <> King,   280| *1837:* need—   *1863:*
need?   281| *1837:* My King—at his great need? am I not here? / . . . .Not in the common
blessed market-place   *1863:* Am I not here? Not in the market place,   *1868:* here? ¶
Not   283| *1837:* from Wentworth! They'll lie   *1868:* from Wentworth! They
lie   284| *1837:* Hungry and say "Why <> day—   *1863:* and smile "Why   *1868:*
Hungry yet smile <> day: 285| *1837:* sake?" ¶—Not   *1868:* sake?" Not
286| *1837:* in Whitehall—the <> sepulchre—   *1863:* in Whitehall, the <>
sepulchre,   287| *1837:* The . . . ¶ [*At the Window, and looking on London*] ¶ Curse
1863: The . . . ¶ Curse   288| *1837:* to-night! Whose   *1863:* to-night. Whose
289| *1837:* kings—set   *1863:* kings? set   291| *1837:* them—supplanting them   *1863:*

55

All love in right of them—supplant them so,
Until you love the man and not the king——
The man with the mild voice and mournful eyes
Which send me forth.
                              —To breast the bloody sea
295 That sweeps before me: with one star for guide.
    Night has its first, supreme, forsaken star.

---

them—supplant them so,   294| *1837:* That send me forth . . . ¶ To   *1863:* Which send
me forth. ¶ —To   295| *1837:* me—with one star to guide—   *1863:* me: with one star
for guide.   296| *1837:* first supreme forsaken star! ¶ [*Exit*]   *1863:* first, supreme,
forsaken star.

ACT III

SCENE I—*Opposite Westminster Hall.*

SIR HENRY VANE, LORD SAVILE, LORD HOLLAND *and others of the Court.*

SIR H. VANE The Commons thrust you out?

SAVILE   And what kept you
From sharing their civility?

SIR H. VANE   Kept me?
Fresh news from Scotland, sir! worse than the last,
If that may be. All's up with Strafford there:

5 Nothing to bar the mad Scots marching hither
Next Lord's-day morning. That detained me, sir!
Well now, before they thrust you out,—go on,—
Their Speaker—did the fellow Lenthal say
All we set down for him?

HOLLAND   Not a word missed.

10 Ere he began, we entered, Savile, I
And Bristol and some more, with hope to breed
A wholesome awe in the new Parliament.
But such a gang of graceless ruffians, Vane,
As glared at us!

VANE   So many?

SAVILE   Not a bench

15 Without its complement of burly knaves;
Your hopeful son among them: Hampden leant

---

³| *1837:* last *1863:* last,   ⁴| *1837:* be! all's <> there!   *1863:* All's <> there:
1868: be. All's   ⁵| *1837:* Nothing's   *1863:* Nothing   ⁶| *1837:* The next fine
morning! That   *1863:* Next Lord's-day morning. That   ⁷| *1837:* out, go on,   *1863:*
out,—go on,—   ⁸| *1837:* Their speaker . . . did <> Lenthall   *1863:* Their
Speaker—did   *1868:* Lenthal   ⁹| *1837:* missed!   *1863:* missed.   ¹¹| *1837:*
more, in hopes   *1863:* more, with hope   ¹²| *1837:* Parliament——   *1863:*
Parliament.   ¹³| *1837:* Vane!   *1863:* Vane,   ¹⁴| *1837:* us. . . . ¶ VANE   *1863:*
us! ¶ VANE   ¹⁵| *1837:* knaves—   *1863:* knaves;   ¹⁶| *1837:* Your son, there,

Upon his shoulder—think of that!

VANE   I'd think
On Lenthal's speech, if I could get at it.
Urged he, I ask, how grateful they should prove
20   For this unlooked-for summons from the King?

HOLLAND Just as we drilled him.

VANE   That the Scots will march
On London?

HOLLAND   All, and made so much of it,
A dozen subsidies at least seemed sure
To follow, when . . .

VANE   Well?

HOLLAND   'Tis a strange thing, now!
25   I've a vague memory of a sort of sound,
A voice, a kind of vast unnatural voice—
Pym, sir, was speaking! Savile, help me out:
What was it all?

SAVILE   , Something about "a matter"—
No,—"work for England."

HOLLAND   "England's great revenge"
30   He talked of.

SAVILE   How should I get used to Pym
More than yourselves?

HOLLAND   However that be,
'Twas something with which we had nought to do,
For we were "strangers" and 'twas "England's work"—
(All this while looking us straight in the face)
35   In other words, our presence might be spared.
So, in the twinkling of an eye, before
I settled to my mind what ugly brute
Was likest Pym just then, they yelled us out,

Vane, among them—Hampden   *1863:* Your hopeful son among them: Hampden
18| Lenthall's <> it . . .   *1863:* it.   *1868:* Lenthall's   **19|** *1837:* He said, I hope, how
<> should be   *1863:* Urged he, I ask, how <> should prove   **21|** *1837:* him . . . ¶
VANE   *1863:* him. ¶ VANE   **22|** *1837:* it   *1863:* it,   **24|** *1837:* thing now!
1888: thing, now!   **25|** *1837:* sound—   *1863:* sound,   **26|** *1837:* A voice—a <>
vast, unnatural   *1863:* A voice, a   *1868:* vast unnatural   **27|** Sir <> out,—   *1863:*
sir <> out: **28|** *1837:* matter" . . .   *1863:* matter"—   **29|** *1837:* No . . "a work
for England." ¶ BRISTOL "England's   *1863:* No,—"a <> England." ¶ HOLLAND "England's
1868: No,—"work   **30|** *1837:* should I be used   *1863:* should I get used
31| *1837:* that may be,   *1868:* that be,   **35|** *1837:* spared: *1863:* spared.

Locked the doors after us, and here are we.

40 VANE Eliot's old method . . .

SAVILE   Prithee, Vane, a truce
To Eliot and his times, and the great Duke,
And how to manage Parliaments! 'Twas you
Advised the Queen to summon this: why, Strafford
(To do him justice) would not hear of it.

45 VANE Say rather, you have done the best of turns
To Strafford: he's at York, we all know why.
I would you had not set the Scots on Strafford
Till Strafford put down Pym for us, my lord!

SAVILE Was it I altered Strafford's plans? did I . . .

A MESSENGER *enters.*

50 MESSENGER The Queen, my lords—she sends me: follow me
At once; 'tis very urgent! she requires
Your counsel: something perilous and strange
Occasions her command.

SAVILE   We follow, friend!
Now, Vane;—your Parliament will plague us all!

55 VANE No Strafford here beside!

SAVILE   If you dare hint
I had a hand in his betrayal, sir . . .

HOLLAND Nay, find a fitter time for quarrels—Pym
Will overmatch the best of you; and, think,
The Queen!

VANE   Come on, then: understand, I loathe

39| *1837:* we! *1863:* we.   40| *1837:* Old Eliot's method . . . ¶ SAVILE Ah, now, Vane
1863: Eliot's old method . . . ¶ SAVILE Prithee, Vane   43| *1837:* this—why Strafford
1863: this: why, Strafford   44| *1837:* To do him justice would <> it! *1863:* (To do
him justice) would <> it.   45| *1837:* Say, rather *1868:* Say rather   46| *1837:*
To Strafford—he's at York—we <> why! *1863:* To Strafford: he's at York, we <>
why.   48| *1837:* Till he had put *1863:* Till Strafford put   49| *1837:* I? did I
alter Strafford's *1863:* SAVILE Was it I altered Strafford's   50| *1837:* lords . . she
sends me . . follow *1863:* lords—she sends me: follow   51| *1837:* once . . 'tis very
urgent . . she would have *1863:* once; 'tis very urgent! she requires   52| *1837:* counsel
. . something *1863:* counsel: something   54| *1837:* Now Vane . . your *1863:* Now,
Vane;—your   56| *1837:* Sir . . . *1863:* sir . . .   57| *1837:* Nay find *1863:* Nay,
find   59| *1837:* on then [*as they go out*] . . . understand *1863:* on, then:

59

Strafford as much as any—but his use!
To keep off Pym, to screen a friend or two,
I would we had reserved him yet awhile.

SCENE II—*Whitehall.*

The QUEEN *and* LADY CARLISLE.

QUEEN It cannot be.
LADY CARLISLE   It is so.
QUEEN   Why, the House
Have hardly met.
LADY CARLISLE   They met for that.
QUEEN   No, no!
Meet to impeach Lord Strafford? 'Tis a jest.
LADY CARLISLE A bitter one.
QUEEN   Consider! 'Tis the House
5 We summoned so reluctantly, which nothing
But the disastrous issue of the war
Persuaded us to summon. They'll wreak all
Their spite on us, no doubt; but the old way
Is to begin by talk of grievances:
10 They have their grievances to busy them.
LADY CARLISLE Pym has begun his speech.
QUEEN   Where's Vane?—That is,
Pym will impeach Lord Strafford if he leaves
His Presidency; he's at York, we know,
Since the Scots beat him: why should he leave York?
15 LADY CARLISLE Because the King sent for him.

---

understand   60| *1837:* but he serves   *1863:* but his use!   61| *1837:* So well to
keep off Pym—to screen us all!   *1863:* To keep <> screen a friend or two!   *1868:* off Pym,
to <> two,   62| *1837:* awhile! [*Exeunt*]   *1863:* awhile.
1| *1837:* be! ¶ LADY CARLISLE <> Why the   *1863:* be. ¶ LADY CARLISLE <> Why, the
2| *1837:* met! ¶ LADY CARLISLE <> No—no—   *1863:* met. ¶ LADY CARLISLE <> No,
no!   3| *1837:* impeach Lord Strafford! 'Tis a jest!   *1863:* impeach Lord Strafford? 'Tis
a jest.   5| *1837:* reluctantly—which   *1863:* reluctantly, which   7| *1837:*
summon; they'll   *1863:* summon. They'll   9| *1837:* grievances!   *1863:*
grievances: 10| *1837:* them!   *1863:* them.   11| *1837:* speech. ¶ QUEEN Where's
Vane? .. That is   *1863:* speech. ¶ QUEEN Where's Vane?—That is,   13| *1837:* His
Presidency—he's at York, you know,   *1863:* His Presidency; he's at York, we know,
14| *1837:* him—why   *1863:* him: why   15| *1837:* sends <> Ah ... but   *1863:* sent

QUEEN   Ah—but if
The King did send for him, he let him know
We had been forced to call a Parliament—
A step which Strafford, now I come to think,
Was vehement against.
LADY CARLISLE   The policy
20 Escaped him, of first striking Parliaments
To earth, then setting them upon their feet
And giving them a sword: but this is idle.
Did the King send for Strafford? He will come.
QUEEN And what am I to do?
LADY CARLISLE   What do? Fail, madam!
25 Be ruined for his sake! what matters how,
So it but stand on record that you made
An effort, only one?
QUEEN   The King away
At Theobald's!
LADY CARLISLE Send for him at once: he must
Dissolve the House.
QUEEN   Wait till Vane finds the truth
30 Of the report: then . . .
LADY CARLISLE   —It will matter little
What the King does. Strafford that lends his arm
And breaks his heart for you!

SIR H. VANE *enters.*

VANE   The Commons, madam,
Are sitting with closed doors. A huge debate,

<> Ah—but   19| *1837:* against . . . ¶ LADY CARLISLE   *1863:* against. ¶ LADY
CARLISLE   20| *1837:* him of   *1863:* him, of   22| *1837:* idle!   *1863:* idle.
23| *1837:*—Did <> Strafford? ¶ He   *1863:* Did <> Strafford? He   24| *1837:*
Madam!   *1863:* madam!   25| *1837:* how   *1863:* how,   27| *1837:* effort—only
<> King's   *1863:* effort, only   *1868:* King   28| *1837:* Theobald's ¶ LADY CARLISLE
<> once—he   *1863:* Theobalds ¶ LADY CARLISLE <> once: he   *1868:* Theobald's! ¶ LADY
CARLISLE   30| *1837:* report—then . . ¶ LADY CARLISLE . . it   *1863:* report: then . . ¶ LADY
CARLISLE—It   *1888:* then . . . ¶ LADY CARLISLE   31| *1837:* king <> that serves you
all—   *1863:* King <> that lends his arm,   *1868:* arm   32| *1837:* That's fighting for
you now! ¶ [VANE *enters*] VANE <> Madam,   *1863:* And breaks his heart for you! ¶ VANE
enters VANE <> madam,   33| *1837:* doors—a huge debate—   *1863:* doors. A huge

61

No lack of noise; but nothing, I should guess,
35 Concerning Strafford: Pym has certainly
Not spoken yet.
QUEEN [*to* LADY CARLISLE]. You hear?
LADY CARLISLE   I do not hear
That the King's sent for!
VANE   Savile will be able
To tell you more.

HOLLAND *enters.*

QUEEN   The last news, Holland?
HOLLAND   Pym
Is raging like a fire. The whole House means
40 To follow him together to Whitehall
And force the King to give up Strafford.
QUEEN   Strafford?
HOLLAND If they content themselves with Strafford! Laud
Is talked of, Cottington and Windebank too.
Pym has not left out one of them—I would
45 You heard Pym raging!
QUEEN   Vane, go find the King!
Tell the King, Vane, the People follow Pym
To brave us at Whitehall!

SAVILE *enters.*

SAVILE   Not to Whitehall—
'Tis to the Lords they go: they seek redress
On Strafford from his peers—the legal way,
50 They call it.
QUEEN   (Wait, Vane!)
SAVILE   But the adage gives

---

debate,   34| *1837:* noise—but   *1863:* noise; but   39| *1837:* Is raving like a
fiend! The   *1863:* Is raging like a fire. The   43| *1837:* too,   *1868:* too.
44| *1837:* them .. I   *1863:* them—I   45| *1837:* heard Pym raving! ¶ QUEEN Vane, find
out the   *1863:* heard Pym raging! ¶ QUEEN Vane, go find the
46| *1837:* king   *1863:* King   48| *1837:* go—they'll seek   *1863:* go: they'll   *1868:* go:
they seek   50| *1837:* it ... ¶ QUEEN <> SAVILE .. But   *1863:* it. ¶ QUEEN <> SAVILE

Long life to threatened men. Strafford can save
Himself so readily: at York, remember,
In his own county: what has he to fear?
The Commons only mean to frighten him
55 From leaving York. Surely, he will not come.
QUEEN Lucy, he will not come!
LADY CARLISLE   Once more, the King
Has sent for Strafford. He will come.
VANE   Oh doubtless!
And bring destruction with him: that's his way.
What but his coming spoilt all Conway's plan?
60 The King must take his counsel, choose his friends,
Be wholly ruled by him! What's the result?
The North that was to rise, Ireland to help,—
What came of it? In my poor mind, a fright
Is no prodigious punishment.
LADY CARLISLE   A fright?
65 Pym will fail worse than Strafford if he thinks
To frighten him. [*To the* QUEEN.] You will not save him then?
SAVILE When something like a charge is made, the King
Will best know how to save him: and 'tis clear,
While Strafford suffers nothing by the matter,
70 The King may reap advantage: this in question,
No dinning you with ship-money complaints!
QUEEN [*to* LADY CARLISLE]. If we dissolve them, who will pay the
    army?
Protect us from the insolent Scots?
LADY CARLISLE   In truth,
I know not, madam. Strafford's fate concerns
75 Me little: you desired to learn what course
Would save him: I obey you.
VANE   Notice, too,

But   51| *1837:* men! Strafford *1863:* men. Strafford   53| *1837:* county, what
1868: county: what   55| *1837:* York. ¶ QUEEN Surely he   *1863:* York. Surely, he
56| *1837:* Carlisle, he   *1863:* Lucy, he   57| *1837:* for Strafford—He <> O
doubtless;   *1863:* for Strafford. He <> Oh, doubtless!   *1868:* Hast <> Oh doubtless!
1888: Has   58| *1837:* him; that's   *1868:* him: that's   62| *1837:* rise—Ireland to
help—   *1863:* rise, Ireland to help,—   63| *1837:* mind a   *1863:* mind, a
66| *1837:* save him, then?   *1868:* save him then?   68| *1837:* clear   *1863:* clear,
69| *1837:* That, while he suffers   *1863:* While Strafford suffers   70| *1837:* The King
will reap   *1863:* The King may reap   73| *1837:* truth   *1868:* truth,   74| *1837:*

There can't be fairer ground for taking full
Revenge—(Strafford's revengeful)—than he'll have
Against his old friend Pym.

QUEEN   Why, he shall claim
80 Vengeance on Pym!

VANE   And Strafford, who is he
To 'scape unscathed amid the accidents
That harass all beside? I, for my part,
Should look for something of discomfiture
Had the King trusted me so thoroughly
85 And been so paid for it.

HOLLAND   He'll keep at York:
All will blow over: he'll return no worse,
Humbled a little, thankful for a place
Under as good a man. Oh, we'll dispense
With seeing Strafford for a month or two!

STRAFFORD *enters.*

90 QUEEN You here!

STRAFFORD   The King sends for me, madam.

QUEEN   Sir,
The King . . .

STRAFFORD   An urgent matter that imports the King!
[*To* LADY CARLISLE.] Why, Lucy, what's in agitation now,
That all this muttering and shrugging, see,
Begins at me? They do not speak!

LADY CARLISLE   'Tis welcome!
95 For we are proud of you—happy and proud
To have you with us, Strafford! You were staunch
At Durham: you did well there! Had you not

not, Madam: Strafford's   *1863:* madam. Strafford's   ^{79|} *1837:* Against this very
Pym   *1863:* Against his old friend Pym   ^{86|} *1837:* worse— *1863:* worse,
^{87|}   *1837:* little—thankful   *1863:* little, thankful   ^{88|} *1837:* man—Oh   *1863:* man.
Oh   ^{90|} *1837:* me, Madam. ¶ QUEEN Sir . . .   *1863:* madam ¶ QUEEN Sir,   *1888:*
madam, ¶ QUEEN   *1889:* madam. ¶ QUEEN   ^{91|} *1837:* imports the King . . .   *1863:*
imports the King.   *1868:* imports the King!   ^{92|} *1837:* now   *1868:* now,
^{94|}   *1837:* speak! ¶ LADY CARLISLE Oh welcome!   *1863:* speak! ¶ LADY CARLISLE 'Tis
welcome!   ^{95|} *1837:* . . And we <> you . . . all very proud   *1863:* For we <>
you—happy and proud   ^{96|} *1837:* us, Strafford . . you were brave   *1863:* us, Strafford!
you were staunch   *1868:* you   ^{97|} *1837:* At Durham . . You <> there . . Had   *1863:*

Been stayed, you might have . . . . we said, even now,
Our hope's in you!

VANE [*to* LADY CARLISLE]. The Queen would speak with you.

100 STRAFFORD Will one of you, his servants here, vouchsafe
To signify my presence to the King?

SAVILE An urgent matter?

STRAFFORD   None that touches you,
Lord Savile! Say, it were some treacherous
Sly pitiful intriguing with the Scots—
105 You would go free, at least! (They half divine
My purpose!) Madam, shall I see the King?
The service I would render, much concerns
His welfare.

QUEEN   But his Majesty, my lord,
May not be here, may . . .

STRAFFORD   Its importance, then,
110 Must plead excuse for this withdrawal, madam,
And for the grief it gives Lord Savile here.

QUEEN [*who has been conversing with* VANE *and* HOLLAND]. The King
will see you, sir!

[*To* LADY CARLISLE.] Mark me: Pym's worst
Is done by now: he has impeached the Earl,
Or found the Earl too strong for him, by now.
115 Let us not seem instructed! We should work
No good to Strafford, but deform ourselves
With shame in the world's eye. [*To* STRAFFORD.] His Majesty
Has much to say with you.

STRAFFORD   Time fleeting, too!

At Durham: you <> there! Had   98| *1837:* stayed you   *1863:* stayed, you
99| *1837:* Our last, last hope's <> speak ¶ A word with you!   *1863:* Our hope's <> speak
with you.   100| *1837:* STRAFFORD [*To* VANE] Will one of you vouchsafe   *1863:*
STRAFFORD Will one of you, his servants here, vouchsafe   102| *1837:* you   *1863:*
you,   103| *1837:* Lord Savile! Say it <> treacherous,   *1863:* Lord Savile! Say, it
1868: treacherous   104| *1837:* Sly, pitiful   *1868:* Sly pitiful   105| *1837:* least!
[*Aside*] They   *1863:* least! (They   106| *1837:* purpose! [*To the* QUEEN]
Madam   *1863:* purpose!) Madam   107| *1837:* render much   *1863:* render,
much   110| *1837:* withdrawal, Madam—   *1863:* withdrawal, madam,
112| *1837:* you, Sir. ¶ [*To*   *1863:* sir   *1868:* sir! ¶ [*To*   113| *1837:* now—he
1863: now: he   114| *1837:* now;   *1863:* now.   117| *1837:* eye! [*To*   *1863:* eye.
[*To*   118| *1837:* you. ¶ STRAFFORD [*Aside*] Time   *1863:* you. ¶ STRAFFORD

65

[*To* LADY CARLISLE.] No means of getting them away? And She—

120 What does she whisper? Does she know my purpose?

What does she think of it? Get them away!

QUEEN [*to* LADY CARLISLE]. He comes to baffle Pym—he thinks the danger

Far off: tell him no word of it! a time

For help will come; we'll not be wanting then.

125 Keep him in play, Lucy—you, self-possessed

And calm! [*To* STRAFFORD.] To spare your lordship some delay

I will myself acquaint the King. [*To* LADY CARLISLE.] Beware!

[*The* QUEEN, VANE, HOLLAND, *and* SAVILE *go out.*]

STRAFFORD She knows it?

LADY CARLISLE   Tell me, Strafford!

STRAFFORD   Afterward!

This moment's the great moment of all time.

130 She knows my purpose?

LADY CARLISLE   Thoroughly: just now

She bade me hide it from you.

STRAFFORD   Quick, dear child,

The whole o' the scheme?

LADY CARLISLE   (Ah, he would learn if they

Connive at Pym's procedure! Could they but

Have once apprised the King! But there's no time

135 For falsehood, now.) Strafford, the whole is known.

STRAFFORD Known and approved?

LADY CARLISLE   Hardly discountenanced.

STRAFFORD And the King—say, the King consents as well?

Time $^{119|}$ *1837:* away, Carlisle?   *1863:* away? And She— $^{123|}$ *1837:* off—tell
<> it—a   *1863:* off: tell <> it! a $^{124|}$ *1837:* come—we'll not be wanting, then!
1863: come; we'll not be wanting then. $^{125|}$ *1837:* play, Carlisle—you   *1863:* play,
Lucy—you $^{126|}$ *1837:* Lordship   *1863:* Lord- ship   *1868:* lordship
$^{128|}$ *1837:* me, Strafford. . . . ¶ STRAFFORD   *1863:* me, Strafford! ¶ STRAFFORD
$^{129|}$ *1837:* The moment's <> time!   *1863:* This moment's <> time.
$^{130|}$ *1837:* purpose? ¶ LADY CARLISLE Thoroughly—just
1863: purpose? ¶ LADY CARLISLE Thoroughly: just $^{131|}$ *1837:*
dear girl . . . *1863:* dear child, $^{132|}$ *1837:* whole grand scheme? ¶ LADY CARLISLE
[*Aside*] Ah   *1863:* whole o' the scheme? ¶ LADY CARLISLE (Ah $^{135|}$ *1837:* now. [*To*
STRAFFORD] Strafford   *1863:* now.) Strafford $^{137|}$ *1837:* king—say the king   *1863:*

LADY CARLISLE The King's not yet informed, but will not dare
To interpose.
STRAFFORD   What need to wait him, then?
140 He'll sanction it! I stayed, child, tell him, long!
It vexed me to the soul—this waiting here.
You know him, there's no counting on the King.
Tell him I waited long!
LADY CARLISLE   (What can he mean?
Rejoice at the King's hollowness?)
STRAFFORD   I knew
145 They would be glad of it,—all over once,
I knew they would be glad: but he'd contrive,
The Queen and he, to mar, by helping it.
An angel's making.
LADY CARLISLE   (Is he mad?) Dear Strafford,
You were not wont to look so happy.
STRAFFORD   Sweet,
150 I tried obedience thoroughly. I took
The King's wild plan: of course, ere I could reach
My army, Conway ruined it. I drew
The wrecks together, raised all heaven and earth,
And would have fought the Scots: the King at once
155 Made truce with them. Then, Lucy, then, dear child,
God put it in my mind to love, serve, die
For Charles, but never to obey him more!
While he endured their insolence at Ripon
I fell on them at Durham. But you'll tell
160 The King I waited? All the anteroom

---

the King—say, the King   138| 1837: king's   1863: King's   140| 1837: stayed,
girl tell   1863: stayed, child, tell   141| 1837: here—   1863: here.   142| 1837:
him—there's <> king!   1863: him, there's <> King.   143| 1837: long! ¶ LADY
CARLISLE [Aside] What   1863: long! ¶ LADY CARLISLE (What   144| 1837: king's
hollowness? ¶ STRAFFORD   1863: the King's hollowness?) ¶ STRAFFORD   146| 1837: glad
... but   1863: glad: but   148| 1837: making! ¶ LADY CARLISLE [Aside] Is he mad?
[To STRAFFORD] Dear   1863: making. ¶ LADY CARLISLE (Is he mad?) Dear   149| 1837:
happy. ¶ STRAFFORD Girl,   1863: happy. ¶ STRAFFORD Sweet,   150| 1837: thoroughly:
I   1863: thoroughly. I   151| 1837: king's wild plan ... of   1863: The King's wild
plan: of   152| 1837: army—Conway <> it: I   1863: army, Conway <> it. I
154| 1837: the Scots—the   1863: the Scots: the   155| 1837: them: then, Lucy, then,
dear girl,   1863: them. Then, Lucy, then, dear child,   157| 1837: For Charles—but
1863: For Charles, but   158| 1837: Rippon   1863: Ripon   159| 1837: at
Durham! ¶ ... But   1863: at Durham. But   160| 1837: king   1863: King

67

Is filled with my adherents.

LADY CARLISLE   Strafford—Strafford,
What daring act is this you hint?

STRAFFORD   No, no!
'Tis here, not daring if you knew? all here!

[*Drawing papers from his breast.*]

Full proof, see, ample proof—does the Queen know
165 I have such damning proof? Bedford and Essex,
Brooke, Warwick, Savile (did you notice Savile?
The simper that I spoilt?), Saye, Mandeville—
Sold to the Scots, body and soul, by Pym!

LADY CARLISLE Great heaven!

STRAFFORD   From Savile and his lords, to Pym
170 And his losels, crushed!—Pym shall not ward the blow
Nor Savile creep aside from it! The Crew
And the Cabal—I crush them!

LADY CARLISLE   And you go—
Strafford,—and now you go?—

STRAFFORD   —About no work
In the background, I promise you! I go
175 Straight to the House of Lords to claim these knaves.
Mainwaring!

LADY CARLISLE Stay—stay, Strafford!

STRAFFORD   She'll return,
The Queen—some little project of her own!
No time to lose: the King takes fright perhaps.

LADY CARLISLE Pym's strong, remember!

STRAFFORD   Very strong, as fits

161| *1837:* adherents. ¶ LADY CARLISLE Strafford—Strafford   *1863:* adherents. ¶ LADY
CARLISLE Strafford—Strafford,   162| *1837:* hint? ¶ STRAFFORD No—No!   *1863:* hint? ¶
STRAFFORD No, no!   163| *1837:* here—not < > knew!—all   *1863:* here, not < > knew!
all   *1888:* knew? all   164| *1837:* proof—see—ample   *1863:* proof, see, ample
166| *1837:* Broke   *1868:* Brooke   167| *1837:* spoilt?) Say   *1863:* Saye   *1888:* spoilt?),
Saye   169| *1837:* to Pym—   *1863:* to Pym   170| *1837:* I crush them,
girl—Pym   *1863:* And his losels, crushed!—Pym   171| *1837:* Nor Savile crawl aside
< > The Court   *1863:* Nor Savile creep aside < > The Crew   172| *1837:* go . . .
1863: go—   173| *1837:* go? . . . ¶ STRAFFORD About   *1863:* go?— ¶
STRAFFORD—About   174| *1837:* back-ground   *1863:* background   175| *1837:*
these men.   *1863:* these knaves.   176| *1837:* return—   *1863:* return,
177| *1837:* own—   *1863:* own!   178| *1837:* lose—the < > perhaps—   *1863:* lose: the
< > perhaps.   179| *1837:* remember! ¶ STRAFFORD Very strong—as   *1863:* remember!

180 The Faction's head—with no offence to Hampden,
    Vane, Rudyard and my loving Hollis: one
    And all they lodge within the Tower to-night
    In just equality. Brian! Mainwaring!

[Many of his ADHERENTS enter.]

    The Peers debate just now (a lucky chance)
185 On the Scots' war; my visit's opportune.
    When all is over, Bryan, you proceed
    To Ireland: these dispatches, mark me, Bryan,
    Are for the Deputy, and these for Ormond:
    We want the army here—my army, raised
190 At such a cost, that should have done such good,
    And was inactive all the time! no matter,
    We'll find a use for it. Willis . . . or, no—you!
    You, friend, make haste to York: bear this, at once . . .
    Or,—better stay for form's sake, see yourself
195 The news you carry. You remain with me
    To execute the Parliament's command,
    Mainwaring! Help to seize these lesser knaves,
    Take care there's no escaping at backdoors:
    I'll not have one escape, mind me—not one!
200 I seem revengeful, Lucy? Did you know
    What these men dare!

LADY CARLISLE   It is so much they dare!

STRAFFORD I proved that long ago; my turn is now.
    Keep sharp watch, Goring, on the citizens!
    Observe who harbours any of the brood
205 That scramble off: be sure they smart for it!

¶ STRAFFORD Very strong, as   180| *1837:* The Faction's Head . . with   *1863:*
head—with   181| *1837:* loving Hollis—one   *1863:* Vane, Rudyard, and   *1868:* Vane,
Rudyard and <> Hollis: one   183| *1837:* Bryan   *1888:* Brian   185| *1837:* the
Scots war—my <> opportune: *1863:* the Scots' war; my <> opportune.
186| *1837:* you'll   *1868:* you   187| *1837:* despatches   *1863:* dispatches
188| *1837:* for Ormond—   *1863:* for Ormond: 189| *1837:* We'll want the Army
here—my Army   *1863:* We want the army here—my army   191| *1837:* matter—
1863: matter,   192| *1837:* it. Willis . . . no—You!   *1863:* it. Willis . . . or, no—You!
1868: you!   193| *1837:* to York—bear   *1863:* to York: bear   194| *1837:*
sake—see   *1868:* sake, see   197| *1837:* Mainwaring—help to seize the lesser knaves:
1863: Mainwaring! Help <> knaves;   *1868:* seize these lesser knaves,   198| *1837:*
backdoors!   *1863:* backdoors: 199| *1837:* To not <> escape—mind   *1863:* I'll not
<> escape, mind   202| *1837:* now!   *1868:* now.   203| *1837:* citizens;   *1868:*

Our coffers are but lean.

                              And you, child, too,
Shall have your task; deliver this to Laud.
Laud will not be the slowest in my praise:
"Thorough" he'll cry!—Foolish, to be so glad!
210 This life is gay and glowing, after all:
'Tis worth while, Lucy, having foes like mine
Just for the bliss of crushing them. To-day
Is worth the living for.

LADY CARLISLE   That reddening brow!
You seem . . .

STRAFFORD   Well—do I not? I would be well—
215 I could not but be well on such a day!
And, this day ended, 'tis of slight import
How long the ravaged frame subjects the soul
In Strafford.

LADY CARLISLE Noble Strafford!

STRAFFORD   No farewell!
I'll see you anon, to-morrow—the first thing.
220 —If She should come to stay me!

LADY CARLISLE   Go—'tis nothing—
Only my heart that swells: it has been thus
Ere now: go, Strafford!

STRAFFORD   To-night, then, let it be.
I must see Him: you, the next after Him.
I'll tell you how Pym looked. Follow me, friends!
225 You, gentlemen, shall see a sight this hour
To talk of all your lives. Close after me!
"My friend of friends!"

                              [STRAFFORD *and the rest go out.*]

LADY CARLISLE   The King—ever the King!

---

citizens!   206| *1837:* you, girl, too,   *1863:* you, child, too,   207| *1837:*
task—deliver <> Laud—   *1863:* task; deliver <> Laud.   208| *1837:* praise!   *1863:*
praise: 209| *1837:* he'll say! ¶ —Foolish   *1863:* say!—Foolish   *1868:* he'll
cry!—Foolish   210| *1837:* This sort of life is vivid, after all!   *1863:* This life is gay and
glowing, after all: 212| *1837:* For the dear bliss <> them! To-day   *1863:* Just for
the bliss <> them.   213| *1837:* for! ¶ LADY CARLISLE   *1863:* for. ¶ LADY
CARLISLE   218| *1837:* In Strafford! ¶ LADY CARLISLE   *1863:* In Strafford. ¶ LADY
CARLISLE   219| *1837:* you, girl, to-morrow   *1863:* you anon, to-morrow
220| *1837:* she   *1863:* She   221| *1837:* swells—it   *1863:* swells: it   222| *1837:*
now—go <> be!   *1863:* now: go <> be.   223| *1837:* see Him . . . I'll see you after
Him . .   *1863:* see Him: you, the next after Him.   227| *1837:* friends!" [STRAFFORD

70

No thought of one beside, whose little word
Unveils the King to him—one word from me,
230 Which yet I do not breathe!
                              Ah, have I spared
Strafford a pang, and shall I seek reward
Beyond that memory? Surely too, some way
He is the better for my love. No, no—
He would not look so joyous—I'll believe
235 His very eye would never sparkle thus,
Had I not prayed for him this long, long while.

SCENE III—*The Antechamber of the House of Lords.*

Many of the Presbyterian Party. The ADHERENTS *of* STRAFFORD, *etc.*

A GROUP OF PRESBYTERIANS—1. I tell you he struck Maxwell: Maxwell sought
To stay the Earl: he struck him and passed on.
2. Fear as you may, keep a good countenance
Before these rufflers.
3.   Strafford here the first,
5 With the great army at his back!
4.   No doubt.
I would Pym had made haste: that's Bryan, hush—
The gallant pointing.
STRAFFORD'S FOLLOWERS—1. Mark these worthies, now!
2. A goodly gathering! "Where the carcass is
There shall the eagles"—what's the rest?
3.   For eagles
10 Say crows.
A PRESBYTERIAN Stand back, sirs!
ONE OF STRAFFORD'S FOLLOWERS Are we in Geneva?
A PRESBYTERIAN No, nor in Ireland; we have leave to breathe.

1863: friends!" ¶ [STRAFFORD   229| *1837:* me—   *1863:* me,   233| *1837:* love . . .
No, no   *1863:* love. No, no—   236| *1837:* while! [*Exit*]   *1863:* while.
1| *1837:* struck Maxwell—Maxwell   *1863:* struck Maxwell: Maxwell   4| *1837:* these
ruffians! ¶ 3 <> first—   *1863:* these rufflers. ¶ 3 <> first,   5| *1837:* doubt!   *1863:*
doubt.   6| *1837:* haste . . . that's   *1863:* haste: that's   7| *1837:* The fellow
pointing   *1863:* The gallant pointing   9| *1837:* eagles" . . what's   *1863:*
eagles"—what's   10| *1837:* Sirs   *1863:* sirs   11| *1837:* No—nor in Ireland, we

ONE OF STRAFFORD'S FOLLOWERS Truly? Behold how privileged we be
That serve "King Pym"! There's Some-one at Whitehall
Who skulks obscure; but Pym struts . . .
THE PRESBYTERIAN   Nearer.
A FOLLOWER OF STRAFFORD   Higher,
15 We look to see him. [*To his* COMPANIONS.] I'm to have St. John
In charge; was he among the knaves just now
That followed Pym within there?
ANOTHER   The gaunt man
Talking with Rudyard. Did the Earl expect
Pym at his heels so fast? I like it not.

MAXWELL *enters.*

20 ANOTHER Why, man, they rush into the net! Here's Maxwell—
Ha, Maxwell? How the brethren flock around
The fellow! Do you feel the Earl's hand yet
Upon your shoulder, Maxwell?
MAXWELL   Gentlemen,
Stand back! a great thing passes here.
A FOLLOWER OF STRAFFORD [*To another.*] The Earl
25 Is at his work! [*To M.*] Say, Maxwell, what great thing!
Speak out! [*To a* PRESBYTERIAN.] Friend, I've a kindness for you!
    Friend,
I've seen you with St. John: O stockishness!
Wear such a ruff, and never call to mind
St. John's head in a charger? How, the plague,
30 Not laugh?
ANOTHER Say, Maxwell, what great thing!
ANOTHER   Nay, wait:

1863: in Ireland; we   *1868:* No, nor   ¹²| *1837:* Really? Behold how grand a thing it
is   *1863:* Truly? Behold how privileged we be   ¹³| *1837:* To serve <> some one
1863: Some-one   *1868:* That serve   ¹⁴| *1837:* That lives obscure, but Pym lives . . . ¶
THE PRESBYTERIAN Nearer! ¶ A FOLLOWER OF STRAFFORD Higher   *1863:* Who skulks obscure;
but Pym struts . . . ¶ THE PRESBYTERIAN Nearer. ¶ A FOLLOWER OF STRAFFORD Higher,
¹⁵| *1837:* him! (*To*   *1863:* him. (*To*   ¹⁹| *1837:* not. [MAXWELL   *1863:* not. ¶
MAXWELL   ²¹| *1837:* Ha, Maxwell?—How   *1863:* Ha, Maxwell? How
²⁴| *1837:* A   *1868:* a   ²⁶| *1837:* Friends <> Friends,   *1863:* Friend <>
Friend,   ²⁷| *1837:* with St. John . . . O   *1863:* with St. John: O   ²⁹| *1837:*
charger? ¶ What—the plague—   *1863:* charger? How, the plague,
³⁰| *1837:* laugh? ¶ ANOTHER Say Maxwell, what it is! ¶ ANOTHER Hush—wait—   *1863:*
laugh? ¶ ANOTHER Say, Maxwell, what great thing! ¶ ANOTHER Nay, wait: ³¹| *1837:*

The jest will be to wait.

FIRST   And who's to bear

These demure hypocrites? You'd swear they came . . .

Came . . . just as we come!

[*A* PURITAN *enters hastily and without observing* STRAFFORD'S FOLLOWERS.]

THE PURITAN   How goes on the work?

Has Pym . . .

A FOLLOWER OF STRAFFORD The secret's out at last. Aha,

35   The carrion's scented! Welcome, crow the first!

Gorge merrily, you with the blinking eye!

"King Pym has fallen!"

THE PURITAN   Pym?

A STRAFFORD   Pym!

A PRESBYTERIAN   Only Pym?

MANY OF STRAFFORD'S FOLLOWERS No, brother, not Pym only; Vane as
      well,

Rudyard as well, Hampden, St. John as well!

40   A PRESBYTERIAN My mind misgives: can it be true?

ANOTHER   Lost! Lost!

A STRAFFORD Say we true, Maxwell?

THE PURITAN   Pride before destruction,

A haughty spirit goeth before a fall.

MANY OF STRAFFORD'S FOLLOWERS Ah now! The very thing! A word in
      season!

A golden apple in a silver picture,

45   To greet Pym as he passes!

          [*The doors at the back begin to open, noise and light issuing.*]

MAXWELL   Stand back, all!

MANY OF THE PRESBYTERIANS I hold with Pym! And I!

STRAFFORD'S FOLLOWERS   Now for the text!

He comes! Quick!

THE PURITAN   How hath the oppressor ceased!

---

wait— ¶ FIRST   *1863:* wait. ¶ FIRST   **32**| *1837:* These quiet hypocrites   *1863:* These
demure hypocrites   **34**| *1837:* last—Aha,   *1863:* last. Aha,   **36**| *1837:* merrily
you   *1863:* merrily, you   **38**| *1837:* brother—not Pym only—Vane as well—   *1863:*
brother, not Pym only; Vane as well,   **39**| *1837:* well—Hampden—Saint John as
well—   *1863:* well, Hampden, St. John as well!   **40**| *1837:* misgives . . can   *1863:*
misgives: can   **42**| *1837:* fall!   *1863:* fall.   **44**| *1837:* picture   *1863:*
picture,   **45**| *1837:* passes! ¶ [*The folding-doors*   *1863:* passes! ¶ [*The doors*
46| *1837:* I'll die with <> text—   *1863:* I hold with <> text!   **47**| comes! Quick! ¶

The Lord hath broken the staff of the wicked!
The sceptre of the rulers, he who smote
50 The people in wrath with a continual stroke,
That ruled the nations in his anger—he
Is persecuted and none hindereth!

> [*The doors open, and* STRAFFORD *issues in the greatest disorder,*
> *and amid cries from within of* "Void the House!"]

STRAFFORD Impeach me! Pym! I never struck, I think,
The felon on that calm insulting mouth
55 When it proclaimed—Pym's mouth proclaimed me . . . God!
Was it a word, only a word that held
The outrageous blood back on my heart—which beats!
Which beats! Some one word—"Traitor," did he say,
Bending that eye, brimful of bitter fire,
60 Upon me?

MAXWELL In the Commons' name, their servant
Demands Lord Strafford's sword.

STRAFFORD   What did you say?

MAXWELL The Commons bid me ask your lordship's sword.

STRAFFORD Let us go forth: follow me, gentlemen!
Draw your swords too: cut any down that bar us.
65 On the King's service! Maxwell, clear the way!

> [*The* PRESBYTERIANS *prepare to dispute his passage.*]

STRAFFORD I stay: the King himself shall see me here.
Your tablets, fellow!

> [*To* MAINWARING.] Give that to the King!

THE PURITAN [*With uplifted arms*] How <> Oppressor   *1863:* comes! Quick! ¶ THE PURITAN
How <> oppressor   48| *1837:* wicked: *1863:* wicked!   49| *1837:* of the
Rulers—he   *1863:* rulers, he   50| *1837:* People <> stroke—   *1863:* people <>
stroke,   51| *1837:* anger . . . He   *1863:* anger—he   52–53| § Stage directions §
1837: [*At the beginning of this speech, the doors* <> STRAFFORD *in* <> House," *staggers*
out. When he reaches the front of the Stage, silence.]   *1863:* Impeach the House." /
Impeach ⟨   55| *1837:* me . . God!   *1868:* me . . . God!   57| *1837:* heart . . which
1863: heart—which   58| *1837:* word . . . "Traitor," did he say   *1863:*
word—"Traitor," did he say,   59| *1863:* brimfull   *1868:* brimful   60| *1837:*
me? ¶ MAXWELL [*Advancing*] In   *1863:* me? ¶ MAXWELL In   62| *1837:* Lordship's
1868: lordship's   63| *1837:* STRAFFORD [*suddenly recovering, and looking round, draws*
it, and turns to his followers] Let us go forth—follow me, gentlemen—   *1863:* STRAFFORD
Let us go forth: follow me, gentlemen!   64| *1837:* too—cut <> us?   *1863:* too: cut
<> us.   66–67| *1837:* STRAFFORD Ha—true! . . . That is, you mistake me, utterly— / I
will stay—the King himself shall see me—here— / Here—I will stay, Mainwaring!—First of
all, / [*To* MAXWELL] Your tablets, fellow! [*He writes on them*] ¶ [*To* MAINWARING
1863: STRAFFORD I stay: the King himself shall see me here. / Your tablets, fellow! ¶ [*To*

74

Yes, Maxwell, for the next half-hour, let be!
Nay, you shall take my sword!

                            [MAXWELL *advances to take it.*]
                Or, no—not that!

70   Their blood, perhaps, may wipe out all thus far,
All up to that—not that! Why, friend, you see
When the King lays your head beneath my foot
It will not pay for that. Go, all of you!
MAXWELL I dare, my lord, to disobey: none stir!

75   STRAFFORD This gentle Maxwell!—Do not touch him, Bryan!
[*To the* PRESBYTERIANS.] Whichever cur of you will carry this
Escapes his fellow's fate. None saves his life?
None?

                      [*Cries from within of* "STRAFFORD!"]
       Slingsby, I've loved you at least: make haste!
Stab me! I have not time to tell you why.

80   You then, my Bryan! Mainwaring, you then!
Is it because I spoke so hastily
At Allerton? The King had vexed me.
[*To the* PRESBYTERIANS.]   You!
—Not even you? If I live over this,
The King is sure to have your heads, you know!

85   But what if I can't live this minute through?
Pym, who is there with his pursuing smile!

                        [*Louder cries of* "STRAFFORD!"]
     The King! I troubled him, stood in the way

MAINWARING   66| *1868:* here   *1888:* here.   68–69| *1837:* half-hour, I will . . . / I
will remain your prisoner, I will! / Nay <> *it*] ¶ No—no—not   *1863:* half- hour, let be! /
Nay <> *it*] ¶ Or, no—not   70| *1837:* far—   *1863:* far,   71| *1863:* see,   *1888:*
see   72| *1837:* lays his head   *1863:* lays your head   73| *1837:* that! Go   *1863:*
that. Go   74| *1837:* I grieve, my <> stir.   *1863:* I dare, my <> stir!
76–78| *1837:* PRESBYTERIAN] <> this / I'll save him from the fate of all the rest— / I'll have
him made a Peer—I'll . . . none will go? / None <> "STRAFFORD." ¶ [*To his* FOLLOWERS]
Slingsby <> least—my friend,   *1863: the* Presbyterians,] <> this / Escapes his fellows'
fate. None saves his life? / None <> "STRAFFORD." ¶ Slingsby <> least: make haste!
77| *1868:* fellow's   79| *1837:* why . . .   *1863:* why.   80| *1837:* then, dear Bryan!
You Mainwaring, then!   *1863:* then, my Bryan! Mainwaring, you then!   81| *1837:* . . .
Ah, that's because   *1863:* Is it because   82–83| *1837:* At Allerton—the King <> me
. . . ¶ (*To* <> You / Miscreants—you then—that I'll exterminate! / —Not <> over it
1863: At Allerton? The King <> me. ¶ [*To* <> You! / —Not <> over this,
84–85| *1837:* heads—you know / I'm not afraid of that—you understand / That if I chose to
wait—made up my mind / To live this minute—he would do me right! / But   *1863:* heads,
you know! / But   85–87| *1837:* through? / If nothing can repay that minute? Pym /

Of his negotiations, was the one
Great obstacle to peace, the Enemy
90 Of Scotland: and he sent for me, from York,
My safety guaranteed—having prepared
A Parliament—I see! And at Whitehall
The Queen was whispering with Vane—I see
The trap!   [*Tearing off the George.*]
          I tread a gewgaw underfoot,
95 And cast a memory from me. One stroke, now!
          [*His own* ADHERENTS *disarm him. Renewed cries of* "STRAFFORD!"]
England! I see thy arm in this and yield.
Pray you now—Pym awaits me—pray you now!
          [STRAFFORD *reaches the doors: they open wide.* HAMPDEN *and a*
              crowd discovered, and, at the bar, PYM *standing apart. As*
                  STRAFFORD *kneels, the scene shuts.*]

With his pursuing smile—Pym to be there! / The   *1863:* through? / Pym, who is there with
his pursuing smile! / The   87| *1837:* him—stood   *1863:* him, stood   88| *1837:*
negotiations—was   *1863:* negotiations, was   89| *1837:* peace—the   *1863:* peace,
the   90| *1837:* Of Scotland—and <> me—from York—   *1863:* Of Scotland: and <>
me, from York,   92| *1837:* A Parliament! I   *1863:* A Parliament—I   93| *1837:*
with Vane ... I   *1863:* with Vane—I   94–97| *1837:* trap! I curse the King! I wish Pym
well! / Wish all his brave friends well! Say, all along / Strafford was with them—all along, at
heart, / I hated Charles and wished them well! and say [*tearing off the George and dashing it
down*] / that as I tread this gew-gaw under foot, / I cast his memory from me! One <>
STRAFFORD"] / I'll not go ... They shall drag me by the hair! / [*Changing suddenly to calm*]
England! I see her arm in this! I yield. / Why—'tis the fairest triumph! Why desire / To cheat
them? I would never stoop to that—— / Be mean enough for that! Let all have end! / Don't
repine, Slingsby .. have they not a right? / They claim me—hearken—lead me to them,
Bryan! / No—I myself should offer up myself. / Pray you now ... Pym <> me ... pray you
now! [*Putting aside those who attempt to support him,* STRAFFORD   *1863:* trap! [*Tearing
off the George*] ¶ I tread a gewgaw underfoot, / And cast a memory from me. One <> /
England! I see Thy arm in this and yield. / Pray you now—Pym <> me—pray you now!
[STRAFFORD   *1868:* thy

ACT IV

S C E N E I—*Whitehall.*

The KING, *the* QUEEN, HOLLIS, LADY CARLISLE. (VANE, HOLLAND, SAVILE, *in the background.*)

LADY CARLISLE Answer them, Hollis, for his sake! One word!

CHARLES [*To* HOLLIS.] You stand, silent and cold, as though I were
Deceiving you—my friend, my playfellow
Of other times. What wonder after all?

5 Just so, I dreamed my People loved me.

HOLLIS   Sir,
It is yourself that you deceive, not me.
You'll quit me comforted, your mind made up
That, since you've talked thus much and grieved thus much,
All you can do for Strafford has been done.

10 QUEEN If you kill Strafford—(come, we grant you leave,
Suppose)—

HOLLIS   I may withdraw, sir?

LADY CARLISLE   Hear them out!
'Tis the last chance for Strafford! Hear them out!

HOLLIS "If we kill Strafford"—on the eighteenth day
Of Strafford's trial—"We!"

CHARLES   Pym, my good Hollis—

15 Pym, I should say!

HOLLIS   Ah, true—sir, pardon me!
You witness our proceedings every day;

---

¹| *1837:* sake!—One   *1863:* sake! One   ⁴| *1837:* times! What   *1863:* times.
What   ⁵| *1837:* so I <> me! ¶ HOLLIS Sire,   *1863:* so, I <> me. ¶ HOLLIS Sir,
⁶| *1837:* me!   *1863:* me.   ⁷| *1837:* comforted—your   *1863:* comforted, your
⁸| *1837:* That since   *1863:* That, since   ¹⁰| *1837:* kill Strafford . . . come   *1863:* kill
Strafford—(come   ¹¹| *1837:* Suppose . . . ¶ HOLLIS <> Sire   *1863:* Suppose)— ¶
HOLLIS <> sir   ¹⁴| *1837:* trial—We! ¶ CHARLES   *1863:* trial—"We!" ¶ CHARLES
1868: trial—"We!" ¶ CHARLES   ¹⁵| *1837:* Sire   *1863:* sir   ¹⁶| *1837:* day,   *1863:*

But the screened gallery, I might have guessed,
Admits of such a partial glimpse at us,
Pym takes up all the room, shuts out the view.
20 Still, on my honour, sir, the rest of the place
Is not unoccupied. The Commons sit
—That's England; Ireland sends, and Scotland too,
Their representatives; the Peers that judge
Are easily distinguished; one remarks
25 The People here and there: but the close curtain
Must hide so much!
QUEEN   Acquaint your insolent crew,
This day the curtain shall be dashed aside!
It served a purpose.
HOLLIS   Think! This very day?
Ere Strafford rises to defend himself?
30 CHARLES I will defend him, sir!—sanction the past
This day: it ever was my purpose. Rage
At me, not Strafford!
LADY CARLISLE   Nobly!—will he not
Do nobly?
HOLLIS   Sir, you will do honestly;
And, for that deed, I too would be a king.
35 CHARLES Only, to do this now!—"deaf" (in your style)
"To subjects' prayers,"—I must oppose them now!
It seems their will the trial should proceed,—
So palpably their will!
HOLLIS   You peril much,

---

day;   **18**| *1837:* us—   *1863:* us,   **19**| *1837:* view!   *1863:* view.   **20**| *1837:*
Sire   *1863:* sir   **21**| *1837:* unoccupied: the   *1863:* unoccupied. The   **23**| *1837:*
representatives: the   *1863:* representatives; the   **25**| *1837:* there . . . but   *1863:*
there: but   **28**| *1837:* purpose! ¶ HOLLIS   *1863:* purpose. ¶ HOLLIS   **30**| *1837:*
him, Sir! sanction the past—   *1863:* sir!—sanction the Past   *1868:* past   **31**| *1837:*
day—it < > purpose! Rage   *1863:* day: it < > purpose. Rage   **32**| *1837:* not
Strafford! Oh I shall be paid / By Strafford's look! ¶ LADY CARLISLE [*To* HOLLIS] Nobly! Oh
will   *1863:* not Strafford! ¶ LADY CARLISLE Nobly!—will   **33**| *1837:* Sire   *1863:*
Sir   **34**| *1837:* that look, I < > king!   *1863:* that deed, I < > king.
35–36| *1837:* CHARLES [*after a pause*] Only < > now—just when they seek / To make me out
a tyrant—one that's deaf / To < > prayers,—shall I oppose them now?   *1863:* CHARLES Only
< > now!—"deaf" (in your style) / "To < > prayers,"—I must oppose them now.   *1888:*
them now!   **37**| *1837:* the Trial should proceed . . .   *1863:* proceed,—   *1868:*
trial   **38**| *1837:* 'Tis palpably < > You'll lose your throne: *1863:* So palpably < >

But it were no bright moment save for that.
40 Strafford, your prime support, the sole roof-tree
Which props this quaking House of Privilege,
(Floods come, winds beat, and see—the treacherous sand!)
Doubtless, if the mere putting forth an arm
Could save him, you'd save Strafford.

CHARLES   And they dare
45 Consummate calmly this great wrong! No hope?
This ineffaceable wrong! No pity then?

HOLLIS No plague in store for perfidy?—Farewell!
You called me, sir—[*To* LADY CARLISLE.] you, lady, bade me come
To save the Earl: I came, thank God for it,
50 To learn how far such perfidy can go!
You, sir, concert with me on saving him
Who have just ruined Strafford!

CHARLES   I?—and how?

HOLLIS Eighteen days long he throws, one after one,.
Pym's charges back: a blind moth-eaten law!
55 —He'll break from it at last: and whom to thank?
The mouse that gnawed the lion's net for him
Got a good friend,—but he, the other mouse,
That looked on while the lion freed himself——
Fared he so well, does any fable say?

60 CHARLES What can you mean?

HOLLIS   Pym never could have proved
Strafford's design of bringing up the troops
To force this kingdom to obedience: Vane—
Your servant, not our friend, has proved it.

CHARLES   Vane?

You peril much   39| *1837:* that!   *1863:* that.   41| *1837:* That props
1888: Which props   43| *1837:* Doubtless if   *1863:* Doubtless, if   44| *1837:* save
Strafford! ¶ CHARLES And they mean   *1863:* save Strafford. ¶ CHARLES   *1889:* they
dare   45| *1837:* Calmly to consummate this wrong   *1868:* Consummate calmly this
great wrong   48| *1837:* You summoned me ... [*To* LADY CARLISLE] You, Lady   *1863:*
You called me, sir—[*To* LADY CARLISLE] you, lady   49| *1837:* the Earl! I   *1863:* the
Earl: I   51| *1837:* ... You dare to talk with me of saving   *1863:* You, sir, concert with
me on saving   52| *1837:* ruined Strafford! ¶ CHARLES I? ¶ HOLLIS See, now!   *1863:*
ruined Strafford! ¶ CHARLES I?—and how?   54| *1837:* Our charges   *1863:* Pym's
charges   55| *1837:* from us at last! And   *1863:* from it at last: and   56| *1837:*
Mouse <> Lion's   *1863:* mouse <> lion's   57| *1837:* Mouse,   *1863:* mouse,
58| *1837:* Lion   *1863:* lion   63| *1837:* servant, Vane ... ¶ QUEEN Well, Sir? ¶ HOLLIS ..

HOLLIS This day. Did Vane deliver up or no
65 Those notes which, furnished by his son to Pym,
Seal Strafford's fate?
CHARLES   Sir, as I live, I know
Nothing that Vane has done! What treason next?
I wash my hands of it. Vane, speak the truth!
Ask Vane himself!
HOLLIS   I will not speak to Vane,
70 Who speak to Pym and Hampden every day.
QUEEN Speak to Vane's master then! What gain to him
Were Strafford's death?
HOLLIS   Ha? Strafford cannot turn
As you, sir, sit there—bid you forth, demand
If every hateful act were not set down
75 In his commission?—whether you contrived
Or no, that all the violence should seem
His work, the gentle ways—your own,—his part,
To counteract the King's kind impulses—
While . . . but you know what he could say! And then
80 He might produce,—mark, sir!—a certain charge
To set the King's express command aside,
If need were, and be blameless. He might add . . .
CHARLES Enough!
HOLLIS   —Who bade him break the Parliament,
Find some pretence for setting up sword-law!

Has *1863:* servant, not our friend, has   64| *1837:* day! Did   *1863:* day. Did
66| *1837:* Have sealed . . . ¶ CHARLES Speak Vane! As I shall live   *1863:* Seal Strafford's fate? ¶
CHARLES Sir, as I live   68| *1837:* it! Vane   *1863:* it. Vane   69| *1837:*—Ask <> to
Vane   *1863:* Ask   *1868:* to Vane,   70| *1837:* day!   *1863:* day.   71| *1837:* then!
Why should he wish   *1863:* then! What gain to him   72| *1837:* For Strafford's death?
¶ HOLLIS Why? Strafford   *1863:* Were Strafford's death? ¶ HOLLIS Ha? Strafford
73| *1837:* you sit <> you come forth and say   *1863:* you, sir, sit <> you forth,
demand   75| *1837:* Whether   *1868:* whether   76| *1837:* no that   *1863:* no,
that   77| *1837:* own, as if   *1863:* own, his part   *1868:* own,—his part,
78| *1837:* He counteracted your kind impulses   *1863:* To counteract the King's kind
impulses—
80| *1837:* Would he produce, mark you, a   *1863:* He might produce,—mark, sir,—a   *1868:*
sir!—a   81| *1837:* set your own express commands   *1863:* set the King's express
command   82| *1837:* blameless! He'd say, then. . . .   *1863:* blameless! He might add
. . .   *1868:* blameless. He   83| *1837:* CHARLES Hold! ¶ HOLLIS. . . . Say who <>
Parliament,—   *1863:* CHARLES Enough! ¶ HOLLIS —Who <> Parliament,   84| Find
out some pretext to set up sword-law . . .   *1863:* Find some pretext for setting up

85 QUEEN Retire!

CHARLES   Once more, whatever Vane dared do,
I know not: he is rash, a fool—I know
Nothing of Vane!

HOLLIS   Well—I believe you. Sir,
Believe me, in return, that . . .
[*Turning to* LADY CARLISLE.] Gentle lady,
The few words I would say, the stones might hear
90 Sooner than these,—I rather speak to you,
You, with the heart! The question, trust me, takes
Another shape, to-day: not, if the King
Or England shall succumb,—but, who shall pay
The forfeit, Strafford or his master. Sir,
95 You loved me once: think on my warning now!

                                        [*Goes out.*]

CHARLES On you and on your warning both!—Carlisle!
That paper!

QUEEN   But consider!

CHARLES   Give it me!
There, signed—will that content you? Do not speak!
You have betrayed me, Vane! See! any day,
100 According to the tenor of that paper,
He bids your brother bring the army up,
Strafford shall head it and take full revenge.
Seek Strafford! Let him have the same, before
He rises to defend himself!

QUEEN   In truth?
105 That your shrewd Hollis should have worked a change

---

sword-law!   *1888:* some pretence for   85| *1837:* QUEEN Retire, Sir! ¶ CHARLES
Vane—once more—what Vane dares do   *1863:* QUEEN Retire! ¶ CHARLES Once more,
whatever Vane dared do,   86| *1837:* not . . . he is rash . . . a fool . . . I   *1863:* not: he is
rash, a fool—I   87| *1837:* you; Sire   *1863:* you. Sir,   88| *1837:* Lady,   *1863:*
lady,   89| *1837:* say the   *1863:* say, the   90| *1837:* these . . . I'll say them all to
1863: these,—I rather speak to   92| *1837:* to-day! 'tis not if Charles   *1863:* to-day: not,
if the King   93| *1837:* but which shall   *1863:* but, who shall   94| *1837:* his
Master: Sire,   *1863:* master. Sir,   95| *1837:* once . . . think <> now! [*Exit*]   *1863:*
once: think <> now! [*Goes out*]   98| *1837:* There—signed <> you?—Do   *1863:*
There, signed <> you? Do   99| *1837:* me, Vane!—See—any day   *1863:* me, Vane!
See! any day,   100| *1837:* (According <> tenour <> paper)   *1863:* According <>
tenor <> paper,   101| *1837:* Army   *1863:* army   102| *1837:* revenge!   *1863:*
revenge.   103| *1837:* have it, look, before   *1863:* have the same, before
105| *1837:* Clever of Hollis, now, to work a   *1863:* That your shrewd Hollis should have

Like this! You, late reluctant . . .

CHARLES   Say, Carlisle,
Your brother Percy brings the army up,
Falls on the Parliament——(I'll think of you,
My Hollis!) say, we plotted long—'tis mine,
110 The scheme is mine, remember! Say, I cursed
Vane's folly in your hearing! If the Earl
Does rise to do us shame, the fault shall lie
With you, Carlisle!

LADY CARLISLE   Nay, fear not me! but still
That's a bright moment, sir, you throw away.
115 Tear down the veil and save him!

QUEEN   Go, Carlisle!

LADY CARLISLE (I shall see Strafford—speak to him: my heart
Must never beat so, then! And if I tell
The truth? What's gained by falsehood? There they stand
Whose trade it is, whose life it is! How vain
120 To gild such rottenness! Strafford shall know,
Thoroughly know them!)

QUEEN   Trust to me! [*To* CARLISLE.] Carlisle,
You seem inclined, alone of all the Court,
To serve poor Strafford: this bold plan of yours
Merits much praise, and yet . . .

LADY CARLISLE   Time presses, madam.
125 QUEEN Yet—may it not be something premature?
Strafford defends himself to-day—reserves
Some wondrous effort, one may well suppose!

LADY CARLISLE Ay, Hollis hints as much.

CHARLES   Why linger then?

worked a   ¹⁰⁶| *1837:* this! You were reluctant <> Carlisle   *1863:* this! You, late
reluctant *1868:* Carlisle,   ¹⁰⁷| *1837:* the Army up—   *1863:* army up,
¹⁰⁸| *1837:* you   *1863:* you,   ¹⁰⁹| *1837:* My Hollis!)—say we <> long . . . 'tis *mine*,
1863: My Hollis!) say, we <> long—'tis mine,   ¹¹⁰| *1837:* remember! Say I *1863:*
remember! Say, I   ¹¹¹| *1837:* hearing! If that man   *1863:* hearing! If the Earl
¹¹⁴| *1837:* Sire <> away . . .   *1863:* sir <> away.   ¹¹⁵| *1837:* Oh, draw the   *1863:*
Tear down the   ¹¹⁶| *1837:* LADY CARLISLE [*aside, and going*] I   *1863:* LADY CARLISLE
(I   ¹¹⁷| *1837:* then! ¶ And   *1863:* then! And   ¹¹⁹| *1837:* is—whose   *1863:* is,
whose   ¹²¹| *1837:* them! ¶ QUEEN [*as she leaves the* KING, &c.] Trust   *1863:* them!)
¶ QUEEN Trust   ¹²⁴| *1837:* Madam. *1863:* madam.   ¹²⁵| *1837:* Yet . . . may
1863: Yet—may   ^{127–128}| *1837:* effort . . one <> suppose— / He'll say some
overwhelming fact, Carlisle! / LADY CARLISLE Aye   *1863:* effort, one <> suppose! / LADY

Haste with the scheme—my scheme: I shall be there
130 To watch his look. Tell him I watch his look!
QUEEN Stay, we'll precede you!
LADY CARLISLE   At your pleasure.
CHARLES   Say—
Say, Vane is hardly ever at Whitehall!
I shall be there, remember!
LADY CARLISLE   Doubt me not.
CHARLES On our return, Carlisle, we wait you here!
135 LADY CARLISLE I'll bring his answer. Sir, I follow you.
(Prove the King faithless, and I take away
All Strafford cares to live for: let it be——
'Tis the King's scheme!
                        My Strafford, I can save,
Nay, I have saved you, yet am scarce content,
140 Because my poor name will not cross your mind.
Strafford, how much I am unworthy you!)

SCENE II—*A Passage adjoining Westminster Hall.*

Many Groups of SPECTATORS *of the Trial.* OFFICERS *of the Court, etc.*

1ST SPECTATOR More crowd than ever! Not know Hampden, man?
That's he, by Pym, Pym that is speaking now.
No, truly, if you look so high you'll see
Little enough of either!
2ND SPECTATOR   Stay: Pym's arm
5   Points like a prophet's rod.
3RD SPECTATOR   Ay, ay, we've heard

CARLISLE Ay   129| *1837:* my scheme—I *1863:* my scheme: I   130| *1837:* look!
Tell *1863:* look. Tell   131| *1837:* Say . . . *1863:* Say—   132| *1837:* Say . .
Vane *1863:* Say, Vane   133| *1837:* not! *1863:* not.   135–136| *1837:* answer;
Sire, I follow You [*Exeunt* K. & c.] / Ah . . . but he would be very sad to find / The King *1863:*
answer. Sir, I follow you. / (Prove the   137| *1837:* All that he cares <> it go——
1863: All Strafford cares <> it be——   138| *1837:* save . . . *1863:* save,
139| *1837:* Nay, I *have* saved you—yet *1863:* you, yet *1868:* have   140| *1837:* mind
. . . *1863:* mind.   141| *1837:* you! [*Exit*] *1863:* you!)
§ Stage Directions §   *1837: the Trial [which is visible from the back of the
Stage]*—OFFICERS   *1863: the Trial.* Officers   1| *1837:* ever! . . . Not *1863:* ever!—
Not   2| *1837:* he—by Pym—Pym <> now! *1863:* he, by Pym, Pym <> now.
3| *1837:* truly—if *1863:* truly, if   4| *1837:* 2nd SPECTATOR Hush . . Pym's *1863:*
2*nd* SPECTATOR Stay: Pym's   5| *1837:* rod! 3rd SPECTATOR Ay—ay—we've *1863:* rod.

Some pretty speaking: yet the Earl escapes.

4TH SPECTATOR I fear it: just a foolish word or two
About his children—and we see, forsooth,
Not England's foe in Strafford, but the man
10   Who, sick, half-blind . . .

2ND SPECTATOR   What's that Pym's saying now
Which makes the curtains flutter? look! A hand
Clutches them. Ah! The King's hand!

5TH SPECTATOR   I had thought
Pym was not near so tall. What said he, friend?

2ND SPECTATOR "Nor is this way a novel way of blood,"
15   And the Earl turns as if to . . . look! look!

MANY SPECTATORS   There!
What ails him? no—he rallies, see—goes on,
And Strafford smiles. Strange!

AN OFFICER   Haselrig!

MANY SPECTATORS   Friend? Friend?

THE OFFICER Lost, utterly lost: just when we looked for Pym
To make a stand against the ill effects
20   Of the Earl's speech! Is Haselrig without?
Pym's message is to him.

3RD SPECTATOR   Now, said I true?
Will the Earl leave them yet at fault or no?

1ST SPECTATOR Never believe it, man! These notes of Vane's
Ruin the Earl.

5TH SPECTATOR A brave end: not a whit
25   Less firm, less Pym all over. Then, the trial
Is closed. No—Strafford means to speak again?

3rd SPECTATOR Ay, ay, we've   6| *1837:* speaking . . yet <> escapes!   *1863:* speaking:
yet <> escapes.   8| *1837:* children . . . and they see   *1863:* children—and we
see   9| *1837:* Not England's Foe in Strafford—but the Man   *1863:* foe in Strafford,
but the man   11| *1837:* That makes <> flutter . . look   *1863:* Which makes <>
flutter? look   12| *1837:* them . . Ah   *1863:* them. Ah   13| *1837:* tall! What
1863: tall. What   14| *1837:* blood" . . .   *1863:* blood,"   15| *1837:* SPECTATORS
Heaven—   *1863:* SPECTATORS There!   16| *1837:* him . . no—he rallies . . see—goes
on   *1863:* him? no—he rallies, see   *1888:* on,   17| *1837:* smiles. Strange! ¶ [*Enter a*
PURITAN] ¶ THE PURITAN Haselrig ¶ MANY   *1863:* smiles. Strange! ¶ AN OFFICER Haselrig! ¶
MANY   18| *1837:* THE PURITAN Lost—utterly lost . . just   *1863:* THE OFFICER Lost,
utterly lost! just   *1868:* lost: just   21| *1837:* him! [*Exit* ¶ 3rd   *1863:* him. ¶
3rd   24| *1837:* the Earl! ¶ 5*th* <> end . . not   *1863:* the Earl. ¶ 5*th* <> end:
not   25| *1837:* firm, less . . . Pym all over! Then the Trial   *1863:* firm, less Pym all
over. Then, the   *1868:* trial   26| *1837:* closed . . . no . . Strafford   *1863:* closed.

AN OFFICER Stand back, there!

5TH SPECTATOR   Why, the Earl is coming hither!
Before the court breaks up! His brother, look,—
You'd say he'd deprecated some fierce act
30 In Strafford's mind just now.

AN OFFICER   Stand back, I say!

2ND SPECTATOR Who's the veiled woman that he talks with?

MANY SPECTATORS Hush—
The Earl! the Earl!

[*Enter* STRAFFORD, SLINGSBY, *and other Secretaries,* HOLLIS,
    LADY CARLISLE, MAXWELL, BALFOUR, *etc.* STRAFFORD *con-
    verses with* LADY CARLISLE.]

HOLLIS   So near the end! Be patient—
Return!

STRAFFORD [*to his Secretaries*]. Here—anywhere—or, 'tis freshest here!
To spend one's April here, the blossom-month:
35 Set it down here!   [*They arrange a table, papers, etc.*]
So, Pym can quail, can cower
Because I glance at him, yet more's to do?
What's to be answered, Slingsby? Let us end!
[*To* LADY CARLISLE.] Child, I refuse his offer; whatsoe'er
It be! Too late! Tell me no word of him!
40 'Tis something, Hollis, I assure you that—
To stand, sick as you are, some eighteen days
Fighting for life and fame against a pack
Of very curs, that lie through thick and thin,
Eat flesh and bread by wholesale, and can't say
45 "Strafford" if it would take my life!

LADY CARLISLE   Be moved!
Glance at the paper!

STRAFFORD   Already at my heels!

No—Strafford   27| *1837: 5th* SPECTATOR Why the   *1863: 5th* SPECTATOR Why,
the   29| *1837: he*   *1868: he'd*   30| *1837: now!* ¶ AN   *1863: now.* ¶ AN
33| *1837: or—'tis* <> *here* ..   *1863: or, 'tis* <> *here!*   34| *1837: (To* <> *here—the
blossom-month!)*   *1863: To* <> *here, the blossom-month!*   *1868: blossom-month:*
35| *1837: papers & c.*] ¶ What, Pym to quail, to sink   *1863: papers, etc.* ¶ So, Pym can quail,
can cower   36| *1837: yet . . .* ¶ Well, to end—   *1863: yet more's to do?*   38| *1837:*
[*To* LADY CARLISLE] Girl, I   *1863:* [*To* LADY CARLISLE] Child, I   40| *1837:* [*To* HOLLIS] 'Tis   *1863:* 'Tis   43| *1837: thro'*   *1868: through*
45–46| *1837:* LADY CARLISLE Be kind / This once! Glance at the paper .. if you will / But glance
at it . . .* ¶ STRAFFORD Already   *1863:* LADY CARLISLE Be moved! / Glance at the paper! ¶

Pym's faulting bloodhounds scent the track again.
Peace, child! Now, Slingsby.

> [MESSENGERS *from* LANE *and other of* STRAFFORD'S COUNSEL
> *within the Hall are coming and going during the Scene.*]

STRAFFORD [*setting himself to write and dictate*]. I shall beat you,
    Hollis!
Do you know that? In spite of St. John's tricks,
50 In spite of Pym—your Pym who shrank from me!
Eliot would have contrived it otherwise.
  [*To a* MESSENGER.] In truth? This slip, tell Lane, contains as much
As I can call to mind about the matter.
Eliot would have disdained . . .
  [*Calling after the* MESSENGER.] And Radcliffe, say,
55 The only person who could answer Pym,
Is safe in prison, just for that.
                    Well, well!
It had not been recorded in that case,
I baffled you.
  [*To* LADY CARLISLE.] Nay, child, why look so grieved?
All's gained without the King! You saw Pym quail?
60 What shall I do when they acquit me, think you,
But tranquilly resume my task as though
Nothing had intervened since I proposed
To call that traitor to account! Such tricks,
Trust me, shall not be played a second time,
65 Not even against Laud, with his grey hair—
Your good work, Hollis! Peace! To make amends,
You, Lucy, shall be here when I impeach
Pym and his fellows.

HOLLIS   Wherefore not protest

STRAFFORD Already   ⁴⁷| *1837:* again! *1863:* again.   ⁴⁸| *1837:* Peace, girl! Now,
Slingsby! ¶ [*Messengers* *1863:* Peace, child! Now *1888:* Slingsby ¶ [Messengers
⁴⁹| *1837:* of all your tricks— *1863:* of St. John's tricks,
⁵⁰| *1837:* of Pym! Your Pym that shrank *1863:* of Pym—your Pym who
shrank   ⁵¹| *1837:* otherwise! *1863:* otherwise.   ⁵⁴| *1837:* [*To* HOLLIS] Eliot
<> say— *1863:* Eliot <> say,   ⁵⁵| *1837:* answer Pym— *1863:* answer
Pym,   ⁵⁶| *1837:* that! ¶ [*Continuing to* HOLLIS] Well—well— *1863:* that. ¶ Well,
well!   ⁵⁸| *1837:* you! ¶ [*To* <> Nay, girl, why *1863:* you. ¶ [*To* <> Nay, child, why
⁶⁰| *1837:* . . . What *1863:* What   ⁶⁴| *1837:* time— *1863:* time,   ⁶⁵| *1837:*
Even against old Laud <> hair . . . *1863:* Say, even against Laud <> hair— *1868:* Not
even   ⁶⁶| *1837:* work, Hollis!—And to make amends *1863:* work, Hollis! Peace! to
1868: amends,   ⁶⁷| *1837:* be there when *1868:* be here when   ⁶⁸| *1837:*

Against our whole proceeding, long ago?
70 Why feel indignant now? Why stand this while
Enduring patiently?
STRAFFORD   Child, I'll tell you—
You, and not Pym—you, the slight graceful girl
Tall for a flowering lily, and not Hollis—
Why I stood patient! I was fool enough
75 To see the will of England in Pym's will;
To fear, myself had wronged her, and to wait
Her judgment: when, behold, in place of it . . .
[*To a* MESSENGER *who whispers.*] Tell Lane to answer no such
    question! Law,—
I grapple with their law! I'm here to try
80 My actions by their standard, not my own!
Their law allowed that levy: what's the rest
To Pym, or Lane, any but God and me?
LADY CARLISLE The King's so weak! Secure this chance! 'Twas Vane,
Never forget, who furnished Pym the notes . . .
85 STRAFFORD Fit,—very fit, those precious notes of Vane,
To close the Trial worthily! I feared
Some spice of nobleness might linger yet
And spoil the character of all the past.
Vane eased me . . . and I will go back and say
90 As much—to Pym, to England! Follow me!
I have a word to say! There, my defence
Is done!
        Stay! why be proud? Why care to own

---

fellows! ¶ HOLLIS   *1863:* fellows. ¶ HOLLIS   **69|** *1837:* proceeding long   *1863:*
proceeding, long   **71|** *1837:* patiently . . . ¶ STRAFFORD [*To* LADY CARLISLE] Girl, I'll
1863: patiently? ¶ STRAFFORD Child, I'll   **72|** *1837:* You—and not Pym . . you   *1863:*
You, and not Pym—you   **73|** *1837:* lily—and not Charles . . .   *1863:* lily, and not
Hollis—   **75|** *1837:* in Pym's will—   *1863:* in Pym's will,   *1868:* in Pym's will;
76| *1837:* To dream that I had wronged her—and   *1863:* To fear, myself had wronged her,
and   **77|** *1837:* judgment,—when   *1868:* judgment: when   **78|** *1837:* question!
Law . . .   *1863:* question! Law,—   **79|** *1837:* Law   *1863:* law   **81|** *1837:* Law
<> levy . . . what's   *1863:* law <> levy: what's   **82–83|** *1837:* or Lane, or any but
myself? / LADY CARLISLE Then cast not thus your only chance away— / The <> weak . . secure
<> Vane   *1863:* or Lane, any but God and me? / LADY CARLISLE The <> weak! Secure <>
Vane,
84| *1837:*—Vane, recollect, who   *1863:* Never forget, who   **85|** *1837:* Fit . . very fit . .
those   *1863:* Fit,—very fit, those   **88|** *1837:* To spoil <> past!   *1863:* And spoil <>
Past.   *1868:* past.   **89|** *1837:* It pleased me . . and [*rising passionately*] I   *1863:* Vane
eased me . . and I   *1888:* me . . . and   **90|** *1837:* to them—to   *1863:* to Pym, to
91| *1837:* say! There! my   *1868:* say! There, my   **92|** *1837:* done! ¶ [*To* LADY

My gladness, my surprise?—Nay, not surprise!
Wherefore insist upon the little pride
95 Of doing all myself, and sparing him
The pain? Child, say the triumph is my King's!
When Pym grew pale, and trembled, and sank down,
One image was before me: could I fail?
Child, care not for the past, so indistinct,
100 Obscure—there's nothing to forgive in it
'Tis so forgotten! From this day begins
A new life, founded on a new belief
In Charles.

HOLLIS   In Charles? Rather believe in Pym!
And here he comes in proof! Appeal to Pym!
105 Say how unfair . . .

STRAFFORD   To Pym? I would say nothing!
I would not look upon Pym's face again.

LADY CARLISLE Stay, let me have to think I pressed your hand!

[STRAFFORD *and his friends go out.*]

Enter HAMPDEN *and* VANE.

VANE O Hampden, save the great misguided man!
Plead Strafford's cause with Pym! I have remarked
110 He moved no muscle when we all declaimed
Against him: you had but to breathe—he turned
Those kind calm eyes upon you.

[*Enter* PYM, *the* SOLICITOR-GENERAL ST. JOHN, *the* MANAGERS *of
the Trial,* FIENNES, RUDYARD, *etc.*]

RUDYARD   Horrible!

CARLISLE] Stay .. why   *1863:* done! ¶ Stay! why   93| *1837:* gladness—my surprise? . .
no—not   *1863:* gladness, my surprise?—Nay, not   94| *1837:* Oh, why insist   *1863:*
Wherefore insist   95| *1837:* myself and   *1863:* myself, and   96| *1837:* pain?
Girl, say   *1863:* pain? Child, say   97| *1837:* down—   *1863:* down,   98| *1837:*
His image <> me . . . could   *1863:* One image <> me: could   99| *1837:* Girl, care
<> past—so indistinct—   *1863:* Child, care <> Past, so indistinct,   *1868:* past
103-105| *1837:* In Charles . . . ¶ HOLLIS Pym comes .. tell Pym it is unfair! / Appeal to Pym!
Hampden—and Vane! see, Strafford! / Say   *1863:* In Charles. ¶ HOLLIS In Charles? Rather,
believe in Pym! / And here he comes in proof! Appeal to Pym! / Say   103| *1868:* Rather
believe   106| *1837:* again!   *1863:* again.   107| *1837:* Stay .. let   *1863:* Stay,
let   108| *1837:* save that great   *1868:* save the great   109| *1837:* with Pym—I
1863: with Pym! I   110| *1837:* all spoke loud   *1863:* all declaimed   111| *1837:*
him . . . you   *1863:* him: you   112| *1837:* kind, large eyes upon you—kind to all / But

88

Till now all hearts were with you: I withdraw
For one. Too horrible! But we mistake
115 Your purpose, Pym: you cannot snatch away
The last spar from the drowning man.

FIENNES   He talks
With St. John of it—see, how quietly!
[*To other* PRESBYTERIANS.] You'll join us? Strafford may deserve the
     worst:
But this new course is monstrous. Vane, take heart!
120 This Bill of his Attainder shall not have
One true man's hand to it.

VANE   Consider, Pym!
Confront your Bill, your own Bill: what is it?
You cannot catch the Earl on any charge,—
No man will say the law has hold of him
125 On any charge; and therefore you resolve
To take the general sense on his desert,
As though no law existed, and we met
Tó found one. You refer to Parliament
To speak its thought upon the abortive mass
130 Of half-borne-out assertions, dubious hints
Hereafter to be cleared, distortions—ay,
And wild inventions. Every man is saved
The task of fixing any single charge
On Strafford: he has but to see in him
135 The enemy of England.

PYM   A right scruple!

Strafford . . whom I murder! ¶ [*Enter* PYM (*conversing with the Solicitor-General*, St. JOHN),
the   *1863:* kind, calm eyes upon you. ¶ [*Enter* PYM, the Solicitor-General St. JOHN, *the*
1868: kind calm   113| *1837:* you . . . I   *1863:* you: I   114| *1837:* one! Too
horrible! Oh we   *1863:* purpose, Pym: you   116| *1837:* man! ¶ FIENNES
1863: man. ¶ FIENNES   117| *1837:* see how   *1863:* see, how
118| *1837:* us? Mind, we own he merits death—   *1863:* us? Strafford may deserve the
worst: 119| *1837:* monstrous! Vane   *1863:* monstrous. Vane
121| *1837:* it! ¶ VANE But hear me, Pym!   *1863:* it. ¶ VANE
Consider, Pym!   122| *1837:* your Bill—your own Bill . . what   *1863:* your Bill, your
own Bill: what   123| *1837:* charge . .   *1863:* charge,—   124| *1837:* Law   *1863:*
law   125| *1837:* charge . . and   *1863:* charge; and   126| *1837:* desert,—   *1863:*
desert,   127| *1837:* Law   *1863:* law   128| *1837:* one!—You refer to every man
1863: one. You refer to Parliament   129| *1837:* speak his thought upon this hideous
mass   *1863:* speak its thought   *1868:* upon the abortive mass   130| *1837:* half- borne
out assertions—dubious   *1863:* assertions, dubious   *1888:* half-borne-out
131| *1837:* cleared—distortions—aye,   *1863:* cleared, distortions—ay,   135| *1837:*

I have heard some called England's enemy
With less consideration.

VANE   Pity me!
Indeed you made me think I was your friend!
I who have murdered Strafford, how remove
140 That memory from me?

PYM   I absolve you, Vane.
Take you no care for aught that you have done!

VANE John Hampden, not this Bill! Reject this Bill!
He staggers through the ordeal: let him go,
Strew no fresh fire before him! Plead for us!
145 When Strafford spoke, your eyes were thick with tears!

HAMPDEN England speaks louder: who are we, to play
The generous pardoner at her expense,
Magnanimously waive advantages,
And, if he conquer us, applaud his skill?

150 VANE He was your friend.

PYM   I have heard that before.

FIENNES And England trusts you.

HAMPDEN   Shame be his, who turns
The opportunity of serving her
She trusts him with, to his own mean account—
Who would look nobly frank at her expense!

155 FIENNES I never thought it could have come to this.

PYM But I have made myself familiar, Fiennes,

The Enemy of England ... ¶ PYM   *1863:* The enemy of England. ¶ PYM   136| *1837:*
Enemy   *1863:* enemy   137–140| *1837:* me! / Me—brought so low—who hoped to do so
much / For England—her true servant—Pym, your friend . . . / Indeed you made me think I
was your friend! / But I have murdered Strafford . . I have been / The instrument of this! who
shall remove / That <> Vane!   *1863:* me! / Indeed you made me think I was your friend! / I
who have murdered Strafford, how remove / That <> Vane.   142| *1837:* Dear
Hampden   *1863:* John Hampden   143| *1837:* thro' the ordeal . . . let him go!   *1863:*
through the ordeal: let him go,   144–146| *1837:* us / With Pym . . what God is he, to
have no heart / Like ours, yet make us love him? ¶ RUDYARD Hampden, plead / For us! When
Strafford spoke your eyes were thick / With tears . . save him, dear Hampden! ¶ HAMPDEN
England speaks / Louder than Strafford! Who   *1863:* us! / When Strafford spoke, your eyes
were thick with tears! / HAMPDEN England speaks louder: who   147| *1837:* expense—
1863: expense,   148| *1837:* advantages—   *1863:* advantages,   149| *1837:* And if
<> us. . . . applaud   *1863:* And, if <> us, applaud   150| *1837:* VANE [*To* PYM] He
<> friend! ¶ PYM   *1863:* VANE He <> friend. ¶ PYM   151| *1837:* But England trusts
you . . . ¶ HAMPDEN   *1863:* And England trusts you. ¶ HAMPDEN   155| *1837:* this!
1863: this.   156| *1837:* PYM [*turning from* ST. JOHN] But   *1863:* PYM But

90

With this one thought—have walked, and sat, and slept,
This thought before me. I have done such things,
Being the chosen man that should destroy
160 The traitor. You have taken up this thought
To play with, for a gentle stimulant,
To give a dignity to idler life
By the dim prospect of emprise to come,
But ever with the softening, sure belief,
165 That all would end some strange way right at last.
FIENNES Had we made out some weightier charge!
PYM   You say
That these are petty charges: can we come
To the real charge at all? There he is safe
In tyranny's stronghold. Apostasy
170 Is not a crime, treachery not a crime:
The cheek burns, the blood tingles, when you speak
The words, but where's the power to take revenge
Upon them? We must make occasion serve,—
The oversight shall pay for the main sin
175 That mocks us.
RUDYARD   But this unexampled course,
This Bill!
PYM   By this, we roll the clouds away
Of precedent and custom, and at once
Bid the great beacon-light God sets in all,
The conscience of each bosom, shine upon

157| *1837:* With that one *1863:* With this one   158| *1837:* That thought before me!
I *1863:* This thought before me. I   160| *1837:* This Strafford! You <> up that
thought   *1863:* The traitor. You <> up this thought   161| *1837:* with—for <>
stimulant— *1863:* with, for <> stimulant,   163| *1837:* of this deed to come . . .
1863: of emprise to come,   165| *1837:* would come some <> last! *1863:* would end
some <> last.   166| *1837:* charge. . . . ¶ PYM *1863:* charge! ¶ PYM   167| *1837:*
charges! Can *1863:* charges: can   168| *1837:* safe! *1863:* safe   169| *1837:*
strong hold! Apostasy *1863:* stronghold. Apostasy   170| *1837:* crime—Treachery not
a crime! *1863:* crime, treachery not a crime: 171| *1837:* you name *1863:* you
speak   172| *1837:* Their names, but *1863:* The words, but   173| *1837:* serve:
serve,—   174| *1837:* The Oversight, pay for the Giant Sin *1863:* oversight here, pay
for the main sin *1868:* oversight shall pay   175| *1837:* us! ¶ RUDYARD <> course——
1863: us. ¶ RUDYARD <> course,   176| *1837:* This Bill. . . . ¶ PYM *1863:* This Bill!
¶ PYM   177| *1837:* Precedent and Custom *1863:* precedent and custom
178| *1837:* great light which God has set in *1863:* great beacon-light God sets in

180 The guilt of Strafford: each man lay his hand
Upon his breast, and judge!

VANE   I only see
Strafford, nor pass his corpse for all beyond!

RUDYARD AND OTHERS Forgive him! He would join us, now he finds
What the King counts reward! The pardon, too,
185 Should be your own. Yourself should bear to Strafford
The pardon of the Commons.

PYM   Meet him? Strafford?
Have we to meet once more, then? Be it so!
And yet—the prophecy seemed half fulfilled
When, at the Trial, as he gazed, my youth,
190 Our friendship, divers thoughts came back at once
And left me, for a time . . . 'Tis very sad!
Tomorrow we discuss the points of law
With Lane—tomorrow?

VANE   Not before tomorrow—
So, time enough! I knew you would relent!

PYM The next day, Haselrig, you introduce
The Bill of his Attainder. Pray for me!

SCENE III—*Whitehall.*

The KING.

CHARLES My loyal servant! To defend himself

180| *1837:* each shall lay   *1868:* each man lay   181–183| *1837:* and say if this one man /
Deserve to die, or no, by those he sought / First to undo. ¶ FIENNES You, Vane— —you answer
him! / VANE Pym, you see farthest . . . I can only see / Strafford . . . I'd not pass over that pale
corse / For all beyond! ¶ RUDYARD AND OTHERS Pym, you would look so great! / Forgive <> us!
now   *1863:* and judge. ¶ VANE I only see / Strafford, nor pass his corpse for all beyond! /
RUDYARD AND OTHERS Forgive <> us, now   *1868:* and judge! ¶ VANE   184| *1837:* How
false the King has been! The   *1863:* What the King counts reward! The   185| *1837:*
own! Yourself   *1863:* own. Yourself   186| *1837:* of the Commons! ¶ PYM [*starting*] Meet
1863: of the Commons. ¶ PYM Meet   189| *1837:* trial <> gazed—my youth—   *1863:*
Trial <> gazed, my youth,   190| *1837:* friendship—all old thoughts   *1863:*
friendship, divers thoughts   191| *1837:* time. . . . ¶ VANE [*aside to* RUDYARD] Moved, is
he not?   *1863:* time . . . 'Tis very sad!   193| *1837:* With Lane . . to-morrow! ¶ VANE
Time enough, dear Pym!   *1863:* With Lane—to-morrow? ¶ VANE Not before
to-morrow—   194| *1837:* See, he relents! I knew he would   *1863:* So, time enough! I
knew you would   195| *1837: you* introduce,   *1863:* you introduce   196| *1837:*
his Attainder. [*After a pause*] Pray   *1863:* his Attainder. Pray
§ 1837 adds two lines before line 1. §   1| *1837:* Strafford, you are a Prince! Not to

Thus irresistibly,—withholding aught
That seemed to implicate us!

                        We have done
Less gallantly by Strafford. Well, the future
5   Must recompense the past.

                         She tarries long.
I understand you, Strafford, now!

                           The scheme—
Carlisle's mad scheme—he'll sanction it, I fear,
For love of me. 'Twas too precipitate:
Before the army's fairly on its march,
10   He'll be at large: no matter.

                         Well, Carlisle?

Enter PYM.

PYM Fear me not, sir:—my mission is to save,
This time.
CHARLES   To break thus on me! Unannounced!
PYM It is of Strafford I would speak.
CHARLES   No more
Of Strafford! I have heard too much from you.
15 PYM I spoke, sir, for the People; will you hear
A word upon my own account?
CHARLES   Of Strafford?
(So turns the tide already? Have we tamed
The insolent brawler?—Strafford's eloquence
Is swift in its effect.) Lord Strafford, sir,
20 Has spoken for himself.
    PYM   Sufficiently

---

reward you / —Nothing does that—but only for a whim! / My noble servant!—To   *1863:* My
loyal servant   *1868:* servant! To   2| *1837:* irresistibly .. withholding *1863:*
irresistibly,—withholding   4| *1837:* by Strafford! Well *1863:* by Strafford. Well, the
Future *1868:* future   5| *1837:* long! *1863:* Past <> long. *1868:* past
8| *1837:* me! 'Twas *1863:* me. 'Twas   9| *1837:* Army's *1863:* army's
10| *1837:* matter .. ¶ Well *1863:* matter. ¶ Well   11| *1837:* not, Sire ... my *1863:*
sir:—my   12| *1837:* time! ¶ CHARLES <> me!—Unannounced ... *1863:* time. ¶
CHARLES <> me! Unannounced!   14| *1837:* you! *1863:* you.   15| *1837:* Sire
<> People: will *1863:* sir *1868:* the People; will   17| *1837:* [*Aside*] So, turns
1863: (So *1868:* (So turns   18| *1837:* brawler?—Strafford's brave defence *1863:*
brawler?—Strafford's eloquence   19| *1837:* effect! [*To* PYM] Lord <> Sir, *1863:*
effect.) Lord <> sir,   20| *1837:* himself! ¶ PYM *1863:* himself. ¶ PYM

I would apprise you of the novel course
The People take: the Trial fails.

CHARLES   Yes, yes
We are aware, sir: for your part in it
Means shall be found to thank you.

PYM   Pray you, read
25 This schedule! I would learn from your own mouth
—(It is a matter much concerning me)—
Whether, if two Estates of us concede
The death of Strafford, on the grounds set forth
Within that parchment, you, sir, can resolve
30 To grant your own consent to it. This Bill
Is framed by me. If you determine, sir.
That England's manifested will should guide
Your judgment, ere another week such will
Shall manifest itself. If not,—I cast
35 Aside the measure.

CHARLES   You can hinder, then,
The introduction of this Bill?

PYM   I can.

CHARLES He is my friend, sir: I have wronged him: mark you,
Had I not wronged him, this might be. You think
Because you hate the Earl . . . (turn not away,
40 We know you hate him)—no one else could love
Strafford: but he has saved me, some affirm.
Think of his pride! And do you know one strange,
One frightful thing? We all have used the man
As though a drudge of ours, with not a source

---

²¹| *1837:* apprize *1863:* apprise   ²²| *1837:* people <> fails, . . . ¶ CHARLES
Yes—yes— *1863:* People <> fails. ¶ CHARLES *1868:* fails. ¶ CHARLES Yes, yes: *1888:* fails.
¶ CHARLES Yes, yes   ²³| *1837:* Sir *1863:* sir   ²⁵| *1837:* schedule! [*as the* KING
reads it] I *1863:* schedule! I   ²⁷| *1837:* of England shall concede *1863:* of us
concede   ²⁹| *1837:* Sire *1863:* sir   ³⁰| *1837:* your full consent to it. That Bill
1863: your own consent *1888:* it. This Bill   ³¹| *1837:* me: if <> Sire, *1863:* me. If
<> sir,   ³²| *1837:* will shall guide *1863:* will should guide   ³³| *1837:* week
that will *1863:* week such will   ³⁵| *1837:* CHARLES . . You *1863:* CHARLES You
³⁶| *1837:* of that Bill *1863:* of this Bill   ³⁷| *1837:* Sir *1863:* sir   ³⁸| *1837:*
him—this might be!—You *1863:* him, this might be. You   ³⁹| *1837:* away— *1863:*
away,   ⁴¹⁻⁴²| *1837:* Strafford . . . but <> me—many times—/ Think what he has
endured . . proud too . . you feel / What he endured!—And, do *1863:* Strafford: but <>
me, some affirm. / Think of his pride! And *1868:* And do   ⁴³| *1837:* used that man
1863: used the man   ⁴⁴| ~~*1837:* though he had been ours . . with~~ *1863:* though a

45 Of happy thoughts except in us; and yet
   Strafford has wife and children, household cares,
   Just as if we had never been. Ah sir,
   You are moved, even you, a solitary man
   Wed to your cause—to England if you will!
50 PYM Yes—think, my soul—to England! Draw not back!
   CHARLES Prevent that Bill, sir! All your course seems fair
   Till now. Why, in the end, 'tis I should sign
   The warrant for his death! You have said much
   I ponder on; I never meant, indeed,
55 Strafford should serve me any more. I take
   The Commons' counsel; but this Bill is yours—
   Nor worthy of its leader: care not, sir,
   For that, however! I will quite forget
   You named it to me. You are satisfied?
60 PYM Listen to me, sir! Eliot laid his hand,
   Wasted and white upon my forehead once;
   Wentworth—he's gone now!—has talked on, whole nights,
   And I beside him; Hampden loves me: sir,
   How can I breathe and not wish England well,
65 And her King well?
   CHARLES   I thank you, sir, who leave
   That King his servant. Thanks, sir!
   PYM   Let me speak!
   —Who may not speak again; whose spirit yearns
   For a cool night after this weary day:

---

drudge of ours, with   **45|** *1837:* us .. and   *1863:* us; and   **46|** *1837:* has
children, and a home as well,   *1863:* has wife and children, household cares,
47| *1837:* been! .. Ah Sir,   *1863:* been. Ah, sir,   *1868:* been. Ah sir,   **48|** *1837:*
moved—you—a   *1863:* moved, even you, a   **50|** *1837:* Yes .. think, my soul .. to
1863: Yes—think, my soul—to   **51|** *1837:* that Bill, Sir .. Oh, your course was fair
1863: sir! All your course seems fair   **52|** *1837:* now! Why   *1863:* now. Why
54| *1837:* That I shall ponder <> meant   *1863:* I ponder <> meant, indeed,
55| *1837:* more: I   *1863:* more. I   **56|** *1837:* counsel: but   *1863:* counsel; but
57| *1837:* Not worthy of its leader .. care not, Sir,   *1863:* Nor worthy of its leader: care not,
sir,   **59|** *1837:* me! You   *1863:* me. You   **60|** *1837:* Sire   *1863:* sir
61| *1837:* white, upon   *1868:* white upon   **62|** *1837:* Wentworth ... he's gone now! ..
has   *1863:* Wentworth—he's gone now!—has   **63|** *1837:* me; Sire,   *1863:* me? sir,
64| *1837:* well—   *1863:* well,   **65|** *1837:* you, Sir! You leave   *1863:* sir! who leave
1868: sir, who   **66|** *1837:* servant! Thanks, Sir <> speak   *1863:* servant. Thanks, sir
<> speak!   **67|** *1837:* again! whose   *1863:* again; whose   **68|** *1837:* day!

—Who would not have my soul turn sicker yet
70 In a new task, more fatal, more august,
More full of England's utter weal or woe.
I thought, sir, could I find myself with you,
After this trial, alone, as man to man—
I might say something, warn you, pray you, save—
75 Mark me, King Charles, save——you!
But God must do it. Yet I warn you, sir—
(With Strafford's faded eyes yet full on me)
As you would have no deeper question moved
—"How long the Many must endure the One,"
80 Assure me, sir, if England give assent
To Strafford's death, you will not interfere!
Or——
CHARLES God forsakes me. I am in a net
And cannot move. Let all be as you say!

Enter LADY CARLISLE.

LADY CARLISLE He loves you—looking beautiful with joy
85 Because you sent me! he would spare you all
The pain! he never dreamed you would forsake
Your servant in the evil day—nay, see
Your scheme returned! That generous heart of his!
He needs it not—or, needing it, disdains
90 A course that might endanger you—you, sir,
Whom Strafford from his inmost soul . . .
[*Seeing* PYM.]   Well met!
No fear for Strafford! All that's true and brave
On your own side shall help us: we are now

1863: day: 69| *1837:* my heart turn   *1863:* my soul turn   70| *1837:* august
1863: august,   71| *1837:* woe . . . *1863:* woe.   72| *1863:* Sire <> you—   *1863:*
sir <> you,   73| *1837:* this Trial—alone—as   *1863:* this Trial, alone, as   *1868:*
trial   74| *1837:* something—warn you—pray you—save you—   *1863:* something,
warn you, pray you, save—   76| *1837:* Sire—   *1863:* sir—   79| *1837:* the Many
shall endure the One" . . .   *1863:* the Many must endure the One,"   80| *1837:* Sire, if
England shall assent   *1863:* sir, if England give assent   82| *1837:* me—I <> net . .
1863: me. I <> net.   *1868:* net   83| *1837:* I cannot move! Let   *1863:* And cannot
move. Let   90| *1837:* Sire,   *1863:* sir,   91| *1837:* soul . . . ¶ [*Seeing* PYM] No
fear—   *1863:* soul . . . ¶ [*Seeing* PYM] Well met!   92| *1837:* all   *1868:* All
93| *1837:* us! we   *1863:* us: we   94| *1837:* ever! ¶ Ha—what, Sire   *1863:* ever. ¶

Stronger than ever.

                Ha—what, sir, is this?

95   All is not well! What parchment have you there?

PYM Sir, much is saved us both.

LADY CARLISLE   This Bill! Your lip

Whitens—you could not read one line to me

Your voice would falter so!

PYM   No recreant yet!

The great word went from England to my soul,

100 And I arose. The end is very near.

LADY CARLISLE I am to save him! All have shrunk beside;

'Tis only I am left. Heaven will make strong

The hand now as the heart. Then let both die!

Ha—what, sir   ⁹⁵| *1837:* there? ¶ [CHARLES *drops it, and exit*]   *1863:* there?
⁹⁶| *1837:* Sire <> both: farewell! ¶ LADY CARLISLE Stay—stay— / This cursed
measure—you'll not dare—you mean / To frighten Charles! This Bill—look— ¶ [*As* PYM
reads it] ¶ Why, your lip   *1863:* Sir <> both. ¶ LADY CARLISLE This Bill! Your lip
⁹⁸| *1837:* so! It shakes you now— / And will you dare . . . ¶ PYM No recreant yet to her!
1863: so! ¶ PYM No recreant yet!   ¹⁰⁰| *1837:* arose! The <> near! [*Exit*]   *1863:*
arose. The <> near.   ¹⁰¹| *1837:* I save <> shrunk from him beside—   *1863:* I am to
save <> shrunk beside—   *1868:* beside;   ¹⁰²| *1837:* left! Heaven   *1868:* left.
Heaven   ¹⁰³| *1837:* hand as the true heart! Then let me die! [*Exit*]   *1863:* hand now
as the heart. Then let both die!

ACT V

Scene I—*Whitehall.*

Hollis, Lady Carlisle.

HOLLIS Tell the King then! Come in with me!

LADY CARLISLE   Not so!

He must not hear till it succeeds.

HOLLIS   Succeed?

No dream was half so vain—you'd rescue Strafford

And outwit Pym! I cannot tell you . . . lady,

5   The block pursues me, and the hideous show.

Today . . . is it today? And all the while

He's sure of the King's pardon. Think, I have

To tell this man he is to die. The King

May rend his hair, for me! I'll not see Strafford!

10 LADY CARLISLE Only, if I succeed, remember——Charles

Has saved him. He would hardly value life

Unless his gift. My staunch friends wait. Go in—

You must go in to Charles!

HOLLIS   And all beside

Left Strafford long ago. The King has signed

15 The warrant for his death! the Queen was sick

Of the eternal subject. For the Court,—

The Trial was amusing in its way,

Only too much of it: the Earl withdrew

---

¹| *1837:* the King, then   *1868:* the King then   ²| *1837:* hear 'till it succeeds! ¶ HOLLIS
Vain! Vain!   *1863:* hear till it succeeds. ¶ HOLLIS Succeed?   ³| *1837:* you'll   *1863:*
you'd   ⁴| *1837:* you . . . girl,   *1863:* you . . . lady,   ⁵| *1837:* me—all the   *1863:*
me, and the   ⁷| *1837:* pardon . . think   *1863:* pardon. Think   ⁸| *1837:* die! ¶
The   *1863:* die. The   ¹¹| *1837:* him! He   *1868:* him. He   ¹²| *1837:* gift. ¶ My
<> wait! Go   *1863:* gift. My <> wait. Go   ¹⁴| *1837:* ago—the   *1863:* ago.
The   ¹⁵| *1837:* death . . the   *1863:* death: the   *1868:* death! the   ¹⁶| *1837:*
subject! For   *1863:* subject. For   ¹⁷| *1837:* way   *1863:* way,   ¹⁸| *1837:* it . .

In time. But you, fragile, alone, so young
20 Amid rude mercenaries—you devise
A plan to save him! Even though it fails,
What shall reward you?

LADY CARLISLE   I may go, you think,
To France with him? And you reward me, friend,
Who lived with Strafford even from his youth
25 Before he set his heart on state-affairs
And they bent down that noble brow of his.
I have learned somewhat of his latter life,
And all the future I shall know: but, Hollis,
I ought to make his youth my own as well.
30 Tell me,——when he is saved!

HOLLIS   My gentle friend,
He should know all and love you, but 'tis vain!

LADY CARLISLE Love? no—too late now! Let him love the King!
'Tis the King's scheme! I have your word, remember!
We'll keep the old delusion up. But, quick!
35 Quick! Each of us has work to do, beside!
Go to the King! I hope—Hollis—I hope!
Say nothing of my scheme! Hush, while we speak
Think where he is! Now for my gallant friends!

HOLLIS Where he is? Calling wildly upon Charles,
40 Guessing his fate, pacing the prison-floor.
Let the King tell him! I'll not look on Strafford.

---

the *1863:* it: the **19|** *1837:* time! But you—fragile—alone—so young! *1863:* time.
But you, fragile, alone, so young, *1888:* young **20|** *1837:* devised *1863:*
devise **21|** *1837:* tho' it fails *1863:* though it fails, **23|** *1837:* friend! *1863:*
friend, **26|** *1837:* his—— *1863:* his. **27|** *1837:* life *1863:* life,
28| *1837:* know—but *1863:* know: but **29|** *1837:* well! *1863:* well.
30| *1837:* me——when <> gentle girl *1863:* me,——when <> gentle friend,
31| *1837:* all—should love you—but *1863:* all and love you, but **32|** *1837:* No—no
1863: Love? no **33|** *1837:* word—remember!— *1863:* word, remember!
34| *1837:* up! But, hush! *1863:* up. But, quick! **35|** *1837:* Hush! Each *1863:*
Quick! Each **38|** *1837:* He <> friends! [*Exit*] *1863:* he <> friends!
39| *1837:* He <> Charles—— *1863:* he <> Charles, **40|** *1837:* fate——pacing
<> prison- floor . . . *1863:* fate, pacing <> prison-floor. **41|** *1837:* on Strafford! ¶
[*Exit*] *1863:* on Strafford.

STRAFFORD *sitting with his* CHILDREN. *They sing.*

> O bell' andare
> Per barca in mare,
> Verso la sera
> Di Primavera!

5   WILLIAM The boat's in the broad moonlight all this while—

> *Verso la sera*
> *Di Primavera!*

And the boat shoots from underneath the moon
Into the shadowy distance; only still
10 You hear the dipping oar—

> *Verso la sera,*

And faint, and fainter, and then all's quite gone,
Music and light and all, like a lost star.
ANNE But you should sleep, father: you were to sleep.
15 STRAFFORD I do sleep, Anne; or if not—you must know
There's such a thing as . . .
WILLIAM   You're too tired to sleep?
STRAFFORD It will come by-and-by and all day long,
In that old quiet house I told you of:
We sleep safe there.
ANNE   Why not in Ireland?
STRAFFORD   No!
20 Too many dreams!—That song's for Venice, William:
You know how Venice looks upon the map—
Isles that the mainland hardly can let go?

---

⁵| *1837:* (The <> while)   *1863:* The <> while—   ⁷| *1837: Di Primavera. 1863:*
Di Primavera!   ⁹| *1837:* distance—only *1863:* distance; only   ¹⁰| *1837:* oar,
1863: oar—   ¹¹| *1837: sera . . . 1863: sera,*   ¹²| *1837:* faint—and
fainter—and *1863:* faint, and fainter, and   ¹⁴| *1837:* to sleep! *1863:* to
sleep.   ¹⁵| *1837:* sleep, dearest; or <> you know *1863:* sleep, Anne; or <> you
must know   ¹⁷| *1837:* by and bye *1863:* by-and-by   ¹⁹| *1837:* We'll sleep <>
STRAFFORD Ah! *1863:* We sleep <> STRAFFORD No!   ²¹| *1837:* map . . . *1863:*

WILLIAM You've been to Venice, father?
STRAFFORD   I was young, then.
WILLIAM A city with no King; that's why I like
25 Even a song that comes from Venice.
STRAFFORD   William!
WILLIAM Oh, I know why! Anne, do you love the King?
But I'll see Venice for myself one day.
STRAFFORD See many lands, boy—England last of all,—
That way you'll love her best.
WILLIAM   Why do men say
30 You sought to ruin her then?
STRAFFORD   Ah,—they say that.
WILLIAM Why?
STRAFFORD   I suppose they must have words to say,
As you to sing.
ANNE   But they make songs beside:
Last night I heard one, in the street beneath,
That called you . . . Oh, the names!
WILLIAM   Don't mind her, father!
35 They soon left off when I cried out to them.
STRAFFORD We shall so soon be out of it, my boy!
'Tis not worth while: who heeds a foolish song?
WILLIAM Why, not the King.
STRAFFORD   Well: it has been the fate
Of better; and yet,—wherefore not feel sure
40 That Time, who in the twilight comes to mend
All the fantastic day's caprice, consign
To the low ground once more the ignoble Term,
And raise the Genius on his orb again,—
That Time will do me right?

map—   **23**| *1837:* young then.   *1868:* young, then.   *1888:* then   **25**| *1837:*
from Venice! ¶ STRAFFORD   *1863:* from Venice. ¶ STRAFFORD   **30**| *1837:* her, then! ¶
STRAFFORD Ah . . . they   *1863:* then? ¶ STRAFFORD Ah,—they   *1888:* her then
31| *1837:* say.   *1863:* say,   **34**| *1837:* That named you   *1863:* That called you
35| *1837:* when I called out to them!   *1863:* when I cried out to them.   **38**| *1837:* the
King! ¶ STRAFFORD   *1863:* the King. ¶ STRAFFORD   **39**| *1837:* better men, and yet. . . .
why not   *1863:* better; and yet,—wherefore not   **40**| *1868:* time
41| *1837:* fantastic Day's caprice—consign   *1863:* day's caprice, consign   **42**| Unto
the ground   *1863:* To the low ground   **43**| *1837:* again—   *1863:* again,—

ANNE   (Shall we sing, William?

45 He does not look thus when we sing.)

STRAFFORD   For Ireland,

Something is done: too little, but enough

To show what might have been.

WILLIAM   (I have no heart

To sing now! Anne, how very sad he looks!

Oh, I so hate the King for all he says!)

50 STRAFFORD Forsook them! What, the common songs will run

That I forsook the People? Nothing more?

Ay, Fame, the busy scribe, will pause, no doubt,

Turning a deaf ear to her thousand slaves

Noisy to be enrolled,—will register

55 The curious glosses, subtle notices,

Ingenious clearings-up one fain would see

Beside that plain inscription of The Name—

The Patriot Pym, or the Apostate Strafford!

              [*The* CHILDREN *resume their song timidly, but break off.*]

Enter HOLLIS *and an* ATTENDANT.

STRAFFORD No,—Hollis? in good time!—Who is he?

HOLLIS   One

60 That must be present.

STRAFFORD   Ah—I understand.

They will not let me see poor Laud alone.

How politic! They'd use me by degrees

To solitude: and, just as you came in,

I was solicitous what life to lead

65 When Strafford's "not so much as Constable

In the King's service." Is there any means

To keep oneself awake? What would you do

44| *1863:* time   45| *1837:* STRAFFORD For Ireland,—   *1863:* STRAFFORD
For Ireland,   46| *1837:* done . . too   *1863:* done: too   47| *1837:* been:— ¶
WILLIAM   *1863:* been. ¶ WILLIAM   49| *1837:* Oh I   *1863:* Oh, I   52| *1837:* . . .
Aye, Fame, the scribe, will pause awhile, no   *1863:* Ay, Fame, the busy scribe, will pause,
no   *1868:* fame   *1888:* Fame   55| *1837:* All curious   *1863:* The curious
59| *1837:* No . . . Hollis   *1863:* No,—Hollis   60| *1837:* understand—   *1863:*
understand.   61| *1837:* alone!   *1863:* alone.   63| *1837:* and just <> in   *1888:*

After this bustle, Hollis, in my place?

HOLLIS Strafford!

STRAFFORD   Observe, not but that Pym and you

70 Will find me news enough—news I shall hear
Under a quince-tree by a fish-pond side
At Wentworth. Garrard must be re-engaged
My newsman. Or, a better project now—
What if when all's consummated, and the Saints

75 Reign, and the Senate's work goes swimmingly,—
What if I venture up, some day, unseen,
To saunter through the Town, notice how Pym,
Your Tribune, likes Whitehall, drop quietly
Into a tavern, hear a point discussed,

80 As, whether Strafford's name were John or James—
And be myself appealed to—I, who shall
Myself have near forgotten!

HOLLIS   I would speak . . .

STRAFFORD Then you shall speak,—not now. I want just now,
To hear the sound of my own tongue. This place

85 Is full of ghosts.

HOLLIS   Nay, you must hear me, Strafford!

STRAFFORD Oh, readily! Only, one rare thing more,—
The minister! Who will advise the King,
Turn his Sejanus, Richelieu and what not,
And yet have health—children, for aught I know—

---

and, just <> in,   69| *1837:* Strafford . . . ¶ STRAFFORD   *1863:* Strafford! ¶
STRAFFORD   72-73| *1837:* At Wentworth. Or   *1863:* At Wentworth. Garrard must be
re-engaged / My newsman. Or   74| *1837:* all is over, and   *1863:* all's consummated,
and   75| *1837:* the Senate goes on swimmingly,—   *1863:* the Senate's work goes
swimmingly,—   76| *1837:* unseen—   *1863:* unseen,   77| *1837:* the
Town—notice   *1863:* the Town, notice   78| *1837:* The Tribune, likes
Whitehall—drop   *1863:* Your Tribune, likes Whitehall, drop   79| *1837:*
tavern—hear <> discussed—   *1863:* tavern, hear <> discussed,   80| *1837:* or
Richard—   *1863:* or James—   81| *1837:* to . . . I   *1863:* to—I   83| *1837:* now: I
want, just   *1863:* want just   *1868:* now. I   85| *1837:* ghosts! ¶ HOLLIS Will you not
hear me, Strafford?   *1863:* ghosts. ¶ HOLLIS Nay, you must hear me, Strafford!
86| *1837:* readily! . . . Only, one droll thing   *1863:* readily! Only, one rare thing   *1868:*
readily! Only one   *1888:* readily! Only, one   87-89| *1837:* the King, / And <>
know!   *1863:* the King, / Turn his Sejanus, Richelieu and what not, / And <>

90 My patient pair of traitors! Ah,—but, William—
Does not his cheek grow thin?

WILLIAM   'Tis you look thin,
Father!

STRAFFORD A scamper o'er the breezy wolds
Sets all to-rights.

HOLLIS   You cannot sure forget
A prison-roof is o'er you, Strafford?

STRAFFORD   No,
95 Why, no. I would not touch on that, the first.
I left you that. Well, Hollis? Say at once,
The King can find no time to set me free!
A mask at Theobald's?

HOLLIS   Hold: no such affair
Detains him.

STRAFFORD   True: what needs so great a matter?
100 The Queen's lip may be sore. Well: when he pleases,—
Only, I want the air: it vexes flesh
To be pent up so long.

HOLLIS   The King—I bear
His message, Strafford: pray you, let me speak!

STRAFFORD Go, William! Anne, try o'er your song again!

[*The* CHILDREN *retire.*]

105 They shall be loyal, friend, at all events.
I know your message: you have nothing new
To tell me: from the first I guessed as much.
I know, instead of coming here himself,
Leading me forth in public by the hand,
110 The King prefers to leave the door ajar
As though I were escaping—bids me trudge
While the mob gapes upon some show prepared

---

know—   90| *1837:*—My <> Ah .. but   *1863:* My <> Ah,—but   93| *1837:*
to-rights! ¶ HOLLIS   *1863:* to-rights. ¶ HOLLIS   96| *1837:* that. Well, Hollis? ¶ . . . .
Say   *1863:* that. Well, Hollis? Say   97| *1837:* The King could find   *1863:* The King
can find   98| *1837:* Hush . . . no   *1863:* Hold: no   100| *1837:* sore!—Well
1863: sore. Well   101| *1837:* vexes one   *1863:* vexes flesh   102| *1837:* long! ¶
HOLLIS The King . . . I   *1863:* long. ¶ HOLLIS The King—I   103| *1837:* message,
Strafford . . . pray   *1863:* message, Strafford: pray   108| *1837:* here at once—   *1863:*
here himself   *1868:* himself,   109| *1837:* forth before them by the hand,—   *1863:*
forth in public by the hand,   110| *1837:* I know the King will leave   *1863:* The King
prefers to leave   111| *1837:* escaping . . . let me fly   *1863:* escaping—bids me

104

On the other side of the river! Give at once
His order of release! I've heard, as well
115 Of certain poor manœuvres to avoid
The granting pardon at his proper risk;
First, he must prattle somewhat to the Lords,
Must talk a trifle with the Commons first,
Be grieved I should abuse his confidence,
120 And far from blaming them, and . . . Where's the order?
HOLLIS Spare me!
STRAFFORD   Why, he'd not have me steal away?
With an old doublet and a steeple hat
Like Prynne's? Be smuggled into France, perhaps?
Hollis, 'tis for my children! 'Twas for them
125 I first consented to stand day by day
And give your Puritans the best of words,
Be patient, speak when called upon, observe
Their rules, and not return them prompt their lie!
What's in that boy of mine that he should prove
130 Son to a prison-breaker? I shall stay
And he'll stay with me. Charles should know as much,
He too has children!
    [*Turning to* HOLLIS's COMPANION.] Sir, you feel for me!
No need to hide that face! Though it have looked
Upon me from the judgment-seat . . . I know
135 Strangely, that somewhere it has looked on me . . .
Your coming has my pardon, nay, my thanks:
For there is one who comes not.
HOLLIS   Whom forgive,

---

trudge   113–114| *1837:* river! ¶ HOLLIS [*to his Companion*] Tell him all; / I knew my
throat would thicken thus . . Speak, you! / STRAFFORD 'Tis all one—I forgive him. Let me have
/ The order <> ¶ . . . I've <> well,   *1863:* river! Give at once / His order <> I've   *1868:*
well   115| *1837:* manoeuvrings *1868:* manoeuvres   117| *1837:* the Lords—
1863: the Lords,   118| *1837:* first— *1863:* first,   120| *1837:* them, and . . . ¶ . . .
Where's *1863:* them, and . . . Where's   121| *1837:* STRAFFORD Why. . . . he'd *1863:*
STRAFFORD Why, he'd   122| *1837:*—With *1863:* With   125| *1837:* I e'er
consented *1863:* I first consented   126| *1837:* give those Puritans <> words—
1863: give your Puritans <> words,   127| *1837:* patient—speak <>
upon—observe *1863:* patient, speak <> upon, observe   128–129| *1837:* rules,—and
not give all of them the lie! / HOLLIS No—Strafford . . no escape . . no . . dearest Strafford! /
STRAFFORD What's <> should be *1863:* rules, and not return them prompt their lie! /
What's <> should prove   131| *1837:* much— *1868:* much,   132| *1837:*
COMPANION] Ah, you *1863:* COMPANION] Sir, you   135–140| *1837:* me . . . /

As one to die!

STRAFFORD   True, all die, and all need

Forgiveness: I forgive him from my soul.

140 HOLLIS 'Tis a world's wonder: Strafford, you must die!

STRAFFORD Sir, if your errand is to set me free

This heartless jest mars much. Ha! Tears in truth?

We'll end this! See this paper, warm—feel—warm

With lying next my heart! Whose hand is there?

145 Whose promise? Read, and loud for God to hear!

"Strafford shall take no hurt"—read it, I say!

"In person, honour, nor estate"—

HOLLIS   The King . . .

STRAFFORD I could unking him by a breath! You sit

Where Loudon sat, who came to prophesy

150 The certain end, and offer me Pym's grace

If I'd renounce the King: and I stood firm

On the King's faith. The King who lives . . .

HOLLIS   To sign

The warrant for your death.

STRAFFORD   "Put not your trust

In princes, neither in the sons of men,

155 In whom is no salvation!"

HOLLIS   Trust in God!

The scaffold is prepared: they wait for you:

Still there is One who does not come—there's One / That shut out Heaven from me . . . ¶
HOLLIS Think on it then! / On Heaven . . and calmly . . as one . . as one to die! / STRAFFORD
Die? True, friend, all must die, and all must need / Forgiveness <> soul. / HOLLIS Be
constant, now . . . be grand and brave . . be now / Just as when . . . Oh, I cannot stay for
words . . . / 'Tis a <> wonder . . but . . you   *1863:* me . . . / Your coming has my pardon,
nay, my thanks. / For there is One who comes not. ¶ HOLLIS Whom forgive, / As one to die!
¶ STRAFFORD True, all die, and all need / Forgiveness <> soul. / HOLLIS 'Tis a <>
wonder: Strafford, you   **136**| *1868:* thanks: **137**| *1868:* one
142–143| *1837:* jest will . . ¶ HOLLIS—you turn white, / And your lip
shivers!—What if . . . ¶ Oh, we'll end, / We'll <> paper—warm . . feel . .
warm   *1863:* jest mars much. Ha! Tears in truth? / We'll <> paper,
warm—feel—warm   **145**| *1837:* promise? Read! Read loud! For   *1863:* promise?
Read, and loud for   **146**| *1837:* hurt" . . read   *1863:* hurt"—read   **147**| *1837:*
estate" . . . . ¶ HOLLIS   *1863:* estate"—¶ HOLLIS   **149**| *1837:* sate . . Loudon, who came to
tell   *1863:* sat, who came to prophesy   **150**| *1837:* me Pym's pardon   *1863:* me Pym's
grace   **151**| *1837:* If I'd forsake the King—and   *1863:* If I'd renounce the King:
and   **152**| *1837:* On my King's faith! The <> lived   *1863:* On the King's faith. The
<> lives   **154**| *1837:* Princes   *1863:* princes   **155–156**| *1837:* salvation!" On

He has consented. Cast the earth behind!

CHARLES You would not see me, Strafford, at your foot!
It was wrung from me! Only, curse me not!

160 HOLLIS [*to* STRAFFORD]. As you hope grace and pardon in your need,
Be merciful to this most wretched man.

> [*Voices from within.*]

Verso la sera
Di Primavera.

STRAFFORD You'll be good to those children, sir? I know
165 You'll not believe her, even should the Queen
Think they take after one they rarely saw.
I had intended that my son should live
A stranger to these matters: but you are
So utterly deprived of friends! He too
170 Must serve you—will you not be good to him?
Or, stay, sir, do not promise—do not swear!
You, Hollis—do the best you can for me!
I've not a soul to trust to: Wandesford's dead,
And you've got Radcliffe safe, Laud's turn comes next:
175 I've found small time of late for my affairs,
But I trust any of you, Pym himself—
No one could hurt them: there's an infant, too.

---

that King——/ Upon his head . . . ¶ CHARLES O Hollis, he will curse me! / The <>
prepared—they <> you— *1863:* salvation!" ¶ HOLLIS Trust in God. / The <> prepared:
they <> you: *1868:* God! 157–158| *1837:* consented . . . ¶ CHARLES No, no—stay
first—Strafford! / You <> me perish at your foot . . . *1863:* consented. Cast the earth
behind! / CHARLES You <> me, Strafford, at your foot! 159–160| *1837:* me! Only curse
me not! / The Queen had cruel eyes! And Vane declared . . / And I believed I could have
rescued you . . / Strafford—they threaten me! and . . well, speak now, / And let me die!— ¶
HOLLIS <> grace from God, *1863:* not! / HOLLIS <> grace and pardon in your need,
1888: me! Only, curse
161| *1837:* man! VOICES *1868:* man [*Voices* *1888:* man. [*Voices* 164| *1837:*
[*after a pause*] You'll <> Sire *1863:* You'll <> sir 165| *1837:* her even *1863:*
her, even 166| *1837:* one they never saw! *1863:* one they rarely saw.
168| *1837:* matters . . . but *1863:* matters: but 171| *1837:* Stay—Sire—stay—do not
promise *1863:* Or, stay, sir, do not promise 172| *1837:* And, Hollis *1863:* You,
Hollis 173| *1837:* dead— *1863:* dead, 174| *1837:* safe—and Laud is here . .
1863: safe, Laud's turn comes next: 175| *1837:* I've had small <> affairs— *1863:*
I've found small <> affairs, 176| *1837:* But I'll trust any of you . . . Pym *1863:* But I
trust any of you, Pym 177| *1837:* too— *1888:* too. 178–179| *1837:* . . . These

These tedious cares! Your Majesty could spare them.
Nay—pardon me, my King! I had forgotten
180 Your education, trials, much temptation,
Some weakness: there escaped a peevish word—
'Tis gone: I bless you at the last. You know
All's between you and me: what has the world
To do with it? Farewell!

CHARLES [*at the door*]. Balfour! Balfour!

Enter BALFOUR.

185 The Parliament!—go to them: I grant all
Demands. Their sittings shall be permanent:
Tell them to keep their money if they will:
I'll come to them for every coat I wear
And every crust I eat: only I choose
190 To pardon Strafford. As the Queen shall choose!
—You never heard the People howl for blood,
Beside!

BALFOUR Your Majesty may hear them now:
The walls can hardly keep their murmurs out:
Please you retire!

CHARLES   Take all the troops, Balfour!
195 BALFOUR There are some hundred thousand of the crowd

CHARLES Come with me, Strafford! You'll not fear, at least!

STRAFFORD Balfour, say nothing to the world of this!
I charge you, as a dying man, forget

<> them—/ But 'tis so awkward—dying in a hurry! / . . . Nay—Pardon *1863:* These <>
them! / Nay—pardon *1888:* them.   **180|** *1837:* trials, and temptations *1863:* trials,
much temptation,   **181|** *1837:* And weakness . . I have said a *1863:* Some weakness:
there escaped a   **182|** *1837:* But, mind I <> last! You *1863:* 'Tis gone: I <> last.
You   **183|** *1837:* 'Tis between <> me . . . what *1863:* All's between <> me:
what   **184–185|** *1837:* door] Balfour! Balfour! / . . . What, die? Strafford to die? This
Strafford here? / Balfour! . . Nay Strafford, do not speak . . Balfour! ¶ *Enter* BALFOUR / The
Parliament . . . go to them—I *1863:* door] Balfour! Balfour! ¶ *Enter* BALFOUR / The
Parliament!—go to them: I   **186|** *1837:* Demands! Their <> permanent— *1863:*
Demands. Their <> permanent: **187|** *1837:* will . . . *1863:* will: **189|** *1837:*
eat, only *1863:* eat: only   **190–191|** *1837:* pardon Strafford—Strafford—my brave
friend! / BALFOUR [*aside*] Is he mad, Hollis? ¶ CHARLES Strafford, now, to die! / . . But the
Queen . . . ah, the Queen!—make haste, Balfour! / —You <> people *1863:* pardon
Strafford. As the Queen shall choose! / —You <> People   **195|** *1837:* crowd. *1888:*
crowd   **196|** *1837:* fear them friend!— *1863:* fear, at least!   **200|** *1837:* one . . or if

108

You gazed upon this agony of one . . .
200 Of one . . . or if . . . why you may say, Balfour,
The King was sorry: 'tis no shame in him:
Yes, you may say he even wept, Balfour,
And that I walked the lighter to the block
Because of it. I shall walk lightly, sir!
205 Earth fades, heaven breaks on me: I shall stand next
Before God's throne: the moment's close at hand
When man the first, last time, has leave to lay
His whole heart bare before its Maker, leave
To clear up the long error of a life
210 And choose one happiness for evermore.
With all mortality about me, Charles,
The sudden wreck, the dregs of violent death—
What if, despite the opening angel-song,
There penetrate one prayer for you? Be saved
215 Through me! Bear witness, no one could prevent
My death! Lead on! ere he awake—best, now!
All must be ready: did you say, Balfour,
The crowd began to murmur? They'll be kept
Too late for sermon at St. Antholin's!
220 Now! But tread softly—children are at play
In the next room. Precede! I follow—

Enter LADY CARLISLE, *with many* ATTENDANTS.

LADY CARLISLE   Me!

. . why   *1888:* one . . . or if . . . why   **201**| *1837:* sorry—very—'tis no shame!   *1863:*
sorry: 'tis no shame in him: **202**| *1837:* wept, Balfour,—   *1863:* wept, Balfour,
204–205| *1837:* lightly, Sire! / —For I shall save you . . save you at the last! / Earth fades,
Heaven dawns on me . . I shall wake next   *1863:* sir! / Earth fades, Heaven breaks on me: I
shall stand next   *1868:* heaven   **207**| *1837:* Man   *1868:* man   **208**| *1837:* its
Maker—leave   *1863:* its Maker, leave   *1868:* maker   *1888:* Maker   **212**| *1837:*
wreck—the dregs—the violent death . . .   *1863:* wreck, the dregs of violent death—
213–215| *1837:* I'll pray for you! Thro' all the Angel-song / Shall penetrate one weak and
quivering prayer— / I'll say how good you are . . inwardly good / And pure . . [*The* KING *falls:*
HOLLIS *raises him*] ¶ Be witness, he could not prevent   *1863:* What if, despite the opening
angel-song, / There penetrate one prayer for you? Be saved / Through me! Bear witness, no
one could prevent   **216**| *1837:* death! I'll go—ere he awakes—go now!   *1863:* death!
Lead on! ere he awake—best, now!   **217**| *1837:* ready—did   *1863:* ready: did
218| *1837:* murmur?—They'll   *1863:* murmur? They'll   **220**| *1837:* Now—but
1863: Now! but   *1868:* Now! But   **221**| *1837:* room—Ah, just my children—Hollis! /

Follow me, Strafford, and be saved! The King?

[*To the* KING.] Well—as you ordered, they are ranged without,

The convoy ... [*seeing the* KING'*s state.*]

[*To* STRAFFORD.] You know all, then! Why, I thought

225 It looked best that the King should save you,—Charles

Alone; 'tis a shame that you should owe me aught.

Or no, not shame! Strafford, you'll not feel shame

At being saved by me?

HOLLIS   All true! Oh Strafford,

She saves you! all her deed! this lady's deed!

230 And is the boat in readiness? You, friend,

Are Billingsley, no doubt. Speak to her, Strafford!

See how she trembles, waiting for your voice!

The world's to learn its bravest story yet.

LADY CARLISLE Talk afterward! Long nights in France enough,

235 To sit beneath the vines and talk of home.

STRAFFORD You love me, child? Ah, Strafford can be loved

As well as Vane! I could escape, then?

LADY CARLISLE   Haste!

Advance the torches, Bryan!

STRAFFORD   I will die.

They call me proud: but England had no right,

240 When she encountered me—her strength to mine—

To find the chosen foe a craven. Girl,

I fought her to the utterance, I fell,

I am hers now, and I will die. Beside,

——Or ... no—support the King! [*a door is unbarred*] ¶ Hark .. they are here! / Stay
Hollis!—Go Balfour! I'll follow. . . . . *Enter   1863:* room. Precede! I follow—*Enter*
²²²| *1837:* saved! ... The   *1863:* saved! The   ²²³| *1837:* ordered .. They <>
without ..   *1863:* ordered, they <> without,   ²²⁴| *1837:* convoy .. [*seeing* <> all
then   *1863:* all, then   *1888:* convoy ... [*seeing*   ²²⁵| *1837:* looked so well that
Charles should save you—Charles   *1863:* looked best that the King should save you,
Charles   *1888:* you,—Charles   ²²⁶| *1837:* Alone .. 'tis shame <> owe it me—   *1863:*
Alone; 'tis <> owe me aught   *1868:* 'tis a shame   ²²⁷| *1837:* Me .. no   *1863:* Or, no,
not shame   *1868:* Or no   ²²⁹| *1837:* deed .. this girl's own deed   *1863:* deed! this
lady's deed!   ²³⁰| *1837:*—And <> readiness? ... You   *1863:* And <> readiness?
You   ²³¹| *1837:* doubt! Speak   *1888:* doubt. Speak   ²³²| *1837:* trembles ..
waiting   *1863:* trembles, waiting   ²³³| *1837:* yet!   *1888:* yet.   ²³⁴| *1837:*
enough   *1863:* enough,   ²³⁵| *1837:* home!   *1868:* home.   ²³⁶| *1837:* me,
girl! . . . . Ah   *1863:* me, child! Ah   *1868:* child? Ah   ²³⁷| *1837:* Haste ..   *1863:*
Haste!   ²³⁸| *1837:* die!   *1863:* die.   ²³⁹| *1837:* proud .. but <> right   *1863:*
proud: but <> right,   ²⁴¹| *1837:* craven! Girl,   *1863:* craven. Girl,   ²⁴²| *1837:*
utterance—I fell—   *1863:* utterance, I fell,   ²⁴³| *1837:* hers now .. and I will die!

The lookers-on! Eliot is all about
245 This place, with his most uncomplaining brow.

LADY CARLISLE Strafford!

STRAFFORD   I think if you could know how much
I love you, you would be repaid, my friend!

LADY CARLISLE Then, for my sake!

STRAFFORD   Even for your sweet sake,
I stay.

HOLLIS For *their* sake!

STRAFFORD   To bequeath a stain?
250 Leave me! Girl, humour me and let me die!

LADY CARLISLE Bid him escape—wake, King! Bid him escape!

STRAFFORD True, I will go! Die, and forsake the King?
I'll not draw back from the last service.

LADY CARLISLE Strafford!

STRAFFORD   And, after all, what is disgrace to me?
255 Let us come, child! That it should end this way!
Lead then! but I feel strangely: it was not
To end this way.

LADY CARLISLE   Lean—lean on me!

STRAFFORD   My King!
Oh, had he trusted me—his friend of friends!

LADY CARLISLE I can support him, Hollis!

STRAFFORD   Not this way!
260 This gate—I dreamed of it, this very gate.

LADY CARLISLE It opens on the river: our good boat
Is moored below, our friends are there.

STRAFFORD   The same:

Beside *1863:* now, and I will die. Beside, *1868:* her's   244| *1868:* looker on   *1888:*
lookers-on   245| *1837:* place with <> brow! *1863:* brow.   *1868:* place, with
247| *1837:* my girl! *1863:* my friend!   248| *1837:* sweet sake . .   *1863:* sweet
sake,   249| *1837:* STRAFFORD I bequeath a stain . . .   *1863:* STRAFFORD To bequeath a
stain?   250–251| *1837:* die! / HOLLIS No way to draw him hence—Carlisle—no way? /
LADY CARLISLE [*suddenly to* CHARLES] Bid him escape . . wake *1863:* die! / LADY CARLISLE Bid
him escape—wake *1868:* die? *1888:* die!   252| *1837:* [*Looks earnestly at him*] Yes,
I *1863:* True, I   255| *1837:* come, girl! . . . That *1863:* come, child! That   *1868:*
way *1888:* way!   256| *1837:* then . . . but <> strangely . . . it *1863:* then! but <>
strangely: it   257| *1837:* way! CHARLES Lean *1863:* way. LADY CARLISLE Lean
258–259| *1837:* his Friend of friends— / Had he but trusted me! ¶ LADY CARLISLE Leave not
the king— / I <> STRAFFORD [*Starting as they approach the door at the back*] Not this
way; *1863:* friend of friends!— / LADY CARLISLE I <> STRAFFORD Not this way! *1868:*
friends!   260| *1837:* gate . . . I <> it . . . this very gate! *1863:* gate—I <> it, this very
gate.   261| *1837:* river—our *1863:* river: our   262| *1837:* below—our <>

111

Only with something ominous and dark,
Fatal, inevitable.

LADY CARLISLE   Strafford! Strafford!

265 STRAFFORD Not by this gate! I feel what will be there!
I dreamed of it, I tell you: touch it not!

LADY CARLISLE To save the King,—Strafford, to save the King!

[*As* STRAFFORD *opens the door,* PYM *is discovered with* HAMPDEN,
VANE, *etc.* STRAFFORD *falls back;* PYM *follows slowly and
confronts him.*]

PYM Have I done well? Speak, England! Whose sole sake
I still have laboured for, with disregard

270 To my own heart,—for whom my youth was made
Barren, my manhood waste, to offer up
Her sacrifice—this friend, this Wentworth here—
Who walked in youth with me, loved me, it may be,
And whom, for his forsaking England's cause,

275 I hunted by all means (trusting that she
Would sanctify all means) even to the block
Which waits for him. And saying this, I feel
No bitterer pang than first I felt, the hour
I swore that Wentworth might leave us, but I

280 Would never leave him: I do leave him now.
I render up my charge (be witness, God!)
To England who imposed it. I have done
Her bidding—poorly, wrongly,—it may be,
With ill effects—for I am weak, a man:

285 Still, I have done my best, my human best,
Not faltering for a moment. It is done.

---

there! ¶ STRAFFORD The same!   *1863:* below, our <> there. ¶ STRAFFORD The same.   *1868:*
same: 264| *1837:* inevitable . . . ¶ LADY CARLISLE   *1863:* inevitable. ¶ LADY
CARLISLE   265| *1837:* gate . . I feel it will   *1863:* gate! I feel what will   266| *1837:*
you . . touch   *1863:* you: touch   § Stage Directions following line 267 §   *1837: back to the
front of the stage:* PYM   *1863:* back: PYM   268| *1837:* well? Speak, England! Whose
great sake   *1863:* well? Speak, England! Whose sole sake   271| *1837:* future dark, to
1863: my Future waste, to   *1868:* my manhood waste   272| *1837:* this man, this
1868: this friend, this   273| *1837:* That walked <> loved me it   *1863:* Who
walked <> me, loved me, it   276| *1837:* the grave   *1863:* the block   277| *1837:*
That yawns for   *1863:* Which waits for   278| *1837:* bitter   *1863:* bitterer
279| *1837:* us,—but   *1863:* us, but   280| *1837:* now!   *1863:* now.   282| *1837:*
it! I   *1863:* it. I   283| *1837:* be   *1863:* be,   284| *1837:* am but a
man. . . . .   *1863:* am weak, a man: 285| *1837:* best, my very best,   *1863:* best, my
human best,   286| *1837:* moment! I have done! ¶ [*After a pause*]   *1863:* moment. It is

112

And this said, if I say . . . yes, I will say
I never loved but one man—David not
More Jonathan! Even thus, I love him now:
290 And look for my chief portion in that world
Where great hearts led astray are turned again,
(Soon it may be, and, certes, will be soon:
My mission over, I shall not live long,)—
Ay, here I know I talk—I dare and must,
295 Of England, and her great reward, as all
I look for there; but in my inmost heart,
Believe, I think of stealing quite away
To walk once more with Wentworth—my youth's friend
Purged from all error, gloriously renewed,
300 And Eliot shall not blame us. Then indeed . . .
This is no meeting, Wentworth! Tears increase
Too hot. A thin mist—is it blood?—enwraps
The face I loved once. Then, the meeting be!
STRAFFORD I have loved England too; we'll meet then, Pym.
305 As well die now! Youth is the only time
To think and to decide on a great course:
Manhood with action follows; but 'tis dreary,
To have to alter our whole life in age—
The time past, the strength gone! As well die now.
310 When we meet, Pym, I'd be set right—not now!
Best die. Then if there's any fault, fault too
Dies, smothered up. Poor grey old little Laud

---

done.   **287|** *1837:* And that said, I will say . . . yes   *1863:* And this said, if I say . . .
yes   **288|** *1837:* but this man   *1863:* but one man   **292|** *1837:* be . . and . . yes . . it
will   *1863:* be, and, certes, will   **293|** *1837:* long!)—   *1863:* long.)—   *1888:*
long,)—   **294|** *1837:* . . . Aye here <> talk—and I will talk   *1863:* Ay, here <>
talk—I dare and must,   **295|** *1837:* Of England—and <> reward—as   *1863:* Of
England, and <> reward, as   **296|** *1837:* heart   *1863:* heart,   **297|** *1837:*
Believe I   *1863:* Believe, I   **298|** *1837:* with Wentworth—with my friend   *1863:* with
Wentworth—my youth's friend   **300|** *1837:* us! Then indeed . .   *1863:* us. Then
indeed . . .   **301|** *1837:* (This <> Tears rise up   *1863:* This <> Tears
increase   **302|** *1837:* hot . . A   *1863:* hot. A   **303–304|** *1837:* loved so!) Then,
shall the <> be! / Then—then—then—I may kiss that hand, I know! ¶ STRAFFORD [*Walks
calmly up to* PYM *and offers his hand*] ¶ I <> Pym!   *1863:* loved once. Then, the <> be! /
STRAFFORD I   *1868:* then, Pym;   *1888:* then, Pym.   **305|** *1837:* well to die! Youth is
the time—our youth,   *1863:* well die now! Youth is the only time   **307|** *1837:* Age
with its action <> dreary   *1863:* Manhood with action   *1868:* dreary,   **308|** *1837:*
alter one's whole   *1863:* alter our whole   **309|** *1837:* as   *1868:* As
310–313| *1837:* now! / I'd die as I have lived . . too late to change! / Best <> any fault, it will /

May dream his dream out, of a perfect Church,
In some blind corner. And there's no one left.
315 I trust the King now wholly to you, Pym!
And yet, I know not: I shall not be there:
Friends fail—if he have any. And he's weak,
And loves the Queen, and . . . Oh, my fate is nothing—
Nothing! But not that awful head—not that!
320 PYM If England shall declare such will to me . . .
STRAFFORD Pym, you help England! I, that am to die,
What I must see! 'tis here—all here! My God,
Let me but gasp out, in one word of fire,
How thou wilt plague him, satiating hell!
325 What? England that you help, become through you
A green and putrefying charnel, left
Our children . . . some of us have children, Pym—
Some who, without that, still must ever wear
A darkened brow, an over-serious look,
330 And never properly be young! No word?
What if I curse you? Send a strong curse forth
Clothed from my heart, lapped round with horror till
She's fit with her white face to walk the world
Scaring kind natures from your cause and you—

Be smothered up: much best! You'll be too busy / With your hereafter, you will have achieved
/ Too many triumphs to be always dwelling / Upon my downfall, Pym? Poor little Laud / May
<> out of <> Church   *1863:* now: / Best <> it too / Dies, smothered up. Poor grey old
little Laud. / May   *1868:* out, of Church,   *1888:* any fault, fault too   **314|** *1837:*
corner? And <> left . . . ¶ [*He glances on the* KING]   *1863:* corner. And <> left.
316–317| *1837:* yet . . I know not! What if with this weakness . . . / And I shall not be there . . .
And he'll betray / His friends—if he has any . . . And he's false . .   *1863:* yet, I know not! I
shall not be there! / Friends fail—if he have any! And he's weak,   *1868:* not: I <> there: /
<> any. And   **318|** *1837:* and . . ¶ Oh   *1863:* and . . Oh   *1888:* and . . . Oh
319–322| *1837:* head . . not that! / § additional space lines 319–320 § Pym, save the King! Pym,
save him! Stay—you shall . . . / For you love England! I, that am dying, think / What I must
see . . 'tis here . . all <> God!   *1863:* head—not that! / § no additional space between lines §
Pym, you help England! I, that am to die, / <> see! 'tis here—all   *1868:* that! / PYM If
England shall declare such will to me . . . / STRAFFORD Pym <> die, / <> God,
324| *1837:* How Thou <> Hell!   *1868:* thou <> hell!   **325|** *1837:* you love—our
land—become   *1863:* you help, become through you   **330–331|** *1837:* young . . . ¶ No
word! / You will not say a word—to me—to Him! [*Turning to* CHARLES] / Speak to him . . . as
you spoke to me . . . that day! / Nay, I will let you pray to him, my King— / Pray to him! He
will kiss your feet, I know! / § additional space between this line and the following § What
<> Curse   *1863:* young! No word? § 1863 drops lines 331–342 §   *1868:* word? / What <>
curse   **332|** *1837:* horror, till   *1868:* horror till   **333|** *1837:* fit, with <> face,

114

335 Then to sit down with you at the board-head,
The gathering for prayer ... O speak, but speak!
... Creep up, and quietly follow each one home,
You, you, you, be a nestling care for each
To sleep with,—hardly moaning in his dreams,
340 She gnaws so quietly,—till, lo he starts,
Gets off with half a heart eaten away!
Oh, shall you 'scape with less if she's my child?
You will not say a word—to me—to Him?
PYM If England shall declare such will to me ...
345 STRAFFORD No, not for England now, not for Heaven now,—
See, Pym, for my sake, mine who kneel to you!
There, I will thank you for the death, my friend!
This is the meeting: let me love you well!
PYM England,—I am thine own! Dost thou exact
350 That service? I obey thee to the end.
STRAFFORD O God, I shall die first—I shall die first!

---

to   *1868:* fit with <> face to   **335|** *1837:* you, at   *1868:* you at   **336|** *1837:*
prayer.... ¶ VANE O speak, Pym! Speak!   *1868:* prayer .. O speak, but speak!   *1888:* prayer
...O   **337|** *1837:* STRAFFORD ...Creep <> home—   *1868:* .. Creep <> home,   *1888:*
...Creep   **338|** *1837:* You—you—you—be <> Care   *1868:* You, you, you, be <>
care   **339|** *1837:* with, hardly <> dreams ...   *1868:* with,—hardly <>
dreams,   **340|** *1837:* quietly ... until he starts—   *1868:* quietly,—till, lo he
starts,   **341|** *1837:* away ...   *1868:* away!   **342-344|** *1837:* Oh you shall 'scape
with less, if she's my child! / VANE [*to* PYM] We never thought of this ... surely not dreamed /
Of this .. it never can ... could come to this! / PYM [*after a pause*] If England should declare
her will   *1863:* You will not say a word—to me—to Him? § 1863 drops lines 344-348 §
1868: Oh shall you 'scape with less if she's my child! / You <> Him? / PYM If England shall
declare such will   *1888:* Oh, shall   **345|** *1837:* No—not for England, now—not for
Heaven, now ...   *1868:* No, not for England now, not for Heaven now,—   **346|** *1837:*
See, Pym—for me! My sake! I kneel   *1868:* See, Pym, for my sake, mine who kneel
347| *1837:* There .. <> death ... my friend,   *1868:* There, I <> death, my friend!
348| *1837:* *This* is the meeting ... you will send me proud / To my chill grave! Dear
Pym—I'll love you well! / Save him for me, and let   *1868:* This is the meeting: let
350| *1837:* end!   *1863:* end.   **349|** *1837:* England——I   *1863:* England—I
351| *1837:* STRAFFORD [*as he totters out*] O § 1863 drops line 351 §   *1868:*
STRAFFORD O   *1837:* § Stage directions § CURTAIN FALLS   *1863:* § Stage direction
omitted §

Nearly Ready

SORDELLO

In Six Books

By
The Author of Paracelsus

§ In 1837 Only §

SORDELLO

Text edited by John Berkey
Annotations by Roma A. King, Jr.

SORDELLO

TO J. MILSAND, OF DIJON.

1 DEAR FRIEND,—Let the next poem be introduced by your name,
therefore remembered along with one of the deepest of my affections,
and so repay all trouble it ever cost me. I wrote it twenty-five years
ago for only a few, counting even in these on somewhat more care
5 about its subject than they really had. My own faults of expression
were many; but with care for a man or book such would be surmounted,
and without it what avails the faultlessness of either? I
blame nobody, least of all myself, who did my best then and since;
for I lately gave time and pains to turn my work into what the many
10 might,—instead of what the few must,—like: but after all, I imagined
another thing at first, and therefore leave as I find it. The historical
decoration was purposely of no more importance than a background
requires; and my stress lay on the incidents in the development of a
soul: little else is worth study. I, at least, always thought so—you,
15 with many known and unknown to me, think so—others may one day
think so; and whether my attempt remain for them or not, I trust,
thought away and past it, to continue ever yours,

R.B.

LONDON: June 9, 1863.

---

§ Not included in 1840 edition § ¹⁻²| *1863:* name, and *1868:* name, therefore
remembered along with one of the deepest of my affections, and ¹⁷| *1863:* yours,
R. B. *1868:* yours, ¶ R. B.

SORDELLO

1840

BOOK THE FIRST

Who will, may hear Sordello's story told:
His story? Who believes me shall behold
The man, pursue his fortunes to the end,
Like me: for as the friendless-people's friend
5 Spied from his hill-top once, despite the din
And dust of multitudes, Pentapolin
Named o' the Naked Arm, I single out
Sordello, compassed murkily about
With ravage of six long sad hundred years.
10 Only believe me. Ye believe?
                              Appears
Verona . . . Never,—I should warn you first,—
Of my own choice had this, if not the worst
Yet not the best expedient, served to tell
A story I could body forth so well
15 By making speak, myself kept out of view,
The very man as he was wont to do,
And leaving you to say the rest for him.

---

§ Not included in 1840 edition §   ¹⁻²| *1863:* name, and   *1868:* name, therefore
remembered along with one of the deepest of my affections, and   ¹⁷| *1863:* yours, R.
B.   *1868:* yours, ¶ R. B.
§ Ed. 1840, 1863, 1868, 1888, 1889. Running Titles 1863, 1868 appear in capitals. §
§ ¹⁻¹⁶| *1863:* A QUIXOTIC ATTEMPT. §   ¹| *1840:* ¶ Who   *1863:* Who
³| *1840:* end   *1863:* end,   ⁴| *1840:* me; for <> friendless people's   *1863:* me: for
<> friendless-people's   ⁹| *1840:* years: *1863:* years.   ¹¹| *1840:* Verona . . .
Never, I <> first,   *1888:* Verona . . . Never,—I <> first,— § ¹⁷⁻⁴⁵| *1863:* WHY THE

Since, though I might be proud to see the dim
Abysmal past divide its hateful surge,
20   Letting of all men this one man emerge
Because it pleased me, yet, that moment past,
I should delight in watching first to last
His progress as you watch it, not a whit
More in the secret than yourselves who sit
25   Fresh-chapleted to listen. But it seems
Your setters-forth of unexampled themes,
Makers of quite new men, producing them,
Would best chalk broadly on each vesture's hem
The wearer's quality; or take their stand,
30   Motley on back and pointing-pole in hand,
Beside him. So, for once I face ye, friends,
Summoned together from the world's four ends,
Dropped down from heaven or cast up from hell,
To hear the story I propose to tell.
35   Confess now, poets know the dragnet's trick,
Catching the dead, if fate denies the quick,
And shaming her; 'tis not for fate to choose
Silence or song because she can refuse
Real eyes to glisten more, real hearts to ache
40   Less oft, real brows turn smoother for our sake:
I have experienced something of her spite;
But there's a realm wherein she has no right
And I have many lovers. Say, but few
Friends fate accords me? Here they are: now view
45   The host I muster! Many a lighted face
Foul with no vestige of the grave's disgrace;
What else should tempt them back to taste our air
Except to see how their successors fare?

POET HIMSELF ADDRESSES §   17| *1840:* him: *1863:* him.   19| *1840:*
Past   *1868:* past   25| *1840:* listen: but   *1863:* listen. But   27| *1840:* them
1863: them,   28| *1840:* Had best <> hem   *1863:* Would best <> hem,   *1888:*
hem   29| *1840:* quality, or take his stand   *1863:* quality; or take their stand,
30| *1840:* hand   *1863:* hand,   31| *1840:* Beside them; so for   *1863:* Beside him. So,
for   33| *1840:* Heaven <> Hell,   *1863:* heaven <> hell,   36| *1840:* dead if
Fate <> quick   *1863:* dead, if fate <> quick,   37| *1840:* Fate   *1863:* fate
43| *1840:* lovers: say but   *1863:* lovers. Say, but   *1888:* Say; but   44| *1840:* Fate <>
are; now   *1863:* fate <> are: now   § 46–73| *1863:* HIS AUDIENCE—FEW LIVING,

My audience! and they sit, each ghostly man
50   Striving to look as living as he can,
Brother by breathing brother; thou art set,
Clear-witted critic, by . . . but I'll not fret
A wondrous soul of them, nor move death's spleen
Who loves not to unlock them. Friends! I mean
55   The living in good earnest—ye elect
Chiefly for love—suppose not I reject
Judicious praise, who contrary shall peep,
Some fit occasion, forth, for fear ye sleep,
To glean your bland approvals. Then, appear,
60   Verona! say—thou, spirit, come not near
Now—not this time desert thy cloudy place
To scare me, thus employed, with that pure face!
I need not fear this audience, I make free
With them, but then this is no place for thee!
65   The thunder-phrase of the Athenian, grown
Up out of memories of Marathon,
Would echo like his own sword's griding screech
Braying a Persian shield,—the silver speech
Of Sidney's self, the starry paladin,
70   Turn intense as a trumpet sounding in
The knights to tilt,—wert thou to hear! What heart
Have I to play my puppets, bear my part
Before these worthies?
                              Lo, the past is hurled
In twain: up-thrust, out-staggering on the world.
75   Subsiding into shape, a darkness rears
Its outline, kindles at the core, appears
Verona. 'Tis six hundred years and more
Since an event. The Second Friedrich wore
The purple, and the Third Honorius filled
80   The holy chair. That autumn eve was stilled:
A last remains of sunset dimly burned

MANY DEAD. §   ⁴⁹| *1840:* audience: and   *1863:* audience! and   ⁵³| *1840:*
Death's   *1863:* death's   ⁵⁷| *1840:* peep   *1863:* peep,   ⁵⁸| *1840:* occasion
forth   *1863:* occasion, forth   ⁶¹| *1840:* Now—nor, this   *1863:* Now—not this
⁷¹| *1840:* tilt—wert <> hear   *1863:* tilt,—wert <> hear! What heart   ⁷³| *1840:*
Past   *1868:* past   § ⁷⁴⁻¹⁰²| *1863:* SHELLEY DEPARTING, VERONA
APPEARS. §   ⁷⁴| *1840:* up thrust   *1863:* up-thrust   ⁸²| *1840:* forests like

O'er the far forests, like a torch-flame turned
By the wind back upon its bearer's hand
In one long flare of crimson; as a brand,
85 The woods beneath lay black. A single eye
From all Verona cared for the soft sky.
But, gathering in its ancient market-place,
Talked group with restless group; and not a face
But wrath made livid, for among them were
90 Death's staunch purveyors, such as have in care
To feast him. Fear had long since taken root
In every breast, and now these crushed its fruit,
The ripe hate, like a wine: to note the way
It worked while each grew drunk! Men grave and grey
95 Stood, with shut eyelids, rocking to and fro,
Letting the silent luxury trickle slow
About the hollows where a heart should be;
But the young gulped with a delirious glee
Some foretaste of their first debauch in blood
100 At the fierce news: for, be it understood,
Envoys apprised Verona that her prince
Count Richard of Saint Boniface, joined since
A year with Azzo, Este's Lord, to thrust
Taurello Salinguerra, prime in trust
105 With Ecelin Romano, from his seat
Ferrara,—over zealous in the feat
And stumbling on a peril unaware,
Was captive, trammelled in his proper snare,
They phrase it, taken by his own intrigue.
110 Immediate succour from the Lombard League
Of fifteen cities that affect the Pope,
For Azzo, therefore, and his fellow-hope
Of the Guelf cause, a glory overcast!
Men's faces, late agape, are now aghast.

115 "Prone is the purple pavis; Este makes
    Mirth for the devil when he undertakes
    To play the Ecelin; as if it cost
    Merely your pushing-by to gain a post
    Like his! The patron tells ye, once for all,
120 There be sound reasons that preferment fall
    On our beloved" . . .

                    "Duke o' the Rood, why not?"
    Shouted an Estian, "grudge ye such a lot?
    The hill-cat boasts some cunning of her own,
    Some stealthy trick to better beasts unknown,
125 That quick with prey enough her hunger blunts,
    And feeds her fat while gaunt the lion hunts."
    "Taurello," quoth an envoy, "as in wane
    Dwelt at Ferrara. Like an osprey fain
    To fly but forced the earth his couch to make
130 Far inland, till his friend the tempest wake,
    Waits he the Kaiser's coming; and as yet
    That fast friend sleeps, and he too sleeps: but let
    Only the billow freshen, and he snuffs
    The aroused hurricane ere it enroughs
135 The sea it means to cross because of him.
    Sinketh the breeze? His hope-sick eye grows dim;
    Creep closer on the creature! Every day
    Strengthens the Pontiff; Ecelin, they say,
    Dozes now at Oliero, with dry lips
140 Telling upon his perished finger-tips
    How many ancestors are to depose
    Ere he be Satan's Viceroy when the doze
    Deposits him in hell. So, Guelfs rebuilt
    Their houses; not a drop of blood was spilt
145 When Cino Bocchimpane chanced to meet

Devil *1863:* devil   ^{121|} *1840:* beloved . . . ¶ Duke <> not? *1863:* beloved" . . . ¶
"Duke <> not?"   ^{122|} *1840:* an Estian, grudge *1863:* an Estian, "grudge
^{124|} *1840:* unknown *1863:* unknown,   ^{125|} *1840:* blunts *1863:* blunts,
^{126|} *1840:* hunts. *1863:* hunts."   ^{127|} *1840:* Taurello, quoth an envoy, as *1863:*
"Taurello," quoth an envoy, "as   ^{130|} *1840:* inland till *1863:* inland, till
§ ^{131–159|} *1863:* WHY THEY ENTREAT THE LOMBARD LEAGUE, §   ^{132|} *1840:*
too sleeps; but *1863:* too sleeps: but   ^{135|} *1840:* him: *1863:* him.   ^{139|} *1840:*
Dozes at *1863:* Dozes now at   ^{143|} *1840:* hell; so Guelfs *1863:* hell. So, Guelfs

Buccio Virtù—God's wafer, and the street
Is narrow! Tutti Santi, think, a-swarm
With Ghibellins, and yet he took no harm!
This could not last. Off Salinguerra went
150 To Padua, Podestà, 'with pure intent,'
Said he, 'my presence, judged the single bar
To permanent tranquillity, may jar
No longer'—so! his back is fairly turned?
The pair of goodly palaces are burned,
155 The gardens ravaged, and our Guelfs laugh, drunk
A week with joy. The next, their laughter sunk
In sobs of blood, for they found, some strange way,
Old Salinguerra back again—I say,
Old Salinguerra in the town once more
160 Uprooting, overturning, flame before,
Blood fetlock-high beneath him. Azzo fled;
Who 'scaped the carnage followed; then the dead
Were pushed aside from Salinguerra's throne,
He ruled once more Ferrara, all alone,
165 Till Azzo, stunned awhile, revived, would pounce
Coupled with Boniface, like lynx and ounce,
On the gorged bird. The burghers ground their teeth
To see troop after troop encamp beneath
I' the standing corn thick o'er the scanty patch
170 It took so many patient months to snatch
Out of the marsh; while just within their walls
Men fed on men. At length Taurello calls
A parley: 'let the Count wind up the war!'
Richard, lighthearted as a plunging star,
175 Agrees to enter for the kindest ends

146| *1840*: Buccio Virtù; God's *1863*: Buccio Virtù—God's   148| *1840*: harm.
1863: harm!   150| *1840*: To Padua, Podestà, with <> intent,   *1863*: To Padua,
Podestà, 'with <> intent,'   151| *1840*: he, my   *1863*: he, 'my   153| *1840*:
longer—so   *1863*: longer'—so   155| *1840*: and your Guelf is drunk   *1863*: and our
Guelfs laugh, drunk   156| *1840*: joy; the next, his laughter   *1863*: joy. The next, their
laughter   157| *1840*: for he found   *1863*: for they found   158| *1840*: again; I
say   *1863*: again—I say,   § 160–187| *1863*: IN THEIR CHANGED FORTUNE AT
FERRARA: §   160| *1840*: before   *1863*: before,   161| *1840*: him; Azzo   *1863*:
him. Azzo   162| *1840*: scaped   *1868*: 'scaped   164| *1863*: alone.   *1888*:
alone,   172| *1840*: on men. Astute Taurello   *1863*: on men. At length Taurello
173| *1840*: parley: let <> war!   *1863*: parley: 'let <> war!'   177| *1840*: more for

Ferrara, flanked with fifty chosen friends,
No horse-boy more, for fear your timid sort
Should fly Ferrara at the bare report.
Quietly through the town they rode, jog-jog;
180 'Ten, twenty, thirty,—curse the catalogue
Of burnt Guelf houses! Strange, Taurello shows
Not the least sign of life'—whereat arose
A general growl: 'How? With his victors by?
I and my Veronese? My troops and I?
185 Receive us, was your word?' So jogged they on,
Nor laughed their host too openly: once gone
Into the trap!—"
              Six hundred years ago!
Such the time's aspect and peculiar woe
(Yourselves may spell it yet in chronicles,
190 Albeit the worm, our busy brother, drills
His sprawling path through letters anciently
Made fine and large to suit some abbot's eye)
When the new Hohenstauffen dropped the mask,
Flung John of Brienne's favour from his casque.
195 Forswore crusading, had no mind to leave
Saint Peter's proxy leisure to retrive
Losses to Otho and to Barbaross,
Or make the Alps less easy to recross;
And, thus confirming Pope Honorius' fear,
200 Was excommunicate that very year.
"The triple-bearded Teuton come to life!"
Groaned the Great League; and, arming for the strife,
Wide Lombardy, on tiptoe to begin,
Took up, as it was Guelf or Ghibellin,
205 Its cry: what cry?
              "The Emperor to come!"

1863: more, for   **180**| *1840:* Ten <> thirty . . . curse *1863:* 'Ten <>
thirty,—curse   **181**| *1840:* houses! Strange Taurello *1863:* houses! Strange,
Taurello   **182**| *1840:* life—whereat *1863:* life'—whereat   **183**| *1840:* growl:
How *1863:* growl: 'How   **185**| *1840:* word? so *1863:* word?' So   **187**| *1840:*
trap . . . ¶ Six *1863:* trap!— ¶ Six *1868:* trap!—" ¶ Six
§ **188–215**| *1863:* FOR THE TIMES GROW STORMY AGAIN. §   **199**| *1840:* And
thus *1863:* And, thus   **201**| *1840:* The <> life! *1863:* "The <> life!"
205| *1840:* cry; what cry? ¶ The <> come! *1863:* what cry? ¶ "The <> come!" *1888:*

His crowd of feudatories, all and some,
That leapt down with a crash of swords, spears, shields,
One fighter on his fellow, to our fields,
Scattered anon, took station here and there,
210 And carried it, till now, with little care—
Cannot but cry for him; how else rebut
Us longer?—cliffs, an earthquake suffered jut
In the mid-sea, each domineering crest
Which nought save such another throe can wrest
215 From out (conceive) a certain chokeweed grown
Since o'er the waters, twine and tangle thrown
Too thick, too fast accumulating round,
Too sure to over-riot and confound
Ere long each brilliant islet with itself,
220 Unless a second shock save shoal and shelf,
Whirling the sea-drift wide: alas, the bruised
And sullen wreck! Sunlight to be diffused
For that!—sunlight, 'neath which, a scum at first,
The million fibres of our chokeweed nurst
225 Dispread themselves, mantling the troubled main,
And, shattered by those rocks, took hold again,
So kindly blazed it—that same blaze to brood
O'er every cluster of the multitude
Still hazarding new clasps, ties, filaments,
230 An emulous exchange of pulses, vents
Of nature into nature; till some growth
Unfancied yet, exuberantly clothe
A surface solid now, continuous, one:
"The Pope, for us the People, who begun
235 The People, carries on the People thus,
To keep that Kaiser off and dwell with us!"
See you?
        Or say, Two Principles that live
Each fitly by its Representative.

---

cry: what   **206|**   *1840:* some   *1863:* some,   **212|**   *1840:* longer? Cliffs an   *1863:*
longer? Cliffs, an   *1888:* longer?—cliffs   **213|**   *1863:* crest,   *1888:* crest
214| *1840:* Nothing save   *1888:* Which nought save   § **216–243|**   *1863:* THE
GHIBELLINS' WISH: THE GUELFS' WISH. §   **219|**   *1840:* itself   *1888:*
itself,   **223|**   *1840:* that! Sunlight   *1888:* that!—sunlight   **226|**   *1840:* again
1863: again,   **232|**   *1840:* yet exuberantly   *1863:* yet, exuberantly   **234|**   *1840:*
The   *1863:* "The   **236|**   *1840:* us!   *1863:* us!"   **238|**   *1840:* its Representative:

"Hill-cat"—who called him so?—the gracefullest
240 Adventurer, the ambiguous stranger-guest
Of Lombardy (sleek but that ruffling fur,
Those talons to their sheath!) whose velvet purr
Soothes jealous neighbours when a Saxon scout
—Arpo or Yoland, is it?—one without
245 A country or a name, presumes to couch
Beside their noblest; until men avouch
That, of all Houses in the Trevisan,
Conrad descries no fitter, rear or van,
Than Ecelo! They laughed as they enrolled
250 That name at Milan on the page of gold,
Godego's lord,—Ramon, Marostica,
Cartiglion, Bassano, Loria,
And every sheep-cote on the Suabian's fief!
No laughter when his son, "the Lombard Chief"
255 Forsooth, as Barbarossa's path was bent
To Italy along the Vale of Trent,
Welcomed him at Roncaglia! Sadness now—
The hamlets nested on the Tyrol's brow,
The Asolan and Euganean hills,
260 The Rhetian and the Julian, sadness fills
Them all, for Ecelin vouchsafes to stay
Among and care about them; day by day
Choosing this pinnacle, the other spot,
A castle building to defend a cot,
265 A cot built for a castle to defend,
Nothing but castles, castles, nor an end
To boasts how mountain ridge may join with ridge
By sunken gallery and soaring bridge.
He takes, in brief, a figure that beseems
270 The griesliest nightmare of the Church's dreams,
—A Signory firm-rooted, unestranged

1863: its Representative.   **239|**   *1840:* Hill-cat . . . who <> so, our gracefullest   *1863:*
"Hill-cat"—who <> so?—the gracefullest   **240|**   *1840:* Adventurer? the   *1863:*
Adventurer, the   § **244–272|**   *1863:* HOW ECELO'S HOUSE GREW HEAD OF
THOSE, §   **244|**   *1840:* . . . Arpo <> it? one   *1863:*—Arpo <> it?—one
247| *1840:* That of <> Trivisan   *1863:* That, of <> Trevisan,   **250|**   *1840:* gold
1863: gold,   **251|**   *1840:* For Godego, Ramon   *1863:* Godego's lord,—Ramon
254| *1840:* son, the <> Chief   *1863:* son, "the <> Chief"   **261|**   *1840:* all that
Ecelin   *1863:* all, for Ecelin   **268|**   *1840:* bridge—   *1863:* bridge.   **271|**   *1840:*

From its old interests, and nowise changed
By its new neighbourhood: perchance the vaunt
Of Otho, "my own Este shall supplant
275 Your Este," come to pass. The sire led in
A son as cruel; and this Ecelin
Had sons, in turn, and daughters sly and tall
And curling and compliant; but for all
Romano (so they styled him) throve, that neck
280 Of his so pinched and white, that hungry cheek
Proved 'twas some fiend, not him, the man's-flesh went
To feed: whereas Romano's instrument,
Famous Taurello Salinguerra, sole
I' the world, a tree whose boughs were slipt the bole
285 Successively, why should not he shed blood
To further a design? Men understood
Living was pleasant to him as he wore
His careless surcoat, glanced some missive o'er,
Propped on his truncheon in the public way,
290 While his lord lifted writhen hands to pray,
Lost at Oliero's convent.
                              Hill-cats, face
Our Azzo, our Guelf Lion! Why disgrace
A worthiness conspicuous near and far
(Atii at Rome while free and consular,
295 Este at Padua who repulsed the Hun)
By trumpeting the Church's princely son?
—Styled Patron of Rovigo's Polesine,
Ancona's march, Ferrara's . . . ask, in fine,
Our chronicles, commenced when some old monk

A   *1863:*—A   § ²⁷³⁻³⁰⁰| *1863:* AS AZZO LORD OF ESTE HEADS THESE. §
²⁷³| *1840:* neighbourhood; perchance   *1863:* neighbourhood: perchance   ²⁷⁷| *1840:*
tall,   *1868:* tall   ²⁷⁹| *1840:* style him) thrives   *1863:* styled him) throve
²⁸¹| *1840:* 'tis <> him, men's flesh is meant   *1863:* 'twas <> him, the man's-flesh
went   ²⁸⁴| *1840:* are   *1863:* were   ²⁸⁵| *1840:* shall   *1863:* should
²⁸⁹| *1840:* way   *1863:* way,   ²⁹⁰| *1840:* Ecelin lifts two writhen <> pray   *1863:*
While his lord lifted writhen <> pray,   ²⁹¹| *1840:* At Oliero's convent now: so,
place   *1863:* Lost at Oliero's convent. ¶ Hill-cats, face   ²⁹²| *1840:* For Azzo, Lion of the
. . . why disgrace   *1863:* With Azzo, our Guelf Lion—nor disgrace   *1868:* Our Azzo, our
Guelf-Lion! Why disgrace   *1888:* Guelf Lion   ²⁹⁵| *1840:* at Padua to repulse   *1863:*
at Padua who repulsed   ²⁹⁶| *1840:* son   *1868:* son?   ²⁹⁷| *1840:* Styled
1868:—Styled   ²⁹⁸| *1840:* March   *1868:* march   ²⁹⁹| *1840:* Your chronicles

134

300 Found it intolerable to be sunk
(Vexed to the quick by his revolting cell)
Quite out of summer while alive and well:
Ended when by his mat the Prior stood,
'Mid busy promptings of the brotherhood,
305 Striving to coax from his decrepit brains
The reason Father Porphyry took pains
To blot those ten lines out which used to stand
First on their charter drawn by Hildebrand.
    The same night wears. Verona's rule of yore
310 Was vested in a certain Twenty-four;
And while within his palace these debate
Concerning Richard and Ferrara's fate,
Glide we by clapping doors, with sudden glare
Of cressets vented on the dark, nor care
315 For aught that's seen or heard until we shut
The smother in, the lights, all noises but
The carroch's booming: safe at last! Why strange
Such a recess should lurk behind a range
Of banquet rooms? Your finger—thus—you push
320 A spring, and the wall opens, would you rush
Upon the banqueters, select your prey,
Waiting (the slaughter-weapons in the way
Strewing this very bench) with sharpened ear
A preconcerted signal to appear;
325 Or if you simply crouch with beating heart,
Bearing in some voluptuous pageant part
To startle them. Nor mutes nor masquers now,
Nor any . . . does that one man sleep whose brow
The dying lamp-flame sinks and rises o'er?
330 What woman stood beside him? not the more
Is he unfastened from the earnest eyes
Because that arras fell between! Her wise
And lulling words are yet about the room,
Her presence wholly poured upon the gloom

1863: Our chronicles   § ³⁰¹⁻³²⁹| *1863:* COUNT RICHARD'S PALACE AT
VERONA. §   ³⁰⁴| *1840:* Mid   *1863:* 'Mid   ³¹⁷| *1840:* booming; safe   *1863:*
booming: safe   ³²²| *1840:* Waiting, the slaughter-weapons   *1868:* Waiting (the
slaughter-weapons   ³²³| *1840:* bench, with   *1868:* bench) with   ³²⁵| *1840:*
heart   *1863:* heart,   § ³³⁰⁻³⁵⁸| *1863:* OF THE COUPLE FOUND THEREIN,

335 Down even to her vesture's creeping stir.
    And so reclines he, saturate with her,
    Until an outcry from the square beneath
    Pierces the charm: he springs up, glad to breathe,
    Above the cunning element, and shakes
340 The stupor off as (look you) morning breaks
    On the gay dress, and, near concealed by it,
    The lean frame like a half-burnt taper, lit
    Erst at some marriage-feast, then laid away
    Till the Armenian bridegroom's dying day,
345 In his wool wedding-robe.
                  For he—for he,
    Gate-vein of this hearts' blood of Lombardy,
    (If I should falter now)—for he is thine!
    Sordello, thy forerunner, Florentine!
    A herald-star I know thou didst absorb
350 Relentless into the consummate orb
    That scared it from its right to roll along
    A sempiternal path with dance and song
    Fulfilling its allotted period,
    Serenest of the progeny of God—
355 Who yet resigns it not! His darling stoops
    With no quenched lights, desponds with no blank troops
    Of disenfranchised brilliances, for, blent
    Utterly with thee, its shy element
    Like thine upburneth prosperous and clear.
360 Still, what if I approach the august sphere
    Named now with only one name, disentwine
    That under-current soft and argentine
    From its fierce mate in the majestic mass
    Leavened as the sea whose fire was mixt with glass
365 In John's transcendent vision,—launch once more

330–357| *1868* §   335| *1840:* stir: *1863:* stir.   338| *1840:* breathe *1868:*
breathe,   344| *1840:* dying-day, *1863:* dying day,   345| *1840:* wedding-robe;
for he—for he— *1863:* wedding-robe. For he—for he, *1868:* wedding-robe. ¶ For he—
for he,   346| *1840:* "Gate-vein <> Lombardy" *1863:* Gate-vein <> Lombardy,
347| *1840:* Thine! *1868:* thine!   353| *1840:* period *1863:* period,
354| *1840:* progeny of God *1863:* progeny of God! *1868:* progeny of God—
355| *1840:* not; his *1863:* not; His *1868:* not! His
§ 359–387| *1863:* ONE BELONGS TO DANTE; HIS BIRTHPLACE.
358–386| *1868* §   359| *1840:* clear: *1868:* clear, *1888:* clear.
362| *1840:* under current *1863:* under-current   365| *1840:* vision,

That lustre? Dante, pacer of the shore
Where glutted hell disgorgeth filthiest gloom,
Unbitten by its whirring sulphur-spume—
Or whence the grieved and obscure waters slope
370 Into a darkness quieted by hope;
Plucker of amaranths grown beneath God's eye
In gracious twilights where his chosen lie,—
I would do this! If I should falter now!
   In Mantua territory half is slough,
375 Half pine-tree forest; maples, scarlet oaks
Breed o'er the river-beds; even Mincio chokes
With sand the summer through: but 'tis morass
In winter up to Mantua walls. There was,
Some thirty years before this evening's coil,
380 One spot reclaimed from the surrounding spoil,
Goito; just a castle built amid
A few low mountains; firs and larches hid
Their main defiles, and rings of vineyard bound
The rest. Some captured creature in a pound,
385 Whose artless wonder quite precludes distress,
Secure beside in its own loveliness,
So peered with airy head, below, above,
The castle at its toils, the lapwings love
To glean among at grape-time. Pass within.
390 A maze of corridors contrived for sin,
Dusk winding-stairs, dim galleries got past,
You gain the inmost chambers, gain at last
A maple-panelled room: that haze which seems
Floating about the panel, if there gleams
395 A sunbeam over it, will turn to gold
And in light-graven characters unfold

The Arab's wisdom everywhere; what shade
Marred them a moment, those slim pillars made,
Cut like a company of palms to prop
400 The roof, each kissing top entwined with top,
Leaning together; in the carver's mind
Some knot of bacchanals, flushed cheek combined
With straining forehead, shoulders purpled, hair
Diffused between, who in a goat-skin bear
405 A vintage; graceful sister-palms! But quick
To the main wonder, now. A vault, see; thick
Black shade about the ceiling, though fine slits
Across the buttress suffer light by fits
Upon a marvel in the midst. Nay, stoop—
410 A dullish grey-streaked cumbrous font, a group
Round it,—each side of it, where'er one sees,—
Upholds it; shrinking Caryatides
Of just-tinged marble like Eve's lilied flesh
Beneath her maker's finger when the fresh
415 First pulse of life shot brightening the snow.
The font's edge burthens every shoulder, so
They muse upon the ground, eyelids half closed;
Some, with meek arms behind their backs disposed,
Some, crossed above their bosoms, some, to veil
420 Their eyes, some, propping chin and cheek so pale,
Some, hanging slack an utter helpless length
Dead as a buried vestal whose whole strength
Goes when the grate above shuts heavily.
So dwell these noiseless girls, patient to see,
425 Like priestesses because of sin impure
Penanced for ever, who resigned endure,
Having that once drunk sweetness to the dregs.
And every eve, Sordello's visit begs
Pardon for them: constant as eve he came

1863: sister-palms! But   **406|**   *1840:* wonder now   *1863:* wonder, now
409| *1840:* midst: nay   *1863:* midst. Nay   **411|**   *1840:* Round it, each <> sees,   *1863:*
Round it,—each <> sees,—   **412|**   *1840:* it—shrinking   *1868:* it; shrinking
414| *1840:* Maker's   *1868:* maker's   **415|**   *1840:* snow: *1863:* snow.
§ **417–445|**   *1863:* AND WHAT SORDELLO WOULD SEE THERE.
416–444| *1868* §   **417|**   *1840:* closed,   *1863:* closed;   **423|**   *1840:* heavily;   *1863:*
heavily.   **427|**   *1840:* dregs;   *1863:* dregs.   **428|**   *1840:* eve Sordello's   *1863:* eve,

430 To sit beside each in her turn, the same
As one of them, a certain space: and awe
Made a great indistinctness till he saw
Sunset slant cheerful through the buttress-chinks,
Gold seven times globed; surely our maiden shrinks
435 And a smile stirs her as if one faint grain
Her load were lightened, one shade less the stain
Obscured her forehead, yet one more bead slipt
From off the rosary whereby the crypt
Keeps count of the contritions of its charge?
440 Then with a step more light, a heart more large,
He may depart, leave her and every one
To linger out the penance in mute stone.
Ah, but Sordello? 'Tis the tale I mean
To tell you.
                    In this castle may be seen,
445 On the hill tops, or underneath the vines,
Or eastward by the mound of firs and pines
That shuts out Mantua, still in loneliness,
A slender boy in a loose page's dress,
Sordello: do but look on him awhile
450 Watching ('tis autumn) with an earnest smile
The noisy flock of thievish birds at work
Among the yellowing vineyards; see him lurk
('Tis winter with its sullenest of storms)
Beside that arras-length of broidered forms,
455 On tiptoe, lifting in both hands a light
Which makes yon warrior's visage flutter bright
—Ecelo, dismal father of the brood,
And Ecelin, close to the girl he wooed,
Auria, and their Child, with all his wives
460 From Agnes to the Tuscan that survives,
Lady of the castle, Adelaide. His face
—Look, now he turns away! Yourselves shall trace
(The delicate nostril swerving wide and fine,

Sordello's   433| *1840:* buttress chinks,   *1863:* buttress-chinks,   444| *1840:* you.
In   *1868:* you. ¶ In   § 446–474| *1863:* HIS BOYHOOD IN THE DOMAIN OF
ECELIN.   444–472| *1868* §   446| *1840:* Or southward by   *1863:* Or eastward
by   458| *1840:* wooed   *1863:* wooed,   459| *1840:*—Auria   *1863:* Auria
461| *1840:* castle, Adelaide: his   *1863:* castle, Adelaide. His   469| *1840:* men and < >

A sharp and restless lip, so well combine
465 With that calm brow) a soul fit to receive
Delight at every sense; you can believe
Sordello foremost in the regal class
Nature has broadly severed from her mass
Of men, and framed for pleasure, as she frames
470 Some happy lands, that have luxurious names,
For loose fertility; a footfall there
Suffices to upturn to the warm air
Half-germinating spices; mere decay
Produces richer life; and day by day
475 New pollen on the lily-petal grows,
And still more labyrinthine buds the rose.
You recognise at once the finer dress
Of flesh that amply lets in loveliness
At eye and ear, while round the rest is furled
480 (As though she would not trust them with her world)
A veil that shows a sky not near so blue,
And lets but half the sun look fervid through.
How can such love?—like souls on each full-fraught
Discovery brooding, blind at first to aught
485 Beyond its beauty, till exceeding love
Becomes an aching weight; and, to remove
A curse that haunts such natures—to preclude
Their finding out themselves can work no good
To what they love nor make it very blest
490 By their endeavour,—they are fain invest
The lifeless thing with life from their own soul,
Availing it to purpose, to control,
To dwell distinct and have peculiar joy
And separate interests that may employ
495 That beauty fitly, for its proper sake.

pleasure as   *1863:* men, and <> pleasure, as   **470|**   *1840:* lands that <> names
1863: lands, that <> names,   **473|**   *1840:* spices, mere   *1863:* spices; mere
474| *1840:* life, and   *1863:* life; and   § **475–503|**   *1863:* **HOW A POET'S SOUL COMES**
INTO PLAY.   **473–501|**   *1868* §   **482|**   *1840:* through: *1863:* through.
483| *1840:* love like   *1863:* love?—like   **485|**   *1840:* beauty; till   *1863:* beauty,
till   **486|**   *1840:* weight, and to   *1863:* weight; and, to   **490|**   *1840:* endeavour,
they   *1863:* endeavour,—they   **491|**   *1840:* soul   *1863:* soul,   **495|**   *1840:* sake;

Nor rest they here; fresh births of beauty wake
Fresh homage, every grade of love is past,
With every mode of loveliness: then cast
Inferior idols off their borrowed crown
500 Before a coming glory. Up and down
Runs arrowy fire, while earthly forms combine
To throb the secret forth; a touch divine—
And the scaled eyeball owns the mystic rod;
Visibly through his garden walketh God.
505   So fare they. Now revert. One character
Denotes them through the progress and the stir,—
A need to blend with each external charm,
Bury themselves, the whole heart wide and warm,—
In something not themselves; they would belong
510 To what they worship—stronger and more strong
Thus prodigally fed—which gathers shape
And feature, soon imprisons past escape
The votary framed to love and to submit
Nor ask, as passionate he kneels to it,
515 Whence grew the idol's empery. So runs
A legend; light had birth ere moons and suns,
Flowing through space a river and alone,
Till chaos burst and blank the spheres were strown
Hither and thither, foundering and blind:
520 When into each of them rushed light—to find
Itself no place, foiled of its radiant chance.
Let such forego their just inheritance!
For there's a class that eagerly looks, too,
On beauty, but, unlike the gentler crew,
525 Proclaims each new revealment born a twin
With a distinctest consciousness within,

.

1863: sake.   **496**| *1840:* here: fresh   *1863:* here; fresh   **497**| *1840:* homage;
every   *1863:* homage, every   **498**| *1840:* loveliness; then   *1863:* loveliness:
then   **500**| *1840:* glory. up   *1863:* glory. Up   **503**| *1840:* rod: *1868:* rod;
§ **504–532**| *1863:* **WHAT DENOTES SUCH A SOUL'S PROGRESS.**
502–530| *1868* §   **504**| *1863:* His   *1868:* his   **505**| *1840:* So fare they—Now
revert: one   *1863:* they. Now revert. One   *1868:* ¶ So   **506**| *1840:* stir;   *1863:*
stir,—   **508**| *1840:* warm,   *1868:* warm,—   **511**| *1840:* fed—that gathers   *1863:*
fed—which gathers   **516**| *1840:* Light   *1863:* light   **519**| *1840:* blind,   *1868:*
blind: **520**| *1840:* Light   *1863:* light   **526**| *1840:* within   *1888:* within,

Referring still the quality, now first
Revealed, to their own soul—its instinct nursed
In silence, now remembered better, shown
530 More thoroughly, but not the less their own;
A dream come true; the special exercise
Of any special function that implies
The being fair, or good, or wise, or strong,
Dormant within their nature all along—
535 Whose fault? So, homage, other souls direct
Without, turns inward. "How should this deject
Thee, soul?" they murmur; "wherefore strength be quelled
Because, its trivial accidents withheld,
Organs are missed that clog the world, inert,
540 Wanting a will, to quicken and exert,
Like thine—existence cannot satiate,
Cannot surprise? Laugh thou at envious fate,
Who, from earth's simplest combination stampt
With individuality—uncrampt
545 By living its faint elemental life,
Dost soar to heaven's complexest essence, rife
With grandeurs, unaffronted to the last,
Equal to being all!"
              In truth? Thou hast
Life, then—wilt challenge life for us: our race
550 Is vindicated so, obtains its place
In thy ascent, the first of us; whom we
May follow, to the meanest, finally,
With our more bounded wills?
                    Ah, but to find

528| *1840:* soul; its *1863:* soul—its § 533-558| *1863:* **HOW POETS CLASS AT
LENGTH—FOR HONOUR,** 531-556| *1868* § 533| *1840:* fair or good or wise
or *1863:* fair, or good, or wise, or 535| *1840:* fault? So homage other *1863:* fault? So,
homage, other 536| *1840:* inward; how *1863:* inward. "How 537| *1840:* soul?
they murmur; wherefore *1863:* soul?" they murmur; "wherefore 541| *1840:*
satiate *1863:* satiate, 542| *1840:* surprise: laugh *1863:* surprise? laugh *1868:*
Laugh 543| *1840:* Who from *1863:* Who, from 548| *1840:* all. ¶ In *1863:*
all!" ¶ In 549| *1840:* us: thy race *1863:* us: our race 558| *1840:* (Too

A certain mood enervate such a mind,
555 Counsel it slumber in the solitude
Thus reached nor, stooping, task for mankind's good
Its nature just as life and time accord
"—Too narrow an arena to reward
Emprize—the world's occasion worthless since
560 Not absolutely fitted to evince
Its mastery!" Or if yet worse befall,
And a desire possess it to put all
That nature forth, forcing our straitened sphere
Contain it,—to display completely here
565 The mastery another life should learn,
Thrusting in time eternity's concern,—
So that Sordello. . . .
                              Fool, who spied the mark
Of leprosy upon him, violet-dark
Already as he loiters? Born just now,
570 With the new century, beside the glow
And efflorescence out of barbarism;
Witness a Greek or two from the abysm
That stray through Florence-town with studious air,
Calming the chisel of that Pisan pair:
575 If Nicolo should carve a Christus yet!
While at Siena is Guidone set,
Forehead on hand; a painful birth must be
Matured ere Saint Eufemia's sacristy
Or transept gather fruits of one great gaze
580 At the moon: look you! The same orange haze,—
The same blue strip round that—and, in the midst,
Thy spectral whiteness, Mother-maid, who didst

1863:"—Too   § 559–586| *1863:* OR SHAME—WHICH MAY THE GODS AVERT
557–583| *1868* §   561| *1840:* mastery) or   *1863:* mastery!" Or   564| *1840:* it;
to   *1863:* it,—to   566| *1840:* concern,   *1863:* concern,—   567| *1840:* that
Sordello . . . Fool   *1868:* that Sordello . . . ¶ Fool   *1888:* that Sordello. . . . ¶ Fool
568| *1840:* violet dark   *1863:* violet-dark   569| *1840:* now—   *1863:* now,
570| *1840:* century—beside   *1863:* century, beside   574| *1840:* pair . . .   *1863:*
pair: 578| *1840:* Eufemio's   *1863:* Eufemia's   580| *1840:* the moon-sun: look
you! An orange haze—   *1863:* the moon: look you! The same orange haze,—
581| *1840:* i'   *1888:* in   582| *1840:* mother-maid   *1863:* Mother-maid

Pursue the dizzy painter!
                              Woe, then, worth
Any officious babble letting forth
585 The leprosy confirmed and ruinous
To spirit lodged in a contracted house!
Go back to the beginning, rather; blend
It gently with Sordello's life; the end
Is piteous, you may see, but much between
590 Pleasant enough. Meantime, some pyx to screen
The full-grown pest, some lid to shut upon
The goblin! So they found at Babylon,
(Colleagues, mad Lucius and sage Antonine)
Sacking the city, by Apollo's shrine,
595 In rummaging among the rarities,
A certain coffer; he who made the prize
Opened it greedily; and out there curled
Just such another plague, for half the world
Was stung. Crawl in then, hag, and couch asquat,
600 Keeping that blotchy bosom thick in spot
Until your time is ripe! The coffer-lid
Is fastened, and the coffer safely hid
Under the Loxian's choicest gifts of gold.
    Who will may hear Sordello's story told,
605 And how he never could remember when
He dwelt not at Goito. Calmly, then,
About this secret lodge of Adelaide's
Glided his youth away; beyond the glades
On the fir-forest border, and the rim
610 Of the low range of mountain, was for him
No other world: but this appeared his own
To wander through at pleasure and alone.

583| *1840:* painter! ¶ Woe then worth   *1863:* painter! ¶ Woe, then, worth
§ 587–615| *1863:* FROM SORDELLO, NOW IN CHILDHOOD.
584–612| *1868* §   587| *1840:* beginning rather   *1863:* beginning, rather
589| *1840:* you shall see   *1863:* you may see   590| *1840:* enough; meantime some
1863: enough. Meantime, some   592| *1840:* goblin! As they   *1863:* goblin! So
they   593| *1840:* (Colleagues mad   *1863:* (Colleagues, mad   594| *1840:* shrine
1863: shrine,   595| *1840:* Its pride, in rummaging the   *1863:* In rummaging among
the   596| *1840:* A cabinet; be sure, who   *1863:* A certain coffer; he who
602| *1840:* fastened and   *1863:* fastened, and   604| *1840:* Who   *1863:* ¶ Who
606| *1840:* at Goito; calmly then   *1863:* at Goito. Calmly, then,   608| *1840:* away:
beyond   *1863:* away; beyond   609| *1840:* fir-forest's   *1868:* fir-forest

The castle too seemed empty; far and wide
Might he disport; only the northern side
615 Lay under a mysterious interdict—
Slight, just enough remembered to restrict
His roaming to the corridors, the vault
Where those font-bearers expiate their fault,
The maple-chamber, and the little nooks
620 And nests, and breezy parapet that looks
Over the woods to Mantua: there he strolled.
Some foreign women-servants, very old,
Tended and crept about him—all his clue
To the world's business and embroiled ado
625 Distant a dozen hill-tops at the most.
And first a simple sense of life engrossed
Sordello in his drowsy Paradise;
The day's adventures for the day suffice—
Its constant tribute of perceptions strange,
630 With sleep and stir in healthy interchange,
Suffice, and leave him for the next at ease
Like the great palmer-worm that strips the trees,
Eats the life out of every luscious plant,
And, when September finds them sere or scant,
635 Puts forth two wondrous winglets, alters quite,
And hies him after unforeseen delight.
So fed Sordello, not a shard dissheathed;
As ever, round each new discovery, wreathed
Luxuriantly the fancies infantine
640 His admiration, bent on making fine
Its novel friend at any risk, would fling
In gay profusion forth: a ficklest king,
Confessed those minions!—eager to dispense

611| *1840:* but that appeared   *1863:* but this appeared   614| *1840:* disport unless
the   *1863:* disport; only the   § 616–644| *1863:* THE DELIGHTS OF HIS CHILDISH
FANCY,   613–641| *1868* §   620| *1840:* nests and   *1863:* nests, and
621| *1840:* to Mantua; there   *1863:* to Mantua: there   626| *1863:* ¶ And   *1888:*
And   629| *1840:* strange   *1863:* strange,   630| *1840:* interchange   *1863:*
interchange,   634| *1840:* And when <> scant   *1863:* And, when <> scant,
636| *1840:* delight;   *1863:* delight.   637| *1840:* disheathed;   *1888:*
dissheathed;   638| *1840:* ever round <> discovery wreathed   *1863:* ever, round <>
discovery, wreathed   642| *1840:* king   *1863:* king,   643| *1840:* minions!

So much from his own stock of thought and sense
645 As might enable each to stand alone
And serve him for a fellow; with his own,
Joining the qualities that just before
Had graced some older favourite. Thus they wore
A fluctuating halo, yesterday
650 Set flicker and to-morrow filched away,—
Those upland objects each of separate name,
Each with an aspect never twice the same,
Waxing and waning as the new-born host
Of fancies, like a single night's hoar-frost,
655 Gave to familiar things a face grotesque;
Only, preserving through the mad burlesque
A grave regard. Conceive! the orpine patch
Blossoming earliest on the log-house thatch
The day those archers wound along the vines—
660 Related to the Chief that left their lines
To climb with clinking step the northern stair
Up to the solitary chambers where
Sordello never came. Thus thrall reached thrall;
He o'er-festooning every interval,
665 As the adventurous spider, making light
Of distance, shoots her threads from depth to height,
From barbican to battlement: so flung
Fantasies forth and in their centre swung
Our architect,—the breezy morning fresh
670 Above, and merry,—all his waving mesh
Laughing with lucid dew-drops rainbow-edged.
   This world of ours by tacit pact is pledged
To laying such a spangled fabric low
Whether by gradual brush or gallant blow.

Eager *1868:* minions!—eager § 645–673| *1863:* WHICH COULD BLOW OUT A
GREAT BUBBLE, 642–670| *1868* § 646| *1840:* own *1863:* own,
648| *1840:* favourite: so they *1863:* favourite. Thus they 650| *1840:* away; *1863:*
away,— 657| *1840:* regard: conceive; the orpine patch *1863:* regard. Conceive! the
orpine-patch *1868:* orpine patch 658| *1840:* on our log-house-thatch *1863:* on the
log-house-thatch *1888:* log-house thatch 664| *1840:* interval *1863:* interval,
667| *1840:* battlement; so *1863:* battlement: so 669| *1840:* architect: the *1863:*
architect,—the 670| *1840:* merry; all *1863:* merry,—all 672| *1840:* This
1868: ¶ This § 674–701| *1863:* BEING SECURE AWHILE FROM INTRUSION.

146

675 But its abundant will was baulked here: doubt
Rose tardily in one so fenced about
From most that nurtures judgment,—care and pain:
Judgment, that dull expedient we are fain,
Less favoured, to adopt betimes and force
680 Stead us, diverted from our natural course
Of joys—contrive some yet amid the dearth,
Vary and render them, it may be, worth
Most we forego. Suppose Sordello hence
Selfish enough, without a moral sense
685 However feeble; what informed the boy
Others desired a portion in his joy?
Or say a ruthful chance broke woof and warp—
A heron's nest beat down by March winds sharp,
A fawn breathless beneath the precipice,
690 A bird with unsoiled breast and unfilmed eyes
Warm in the brake—could these undo the trance
Lapping Sordello? Not a circumstance
That makes for you, friend Naddo! Eat fern-seed
And peer beside us and report indeed
695 If (your word) "genius" dawned with throes and stings
And the whole fiery catalogue, while springs,
Summers, and winters quietly came and went.
    Time put at length that period to content,
By right the world should have imposed: bereft
700 Of its good offices, Sordello, left
To study his companions, managed rip
Their fringe off, learn the true relationship,
Core with its crust, their nature with his own:
Amid his wild-wood sights he lived alone.
705 As if the poppy felt with him! Though he

671–698| *1868* §   674| *1840:* blow: *1863:* blow.   675| *1840:* balked *1863:*
baulked   677| *1840:* judgment, care *1888:* judgment,—care   681| *1840:* joys,
contrive *1863:* joys,—contrive *1868:* joys—contrive   683| *1840:* forego: suppose
1863: forego. Suppose
690| *1840:* and filmless eyes *1888:* and unfilmed eyes   695| *1840:* Genius *1863:*
"genius"   696| *1840:* springs *1888:* springs,   697| *1840:* Summers and winters
<> went, *1863:* went. *1888:* Summers, and winters   698| *1840:* Putting at <>
content *1863:* ¶ Time put at <> content, § 702–729| *1863:* BUT IT COMES; AND
NEW-BORN JUDGMENT   699–727| *1868* §   703| *1840:* natures <> own;
1863: own. *1868:* nature   704| *1840:* alone: *1863:* alone.   707| *1840:* spoils

Partook the poppy's red effrontery
Till Autumn spoiled their fleering quite with rain,
And, turbanless, a coarse brown rattling crane
Lay bare. That's gone: yet why renounce, for that,
710 His disenchanted tributaries—flat
Perhaps, but scarce so utterly forlorn,
Their simple presence might not well be borne
Whose parley was a transport once: recall
The poppy's gifts, it flaunts you, after all,
715 A poppy:—why distrust the evidence
Of each soon satisfied and healthy sense?
The new-born judgment answered, "little boots
Beholding other creatures' attributes
And having none!" or, say that it sufficed,
720 "Yet, could one but possess, oneself," (enticed
Judgment) "some special office!" Nought beside
Serves you? "Well then, be somehow justified
For this ignoble wish to circumscribe
And concentrate, rather than swell, the tribe
725 Of actual pleasures: what, now, from without
Effects it?—proves, despite a lurking doubt,
Mere sympathy sufficient, trouble spared?
That, tasting joys by proxy thus, you fared
The better for them?" Thus much craved his soul.
730 Alas, from the beginning love is whole
And true; if sure of nought beside, most sure
Of its own truth at least; nor may endure
A crowd to see its face, that cannot know
How hot the pulses throb its heart below:

1863: spoiled   **709|**   *1840:* Protrudes: that's gone! yet   *1863:* Lay bare. That's   *1868:*
gone: yet   **711|**   *1840:* forlorn   *1863:* forlorn,   **715|**   *1840:* poppy: why   *1868:*
poppy:—why   **717|**   *1840:* new- born Judgment answered: little   *1863:* judgment
answered: "little   *1868:* answered, "little   **719|**   *1840:* none: or say   *1863:* none!" or,
say   **720|**   *1840:* Yet <> oneself, (enticed   *1863:* "Yet <> oneself," (enticed
721| *1840:* Judgment) some <> office! Nought   *1863:* Judgment) "some <> office!"
Nought   **722|**   *1840:* you? Well   *1863:* you? "Well   **725|**   *1840:* what now from
1863: what, now, from   **727|**   *1840:* spared;   *1863:* spared?   **728|**   *1840:*—He
tasted joys by proxy, clearly fared   *1863:* That tasting joys by proxy thus, you fared   *1868:*
That, tasting   **729|**   *1840:* them; thus <> soul.   *1863:* them?" Thus   *1868:* soul,
§ **730–757|**   *1863:* **DECIDES THAT HE NEEDS SYMPATHIZERS.**
728–755| *1868* §   **730|**   *1840:* Love   *1868:* love   **734|**   *1840:* below;   *1863:*

735 While its own helplessness and utter want
Of means to worthily be ministrant
To what it worships, do but fan the more
Its flame, exalt the idol far before
Itself as it would have it ever be.
740 Souls like Sordello, on the contrary,
Coerced and put to shame, retaining will,
Care little, take mysterious comfort still,
But look forth tremblingly to ascertain
If others judge their claims not urged in vain,
745 And say for them their stifled thoughts aloud.
So, they must ever live before a crowd:
—"Vanity," Naddo tells you.
                              Whence contrive
A crowd, now? From these women just alive,
That archer-troop? Forth glided—not alone
750 Each painted warrior, every girl of stone,
Nor Adelaide (bent double o'er a scroll,
One maiden at her knees, that eve, his soul
Shook as he stumbled through the arras'd glooms
On them, for, 'mid quaint robes and weird perfumes,
755 Started the meagre Tuscan up,—her eyes,
The maiden's, also, bluer with surprise)
—But the entire out-world: whatever, scraps
And snatches, song and story, dreams perhaps,
Conceited the world's offices, and he
760 Had hitherto transferred to flower or tree,
Not counted a befitting heritage
Each, of its own right, singly to engage
Some man, no other,—such now dared to stand

---

below. *1888:* below: **739|** *1840:* would ever have it be; *1863:* would have it ever
be.   **741|** *1840:* retaining Will, *1863:* will,   **744|** *1840:* vain *1863:* vain,
745| *1840:*—Will say <> aloud; *1863:* And say <> aloud.   **746|** *1840:* So they
1863: So, they   **747|** *1840:* Vanity, Naddo *1863:*—"Vanity," Naddo   **748|** *1840:*
now? These brave women *1863:* now? From these women   **751|** *1840:*—Nor Adelaide
bent *1863:* Nor Adelaide (bent   **752|** *1840:* eve his *1863:* eve, his   **755|** *1840:*
up (her eyes *1863:* up,—her eyes,   **756|** *1840:* maiden's also *1863:* maiden's,
also   **757|** *1840:* whatever scraps *1863:* whatever, scraps § **758–786|** *1863:* HE
THEREFORE CREATES SUCH A COMPANY,   **756–784|** *1868:*
COMPANY; §   **760|** *1840:* Transferred to the first comer, flower *1863:* Had hitherto
transferred to flower   **761|** *1840:* Nor counted *1888:* Not counted   **763|** *1840:*

Alone. Strength, wisdom, grace on every hand
765　Soon disengaged themselves, and he discerned
A sort of human life: at least, was turned
A stream of lifelike figures through his brain.
Lord, liegeman, valvassor and suzerain,
Ere he could choose, surrounded him; a stuff
770　To work his pleasure on; there, sure enough:
But as for gazing, what shall fix that gaze?
Are they to simply testify the ways
He who convoked them sends his soul along
With the cloud's thunder or a dove's brood-song?
775　—While they live each his life, boast each his own
Peculiar dower of bliss, stand each alone
In some one point where something dearest loved
Is easiest gained—far worthier to be proved
Than aught he envies in the forest-wights!
780　No simple and self-evident delights,
But mixed desires of unimagined range,
Contrasts or combinations, new and strange,
Irksome perhaps, yet plainly recognized
By this, the sudden company—loves prized
785　By those who are to prize his own amount
Of loves. Once care because such make account,
Allow that foreign recognitions stamp
The current value, and his crowd shall vamp
Him counterfeits enough; and so their print
790　Be on the piece, 'tis gold, attests the mint,
And "good," pronounce they whom his new appeal
Is made to: if their casual print conceal—
This arbitrary good of theirs o'ergloss

Man, no other; such availed to　*1863:* man, no other,—such now dared to　**764|**　*1840:*
Alone: strength　*1863:* Alone. Strength　**765|**　*1840:* themselves; and　*1863:*
themselves, and　**767|**　*1840:* life-like <> brain　*1863:* lifelike <> brain.
768|　*1840:*—Lord, Liegeman, Valvassor and Suzerain,　*1863:* Lord, liegeman, valvassor and
suzerain,　**770|**　*1840:* enough,　*1863:* enough:　**775|**　*1840:* While <> each its
life <> each its own　*1863:*—While <> each his life <> each his own　**783|**　*1840:*
recognised　*1863:* recognized　*1868:* recognised　*1888:* recognized　§ **787–815|**　*1863:*
EACH OF WHICH, LEADING ITS OWN LIFE,　**785–813|**　*1868* §　**787|**　*1840:*
Allow a foreign recognition　*1863:* Allow that foreign recognitions　**788|**　*1840:* and
your crowd　*1863:* and his crowd　**789|**　*1840:* You counterfeits　*1863:* Him
counterfeits　**790|**　*1840:* mint　*1863:* mint,　**791|**　*1840:* And good, pronounce

What he has lived without, nor felt the loss—
795 Qualities strange, ungainly, wearisome,
   —What matter? So must speech expand the dumb
Part-sight, part-smile with which Sordello, late
Whom no poor woodland-sights could satiate,
Betakes himself to study hungrily
800 Just what the puppets his crude phantasy
Supposes notablest,—popes, kings, priests, knights,—
May please to promulgate for appetites;
Accepting all their artificial joys
Not as he views them, but as he employs
805 Each shape to estimate the other's stock
Of attributes, whereon—a marshalled flock
Of authorized enjoyments—he may spend
Himself, be men, now, as he used to blend
With tree and flower—nay more entirely, else
810 'Twere mockery: for instance, "How excels
My life that chieftain's?" (who apprised the youth
Ecelin, here, becomes this month, in truth,
Imperial Vicar?) "Turns he in his tent
Remissly? Be it so—my head is bent
815 Deliciously amid my girls to sleep.
What if he stalks the Trentine-pass? Yon steep
I climbed an hour ago with little toil:
We are alike there. But can I, too, foil
The Guelf's paid stabber, carelessly afford
820 Saint Mark's a spectacle, the sleight o' the sword

---

they whom my new *1863:* And "good," pronounce they whom his new ^{794|} *1840:*
What I have <> felt my loss— *1863:* What he have <> felt the loss— *1888:* has
^{796|} *1840:* so *1868:* So ^{797|} *1840:* Part sigh, part smile *1863:* Part-sigh,
part-smile ^{798|} *1840:* No foolish woodland-sights *1888:* Whom no poor
woodland-sights ^{800|} *1840:* fantasy *1888:* phantasy ^{801|} *1840:* notablest,
popes <> knights, *1888:* notablest,—popes <> knights,— ^{806|} *1840:* attributes,
that on a *1888:* attributes, whereon—a ^{807|} *1840:* enjoyments he *1888:*
enjoyments—he ^{808|} *1840: be* Men now *1863: be* men, now ^{810|} *1840:*
instance, how *1863:* instance, "how *1888:* How ^{811|} *1840:* Chieftain's? (who
1863: chieftain's?" (who ^{812|} *1840:* month in *1863:* month, in ^{813|} *1840:*
Imperial Vicar?) Turns *1863:* Imperial Vicar?) "Turns ^{815|} *1840:* sleep: *1863:*
sleep. § ^{816–843|} *1863:* HAS QUALITIES IMPOSSIBLE TO A BOY,
^{814–842|} *1868* § ^{817|} *1840:* toil— *1868:* toil: ^{818|} *1840:* there: but *1863:*
there. But ^{819|} *1840:* Guelfs' *1868:* Guelf's ^{820|} *1840:* St. *1863:*

Baffling the treason in a moment?" Here
No rescue! Poppy he is none, but peer
To Ecelin, assuredly: his hand,
Fashioned no otherwise, should wield a brand
825 With Ecelin's success—try, now! He soon
Was satisfied, returned as to the moon
From earth; left each abortive boy's-attempt
For feats, from failure happily exempt,
In fancy at his beck. "One day I will
830 Accomplish it! Are they not older still
—Not grown-up men and women? 'Tis beside
Only a dream; and though I must abide
With dreams now, I may find a thorough vent
For all myself, acquire an instrument
835 For acting what these people act; my soul
Hunting a body out may gain its whole
Desire some day!" How else express chagrin
And resignation, show the hope steal in
With which he let sink from an aching wrist
840 The rough-hewn ash-bow? Straight, a gold shaft hissed
Into the Syrian air, struck Malek down
Superbly! "Crosses to the breach! God's Town
Is gained him back!" Why bend rough ash-bows more?
      Thus lives he: if not careless as before,
845 Comforted: for one may anticipate,
Rehearse the future, be prepared when fate
Shall have prepared in turn real men whose names
Startle, real places of enormous fames,
Este abroad and Ecelin at home
850 To worship him,—Mantua, Verona, Rome
To witness it. Who grudges time so spent?

Saint   821| *1840:* Baffling their project in a moment? Here   *1863:* moment?" Here
1868: Baffling the treason in   829| *1840:* beck. One   *1863:* beck. "One
831| *1840:* grown up   *1868:* grown-up   836| *1840:* out, obtain its   *1863:* out, may
gain its   *1868:* out may   837| *1840:* day! How   *1863:* day!" How   840| *1840:*
ash bow, and a <> hiss'd   *1863:* bow? straight, a <> hissed   *1868:* ash-bow?
Straight   842| *1840:* Superbly! Crosses   *1863:* Superbly! "Crosses   843| *1840:*
Was <> Him back! Why   *1863:* Is <> back!" Why   *1868:* him   § 844–871| *1863:* SO
ONLY TO BE APPROPRIATED IN FANCY,   843–870| *1868* §   844| *1840:* So
lives   *1863:* Thus lives   846| *1840:* future; be   *1863:* Future, be   *1868:* future
849| *1840:* Estes <> Ecelins   *1863:* Este <> Ecelin   850| *1840:* him, Mantuas,

Rather test qualities to heart's content—
Summon them, thrice selected, near and far—
Compress the starriest into one star,
855 And grasp the whole at once!
                              The pageant thinned
Accordingly; from rank to rank, like wind
His spirit passed to winnow and divide;
Back fell the simpler phantasms; every side
The strong clave to the wise; with either classed
860 The beauteous; so, till two or three amassed
Mankind's beseemingnesses, and reduced
Themselves eventually,—graces loosed,
Strengths lavished,—all to heighten up One Shape
Whose potency no creature should escape.
865 Can it be Friedrich of the bowmen's talk?
Surely that grape-juice, bubbling at the stalk,
Is some grey scorching Saracenic wine
The Kaiser quaffs with the Miramoline—
Those swarthy hazel-clusters, seamed and chapped,
870 Or filberts russet-sheathed and velvet-capped,
Are dates plucked from the bough John Brienne sent
To keep in mind his sluggish armament
Of Canaan:—Friedrich's, all the pomp and fierce
Demeanour! But harsh sounds and sights transpierce
875 So rarely the serene cloud where he dwells
Whose looks enjoin, whose lightest words are spells
On the obdurate! That right arm indeed
Has thunder for its slave; but where's the need
Of thunder if the stricken multitude
880 Hearkens, arrested in its angriest mood,
While songs go up exulting, then dispread,
Dispart, disperse, lingering overhead
Like an escape of angels? 'Tis the tune,

Veronas   *1863:* him,—Mantua, Verona   ^{854|} *1840:* star   *1863:* star,
^{855|}   *1840:* So grasp <> once! The pageant's   *1863:* And grasp <> once! ¶ The
pageant   ^{862|} *1840:* eventually, graces   *1888:* eventually,—graces   ^{863|} *1840:*
And lavished strengths, to   *1888:* Strengths lavished,—all to   ^{864|} *1840:* escape:
1863: escape.   ^{871|} *1863:* sent,   *1888:* sent   § ^{872–900|} *1863:* AND PRACTISED ON
TILL THE REAL COME.   ^{871–899|} *1868* §   ^{873|} *1840:* Of Canaan . . .
Friedrich's   *1863:* Of Canaan.—Friedrich's   *1868:* Of Canaan:—Friedrich's
^{875|} *1863:* dwells,   *1888:* dwells   ^{877|} *1840:* Upon the obdurate; that arm   *1863:* On

Nor much unlike the words his women croon
885 Similingly, colourless and faint-designed
Each, as a worn-out queen's face some remind
Of her extreme youth's love-tales. "Eglamor
Made that!" Half minstrel and half emperor,
What but ill objects vexed him? Such he slew.
890 The kinder sort were easy to subdue
By those ambrosial glances, dulcet tones;
And these a gracious hand advanced to thrones
Beneath him. Wherefore twist and torture this,
Striving to name afresh the antique bliss,
895 Instead of saying, neither less nor more,
He had discovered, as our world before,
Apollo? That shall be the name; nor bid
Me rag by rag expose how patchwork hid
The youth—what thefts of every clime and day
900 Contributed to purfle the array
He climbed with (June at deep) some close ravine
Mid clatter of its million pebbles sheen,
Over which, singing soft, the runnel slipped
Elate with rains: into whose streamlet dipped
905 He foot, yet trod, you thought, with unwet sock—
Though really on the stubs of living rock
Ages ago it crenelled; vines for roof,
Lindens for wall; before him, aye aloof,
Flittered in the cool some azure damsel-fly,
910 Born of the simmering quiet, there to die.
Emerging whence, Apollo still, he spied
Mighty descents of forest; multiplied
Tuft on tuft, here, the frolic myrtle-trees,
There gendered the grave maple stocks at ease.

the obdurate! That right arm   884| *1840:* words the women   *1888:* words his
women   885| *1840:* faint designed   *1863:* faint-designed   886| *1840:* Each as
1863: Each, as   887| *1840:* love-tales. Eglamor   *1863:* love-tales. "Eglamor
888| *1840:* that! Half   *1863:* that!" Half   889| *1840:* Who but   *1863:* What
but   899| *1840:* The man—what   *1863:* The youth—what   § 901–928| *1863:* HE
MEANS TO BE PERFECT—SAY, APOLLO: 900–927| *1868* §   901| *1840:*
climbs with (June's   *1863:* climbed with (June   902| *1840:* 'Mid   *1888:* Mid
903| *1840:* which singing soft the <> slipt   *1863:* which, singing soft, the   *1868:*
slipped   904| *1840:* dipt   *1868:* dipped   907| *1840:* crenneled   *1888:*
crenelled   910| *1840:* Child of <> die: *1868:* Born of <> die.   913| *1840:*

₉₁₅ And, proud of its observer, straight the wood
Tried old surprises on him; black it stood
A sudden barrier ('twas a cloud passed o'er)
So dead and dense, the tiniest brute no more
Must pass; yet presently (the cloud dispatched)
₉₂₀ Each clump, behold, was glistering detached
A shrub, oak-boles shrunk into ilex-stems!
Yet could not he denounce the stratagems
He saw thro', till, hours thence, aloft would hang
White summer-lightnings; as it sank and sprang
₉₂₅ To measure, that whole palpitating breast
Of heaven, 'twas Apollo, nature prest
At eve to worship.
                              Time stole: by degrees
The Pythons perish off; his votaries
Sink to respectful distance; songs redeem
₉₃₀ Their pains, but briefer; their dismissals seem
Emphatic; only girls are very slow
To disappear—his Delians! Some that glow
O' the instant, more with earlier loves to wrench
Away, reserves to quell, disdains to quench;
₉₃₅ Alike in one material circumstance—
All soon or late adore Apollo! Glance
The bevy through, divine Apollo's choice,
His Daphne! "We secure Count Richard's voice
In Este's counsels, good for Este's ends
₉₄₀ As our Taurello," say his faded friends,
"By granting him our Palma!"—the sole child,
They mean, of Agnes Este who beguiled
Ecelin, years before this Adelaide
Wedded and turned him wicked: "but the maid

---

myrtle-trees; *1863:* myrtle-trees,   ⁹¹⁸| *1840:* dense the   *1863:* dense, the
⁹¹⁹| *1840:* despatched) *1863:* dispatched)   ⁹²⁰| *1840:* clump, forsooth, was *1863:*
clump, behold, was   ⁹²⁵| *1840:* In measure   *1863:* To measure   ⁹²⁶| *1840:* Of
Heaven, 'twas Apollo nature   *1863:* heaven, 'twas Apollo, nature   ⁹²⁸| *1840:*
perished   *1863:* perish   § ^{929–957}| *1863:* AND APOLLO MUST ONE DAY FIND
DAPHNE   ^{928–956}| *1868* §   ⁹²⁹| *1840:* Sunk   *1863:* Sink   ⁹³²| *1840:*
disappear: his   *1863:* disappear—his   ⁹³⁸| *1840:* A Daphne! We   *1863:* His Daphne!
"We   ⁹³⁹| *1840:* counsels, one for   *1863:* counsels, good for   ⁹⁴⁰| *1840:* our
Taurello, say   *1863:* our Taurello," say   ⁹⁴¹| *1840:* By <> Palma! The   *1863:* "By
<> Palma!"—The   *1868:* the   ⁹⁴⁴| *1840:* wicked; but   *1863:* wicked: "but

945 Rejects his suit," those sleepy women boast.
She, scorning all beside, deserves the most
Sordello: so, conspicuous in his world
Of dreams sat Palma. How the tresses curled
Into a sumptuous swell of gold and wound
950 About her like a glory! even the ground
Was bright as with spilt sunbeams; breathe not, breathe
Not!—poised, see, one leg doubled underneath,
Its small foot buried in the dimpling snow,
Rests, but the other, listlessly below,
955 O'er the couch-side swings feeling for cool air,
The vein-streaks swollen a richer violet where
The languid blood lies heavily; yet calm
On her slight prop, each flat and outspread palm,
As but suspended in the act to rise
960 By consciousness of beauty, whence her eyes
Turn with so frank a triumph, for she meets
Apollo's gaze in the pine glooms.
                                    Time fleets:
That's worst! Because the pre-appointed age
Approaches. Fate is tardy with the stage
965 And crowd she promised. Lean he grows and pale,
Though restlessly at rest. Hardly avail
Fancies to soothe him. Time steals, yet alone
He tarries here! The earnest smile is gone.
How long this might continue matters not;
970 —For ever, possibly; since to the spot
None come: our lingering Taurello quits
Mantua at last, and light our lady flits
Back to her place disburthened of a care.
Strange—to be constant here if he is there!
975 Is it distrust? Oh, never! for they both

945| *1840:* suit, those   *1863:* suit," those   947| *1840:* so conspicuous   *1863:* so,
conspicuous   948| *1840:* sate   *1863:* sat   950| *1840:* glory, even   *1863:* glory!
even   951| *1840:* with shed sunbeams; (breathe   *1863:* with split sunbeams;
breathe   952| *1840:* Not)—poised   *1863:* Not!—poised   956| *1840:* swoln
1863: swollen   *1868:* swoln   *1888:* swollen   957| *1840:* heavily; and calm   *1863:*
heavily; yet calm   § 958–985| *1863:* BUT WHEN WILL THIS DREAM TURN
TRUTH?   957–984| *1868* §   962| *1840:* fleets   *1863:* fleets: 965| *1840:*
She all but promised   *1863:* And crowd she promised   969| *1840:* not: *1863:*
not;   970| *1840:* For   *1863:*—For   971| *1840:* come: for lingering   *1863:* come:

Goad Ecelin alike, Romano's growth
Is daily manifest, with Azzo dumb
And Richard wavering: let but Friedrich come,
Find matter for the minstrelsy's report
980 —Lured from the Isle and its young Kaiser's court
To sing us a Messina morning up,
And, double rillet of a drinking cup,
Sparkle along to ease the land of drouth,
Northward to Provence that, and thus far south
985 The other! What a method to apprise
Neighbours of births, espousals, obsequies,
Which in their very tongue the Troubadour
Records! and his performance makes a tour,
For Trouveres bear the miracle about,
990 Explain its cunning to the vulgar rout,
Until the Formidable House is famed
Over the country—as Taurello aimed,
Who introduced, although the rest adopt,
The novelty. Such games, her absence stopped,
995 Begin afresh now Adelaide, recluse
No longer, in the light of day pursues
Her plans at Mantua: whence an accident
Which, breaking on Sordello's mixed content
Opened, like any flash that cures the blind,
1000 The veritable business of mankind.

BOOK THE SECOND

The woods were long austere with snow: at last
Pink leaflets budded on the beech, and fast

---

our lingering   976| _1840:_ alike—Romano's   _1868:_ alike, Romano's   977| _1840:_
So daily manifest that Azzo's dumb   _1863:_ manifest, that   _1868:_ Is daily manifest, and
Azzo's   _1888:_ manifest, with Azzo dumb   978| _1840:_ wavers . . . let <> come!   _1863:_
wavers: let   _1868:_ come,   _1888:_ wavering   979| _1840:_—Find   _1863:_ report,   _1868:_
Find <> report!   _1888:_ report   980| _1840:_ Lured   _1868:_—Lured   981| _1840:_
up;   _1863:_ up,   982| _1840:_ Who, double rillets   _1863:_ And, double rillet
985| _1840:_ other: what   _1863:_ other. What   _1888:_ other! What   § 986-1000| _1863:_ FOR
THE TIME IS RIPE, AND HE READY.   985-1000| _1868_ §   986| _1840:_
obsequies!   _1888:_ obsequies,   988| _1840:_ Records; and   _1888:_ Records! and
992| _1840:_ aimed   _1863:_ aimed,   994| _1840:_ novelty. Their games her <> stopped
_1863:_ novelty. Such games, her <> stopped,   997| _1840:_ at Mantua—whence   _1863:_
at Mantua: whence   998| _1840:_ That breaking   _1863:_ Which, breaking <>
content,   _1888:_ content
§ 1-23| _1863:_ THIS BUBBLE OF FANCY, §   1| _1840:_ ¶ The   _1888:_ The

Larches, scattered through pine-tree solitudes,
Brightened, "as in the slumbrous heart o' the woods
5 Our buried year, a witch, grew young again
To placid incantations, and that stain
About were from her cauldron, green smoke blent
With those black pines"—so Eglamor gave vent
To a chance fancy. Whence a just rebuke
10 From his companion; brother Naddo shook
The solemnest of brows: "Beware," he said,
"Of setting up conceits in nature's stead!"
Forth wandered our Sordello. Nought so sure
As that to-day's adventure will secure
15 Palma, the visioned lady—only pass
O'er yon damp mound and its exhausted grass,
Under that brake where sundawn feeds the stalks
Of withered fern with gold, into those walks
Of pine and take her! Buoyantly he went.
20 Again his stooping forehead was besprent
With dew-drops from the skirting ferns. Then wide
Opened the great morass, shot every side
With flashing water through and through; a-shine,
Thick-steaming, all-alive. Whose shape divine,
25 Quivered i' the farthest rainbow-vapour, glanced
Athwart the flying herons? He advanced,
But warily; though Mincio leaped no more,
Each foot-fall burst up in the marish-floor
A diamond jet: and if he stopped to pick
30 Rose-lichen, or molest the leeches quick,
And circling blood-worms, minnow, newt or loach,
A sudden pond would silently encroach
This way and that. On Palma passed. The verge
Of a new wood was gained. She will emerge

7| *1840:* caldron   *1863:* cauldron   9| *1840:* fancy: whence   *1863:* fancy. Whence
11| *1840:* brows; Beware, he   *1863:* brows; "Beware," he   *1888:* brows: "Beware
12| *1840:* Nature's stead!   *1863:* nature's stead!"   15| *1840:* the forest-lady—only
1863: the visioned lady   19| *1840:* pine, and   *1868:* pine and   § 24–51| *1863:*
WHEN GREATEST AND BRIGHTEST, BURSTS. §   24| *1840:* Thick steaming
<> divine   *1863:* Thick-steaming   *1868:* divine,   29| *1840:* if you stopped   *1863:*

35 Flushed, now, and panting,—crowds to see,—will own
She loves him—Boniface to hear, to groan,
To leave his suit! One screen of pine-trees still
Opposes: but—the startling spectacle—
Mantua, this time! Under the walls—a crowd
40 Indeed, real men and women, gay and loud
Round a pavilion. How he stood!

                                        In truth
No prophecy had come to pass: his youth
In its prime now—and where was homage poured
Upon Sordello?—born to be adored,
45 And suddenly discovered weak, scarce made
To cope with any, cast into the shade
By this and this. Yet something seemed to prick
And tingle in his blood; a sleight—a trick—
And much would be explained. It went for nought—
50 The best of their endowments were ill bought
With his identity: nay, the conceit,
That this day's roving led to Palma's feet
Was not so vain—list! The word, "Palma!" Steal
Aside, and die, Sordello; this is real,
55 And this—abjure!

                         What next? The curtains see
Dividing! She is there; and presently
He will be there—the proper You, at length—
In your own cherished dress of grace and strength:
Most like, the very Boniface!

                                        Not so.
60 It was a showy man advanced; but though
A glad cry welcomed him, then every sound
Sank and the crowd disposed themselves around,
—"This is not he," Sordello felt; while, "Place

---

if he stopped   **35|** *1840:* panting; crowds to see; will   *1863:* panting,—crowds to
see,—will   **40|** *1840:* Indeed—real <> women—gay   *1863:* Indeed, real <>
women, gay   **49|** *1840:* naught—   *1863:* nought—   **51|** *1840:* conceit   *1863:*
conceit,   § **52-78|**   *1863:* AT A COURT OF LOVE, A MINSTREL SINGS §
52| *1840:* This present roving leads. to   *1863:* That this day's roving led to   **53|** *1840:*
vain ... list! The word, Palma? Steal   *1863:* vain—list! The word, "Palma!" Steal
55| *1840:* curtains, see,   *1868:* curtains see   **59|** *1840:* like the very Boniface ... ¶
Not   *1863:* like, the very Boniface! ¶ Not   **63|** *1840:*—This <> he, Sordello <>

For the best Troubadour of Boniface!"
65　Hollaed the Jongleurs,—"Eglamor, whose lay
Concludes his patron's Court of Love to-day!"
Obsequious Naddo strung the master's lute
With the new lute-string, "Elys," named to suit
The song: he stealthily at watch, the while,
70　Biting his lip to keep down a great smile
Of pride: then up he struck. Sordello's brain
Swam; for he knew a sometime deed again;
So, could supply each foolish gap and chasm
The minstrel left in his enthusiasm,
75　Mistaking its true version—was the tale
Not of Apollo? Only, what avail
Luring her down, that Elys an he pleased,
If the man dared no further? Has he ceased
And, lo, the people's frank applause half done,
80　Sordello was beside him, had begun
(Spite of indignant twitchings from his friend
The Trouvere) the true lay with the true end,
Taking the other's names and time and place
For his. On flew the song, a giddy race,
85　After the flying story; word made leap
Out word, rhyme—rhyme; the lay could barely keep
Pace with the action visibly rushing past:
Both ended. Back fell Naddo more aghast
Than some Egyptian from the harassed bull
90　That wheeled abrupt and, bellowing, fronted full
His plague, who spied a scarab 'neath the tongue,
And found 'twas Apis' flank his hasty prong
Insulted. But the people—but the cries,
The crowding round, and proffering the prize!

---

while "Place　　1863:—"This <> he," Sordello <> while, "Place　　⁶⁴| 1840:
Boniface," 1863: Boniface!"　　⁶⁵| 1840: the Jongleurs, "Eglamor whose 1863: the
Jongleurs,—"Eglamor, whose　　⁶⁶| 1840: to-day." 1863: to-day!"　　⁶⁷| 1840:
strung his master's 1863: strung the master's　　⁶⁸| 1840: lute-string, Elys, named
1863: lute-string, "Elys," named　　⁶⁹| 1840: He 1863: he　　⁷³| 1840: So could
1863: So, could　　⁷⁸| 1840: dares <> ceased? 1888: dared <> ceased
§ ⁷⁹⁻¹⁰⁷| 1863: SORDELLO, BEFORE PALMA, CONQUERS HIM, §　　⁸⁶| 1840:
word; rhyme—rhyme 1863: word, rhyme—rhyme　　⁸⁹| 1840: Than your Egyptian
1863: Than some Egyptian　　⁹⁰| 1840: wheels <> fronts 1863: wheeled <>
fronted　　⁹¹| 1840: spies <> 'neath his tongue, 1863: spied 1868: 'neath the
tongue,　　⁹²| 1840: finds 1863: found　　⁹⁴| 1840: And crowding 1863: The

95   —For he had gained some prize. He seemed to shrink
Into a sleepy cloud, just at whose brink
One sight withheld him. There sat Adelaide,
Silent; but at her knees the very maid
Of the North Chamber, her red lips as rich,
100 The same pure fleecy hair; one weft of which,
Golden and great, quite touched his cheek as o'er
She leant, speaking some six words and no more.
He answered something, anything; and she
Unbound a scarf and laid it heavily
105 Upon him, her neck's warmth and all. Again
Moved the arrested magic; in his brain
Noises grew, and a light that turned to glare,
And greater glare, until the intense flare
Engulfed him, shut the whole scene from his sense.
110 And when he woke 'twas many a furlong thence,
At home; the suñ shining his ruddy wont;
The customary birds'-chirp; but his front
Was crowned—was crowned! Her scented scarf around
His neck! Whose gorgeous vesture heaps the ground?
115 A prize? He turned, and peeringly on him
Brooded the women-faces, kind and dim,
Ready to talk—"The Jongleurs in a troop
Had brought him back, Naddo and Squarcialupe
And Tagliafer; how strange! a childhood spent
120 In taking, well for him, so brave a bent!
Since Eglamor," they heard, "was dead with spite,
And Palma chose him for her minstrel."

                                   Light

Sordello rose—to think, now; hitherto
He had perceived. Sure, a discovery grew

---

crowding   95| *1840:* (For <> prize)—He   *1863:*—For <> prize. He
97| *1840:* him; there   *1863:* him. There   100| *1840:* one curl of   *1863:* one weft
of   102| *1840:* more;   *1863:* more.   105| *1840:* all; again   *1863:* all. Again
§ 108–135| *1863:* RECEIVES THE PRIZE, AND RUMINATES. §   109| *1840:*
sense,   *1863:* sense.   111| *1840:* home: the   *1863:* home; the   116| *1840:*
women faces   *1863:* women-faces   117| *1840:* talk. The   *1863:* talk.—"The   *1888:*
talk—"The   120| *1840:* Assuming, well   *1863:* In taking, well   121| *1840:* Since
Eglamor, they heard, was   *1863:* Since Eglamor," they heard, "was   122| *1840:*
minstrel. ¶ Light   *1863:* minstrel." ¶ Light   124| *1840:* perceived. Sure a   *1863:*

125 Out of it all! Best live from first to last
The transport o'er again. A week he passed,
Sucking the sweet out of each circumstance,
From the bard's outbreak to the luscious trance
Bounding his own achievement. Strange! A man
130 Recounted an adventure, but began
Imperfectly; his own task was to fill
The frame-work up, sing well what he sung ill,
Supply the necessary points, set loose
As many incidents of little use
135 —More imbecile the other, not to see
Their relative importance clear as he!
But, for a special pleasure in the act
Of singing—had he ever turned, in fact,
From Elys, to sing Elys?—from each fit
140 Of rapture to contrive a song of it?
True, this snatch or the other seemed to wind
Into a treasure, helped himself to find
A beauty in himself; for, see, he soared
By means of that mere snatch, to many a hoard
145 Of fancies; as some falling cone bears soft
The eye along the fir-tree-spire, aloft
To a dove's nest. Then, how divine the cause
Why such performance should exact applause
From men, if they had fancies too? Did fate
150 Decree they found a beauty separate
In the poor snatch itself?—"Take Elys, there,
—'Her head that's sharp and perfect like a pear,
So close and smooth are laid the few fine locks
Coloured like honey oozed from topmost rocks

perceived. Sure, a   126| *1840:* passed   *1863:* passed,   130| *1840:* Recounted that
adventure, and began   *1863:* Recounted an adventure, but began   132| *1840:* sang
1868: sung   § 136–164| *1863:* **HOW HAD HE BEEN SUPERIOR TO**
EGLAMOR? §   137| *1840:* But for   *1863:* But, for   140| *1868:* rapture, to
1888: rapture to   144| *1840:* snatch to   *1868:* snatch,   145| *1840:* bears oft
1863: bears soft   146| *1840:* eye, along   *1868:* eye along   147| *1840:* nest. Then
how   *1863:* nest. Then, how   148| *1840:* Such a performance   *1888:* Why such
performance   149| *1840:* men if they have fancies too? Can Fate   *1863:* men, if they
had fancies too? Could fate   *1888:* too? Did fate   150| *1840:* find   *1863:* found
151| *1840:* itself . . . our Elys   *1863:* itself?—"Take Elys   152| *1840:* ("Her

155 Sun-blanched the livelong summer'—if they heard
   Just those two rhymes, assented at my word,
   And loved them as I love them who have run
   These fingers through those pale locks, let the sun
   Into the white cool skin—who first could clutch,
160 Then praise—I needs must be a god to such.
   Or what if some, above themselves, and yet
   Beneath me, like their Eglamor, have set
   An impress on our gift? So, men believe
   And worship what they know not, nor receive
165 Delight from. Have they fancies—slow, perchance,
   Not at their beck, which indistinctly glance
   Until, by song, each floating part be linked
   To each, and all grow palpable, distinct?"
   He pondered this.
                    Meanwhile, sounds low and drear
170 Stole on him, and a noise of footsteps, near
   And nearer, while the underwood was pushed
   Aside, the larches grazed, the dead leaves crushed
   At the approach of men. The wind seemed laid;
   Only, the trees shrunk slightly and a shade
175 Came o'er the sky although 'twas midday yet:
   You saw each half-shut downcast floweret
   Flutter—"a Roman bride, when they'd dispart
   Her unbound tresses with the Sabine dart,
   Holding that famous rape in memory still,
180 Felt creep into her curls the iron chill,
   And looked thus," Eglamor would say—indeed
   'Tis Eglamor, no other, these precede
   Home hither in the woods. "'Twere surely sweet

1863:—'Her   155| 1840: summer")—if 1863: summer'—if   159| 1840: skin . . .
nay, thus I clutch   1863: skin—who first could clutch,   160| 1840: Those locks!—I
< > God   1863: Then praise—I   1868: god   161| 1840: Or if some few, above
1888: Or what if some, above   163| 1840: gift? So men   1863: gift? So, men
§ 165–192| 1863: THIS IS ANSWERED BY EGLAMOR HIMSELF: §   167| 1840:
Until by song each   1863: Until, by song, each   168| 1840: distinct?   1863:
distinct?"   169| 1840: this. ¶ Meanwhile sounds   1863: this. ¶ Meanwhile,
sounds   171| 1840: nearer, and the   1888: nearer, while the   176| 1840:
downcast violet   1863: downcast floweret   177| 1840: Flutter—a < > they   1863:
Flutter—"a < > they'd   181| 1840: thus, Eglamor   1863: thus," Eglamor
183| 1840: woods. 'Twere   1863: woods. "'Twere   185| 1840: sleep! thought

163

Far from the scene of one's forlorn defeat
185 To sleep!" judged Naddo, who in person led
Jongleurs and Trouveres, chanting at their head.
A scanty company; for, sooth to say,
Our beaten Troubadour had seen his day.
Old worshippers were something shamed, old friends
190 Nigh weary; still the death proposed amends.
"Let us but get them safely through my song
And home again!" quoth Naddo.
                                    All along,
This man (they rest the bier upon the sand)
—This calm corpse with the loose flowers in his hand,
195 Eglamor, lived Sordello's opposite.
For him indeed was Naddo's notion right,
And verse a temple-worship vague and vast,
A ceremony that withdrew the last
Opposing bolt, looped back the lingering veil
200 Which hid the holy place: should one so frail
Stand there without such effort? or repine
If much was blank, uncertain at the shrine
He knelt before, till, soothed by many a rite,
The power responded, and some sound or sight
205 Grew up, his own forever, to be fixed,
In rhyme, the beautiful, forever!—mixed
With his own life, unloosed when he should please,
Having it safe at hand, ready to ease
All pain, remove all trouble; every time
210 He loosed that fancy from its bonds of rhyme,
(Like Perseus when he loosed his naked love)
Faltering; so distinct and far above
Himself, these fancies! He, no genius rare,
Transfiguring in fire or wave or air

Naddo   *1863:* sleep!" judged Naddo   **188|**   *1840:* day: *1863:* day.   **190|** *1840:*
amends: *1863:* amends.   **191|** *1840:* Let   *1863:* "Let   **192|** *1840:* again,
quoth   *1863:* again!" quoth   § **192–220|**   *1863:* ONE WHO BELONGED TO WHAT HE
LOVED, §   **194|**   *1840:* in its hand,   *1863:* in his hand   *1868:* hand,   **195|** *1840:*
opposite: *1863:* opposite.   **196|** *1840:* right   *1863:* right,   **197|** *1840:* Verse
1863: verse   **200|** *1840:* place—should   *1868:* place: should   **202|** *1840:* That
much   *1888:* If much   **204|** *1840:* Power   *1868:* power   **205|** *1840:* forever! to
be fixed   *1863:* forever, to   *1888:* fixed,   **206|** *1840:* forever; mixed   *1863:* forever!
mixed   *1888:* forever!—mixed   **211|**   *1840:* Like <> love,   *1868:* (Like <>

215 At will, but a poor gnome that, cloistered up
    In some rock-chamber with his agate cup,
    His topaz rod, his seed-pearl, in these few
    And their arrangement finds enough to do
    For his best art. Then, how he loved that art!
220 The calling marking him a man apart
    From men—one not to care, take counsel for
    Cold hearts, comfortless faces—(Eglamor
    Was neediest of his tribe)—since verse, the gift,
    Was his, and men, the whole of them, must shift
225 Without it, e'en content themselves with wealth
    And pomp and power, snatching a life by stealth.
    So, Eglamor was not without his pride!
    The sorriest bat which cowers throughout noontide
    While other birds are jocund, has one time
230 When moon and stars are blinded, and the prime
    Of earth is his to claim, nor find a peer;
    And Eglamor was noblest poet here—
    He well knew, 'mid those April woods he cast
    Conceits upon in plenty as he passed,
235 That Naddo might suppose him not to think
    Entirely on the coming triumph: wink
    At the one weakness! 'Twas a fervid child,
    That song of his; no brother of the guild
    Had e'er conceived its like. The rest you know,
240 The exaltation and the overthrow:
    Our poet lost his purpose, lost his rank,
    His life—to that it came. Yet envy sank
    Within him, as he heard Sordello out,
    And, for the first time, shouted—tired to shout
245 Like others, not from any zeal to show

love)   215| 1840: up,   1863: up   § 221–249| 1863: LOVING HIS ART AND
REWARDED BY IT, §   222| 1840: faces (Eglamor   1863: faces—(Eglamor
223| 1840: tribe) since   1863: tribe)—since   227| 1840: So Eglamor   1863: So,
Eglamor   228| 1840: cowers through noontide   1888: cowers throughout
noontide   231| 1840: is its to   1863: is his to   232| 1840: here,   1863: here
1868: here—   233| 1840: He knew, among the April   1863: He knew that, 'mid the
April woods, he   1888: He well knew, 'mid those April woods he   234| 1840: past,
1868: passed,   236| 1840: triumph; wink   1863: triumph: wink   237| 1840:
child   1863: child,   238| 1840: his—no   1868: his; no   239   1840: know;
1863: know,   240| 1840: overthrow;   1863: overthrow:

Pleasure that way: the common sort did so,
What else was Eglamor? who, bending down
As they, placed his beneath Sordello's crown,
Printed a kiss on his successor's hand,
250 Left one great tear on it, then joined his band
—In time; for some were watching at the door:
Who knows what envy may effect? "Give o'er,
Nor charm his lips, nor craze him!" (here one spied
And disengaged the withered crown)—"Beside
255 His crown? How prompt and clear those verses rang
To answer yours! nay, sing them!" And he sang
Them calmly. Home he went; friends used to wait
His coming, zealous to congratulate;
But, to a man—so quickly runs report—
260 Could do no less than leave him, and escort
His rival. That eve, then, bred many a thought:
What must his future life be? was he brought
So low, who stood so lofty this Spring morn?
At length he said, "Best sleep now with my scorn.
265 And by to-morrow I devise some plain
Expedient!" So, he slept, nor woke again.
They found as much, those friends, when they returned
O'erflowing with the marvels they had learned
About Sordello's paradise, his roves
270 Among the hills and vales and plains and groves,
Wherein, no doubt, this lay was roughly cast,
Polished by slow degrees, completed last
To Eglamor's discomfiture and death.
    Such form the chanters now, and, out of breath,

---

²⁴⁷| *1840:* And what was   *1888:* What else was   ²⁴⁸| *1840:* The same, placed   *1888:*
As they, placed   § ²⁵⁰⁻²⁷⁸| *1863:* ENDING WITH WHAT HAD POSSESSED
HIM. §   ²⁵¹| *1840:* door—   *1863:* door: ²⁵²| *1840:* effect? Give   *1863:* effect?
"Give   ²⁵³| *1840:* him! (here   *1863:* him!" (here   ²⁵⁴| *1840:* crown)—Beside
1863: crown)—"Beside   ²⁵⁵| *1840:* crown! How <> rung   *1868:* crown? how
1888: rang   ²⁵⁶| *1840:* nay sing them! And he sung   *1863:* nay, sing them!" And
1888: he sang   ²⁵⁸| *1840:* coming, anxious to congratulate,   *1863:* coming, zealous
to   *1868:* congratulate;   ²⁵⁹| *1840:* man, so <> report,   *1888:* man—so <>
report—   ²⁶¹| *1840:* thought   *1863:* thought: ²⁶²| *1840:* be: was   *1863:* be?
was   ²⁶³| *1840:* who was so <> spring   *1863:* Spring   *1888:* who stood so
²⁶⁴| *1840:* said, Best   *1863:* said, "Best   ²⁶⁶| *1840:* Expedient! So he   *1863:*
Expedient!" So, he   ²⁷⁰| *1840:* and valleys, plains   *1888:* and vales and plains

275 They lay the beaten man in his abode,
     Naddo reciting that same luckless ode,
     Doleful to hear. Sordello could explore
     By means of it, however, one step more
     In joy; and, mastering the round at length,
280 Learnt how to live in weakness as in strength,
     When from his covert forth he stood, addressed
     Eglamor, bade the tender ferns invest,
     Primæval pines o'ercanopy his couch,
     And, most of all, his fame—(shall I avouch
285 Eglamor heard it, dead though he might look,
     And laughed as from his brow Sordello took
     The crown, and laid on the bard's breast, and said
     It was a crown, now, fit for poet's head?)
     —Continue. Nor the prayer quite fruitless fell.
290 A plant they have, yielding a three-leaved bell
     Which whitens at the heart ere noon, and ails
     Till evening; evening gives it to her gales
     To clear away with such forgotten things
     As are an eyesore to the morn: this brings
295 Him to their mind, and bears his very name.
         So much for Eglamor. My own month came;
     'Twas a sunrise of blossoming and May.
     Beneath a flowering laurel thicket lay
     Sordello; each new sprinkle of white stars
300 That smell fainter of wine than Massic jars
     Dug up at Baiæ, when the south wind shed
     The ripest, made him happier; filleted
     And robed the same, only a lute beside
     Lay on the turf. Before him far and wide
305 The country stretched: Goito slept behind
     —The castle and its covert, which confined
     Him with his hopes and fears; so fain of old
     To leave the story of his birth untold.
     At intervals, 'spite the fantastic glow

277| *1840:* hear: Sordello *1863:* hear. Sordello § 279–307| *1863:* EGLAMOR DONE
WITH, SORDELLO BEGINS. §   283| *1840:* Primeval *1863:* Primæval
287| *1840:* laid it on his breast, and said, *1868:* laid on the bard's breast, and said
289| *1840:* fell; *1863:* fell.   290| *1840:* have yielding *1868:* have, yielding
306| *1840:* covert which *1863:* covert, which § 308–336| *1863:* WHO HE REALLY WAS,

310 Of his Apollo-life, a certain low
And wretched whisper, winding through the bliss,
Admonished, no such fortune could be his,
All was quite false and sure to fade one day:
The closelier drew he round him his array
315 Of brilliance to expel the truth. But when
A reason for his difference from men
Surprised him at the grave, he took no rest
While aught of that old life, superbly dressed
Down to its meanest incident, remained
320 A mystery: alas, they soon explained
Away Apollo! and the tale amounts
To this: when at Vicenza both her counts
Banished the Vivaresi kith and kin,
Those Maltraversi hung on Ecelin,
325 Reviled him as he followed; he for spite
Must fire their quarter, though that self-same night
Among the flames young Ecelin was born
Of Adelaide, there too, and barely torn
From the roused populace hard on the rear,
330 By a poor archer when his chieftain's fear
Grew high; into the thick Elcorte leapt,
Saved her, and died; no creature left except
His child to thank. And when the full escape
Was known—how men impaled from chine to nape
335 Unlucky Prata, all to pieces spurned
Bishop Pistore's concubines, and burned
Taurello's entire household, flesh and fell,
Missing the sweeter prey—such courage well
Might claim reward. The orphan, ever since,
340 Sordello, had been nurtured by his prince
Within a blind retreat where Adelaide—
(For, once this notable discovery made,
The past at every point was understood)

AND WHY AT GOITO. §   311| *1840:* whisper winding <> bliss *1863:* whisper,
winding <> bliss,   318| *1840:* drest *1868:* dressed   320| *1840:*
mystery—alas *1868:* mystery: alas   322| *1840:* Counts *1868:* counts
325| *1840:* Reviling as *1863:* Reviled him as   329| *1840:* rear *1863:* rear,
331| *1840:* Was high *1863:* Grew high § 337–365| *1863:* HE, SO LITTLE, WOULD
FAIN BE SO MUCH: §   341| *1840:* where Adelaide *1863:* where Adelaide—

—Might harbour easily when times were rude,
345 When Azzo schemed for Palma, to retrieve
That pledge of Agnes Este—loth to leave
Mantua unguarded with a vigilant eye,
While there Taurello bode ambiguously—
He who could have no motive now to moil
350 For his own fortunes since their utter spoil—
As it were worth while yet (went the report)
To disengage himself from her. In short,
Apollo vanished; a mean youth, just named
His lady's minstrel, was to be proclaimed
355 —How shall I phrase it?—Monarch of the World!
For, on the day when that array was furled
Forever, and in place of one a slave
To longings, wild indeed, but longings save
In dreams as wild, suppressed—one daring not
360 Assume the mastery such dreams allot,
Until a magical equipment, strength,
Grace, wisdom, decked him too,—he chose at length,
Content with unproved wits and failing frame,
In virtue of his simple will, to claim
365 That mastery, no less—to do his best
With means so limited, and let the rest
Go by,—the seal was set: never again
Sordello could in his own sight remain
One of.the many, one with hopes and cares
370 And interests nowise distinct from theirs,
Only peculiar in a thriveless store

344| *1840:* Can harbour <> are   *1863:*—Might harbour <> were   345| *1840:*
When Este schemes for Palma—would retrieve   *1863:* When Azzo schemed for Palma, to
retrieve   346| *1840:* pledge, when Mantua is not fit to   *1863:* pledge of Agnes
Este—loth to   347| *1840:* Longer unguarded   *1863:* Mantua unguarded
348| *1840:* Taurello bides there so ambiguously   *1863:* biding there ambiguously—   *1888:*
While there Taurello bode ambiguously—   349| *1840:* (He who can   *1863:* He who
could   350| *1840:* spoil)   *1863:* spoil—   351| *1840:* goes   *1863:* went
352| *1840:* from us. In   *1863:* from her. In   355| *1840:* it? Monarch <> world.
1863: it?—Monarch <> world!   356| *1840:* But on the morning that   *1863:* For,
on   *1888:* the day when that   357| *1840:* For ever   *1868:* Forever   358| *1840:*
wild, indeed   *1863:* wild indeed   361| *1840:* strength   *1868:* strength,
362| *1840:* length   *1863:* length,   363| *1840:* (Content <> frame)   *1863:* Content
<> frame,   364| *1840:* Will   *1863:* will   § 366–394| *1863:* LEAVES THE DREAM

Of fancies, which were fancies and no more;
Never again for him and for the crowd
A common law was challenged and allowed
375 If calmly reasoned of, howe'er denied
By a mad impulse nothing justified
Short of Apollo's presence. The divorce
Is clear: why needs Sordello square his course
By any known example? Men no more
380 Compete with him than tree and flower before.
Himself, inactive, yet is greater far
Than such as act, each stooping to his star,
Acquiring thence his function; he has gained
The same result with meaner mortals trained
385 To strength or beauty, moulded to express
Each the idea that rules him; since no less
He comprehends that function, but can still
Embrace the others, take of might his fill
With Richard as of grace with Palma, mix
390 Their qualities, or for a moment fix
On one; abiding free meantime, uncramped
By any partial organ, never stamped
Strong, and to strength turning all energies—
Wise, and restricted to becoming wise—
395 That is, he loves not, nor possesses One
Idea that, star-like over, lures him on
To its exclusive purpose. "Fortunate!
This flesh of mine ne'er strove to emulate
A soul so various—took no casual mould
400 Of the first fancy and, contracted, cold,
Clogged her forever—soul averse to change
As flesh: whereas flesh leaves soul free to range,
Remains itself a blank, cast into shade,

HE MAY BE SOMETHING, §   377| *1840:* presence: the   *1863:* presence. The
380| *1840:* before;   *1888:* before.   387| *1840:* function but   *1863:* function,
but   388| *1840:* Might   *1863:* might   389| *1840:* Grace   *1863:* grace
391| *1840:* one, abiding   *1863:* one; abiding   393| *1840:* Strong, so to Strength
1863: Strong, and to strength   394| *1840:* Wise—   *1863:* wise—   § 395–422| *1863:*
FOR THE FACT THAT HE CAN DO NOTHING, §   397| *1840:* purpose.
Fortunate   *1863:* purpose. "Fortunate!   400| *1840:* and contracted cold   *1863:* and,
contracted, cold,   401| *1840:* Lay clogged forever thence, averse   *1888:* Clogged her
forever—soul averse   402| *1840:* As that. Whereas it left her free   *1863:* that:

Encumbers little, if it cannot aid.
405 So, range, free soul!—who, by self-consciousness,
The last drop of all beauty dost express—
The grace of seeing grace, a quintessence
For thee: while for the world, that can dispense
Wonder on men who, themselves, wonder—make
410 A shift to love at second-hand, and take
For idols those who do but idolize,
Themselves,—the world that counts men strong or wise,
Who, themselves, court strength, wisdom,—it shall bow
Surely in unexampled worship now,
415 Discerning me!"—
　　　　　　　(Dear monarch, I beseech,
Notice how lamentably wide a breach
Is here: discovering this, discover too
What our poor world has possibly to do
With it! As pigmy natures as you please—
420 So much the better for you; take your ease,
Look on, and laugh; style yourself God alone;
Strangle some day with a cross olive-stone!
All that is right enough: but why want us
To know that you yourself know thus and thus?)
425 "The world shall bow to me conceiving all
Man's life, who see its blisses, great and small,
Afar—not tasting any; no machine
To exercise my utmost will is mine:
Be mine mere consciousness! Let men perceive

whereas   *1888:* As flesh: whereas flesh leaves soul free   405| *1840:* range, my soul!
Who by self-consciousness   *1863:* soul!—who, by self-consciousness,   *1888:* range, free
soul   408| *1840:* thee: but for   *1888:* thee: while for   409| *1840:* men,
themselves that wonder   *1863:* men who, themselves, wonder   410| *1840:* second
hand and   *1863:* second-hand, and   411| *1840:* Those for its idols who   *1888:* For
idols those who   412| *1840:* Themselves,—that loves the soul as strong, as wise,   *1863:*
Themselves,—would that loves souls as strong or wise,   *1888:* Themselves,—the world that
counts men strong   413| *1840:* Whose love is Strength, is Wisdom,—such shall   *1863:*
Who, themselves, loves strength, wisdom,—it shall   *1888:* themselves, court strength
415| *1840:* me!— ¶ (Dear   *1863:* me!"— ¶ (Dear   417| *1840:* here! discovering   *1868:*
here: discovering   420| *1840:* ease;   *1888:* ease,   422| *1840:* olive-stone;   *1863:*
olive-stone: *1888:* olive-stone! § 423–451| *1863:* YET IS ABLE TO IMAGINE
EVERYTHING, §   424| *1840:* and thus?   *1863:* and thus?)   425| *1840:* Nay
finish—) ¶ —Bow to   *1863:* "The world shall bow to   427| *1840:* any: no   *1863:* any;
no   428| *1840:* mine,   *1863:* mine: 429| *1840:* Therefore mere consciousness

430 What I could do, a mastery believe,
Asserted and established to the throng
By their selected evidence of song
Which now shall prove, whate'er they are, or seek
To be, I am—whose words, not actions speak,
435 Who change no standards of perfection, vex
With no strange forms created to perplex,
But just perform their bidding and no more,
At their own satiating-point give o'er,
While each shall love in me the love that leads
440 His soul to power's perfection." Song, not deeds,
For we get tired was chosen. Fate would brook
Mankind no other organ; he would look
For not another channel to dispense
His own volition by, receive men's sense
445 Of its supremacy—would live content,
Obstructed else, with merely verse for vent.
Nor should, for instance, strength an outlet seek
And, striving, be admired: nor grace bespeak
Wonder, displayed in gracious attitudes:
450 Nor wisdom, poured forth, change unseemly moods;
But he would give and take on song's one point.
Like some huge throbbing stone that, poised a-joint,
Sounds, to affect on its basaltic bed,
Must sue in just one accent; tempests shed

for me!—Perceive   *1863:* Be mine mere consciousness! Let men perceive   ^{432|}   *1840:*
Song   *1863:* song   ^{433|}   *1840:* prove whate'er   *1863:* prove, whate'er
^{434|}   *1840:* who take no pains to speak,   *1888:* whose words, not actions speak,
^{435|}   *1840:* Change no old standards   *1888:* Who change no standards   ^{437|}   *1840:*
But mean perform   *1863:* But will perform   *1888:* But just perform   ^{439|}   *1840:* And
each   *1863:* While each   ^{440|}   *1840:* to its perfection. Song, not Deeds,   *1863:*
perfection." Song, not deeds,   *1888:* to power's perfection   ^{442|}   *1840:* He   *1863:*
he   ^{444|}   *1840:* volition and receive their sense   *1863:* volition, and   *1888:* volition
by, receive men's sense   ^{445|}   *1840:* its existing, but would be content,   *1863:* existing;
but   *1888:* its supremacy—would live content,   ^{446|}   *1840:* vent—   *1863:*
vent.   ^{447|}   *1840:* Strength   *1863:* strength   ^{448|}   *1840:* And striving be
admired, nor Grace   *1863:* And, striving, be <> grace   *1868:* admired; nor   *1888:*
admired: nor   ^{449|}   *1840:* attitudes,   *1863:* attitudes;   *1888:* attitudes:
^{450|}   *1840:* Nor Wisdom   *1863:* wisdom <> moods: *1888:* moods;   ^{451|}   *1840:* on
Song's one point.   *1863:* on song's one point.   § ^{452–478|}   *1863:* IF THE WORLD
ESTEEM THIS EQUIVALENT. §   ^{452|}   *1840:* throbbing-stone   *1863:* throbbing
stone   ^{453|}   *1840:* Sounds to <> bed   *1863:* Sounds, to <> bed,   ^{454|}   *1840:*

455 Thunder, and raves the windstorm: only let
That key by any little noise be set—
The far benighted hunter's halloo pitch
On that, the hungry curlew chance to scritch
Or serpent hiss it, rustling through the rift,
460 However loud, however low—all lift
The groaning monster, stricken to the heart.
    Lo ye, the world's concernment, for its part,
And this, for his, will hardly interfere!
Its businesses in blood and blaze this year
465 But wile the hour away—a pastime slight
Till he shall step upon the platform: right!
And, now thus much is settled, cast in rough,
Proved feasible, be counselled! thought enough,—
Slumber, Sordello! any day will serve:
470 Were it a less digested plan! how swerve
To-morrow? Meanwhile eat these sun-dried grapes,
And watch the soaring hawk there! Life escapes
Merrily thus.
                He thoroughly read o'er
His truchman Naddo's missive six times more,
475 Praying him visit Mantua and supply
A famished world.
                The evening star was high
When he reached Mantua, but his fame arrived
Before him: friends applauded, foes connived,
And Naddo looked an angel, and the rest
480 Angels, and all these angels would be blest
Supremely by a song—the thrice-renowned
Goito-manufacture. Then he found
(Casting about to satisfy the crowd)
That happy vehicle, so late allowed,
485 A sore annoyance; 'twas the song's effect
He cared for, scarce the song itself: reflect!
In the past life, what might be singing's use?

---

accent: tempests   *1863:* accent; tempests   ⁴⁵⁵| *1840:* the landstorm: only   *1888:* the
windstorm: only   ⁴⁶⁵| *1840:*—But   *1863:* But   ⁴⁶⁷| *1840:* And now   *1863:*
And, now   ⁴⁶⁸| *1840:* enough,   *1863:* enough,—   ⁴⁷¹| *1840:* grapes   *1863:*
grapes,   § ^{479–507}| *1863:* HE HAS LOVED SONG'S RESULTS, NOT SONG: §
⁴⁸²| *1840:* Goito manufacture   *1888:* Goito-manufacture   ⁴⁸⁷| *1840:* life what

Just to delight his Delians, whose profuse
Praise, not the toilsome process which procured
490 That praise, enticed Apollo: dreams abjured,
No overleaping means for ends—take both
For granted or take neither! I am loth
To say the rhymes at last were Eglamor's;
But Naddo, chuckling, bade competitors
495 Go pine; "the master certes meant to waste
No effort, cautiously had probed the taste
He'd please anon: true bard, in short,—disturb
His title if they could; nor spur nor curb,
Fancy nor reason, wanting in him; whence
500 The staple of his verses, common sense:
He built on man's broad nature—gift of gifts,
That power to build! The world contented shifts
With counterfeits enough, a dreary sort
Of warriors, statesmen, ere it can extort
505 Its poet-soul—that's, after all, a freak
(The having eyes to see and tongue to speak)
With our herd's stupid sterling happiness
So plainly incompatible that—yes—
Yes—should a son of his improve the breed
510 And turn out poet, he were cursed indeed!"
"Well, there's Goito and its woods anon,
If the worst happen; best go stoutly on
Now!" thought Sordello.
                              Ay, and goes on yet!
You pother with your glossaries to get
515 A notion of the Troubadour's intent
In rondel, tenzon, virlai or sirvent—
Much as you study arras how to twirl
His angelot, plaything of page and girl

1863: life, what   491| *1840:* over-leaping   *1863:* overleaping   495| *1840:* pine;
the Master   *1863:* pine; "the master   497| *1840:* short, disturb   *1888:*
short,—disturb   501| *1840:* on Man's <> gifts   *1863:* on man's <> gifts,
§ 508–535| *1863:* SO, MUST EFFECT THIS TO OBTAIN THOSE. §   510| *1840:*
poet he <> indeed.   *1863:* poet, he <> indeed!"   511| *1840:* Well, there's Goito to
retire upon   *1863:* "Well, there's Goito and its woods anon,   513| *1840:* Now!
thought   *1863:* Now!" thought   515| *1840:* intent—   *1863:* intent   516| *1840:*
His Rondels, Tenzons, Virlai or Sirvent—   *1863:* In rondel, tenzon, virlai or
sirvent—   518| *1840:* Angelot <> girl,   *1863:* angelot   *1868:* girl   523| *1840:*

174

Once; but you surely reach, at last,—or, no!
520 Never quite reach what struck the people so,
As from the welter of their time he drew
Its elements successively to view,
Followed all actions backward on their course,
And catching up, unmingled at the source,
525 Such a strength, such a weakness, added then
A touch or two, and turned them into men.
Virtue took form, nor vice refused a shape;
Here heaven opened, there was hell agape,
As Saint this simpered past in sanctity,
530 Sinner the other flared portentous by
A greedy people. Then why stop, surprised
At his success? The scheme was realized
Too suddenly in one respect: a crowd
Praising, eyes quick to see, and lips as loud
535 To speak, delicious homage to receive,
The woman's breath to feel upon his sleeve,
Who said, "But Anafest—why asks he less
Than Lucio, in your verses? how confess,
It seemed too much but yestereve!"—the youth,
540 Who bade him earnestly, "Avow the truth!
You love Bianca, surely, from your song;
I knew I was unworthy!"—soft or strong,
In poured such tributes ere he had arranged
Ethereal ways to take them, sorted, changed,
545 Digested. Courted thus at unawares,
In spite of his pretensions and his cares,
He caught himself shamefully hankering
After the obvious petty joys that spring

course 1863: course, 525| 1840: Strength <> Weakness 1863: strength <>
weakness 526| 1840: Men. 1863: men. 527| 1840: Vice 1863: vice
528| 1840: Heaven <> Hell 1863: heaven <> hell 531| 1840: People: then
1863: people. Then § 536–563| 1863: HE SUCCEEDS A LITTLE, BUT FALLS
MORE; § 536| 1840: Bianca's breath <> sleeve 1863: The woman's breath <>
sleeve, 538| 1840: confess 1863: confess, 539| 1840: yestereve!" The youth
1863: yestereve!"—the youth, 540| 1840: earnestly "avow the truth, 1863: earnestly,
"Avow the truth! 542| 1840: unworthy!" soft 1863: unworthy!"—soft
544| 1840: Etherial 1863: Ethereal 545| 1840: Digested: courted 1863: Digested.
Courted 546| 1840: cares 1863: cares, 548| 1840: After your obvious 1863:

From true life, fain relinquish pedestal
550 And condescend with pleasures—one and all
To be renounced, no doubt; for, thus to chain
Himself to single joys and so refrain
From tasting their quintessence, frustrates, sure,
His prime design; each joy must he abjure
555 Even for love of it.
                        He laughed: what sage
But perishes if from his magic page
He look because, at the first line, a proof
'Twas heard salutes him from the cavern roof?
"On! Give yourself, excluding aught beside,
560 To the day's task; compel your slave provide
Its utmost at the soonest; turn the leaf
Thoroughly conned. These lays of yours, in brief—
Cannot men bear, now, something better?—fly
A pitch beyond this unreal pageantry
565 Of essences? the period sure has ceased
For such: present us with ourselves, at least,
Not portions of ourselves, mere loves and hates
Made flesh: wait not!"
                        Awhile the poet waits
However. The first trial was enough:
570 He left imagining, to try the stuff
That held the imaged thing, and, let it writhe
Never so fiercely, scarce allowed a tithe
To reach the light—his Language. How he sought
The cause, conceived a cure, and slow re-wrought
575 That Language,—welding words into the crude
Mass from the new speech round him, till a rude
Armour was hammered out, in time to be
Approved beyond the Roman panoply

After the obvious   549| _1840:_ From real life   _1868:_ From true life   551| _1840:_
for thus   _1863:_ for, thus   553| _1840:_ frustrated   _1863:_ frustrates   559| _1840:_
On! Give thyself, excluding   _1863:_ "On! Give yourself, excluding   560| _1840:_ compel
thy slave   _1863:_ compel your slave   562| _1840:_ conned; these lays of thine, in   _1863:_
conned. These lays of yours, in   563| _1840:_ now, somewhat better   _1863:_ now,
something better   § 564–591| _1863:_ TRIES AGAIN, IS NO BETTER SATISFIED, §
568| _1840:_ not! ¶ Awhile   _1863:_ not!" ¶ Awhile   571| _1840:_ thing and   _1863:_ thing,
and   575| _1840:_ That Language, welding   _1863:_ That Language,—welding

Melted to make it,—boots not. This obtained
580 With some ado, no obstacle remained
To using it; accordingly he took
An action with its actors, quite forsook
Himself to live in each, returned anon
With the result—a creature, and, by one
585 And one, proceeded leisurely to equip
Its limbs in harness of his workmanship.
"Accomplished! Listen, Mantuans!" Fond essay!
Piece after piece that armour broke away,
Because perceptions whole, like that he sought
590 To clothe, reject so pure a work of thought
As language: thought may take perception's place
But hardly co-exist in any case,
Being its mere presentment—of the whole
By parts, the simultaneous and the sole
595 By the successive and the many. Lacks
The crowd perception? painfully it tacks
Thought to thought, which Sordello, needing such,
Has rent perception into: it's to clutch
And reconstruct—his office to diffuse,
600 Destroy: as hard, then, to obtain a Muse
As to become Apollo. "For the rest,
E'en if some wondrous vehicle expressed
The whole dream, what impertinence in me
So to express it, who myself can be
605 The dream! nor, on the other hand, are those
I sing to, over-likely to suppose

579| *1840:* it, boots *1863:* it,—boots   584| *1840:* and by *1863:* and, by
585| *1840:* one proceeded leisurely equip   *1863:* one, proceeded leisurely to equip
587| *1840:* Accomplished! Listen Mantuans! Fond   *1863:* "Accomplished! Listen,
Mantuans!" Fond   588| *1840:* away *1863:* away,   591| *1840:* Thought <>
Perception's   *1863:* thought <> perception's   § 592–619| *1863:* AND DECLINES FROM
THE IDEAL OF SONG. §   593| *1840:* Whole *1863:* whole   594| *1840:* By
Parts, the Simultaneous <> Sole   *1863:* parts, the simultaneous <> sole
595| *1840:* Successive <> Many   *1863:* successive <> many   596| *1840:*
perceptions *1863:* perception   597| *1840:* Together thoughts Sordello *1863:*
Thought to thought, which Sordello   600| *1840:* as difficult obtain *1863:* as hard,
then, to obtain   601| *1840:* In short, as be Apollo. For   *1863:* As to become Apollo.
"For   602| *1840:* exprest *1863:* expressed   605| *1840:* those, *1863:*
those   606| *1840:* to over-likely *1863:* to, over-likely   608| *1840:* Now, and

A higher than the highest I present
Now, which they praise already: be content
Both parties, rather—they with the old verse,
610 And I with the old praise—far go, fare worse!"
A few adhering rivets loosed, upsprings
The angel, sparkles off his mail, which rings
Whirled from each delicatest limb it warps;
So might Apollo from the sudden corpse
615 Of Hyacinth have cast his luckless quoits.
He set to celebrating the exploits
Of Montfort o'er the Mountaineers.

                    Then came
The world's revenge: their pleasure, now his aim
Merely,—what was it? "Not to play the fool
620 So much as learn our lesson in your school!"
Replied the world. He found that, every time
He gained applause by any ballad-rhyme.
His auditory recognized no jot
As he intended, and, mistaking not
625 Him for his meanest hero, ne'er was dunce
Sufficient to believe him—all, at once.
His will . . . conceive it caring for his will!
—Mantuans, the main of them, admiring still
How a mere singer, ugly, stunted, weak,
630 Had Montfort at completely (so to speak)
His fingers' ends; while past the praise-tide swept
To Montfort, either's share distinctly kept:
The true meed for true merit!—his abates
Into a sort he most repudiates,
635 And on them angrily he turns. Who were

---

they   *1863:* Now, which they   609| *1840:* rather; they   *1863:* rather—they
610| *1840:* worse!   *1863:* worse!"   612| *1840:* mail, and rings   *1888:* mail, which
rings   613| *1840:* warps,   *1888:* warps;   614| *1840:* As might   *1888:* So
might   618| *1840:* pleasure now   *1863:* pleasure, now   619| *1840:*
Merely—what <> Not   *1863:* Merely,—what <> "Not   § 620-648| *1863:* WHAT IS THE
WORLD'S RECOGNITION WORTH? §   620| *1840:* school,   *1863:* school!"
621| *1840:* world: he found that every   *1863:* world. He found that, every   622| *1840:*
any given rhyme   *1863:* any ballad-rhyme,   626| *1840:* him—All at   *1863:* him—all,
at   627| *1840:* Will <> Will!   *1863:* will <> will!   632| *1840:* kept,   *1863:*
kept: 633| *1840:* merit—His   *1863:* merit!—his   639| *1840:* truth) was   *1863:*

The Mantuans, after all, that he should care
About their recognition, ay or no?
In spite of the convention months ago,
(Why blink the truth?) was not he forced to help
640   This same ungrateful audience, every whelp
Of Naddo's litter, make them pass for peers
With the bright band of old Goito years,
As erst he toiled for flower or tree? Why, there
Sat Palma! Adelaide's funereal hair
645   Ennobled the next corner. Ay, he strewed
A fairy dust upon that multitude,
Although he feigned to take them by themselves;
His giants dignified those puny elves,
Sublimed their faint applause. In short, he found
650   Himself still footing a delusive round,
Remote as ever from the self-display
He meant to compass, hampered every way
By what he hoped assistance. Wherefore then
Continue, make believe to find in men
655   A use he found not?
                            Weeks, months, years went by
And lo, Sordello vanished utterly,
Sundered in twain; each spectral part at strife
With each; one jarred against another life;
The Poet thwarting hopelessly the Man—
660   Who, fooled no longer, free in fancy ran
Here, there: let slip no opportunities
As pitiful, forsooth, beside the prize
To drop on him some no-time and acquit
His constant faith (the Poet-half's to wit—
665   That waiving any compromise between
No joy and all joy kept the hunger keen

truth?) was   642| *1840:* of those Goito   *1863:* of old Goito   643| *1840:* tree?
Why there   *1863:* tree? Why, there   644| *1840:* Sate   *1863:* Sat   646| *1840:*
multitude   *1863:* multitude,   § 649–676| *1863:* HOW, POET NO LONGER IN UNITY
WITH MAN, §   649| *1840:* short he   *1863:* short, he   655| *1840:* by;   *1888:*
by   656| *1840:* And, lo   *1868:* And lo   659| *1840:* hopelessly the Man   *1888:*
hopelessly the Man—   661| *1840:* there; let   *1888:* there: let   662| *1840:*
Forsooth, as pitiful beside   *1863:* As pitiful, forsooth, beside   664| *1840:* wit)   *1863:*

Beyond most methods)—of incurring scoff
From the Man-portion—not to be put off
With self-reflectings by the Poet's scheme,
670 Though ne'er so bright. Who sauntered forth in dream,
Dressed any how, nor waited mystic frames,
Immeasurable gifts, astounding claims,
But just his sorry self?—who yet might be
Sorrier for aught he in reality
675 Achieved, so pinioned Man's the Poet-part,
Fondling, in turn of fancy, verse; the Art
Developing his soul a thousand ways—
Potent, by its assistance, to amaze
The multitude with majesties, convince
680 Each sort of nature that the nature's prince
Accosted it. Language, the makeshift, grew
Into a bravest of expedients, too;
Apollo, seemed it now, perverse had thrown
Quiver and bow away, the lyre alone
685 Sufficed. While, out of dream, his day's work went
To tune a crazy tenzon or sirvent—
So hampered him the Man-part, thrust to judge
Between the bard and the bard's audience, grudge
A minute's toil that missed its due reward!
690 But the complete Sordello, Man and Bard,
John's cloud-girt angel, this foot on the land,
That on the sea, with, open in his hand,
A bitter-sweeting of a book—was gone.
Then, if internal struggles to be one,
695 Which frittered him incessantly piecemeal,

wit—   667| 1840: methods—of   1863: methods)—of   668| 1840: the
Man-portion not   1863: the Man-portion—not   669| 1840: scheme   1863:
scheme,   670| 1840: bright; which sauntered   1863: bright; that sauntered   1868:
bright;—that   1888: bright. Who sauntered   671| 1840: Dress'd   1863: Drest
1888: Dressed   673| 1840: self; who   1863: self—who   1888: self?—who
675| 1840: piinioned that the   1863: That   1888: pinioned Man's the   676| 1840:
Verse   1863: verse   § 677–705| 1863: THE WHOLE VISIBLE SORDELLO GOES
WRONG §   677| 1840: ways;   1863: ways—   680| 1840: that same nature's
1863: nature, that   1888: nature that the nature's   681| 1840: it: language   1863: it.
Language   685| 1840: Sufficed: while   1863: Sufficed. While   692| 1840: with
open <> hand   1868: with, open <> hand,   694| 1840: ¶ And if <> one   1868: ¶
Then, if   1888: one,   695| 1840: That frittered <> piece-meal,   1863: piecemeal,

Referred, ne'er so obliquely, to the real
Intruding Mantuans! ever with some call
To action while he pondered, once for all,
Which looked the easier effort—to pursue
700 This course, still leap o'er paltry joys, yearn through
The present ill-appreciated stage
Of self-revealment, and compel the age
Know him—or else, forswearing bard-craft, wake
From out his lethargy and nobly shake
705 Off timid habits of denial, mix
With men, enjoy like men. Ere he could fix
On aught, in rushed the Mantuans; much they cared
For his perplexity! Thus unprepared,
The obvious if not only shelter lay
710 In deeds, the dull conventions of his day
Prescribed the like of him: why not be glad
'Tis settled Palma's minstrel, good or bad,
Submits to this and that established rule?
Let Vidal change, or any other fool,
715 His murrey-coloured robe for filamot,
And crop his hair; too skin-deep, is it not,
Such vigour? Then, a sorrow to the heart,
His talk! Whatever topics they might start
Had to be groped for in his consciousness
720 Straight, and as straight delivered them by guess.
Only obliged to ask himself, "What was,"
A speedy answer followed; but, alas,
One of God's large ones, tardy to condense
Itself into a period; answers whence
725 A tangle of conclusions must be stripped
At any risk ere, trim to pattern clipped,

1888: Which frittered   697| *1840:* Mantuans! intruding ever   *1888:* Intruding
Mantuans! ever   702| *1840:* self-revealment and   *1863:* self-revealment, and
703| *1840:* him; or   *1888:* him—or § 706–734| *1863:* WITH THOSE TOO HARD FOR
HALF OF HIM, §   706| *1840:* like men: ere   *1863:* like men. Ere   710| *1840:*
deeds the   *1863:* deeds, the   714| *1840:* change or <> fool   *1863:* change, or <>
fool,   715| *1840:* philamot   *1863:* philamot,   *1868:* filamot,   716| *1840:* hair;
so skin-deep   *1863:* hair; too skin-deep   718| *1863:* start,   *1868:* start
720| *1840:* Strait <> strait <> guess: *1863:* Straight <> straight <> guess.
722| *1840:* followed, but   *1863:* followed; but   725| *1840:* stripp'd   *1863:*
stripped   726| *1840:* clipp'd,   *1863:* clipped,   729| *1840:* sorted o'er   *1863:*

They matched rare specimens the Mantuan flock
Regaled him with, each talker from his stock
Of sorted-o'er opinions, every stage,
730 Juicy in youth or desiccate with age,
Fruits like the fig tree's, rathe-ripe, rotten-rich,
Sweet-sour, all tastes to take: a practice which
He too had not impossibly attained,
Once either of those fancy-flights restrained;
735 (For, at conjecture how might words appear
To others, playing there what happened here,
And occupied abroad by what he spurned
At home, 'twas slipped, the occasion he returned
To seize:) he'd strike that lyre adroitly—speech,
740 Would but a twenty-cubit plectre reach;
A clever hand, consummate instrument,
Were both brought close; each excellency went
For nothing, else. The question Naddo asked,
Had just a lifetime moderately tasked
745 To answer, Naddo's fashion. More disgust
And more: why move his soul, since move it must
At minute's notice or as good it failed
To move at all? The end was, he retailed
Some ready-made opinion, put to use
750 This quip, that maxim, ventured reproduce
Gestures and tones—at any folly caught
Serving to finish with, nor too much sought
If false or true 'twas spoken; praise and blame
Of what he said grew pretty nigh the same
755 —Meantime awards to meantime acts: his soul,
Unequal to the compassing a whole,
Saw, in a tenth part, less and less to strive

sorted-o'er § 735–762| 1863: OF WHOM HE IS ALSO TOO CONTEMPTUOUS. §
735| 1840: For <> how the words   1863: how might words   1868: (For   736| 1840:
what passes here,   1863: what happened here,   738| 1840: slipt the   1863: slipt,
the 1868: slipped   739| 1840: seize: he'd 1868: seize:) he'd   740| 1840:
twenty cubit 1863: twenty-cubit   742| 1840: close! each 1863: close; each
743| 1840: asked 1863: asked,   744| 1840: life-time 1863: lifetime
745| 1840: fashion; more 1863: fashion. More   746| 1840: more; why 1863: more!
why 1868: more: why   747| 1840: minutes' 1863: minute's   754| 1840:
pretty well the 1888: pretty nigh the   756| 1840: Whole, 1863: whole,
757| 1840: Saw in <> part less and 1863: Saw, in <> part, less and   758| 1840:

About. And as for men in turn . . . contrive
Who could to take eternal interest
760 In them, so hate the worst, so love the best,
Though, in pursuance of his passive plan,
He hailed, decried, the proper way.

                                        As Man
So figured he; and how as Poet? Verse
Came only not to a stand-still. The worse,
765 That his poor piece of daily work to do
Was—not sink under any rivals; who
Loudly and long enough, without these qualms,
Turned, from Bocafoli's stark-naked psalms,
To Plara's sonnets spoilt by toying with,
770 "As knops that stud some almug to the pith
Prickèd for gum, wry thence, and crinklèd worse.
Than pursèd eyelids of a river-horse
Sunning himself o' the slime when whirrs the breese"—
Gad-fly, that is. He might compete with these!
775 But—but—
                    "Observe a pompion-twine afloat;
Pluck me one cup from off the castle-moat!
Along with cup you raise leaf, stalk and root,
The entire surface of the pool to boot.
So could I pluck a cup, put in one song
780 A single sight, did not my hand, too strong,
Twitch in the least the root-strings of the whole.
How should externals satisfy my soul?"
"Why that's precise the error Squarcialupe"
(Hazarded Naddo) "finds; 'the man can't stoop
785 To sing us out,' quoth he, 'a mere romance;
He'd fain do better than the best, enhance

Men   *1863:* men   761| *1840:* Though in <> plan   *1863:* Though, in <>
plan,   762| *1840:* decried the   *1868:* decried, the   § 763–789| *1863:* HE PLEASES
NEITHER HIMSELF NOR THEM: 763–790| *1868* §   766| *1840:* Was not
1863: Was, not   *1888:* Was—not   768| *1840:* Tuned, from   *1888:* Turned,
from   772| *1840:* pursed-up   *1863:* pursèd   773| *1840:* breese"   *1863:*
breeze"—   *1888:* breese"—   774| *1840:* Ha, ha! Of course he <> these   *1863:*
Gad-fly, that is. He <> these!   775| *1840:* But—but— ¶ Observe   *1863:* But—but—
¶ "Observe   776| *1840:* castle-moat—   *1863:* castle-moat!   782| *1840:* soul?
1863: soul?"   783| *1840:* Why <> Squarcialupe   *1863:* "Why <>
Squarcialupe"   784| *1840:* Naddo) finds; the   *1863:* Naddo) "finds; 'the
785| *1840:* out, quoth he, a   *1863:* out,' quoth he, 'a   788| *1840:* Therewith: now

183

The subjects' rarity, work problems out
Therewith.' Now, you're a bard, a bard past doubt,
And no philosopher; why introduce
790 Crotchets like these? fine, surely, but no use
In poetry—which still must be, to strike,
Based upon common sense; there's nothing like
Appealing to our nature! what beside
Was your first poetry? No tricks were tried
795 In that, no hollow thrills, affected throes!
'The man,' said we, 'tells his own joys and woes:
We'll trust him.' Would you have your songs endure?
Build on the human heart!—why, to be sure
Yours is one sort of heart—but I mean theirs,
800 Ours, every one's, the healthy heart one cares
To build on! Central peace, mother of strength,
That's father of . . . nay, go yourself that length,
Ask those calm-hearted doers what they do
When they have got their calm! And is it true,
805 Fire rankles at the heart of every globe?
Perhaps. But these are matters one may probe
Too deeply for poetic purposes:
Rather select a theory that . . . yes,
Laugh! what does that prove?—stations you midway
810 And saves some little o'er-refining. Nay,
That's rank injustice done me! I restrict
The poet? Don't I hold the poet picked
Out of a host of warriors, statesmen . . . did
I tell you? Very like! As well you hid
815 That sense of power, you have! True bards believe
All able to achieve what they achieve—
That is, just nothing—in one point abide
Profounder simpletons than all beside.

---

you're   *1863:* Therewith:' now, you're   *1888:* Therewith.' Now   § ⁷⁹⁰⁻⁸¹⁸| *1863:* WHICH
THE BEST JUDGES ACCOUNT FOR.   ⁷⁹¹⁻⁸¹⁹| *1868* §   ⁷⁹⁶| *1840:* The man,
said we, tells <> woes—   *1863:* 'The man,' said we, 'tells   *1888:* woes: ⁷⁹⁷| *1840:*
him. Would   *1863:* him.' Would   ⁷⁹⁸| *1840:* heart!—Why to   *1863:* heart!—Why,
to   *1888:* why   ⁸⁰⁴| *1840:* calm! Nay, is it true   *1863:* calm! And is it true
⁸⁰⁶| *1840:* Perhaps! But   *1868:* Perhaps. But   ⁸⁰⁸| *1840:* yes   *1863:* yes,
⁸⁰⁹| *1840:* prove? . . . stations   *1863:* prove?—stations   ⁸¹³| *1840:* statesmen—did
1863: statesmen . . . did   ⁸¹⁴| *1840:* as   *1863:* As   ⁸¹⁵| *1840:* power you   *1863:*
power, you   ⁸¹⁶| *1840:* Us able   *1863:* All able   ⁸¹⁸| *1840:* beside: *1863:*

184

Oh, ay! The knowledge that you are a bard
820 Must constitute your prime, nay sole, reward!"
So prattled Naddo, busiest of the tribe
Of genius-haunters—how shall I describe
What grubs or nips or rubs or rips—your louse
For love, your flea for hate, magnanimous,
825 Malignant, Pappacoda, Tagliafer,
Picking a sustenance from wear and tear
By implements it sedulous employs
To undertake, lay down, mete out, o'er-toise
Sordello? Fifty creepers to elude
830 At once! They settled staunchly; shame ensued:
Behold the monarch of mankind succumb
To the last fool who turned him round his thumb,
As Naddo styled it! 'Twas not worth oppose
The matter of a moment, gainsay those
835 He aimed at getting rid of; better think
Their thoughts and speak their speech, secure to slink
Back expeditiously to his safe place,
And chew the cud—what he and what his race
Were really, each of them. Yet even this
840 Conformity was partial. He would miss
Some point, brought into contact with them ere
Assured in what small segment of the sphere
Of his existence they attended him;
Whence blunders, falsehoods rectified—a grim
845 List—slur it over! How? If dreams were tried,
His will swayed sicklily from side to side,
Nor merely neutralized his waking act
But tended e'en in fancy to distract
The intermediate will, the choice of means.
850 He lost the art of dreaming: Mantuan scenes

beside.   § 819–847| 1863: THEIR CRITICISMS GIVE SMALL COMFORT:
820–848| 1868 §   819| 1840: Oh ay   1863: Oh, ay   820| 1840: reward!   1863:
reward!"   823| 1840: nips, or rubs, or rips   1863: nips or rubs or rips
829| 1840: fifty   1863: Fifty   830| 1840: stanchly   1868: staunchly   844| 1840:
blunders—falsehoods   1868: blunders, falsehoods   846| 1840: to side   1863: to side,
§ 848–876| 1863: AND HIS OWN DEGRADATION IS COMPLETE.
849–877| 1868 §   849| 1840: means: 1863: means.   850| 1840: Mantua   1863:

Supplied a baron, say, he sang before,
Handsomely reckless, full to running-o'er
Of gallantries; "abjure the soul, content
"With body, therefore!" Scarcely had he bent
855 Himself in dream thus low, when matter fast
Cried out, he found, for spirit to contrast
And task it duly; by advances slight,
The simple stuff becoming composite,
Count Lori grew Apollo: best recall
860 His fancy! Then would some rough peasant-Paul,
Like those old Ecelin confers with, glance
His gay apparel o'er; that countenance
Gathered his shattered fancies into one,
And, body clean abolished, soul alone
865 Sufficed the grey Paulician: by and by,
To balance the ethereality,
Passions were needed; foiled he sank again.
    Meanwhile the world rejoiced ('tis time explain)
Because a sudden sickness set it free
870 From Adelaide. Missing the mother-bee,
Her mountain-hive Romano swarmed; at once
A rustle-forth of daughters and of sons
Blackened the valley. "I am sick too, old,
Half-crazed I think; what good's the Kaiser's gold
875 To such an one? God help me! for I catch
My children's greedy sparkling eyes at watch—
'He bears that double breastplate on,' they say,
'So many minutes less than yesterday!'
Beside, Monk Hilary is on his knees

Mantuan   851| 1840: sung   1868: sang   852| 1840: running o'er   1888:
running-o'er   853| 1840: gallantries; abjure   1863: gallantries; "abjure
854| 1840: therefore! Scarcely   1863: therefore!" Scarcely   855| 1840: low when
1863: low, when   859| 1840: grew Apollo—best   1888: grew Apollo: best
860| 1840: peasant-Paul   1863: peasant-Paul,   863| 1840: fancy   1888: fancies
865| 1840: and by   1863: and by,   866| 1840: ethereality   1863: ethereality,
867| 1840: sunk   1888: sank   870| 1840: mother bee   1863: mother-bee,
871| 1840: mountain hive   1863: mountain-hive   873| 1840: valley. I   1863: valley.
"I   874| 1840: Half crazed   1863: Half-crazed   § 877–905| 1863: ADELAIDE'S
DEATH; WHAT HAPPENS ON IT: 878–905| 1868: DEATH: WHAT §
877| 1840: He <> on, they   1868: 'He <> on,' they   878| 1840: So <>
yesterday!   1868: 'So <> yesterday!'   879| 1840: Beside Monk   1863: Beside,

880 Now, sworn to kneel and pray till God shall please
Exact a punishment for many things
You know, and some you never knew; which brings
To memory, Azzo's sister Beatrix
And Richard's Giglia are my Alberic's
385 And Ecelin's betrothed; the Count himself
Must get my Palma: Ghibellin and Guelf
Mean to embrace each other." So began
Romano's missive to his fighting man
Taurello—on the Tuscan's death, away
890 With Friedrich sworn to sail from Naples' bay
Next month for Syria. Never thunder-clap
Out of Vesuvius' throat, like this mishap
Startled him. "That accursed Vicenza! I
Absent, and she selects this time to die!
895 Ho, fellows, for Vicenza!" Half a score
Of horses ridden dead, he stood before
Romano in his reeking spurs: too late—
"Boniface urged me, Este could not wait,"
The chieftain stammered; "let me die in peace—
900 Forget me! Was it I who craved increase
Of rule? Do you and Friedrich plot your worst
Against the Father: as you found me first
So leave me now. Forgive me! Palma, sure,
Is at Goito still. Retain that lure—
905 Only be pacified!"
                     The country rung
With such a piece of news: on every tongue,
How Ecelin's great servant, congeed off,
Had done a long day's service, so, might doff
The green and yellow, and recover breath

Monk   882| *1840:* know and   *1863:* know, and   887| *1840:* other. So   *1863:*
other." So   888| *1840:* fighting-man   *1868:* fighting man   889| *1840:* Taurello
on   *1863:* Taurello—on   892| *1840:* of Vesuvius' mount like   *1863:* of Vesuvius'
throat, like   893| *1840:* him. That   *1863:* him. "That   895| *1840:* for Vicenza!
Half   *1863:* for Vicenza!" Half   896| *1840:* dead he   *1863:* dead, he   898| *1840:*
Boniface <> wait,   *1863:* "Boniface <> wait,"   899| *1840:* stammered; let   *1863:*
stammered; "let   900| *1840:* it I e'er craved   *1888:* it I who craved   905| *1840:*
pacified! ¶ The   *1863:* pacified!" ¶ The § 905-934| *1863:* AND A TROUBLE IT
OCCASIONS SORDELLO. §   906| *1840:* tongue   *1863:* tongue,   908| *1840:* so
might   *1863:* so, might   909| *1840:* yellow to recover   *1863:* yellow, and

910 At Mantua, whither,—since Retrude's death,
(The girlish slip of a Sicilian bride
From Otho's house, he carried to reside
At Mantua till the Ferrarese should pile
A structure worthy her imperial style,
915 The gardens raise, the statues there enshrine,
She never lived to see)—although his line
Was ancient in her archives and she took
A pride in him, that city, nor forsook
Her child when he forsook himself and spent
920 A prowess on Romano surely meant
For his own growth—whither he ne'er resorts
If wholly satisfied (to trust reports)
With Ecelin. So, forward in a trice
Were shows to greet him. "Take a friend's advice,"
925 Quoth Naddo to Sordello, "nor be rash
Because your rivals (nothing can abash
Some folks) demur that we pronounced you best
To sound the great man's welcome; 'tis a test,
Remember! Strojavacca looks asquint,
930 The rough fat sloven; and there's plenty hint
Your pinions have received of late a shock—
Outsoar them, cobswan of the silver flock!
Sing well!" A signal wonder, song's no whit
Facilitated.
                    Fast the minutes flit;
935 Another day, Sordello finds, will bring
The soldier, and he cannot choose but sing;
So, a last shift, quits Mantua—slow, alone:
Out of that aching brain, a very stone,

---

recover   910| *1840:* whither, since   *1863:* whither,—since   912| *1840:* From
Otho's House he   *1863:* From Otho's House, he   *1868:* house   915| *1840:* raise, their
tenantry enshrine   *1863:* raise, the statues there enshrine,   916| *1840:* see)
although   *1863:* see)—although   919| *1840:* child though he   *1863:* child when
he   921| *1840:* own purposes—he   *1863:* own growth—whither he   923| *1840:*
With Ecelin. So forward   *1863:* With Ecelin. So, forward   924| *1840:* him. Take <>
advice,   *1863:* him. "Take <> advice,"   925| *1840:* to Sordello, nor   *1863:* to
Sordello, "nor   928| *1840:* test   *1863:* test,   932| *1840:* Out-soar   *1868:*
Outsoar   933| *1840:* well! A signal wonder song's   *1863:* well!" A signal wonder,
song's   § 934–962| *1863:* HE CHANCES UPON HIS OLD ENVIRONMENT, §
937| *1840:* So quits, a last shift, Mantua   *1863:* So, a last shift, quits Mantua

188

Song must be struck. What occupies that front?
940 Just how he was more awkward than his wont
The night before, when Naddo, who had seen
Taurello on his progress, praised the mien
For dignity no crosses could affect—
Such was a joy, and might not he detect
945 A satisfaction if established joys
Were proved imposture? Poetry annoys
Its utmost: wherefore fret? Verses may come
Or keep away! And thus he wandered, dumb
Till evening, when he paused, thoroughly spent,
950 On a blind hill-top: down the gorge he went,
Yielding himself up as to an embrace.
The moon came out; like features of a face,
A querulous fraternity of pines,
Sad blackthorn clumps, leafless and grovelling vines
955 Also came out, made gradually up
The picture; 'twas Goito's mountain-cup
And castle. He had dropped through one defile
He never dared explore, the Chief erewhile
Had vanished by. Back rushed the dream, enwrapped
960 Him wholly. 'Twas Apollo now they lapped,
Those mountains, not a pettish minstrel meant
To wear his soul away in discontent,
Brooding on fortune's malice. Heart and brain
Swelled; he expanded to himself again,
965 As some thin seedling spice-tree starved and frail,
Pushing between cat's head and ibis' tail
Crusted into the porphyry pavement smooth,
—Suffered remain just as it sprung, to soothe
The Soldan's pining daughter, never yet
970 Well in her chilly green-glazed minaret,—

950| *1840:* hill-top; down *1863:* hill-top: down   951| *1840:* embrace; *1863:*
embrace.   952| *1840:* face *1868:* face,   959| *1840:* enwrapt *1863:*
enwrapped   960| *1840:* lapped *1863:* lapped,   962| *1840:* discontent *1863:*
discontent, § 963–991| *1863:* SEES BUT FAILURE IN ALL DONE SINCE, §
963| *1840:* malice; heart *1863:* malice. Heart   964| *1840:* again *1863:* again,
965| *1840:* As that thin <> frail *1863:* As some thin <> frail,   966| *1840:* head or
ibis' *1863:* head and ibis'   967| *1840:* smooth *1863:* smooth,   968| *1840:*
sprung to *1863:* sprung, to   970| *1840:* in the chilly <> minaret— *1863:* in her

When rooted up, the sunny day she died,
And flung into the common court beside
Its parent tree. Come home, Sordello! Soon
Was he low muttering, beneath the moon,
975 Of sorrow saved, of quiet evermore,—
Since from the purpose, he maintained before,
Only resulted wailing and hot tears.
Ah, the slim castle! dwindled of late years,
But more mysterious; gone to ruin—trails
980 Of vine through every loop-hole. Nought avails
The night as, torch in hand, he must explore
The maple chamber: did I say, its floor
Was made of intersecting cedar beams?
Worn now with gaps so large, there blew cold streams
985 Of air quite from the dungeon; lay your ear
Close and 'tis like, one after one, you hear
In the blind darkness water drop. The nests
And nooks retain their long ranged vesture-chests
Empty and smelling of the iris root
990 The Tuscan grated o'er them to recruit
Her wasted wits. Palma was gone that day,
Said the remaining women. Last, he lay
Beside the Carian group reserved and still.
    The Body, the Machine for Acting Will,
995 Had been at the commencement proved unfit;
That for Demonstrating, Reflecting it,
Mankind—no fitter: was the Will Itself
In fault?
        His forehead pressed the moonlit shelf
Beside the youngest marble maid awhile;
1000 Then, raising it, he thought, with a long smile,

---

chilly <> minaret,—   971| *1840:* up the <> died   *1863:* up, the <> died,
974| *1840:* muttering beneath the moon   *1863:* muttering, beneath the moon,
975| *1840:* evermore,   *1863:* evermore,—   976| *1840:* How from his purposes
maintained before   *1863:* Since from the purpose, he maintained before,   980| *1840:*
thro'   *1863:* through   982| *1840:* chamber—did I say its   *1863:* chamber: did I say,
its   984| *1840:* large there   *1863:* large, there   987| *1840:* water-drops   *1863:*
water drop   988| *1840:* retained   *1868:* retain   989| *1840:* iris-root   *1868:* iris
root   § 992–1016| *1863:* AND RESOLVES TO DESIST FROM THE LIKE. §
994| *1840:* for Acting Will   *1863:* for Acting Will,   996| *1840:* for Reflecting,

"I shall be king again!" as he withdrew
The envied scarf; into the font he threw
His crown.
                    Next day, no poet! "Wherefore?" asked
Taurello, when the dance of Jongleurs, masked
1005 As devils, ended; "don't a song come next?"
The master of the pageant looked perplexed
Till Naddo's whisper came to his relief.
"His Highness knew what poets were: in brief,
Had not the tetchy race percriptive right
1010 To peevishness, caprice? or, call it spite,
One must receive their nature in its length
And breadth, expect the weakness with the strength!"
—So phrasing, till, his stock of phrases spent,
The easy-natured soldier smiled assent,
1015 Settled his portly person, smoothed his chin,
And nodded that the bull-bait might begin.

BOOK THE THIRD

And the font took them: let our laurels lie!
Braid moonfern now with mystic trifoly
Because once more Goito gets, once more,
Sordello to itself! A dream is o'er,
5   And the suspended life begins anew;
Quiet those throbbing temples, then, subdue
That cheek's distortion! Nature's strict embrace,
Putting aside the past, shall soon efface

Demonstrating it,   *1868:* for Demonstrating, Reflecting it,   1001| *1840:* I <> again!
as   *1863:* "I <> again!" as   1003| *1840:* poet! Wherefore? asked   *1863:* poet!
"Wherefore!" asked   *1888:* crown ¶ Next   *1889:* crown. ¶ Next   1004| *1840:* of
Jongleurs masked   *1863:* of Jongleurs, masked   1005| *1840:* devils ended; don't <>
next?   *1863:* devils, ended; "don't <> next?"   1006| *1840:* perplext   *1868:*
perplexed   1007| *1840:* relief;   *1863:* relief.   1008| *1840:* His   *1863:*
"His   1012| *1840:* strength!   *1863:* strength!"   1013| *1840:* So
1863:—So   1016| *1840:* the bull-chase might   *1863:* the bull-bait might
§ 1–23| *1863:* NATURE MAY TRIUMPH THEREFORE: §   1| *1840:* ¶ And   *1863:*
And   4| *1840:* o'er   *1863:* o'er,   8| *1863:* Past   *1868:* past   15| *1840:* sea

Its print as well—factitious humours grown
10 Over the true—loves, hatreds not his own—
And turn him pure as some forgotten vest
Woven of painted byssus, silkiest
Tufting the Tyrrhene whelk's pearl-sheeted lip,
Left welter where a trireme let it slip
15 I' the sea, and vexed a satrap; so the stain
O' the world forsakes Sordello, with its pain,
Its pleasure: how the tinct loosening escapes,
Cloud after cloud! Mantua's familiar shapes
Die, fair and foul die, fading as they flit,
20 Men, women, and the pathos and the wit,
Wise speech and foolish, deeds to smile or sigh
For, good, bad, seemly or ignoble, die.
The last face glances through the eglantines,
The last voice murmurs, 'twixt the blossomed vines,
25 Of Men, of that machine supplied by thought
To compass self-perception with, he sought
By forcing half himself—an insane pulse
Of a god's blood, on clay it could convulse,
Never transmute—on human sights and sounds,
30 To watch the other half with; irksome bounds
It ebbs from to its source, a fountain sealed
Forever. Better sure be unrevealed
Than part revealed: Sordello well or ill
Is finished: then what further use of Will,
35 Point in the prime idea not realized,
An oversight? inordinately prized,
No less, and pampered with enough of each
Delight to prove the whole above its reach.

---

and <> Satrap   *1863:* sea, and <> satrap   [16]   *1840:* forsakes Sordello with its
pain   *1863:* forsakes Sordello, with its pain,   [17]   *1840:* escapes   *1863:* escapes,
[22]   *1840:* die: *1863:* die.   § [24-52]   *1863:* FOR HER SON, LATELY ALIVE, DIES
AGAIN, §   [24]   *1840:* murmurs 'twixt <> vines   *1888:* murmurs, 'twixt <>
vines,   [25]   *1840:* This May of the Machine <> Thought   *1863:* Of Men, of that
machine <> thought   [26]   *1840:* Self-perception idly sought   *1863:* self-perception
with, he sought   [28]   *1840:* a God's blood on <> convulse   *1863:* god's blood, on <>
convulse,   [29]   *1840:* sounds   *1863:* sounds,   [33]   *1840:* part-revealed   *1888:*
part revealed   [34]   *1840:* finished with: what <> Will?   *1863:* finished: then what
<> Will,   [35]   *1840:*—Point   *1863:* A point   *1868:* Point   [36]   *1840:*

"To need become all natures, yet retain
40   The law of my own nature—to remain
Myself, yet yearn . . . as if that chestnut, think,
Should yearn for this first larch-bloom crisp and pink,
Or those pale fragrant tears where zephyrs stanch
March wounds along the fretted pine-tree branch!
45   Will and the means to show will, great and small,
Material, spiritual,—abjure them all
Save any so distinct, they may be left
To amuse, not tempt become! and, thus bereft,
Just as I first was fashioned would I be!
50   Nor, moon, is it Apollo now, but me
Thou visitest to comfort and befriend!
Swim thou into my heart, and there an end,
Since I possess thee!—nay, thus shut mine eyes
And know, quite know, by this heart's fall and rise,
55   When thou dost bury thee in clouds, and when
Out-standest: wherefore practise upon men
To make that plainer to myself?"

                                    Slide here

Over a sweet and solitary year
Wasted; or simply notice change in him—
60   How eyes, once with exploring bright, grew dim
And satiate with receiving. Some distress
Was caused, too, by a sort of consciousness

---

oversight, inordinately prized   *1863:* oversight? inordinatley prized,   ³⁹| *1840:* To
<> natures yet   *1863:* "To <> natures, yet   ⁴⁰| *1840:* of one's own   *1863:* of my
own   ⁴¹| *1840:* Oneself, yet yearn . . . aha, that   *1863:* Myself, yet yearn . . . as if
that   ⁴²| *1840:* To yearn   *1863:* Should yearn   ⁴³| *1840:* With those <>
staunch   *1863:* Or those <> stanch   ⁴⁵| *1840:* show it, great and small   *1863:* show
will, great and small,   ⁴⁶| *1840:* spiritual, abjure   *1863:* spiritual,—abjure
⁴⁷| *1840:* distinct as to be   *1863:* distinct, they may be   ⁴⁸| *1840:* Amuse <>
become: and   *1863:* To amuse <> become! and   ⁴⁹| *1840:* Say, just as I am
fashioned   *1863:* Just as I first was fashioned   ⁵⁰| *1840:* Nor, Moon <> now but
1863: now, but   *1868:* moon   ⁵¹| *1840:* befriend;   *1863:* befriend!   ⁵²| *1840:*
heart and <> end   *1863:* heart, and <> end,   § ^{53–80}| *1863:*—WAS FOUND AND IS
LOST. §   ⁵³| *1840:* thee! nay thus   *1863:* thee!—nay, thus   ⁵⁴| *1840:* by that
heart's <> rise   *1863:* by this heart's <> rise,   ⁵⁵| *1840:* If thou <> clouds and
1863: When thou <> clouds, and   ⁵⁶| *1840:* Men   *1863:* men   ⁵⁷| *1840:*
myself? ¶ Slide   *1863:* myself?" ¶ Slide   ⁵⁹| *1840:* Wasted: or   *1868:* Wasted;
or   ⁶⁰| *1840:* eyes, bright with exploring once, grew   *1888:* eyes, once with exploring
bright, grew   ⁶¹| *1840:* As satiate   *1863:* And satiate   ⁶²| *1840:* Occasioned,

Under the imbecility,—nought kept
That down; he slept, but was aware he slept,
65 So, frustrated: as who brainsick made pact
Erst with the overhanging cataract
To deafen him, yet still distinguished plain
His own blood's measured clicking at his brain.
     To finish. One declining Autumn day—
70 Few birds about the heaven chill and grey,
No wind that cared trouble the tacit woods—
He sauntered home complacently, their moods
According, his and nature's. Every spark
Of Mantua life was trodden out; so dark
75 The embers, that the Troubadour, who sung
Hundreds of songs, forgot, its trick his tongue,
Its craft his brain, how either brought to pass
Singing at all; that faculty might class
With any of Apollo's now. The year
80 Began to find its early promise sere
As well. Thus beauty vanishes; thus stone
Outlingers flesh: nature's and his youth gone,
They left the world to you, and wished you joy.
When, stopping his benevolent employ,
85 A presage shuddered through the welkin; harsh
The earth's remonstrance followed. 'Twas the marsh
Gone of a sudden. Mincio, in its place,
Laughed, a broad water, in next morning's face,
And, where the mists broke up immense and white

---

too, a *1863:* Was caused, too, by a   63| *1840:* imbecility; nought *1863:*
imbecility,—nought   64| *1840:* down: he <> he slept *1863:* down; he <> he
slept,   65| *1840:* And frustrate so: as *1863:* So, frustrated: as   67| *1840:* yet may
distinguish now *1863:* yet still distinguished slow *1888:* distinguished plain
68| *1840:* at his brow. *1888:* at his brain.   73| *1840:* Nature's *1868:* nature's
75| *1840:* embers that the Troubadour who *1863:* embers, that the Troubadour,
who   76| *1840:* songs forgot, its trick the tongue, *1863:* songs, forgot, its trick his
tongue,   77| *1840:* craft the brain *1863:* craft his brain   78| *1840:* Singing so
e'er; that *1863:* Singing at all; that § 81–108| *1863:* BUT NATURE IS ONE THING,
MAN ANOTHER— §   81| *1840:* vanishes! Your stone *1863:* vanishes; thus
stone   82| *1840:* Outlasts your flesh. Nature's *1863:* Outlingers flesh: nature's
83| *1840:* you and *1863:* you, and   84| *1840:* When stopping <> employ *1863:*
When, stopping <> employ,   87| *1840:* sudden. Mincio in its place *1863:* sudden.
Mincio, in its place,   88| *1840:* Laughed a broad water in <> face *1863:* Laughed, a

90 I' the steady wind, burned like a spilth of light
    Out of the crashing of a myriad stars.
    And here was nature, bound by the same bars
    Of fate with him!
                    "No! youth once gone is gone:
    Deeds, let escape, are never to be done.
95 Leaf-fall and grass-spring for the year; for us—
    Oh forfeit I unalterably thus
    My chance? nor two lives wait me, this to spend,
    Learning save that? Nature has time, may mend
    Mistake, she knows occasion will recur;
100 Landslip or seabreach, how affects it her
    With her magnificent resources?—I
    Must perish once and perish utterly.
    Not any strollings now at even-close
    Down the field-path, Sordello! by thorn-rows
105 Alive with lamp-flies, swimming spots of fire
    And dew, outlining the black cypress' spire
    She waits you at, Elys, who heard you first
    Woo her, the snow-month through, but ere she durst
    Answer 'twas April. Linden-flower-time-long
110 Her eyes were on the ground; 'tis July, strong
    Now; and because white dust-clouds overwhelm
    The woodside, here or by the village elm
    That holds the moon, she meets you, somewhat pale,
    But letting you lift up her coarse flax veil
115 And whisper (the damp little hand in yours)
    Of love, heart's love, your heart's love that endures
    Till death. Tush! No mad mixing with the rout

---

broad water, in <> face, 90| *1840:* burnt *1863:* burned 92| *1840:* Nature
1868: nature 93| *1840:* him! ¶ No: youth *1863:* him! ¶ "No! youth 94| *1840:*
Deeds let escape are <> done: *1863:* done. *1888:* Deeds, let escape, are 95| *1840:*
year, but us— *1863:* year; for us— 97| *1840:* spend *1863:* spend, 98| *1840:*
has leisure mend *1863:* has time to mend *1868:* time, may mend 99| *1840:*
Mistake, occasion, knows she, will recur— *1863:* Mistake, she knows occasion will recur—
1868: recur; 100| *1840:* seabreach how *1863:* seabreach, how 101| *1840:*
resources? I *1863:* resources?—I 102| *1840:* utterly *1868:* utterly.
104| *1840:* field-path, Sordello, by *1863:* field-path, Sordello! by 108| *1840:* her the
snow-month—ah, but *1863:* her, the snow-month through, but § 109–137| *1863:* HAVING
MULTIFARIOUS SYMPATHIES, 109–136| *1868* § 109| *1840:* 'twas April!
Linden-flower-time-long *1863:* 'twas April. Linden-flower-time-long 113| *1840:*
moon she *1863:* moon, she 116| *1840:* Of love—heart's love—your *1863:* Of love,

195

Of haggard ribalds wandering about
The hot torchlit wine-scented island-house
120 Where Friedrich holds his wickedest carouse,
Parading,—to the gay Palermitans,
Soft Messinese, dusk Saracenic clans
Nuocera holds,—those tall grave dazzling Norse,
High-cheeked, lank-haired, toothed whiter than the morse,
125 Queens of the caves of jet stalactites,
He sent his barks to fetch through icy seas,
The blind night seas without a saving star,
And here in snowy birdskin robes they are,
Sordello!—here, mollitious alcoves gilt
130 Superb as Byzant domes that devils built!
—Ah, Byzant, there again! no chance to go
Ever like august cheery Dandolo,
Worshipping hearts about him for a wall,
Conducted, blind eyes, hundred years and all,
135 Through vanquished Byzant where friends note for him
What pillar, marble massive, sardius slim,
'Twere fittest he transport to Venice' Square—
Flattered and promised life to touch them there
Soon, by those fervid sons of senators!
140 No more lifes, deaths, loves, hatreds, peaces, wars!
Ah, fragments of a whole ordained to be,
Points in the life I waited! what are ye
But roundels of a ladder which appeared
Awhile the very platform it was reared
145 To lift me on?—that happiness I find
Proofs of my faith in, even in the blind

heart's love, your   120| *1840:* carouse   *1863:* carouse,   121| *1840:* Parading to
1863: Parading,—to   123| *1840:* From Nuocera, those   *1863:* Nuocera
holds,—those   124| *1840:* Clear-cheeked   *1863:* High-cheeked   125| *1840:*
stalactites   *1863:* stalactites,   127| *1840:* saving-star,   *1863:* saving star,
129| *1840:* Sordello, here   *1863:* Sordello!—here   130| *1840:* as Byzant-domes the
devils built   *1863:* as Byzant domes that devils built!   132| *1840:* august pleasant
Dandolo,   *1888:* august cheery Dandolo,   135| *1840:* vanquished Byzant to have
noted him   *1863:* vanquished Byzant where friends note for him   137| *1840:* fittest we
transport   *1863:* fittest he transport   § 138–167| *1863:* HE MAY NEITHER RENOUNCE
NOR SATISFY;   137–165| *1868* §   139| *1840:* by his fervid   *1868:* by those
fervid   140| *1840:* wars—   *1868:* wars!   141| *1840:* Whole <> be!   *1863:*
whole   *1868:* be,   145| *1840:* on—that Happiness   *1863:* on?—that happiness

Instinct which bade forego you all unless
Ye led me past yourselves. Ay, happiness
Awaited me; the way life should be used
150 Was to acquire, and deeds like you conduced
To teach it by a self-revealment, deemed
Life's very use, so long! Whatever seemed
Progress to that, was pleasure; aught that stayed
My reaching it—no pleasure. I have laid
155 The ladder down; I climb not; still, aloft
The platform stretches! Blisses strong and soft,
I dared not entertain, elude me; yet
Never of what they promised could I get
A glimpse till now! The common sort, the crowd,
160 Exist, perceive; with Being are endowed,
However slight, distinct from what they See,
However bounded; Happiness must be,
To feed the first by gleanings from the last,
Attain its qualities, and slow or fast
165 Become what they behold; such peace-in-strife,
By transmutation, is the Use of Life,
The Alien turning Native to the soul
Or body—which instructs me; I am whole
There and demand a Palma; had the world
170 Been from my soul to a like distance hurled,
'Twere Happiness to make it one with me:
Whereas I must, ere I begin to Be,
Include a world, in flesh, I comprehend
In spirit now; and this done, what's to blend
175 With? Nought is Alien in the world— my Will

148| *1840:* yourselves? Ay, Happiness   *1863:* yourselves. Ay, happiness   151| *1840:*
self-revealment (deemed   *1863:* self-revealment, deemed   152| *1840:* That very use
too long). Whatever   *1863:* The very use, so long! Whatever   *1888:* Life's very
153| *1840:* that was Pleasure   *1863:* that, was pleasure   154| *1840:* Me reaching
it—No Pleasure   *1863:* My reaching it—no pleasure   155| *1840:* The roundels down
<> still aloft   *1863:* The ladder down <> still, aloft   156| *1840:* soft   *1863:*
soft,   157| *1840:* entertain elude   *1863:* entertain, elude   162| *1840:* bounded:
Happiness must be   *1863:* bounded; Happiness must be,   165| *1840:* what one
beholds; such place-in-strife   *1863:* what they behold   *1888:* such peace-in-strife,
166| *1840:* transmutation is   *1863:* transmutation, is   § 168-196| *1863:* IN THE PROCESS
TO WHICH IS PLEASURE,   166-194| *1868* §   170| *1840:* hurled   *1863:*
hurled,   171| *1840:* me—   *1868:* me: 175| *1840:* is Alien here—my   *1863:* is

Owns all already; yet can turn it—still
Less—Native, since my Means to correspond
With Will are so unworthy, 'twas my bond
To tread the very joys that tantalize
180 Most now, into a grave, never to rise.
I die then! Will the rest agree to die?
Next Age or no? Shall its Sordello try
Clue after clue, and catch at last the clue
I miss?—that's underneath my finger too,
185 Twice, thrice a day, perhaps,—some yearning traced
Deeper, some petty consequence embraced
Closer! Why fled I Mantua, then?—complained
So much my Will was fettered, yet remained
Content within a tether half the range
190 I could assign it?—able to exchange
My ignorance (I felt) for knowledge, and
Idle because I could thus understand—
Could e'en have penetrated to its core
Our mortal mystery, yet—fool—forbore,
195 Preferred elaborating in the dark
My casual stuff, by any wretched spark
Born of my predecessors, though one stroke
Of mine had brought the flame forth! Mantua's yoke,
My minstrel's-trade, was to behold mankind,—
200 My own concern was just to bring my mind
Behold, just extricate, for my acquist,
Each object suffered stifle in the mist
Which hazard, custom, blindness interpose

Alien in the world—my $^{176}|$ *1840:* Owns it already <> it still   *1863:* Owns all
already   *1888:* it—still $^{177}|$ *1840:* Less Native   *1888:* Less—Native
$^{178}|$ *1840:* unworthy 'twas   *1863:* unworthy, 'twas $^{179}|$ *1840:* very ones that   *1863:*
very joys that $^{180}|$ *1840:* Me now into <> rise—   *1863:* Most now, into <>
rise. $^{183}|$ *1840:* after clue and   *1863:* after clue, and $^{184}|$ *1840:* miss, that's
1863: miss?—that's $^{187}|$ *1840:* fled I Mantua then? Complained   *1863:* fled I
Mantua, then?—complained $^{191}|$ *1840:* ignorance, I felt, for   *1863:* ignorance (I felt)
for $^{194}|$ *1840:* mystery, and yet forbore,   *1888:* mystery, yet—fool—forbore,
§ $^{197-222}|$ *1863:* WHILE RENUNCIATION ENSURES DESPAIR.
$^{195-221}|$ *1868* § $^{197}|$ *1840:* tho'   *1863:* though $^{199}|$ *1840:* mankind,   *1863:*
mankind,— $^{200}|$ *1840:* And my own matter—just   *1863:* My own concern was
just $^{203}|$ *1840:* Convention, hazard, blindness could impose   *1863:* What hazard, use
and blindness   *1888:* Which hazard, custom, blindness interpose $^{204}|$ *1840:* In their

Betwixt things and myself."

Whereat he rose.

205 The level wind carried above the firs
Clouds, the irrevocable travellers,
Onward.

"Pushed thus into a drowsy copse,
Arms twine about my neck, each eyelid drops
Under a humid finger; while there fleets,
210 Outside the screen, a pageant time repeats
Never again! To be deposed, immured
Clandestinely—still petted, still assured
To govern were fatiguing work—the Sight
Fleeting meanwhile! 'Tis noontide: wreak ere night
215 Somehow my will upon it, rather! Slake
This thirst somehow, the poorest impress take
That serves! A blasted bud displays you, torn,
Faint rudiments of the full flower unborn;
But who divines what glory coats o'erclasp
220 Of the bulb dormant in the mummy's grasp
Taurello sent?" . . .

"Taurello? Palma sent
Your Trouvere," (Naddo interposing leant
Over the lost bard's shoulder)—"and, believe,
You cannot more reluctantly receive
225 Than I pronounce her message: we depart
Together. What avail a poet's heart
Verona's pomps and gauds? five blades of grass
Suffice him. News? Why, where your marish was,

---

relation to myself. ¶ He rose.   *1863:* myself." ¶ He   *1888:* Betwixt things and myself." ¶
Whereat he   207| *1840:* ¶ Pushed   *1863:* ¶ "Pushed   209| *1840:* fleets   *1863:*
fleets,   210| *1840:* screen a   *1863:* screen, a   211| *1840:* deposed—immured
1868: deposed, immured   214| *1840:* noontide—wreak   *1863:* noontide: wreak
215| *1840:* Somehow one's will upon it rather   *1863:* Somehow my will upon it,
rather   219| *1840:* what petal coats   *1863:* what glory coats   220| *1840:*
Mummy's   *1863:* mummy's   221| *1840:* sent . . . ¶ Taurello   *1863:* sent" . . . ¶
"Taurello   *1868:* sent?" . . . ¶ "Taurello   222| *1840:* Your Trouvere (Naddo   *1863:*
Your Trouvere," (Naddo   § *223–250| *1863:* THERE IS YET A WAY OF ESCAPING
THIS;   221–248| *1868* §   223| *1840:* shoulder) and believe   *1863:*
shoulder)—"and, believe,   224| *1840:* reluctantly conceive   *1863:* reluctantly
receive   226| *1840:* Together: what   *1863:* Together. What   227| *1840:* Verona

On its mud-banks smoke rises after smoke
230 I' the valley, like a spout of hell new-broke.
Oh, the world's tidings! small your thanks, I guess,
For them. The father of our Patroness,
Has played Taurello an astounding trick,
Parts between Ecelin and Alberic
235 His wealth and goes into a convent: both
Wed Guelfs: the Count and Palma plighted troth
A week since at Verona: and they want
You doubtless to contrive the marriage-chant
Ere Richard storms Ferrara." Then was told
240 The tale from the beginning—how, made bold
By Salinguerra's absence, Guelfs had burned
And pillaged till he unawares returned
To take revenge: how Azzo and his friend
Were doing their endeavour, how the end
245 O' the siege was nigh, and how the Count, released
From further care, would with his marriage-feast
Inaugurate a new and better rule,
Absorbing thus Romano.
                              "Shall I school
My master," added Naddo, "and suggest
250 How you may clothe in a poetic vest
These doings, at Verona? Your response
To Palma! Wherefore jest? 'Depart at once?'
A good resolve! In truth, I hardly hoped
So prompt an acquiescence. Have you groped
255 Out wisdom in the wilds here?—thoughts may be
Over-poetical for poetry.
            Pearl-white, you poets liken Palma's neck;

---

and her gauds   *1863:* Verona's pomps and gauds   229| *1863:* smoke fast rises after
1888: smoke rises after   230| *1840:* valley like   *1863:* valley, like   231| *1840:*
tidings! little thanks   *1863:* tidings! small your thanks   232| *1840:* our Patroness
1863: our Patroness,   233| *1840:* Playing Taurello <> trick   *1863:* Has played
Taurello <> trick,   237| *1840:* and she wants   *1863:* and they want
238| *1840:* marriage-chants   *1863:* marriage-chant   239–251| *1840:* Ferrara ¶ At
Verona? Your   *1863:* § adds 239–251 §   239| *1840:* Ferrara. Your   *1863:* Ferrara."
Here was   *1888:* Ferrara." Then was   245| *1863:* Of   *1888:* O' § 251–277| *1863:*
WHICH HE NOW TAKES BY OBEYING PALMA: 249–275| *1868* §
252| *1840:* To Palma? Wherefore jest? 'Depart at once?   *1863:* To Palma! Wherefore jest?
'Depart at once?'   253| *1840:* truth I   *1863:* truth, I   255| *1840:* Thoughts
1888: thoughts   256| *1840:* poetry?   *1863:* poetry.   257| *1840:* Pearl-white you

And yet what spoils an orient like some speck
Of genuine white, turning its own white grey?
260 You take me? Curse the cicala!"
                                        One more day,
One eve—appears Verona! Many a group,
(You mind) instructed of the osprey's swoop
On lynx and ounce, was gathering—Christendom
Sure to receive, whate'er the end was, from
265 The evening's purpose cheer or detriment,
Since Friedrich only waited some event
Like this, of Ghibellins establishing
Themselves within Ferrara, ere, as King
Of Lombardy, he'd glad descend there, wage
270 Old warfare with the Pontiff, disengage
His barons from the burghers, and restore
The rule of Charlemagne, broken of yore
By Hildebrand.
                        I' the palace, each by each,
Sordello sat and Palma: little speech
275 At first in that dim closet, face with face
(Despite the tumult in the market-place)
Exchanging quick low laughters: now would rush
Word upon word to meet a sudden flush,
A look left off, a shifting lips' surmise—
280 But for the most part their two histories
Ran best thro' the locked fingers and linked arms.
And so the night flew on with its alarms
Till in burst one of Palma's retinue;
"Now, Lady!" gasped he. Then arose the two
285 And leaned into Verona's air, dead-still.

---

minstrels liken Palma's neck,   *1863:* Pearl-white, you poets liken Palma's neck;
259| *1840:* white turning *1863:* white, turning   260| *1840:* cicales! ¶ One more
day—   *1863:* cicale!" ¶ One more day.   *1868:* cicala <> day   *1888:* day,   263| *1840:*
l nx   *1863:* lynx   264| *1840:* whate'er it might be, from   *1863:* whate'er the end was,
from   265| *1840:* detriment   *1863:* detriment,   267| *1840:* this of   *1863:* this,
of   272| *1840:* of Charlemagne broken   *1863:* of Charlemagne, broken
273| *1840:* By Hildebrand. That eve-long each by each   *1863:* By Hildebrand. ¶ In the
palace, each by each,   *1888:* I'   274| *1840:* sate   *1863:* sat   276| *1840:* Despite
<> market place   *1863:* (Despite <> market-place)   277| *1840:* would gush   *1863:*
would rush   § 278-303| *1863:* WHO THEREUPON BECOMES HIS ASSOCIATE;
276-301| *1868* §   284| *1840:* Now Lady, gasped   *1863:* "Now, Lady!" gasped
285| *1840:* air dead still.   *1863:* air, dead-still.   287| *1840:* Out 'mid <> torchfire

A balcony lay black beneath until
Out, 'mid a gush of torchfire, grey-haired men
Came on it and harangued the people: then
Sea-like that people surging to and fro
290 Shouted, "Hale forth the carroch—trumpets, ho,
A flourish! Run it in the ancient grooves!
Back from the bell! Hammer—that whom behoves
May hear the League is up! Peal—learn who list,
Verona means not first of towns break tryst
295 To-morrow with the League!"
                                    Enough. Now turn—
Over the eastern cypresses: discern!
Is any beacon set a-glimmer?
                                    Rang
The air with shouts that overpowered the clang
Of the incessant carroch, even: "Haste—
300 The candle's at the gateway! ere it waste,
Each soldier stand beside it, armed to march
With Tiso Sampier through the eastern arch!"
Ferrara's succoured, Palma!
                                    Once again
They sat together; some strange thing in train
305 To say, so difficult was Palma's place
In taking, with a coy fastidious grace
Like the bird's flutter ere it fix and feed.
But when she felt she held her friend indeed
Safe, she threw back her curls, began implant
310 Her lessons; telling of another want
Goito's quiet nourished than his own;

---

grey-haired   *1863:* Out, 'mid <> torchfire, grey-haired   ²⁹⁰| *1840:* Shouted, Hale
<> Carroch   *1863:* Shouted, "Hale   *1868:* carroch   ²⁹¹| *1840:* run <>
grooves—   *1863:* Run <> grooves!   ²⁹²| *1840:* bell! Hammer! that   *1868:* bell!
Hammer—that   ²⁹³| *1840:* up! Peal! learn who list   *1863:* list,   *1868:* up!
Peal—learn   ²⁹⁴| *1840:* not be the first break   *1888:* not first of towns break
²⁹⁵| *1840:* the League! ¶ Enough   *1863:* the League!" ¶ Enough   ²⁹⁶| *1840:* Eastern
<> discern   *1863:* eastern <> discern—   *1868:* discern!   ²⁹⁷| *1840:* You any
1863: Is any   ²⁹⁹| *1840:* carroch even. Haste—   *1863:* carroch, even: "Haste—
³⁰⁰| *1840:* waste   *1863:* waste,   ³⁰¹| *1840:* stands beside, armed fit to   *1863:* stand
beside it, armed to   ³⁰²| *1840:* thro' that Eastern arch!   *1863:* through the eastern
arch!"   § ³⁰⁴⁻³³²| *1863:* AS HER OWN HISTORY WILL ACCOUNT FOR,
³⁰²⁻³²⁹| *1868* §   ³⁰⁴| *1840:* sate   *1863:* sat   ³⁰⁷| *1840:* feed;   *1863:*

Palma—to serve him—to be served, alone
Importing; Agnes' milk so neutralized
The blood of Ecelin. Nor be surprised
315 If, while Sordello fain had captive led
Nature, in dream was Palma subjected
To some out-soul, which dawned not though she pined
Delaying, till its advent, heart and mind
Their life. "How dared I let expand the force
320 Within me, till some out-soul, whose resource
It grew for, should direct it? Every law
Of life, its every fitness, every flaw,
Must One determine whose corporeal shape
Would be no other than the prime escape
325 And revelation to me of a Will
Orb-like o'ershrouded and inscrutable
Above, save at the point which, I should know,
Shone that myself, my powers, might overflow
So far, so much; as now it signified
330 Which earthly shape it henceforth chose my guide,
Whose mortal lip selected to declare
Its oracles, what fleshly garb would wear
—The first of intimations, whom to love;
The next, how love him. Seemed that orb, above
335 The castle-covert and the mountain-close,
Slow in appearing?—if beneath it rose
Cravings, aversions,—did our green precinct

---

feed.   312| 1840: serve, as him—be served   1863: serve him—to be served
315| 1840: while Sordello nature captive led,   1863: while Sordello fain had captive
led   316| 1840: In dream was Palma wholly subjected   1863: Nature, in dream was
Palma wholly subjected   1868: Palma subjected   317| 1840: out-soul which   1863:
out-soul, which   318| 1840: Delyaing still (pursued she) heart   1863: Delaying till its
advent, heart and mind,   1888: Delaying, till <> mind   319| 1840: To live: how
1863: Their life. "How   320| 1840: me till some out soul whose   1863: me, till some
out-soul, whose   321| 1840: for should   1863: for, should   322| 1840: its
fitnesses and every   1863: its every fitness, every   323| 1840: Must that determine
1863: Must One determine
327| 1840: Above except the point I was to know   1863: Above, save at the point which, I
should know,   330| 1840: chose to guide   1863: chose my guide,   331| 1840: Me
by, whose lip   1863: Whose mortal lip   332| 1840: wear: 1863: wear;   1868: wear
§ 333–359| 1863:—A REVERSE TO, AND COMPLETION OF, HIS.
330–357| 1868 §   334| 1840: him. And that orb above   1863: him. Seemed that orb,
above   335| 1840: mountain-close   1863: mountain-close,   336| 1840:
appearing, if beneath arose   1863: appearing?—if beneath it rose   337| 1840:

203

Take pride in me, at unawares distinct
With this or that endowment,—how, repressed
340 At once, such jetting power shrank to the rest!
Was I to have a chance touch spoil me, leave
My spirit thence unfitted to receive
The consummating spell?—that spell so near
Moreover! 'Waits he not the waking year?
345 His almond-blossoms must be honey-ripe
By this; to welcome him, fresh runnels stripe
The thawed ravines; because of him, the wind
Walks like a herald. I shall surely find
Him now!'
        "And chief, that earnest April morn
350 Of Richard's Love-court, was it time, so worn
And white my cheek, so idly my blood beat,
Sitting that morn beside the Lady's feet
And saying as she prompted; till outburst
One face from all the faces. Not then first
355 I knew it; where in maple chamber glooms,
Crowned with what sanguine-heart pomegranate blooms,
Advanced it ever? Men's acknowledgment
Sanctioned my own: 'twas taken, Palma's bent,—
Sordello,—recognized, accepted.
                      "Dumb
360 Sat she still scheming. Ecelin would come
Gaunt, scared, 'Cesano baffles me,' he'd say:
'Better I fought it out, my father's way!

---

aversions, and our   *1863:* aversions,—did our   ³³⁸| *1840:* Took <> me at   *1863:*
Take <> me, at   ³³⁹| *1840:* endowment, how represt,   *1863:* endowment,—how,
represt   *1868:* repressed   ³⁴⁰| *1840:* once such <> shrunk   *1863:* once, such   *1888:*
shrank   ³⁴⁴| *1840:* Moreover: waits   *1863:* Moreover! 'Waits   ³⁴⁶| *1840:* him
fresh   *1863:* him, fresh   ³⁴⁷| *1840:* him the   *1863:* him, the   ³⁴⁹| *1840:* now! ¶
And chief that   *1863:* now!' ¶ "And chief, that   ³⁵⁰| *1840:* Of Richard's Love-court
was   *1863:* Of Richard's Love-court, was   ³⁵¹| *1840:* white her cheek, so idly her
blood   *1863:* white my cheek, so idly my blood   ³⁵⁴| *1840:* faces—not   *1888:* faces.
Not   ³⁵⁵| *1840:* She knew <> maple-chamber   *1863:* I knew <> maple
chamber   ³⁵⁶| *1840:* blooms   *1888:* blooms,   ³⁵⁸| *1840:* Sanctioned her own
<> bent,   *1863:* Sanctioned my own <> bent,—   ³⁵⁹| *1840:* She said. ¶ And day by
day the Tuscan dumb   *1863:* Sordello, accepted. ¶ And the Tuscan dumb   *1888:*
Sordello,—recognized, accepted. ¶ "Dumb   § ³⁶⁰⁻³⁸⁸   *1863:* HOW SHE EVER ASPIRED
FOR HIS SAKE,   ³⁵⁸⁻³⁸⁵| *1868* §   ³⁶⁰| *1840:* Sat scheming, scheming; Ecelin
1863: Sat scheming, scheming. Ecelin   *1888:* Sat she still scheming   ³⁶¹| *1840:* scared,
Cesano baffles me, he'd   *1863:* scared, 'Cesano baffles me,' he'd   ³⁶²| *1840:* Better

Strangle Ferrara in its drowning flats,
And you and your Taurello yonder!—what's
365 Romano's business there?' An hour's concern
To cure the froward Chief!—induce return
As heartened from those overmeaning eyes,
Wound up to persevere,—his enterprise
Marked out anew, its exigent of wit
370 Apportioned,—she at liberty to sit
And scheme against the next emergence, I—
To covet her Taurello-sprite, made fly
Or fold the wing—to con your horoscope
For leave command those steely shafts shoot ope,
375 Or straight assuage their blinding eagerness
In blank smooth snow. What semblance of success
To any of my plans for making you
Mine and Romano's? Break the first wall through,
Tread o'er the ruins of the Chief, supplant
380 His sons beside, still, vainest were the vaunt:
There, Salinguerra would obstruct me sheer,
And the insuperable Tuscan, here,
Stay me! But one wild eve that Lady died
In her lone chamber: only I beside:
385 Taurello far at Naples, and my sire
At Padua, Ecelin away in ire
With Alberic. She held me thus—a clutch
To make our spirits as our bodies touch—
And so began flinging the past up, heaps

<> out my   *1863:* 'Better <> out, my   363| *1840:* flats   *1863:* flats,
364| *1840:* yonder—what's   *1888:* yonder!—what's   365| *1840:* there? An   *1863:*
there?' An   366| *1840:* froward Chief! induced   *1863:* froward Chief!—induced
1888: induce   367| *1840:* Much heartened   *1888:* As heartened   368| *1840:*
persevere, his   *1863:* persevere,—his   370| *1840:* Apportioned, she   *1863:*
Apportioned,—she   372| *1840:* covet what I deemed their sprite, made   *1863:* covet
her Taurello-sprite, made   374| *1840:* ope   *1863:* ope,   376| *1840:* To blank
smooth snow: what   *1863:* snow. What   *1888:* In blank smooth snow What
378| *1840:* Romano's lord? That Chief—her children too—   *1863:* Mine and Romano's?
Break the first wall through,   378–381| *1840:* too— ¶ There   *1863:* § adds
379–380 §   381| *1840:* There Salinguerra   *1863:* There, Salinguerra   382| *1840:*
insuperable Tuscan here   *1863:* insuperable Tuscan, here,   383| *1840:* Stayed   *1868:*
Stay   387| *1840:* With Alberic: she   *1863:* With Alberic. She   § 389–416| *1863:*
CIRCUMSTANCES HELPING OR HINDERING.   386–413| *1868* §

390 Of uncouth treasure from their sunless sleeps
    Within her soul; deeds rose along with dreams,
    Fragments of many miserable schemes,
    Secrets, more secrets, then—no, not the last—
    'Mongst others, like a casual trick o' the past,
395 How . . . ay, she told me, gathering up her face,
    All left of it, into one arch-grimace
    To die with . . .
                    "Friend, 'tis gone! but not the fear
    Of that fell laughing, heard as now I hear.
    Nor faltered voice, nor seemed her heart grow weak
400 When i' the midst abrupt she ceased to speak
    —Dead, as to serve a purpose, mark!—for in
    Rushed o' the very instant Ecelin
    (How summoned, who divines?)—looking as if
    He understood why Adelaide lay stiff
405 Already in my arms; for 'Girl, how must
    I manage Este in the matter thrust
    Upon me, how unravel your bad coil?—
    Since' (he declared) "tis on your brow—a soil
    Like hers there!' then in the same breath, 'he lacked
410 No counsel after all, had signed no pact
    With devils, nor was treason here or there,
    Goito or Vicenza, his affair:
    He buried it in Adelaide's deep grave,
    Would begin life afresh, now,—would not slave
415 For any Friedrich's nor Taurello's sake!
    What booted him to meddle or to make

389| *1863:* Past *1868:* past *1888:* up heaps   394| *1863:* Past, *1868:* past,
395| *1840:* gathering her face *1863:* gathering up her *1868:* face,
396| *1840:*—That face of hers into *1863:*—All left of it, into *1868:* All   399| *1840:*
seemed herself grow weak, *1863:* seemed her heart grow *1868:* weak   401| *1840:'*
mark, for *1863:* mark!—for   403| *1840:* summoned who divines?) looking *1863:*
summoned, who divines?)—looking   404| *1840:* Part understood he why his mate
lay *1863:* He understood why Adelaide lay   405| *1840:* arms for, Girl *1863:* arms;
for, 'Girl *1888:* for 'Girl   407| *1840:* unravel their bad coil? *1863:* unravel your bad
coil?—   408| *1840:* Since (he declared) 'tis *1863:* Since' (he declared)' 'tis
409| *1840:* there! then said in a breath he *1863:* there!' then in the same breath, 'he
413| *1840:* He'd bury it <> grave *1863:* He buried it <> grave,   414| *1840:* And
begin life afresh, nor, either, slave *1863:* Would begin life afresh, now,—would not
slave   415| *1840:* any Friedrich's or Taurello's *1863:* any Friedrich's nor Taurello's
§ 417–444| *1863:* HOW SUCCESS AT LAST SEEMED POSSIBLE,   414–441| *1868* §

In Lombardy?' And afterward I knew
The meaning of his promise to undo
All she had done—why marriages were made,
420 New friendships entered on, old followers paid
With curses for their pains,—new friends' amaze
At height, when, passing out by Gate Saint Blaise,
He stopped short in Vicenza, bent his head
Over a friar's neck,—'had vowed,' he said,
425 'Long since, nigh thirty years, because his wife
And child were saved there, to bestow his life
On God, his gettings on the Church.'

       "Exiled
Within Goito, still one dream beguiled
My days and nights; 'twas found, the orb I sought
430 To serve, those glimpses came of Fomalhaut,
No other: but how serve it?—authorize
You and Romano mingle destinies?
And straight Romano's angel stood beside
Me who had else been Boniface's bride,
435 For Salinguerra 'twas, with neck low bent,
And voice lightened to music, (as he meant
To learn, not teach me,) who withdrew the pall
From the dead past and straight revived it all,
Making me see how first Romano waxed,
440 Wherefore he waned now, why, if I relaxed
My grasp (even I!) would drop a thing effete,
Frayed by itself, unequal to complete

417| *1840:* In Lombardy? 'Twas afterward *1863:* In Lombardy?' And afterward
421| *1840:* In curses <> pains, people's amaze *1863:* With curses <> pains,—new
friends' amaze   422| *1840:* when passing <> Blaise *1863:* when, passing <>
Blaise,   424| *1840:* neck, had vowed, he *1863:* neck,—'had vowed,' he
425| *1840:* Long *1863:* 'Long   427| *1840:* the Church. ¶ "Exiled *1863:* the Church.'
¶ "Exiled   428| *1840:* still that dream *1863:* still one dream   429| *1840:* Her
days <> found the orb she sought *1863:* My days <> found, the orb I sought
430| *1840:* of Fomalhaut *1863:* of Fomalhaut,   431| *1840:* other: how then serve
1863: other: but how serve   432| *1840:* Him and *1863:* You and   434| *1840:*
Her who *1863:* Me who   435| *1840:* 'twas, the neck *1863:* 'twas, with neck
436| *1840:* The voice <> music as *1863:* And voice <> music, (as § 437–439| *1840:* me /
see *1863:* § adds 437–439   437| *1840:* me *1863:* me,)   438| *1863:* Past *1868:* past
439| *1840:* how Romano *1863:* how first Romano   440| *1840:* Wherefore it waned,
and why if *1863:* Wherefore he waned now, why, if   441| *1840:* grasp (think, I

207

Its course, and counting every step astray
A gain so much. Romano, every way
445 Stable, a Lombard House now—why start back
Into the very outset of its track?
This patching principle which late allied
Our House with other Houses—what beside
Concerned the apparition, the first Knight
450 Who followed Conrad hither in such plight
His utmost wealth was summed in his one steed?
For Ecelo, that prowler, was decreed
A task, in the beginning hazardous
To him as ever task can be to us;
455 But did the weather-beaten thief despair
When first our crystal cincture of warm air
That binds the Trevisan,—as its spice-belt
(Crusaders say) the tract where Jesus dwelt,—
Furtive he pierced, and Este was to face—
460 Despaired Saponian strength of Lombard grace?
Tried he at making surer aught made sure,
Maturing what already was mature?
No; his heart prompted Ecelo, 'Confront
Este, inspect yourself. What's nature? Wont.
465 Discard three-parts your nature, and adopt
The rest as an advantage!' Old strength propped
The man who first grew Podestà among
The Vicentines, no less than, while there sprung

1863: grasp (even I   443| *1840:* The course and   *1863:* Its course, and
444| *1840:* much. Romano every   *1863:* much. Romano, every   § 445–473| *1863:* BY THE
INTERVENTION OF SALINGUERRA: 442–470| *1868* §   445| *1840:* a House
now—why this starting back   *1863:* a Lombard House now—why start back
447| *1840:* This recent patching-principle allied   *1863:* This patching-principle which late
allied   *1868:* patching principle   449| *1840:* apparition, yon grim Knight   *1863:*
apparition, the first Knight   451| *1840:* was reckoned in his steed?   *1863:* was
summed in his one steed?   453| *1840:* task in   *1863:* task, in   454| *1840:* us,
1863: us;   456| *1840:* air,   *1863:* air,—   *1888:* air   457| *1840:* the Trivisan as
1863: the Trevisan,—as   458| *1840:* dwelt,   *1863:* dwelt,—   459| *1840:* pierced
and   *1863:* pierced, and   460| *1840:* Strength <> Grace?   *1863:* strength <>
grace?   461| *1840:* Said he for making   *1863:* Tried he at making   463| *1840:*
prompted Ecelo, Confront   *1863:* prompted Ecelo, 'Confront   465| *1840:* nature
and   *1863:* nature, and   466| *1840:* advantage! Old Strength   *1863:* advantage!' Old
strength   467| *1840:* The earliest of Podestàs   *1863:* The man who first grew

His palace up in Padua like a threat,
470 Their noblest spied a grace, unnoticed yet
In Conrad's crew. Thus far the object gained,
Romano was established—has remained—
'For are you not Italian, truly peers
With Este? *Azzo* better soothes our ears
475 Than *Alberic*? or is this lion's-crine
From over-mounts' (this yellow hair of mine)
'So weak a graft on Agnes Este's stock?'
(Thus went he on with something of a mock)
'Wherefore recoil, then, from the very fate
480 Conceded you, refuse to imitate
Your model farther? Este long since left
Being mere Este: as a blade its heft,
Este required the Pope to further him:
And you, the Kaiser—whom your father's whim
485 Foregoes or, better, never shall forego
If Palma dare pursue what Ecelo
Commenced, but Ecelin desists from: just
As Adelaide of Susa could intrust
Her donative,—her Piedmont given the Pope,
490 Her Alpine-pass for him to shut or ope
'Twixt France and Italy,—to the superb
Matilda's perfecting,—so, lest aught curb
Our Adelaide's great counter-project for
Giving her Trentine to the Emperor
495 With passage here from Germany,—shall you

Podestà 469| *1840:* Palace *1863:* palace 470| *1840:* Grace unnoticed *1863:*
grace, unnoticed 472| *1840:* established; has *1863:* established—has
473| *1840:* For < > peer *1863:* peers *1888:* 'For § 474–501| *1863:* WHO REMEDIED
ILL WROUGHT BY ECELIN, 471–498| *1868* § 474| *1840:* With Este? Azzo
better soothes it ear *1863:* With Estè? 'Azzo' better soothes our ears *1888:* Azzo
475| *1840:* Alberic *1863:* Than 'Alberic?' *1888: Alberic* 476| *1840:* over-mount
1863: over-mounts' 477| *1840:* So < > stock? *1863:* 'So < > stock?' 479| *1840:*
Wherefore recoil then from *1863:* 'Wherefore recoil, then, from 483| *1840:*
requires *1863:* required 484| *1840:* the Kaiser: whom *1863:* the
Kaiser—whom 486| *1840:* dares *1863:* dare 487| *1840:* Commenced but
1863: Commenced, but 489| *1840:* donative (that's Piedmont to the Pope, *1863:*
donative,—her Piedmont given the Pope, 490| *1840:* The Alpine-pass *1863:* Her
Alpine-pass 491| *1840:* and Italy) to *1863:* and Italy,—to 492| *1840:*
perfecting,—lest aught disturb *1863:* perfecting,—so, lest aught curb 495| *1840:*
And passage < > Germany, shall *1863:* With passage < > Germany,—shall

Take it,—my slender plodding talent, too!'
—Urged me Taurello with his half-smile

                                        "He
As Patron of the scattered family
Conveyed me to his Mantua, kept in bruit
500 Azzo's alliances and Richard's suit
Until, the Kaiser excommunicate,
'Nothing remains,' Taurello said, 'but wait
Some rash procedure: Palma was the link,
As Agnes' child, between us, and they shrink
505 From losing Palma: judge if we advance,
Your father's method, your inheritance!'
The day I was betrothed to Boniface
At Padua by Taurello's self, took place
The outrage of the Ferrarese: again,
510 The day I sought Verona with the train
Agreed for,—by Taurello's policy
Convicting Richard of the fault, since we
Were present to annul or to confirm,—
Richard, whose patience had outstayed its term,
515 Quitted Verona for the siege.
                              "And now
What glory may engird Sordello's brow
Through this? A month since at Oliero slunk
All that was Ecelin into a monk;
But how could Salinguerra so forget
520 His liege of thirty years as grudge even yet
One effort to recover him? He sent
Forthwith the tidings of this last event

496| *1840:* it, my <> too— *1863:* it,—my <> too!' **497|** *1840:* half-smile.
1863:—Urged *1888:* half-smile **499|** *1840:* Conveyed her to *1863:* Conveyed me to
§ **502–529|** *1863:* AND HAD A PROJECT FOR HER OWN GLORY,
499–526| *1868* § **502|** *1840:* Nothing remains, Taurello said, but *1863:* 'Nothing
remains,' Taurello said, 'but **505|** *1840:* advance *1863:* advance, **506|** *1840:*
method your inheritance! *1863:* method, your inheritance!' **507|** *1840:* That day
she was *1863:* day I was *1888:* The day **510|** *1840:* That day she sought *1863:* day
I sought *1888:* The day **511|** *1840:* for, by *1863:* for,—by **512|** *1840:* since
she *1863:* since we **513|** *1840:* Was <> confirm, *1863:* Were <>
confirm,— **517|** *1840:* For this <> since Oliero sunk *1863:* Through this <> since
at Oliero slunk **518|** *1840:* All Ecelin that was into a Monk; *1863:* All that was
Ecelin into a monk; **520|** *1840:* thirty summers as grudge yet *1863:* thirty years as
grudge even yet **522|** *1840:* of the Town's event *1863:* of this last event

To Ecelin—declared that he, despite
The recent folly, recognized his right
525 To order Salinguerra: 'Should he wring
Its uttermost advantage out, or fling
This chance away? Or were his sons now Head
O' the House?' Through me Taurello's missive sped;
My father's answer will by me return.
530 Behold! 'For him,' he writes, 'no more concern
With strife than, for his children, with fresh plots
Of Friedrich. Old engagements out he blots
For aye: Taurello shall no more subserve,
Nor Ecelin impose.' Lest this unnerve
535 Taurello at this juncture, slack his grip
Of Richard, suffer the occasion slip,—
I, in his sons' default (who, mating with
Este, forsake Romano as the frith
Its mainsea for that firmland, sea makes head
540 Against) I stand, Romano,—in their stead
Assume the station they desert, and give
Still, as the Kaiser's representative,
Taurello licence he demands. Midnight—
Morning—by noon to-morrow, making light
545 Of the League's issue, we, in some gay weed
Like yours, disguised together, may precede
The arbitrators to Ferrara: reach
Him, let Taurello's noble accents teach
The rest! Then say if I have misconceived
550 Your destiny, too readily believed

523| *1840:* To Oliero, adding, he   *1863:* To Ecelin—declared that he   525| *1840:*
order such proceedings: should   *1863:* order Salinguerra: 'Should   527| • *1840:* away?
If not him, who was Head   *1863:* away? Or were his sons now Head   528| *1840:* Now
of the House? Through me that missive   *1863:* Of the House?' Through me Taurello's
missive   *1888:* O'   § 530–557| *1863:* WHICH SHE WOULD CHANGE TO
SORDELLO'S.   527–554| *1868* §   530| *1840:* Behold! For him, he writes, no
1863: Behold! 'For him,' he writes, 'no   531| *1840:* than for his children with the
plots   *1863:* than, for his children, with fresh plots   533| *1840:* subserve   *1863:*
subserve,   534| *1840:* impose. Lest   *1863:* impose,' Lest   535| *1840:* Him
therefore at   *1863:* Taurello at   536| *1840:* slip,   *1863:* slip,—   539| *1840:* for
the firmland that makes   *1863:* firmland, sea makes   *1888:* for that firmland
540| *1840:* stand, Romano; in   *1863:* stand, Romano,—in   542| *1840:*
Representative,   *1863:* representative,   546| *1840:* yours disguised   *1863:* yours,
disguised   547| *1840:* to Ferrara; reach   *1863:* to Ferrara: reach   549| *1840:*

The Kaiser's cause your own!"

                      And Palma's fled.

Though no affirmative disturbs the head,
A dying lamp-flame sinks and rises o'er,
Like the alighted planet Pollux wore,
555 Until, morn breaking, he resolves to be
Gate-vein of this heart's blood of Lombardy,
Soul of this body—to wield this aggregate
Of souls and bodies, and so conquer fate
Though he should live—a centre of disgust
560 Even—apart, core of the outward crust
He vivifies, assimilates. For thus
I bring Sordello to the rapturous
Exclaim at the crowd's cry, because one round
Of life was quite accomplished; and he found
565 Not only that a soul, whate'er its might,
Is insufficient to its own delight,
Both in corporeal organs and in skill
By means of such to body forth its Will—
And, after, insufficient to apprise
570 Men of that Will, oblige them recognize
The Hid by the Revealed—but that,—the last
Nor lightest of the struggles overpast,—
Will, he bade abdicate, which would not void
The throne, might sit there, suffer he enjoyed
575 Mankind, a varied and divine array
Incapable of homage, the first way,
Nor fit to render incidentally

---

then   *1868:* Then   ⁵⁵¹| *1840:* own! ¶ And   *1863:* own!" ¶ And   ⁵⁵²| *1840:*
head   *1863:* head,   ⁵⁵³| *1840:* o'er   *1863:* o'er,   ⁵⁵⁷| *1840:* Soul to their
body—have their aggregate   *1863:* Soul of this body—to wield this aggregate
§ ⁵⁵⁸⁻⁵⁸⁶| *1863:* THUS THEN, HAVING COMPLETED A CIRCLE,
⁵⁵⁵⁻⁵⁸³| *1868* §   ⁵⁵⁹| *1840:* live, a   *1863:* live—a   ⁵⁶⁰| *1840:* Even, apart
1863: Even—apart   ⁵⁶¹| *1863:* vivified, assimilated. Thus   *1868:* vivifies, assimilates.
For thus   ⁵⁶²| *1840:* Bring I Sordello   *1863:* I bring Sordello   ⁵⁶⁴| *1840:*
accomplished and   *1863:* accomplished; and   ⁵⁶⁵| *1840:* soul, howe'er its   *1863:*
soul, whate'er its   ⁵⁶⁷| *1840:* delight   *1863:* delight,   ⁵⁷¹| *1840:* that, the
1888: that,—the   ⁵⁷²| *1840:* overpast,   *1888:* overpast,—   ⁵⁷³| *1840:* His Will,
bade   *1888:* Will, he bade   ⁵⁷⁴| *1840:* suffer be enjoyed   *1888:* suffer he
enjoyed   ⁵⁷⁵| *1840:* The same a   *1863:* Mankind, a   ⁵⁷⁶| *1840:* homage the first
way   *1863:* homage, the first way,

Tribute connived at, taken by the by,
In joys. If thus with warrant to rescind
580 The ignominious exile of mankind—
Whose proper service, ascertained intact
As yet, (to be by him themselves made act,
Not watch Sordello acting each of them)
Was to secure—if the true diadem
585 Seemed imminent while our Sordello drank
The wisdom of that golden Palma,—thank
Verona's Lady in her citadel
Founded by Gaulish Brennus, legends tell:
And truly when she left him, the sun reared
590 A head like the first clamberer's who peered
A-top the Capitol, his face on flame
With triumph, triumphing till Manlius came.
Nor slight too much my rhymes—that spring, dispread,
Dispart, disperse, lingering over head
595 Like an escape of angels! Rather say,
My transcendental platan! mounting gay
(An archimage so courts a novice-queen)
With tremulous silvered trunk, whence branches sheen
Laugh out, thick-foliaged next, a-shiver soon
600 With coloured buds, then glowing like the moon
One mild flame,—last a pause, a burst, and all
Her ivory limbs are smothered by a fall,
Bloom-flinders and fruit-sparkles and leaf-dust,
Ending the weird work prosecuted just
605 For her amusement; he decrepit, stark,
Dozes; her uncontrolled delight may mark

579| *1840:* joys: and if, thus warranted rescind   *1863:* joys. If thus with warrant to
rescind   580| *1840:* mankind   *1863:* mankind—   582| *1840:* yet (by Him to be
themselves   *1863:* yet, (to be by him themselves   586| *1840:* golden Palma, thank
1863: golden Palma,—thank   § 587–615| *1863:* THE POET MAY PAUSE AND
BREATHE,   584–611| *1868* §   587| *1840:* Citadel   *1868:* citadel
588| *1840:* by Gaulish Brennus legends tell—   *1863:* by Gaulish Brennus, legends
tell: 589| *1840:* him the   *1863:* him, the   590| *1840:* clamberer's that peered
1888: clamberer's who peered   593| *1840:* rhymes—"that   *1863:* rhymes—that
594| *1840:* overhead   *1868:* over head   595| *1840:* angels?" Rather say   *1863:* angels?
Rather say,   *1888:* angels! Rather   599| *1840:* thick foliaged   *1863:*
thick-foliaged   601| *1840:* flame, last   *1863:* flame,—last   607| *1840:* never

Apart—
          Yet not so, surely never so
Only, as good my soul were suffered go
O'er the lagune: forth fare thee, put aside—
610 Entrance thy synod, as a god may glide
Out of the world he fills, and leave it mute
For myriad ages as we men compute,
Returning into it without a break
O' the consciousness! They sleep, and I awake
615 O'er the lagune, being at Venice.
                      Note,
In just such songs as Eglamor (say) wrote
With heart and soul and strength, for he believed
Himself achieving all to be achieved
By singer—in such songs you find alone
620 Completeness, judge the song and singer one,
And either purpose answered, his in it
Or its in him: while from true works (to wit
Sordello's dream-performances that will
Never be more than dreamed) escapes there still
625 Some proof, the singer's proper life was 'neath
The life his song exhibits, this a sheath
To that; a passion and a knowledge far
Transcending these, majestic as they are,
Smouldered; his lay was but an episode
630 In the bard's life: which evidence you owed
To some slight weariness, some looking-off
Or start-away. The childish skit or scoff
In "Charlemagne," (his poem, dreamed divine

so! _1888:_ never so   [608] _1840:_ Only as _1863:_ Only, as   [609] _1840:_ aside
_1868:_ aside—   [610] _1840:_ God _1863:_ god   [611] _1840:_ fills and _1863:_ fills,
and   [612] _1840:_ A myriad _1863:_ For myriad   [614] _1840:_ I' the _1863:_ O' the
§ [615–643] _1863:_ BEING REALLY IN THE FLESH AT VENICE,
[612–639] _1868_ §   [615] _1840:_ lagune. ¶ Sordello said once, note _1863:_ once, "Note,
_1888:_ lagune, being at Venice. ¶ Note,   [616] _1840:_ as Eglamor, say, wrote _1863:_ as
Eglamor (say) wrote   [620] _1840:_ One _1863:_ one,   [621] _1840:_ either's _1868:_
either   [624] _1840:_ Be never more than dream _1863:_ dreamed _1888:_ Never be
more   [625] _1840:_ proof the <> life's beneath _1863:_ proof, the <> life was
'neath   [629] _1840:_ Smoulder _1863:_ Smouldered   [630] _1840:_ life. Which
_1863:_ life: which   [631] _1840:_ weariness, a looking-off _1863:_ weariness, some
looking-off   [632] _1840:_ start-away, the _1863:_ start-away. The   [633] _1840:_ In

In every point except one silly line
635 About the restiff daughters)—what may lurk
In that? "My life commenced before this work,"
(So I interpret the significance
Of the bard's start aside and look askance)
"My life continues after: on I fare
640 With no more stopping, possibly, no care
To note the undercurrent, the why and how,
Where, when, o' the deeper life, as thus just now.
But, silent, shall I cease to live? Alas
For you! who sigh, 'When shall it come to pass
645 We read that story? How will he compress
The future gains, his life's true business,
Into the better lay which—that one flout,
Howe'er inopportune it be, lets out—
Engrosses him already, though professed
650 To meditate with us eternal rest,
And partnership in all his life has found?' "
'Tis but a sailor's promise, weather-bound:
"Strike sail, slip cable, here the bark be moored
For once, the awning stretched, the poles assured!
655 Noontide above; except the wave's crisp dash,
Or buzz of colibri, or tortoise' splash,

"Charlemagne," for instance, dreamed   *1863:* In "Charlemagne," (his poem,
dreamed   **634|**   *1840:* one restive line   *1863:* one silly line   **635|**   *1840:* (Those
daughters!)—what significance may   *1863:* About the restiff daughters!)—what may
1868: daughters)—what   **636|**   *1840:* that? My <> before that work,   *1863:* that? 'My
<> work,'   *1868:* that? "My <> before this work,"   § **636–639|**   *1840:* work, / Continues
1863: § adds **637–638** §   **637|**   *1863:* (Thus I   *1868:* (So I   **639|**   *1840:* Continues
after it, as on   *1863:* 'My life continues after: on   *1868:* "My   **640|**   *1840:* stopping
possibly   *1863:* stopping, possibly   **641|**   *1840:* To jot down (says the bard) the <>
how   *1863:* To note the undercurrent, the <> how,   **642|**   *1840:* And where and
when of life as I do now: *1863:* Where, when, of the deeper life, as thus just now.   *1868:*
o'   **643|**   *1840:* But shall I cease to live for that? Alas   *1863:* But, silent, shall I cease to
live? Alas   § **644–672|**   *1863:* AND WATCHING HIS OWN LIFE SOMETIMES,
640–668| *1868* §   **644|**   *1840:* sigh, when   *1863:* sigh, 'When   **645|**   *1840:* story,
when will   *1863:* story? How will   **646|**   *1840:* future years, his whole life's business,
1863: future gains, his life's true business,   **647|**   *1840:* Into another lay which that
1863: Into the better lay which—that   **648|**   *1840:* out   *1863:* out—   **649|**   *1840:*
already while professed   *1863:* already, though professed   **650|**   *1840:* rest?   *1863:*
rest,   **650–653|**   *1840:* rest? / Strike   *1863:* § adds **651–652** §   **651|**   *1863:*
found?   *1868:* found?' "   **653|**   *1840:* Strike <> cable! here the galley's moored
1863: 'Strike <> cable, here the bark be moored   *1868:* "Strike   **654|**   *1840:* awning's

The margin's silent: out with every spoil
Made in our tracking, coil by mighty coil,
This serpent of a river to his head
660 I' the midst! Admire each treasure, as we spread
The bank, to help us tell our history
Aright: give ear, endeavour to descry
The groves of giant rushes, how they grew
Like demons' endlong tresses we sailed through,
665 What mountains yawned, forests to give us vent
Opened, each doleful side, yet on we went
Till . . . may that beetle (shake your cap) attest
The springing of a land-wind from the West!"
—Wherefore? Ah yes, you frolic it to-day!
670 To-morrow, and, the pageant moved away
Down to the poorest tent-pole, we and you
Part company: no other may pursue
Eastward your voyage, be informed what fate
Intends, if triumph or decline await
675 The tempter of the everlasting steppe.
I muse this on a ruined palace-step
At Venice: why should I break off, nor sit
Longer upon my step, exhaust the fit
England gave birth to! Who's adorable
680 Enough reclaim a —— no Sordello's Will
Alack!—be queen to me? That Bassanese
Busied among her smoking fruit-boats? These
Perhaps from our delicious Asolo
Who twinkle, pigeons o'er the portico
685 Not prettier, bind June lilies into sheaves
To deck the bridge-side chapel, dropping leaves

<> assured;   *1863:* awning <> assured!   657| *1840:* silent; out   *1863:* silent:
out   660| *1840:* treasure as   *1863:* treasure, as   661| *1840:* The turf to   *1863:*
The bank, to   662| *1840:* ear then gentles, and descry   *1863:* ear, endeavour to
descry   663| *1840:* rushes how   *1863:* rushes, how   665| *1840:* How
mountains   *1863:* What mountains   668| *1840:* the West!   *1863:* the West!'   *1868:*
the West!"   669| *1840:* Wherefore? Ah yes, we frolic it to-day: *1863:*—'Wherefore?
Ah yes, you frolic it to-day!   *1868:*—Wherefore   670| *1840:* and the pageant's   *1888:*
and, the pageant   671| *1840:* tent-pole: we   *1868:* tent-pole, we   § 673–700| *1863:*
BECAUSE IT IS PLEASANT TO BE YOUNG,   669–696| *1868* §   675| *1863:*
steppe.'   *1868:* steppe.   676| *1840:* ¶ I sung this on an empty palace-step   *1863:* ¶ I
muse this on a ruined palace-step   685| *1840:* bind late lilies   *1863:* bind June

Soiled by their own loose gold-meal? Ah, beneath
The cool arch stoops she, brownest cheek! Her wreath
Endures a month—a half-month—if I make
690 A queen of her, continue for her sake
Sordello's story? Nay, that Paduan girl
Splashes with barer legs where a live whirl
In the dead black Giudecca proves sea-weed
Drifting has sucked down three, four, all indeed
695 Save one pale-red striped, pale-blue turbaned post
For gondolas.
            You sad dishevelled ghost
That pluck at me and point, are you advised
I breathe? Let stay those girls (e'en her disguised
—Jewels i' the locks that love no crownet like
700 Their native field-buds and the green wheat-spike,
So fair!—who left this end of June's turmoil,
Shook off, as might a lily its gold soil,
Pomp, save a foolish gem or two, and free
In dream, came join the peasants o'er the sea.)
705 Look they too happy, too tricked out? Confess
There is such niggard stock of happiness
To share, that, do one's uttermost, dear wretch,
One labours ineffectually to stretch
It o'er you so that mother and children, both
710 May equitably flaunt the sumpter-cloth!
Divide the robe yet farther: be content
With seeing just a score pre-eminent
Through shreds of it, acknowledged happy wights,
Engrossing what should furnish all, by rights!
715 For, these in evidence, you clearlier claim
A like garb for the rest,—grace all, the same

lilies   688| *1840:* brownest-cheek   *1888:* brownest cheek   689| *1840:* half
month   *1888:* half-month   699| *1840:* in   *1888:* i' § 701-729| *1863:* WOULD BUT
SUFFERING HUMANITY ALLOW!   697-725| *1868* §   700| *1840:* wheat
spike,   *1888:* wheat-spike,   701| *1840:* Who   *1863:* who   704| *1840:* Came join
the peasants o'er the kissing sea.)   *1863:* In dream, came < > the sea.)   706| *1840:* You
have so niggard   *1863:* There is such niggard   707| *1840:* share that   *1863:* share,
that   708| *1840:* ineffectually stretch   *1863:* ineffectually to stretch   709| *1840:*
mother, children   *1863:* mother and children   711| *1840:* No: tear the   *1863:* Divide
the   712| *1840:* seeing some few score   *1863:* seeing just a score   714| *1840:*
rights—   *1868:* rights!   714-721| *1840:* rights—/ (At   *1863:* § adds

As these my peasants. I ask youth and strength
And health for each of you, not more—at length
Grown wise, who asked at home that the whole race
720 Might add the spirit's to the body's grace,
And all be dizened out as chiefs and bards.
But in this magic weather one discards
Much old requirement. Venice seems a type
Of Life—'twixt blue and blue extends, a stripe,
725 As Life, the somewhat, hangs 'twixt nought and nought:
'Tis Venice, and 'tis Life—as good you sought
To spare me the Piazza's slippery stone
Or keep me to the unchoked canals alone,
As hinder Life the evil with the good
730 Which make up Living, rightly understood.
Only, do finish something! Peasants, queens,
Take them, made happy by whatever means,
Parade them for the common credit, vouch
That a luckless residue, we send to crouch
735 In corners out of sight, was just as framed
For happiness, its portion might have claimed
As well, and so, obtaining joy, had stalked
Fastuous as any!—such my project, baulked
Already; I hardly venture to adjust
740 The first rags, when you find me. To mistrust

715–720 §   721| 1840: (At home we dizen scholars, chiefs and kings,   1863: And all be
dizened out as chiefs and bards.   722| 1840: weather hardly clings   1863: weather one
discards   723| 1840: The old garb gracefully: Venice, a type   1863: Much old
requirement—Venice seems a type   1868: requirement. Venice   724| 1840: Of Life,
'twixt   1863: Of Life,— 'twixt   1888: Of Life—'twixt   725| 1863: and nought
1868: and nought: 727| 1840: stone,   1868: stone   728| 1840: Or stay me third
her cross canals   1863: Or keep me to the unchoked canals   729| 1840: hinder Life
what seems the single good   1863: hinder Life the evil with the good
§ 730–758| 1863:—WHICH INSTIGATES TO TASKS LIKE THIS,
726–754| 1868 §   730| 1840: Sole purpose, one thing to be understood   1863: Which
make up Living, rightly understood.   731| 1840: Of Life)—best, be they Peasants, be
they Queens,   1863: Only, do finish something! Peasants or queens,   1868: something!
Peasants, queens,   732| 1840: them, I say, made happy any means,   1863: them, made
happy by whatever means,   734| 1840: A luckless residue we   1863: That a luckless
residue, we   735| 1840: sight was   1863: sight, was   737| 1840: And so, could we
concede that portion, stalked   1863: As well, and so, obtaining it, had stalked   1868:
obtaining joy, had   738| 1840: any—such   1863: any!—such   739| 1840:
Already; hardly venture I adjust   1863: Already; I hardly venture to adjust
740| 1840: A lappet when I find you! To   1863: The first rags, when you find me. To

Me!—nor unreasonably. You, no doubt,
Have the true knack of tiring suitors out
With those thin lips on tremble, lashless eyes
Inveterately tear-shot: there, be wise,
745 Mistress of mine, there, there, as if I meant
You insult!—shall your friend (not slave) be shent
For speaking home? Beside, care-bit erased
Broken-up beauties ever took my taste
Supremely; and I love you more, far more
750 Than her I looked should foot Life's temple-floor.
Years ago, leagues at distance, when and where
A whisper came, "Let others seek!—thy care
Is found, thy life's provision; if thy race
Should be thy mistress, and into one face
755 The many faces crowd?" Ah, had I, judge,
Or no, your secret? Rough apparel—grudge
All ornaments save tag or tassel worn
To hint we are not thoroughly forlorn—
Slouch bonnet, unloop mantle, careless go
760 Alone (that's saddest, but it must be so)
Through Venice, sing now and now glance aside,
Aught desultory or undignified,—
Then, ravishingest lady, will you pass
Or not each formidable group, the mass
765 Before the Basilic (that feast gone by,
God's great day of the Corpus Domini)
And, wistfully foregoing proper men,
Come timid up to me for alms? And then
The luxury to hesitate, feign do

741| *1840:* Me! nor   *1863:* Me!—nor   744| *1840:* tear-shot—there, be wise   *1868:*
wise,   *1888:* tear-shot: there   746| *1840:* insult! Shall   *1868:* insult!—shall
747| *1840:* home? Beside care-bit   *1863:* home? Beside, care-bit, erased,   *1868:* care-bit
erased   749| *1840:* Supremely, and   *1868:* Supremely; and   750| *1840:* That she
I <> temple-floor—   *1863:* Than her I <> temple-floor.   752| *1840:* came, Seek
others, since thy   *1863:* came, "Let others seek!—thy   753| *1840:* found, a life's <> if
a race   *1863:* found, thy life's <> if thy race   755| *1840:* crowd? Ah   *1863:* crowd?"
Ah   § 759–787| *1863:* AND DOUBTLESSLY COMPENSATES THEM,
755–783| *1868* §   760| *1840:* saddest but   *1863:* saddest,   762| *1840:*
undignified,   *1863:* undignified,—   763| *1840:* And, ravishingest   *1863:* Then,
ravishingest   765| *1840:* Basilike   *1863:* Basilic   766| *1840:* God's day, the great
June Corpus   *1863:* God's great day of the Corpus   767| *1840:* And wistfully <>

770 Some unexampled grace!—when, whom but you
Dare I bestow your own upon? And hear
Further before you say, it is to sneer
I call you ravishing; for I regret
Little that she, whose early foot was set
775 Forth as she'd plant it on a pedestal,
Now, i' the silent city, seems to fall
Toward me—no wreath, only a lip's unrest
To quiet, surcharged eyelids to be pressed
Dry of their tears upon my bosom. Strange
780 Such sad chance should produce in thee such change,
My love! Warped souls and bodies! yet God spoke
Of right-hand, foot and eye—selects our yoke,
Sordello, as your poetship may find!
So, sleep upon my shoulder, child, nor mind
785 Their foolish talk; we'll manage reinstate
Your old worth; ask moreover, when they prate
Of evil men past hope, "Don't each contrive,
Despite the evil you abuse, to live?—
Keeping, each losel, through a maze of lies,
790 His own conceit of truth? to which he hies
By obscure windings, tortuous, if you will,
But to himself not inaccessible;
He sees truth, and his lies are for the crowd
Who cannot see; some fancied right allowed
795 His vilest wrong, empowered the losel clutch
One pleasure from a multitude of such

men   *1863:* And, wistfully <> men,   770| *1840:* grace, when whom   *1863:*
grace!—when, whom   772| *1840:* Me out before you say it   *1863:* Further before you
say, it   773| *1840:* ravishing, for   *1863:* ravishing; for   776| *1840:* Now i'
1863: Now, i'   777| *1840:* Towards   *1863:* Toward   779| *1840:* bosom:
strange   *1863:* bosom. Strange   781| *1840:* warped men, souls, bodies   *1863:* warped
souls and bodies   *1868:* Warped   782| *1840:* right-hand foot <> yoke   *1863:*
right-hand, foot <> yoke,   783| *1840:* Sordello! as <> find: *1863:* Sordello, as <>
find!   784| *1840:* So sleep   *1863:* So, sleep   786| *1840:* The matter; ask   *1863:*
Your old worth; ask   787| *1840:* hope, don't each contrive   *1863:* hope, "don't each
contrive,   *1868:* hope, "Don't   § 788–816| *1863:* AS THOSE WHO DESIST SHOULD
REMEMBER.   784–812| *1868* §   788| *1840:* abuse to live?   *1863:* abuse, to
live?—   789| *1840:* thro'   *1863:* through   791| *1840:* obscure tortuous
windings, if   *1863:* obscure windings, tortuous, if   793| *1840:* sees it, and   *1863:* sees
truth, and   795| *1840:* the fellow cluth   *1888:* the losel clutch   796| *1840:* from

Denied him." Then assert, "All men appear
To think all better than themselves, by here
Trusting a crowd they wrong; but really," say,
800 "All men think all men stupider than they,
Since, save themselves, no other comprehends
The complicated scheme to make amends
—Evil, the scheme by which, thro' Ignorance,
Good labours to exist." A slight advance,—
805 Merely to find the sickness you die through,
And nought beside! but if one can't eschew
One's portion in the common lot, at least
One can avoid an ignorance increased
Tenfold by dealing out hint after hint
810 How nought were like dispensing without stint
The water of life—so easy to dispense
Beside, when one has probed the centre whence
Commotion's born—could tell you of it all!
"—Meantime, just meditate my madrigal
815 O' the mugwort that conceals a dewdrop safe!"
What, dullard? we and you in smothery chafe,
Babes, baldheads, stumbled thus far into Zin
The Horrid, getting neither out nor in,
A hungry sun above us, sands that bung
820 Our throats,—each dromedary lolls a tongue,
Each camel churns a sick and frothy chap,
And you, 'twixt tales of Potiphar's mishap,
And sonnets on the earliest ass that spoke,
—Remark, you wonder any one needs choke
825 With founts about! Potsherd him, Gibeonites!

---

the multitude   *1863:* from a multitude   ⁷⁹⁷| *1840:* him: then assert, all   *1863:* him."
Then assert, "all   *1868:* All   ⁷⁹⁹| *1840:* really, say,   *1863:* really," say,
⁸⁰⁰| *1840:* All <> they   *1863:* "All <> they,   ⁸⁰¹| *1840:* Since save themselves
no   *1863:* Since, save themselves, no   ⁸⁰³| *1840:* thro' Ignorance   *1863:* thro'
Ignorance,   ⁸⁰⁴| *1840:* exist. A slight advance   *1863:* exist." A slight
advance,—   ⁸⁰⁵| *1840:* through   *1863:* through,   ⁸⁰⁶| *1840:* beside: but
1863: beside! but   ⁸¹⁰| *1840:* is   *1863:* were   ⁸¹³| *1840:* all   *1863:* all!
⁸¹⁴| *1840:*—Meantime   *1863:*"—Meantime   ⁸¹⁵| *1840:* safe!   *1863:* safe!"
⁸¹⁶| *1840:* chafe   *1863:* chafe,   § ^{817–845}| *1863:* LET THE POET TAKE HIS OWN
PART, THEN,   ^{813–841}| *1868* §   ⁸¹⁹| *1840:* sands among   *1863:* sands that
bung   ⁸²⁰| *1840:* throats, each   *1863:* throats,—each   ⁸²²| *1840:* mishap
1863: mishap,   ⁸²⁴| *1840:* Remark you   *1863:*—Remark, you   ⁸²⁵| *1840:* him,

While awkwardly enough your Moses smites
The rock, though he forego his Promised Land
Thereby, have Satan claim his carcass, and
Figure as Metaphysic Poet . . . ah,
830 Mark ye the dim first oozings? Meribah!
Then, quaffing at the fount my courage gained,
Recall—not that I prompt ye—who explained . . .
    "Presumptuous!" interrupts one. You, not I
'Tis brother, marvel at and magnify
835 Such office: "office," quotha? can we get
To the beginning of the office yet?
What do we here? simply experiment
Each on the other's power and its intent
When elsewhere tasked,—if this of mine were trucked
840 For yours to either's good,—we watch construct,
In short, an engine: with a finished one,
What it can do, is all,—nought, how 'tis done.
But this of ours yet in probation, dusk
A kernel of strange wheelwork through its husk
845 Grows into shape by quarters and by halves;
Remark this tooth's spring, wonder what that valve's
Fall bodes, presume each faculty's device,
Make out each other more or less precise—
The scope of the whole engine's to be proved;
850 We die: which means to say, the whole's removed,
Dismounted wheel by wheel, this complex gin,—
To be set up anew elsewhere, begin

Gibeonites, *1863:* him, Gibeonites!   ⁸²⁷| *1840:* rock though *1863:* rock, though
<> Land, *1868:* Land   ⁸²⁹| *1840:* Dance, forsooth, Metaphysic Poet . . . Ah, *1863:*
Figure as Metaphysic *1868:* ah,   ⁸³¹| *1840:* And quaffing <> gained *1863:* Then,
quaffing <> gained,   ⁸³³| *1840:* Presumptuous! interrupts one. You not *1863:*
"Presumptuous!" interrupts one. You, not *1888:* ¶ "Presumptuous   ⁸³⁴| *1840:* 'Tis,
Brother *1863:* brother *1888:* 'Tis brother   ⁸³⁵| *1840:* Mine office: office, quotha
1863: Such office: "office," quotha   ⁸³⁹| *1840:* tasked, if *1863:* tasked,—if
⁸⁴⁰| *1840:* For thine to either's profit,—watch *1863:* For yours to either's good,—we
watch   ⁸⁴¹| *1840:* one *1863:* one,   ⁸⁴²| *1840:* do is all, nought how 'tis done;
1863: do, is all,—nought, how 'tis done.   ⁸⁴⁴| *1840:* thro' *1863:* through
§ ^{846–874}| *1863:* SHOULD ANY OBJECT THAT HE WAS DULL
^{842–870}| *1868* §   ⁸⁴⁹| *1840:* proved— *1863:* proved;   ⁸⁵⁰| *1840:* say the
1863: say, the   ⁸⁵¹| *1840:* by wheel that complex gin, *1863:* by wheel, this complex

A task indeed, but with a clearer clime
Than the murk lodgment of our building-time.
855 And then, I grant you, it behoves forget
How 'tis done—all that must amuse us yet
So long: and, while you turn upon your heel,
Pray that I be not busy slitting steel
Or shredding brass, camped on some virgin shore
860 Under a cluster of fresh stars, before
I name a tithe o' the wheels I trust to do!
   So occupied, then, are we: hitherto,
At present, and a weary while to come,
The office of ourselves,—nor blind nor dumb,
865 And seeing somewhat of man's state,—has been,
For the worst of us, to say they so have seen;
For the better, what it was they saw; the best
Impart the gift of seeing to the rest:
"So that I glance," says such an one, "around,
870 And there's no face but I can read profound
Disclosures in; this stands for hope, that—fear,
And for a speech, a deed in proof, look here!
'Stoop, else the strings of blossom, where the nuts
O'erarch, will blind thee! Said I not? She shuts
875 Both eyes this time, so close the hazels meet!
Thus, prisoned in the Piombi, I repeat
Events one rove occasioned, o'er and o'er,
Putting 'twixt me and madness evermore
Thy sweet shape, Zanze! Therefore stoop!'
                        " 'That's truth!'
880 (Adjudge you) 'the incarcerated youth

gin,—   853| *1840:* indeed but   *1863:* indeed, but   854| *1840:* building-time:
1863: building-time.   857| *1840:* and while thou turnest on thy heel   *1863:* and, while
you turn upon your heel,   859| *1840:* brass upon a virgin   *1863:* brass, camped on
some virgin   861| *1840:* tithe the   *1863:* tithe o' the   862| *1840:* So   *1888:* ¶
So   864| *1840:* ourselves nor blind nor dumb   *1863:* ourselves,—nor blind nor
dumb,   865| *1840:* state, has   *1863:* state,—has   866| *1840:* The worst   *1863:*
For the worst   867| *1840:* The <> best,   *1863:* For the <> best   869| *1840:* So
<> glance, says <> one, around,   *1863:* "So <> glance," says <> one, "around,
873| *1840:* Stoop <> blossom   *1863:* 'Stoop   874| *1840:* said <>
she   *1868:* Said <> She   § 875–901| *1863:* BESIDE HIS SPRIGHTLIER
PREDECESSORS.   871–896| *1868* §   879| *1840:* shape, Elys! therefore stoop— ¶
That's truth!   *1863:* shape, Zanze! Therefore stoop!' ¶ 'That's truth!'   *1868:* stoop!' ¶
" 'That's   880| *1840:* (Applaud you) the   *1863:* (Adjudge you) 'the   881| *1840:*

Would say that!'
              "Youth? Plara the bard? Set down
That Plara spent his youth in a grim town
Whose cramped ill-featured streets huddled about
The minster for protection, never out
885 Of its black belfry's shade and its bells' roar.
The brighter shone the suburb,—all the more
Ugly and absolute that shade's reproof
Of any chance escape of joy,—some roof,
Taller than they, allowed the rest detect,—
890 Before the sole permitted laugh (suspect
Who could, 'twas meant for laughter, that ploughed cheek's
Repulsive gleam!) when the sun stopped both peaks
Of the cleft belfry like a fiery wedge,
Then sank, a huge flame on its socket edge,
895 With leavings on the grey glass oriel-pane
Ghastly some minutes more. No fear of rain—
The minster minded that! in heaps the dust
Lay everywhere. This town, the minster's trust,
Held Plara; who, its denizen, bade hail
900 In twice twelve sonnets, Tempe's dewy vale."
    " 'Exact the town, the minster and the street!' "
"As all mirth triumphs, sadness means defeat:
Lust triumphs and is gay, Love's triumphed o'er
And sad: but Lucio's sad. I said before,
905 Love's sad, not Lucio; one who loves may be
As gay his love has leave to hope, as he

---

that! ¶ Youth <> set   *1863:* that!' ¶ 'Youth <> Set   *1868:* that!' ¶ "Youth
885| *1840:* belfry's shadow or bells' roar: *1863:* belfry's shade and its bells' roar
886| *1840:* Brighter the sun illumed the suburbs, more
1863: The brighter shone the suburb,—all the more   **888|** *1840:* For any <>
joy some roof   *1863:* Of any <> joy,—some roof,   **889|** *1840:* they allowed <>
detect   *1863:* they, allowed   *1868:* detect,—   **894|** *1840:* sunk <> socket's   *1868:*
socket   *1888:* sank   **895|** *1840:* Whose leavings   *1863:* With leavings
896| *1840:* Were ghastly some few minutes more: no rain—   *1863:* Ghastly some minutes
more. No fear of rain—   **897|** *1840:* The Minster   *1863:* minster
898| *1840:* every where: that town, the Minster's   *1863:* everywhere. This
town, the minster's   **900|** *1840:* sonnets, Naddo, Tempe's vale.
1863: sonnets, Tempe's dewy vale.'   *1868:* vale."   **901|** *1840:* Exact <> street!   *1863:*
'Exact <> street!'   *1868:* " 'Exact <> street!' "   § **902–930|** *1863:* ONE OUGHT NOT
BLAME BUT PRAISE THIS;   **897–924|** *1868* §   **902|** *1840:* ¶ As   *1863:* 'As
1868: "As   **904|** *1840:* but Lucio's sad. I said before   *1863:* but

Downcast that lusts' desire escapes the springe:
'Tis of the mood itself I speak, what tinge
Determines it, else colourless,—or mirth,
910 Or melancholy, as from heaven or earth."
" 'Ay, that's the variation's gist!'
                              "Indeed?
Thus far advanced in safety then, proceed!
And having seen too what I saw, be bold
And next encounter what I do behold
915 (That's sure) but bid you take on trust!"
                              Attack
The use and purpose of such sights! Alack,
Not so unwisely does the crowd dispense
On Salinguerras praise in preference
To the Sordellos: men of action, these!
920 Who, seeing just as little as you please,
Yet turn that little to account,—engage
With, do not gaze at,—carry on, a stage,
The work o' the world, not merely make report
The work existed ere their day! In short,
925 When at some future no-time a brave band
Sees, using what it sees, then shake my hand
In heaven, my brother! Meanwhile where's the hurt
Of keeping the Makers-see on the alert,
At whose defection mortals stare aghast
930 As though heaven's bounteous windows were slammed fast
Incontinent? Whereas all you, beneath,

Lucio's sad. I said before,   907| *1840:* Downcast his lusts'   *1863:* Downcast that
lusts'   909| *1840:* colourless, or   *1863:* colourless,—or   910| *1840:* Heaven or
Earth.   *1863:* heaven or earth.'   *1868:* earth."   911| *1840:* ¶ Ay <> gist! Indeed?
1863: 'Ay <> gist!' Indeed?   *1868:* " 'Ay   *1888:* gist!' ¶ "Indeed?   914| *1840:* Enough
encounter   *1863:* And next encounter   915| *1840:* but you must take on trust!
Attack   *1863:* but bid you take   *1868:* trust!" ¶ Attack   916| *1863:* sights? Alack,
1888: sights! Alack,   917| *1840:* unwisely hasts the   *1863:* unwisely does the
919| *1840:* action these!   *1863:* action, these!   920| *1840:* Who seeing <> please
1863: Who, seeing <> please,   921| *1840:* account; engage   *1863:*
account,—engage   922| *1840:* at; carry on a stage   *1863:* at,—carry on, a stage,
924| *1840:* their time—In   *1863:* their day! In   928| *1840:* To keep the <> alert
1863: Of keeping the <> alert,   930| *1840:* Heaven's   *1863:* heaven's
§ 931–959| *1863:* AT ALL EVENTS, HIS OWN AUDIENCE MAY:
925–952| *1868* §   931| *1840:* whereas all you beneath   *1863:* you, beneath,   *1868:*

Should scowl at, bruise their lips and break their teeth
Who ply the pullies, for neglecting you:
And therefore have I moulded, made anew
935 A Man, and give him to be turned and tried,
Be angry with or pleased at. On your side,
Have ye times, places, actors of your own?
Try them upon Sordello when full-grown,
And then—ah then! If Hercules first parched
940 His foot in Egypt only to be marched
A sacrifice for Jove with pomp to suit,
What chance have I? The demigod was mute
Till, at the altar, where time out of mind
Such guests became oblations, chaplets twined
945 His forehead long enough, and he began
Slaying the slayers, nor escaped a man.
Take not affront, my gentle audience! whom
No Hercules shall make his hecatomb,
Believe, nor from his brows your chaplet rend—
950 That's your kind suffrage, yours, my patron-friend,
Whose great verse blares unintermittent on
Like your own trumpeter at Marathon,—
You who, Platæa and Salamis being scant,
Put up with Ætna for a stimulant—
955 And did well, I acknowledged, as he loomed
Over the midland sea last month, presumed
Long, lay demolished in the blazing West
At eve, while towards him tilting cloudlets pressed

Whereas   932| *1840:* at, curse them, bruise lips, break   *1888:* at, bruise their lips and
break   933| *1840:* pullies for   *1863:* pullies, for
935| *1840:* A Man, delivered to   *1863:* A Man, and give him to   936| *1840:* side
1863: side,   938| *1840:* upon Sordello once full-grown,   *1863:* upon Sordello when
full-grown,   943| *1840:* Till at   *1863:* Till, at   946| *1840:* man—   *1863:*
man.   948| *1840:* hecatomb   *1863:* hecatomb,   950| *1840:* yours, nay, yours, my
friend   *1863:* yours, my patron-friend,   952| *1840:* Like any trumpeter at
Marathon,   *1863:* Like your own trumpeter at Marathon,—   953| *1840:* He'll testify
who when Platæas grew scant   *1863:* You who, Platæa and Salamis being scant,
954| *1840:* stimulant!   *1863:* stimulant—   955| *1840:* And well too, I <> as it
loomed   *1863:* And did well, I <> as he loomed   956| *1840:* the Midland sea that
morn, presumed   *1863:* midland sea last month, presumed
957| *1840:* All day, demolished by the   *1863:* Long, lay demolished in the   958| *1840:*
towards it tilting cloudlets prest   *1863:* towards him tilting   *1868:* pressed

Like Persian ships at Salamis. Friend, wear
960 A crest proud as desert while I declare
Had I a flawless ruby fit to wring
Tears of its colour from that painted king
Who lost it, I would, for that smile which went
To my heart, fling it in the sea, content,
965 Wearing your verse in place, an amulet
Sovereign against all passion, wear and fret!
My English Eyebright, if you are not glad
That, as I stopped my task awhile, the sad
Dishevelled form, wherein I put mankind
970 To come at times and keep my pact in mind,
Renewed me,—hear no crickets in the hedge,
Nor let a glowworm spot the river's edge
At home, and may the summer showers gush
Without a warning from the missel thrush!
975 So, to our business, now—the fate of such
As find our common nature—overmuch
Despised because restricted and unfit
To bear the burthen they impose on it—
Cling when they would discard it; craving strength
980 To leap from the allotted world, at length
They do leap,—flounder on without a term,
Each a god's germ, doomed to remain a germ
In unexpanded infancy, unless . . .
But that's the story—dull enough, confess!
985 There might be fitter subjects to allure;
Still, neither misconceive my portraiture

959| *1840:* ships for Salamis   *1863:* ships at Salamis   § 960–988| *1863:* WHAT IF THINGS
BRIGHTEN, WHO KNOWS?   953–981| *1868* §   962| *1840:* A tear its   *1863:*
Tears of its   963| *1840:* To lose, I would, for that one smile   *1863:* Who lost it, I
would, for that smile   964| *1840:* sea content   *1863:* sea, content,   966| *1840:*
against low-thoughtedness and fret!   *1863:* against all passion, wear and fret!
969| *1840:* form wherein   *1863:* form, wherein   970| *1840:* mind   *1863:*
mind,   971| *1840:* hedge   *1863:* hedge,   975| *1840:* For, Eyebright, what I sing's
the   *1863:* So, to our business, now—the   976| *1840:* nature (overmuch   *1863:*
nature—overmuch   978| *1840:* it)   *1863:* it—   981| *1840:* 'Tis left—they
floundering without a term   *1863:* They do leap,—flounder on without a term,
982| *1840:* a God's germ, but doomed remain   *1863:* god's germ, doomed to remain
983| *1840:* infancy, assure   *1863:* infancy, unless . . .   983–986| *1840:* assure /
Yourself   *1863:* § adds 984–985 §   986| *1840:* Yourself, nor misconceive   *1863:* Still,

Nor undervalue its adornments quaint:
What seems a fiend perchance may prove a saint.
Ponder a story ancient pens transmit,
990 Then say if you condemn me or acquit.
   John the Beloved, banished Antioch
For Patmos, bade collectively his flock
Farewell, but set apart the closing eve
To comfort those his exile most would grieve,
995 He knew: a touching spectacle, that house
In motion to receive him! Xanthus' spouse
You missed, made panther's meat a month since; but
Xanthus himself (his nephew 'twas, they shut
'Twixt boards and sawed asunder) Polycarp,
1000 Soft Charicle, next year no wheel could warp
To swear by Cæsar's fortune, with the rest
Were ranged; thro' whom the grey disciple pressed,
Busily blessing right and left, just stopped
To pat one infant's curls, the hangman cropped
1005 Soon after, reached the portal. On its hinge
The door turns and he enters: what quick twinge
Ruins the smiling mouth, those wide eyes fix
Whereon, why like some spectral candlestick's
Branch the disciple's arms? Dead swooned he, woke
1010 Anon, heaved sigh, made shift to gasp, heart-broke,
"Get thee behind me, Satan! Have I toiled
To no more purpose? Is the gospel foiled
Here too, and o'er my son's, my Xanthus' hearth,
Portrayed with sooty garb and features swarth—

---

neither misconceive   987| *1840:* quaint!   *1863:* quaint: 988| *1840:* saint!
1863: saint.   § 989–1017| *1863:* WHERE UPON, WITH A STORY TO THE POINT,
982–1010| *1868* §   991| *1840:* John   *1868:* ¶ John   993| *1840:* Farewell but
1863: Farewell, but   994| *1840:* comfort some his <> grieve   *1863:* comfort those his
<> grieve,   998| *1840:* himself (for 'twas his nephew shut   *1863:* himself (his
nephew 'twas, they shut   999| *1840:* sawn   *1863:* sawed   1002| *1840:* prest
1863: prest,   *1868:* pressed,   1003| *1840:* stopt   *1868:* stopped   1004| *1840:*
curls the <> cropt   *1863:* curls, the   *1868:* cropped   1005| *1840:* portal; on   *1863:*
portal—on   *1868:* portal. On   1006| *1840:* enters—what deep twinge   *1863:* what
quick twinge   *1868:* enters: what   1008| *1840:* Whereon? How like   *1863:* Whereon,
why like   1009| *1840:* arms! Dead   *1863:* arms? Dead   1010| *1840:* gasp
heart-broke   *1863:* gasp, heart-broke,   1011| *1840:* Get <> me Satan! have   *1863:*
"Get <> me, Satan   *1868:* Have   1012| *1840:* is   *1863:* Is   1014| *1840:*

228

1015 Ah Xanthus, am I to thy roof beguiled
      To see the—the—the Devil domiciled?"
      Whereto sobbed Xanthus, "Father, 'tis yourself
      Installed, a limning which our utmost pelf
      Went to procure against to-morrow's loss;
1020 And that's no twy-prong, but a pastoral cross,
      You're painted with!"
                            His puckered brows unfold—
      And you shall hear Sordello's story told.

BOOK THE FOURTH

    Meantime Ferrara lay in rueful case;
    The lady-city, for whose sole embrace
    Her pair of suitors struggled, felt their arms
    A brawny mischief to the fragile charms
5   They tugged for—one discovering that to twist
    Her tresses twice or thrice about his wrist
    Secure a point of vantage—one, how best
    He'd parry that by planting in her breast
    His elbow spike—each party too intent
10 For noticing, howe'er the battle went,
    The conqueror would but have a corpse to kiss.
    "May Boniface be duly damned for this!"
    —Howled some old Ghibellin, as up he turned,
    From the wet heap of rubbish where they burned
15 His house, a little skull with dazzling teeth:
    "A boon, sweet Christ—let Salinguerra seethe

Pourtrayed   *1863:* Portrayed   ¹⁰¹⁶| *1840:* domiciled?   *1863:* domiciled?"
¹⁰¹⁷| *1840:* sobbed Xanthus, Father   *1863:* sobbed Xanthus, "Father   § ^{1018–1022}| *1863:*
HE TAKES UP THE THREAD OF DISCOURSE.   ^{1011–1022}| *1868* §
¹⁰¹⁹| *1840:* loss,   *1863:* loss;   ¹⁰²⁰| *1840:* twy-prong but <> cross   *1863:*
twy-prong, but <> cross,   ¹⁰²¹| *1840:* with! The puckered   *1863:* with!" His
puckered   *1868:* with!" ¶ His
§ ^{1–23}| *1863:* MEN SUFFERED MUCH, §   ⁵| *1840:* Each tugged <> discovering
to   *1863:* They tugged <> discovering that to   ¹¹| *1840:* Its conqueror would
have   *1863:* The conqueror but have   ¹²| *1840:* May <> this!   *1863:* "May
<> this!"   ¹³| *1840:* Howled <> Ghibellin as   *1863:*—Howled <> Ghibellin,

In hell for ever, Christ, and let myself
Be there to laugh at him!"—moaned some young Guelf
Stumbling upon a shrivelled hand nailed fast
20 To the charred lintel of the doorway, last
His father stood within to bid him speed.
The thoroughfares were overrun with weed
—Docks, quitchgrass, loathy mallows no man plants.
      The stranger, none of its inhabitants
25 Crept out of doors to taste fresh air again,
And ask the purpose of a splendid train
Admitted on a morning; every town
Of the East League was come by envoy down
To treat for Richard's ransom: here you saw
30 The Vicentine, here snowy oxen draw
The Paduan carroch, its vermilion cross
On its white field. A-tiptoe o'er the fosse
Looked Legate Montelungo wistfully
After the flock of steeples he might spy
35 In Este's time, gone (doubts he) long ago
To mend the ramparts: sure the laggards know
The Pope's as good as here! They paced the streets
More soberly. At last, "Taurello greets
The League," announced a pursuivant,—"will match
40 Its courtesy, and labours to dispatch
At earliest Tito, Friedrich's Pretor, sent
On pressing matters from his post at Trent,
With Mainard Count of Tyrol,—simply waits
Their going to receive the delegates."
45 "Tito!" Our delegates exchanged a glance,
And, keeping the main way, admired askance
The lazy engines of outlandish birth,

as   16| 1840: A   1863: "A   18| 1840: him! moaned   1863:
him!"—moaned   20| 1840: doorway last   1863: doorway, last   § 24-52| 1863:
WHICHEVER OF THE PARTIES WAS VICTOR. §   24| 1840: stranger none
1863: stranger, none   26| 1840: Or ask < > a sumptuous train   1863: And ask   1868:
a splendid train   32| 1840: field: a-tiptoe   1863: field. A-tiptoe   36| 1840:
ramparts—sure   1868: ramparts: sure   38| 1840: last, Taurello   1863: last,
"Taurello   39| 1840: The League, announced a pursuivant,—will   1863: The
League," announced a pursuivant,—"will   42| 1840: at Trent   1863: at Trent,
44| 1840: delegates.   1863: delegates."   45| 1840: Tito! Our   1863: "Tito!"
Our   47| 1840: birth   1863: birth,   49| 1840: mangenel, and   1868: mangenel

Couched like a king each on its bank of earth—
Arbalist, manganel and catapult;
50 While stationed by, as waiting a result,
Lean silent gangs of mercenaries ceased
Working to watch the strangers. "This, at least,
Were better spared; he scarce presumes gainsay
The League's decision! Get our friend away
55 And profit for the future: how else teach
Fools 'tis not safe to stray within claw's reach
Ere Salinguerra's final gasp be blown?
Those mere convulsive scratches find the bone.
Who bade him bloody the spent osprey's nare?"
60 The carrochs halted in the public square.
Pennons of every blazon once a-flaunt,
Men prattled, freelier than the crested gaunt
White ostrich with a horse-shoe in her beak
Was missing, and whoever chose might speak
65 "Ecelin" boldly out: so,—"Ecelin
Needed his wife to swallow half the sin
And sickens by himself: the devil's whelp,
He styles his son, dwindles away, no help
From conserves, your fine triple-curded froth
70 Of virgin's blood, your Venice viper-broth—
Eh? Jubilate!"—"Peace! no little word
You utter here that's not distinctly heard
Up at Oliero: he was absent sick
When we besieged Bassano—who, i' the thick
75 O' the work, perceived the progress Azzo made,
Like Ecelin, through his witch Adelaide?

---

and   52| 1840: strangers—this   1863: strangers. "This   § 53–81| 1863: HOW GUELFS
CRITICISE GHIBELLIN WORK   1868: CRITICIZE §   56| 1840: Azzo 'tis so safe
within   1863: Fools 'tis not safe to stray within   57| 1840: Till Salinguerra's   1863:
Ere Salinguerra's   58| 1840: bone   1863: bone.   59| 1840:—Who <> nare?
1863: Who <> nare?"   62| 1840: freelier that the   1888: freelier than the
64| 1840: missing; whosoever   1868: "Was missing, and whoever   1888: Was
65| 1840: Ecelin boldly out: so, Ecelin   1863: so,—"Ecelin   1868: "Ecelin" boldly
67| 1840: whelp   1863: whelp,   68| 1840: son dwindles   1863: son, dwindles
71| 1840: Eh? Jubilate! Tusk! no   1863: Eh? Jubilate!"—"Peace! no   73| 1840: At
Oliero   1863: Up at Oliero   74| 1840: who i' the   1863: who, i' the   75| 1840:
work perceived <> made   1863: work, perceived <> made,   76| 1840: Like Ecelin?

She managed it so well that, night by night
At their bed-foot stood up a soldier-sprite,
First fresh, pale by and by without a wound,
80 And, when it came with eyes filmed as in swound,
They knew the place was taken."—"Ominous
That Ghibellins should get what cautelous
Old Redbeard sought from Azzo's sire to wrench
Vainly; Saint George contrived his town a trench
85 O' the marshes, an impermeable bar."
"—Young Ecelin is meant the tutelar
Of Padua, rather; veins embrace upon
His hand like Brenta and Bacchiglion."
What now?—"The founts! God's bread, touch not a plank!
90 A crawling hell of carrion—every tank
Choke-full!—found out just now to Cino's cost—
The same who gave Taurello up for lost,
And, making no account of fortune's freaks,
Refused to budge from Padua then, but sneaks
95 Back now with Concorezzi; 'faith! they drag
Their carroch to San Vitale, plant the flag
On his own palace, so adroitly razed
He knew it not; a sort of Guelf folk gazed
And laughed apart; Cino disliked their air—
100 Must pluck up spirit, show he does not care—
Seats himself on the tank's edge—will begin
To hum, za, za, Cavaler Ecelin—
A silence; he gets warmer, clinks to chime,

---

through <> Adelaide   1863: Like Ecelin, through <> Adelaide?   77| 1840: Who
managed <> that night by   1863: She managed <> that, night by night,   1888: by
night   78| 1840: soldier-sprite   1868: soldier-sprite,   80| 1840: And when he
came <> swound   1863: And, when it came <> swound,   81| 1840:
taken—Ominous   1863: taken. Ominous   1868: taken."—"Ominous   § 82–109| 1863: AS
UNUSUALLY ENERGETIC IN THIS CASE.   82–108| 1868 §   82| 1840: Your
Ghibellin   1863: That Ghibellins   84| 1840: St.   1863: Saint   85| 1840:
bar: 1863: bar.   1868: bar."   86| 1840: Young   1868: "—Young   87| 1840:
Of Padua rather   1863: Of Padua, rather   88| 1840: and Bacchiglion . . .   1863: and
Bacchiglion.   1868: and Bacchiglion."   89| 1840: now? The   1868:
now?—"The   91| 1840: Choke full! found   1863: full!—found   1888:
Choke-full   95| 1840: with Concorezzi—'faith   1888: with Concorezzi: 'faith
96| 1840: Vital   1868: Vitale   97| 1840: Palace so   1863: palace   1868: palace,
so   102| 1840: za za   1863: za, za   105| 1840: za, and   1863: za za   1888: za, za

Now both feet plough the ground, deeper each time,
105 At last, *za, za* and up with a fierce kick
Comes his own mother's face caught by the thick
Grey hair about his spur!"
               Which means, they lift
The covering, Salinguerra made a shift
To stretch upon the truth; as well avoid
110 Further disclosures; leave them thus employed.
Our dropping Autumn morning clears apace,
And poor Ferrara puts a softened face
On her misfortunes. Let us scale this tall
Huge foursquare line of red brick garden-wall
115 Bastioned within by trees of every sort
On three sides, slender, spreading, long and short;
Each grew as it contrived, the poplar ramped,
The fig-tree reared itself,—but stark and cramped,
Made fools of, like tamed lions: whence, on the edge,
120 Running 'twixt trunk and trunk to smooth one ledge
Of shade, were shrubs inserted, warp and woof,
Which smothered up that variance. Scale the roof
Of solid tops, and o'er the slope you slide
Down to a grassy space level and wide,
125 Here and there dotted with a tree, but trees
Of rarer leaf, each foreigner at ease,
Set by itself: and in the centre spreads,
Borne upon three uneasy leopards' heads,
A laver, broad and shallow, one bright spirt
130 Of water bubbles in. The walls begirt
With trees leave off on either hand; pursue
Your path along a wondrous avenue

---

and   **107|**   *1840:* spur! Which   *1863:* spur!" Which   **108|**   *1840:* covering
Taurello made   *1863:* covering, Salinguerra made   **§ 110–38|**   HOW, PASSING THROUGH
THE RARE GARDEN,   **109–37|**   *1868* §   **113|**   *1840:* misfortunes, save one
spot—this   *1863:* misfortunes. Let us scale this   **116|**   *1840:* short,   *1868:*
short;   **117|**   *1840:* (Each   *1863:*—Each   *1868:* Each   **118|**   *1840:* itself,) but
1863: itself,—but   **119|**   *1840:* of; whence upon the very edge,   *1863:* of, like tamed
lions; whence, on the edge,   *1868:* lions: whence   **121|**   *1840:* are   *1863:* were
122| *1840:* smother   *1863:* smothered   **123|**   *1840:* tops and   *1863:* tops, and
127| *1840:* itself; and   *1863:* itself: and   **128|**   *1840:* Born   *1868:* Borne
130| *1840:* in: the   *1863:* in. The   **131|**   *1840:* hand: pursue   *1863:* hand;

Those walls abut on, heaped of gleamy stone,
With aloes leering everywhere, grey-grown
135 From many a Moorish summer: how they wind
Out of the fissures! likelier to bind
The building than those rusted cramps which drop
Already in the eating sunshine. Stop,
You fleeting shapes above there! Ah, the pride
140 Or else despair of the whole country-side!
A range of statues, swarming o'er with wasps,
God, goddess, woman, man, the Greek rough-rasps
In crumbling Naples marble—meant to look
Like those Messina marbles Constance took
145 Delight in, or Taurello's self conveyed
To Mantua for his mistress, Adelaide,—
A certain font with caryatides
Since cloistered at Goito; only, these
Are up and doing, not abashed, a troop
150 Able to right themselves—who see you, stoop
Their arms o' the instant after you! Unplucked
By this or that, you pass; for they conduct
To terrace raised on terrace, and, between,
Creatures of brighter mould and braver mien
155 Than any yet, the choicest of the Isle
No doubt. Here, left a sullen breathing-while,
Up-gathered on himself the Fighter stood
For his last fight, and, wiping treacherous blood
Out of the eyelids just held ope beneath
160 Those shading fingers in their iron sheath,
Steadied his strengths amid the buzz and stir
Of the dusk hideous amphitheatre

pursue   133| *1840:* The walls   *1863:* Those walls   135| *1840:* summer; how
1863: summer: how   138| *1840:* sunshine. Stop   *1863:* sunshine. Stop,   § 139–67| *1863:*
SALINGUERRA CONTRIVED FOR A PURPOSE,   138–66| *1868* §
139| *1840:* Yon fleeting   *1863:* You fleeting   140| *1840:* country-side—   *1863:*
country-side!   142| *1840:* man, your Greek   *1863:* man, the Greek   143| *1840:*
marble! meant   *1868:* marble—meant   146| *1840:* mistress, Adelaide,   *1888:*
mistress, Adelaide,—   151| *1840:* O' the instant after you their arms! unplucked
1863: Unplucked   *1888:* Their arms o' the instant after you! Unplucked   152| *1840:*
that you pass, for   *1863:* that, you   *1868:* pass; for   156| *1840:* doubt; here   *1863:*
doubt. Here   161| *1840:* buz   *1888:* buzz   162| *1840:* Of a dusk   *1863:* Of the

234

At the announcement of his over-match
To wind the day's diversion up, dispatch
165 The pertinacious Gaul: while, limbs one heap,
The Slave, no breath in her round mouth, watched leap
Dart after dart forth, as her hero's car
Clove dizzily the solid of the war
—Let coil about his knees for pride in him.
170 We reach the farthest terrace, and the grim
San Pietro Palace stops us.
                                    Such the state
Of Salinguerra's plan to emulate
Sicilian marvels, that his girlish wife
Retrude still might lead her ancient life
175 In her new home: whereat enlarged so much
Neighbours upon the novel princely touch
He took,—who here imprisons Boniface.
Here must the Envoys come to sue for grace;
And here, emerging from the labyrinth
180 Below, Sordello paused beside the plinth
Of the door-pillar.
                              He had really left
Verona for the cornfields (a poor theft
From the morass) where Este's camp was made;
The Envoys' march, the Legate's cavalcade—
185 All had been seen by him, but scarce as when,—
Eager for cause to stand aloof from men
At every point save the fantastic tie
Acknowledged in his boyish sophistry,—
He made account of such. A crowd,—he meant
190 To task the whole of it; each part's intent
Concerned him therefore: and, the more he pried,

---

dusk   164| *1840:* despatch   *1863:* dispatch   165| *1840:* Their pertinacious
friend: while   *1863:* The pertinacious Gaul: while   167| *1840:* forth as   *1863:* forth,
as   § 168–94| *1863:* SORDELLO PONDERS ALL SEEN AND HEARD,
167–93| *1868* §   170| *1840:* terrace and   *1863:* terrace, and   173| *1840:* marvels
that   *1863:* marvels, that   175| *1840:* home—whereat   *1868:* home: whereat
177| *1840:* took who   *1863:* took,—who   180| *1840:* Below, two minstrels pause
beside   *1863:* Below, Sordello paused beside   181| *1840:* door-pillar. ¶ One had <>
left   *1863:* door-pillar. ¶ He had <> left.   *1868:* left   183| *1840:* made,   *1863:*
made;   185| *1840:* Looked cursorily o'er, but <> when,   *1863:* All had been seen by
him, but   *1868:* when,—   188| *1840:* sophistry,   *1868:* sophistry,—
189| *1840:* crowd; he   *1863:* crowd,—he   191| *1840:* therefore, and the <> pried

The less became Sordello satisfied
With his own figure at the moment. Sought
He respite from his task? Descried he aught
195 Novel in the anticipated sight
Of all these livers upon all delight?
This phalanx, as of myriad points combined,
Whereby he still had imaged the mankind
His youth was passed in dreams of rivalling,
200 His age—in plans to prove at least such thing
Had been so dreamed,—which now he must impress
With his own will, effect a happiness
By theirs,—supply a body to his soul
Thence, and become eventually whole
205 With them as he had hoped to be without—
Made these the mankind he once raved about?
Because a few of them were notable,
Should all be figured worthy note? As well
Expect to find Taurello's triple line
210 Of trees a single and prodigious pine.
Real pines rose here and there; but, close among,
Thrust into and mixed up with pines, a throng
Of shrubs, he saw,—a nameless common sort
O'erpast in dreams, left out of the report
215 And hurried into corners, or at best
Admitted to be fancied like the rest.
Reckon that morning's proper chiefs—how few!
And yet the people grew, the people grew,
Grew ever, as if the many there indeed,
220 More left behind and most who should succeed,—

1888: therefore: and, the <> pried,   194| *1840:* descried   *1863:* Descried
§ 195–223| *1863:* FINDS IN MEN NO MACHINE FOR HIS SAKE,
194–222| *1868* §   196| *1840:* Of all those livers   *1863:* Of all these livers
197| *1840:* A phalanx as <> combined   *1863:* This phalanx, as <> combined,
198| *1840:* imaged that mankind   *1868:* imaged the mankind   200| *1840:* least the
thing   *1863:* least such thing   201| *1840:* So dreamed, but now he hastened to
impress   *1863:* Had been so dreamed,—which now he must impress   203| *1840:* From
theirs, supply   *1863:* By theirs,—supply   206| *1840:* he was made about?   *1863:* he
once raved about?   207| *1840:* notable   *1863:* notable,   208| *1840:* Must all
1863: Should all   211| *1840:* there, but   *1863:* there; but   213| *1840:* shrubs you
saw, a   *1863:* shrubs, he saw,—a   214| *1840:* report,   *1863:* report   215| *1840:*
Fast hurried   *1863:* And hurried   217| *1840:* chiefs; how   *1863:* chiefs—how
219| *1840:* as with many   *1863:* as if the many   220| *1840:* succeed,   *1863:*

Simply in virtue of their mouths and eyes,
Petty enjoyments and huge miseries,—
Mingled with, and made veritably great
Those chiefs: he overlooked not Mainard's state
225 Nor Concorezzi's station, but instead
Of stopping there, each dwindled to be head
Of infinite and absent Tyrolese
Or Paduans; startling all the more, that these
Seemed passive and disposed of, uncared for,
230 Yet doubtless on the whole (like Eglamor)
Smiling; for if a wealthy man decays
And out of store of robes must wear, all days,
One tattered suit, alike in sun and shade,
'Tis commonly some tarnished gay brocade
235 Fit for a feast-night's flourish and no more:
Nor otherwise poor Misery from her store
Of looks is fain upgather, keep unfurled
For common wear as she goes through the world,
The faint remainder of some worn-out smile
240 Meant for a feast-night's service merely. While
Crowd upon crowd rose on Sordello thus,—
(Crowds no way interfering to discuss,
Much less dispute, life's joys with one employed
In envying them,—or, if they aught enjoyed,
245 Where lingered something indefinable
In every look and tone, the mirth as well
As woe, that fixed at once his estimate

---

succeed,—   221| *1840:* their faces, eyes,   *1863:* their mouths and eyes,
222| *1840:* miseries,   *1863:* miseries,—   223| *1840:* Were veritably mingled with,
made great   *1863:* Mingled with, and made veritably great   § 224–52| *1863:* BUT A THING
WITH A LIFE OF ITS OWN,   223–51| *1868* §   224| *1840:* chiefs: no
overlooking Mainard's   *1863:* chiefs: he overlooked not Mainard's   228| *1840:*
startling too the more that   *1863:* startling all the more, that   230| *1840:* whole
(quoth Eglamor)   *1863:* "Yet <> whole" (quoth   *1868:* Yet <> whole (like
Eglamor)   231| *1840:* Smiling—for   *1863:* "Smiling   *1868:* Smiling; for
232| *1840:* store of such must wear all days   *1863:* store of robes must wear, all days,
233| *1840:* suit alike   *1863:* suit, alike   234| *1840:* tarnished fine brocade   *1863:*
tarnished gay brocade   235| *1840:* more;   *1863:* more: 238| *1840:* world
1863: world,   240| *1863:* merely." While   *1868:* merely. While   242| *1840:*
Crowds <> discuss   *1863:* (Crowds <> discuss,   243| *1840:* dispute life's   *1863:*
dispute, life's   244| *1840:* them, or, if they enjoyed   *1863:* them,—or, if they aught
enjoyed,   245| *1840:* There lingered somewhat indefinable   *1863:* Where lingered

Of the result, their good or bad estate)—
Old memories returned with new effect:
250 And the new body, ere he could suspect,
Cohered, mankind and he were really fused,
The new self seemed impatient to be used
By him, but utterly another way
Than that anticipated: strange to say,
255 They were too much below him, more in thrall
Than he, the adjunct than the principal.
What booted scattered units?—here a mind
And there, which might repay his own to find,
And stamp, and use?—a few, howe'er august,
260 If all the rest were grovelling in the dust?
No: first a mighty equilibrium, sure,
Should he establish, privilege procure
For all, the few had long possessed! He felt
An error, an exceeding error melt:
265 While he was occupied with Mantuan chants,
Behoved him think of men, and take their wants
Such as he now distinguished every side,
As his own want which might be satisfied,—
And, after that, think of rare qualities
270 Of his own soul demanding exercise.
It followed naturally, through no claim
On their part, which made virtue of the aim

---

something indefinable   248| *1840:* estate,—   *1863:* estate)—   249| *1840:*
memories flocked but with a new   *1863:* memories returned with new   § 253–81| *1863:* AND
RIGHTS HITHERTO IGNORED BY HIM,   252–80| *1868* §   254| *1840:* To
that   *1868:* Than that   257| *1840:* scattered brilliances? the mind   *1863:* scattered
units?—here a mind   258| *1840:* Of any number he might hope to bind   *1863:* And
there, which might repay his own to find,   259| *1840:* stamp with his own thought,
howe'er   *1863:* stamp, and use?—a few, howe'er   260| *1840:* rest should grovel in
1863: rest were grovelling in   261| *1840:* equilibrium sure   *1863:* equilibrium,
sure,   262| *1840:* To be established, privilege   *1863:* Should he establish,
privilege   263| *1840:* For them himself had <> he   *1863:* For all, the few had   *1868:*
He   264| *1840:* melt—   *1888:* melt: 265| *1840:* chants   *1863:* chants,
266| *1840:* men and   *1863:* men, and <> wants,   268| *1840:* want that
might be satisfied,   *1863:* want which might be satisfied,—   269| *1840:* that, of
wondrous qualities   *1863:* that, think of rare qualities   270| *1840:* exercise,   *1863:*
exercise.   271| *1840:* And like demand it longer: nor a claim   *1863:* exercise.
271| *1840:* And like demand it longer: nor a claim   *1863:* It followed naturally, through no
claim   272| *1840:* part, nor was virtue in the   *1863:* part, which made virtue of

At serving them, on his,—that, past retrieve,
He felt now in their toils, theirs—nor could leave
275 Wonder how, in the eagerness of rule,
Impress his will on mankind, he (the fool!)
Had never even entertained the thought
That this his last arrangement might be fraught
With incidental good to them as well,
280 And that mankind's delight would help to swell
His own. So, if he sighed, as formerly
Because the merry time of life must fleet,
'Twas deeplier now,—for could the crowds repeat
Their poor experiences? His hand that shook
285 Was twice to be deplored. "The Legate, look!
With eyes, like fresh-blown thrush-eggs on a thread,
Faint-blue and loosely floating in his head,
Large tongue, moist open mouth; and this long while
That owner of the idiotic smile
290 Serves them!"
                    He fortunately saw in time
His fault however, and since the office prime
Includes the secondary—best accept
Both offices; Taurello, its adept,
Could teach him the preparatory one,
295 And how to do what he had fancied done
Long previously, ere take the greater task.
How render first these people happy? Ask

the   273| 1840: them on his, but, past   1863: them, on his,—that, past
274| 1840: He in their toils felt with them, nor could leave,   1863: He felt now in their toils,
theirs—nor could leave   275| 1840: Wonder that in   1863: Wonder how, in
276| 1840: will upon them, he the fool   1863: will on mankind, he (the fool!)
277| 1840: never entertained the obvious thought   1863: never even entertained the
thought   278| 1840: This last of his arrangements would be   1863: That this his last
arrangement might be   279| 1840: With good to them as well, and he should be
1863: With incidental good to them as well,   279–281| 1863: well, / And that mankind's
delight would help to swell / His   281| 1840: Rejoiced thereat; and if, as formerly,
1863: His own. So he he sighed, as formerly   § 282–310| 1863:—A FAULT HE IS NOW
ANXIOUS TO REPAIR,   281–308| 1868 §   282| 1840: He sighed the   1863:
Because the
283| 1840: now, for   1863: now,—for   285| 1840: deplored. The   1863: deplored.
"The   290| 1840: them! He   1863: them!" He   1868: them!" ¶ He   291| 1840:
and the   1863: and since the   293| 1840: offices; Taurello its adept   1863: offices;
Taurello, its adept,   297| 1840: render then these <> ask   1863: render first these

The people's friends: for there must be one good
One way to it—the Cause! He understood
300 The meaning now of Palma; why the jar
Else, the ado, the trouble wide and far
Of Guelfs and Ghibellins, the Lombard hope
And Rome's despair?—'twixt Emperor and Pope
The confused shifting sort of Eden tale—
305 Hardihood still recurring, still to fail—
That foreign interloping fiend, this free
And native overbrooding deity:
Yet a dire fascination o'er the palms
The Kaiser ruined, troubling even the calms
310 Of paradise; or, on the other hand,
The Pontiff, as the Kaisers understand,
One snake-like cursed of God to love the ground,
Whose heavy length breaks in the noon profound
Some saving tree—which needs the Kaiser, dressed
315 As the dislodging angel of that pest:
Yet flames that pest bedropped, flat head, full fold,
With coruscating dower of dyes. "Behold
The secret, so to speak, and master-spring
O' the contest!—which of the two Powers shall bring
320 Men good, perchance the most good: ay, it may

1868: Ask   298| *1840:* good,   *1888:* good   299| *1840:* he   *1863:* the
Cause!—he   *1888:* the Cause! He   300| *1840:* of Palma; else why are   *1863:* of Palma;
why the jar   301| *1840:* The great ado <> far,   *1863:* Else, the ado <> far
302| *1840:* These Guelfs <> Lombard's   *1863:* Of Guelfs   *1888:* Lombard
303| *1840:* Or its despair! 'twixt Emperor or Pope   *1863:* And Rome's despair?—'twixt
Emperor and Pope   305| *1840:* Of hardihood recurring still   *1863:* Still hardihood
recurring, still   *1888:* Hardihood still recurring   307| *1840:* Deity—   *1863:*
deity—   *1888:* deity: 309| *1840:* His presence ruined troubling thorough calms
1863: The Kaiser ruined, troubling even the calms   310| *1840:* Of Paradise—or   *1868:*
paradise   *1888:* paradise; or   § 311–38| *1863:* SINCE HE APPREHENDS ITS FULL
EXTENT,   309–36| *1868:* §   311| *1840:* as your Kaisers   *1863:* as the
Kaisers   312| *1840:* That, snake-like   *1863:* One snake-like   313| *1840:* With
lulling eye breaks   *1863:* Whose heavy length breaks   314| *1840:* tree—who but the
Kaiser drest   *1863:* tree—which needs the Kaiser, drest   *1868:* dressed   315| *1840:* of
the pest   *1863:* of that pest,   *1888:* pest: 316| *1840:* Then? yet that pest bedrop
1863: Then—yet   *1868:* bedropped   *1888:* Yet flames that   317| *1840:* dyes;
behold   *1863:* dyes. "Behold   319| *1840:* Of the whole contest! which of them shall
1863: the contest! which of the two Powers shall   *1868:* contest!—which   *1888:* O'
320| *1840:* good—perchance <> good—ay   *1888:* good, perchance <> good: ay

Be that!—the question, which best knows the way."
 And hereupon Count Mainard strutted past
Out of San Pietro; never seemed the last
Of archers, slingers: and our friend began
325 To recollect strange modes of serving man—
Arbalist, catapult, brake, manganel,
And more. "This way of theirs may,—who can tell?—
Need perfecting," said he: "let all be solved
At once! Taurello 'tis, the task devolved
330 On late: confront Taurello!"
                                And at last
He did confront him. Scarce an hour had past
When forth Sordello came, older by years
Than at his entry. Unexampled fears
Oppressed him, and he staggered off, blind, mute
335 And deaf, like some fresh-mutilated brute,
Into Ferrara—not the empty town
That morning witnessed: he went up and down
Streets whence the veil had been stript shred by shred,
So that, in place of huddling with their dead
340 Indoors, to answer Salinguerra's ends,
Townsfolk make shift to crawl forth, sit like friends
With any one. A woman gave him choice
Of her two daughters, the infantile voice
Or the dimpled knee, for half a chain, his throat
345 Was clasped with; but an archer knew the coat—
Its blue cross and eight lilies,—bade beware

321| *1840:* that; the question is which knows the way.   *1863:* that! the question, which best knows the way."   *1868:* that!—the   323| *1840:* never looked the   *1863:* never seemed the   324| *1840:* slingers; and   *1863:* slingers: and   325| *1868:* man   *1888:* man—   327| *1840:* more: this <> may, who can tell,   *1863:* more. "This <> may,—who can tell?—   328| *1840:* perfecting, said he: all's better solved   *1863:* perfecting," said he: "let all be solved   329| *1840:* once: Taurello 'twas the   *1863:* once! Taurello 'tis, the   330| *1840:* late—confront Taurello! ¶ And   *1863:* Taurello!" ¶ And   *1888:* late: confront   331| *1840:* They did <> him. Scarcely an hour past   *1863:* He did   *1888:* him. Scarce an hour had past   338| *1840:* veil was stripped shred after shred,   *1863:* veil had been stripped shred by shred,   *1888:* stript   § 339–67| *1863:* AND WOULD FAIN HAVE HELPED SOME WAY.   337–65| *1868* §   339| *1840:* that in   *1863:* that, in   340| *1840:* Indoors to   *1863:* Indoors, to   341| *1840:* Its folk make <> crawl and sit   *1863:* crawl forth, sit   *1888:* Townsfolk make   344| *1840:* Or dimpled <> chain his   *1863:* Or the dimpled <> chain, his   346| *1840:* lilies, bade   *1863:* lilies,—bade   349| *1840:* dews fell rife,

One dogging him in concert with the pair
Though thrumming on the sleeve that hid his knife.
Night set in early, autumn dews were rife,
350 They kindled great fires while the Leaguers' mass
Began at every carroch: he must pass
Between the kneeling people. Presently
The carroch of Verona caught his eye
With purple trappings; silently he bent
355 Over its fire, when voices violent
Began, "Affirm not whom the youth was like
That struck me from the porch: I did not strike
Again: I too have chestnut hair; my kin
Hate Azzo and stand up for Ecelin.
360 Here, minstrel, drive bad thoughts away! Sing! Take
My glove for guerdon!" And for that man's sake
He turned: "A song of Eglamor's!"—scarce named,
When, "Our Sordello's rather!"—all exclaimed;
"Is not Sordello famousest for rhyme?"
365 He had been happy to deny, this time,—
Profess as heretofore the aching head
And failing heart,—suspect that in his stead
Some true Apollo had the charge of them,
Was champion to reward or to condemn,
370 So his intolerable risk might shift
Or share itself; but Naddo's precious gift
Of gifts, he owned, be certain! At the close—
"I made that," said he to a youth who rose

1863: dews were rife,   350| *1840:* And fires were kindled while the
Leaguer's   *1863:* They kindled great fires while   *1888:* Leaguers'   351| *1840:*
carroch—he   *1888:* carroch: he   352| *1840:* Between that kneeling people:
presently   *1863:* Between the kneeling people. Presently   356| *1840:* Began, Affirm
1863: Began, "Affirm   357| *1840:* That, striking from the porch, I   *1888:* That struck
me from the porch: I   358| *1840:* Again; I   *1868:* Again: I   359| *1840:* for
Ecelin;   *1863:* for Ecelin.   360| *1840:* away; sing; take   *1863:* away! sing! take   *1868:*
Sing! Take   361| *1840:* guerdon! and   *1863:* guerdon!" and   *1868:* And
362| *1840:* turned: A <> Eglamor's! scarce   *1863:* turned: "A <>
Eglamor's!"—scarce   363| *1840:* When Our Sordello's, rather! all   *1863:* When, "Our
Sordello's rather!" all   *1868:* rather!"—all   364| *1840:* Is <> rhyme?   *1863:* "Is
<> rhyme?"   365| *1840:* time;   *1863:* time,—   366| *1840:* head,   *1863:*
head   367| *1840:* The failing heart; suspect   *1863:* And failing heart,—suspect
§ 368–96| *1863:* BUT SALINGUERRA IS ALSO PRE-OCCUPIED;
366–94| *1868* §   369| *1840:* condemn   *1863:* condemn,   372| *1840:* gifts
returned, be <> at   *1863:* gifts, he owned, be <> at   373| *1840:* I made that, said

As if to hear: 'twas Palma through the band
375 Conducted him in silence by her hand.
　　　　Back now for Salinguerra. Tito of Trent
Gave place to Palma and her friend, who went
In turn at Montelungo's visit: one
After the other were they come and gone,—
380 These spokesmen for the Kaiser and the Pope,
This incarnation of the People's hope,
Sordello,—all the say of each was said;
And Salinguerra sat,—himself instead
Of these to talk with, lingered musing yet.
385 'Twas a drear vast presence-chamber roughly set
In order for the morning's use; full face,
The Kaiser's ominous sign-mark had first place,
The crowned grim twy-necked eagle, coarsely-blacked
With ochre on the naked wall; nor lacked
390 Romano's green and yellow either side;
But the new token Tito brought had tried
The Legate's patience—nay, if Palma knew
What Salinguerra almost meant to do
Until the sight of her restored his lip
395 A certain half-smile, three months' chieftainship
Had banished! Afterward, the Legate found
No change in him, nor asked what badge he wound
And unwound carelessly. Now sat the Chief
Silent as when our couple left, whose brief

1863: "I made that," said 　　 375| 　*1840:* by the hand. 　*1863:* by her hand.
377| 　*1840:* place, remember, to the pair; who 　*1863:* place to Palma and her friend; who
1888: friend, who 　　 378| 　*1840:* visit—one 　*1888:* visit: one 　　 379| 　*1840:* are <>
gone. 　*1863:* were <> gone,— 　　 379–385| 　*1840:* gone. / A 　*1863:* § adds 380–84 §
382| 　*1863:* said, 　*1868:* said 　*1888:* said; 　　 383| 　*1863:* sat, himself 　*1888:*
sat,—himself 　　 385| 　*1840:* A drear 　*1863:* 'Twas a drear 　　 386| 　*1840:* for this
morning's use: you met 　*1863:* for the morning's use; full face, 　　 386–88| 　*1863:* face, /
The Kaiser's ominous sign-mark had first place, / The 　　 388| 　*1840:* The grim black
twy-necked eagle, coarsely blacked 　*1863:* The crowned grim twy-necked eagle,
coarsely-blacked 　　 389| 　*1840:* walls, nor 　*1863:* wall; nor 　　 390| 　*1840:* There
green and yellow tokens either 　*1863:* Romano's green and yellow either 　　 391| 　*1840:*
new symbol Tito 　*1863:* new token Tito 　　 395| 　*1840:* half-smile three 　*1863:*
half-smile, three 　　 396| 　*1840:* banished? Afterward the 　*1863:* banished! Afterward,
the 　§ 397–425| 　*1863:* RESEMBLING SORDELLO IN NOTHING ELSE.
395–423| 　*1868* § 　　 398| 　*1840:* carelessly! Now sate 　*1863:* carelessly. Now sat
399| 　*1840:* left whose 　*1863:* left, whose 　　 401| 　*1840:* reject— 　*1863:* reject. 　*1888:*

400 Encounter wrought so opportune effect
In thoughts he summoned not, nor would reject,
Though time 'twas now if ever, to pause—fix
On any sort of ending: wiles and tricks
Exhausted, judge! his charge, the crazy town,
405 Just managed to be hindered crashing down—
His last sound troops ranged—care observed to post
His best of the maimed soldiers innermost—
So much was plain enough, but somehow struck
Him not before. And now with this strange luck
410 Of Tito's news, rewarding his address
So well, what thought he of?—how the success
With Friedrich's rescript there, would either hush
Old Ecelin's scruples, bring the manly flush
To his young son's white cheek, or, last, exempt
415 Himself from telling what there was to tempt?
No: that this minstrel was Romano's last
Servant—himself the first! Could he contrast
The whole!—that minstrel's thirty years just spent
In doing nought, their notablest event
420 This morning's journey hither, as I told—
Who yet was lean, outworn and really old,
A stammering awkward man that scarce dared raise
His eye before the magisterial gaze—
And Salinguerra with his fears and hopes
425 Of sixty years, his Emperors and Popes,
Cares and contrivances, yet, you would say,
'Twas a youth nonchalantly looked away
Through the embrasure northward o'er the sick

---

reject, ⁴⁰²| *1840:* time, if ever, 'twas to pause now—fix   *1863:* time 'twas now if ever,
to pause—fix   ⁴⁰⁷| *1840:* His last of   *1863:* His best of   ⁴⁰⁹| *1840:* before:
and   *1863:* before. And   ⁴¹¹| *1840:* of? How   *1863:* of?—how   ⁴¹²| *1840:* there
would   *1863:* there, would   ⁴¹³| *1840:* Ecelin's fiercest scruple up, or flush   *1863:*
Old Ecelin's scruples, bring the manly flush   ⁴¹⁴| *1840:* Young Ecelin's white   *1863:*
To his young son's white   ⁴¹⁸| *1840:* whole! that <> thirty autumns spent   *1863:*
thirty years just spent   *1868:* whole!—that   ⁴¹⁹| *1840:* nought, his notablest   *1863:*
nought, their notablest   ⁴²⁰| *1840:* as we told—   *1863:* as I told—   ⁴²²| *1840:*
awkward youth (scarce dared he raise   *1863:* awkward man that scarce dared raise
⁴²³| *1840:* before that magisterial gaze)   *1863:* before the magisterial gaze
⁴²⁴| *1840:* —And Salinguerra   *1863:* And Salinguerra   ⁴²⁶⁻⁵⁴| *1863:* HOW HE
WAS MADE IN BODY AND SPIRIT,   ³²⁴⁻⁵²| *1868* §   ⁴²⁶| *1840:* yet you <>
say   *1863:* yet, you <> say,   ⁴²⁷| *1840:* A youth 'twas nonchalantly   *1863:* 'Twas a

244

Expostulating trees—so agile, quick
430 And graceful turned the head on the broad chest
Encased in pliant steel, his constant vest,
Whence split the sun off in a spray of fire
Across the room; and, loosened of its tire
Of steel, that head let breathe the comely brown
435 Large massive locks discoloured as if a crown
Encircled them, so frayed the basnet where
A sharp white line divided clean the hair;
Glossy above, glossy below, it swept
Curling and fine about a brow thus kept
440 Calm, laid coat upon coat, marble and sound:
This was the mystic mark the Tuscan found,
Mused of, turned over books about. Square-faced,
No lion more; two vivid eyes, enchased
In hollows filled with many a shade and streak
445 Settling from the bold nose and bearded cheek.
Nor might the half-smile reach them that deformed
A lip supremely perfect else—unwarmed,
Unwidened, less or more; indifferent
Whether on trees or men his thought were bent,
450 Thoughts rarely, after all, in trim and train
As now a period was fulfilled again:
Of such, a series made his life, compressed
In each, one story serving for the rest—
How his life-streams rolling arrived at last
455 At the barrier, whence, were it once overpast,
They would emerge, a river to the end,—
Gathered themselves up, paused, bade fate befriend,
Took the leap, hung a minute at the height,
Then fell back to oblivion infinite:
460 Therefore he smiled. Beyond stretched garden-grounds
Where late the adversary, breaking bounds,
Had gained him an occasion, That above,

---

youth nonchalantly   429| *1840:* agile quick   *1863:* agile, quick   432| *1840:*
thesun   *1863:* the sun   434| *1840:* let see the   *1863:* let breathe the   435| *1840:*
as a   *1863:* as if a   445| *1840:* cheek;   *1868:* cheek.   449| *1840:* bent—   *1863:*
bent,   451| *1840:* now: a < > again;   *1863:* now a   *1868:* again: 452| *1840:*
Such in a   *1863:* Of such, a   453–60| *1840:* rest—/ Therefore   *1863:* § adds
454–59 §   455–83| *1863:* AND WHAT HAD BEEN HIS CAREER OF OLD.
453–81| *1868* §   462| *1840:* Procured him an occasion That   *1863:* Had gained him an

That eagle, testified he could improve
Effectually. The Kaiser's symbol lay
465 Beside his rescript, a new badge by way
Of baldric; while,—another thing that marred
Alike emprise, achievement and reward,—
Ecelin's missive was conspicuous too.
     What past life did those flying thoughts pursue?
470 As his, few names in Mantua half so old;
But at Ferrara, where his sires enrolled
It latterly, the Adelardi spared
No pains to rival them: both factions shared
Ferrara, so that, counted out, 'twould yield
475 A product very like the city's shield,
Half black and white, or Ghibellin and Guelf
As after Salinguerra styled himself
And Este who, till Marchesalla died,
(Last of the Adelardi)—never tried
480 His fortune there: with Marchesalla's child
Would pass,—could Blacks and Whites be reconciled
And young Taurello wed Linguetta,—wealth
And sway to a sole grasp. Each treats by stealth
Already: when the Guelfs, the Ravennese
485 Arrive, assault the Pietro quarter, seize
Linguetta, and are gone! Men's first dismay
Abated somewhat, hurries down, to lay
The after indignation, Boniface,
This Richard's father. "Learn the full disgrace
490 Averted, ere you blame us Guelfs, who rate

occasion, That   464| *1840:* Effectually; the   *1863:* Effectually. The   466| *1840:*
while another   *1863:* while,—another   467| *1840:* emprize <> reward,   *1863:*
emprise <> reward,—   469| *1840:* What a past life those <> pursue!   *1863:* What
past life did those <> pursue?   470| *1840:* his no name   *1863:* his, few names
473| *1840:* Few means to   *1863:* No pains to   476| *1840:* or Ghibellin and Guelf,
1888: or Ghibellin and Guelf   478| *1840:* died   *1863:* died,   479| *1840:*—Last
<> Adelardi, never   *1863:* (Last <> Adelardi)—never   480| *1840:* there; but
Marchesalla's   *1863:* there: with Marchesalla's   481| *1840:* Transmits (can Blacks
1863: Would pass,—could Blacks   482| *1840:* wed Linguetta) wealth   *1863:* wed
Linguetta,—wealth   483| *1840:* grasp: each   *1863:* grasp. Each   § 484–512| THE
ORIGINAL CHECK TO HIS FORTUNES,   482–510| *1868* §   486| *1840:* gone!
Our first   *1863:* gone! Men's first   487| *1840:* down to   *1863:* down, to
488| *1840:* indignation Boniface,   *1863:* indignation, Boniface,   489| *1840:* No
meaner spokesman: Learn   *1863:* This Richard's father. "Learn   490| *1840:* Averted

Your Salinguerra, your sole potentate
That might have been, 'mongst Este's valvassors—
Ay, Azzo's—who, not privy to, abhors
Our step; but we were zealous." Azzo then
495 To do with! Straight a meeting of old men:
"Old Salinguerra dead, his heir a boy,
What if we change our ruler and decoy
The Lombard Eagle of the azure sphere
With Italy to build in, fix him here,
500 Settle the city's troubles in a trice?
For private wrong, let public good suffice!"
In fine, young Salinguerra's staunchest friends
Talked of the townsmen making him amends,
Gave him a goshawk, and affirmed there was
505 Rare sport, one morning, over the green grass
A mile or so. He sauntered through the plain,
Was restless, fell to thinking, turned again
In time for Azzo's entry with the bride;
Count Boniface rode smirking at their side;
510 "She brings him half Ferrara," whispers flew,
"And all Ancona! If the stripling knew!"
    Anon the stripling was in Sicily
Where Heinrich ruled in right of Constance; he
Was gracious nor his guest incapable;
515 Each understood the other. So it fell,
One Spring, when Azzo, thoroughly at ease,
Had near forgotten by what precise degrees
He crept at first to such a downy seat,

ere <> us—wont to rate   *1863:* Averted, ere <> us Guelfs, who rate   **491|**   *1840:*
Your Salinguerra, and sole   *1863:* Your Salinguerra, your sole   **494|**   *1840:* step—but
<> zealous. Azzo's then   *1863:* zealous." Azzo's   *1868:* step; but   *1888:* Azzo
495–98| *1863:* men: / "Old Salinguerra dead, his heir a boy, / What if we change our ruler and
decoy / The   **498|**   *1863:* sphere,   *1888:* sphere   **499|**   *1840:* in, builds he here?
1863: in, fix him here,   **500|**   *1840:* This deemed—the other owned upon advice—
1863: Settle the city's troubles in a trice?   **501|**   *1840:* A third reflected on the matter
twice—   *1863:* For private wrong, let public good suffice!"   **505|**   *1840:* the morass
1863: the green grass   **509|**   *1840:* at his side;   *1863:* at their side;   **510|**   *1840:*
There's half Ferrara with her, whispers   *1863:* "She brings him half Ferrara,"
whispers   **511|**   *1840:* And <> knew!   *1863:* "And <> knew!"   § **513–41|**   *1863:*
WHICH HE WAS IN THE WAY TO RETRIEVE,   **511–39|**   *1868* §   **517|**   *1840:*
forgotten what   *1863:* forgotten by what   **518|**   *1840:* crept by into such   *1863:* crept

The Count trudged over in a special heat
520　To bid him of God's love dislodge from each
Of Salinguerra's palaces,—a breach
Might yawn else, not so readily to shut,
For who was just arrived at Mantua but
The youngster, sword on thigh and tuft on chin,
525　With tokens for Celano, Ecelin,
Pistore, and the like! Next news,—no whit
Do any of Ferrara's domes befit
His wife of Heinrich's very blood: a band
Of foreigners assemble, understand
530　Garden-constructing, level and surround,
Build up and bury in. A last news crowned
The consternation: since his infant's birth,
He only waits they end his wondrous girth
Of trees that link San Pietro with Tomà,
535　To visit Mantua. When the Podestà
Ecelin, at Vicenza, called his friend
Taurello thither, what could be their end
But to restore the Ghibellins' late Head,
The Kaiser helping? He with most to dread
540　From vengeance and reprisal, Azzo, there
With Boniface beforehand, as aware
Of plots in progress, gave alarm, expelled
Both plotters: but the Guelfs in triumph yelled
Too hastily. The burning and the flight,
545　And how Taurello, occupied that night
With Ecelin, lost wife and son, I told:

at first to such   519|　1840: Over the Count trudged in　1863: The Count trudged over
in   521|　1840: Of <> Palaces; a　1863: palaces,—a   522|　1840: else not　1863:
else, not   524|　1840: sword to thigh, tuft upon chin,　1863: sword on thigh, and tuft
on chin,   526|　1840: Pistore and <> news: no　1868: Pistore, and <> news,—no
1868: Pistore, and   532|　1840: birth　1863: birth,   534|　1840: with Tomà
1863: with Tomà,   535|　1840: visit us. When, as its Podestà　1863: visit Mantua.
When the Podestà   535–40|　1863: Podestà / Ecelin, at Vicenza, called his friend /
Taurello thither, what could be their end / But to restore the Ghibellins' late Head, / The
Kaiser helping? He with most to dread / From   540|　1840: Regaled him at Vicenza,
Este, there　1863: From vengeance and reprisal, Azzo, there   541|　1840: beforehand,
each aware　1863: beforehand, as aware　§ 542–70|　1863: WHEN A FRESH CALAMITY
DESTROYED ALL.   540–68|　1868 §   543|　1840: A party which abetted him,
but yelled　1863: Both plotters: but the Guelfs in triumph yelled   546|　1840: son,

—Not how he bore the blow, retained his hold,
Got friends safe through, left enemies the worst
O' the fray, and hardly seemed to care at first:
550 But afterward men heard not constantly
Of Salinguerra's House so sure to be!
Though Azzo simply gained by the event
A shifting of his plagues—the first, content
To fall behind the second and estrange
555 So far his nature, suffer such a change
That in Romano sought he wife and child,
And for Romano's sake seemed reconciled
To losing individual life, which shrunk
As the other prospered—mortised in his trunk;
560 Like a dwarf palm which wanton Arabs foil
Of bearing its own proper wine and oil,
By grafting into it the stranger-vine,
Which sucks its heart out, sly and serpentine,
Till forth one vine-palm feathers to the root,
565 And red drops moisten the insipid fruit.
Once Adelaide set on,—the subtle mate
Of the weak soldier, urged to emulate
The Church's valiant women deed for deed,
And paragon her namesake, win the meed
570 O' the great Matilda,—soon they overbore
The rest of Lombardy,—not as before

were told   *1863:* son, I told   ⁵⁴⁹| *1840:* first—   *1888:* first: ⁵⁵⁰| *1840:*
afterward you heard   *1863:* afterward men heard   ⁵⁵³| *1840:* plagues—this one
content   *1863:* plagues—the first, content   ⁵⁵⁴| *1840:* the other and estrange,   *1863:*
the second and estrange   ⁵⁵⁵| *1840:* You will not say, his nature, but so change   *1863:*
So far his nature, suffer such a change   ⁵⁵⁶| *1868:* child   *1888:* child,
⁵⁵⁷| *1840:* sake was reconciled   *1863:* sake seemed reconciled   ⁵⁵⁸| *1840:* life, deep
sunk,   *1863:* life, which shrunk   ⁵⁵⁹| *1840:* A very pollard mortised in a trunk   *1863:*
As the other prospered—mortised in his trunk;   ⁵⁶⁰| *1840:* Which Arabs out of
wantonness contrive   *1863:* Like a dwarf palm which wanton Arabs foil   ⁵⁶¹| *1840:*
Shall dwindle that the alien stock may thrive   *1863:* Of bearing its own proper wine and
oil,   ⁵⁶¹⁻⁶⁴| *1863:* oil, / By grafting into it the stranger-vine, / Which sucks its heart
out, sly and serpentine, / Till   ⁵⁶⁴| *1840:* forth that vine-palm <> root   *1863:* forth
one vine-palm <> root,   ⁵⁶⁶| *1840:* Once set on Adelaide, the   *1863:* Once Adelaide
set on,—the   ⁵⁶⁷| *1840:* And wholly at his beck, to   *1863:* Of the weak soldier, urged
to   ⁵⁶⁸| *1840:* Churches   *1863:* Church's   ⁵⁶⁹| *1840:* To paragon   *1863:* And
paragon   ⁵⁷⁰| *1840:* Of its Matilda,—and they   *1863:* O' the great Matilda,—soon
they § ⁵⁷¹⁻⁹⁸| *1863:* HE SANK INTO A SECONDARY PERSONAGE,
⁵⁶⁹⁻⁹⁷| *1868* §   ⁵⁷¹| *1840:* of Lombardy—not   *1863:* of Lombardy,—not

By an instinctive truculence, but patched
The Kaiser's strategy until it matched
The Pontiff's, sought old ends by novel means.
575 "Only, why is it Salinguerra screens
Himself behind Romano?—him we bade
Enjoy our shine i' the front, not seek the shade!"
—Asked Heinrich, somewhat of the tardiest
To comprehend. Nor Philip acquiesced
580 At once in the arrangement; reasoned, plied
His friend with offers of another bride,
A statelier function—fruitlessly: 'twas plain
Taurello through some weakness must remain
Obscure. And Otho, free to judge of both
585 —Ecelin the unready, harsh and loth,
And this more plausible and facile wight
With every point a-sparkle—chose the right,
Admiring how his predecessors harped
On the wrong man: "thus," quoth he, "wits are warped
590 By outsides!" Carelessly, meanwhile, his life
Suffered its many turns of peace and strife
In many lands—you hardly could surprise
The man; who shamed Sordello (recognize!)
In this as much beside, that, unconcerned
595 What qualities were natural or earned,
With no ideal of graces, as they came
He took them, singularly well the same—
Speaking the Greek's own language, just because
Your Greek eludes you, leave the least of flaws

574| *1840:* means: *1863:* means. 575| *1840:* Only, Romano Salinguerra screens.
1863: "Only, why is it Salinguerra screens 575–78| *1863:* screens / Himself behind
Romano?—him we bade / Enjoy our shine i' the front, not seek the shade!" / —Asked
578| *1840:* Heinrich was somewhat *1863:*—Asked Heinrich, somewhat 579| *1840:*
comprehend, nor *1863:* comprehend. Nor 582| *1840:* 'tis *1863:* 'twas
583| *1840:* Taurello's somehow one to let remain *1863:* Taurello through some weakness
must remain 584| *1840:* Obscure; and <> both, *1863:* Obscure. And <>
both 589| *1840:* man: thus, quoth he, wits *1863:* man: "thus," quoth he, "wits
590| *1840:* outsides! Carelessly, withal, his *1863:* outsides!" Carelessly, meanwhile,
his 593| *1840:* A man who <> recognise) *1863:* The man;—who <> recognise!)
1868: man; who *1888:* recognize!) 595| *1840:* are *1863:* were
598| *1840:* Speaking a dozen languages because *1863:* Speaking the Greek's own language,
just because § 599–626| *1863:* WITH THE APPROPRIATE GRACES OF SUCH.
598–625| *1868* § 599| *1868:* least to flaws *1888:* least of flaws 600| *1840:*

600 In contracts with him; while, since Arab lore
Holds the stars' secret—take one trouble more
And master it! 'Tis done, and now deter
Who may the Tuscan, once Jove trined for her,
From Friedrich's path!—Friedrich, whose pilgrimage
605 The same man puts aside, whom he'll engage
To leave next year John Brienne in the lurch,
Come to Bassano, see Saint Francis' church
And judge of Guido the Bolognian's piece
Which,—lend Taurello credit,—rivals Greece—
610 Angels, with aureoles like golden quoits
Pitched home, applauding Ecelin's exploits.
For elegance, he strung the angelot,
Made rhymes thereto; for prowess, clove he not
Tiso, last siege, from crest to crupper? Why
615 Detail you thus a varied mastery
But to show how Taurello, on the watch
For men, to read their hearts and thereby catch
Their capabilities and purposes,
Displayed himself so far as displayed these:
620 While our Sordello only cared to know
About men as a means whereby he'd show
Himself, and men had much or little worth
According as they kept in or drew forth
That self; the other's choicest instruments
625 Surmised him shallow.
                        Meantime, malcontents
Dropped off, town after town grew wiser. "How

---

contracts, while, through Arab lore, deter   *1863:* contracts with him; while, since Arab
lore   600–603| *1863:* lore / Holds the stars' secret—take one trouble more / And master
it! 'Tis done, and now deter / Who   604| *1840:* path! Friedrich   *1863:*
path!—Friedrich   607| *1840:* And see Bassano for Saint   *1863:* Come to Bassano, see
Saint   608| *1840:*—Profound on Guido   *1863:* And judge of Guido   609| *1840:*
That, if you lend him credit, rivals   *1863:* Which, lend Taurello credit   *1868:*
Which,—lend <> credit,—rivals   611| *1840:* exploits   *1863:* exploits.
612| *1840:* In Painimrie. He <> angelot;   *1863:* For elegance, he <> angelot,
614| *1840:* why   *1863:* Why   616| *1840:* But that Taurello, ever on   *1863:* But to
show how Taurello, on   621| *1840:* means for him to show   *1863:* means whereby he'd
show   622| *1840:* men were much   *1863:* men had much   624| *1863:* self;
Taurello's choicest   *1868:* self; the other's choicest   625| *1840:* shallow. Meantime
malcontents   *1863:* shallow. ¶ Meantime, malcontents   626| *1840:* wise; how   *1863:*

251

"Change the world's face?" asked people; "as 'tis now
It has been, will be ever: very fine
Subjecting things profane to things divine,
630 In talk! This contumacy will fatigue
The vigilance of Este and the League!
The Ghibellins gain on us!"—as it happed.
Old Azzo and old Boniface, entrapped
By Ponte Alto, both in one month's space
635 Slept at Verona: either left a brace
Of sons—but, three years after, either's pair
Lost Guglielm and Aldobrand its heir:
Azzo remained and Richard—all the stay
Of Este and Saint Boniface, at bay
640 As 'twere. Then, either Ecelin grew old
Or his brain altered—not o' the proper mould
For new appliances—his old palm-stock
Endured no influx of strange strengths. He'd rock
As in a drunkenness, or chuckle low
645 As proud of the completeness of his woe,
Then weep real tears;—now make some mad onslaught
On Este, heedless of the lesson taught
So painfully,—now cringe for peace, sue peace
At price of past gain, bar of fresh increase
650 To the fortunes of Romano. Up at last
Rose Este, down Romano sank as fast.
And men remarked these freaks of peace and war

wiser. "How   § 627-55| 1840: BUT ECELIN, HE SET IN FRONT, FALLING,
626-54| 1868 §   627| 1840: face? said people; as   1863: face?" asked people; "as
629| 1840: divine   1863: divine,   630| 1840: talk: This   1863: talk! this   1868:
This   631| 1840: And the League,   1863: and the League!   632| 1840: Observe!
accordingly, their basement sapped,   1863: The Ghibellins gain on us!"—as it
happed.   633| 1840: Azzo and Boniface were soon entrapped   1863: Old Azzo and old
Boniface, entrapped   634| 1840: By Ponte Alto, and in   1863: By Ponte Alto, both
in   636| 1840: sons—so three   1863: sons—but, three   639| 1840: St.   1863:
Saint   640| 1840: 'twere; when either   1863: 'twere. Then, either   641| 1840:
not the   1863: not of the   1888: o'   642| 1840: palm stock   1863: palm-stock
643| 1840: strengths: he'd   1863: strengths. He'd   646| 1840: weep—real tears!
Now   1863: weep real tears;—now   648| 1840: painfully—now cringe, sue peace, but
peace   1863: painfully,—now cringe for peace, sue peace   649| 1840: of all advantage;
therefore cease   1863: of past gain,—much more, fresh increase   1868: gain, bar of
fresh   650| 1840: The fortunes of Romano! Up   1863: To the <> Romano.
Up   651| 1840: Rose Este and Romano   1863: Rose Este, down Romano
652| 1840: remarked this sort of   1863: remarked these freaks of   653| 1840:

Happened while Salinguerra was afar:
Whence every friend besought him, all in vain,

655 To use his old adherent's wits again.
Not he!—"who had advisers in his sons,
Could plot himself, nor needed any one's
Advice." 'Twas Adelaide's remaining staunch
Prevented his destruction root and branch

660 Forthwith; but when she died, doom fell, for gay
He made alliances, gave lands away
To whom it pleased accept them, and withdrew
For ever from the world. Taurello, who
Was summoned to the convent, then refused

665 A word at the wicket, patience thus abused,
Promptly threw off alike his imbecile
Ally's yoke, and his own frank, foolish smile.
Soon a few movements of the happier sort
Changed matters, put himself in men's report

670 As heretofore; he had to fight, beside,
And that became him ever. So, in pride
And flushing of this kind of second youth,
He dealt a good-will blow. Este in truth
Lay prone—and men remembered, somewhat late,

675 A laughing old outrageous stifled hate
He bore to Este—how it would outbreak
At times spite of disguise, like an earthquake
In sunny weather—as that noted day
When with his hundred friends he tried to slay

Commenced while   1863: Happened while   654| 1840: And every <> him, but in
1863: Whence every <> him, all in   655| 1840: To wait his old adherent, call again
1863: To use his old adherent's wits again.   § 656-84| 1863: SALINGUERRA MUST AGAIN
COME FORWARD,   655-83| 1868 §   656| 1840: Taurello: not he—who had
daughters, sons,   1863: Not he!—"who had advisers in his sons,   658| 1840: Advice,
'Twas   1863: Advice." 'Twas   660| 1840: Forthwith; Goito green above her, gay
1863: Forthwith; but when she died, doom fell, for gay   665| 1840: word,—however
patient, thus   1863: word at the wicket, patience thus   666| 1840: At Este's mercy
through his   1863: Promptly threw off alike his   667| 1840: Ally, was fain dismiss the
foolish smile,   1863: Ally's yoke, and his own frank, foolish smile.   668| 1840: And a
1863: Soon a   671| 1840: ever. So in   1863: ever. So, in   672| 1840: youth   1863:
youth,   673| 1840: blow: Este   1863: blow. Este   674| 1840: Was prone—and
you remembered   1863: Lay prone—and men remembered   676| 1840: bore that
Este   1863: bore to Este   679| 1840: he offered slay   1863: he tried to slay

680 Azzo before the Kaiser's face: and how,
     On Azzo's calm refusal to allow
     A liegeman's challenge, straight he too was calmed:
     As if his hate could bear to lie embalmed,
     Bricked up, the moody Pharaoh, and survive
685 All intermediate crumblings, to arrive
     At earth's catastrophe—'twas Este's crash
     Not Azzo's he demanded, so, no rash
     Procedure! Este's true antagonist
     Rose out of Ecelin: all voices whist,
690 All eyes were sharpened, wits predicted. He
     'Twas, leaned in the embrasure absently,
     Amused with his own efforts, now, to trace
     With his steel-sheathed forefinger Friedrich's face
     I' the dust: but as the trees waved sere, his smile
695 Deepened, and words expressed its thought erewhile.
          "Ay, fairly housed at last, my old compeer?
     That we should stick together, all the year
     I kept Vicenza!—How old Boniface,
     Old Azzo caught us in its market-place,
700 He by that pillar, I at this,—caught each
     In mid swing, more than fury of his speech,
     Egging the rabble on to disavow
     Allegiance to their Marquis—Bacchus, how
     They boasted! Ecelin must turn their drudge,
705 Nor, if released, will Salinguerra grudge
     Paying arrears of tribute due long since—
     Bacchus! My man could promise then, nor wince:

680| *1840:* how   *1863:* how,   682| *1840:* challenge straight   *1863:* challenge,
straight   683| *1840:* His hate, no doubt, would bear   *1863:* As if his hate could
bear   684| *1840:* moody Pharaoh, to survive   *1863:* moody Pharaoh, and survive
§ 685–713| *1863:*—WHY AND HOW, IS LET OUT IN SOLILOQUY.
684–712| *1868* §   685| *1840:* crumblings, be alive   *1863:* crumblings, and arrive
1888: crumblings, to arrive   687| *1840:* so no   *1863:* so, no   690| *1840:* Each
glance was sharpened, wit   *1863:* All eyes were sharpened, wits   691| *1840:* 'Twas
leaned <> embrasure presently,   *1863:* 'Twas, leaned <> embrasure absently,
694| *1840:* dust: and as   *1863:* dust: but as   696| *1840:* Ay   *1863:* "Ay
697| *1840:* together all   *1863:* together, all   698| *1840:* kept Verona!—How   *1863:*
kept Vicenza!—How   700| *1840:* pillar, I this pillar, each   *1863:* pillar, I at
this,—caught each   702| *1840:* Egging our rabble   *1863:* Egging the rabble
703| *1840:* to the Marquis   *1863:* to their Marquis   704| *1840:* They caught us!
Ecelin <> drudge;   *1863:* They boasted! Ecelin <> drudge,   707| *1840:* man, could

The bones-and-muscles! Sound of wind and limb,
Spoke he the set excuse I framed for him:
710 And now he sits me, slavering and mute,
Intent on chafing each starved purple foot
Benumbed past aching with the altar slab:
Will no vein throb there when some monk shall blab
Spitefully to the circle of bald scalps,
715 'Friedrich's affirmed to be our side the Alps'
—Eh, brother Lactance, brother Anaclet?
Sworn to abjure the world, its fume and fret,
God's own now? Drop the dormitory bar,
Enfold the scanty grey serge scapular
720 Twice o'er the cowl to muffle memories out!
So! But the midnight whisper turns a shout,
Eyes wink, mouths open, pulses circulate
In the stone walls: the past, the world you hate
Is with you, ambush, open field—or see
725 The surging flame—we fire Vicenza—glee!
Follow, let Pilio and Bernardo chafe!
Bring up the Mantuans—through San Biagio—safe!
Ah, the mad people waken? Ah, they writhe
And reach us? If they block the gate? No tithe
730 Can pass—keep back, you Bassanese! The edge,
Use the edge—shear, thrust, hew, melt down the wedge,
Let out the black of those black upturned eyes!
Hell—are they sprinkling fire too? The blood fries
And hisses on your brass gloves as they tear
735 Those upturned faces choking with despair.
Brave! Slidder through the reeking gate! 'How now?

<> wince,   *1868:* man could   *1888:* wince   ⁷⁰⁸| *1840:* sound   *1868:* Sound
⁷⁰⁹| *1840:* him;   *1863:* him: ⁷¹²| *1840:* slab—   *1888:* slab: § ⁷¹⁴⁻⁴⁰| *1863:*
ECELIN, HE DID ALL FOR, IS A MONK NOW,   ⁷¹³⁻⁴⁰| *1868* §   ⁷¹⁴| *1840:*
scalps   *1863:* scalps,   ⁷¹⁵| *1840:* "Friedrich's <> Alps"   *1863:* 'Friedrich's <>
Alps'   ⁷¹⁷| *1840:* world and the world's fret,   *1863:* world, its fume and fret,
⁷¹⁸| *1840:* drop   *1863:* Drop   ⁷²⁰| *1840:* out—   *1868:* out!   ⁷²¹| *1840:* but
1868: But   ⁷²³| *1840:* Past   *1863:* past   ⁷²⁵| *1840:* flame—they fire   *1863:*
flame—we fire   ⁷²⁶| *1840:* and Bernardi chafe—   *1863:* and Bernardo chafe—
1868: chafe!   ⁷²⁹| *1840:* reach you? if <> gate—no   *1863:* reach us? if   *1868:* gate?
No   *1888:* If   ⁷³⁰| *1840:* back you <> the   *1863:* back, you   *1868:* The
⁷³³| *1840:* the   *1868:* The   ⁷³⁶| *1840:* gate—how now!   *1863:* gate—'how now?

255

You six had charge of her?' And then the vow
Comes, and the foam spirts, hair's plucked, till one shriek
(I hear it) and you fling—you cannot speak—
740 Your gold-flowered basnet to a man who haled
The Adelaide he dared scarce view unveiled
This morn, naked across the fire: how crown
The archer that exhausted lays you down
Your infant, smiling at the flame, and dies?
745 While one, while mine . . .

                            "Bacchus! I think there lies
More than one corpse there" (and he paced the room)
—Another cinder somewhere: 'twas my doom
Beside, my doom! If Adelaide is dead,
I live the same, this Azzo lives instead
750 Of that to me, and we pull, any how,
Este into a heap: the matter's now
At the true juncture slipping us so oft.
Ay, Heinrich died and Otho, please you, doffed
His crown at such a juncture! Still, if holds
755 Our Friedrich's purpose, if this chain enfolds
The neck of . . . who but this same Ecelin
That must recoil when the best days begin!
Recoil? that's nought; if the recoiler leaves
His name for me to fight with, no one grieves:
760 But he must interfere, forsooth, unlock
His cloister to become my stumbling-block
Just as of old! Ay, ay, there 'tis again—
The land's inevitable Head—explain
The reverences that subject us! Count
765 These Ecelins now! Not to say as fount,
Originating power of thought,—from twelve

1868: gate! 'How   737| *1840:* her? And   *1863:* her?' And   § 741–68| *1863:* JUST
WHEN THE PRIZE AWAITS SOMEBODY §   746| *1840:* there (and   *1863:* there"
(and   747| *1840:* somewhere—'twas   *1863:* "—Another   *1868:* somewhere:
'twas   748| *1840:* doom: if <> dead   *1863:* doom! If   *1868:* dead,   749| *1840:*
I am the   *1868:* I live the   750| *1840:* pull any how   *1863:* pull, any how,
751| *1840:* heap—the   *1868:* heap: the   752| *1840:* oft;   *1863:* oft.   754| *1840:*
juncture: let but hold   *1863:* juncture! still, if hold   *1868:* Still
755| *1840:* purpose, let this   *1863:* purpose, if this   756| *1840:* same Ecelin?   *1863:*
same Ecelin   757| *1840:* begin—   *1863:* begin!   758| *1840:* nought; so the
1863: nought; if the   759| *1840:* grieves!   *1868:* grieves: 765| *1840:* not   *1863:*
Not   766| *1840:* thought, from   *1863:* thought,—from   767| *1840:* delve

That drop i' the trenches they joined hands to delve,
Six shall surpass him, but . . . why men must twine
Somehow with something! Ecelin's a fine
770 Clear name! 'Twere simpler, doubtless, twine with me
At once: our cloistered friend's capacity
Was of a sort! I had to share myself
In fifty portions, like an o'ertasked elf
That's forced illume in fifty points the vast
775 Rare vapour he's environed by. At last
My strengths, though sorely frittered, e'en converge
And crown . . . no, Bacchus, they have yet to urge
The man be crowned!
              "That aloe, an he durst,
Would climb! Just such a bloated sprawler first
780 I noted in Messina's castle-court
The day I came, when Heinrich asked in sport
If I would pledge my faith to win him back
His right in Lombardy: 'for, once bid pack
Marauders,' he continued, 'in my stead
785 You rule, Taurello!' and upon this head
Laid the silk glove of Constance—I see her
Too, mantled head to foot in miniver,
Retrude following!
           "I am absolved
From further toil: the empery devolved
790 On me, 'twas Tito's word: I have to lay
For once my plan, pursue my plan my way,
Prompt nobody, and render an account
Taurello to Taurello! Nay, I mount
To Friedrich: he conceives the post I kept,
795 —Who did true service, able or inept,

1863: delve,   768| 1840: why, men   1888: why men § 769-95| 1863:—HIMSELF, IF
IT WERE ONLY WORTH WHILE, §   769| 1863: Ecelin's   1868: Ecelin's
775| 1840: by: at   1863: by. At   777| 1840: crown—no   1863: crown . . . no
779| 1840: just 1868: Just   780| 1840: castle court   1863: castle-court
781| 1840: came, and Heinrich   1863: came, when Heinrich   783| 1840: in
Lombardy; for 1863: in Lombardy: 'for   784| 1840: Marauders, he continued, in
1863: Marauders', he continued, 'in   785| 1840: rule, Taurello! and   1863: rule,
Taurello!' and   790| 1840: word: and think, to   1863: word: I have to
793| 1840: nay 1868: Nay   794| 1840: To Friedrich—he   1868: To Friedrich:
he   795| 1840: Who 1868:—Who § 796-824| 1863: AS IT MAY BE—BUT ALSO, AS

Who's worthy guerdon, Ecelin or I.
Me guerdoned, counsel follows: would he vie
With the Pope really? Azzo, Boniface
Compose a right-arm Hohenstauffen's race
800 Must break ere govern Lombardy. I point
How easy 'twere to twist, once out of joint,
The socket from the bone: my Azzo's stare
Meanwhile! for I, this idle strap to wear,
Shall—fret myself abundantly, what end
805 To serve? There's left me twenty years to spend
—How better than my old way? Had I one
Who laboured to o'erthrow my work—a son
Hatching with Azzo superb treachery,
To root my pines up and then poison me,
810 Suppose—'twere worth while frustrate that! Beside
Another life's ordained me: the world's tide
Rolls, and what hope of parting from the press
Of waves, a single wave through weariness
Gently lifted aside, laid upon shore?
815 My life must be lived out in foam and roar,
No question. Fifty years the province held
Taurello; troubles raised, and troubles quelled,
He in the midst—who leaves this quaint stone place,
These trees a year or two, then not a trace
820 Of him! How obtain hold, fetter men's tongues
Like this poor minstrel with the foolish songs—
To which, despite our bustle, he is linked?
—Flowers one may teaze, that never grow extinct.
Ay, that patch, surely, green as ever, where
825 I set Her Moorish lentisk, by the stair,
To overawe the aloes; and we trod
Those flowers, how call you such?—into the sod;

<hr>

IT MAY NOT BE §   ⁷⁹⁶| *1840:* or I: *1863:* or I.   ⁷⁹⁷| *1840:* follows; would
1868: follows: would   ⁸⁰⁰| *1840:* govern Lombardy; I   *1863:* govern Lombardy.
I   ⁸⁰²| *1840:* bone; my   *1863:* bone:—my   *1888:* bone: my   ⁸¹⁰| *1863:* that!
Beside,   ⁸¹³| *1888:* though   ⁸¹⁴| *1840:* That's gently led aside   *1863:* Gently
lifted aside   ⁸¹⁹| *1840:* Those trees <> then, not   *1863:* These trees   *1868:* then
not   ⁸²¹| *1840:* Like that Sordello with his foolish   *1863:* Like this poor minstrel with
the foolish   ⁸²³| *1840:* never seem extinct;   *1863:* never grow extinct.
§ 825–51| *1863:*— THE SUPPOSITION HE MOST INCLINES TO; §   ⁸²⁶| *1840:*
aloes—and   *1863:* aloes; and   ⁸²⁷| *1840:* such? into   *1863:* such?—into

A stately foreigner—a world of pain
To make it thrive, arrest rough winds—all vain!
830 It would decline; these would not be destroyed:
And now, where is it? where can you avoid
The flowers? I frighten children twenty years
Longer!—which way, too, Ecelin appears
To thwart me, for his son's besotted youth
835 Gives promise of the proper tiger-tooth:
They feel it at Vicenza! Fate, fate, fate,
My fine Taurello! Go you, promulgate
Friedrich's decree, and here's shall aggrandise
Young Ecelin—your Prefect's badge! a prize
840 Too precious, certainly.

               How now? Compete
With my old comrade? shuffle from their seat
His children? Paltry dealing! Don't I know
Ecelin? now, I think, and years ago!
What's changed—the weakness? did not I compound
845 For that, and undertake to keep him sound
Despite it? Here's Taurello hankering
After a boy's preferment—this plaything
To carry, Bacchus!" And he laughed.

                      Remark
Why schemes wherein cold-blooded men embark
850 Prosper, when your enthusiastic sort
Fail: while these last are ever stopping short—
(So much they should—so little they can do!)
The careless tribe see nothing to pursue
If they desist; meantime their scheme succeeds.

828| *1840:* foreigner—and worlds *1863:* foreigner—a world 830| *1840:* decline—these <> destroyed— *1863:* decline; these <> destroyed: 831| *1840:* it—where *1863:* it? where 835| *1840:* tiger-tooth, *1863:* tiger-tooth: 836| *1840:* They prattle, at *1863:* They feel it at 837| *1840:* go *1868:* Go 839| *1840:* Young Ecelin—our Prefect's *1863:* Young Ecelin—your Prefect's 842| *1840:* don't *1863:* Don't 845| *1840:* undertake preserve him *1863:* undertake to keep him 846| *1840:* it? Say Taurello's *1863:* it? Here's Taurello 847| *1840:* After the boy's <> play-thing *1863:* After a boy's <> plaything 848| *1840:* carry, Bacchus! And *1863:* carry, Bacchus!" And 851| *1840:* Fails: for these *1863:* Fail: while these § 852–80| *1863:* SORDELLO, TAUGHT WHAT GHIBELLINS ARE, § 852| *1840:* (Much to be done—so *1863:* (So much they should—so 854| *1840:* Should they *1863:* If they 856| *1840:* so he turned,

855   Thoughts were caprices in the course of deeds
      Methodic with Taurello; so, he turned,—
      Enough amused by fancies fairly earned
      Of Este's horror-struck submitted neck,
      And Richard, the cowed braggart, at his beck,—
860 To his own petty but immediate doubt
      If he could pacify the League without
      Conceding Richard; just to this was brought
      That interval of vain discursive thought!
      As, shall I say, some Ethiop, past pursuit
865 Of all enslavers, dips a shackled foot
      Burnt to the blood, into the drowsy black
      Enormous watercourse which guides him back
      To his own tribe again, where he is king;
      And laughs because he guesses, numbering
870 The yellower poison-wattles on the pouch
      Of the first lizard wrested from its couch
      Under the slime (whose skin, the while, he strips
      To cure his nostril with, and festered lips,
      And eyeballs bloodshot through the desert-blast)
875 That he has reached its boundary, at last
      May breathe;—thinks o'er enchantments of the South
      Sovereign to plague his enemies, their mouth,
      Eyes, nails, and hair; but, these enchantments tried
      In fancy, puts them soberly aside
880 For truth, projects a cool return with friends,
      The likelihood of winning mere amends
      Ere long; thinks that, takes comfort silently,
      Then, from the river's brink, his wrongs and he,
      Hugging revenge close to their hearts, are soon
885 Off-striding for the Mountains of the Moon.
      Midnight: the watcher nodded on his spear,

1863: so, he   *1888:* turned,—   859| *1840:* And Boniface completely at his beck,
1863: And Richard, the cowed braggart, at his beck,—   865| *1840:* foot,   *1863:*
foot   867| *1840:* Enormous water current, his sole track   *1863:* Enormous watercourse
which guides him back   868| *1840:* King;   *1863:* king;   874| *1840:* desert
blast)   *1888:* desert-blast)   877| *1840:* mouth   *1863:* mouth,   878| *1840:* And
nails,   *1863:* Eyes, nails   880| *1840:* truth, cool projects, a return   *1863:* truth,
projects a cool return   881| *1840:* winning wild amends   *1863:* winning mere
amends   883| *1840:* And from <> brink his   *1863:* Then, from <> brink, his

Since clouds dispersing left a passage clear
For any meagre and discoloured moon
To venture forth; and such was peering soon
890　Above the harassed city—her close lanes
Closer, not half so tapering her fanes,
As though she shrunk into herself to keep
What little life was saved, more safely. Heap
By heap the watch-fires mouldered, and beside
895　The blackest spoke Sordello and replied
Palma with none to listen. " 'Tis your cause:
What makes a Ghibellin? There should be laws—
(Remember how my youth escaped! I trust
To you for manhood, Palma! tell me just
900　As any child)—there must be laws at work
Explaining this. Assure me, good may lurk
Under the bad,—my multitude has part
In your designs, their welfare is at heart
With Salinguerra, to their interest
905　Refer the deeds he dwelt on,—so divest
Our conference of much that scared me. Why
Affect that heartless tone to Tito? I
Esteemed myself, yes, in my inmost mind
This morn, a recreant to my race—mankind
910　O'erlooked till now: why boast my spirit's force,
—Such force denied its object? why divorce
These, then admire my spirit's flight the same
As though it bore up, helped some half-orbed flame
Else quenched in the dead void, to living space?
915　That orb cast off to chaos and disgrace,

887|　*1840:* clear,　*1888:* clear　　　888|　*1840:* If any　*1863:* For any　　　889|　*1840:*
Should venture　*1863:* To venture　　　893|　*1840:* saved more　*1863:* saved, more
896|　*1840:* listen. 'Tis your Cause—　*1863:* listen. " 'Tis your Cause:　*1888:* cause:
899|　*1840:* manhood, Palma; tell　*1888:* manhood, Palma! tell　　　900|　*1840:*
child)—laws secretly at work　*1863:* child)—there must be laws at work　　　901|　*1840:*
me good　*1863:* me, good　　　902|　*1840:* bad; my　*1863:* bad,—my　　　905|　*1840:*
on—so　*1863:* on,—so　　　906|　*1840:* me: why　*1863:* me. Why　　　909|　*1840:* to that
wide mankind　*1863:* to my race—mankind　§ 910-36|　*1863:* AND WHAT GUELFS,
APPROVES OF NEITHER. §　　　911|　*1840:*—That force　*1863:*—Such force
912|　*1840:* same,　*1863:* same　　　913|　*1840:* bore a burden, which could tame　*1863:*
bore up, helped some half-orbed flame　　　914|　*1840:* No pinion, from dead void to
1863: Else quenched in the dead void, to　　　915|　*1840:*—That orb consigned to　*1863:*

Why vaunt so much my unencumbered dance,
Making a feat's facilities enhance
Its marvel? But I front Taurello, one
Of happier fate, and all I should have done,
920 He does; the people's good being paramount
With him, their progress may perhaps account
For his abiding still; whereas you heard
The talk with Tito—the excuse preferred
For burning those five hostages,—and broached
925 By way of blind, as you and I approached,
I do believe."

               She spoke: then he, "My thought
Plainlier expressed! All to your profit—nought
Meantime of these, of conquests to achieve
For them, of wretchedness he might relieve
930 While profiting your party. Azzo, too,
Supports a cause: what cause? Do Guelfs pursue
Their ends by means like yours, or better?"

                              When
The Guelfs were proved alike, men weighed with men,
And deed with deed, blaze, blood, with blood and blaze,
935 Morn broke: "Once more, Sordello, meet its gaze
Proudly—the people's charge against thee fails
In every point, while either party quails!
These are the busy ones: be silent thou!

---

orb cast off to   *1868:* That   ⁹¹⁶| *1840:* vaunt complacently my frantic dance,   *1863:*
vaunt so much my unencumbered dance,   ⁹¹⁸| *1840:* The marvel   *1863:* Its
marvel   ⁹¹⁹| *1840:* and what I < > done   *1863:* and all I < > done,   ⁹²⁰| *1840:*
the multitude aye paramount   *1863:* the people's good being paramount   ⁹²¹| *1840:*
him, its making progress may account   *1863:* him, their progress may perhaps
account   ⁹²²| *1840:* still: when . . . but you   *1863:* still: whereas you   *1888:* still;
whereas   ⁹²³| *1840:* His talk   *1863:* The talk   ⁹²⁴| *1840:* hostages—and
1863: hostages,—and   ⁹²⁶| *1840:* believe. / She < > he, My   *1863:* believe." / She,
"My   ⁹²⁷| *1840:* Plainer expressed! All Friedrich's profit   *1863:* Plainlier expressed!
All to your profit   ⁹²⁸| *1840:* Of these meantime, of   *1863:* Meantime of these,
of   ⁹²⁹| *1840:* of wretchednesses to relieve   *1863:* of wretchedness he might
relieve   ⁹³⁰| *1840:* profiting that Friedrich. Azzo   *1863:* profiting your party.
Azzo   ⁹³¹| *1840:* what is it? Guelfs   *1863:* what cause? Do Guelfs   ⁹³²| *1840:*
better? / When   *1863:* better?" / When   ⁹³³| *1840:* were shown alike, men ranged
with   *1863:* were proved alike, men weighed with   ⁹³⁵| *1840:* broke: once   *1863:*
broke: "Once   § ⁹³⁷⁻⁶⁴| *1863:* HAVE MEN A CAUSE DISTINCT FROM BOTH? §
⁹³⁸| *1840:* ones—be   *1868:* ones: be   ⁹⁴¹| *1840:* same method; whoso   *1863:* same

262

Two parties take the world up, and allow
940 No third, yet have one principle, subsist
By the same injustice; whoso shall enlist
With either, ranks with man's inveterate foes.
So there is one less quarrel to compose:
The Guelf, the Ghibellin may be to curse—
945 I have done nothing, but both sides do worse
Than nothing. Nay, to me, forgotten, reft
Of insight, lapped by trees and flowers, was left
The notion of a service—ha? What lured
Me here, what mighty aim was I assured
950 Must move Taurello? What if there remained
A cause, intact, distinct from these, ordained
For me, its true discoverer?"

                      Some one pressed
Before them here, a watcher, to suggest
The subject for a ballad: "They must know
955 The tale of the dead worthy, long ago
Consul of Rome—that's long ago for us,
Minstrels and bowmen, idly squabbling thus
In the world's corner—but too late no doubt,
For the brave time he sought to bring about.
960 —Not know Crescentius Nomentanus?" Then
He cast about for terms to tell him, when
Sordello disavowed it, how they used
Whenever their Superior introduced
A novice to the Brotherhood—("for I
965 Was just a brown-sleeve brother, merrily
Appointed too," quoth he, "till Innocent

---

injustice; whoso   ⁹⁴⁴| *1840:* 'Twixt us: the Guelf's, the Ghibellin's to   *1863:* The
Guelf, the Ghibellin may be to   ⁹⁴⁶| *1840:* nothing; nay to   *1863:* nothing. Nay,
to   ⁹⁵⁰| *1840:* Moved Salinguerra? If a Cause remained   *1863:* Must move Taurello?
What if there remained   ⁹⁵¹| *1840:* Intact, distinct from these, and fate ordained,
1863: A Cause, intact <> these, ordained,   *1868:* cause <> ordained   ⁹⁵²| *1840:* For
all the past, that Cause for me? ¶ One pressed   *1863:* For me, its true discoverer?" ¶ Some one
pressed   ⁹⁵⁴| *1840:* ballad: he must   *1863:* ballad: "They must   ⁹⁵⁸| *1840:*
corners <> late, no   *1863:* corner   *1888:* late no   ⁹⁵⁹| *1840:* about   *1863:*
about.   ⁹⁶⁰| *1840:* know Crescentius Nomentanus? Then   *1863:* know Crescentius
Nomentanus?" Then   ⁹⁶⁴| *1840:* the Brotherhood (for   *1863:* the
Brotherhood—("for   § ^{965–93}| *1863:* WHO WAS THE FAMED ROMAN
CRESCENTIUS? §   ⁹⁶⁶| *1840:* too, quoth he, till   *1863:* too," quoth he, "till

Bade me relinquish, to my small content,
My wife or my brown sleeves")—some brother spoke
Ere nocturns of Crescentius, to revoke
970 The edict issued, after his demise,
Which blotted fame alike and effigies,
All out except a floating power, a name
Including, tending to produce the same
Great act. Rome, dead, forgotten, lived at least
975 Within that brain, though to a vulgar priest
And a vile stranger,—two not worth a slave
Of Rome's, Pope John, King Otho,—fortune gave
The rule there: so, Crescentius, haply dressed
In white, called Roman Consul for a jest,
980 Taking the people at their word, forth stepped
As upon Brutus' heel, nor ever kept
Rome waiting,—stood erect, and from his brain
Gave Rome out on its ancient place again,
Ay, bade proceed with Brutus' Rome, Kings styled
985 Themselves mere citizens of, and, beguiled
Into great thoughts thereby, would choose the gem
Out of a lapfull, spoil their diadem
—The Senate's cypher was so hard to scratch!
He flashes like a phanal, all men catch
990 The flame, Rome's just accomplished! when returned
Otho, with John, the Consul's step had spurned,
And Hugo Lord of Este, to redress

968| *1840:* sleeves) out some one spoke   *1863:* sleeves")—some brother spoke
970| *1840:* issued after his demise   *1863:* issued, after his demise,   971| *1840:* That
blotted memory, and   *1863:* Which blotted fame alike and   975| *1840:* that man,
though   *1863:* that brain, though   976| *1840:* stranger, fit to be a   *1863:*
stranger,—two not worth a   977| *1840:* Of Rome's, Pope John, King Otho, fortune
1863: Of Rome's, Pope John, King Otho,—fortune   978| *1840:* there: but, Crescentius
<> drest   *1863:* there: so, Crescentius   *1868:* dressed   980| *1840:* stept   *1868:*
stepped   982| *1840:* Us waiting; stept he forth and   *1863:* Rome waiting,—stood
erect, and   984| *1840:* with Brutus' Rome kings   *1863:* with Brutus' Rome, kings
1868: Kings   985| *1840:* Themselves the citizens   *1863:* Themselves mere
citizens   986| *1840:* Thereby, were fain select the lustrous gem   *1863:* Into great
thoughts thereby, would choose the gem   988| *1888:* scratch   989| *1840:* phanal,
men too catch   *1863:* phanal, all men catch   990| *1840:* flame, and Rome's
accomplished; when ·   *1863:* flame, Rome's just accomplished! when   991| *1840:* Otho
and John the   *1863:* Otho, with John, the   992| *1840:* With Hugo   *1863:* And Hugo

The wrongs of each. Crescentius in the stress
Of adverse fortune bent. "They crucified
995 Their Consul in the Forum; and abide
E'er since such slaves at Rome, that I—(for I
Was once a brown-sleeve brother, merrily
Appointed)—I had option to keep wife
Or keep brown sleeves, and managed in the strife
1000 Lose both. A song of Rome!"

              And Rome, indeed,
Robed at Goito in fantastic weed,
The Mother-City of his Mantuan days,
Looked an established point of light whence rays
Traversed the world: for, all the clustered homes
1005 Beside of men, seemed bent on being Romes
In their degree; the question was, how each
Should most resemble Rome, clean out of reach.
Nor, of the Two, did either principle
Struggle to change, but to possess Rome,—still
1010 Guelf Rome or Ghibellin Rome.

                 Let Rome advance!
Rome, as she struck Sordello's ignorance—
How could he doubt one moment? Rome's the Cause!
Rome of the Pandects, all the world's new laws—
Of the Capitol, of Castle Angelo;
1015 New structures, that inordinately glow,
Subdued, brought back to harmony, made ripe

§ 994–1020| *1863:* HOW IF, IN THE RE-INTEREGATION OF ROME, §   994| *1840:*
bent. They   *1863:* bent. "They   995| *1840:* the Forum and   *1863:* the Forum, and
1868: the Forum; and   996| *1840:* Such slaves at Rome e'er since, that   *1863:* E'er since
such slaves at Rome, that   1000| *1840:* of Rome! / And   *1863:* of Rome!" / And
1002| *1840:* of those Mantuan   *1863:* of his Mantuan   1004| *1840:* world; and all
1863: world; for, all   1005| *1840:* of men were bent   *1863:* of men, seemed bent
1006| *1840:* was how   *1863:* was, how   1007| *1840:* reach   *1863:* reach.
1008| *1840:* Herself; nor struggled either   *1863:* Nor, of the great Two, either principle,
1888: the Two, did either principle   1009| *1840:* To change what it aspired
possess—Rome, still   *1863:* Struggled to change—but to possess—Rome, still,   *1888:*
change, but to possess Rome,—still   1010| *1840:* For Friedrich or Honorius. / Rome's
the Cause!   *1863:* Guelf Rome or Ghibellin Rome. / Let Rome advance!
1010–13| *1863:* advance! / Rome, as she struck Sordello's ignorance— / How could he doubt
one moment? Rome's the Cause! / Rome   1013| *1840:* The Rome of the old Pandects,
our new   *1863:* Rome of the Pandects, all the world's new   1014| *1840:* The Capitol
turned Castle Angelo   *1863:* Of the Capitol, of Castle Angelo;   1015| *1840:* And
structures that <> glow   *1863:* New structures, that <> glow,   1015–20| *1863:* glow,

By many a relic of the archetype
Extant for wonder; every upstart church
That hoped to leave old temples in the lurch,
1020 Corrected by the Theatre forlorn
That,—as a mundane shell, its world late born,—
Lay and o'ershadowed it. These hints combined,
Rome typifies the scheme to put mankind
Once more in full possession of their rights.
1025 "Let us have Rome again! On me it lights
To build up Rome—on me, the first and last:
For such a future was endured the past!"
And thus, in the grey twilight, forth he sprung
To give his thought consistency among
1030 The very People—let their facts avail
Finish the dream grown from the archer's tale.

BOOK THE FIFTH

Is it the same Sordello in the dusk
As at the dawn?—merely a perished husk
Now, that arose a power fit to build
Up Rome again? The proud conception chilled
5 So soon? Ay, watch that latest dream of thine
—A Rome indebted to no Palatine—

/ Subdued, brought back to harmony, made ripe / By many a relic of the archetype / Extant
for wonder; every upstart church / That hoped to leave old temples in the lurch, / Corrected
§ 1021-31| 1863: HE TYPIFIED THE TRIUMPH OF MANKIND? §   1021| 1840: As
a black mundane <> born   1863: That,—as a mundane <> born,—
1022| 1840:—Verona, that's beside it. These combined,   1863: Lay and o'ershadowed it.
These hints combined,   1023| 1840: We typify the   1863: Rome typifies the
1024| 1840: rights 1863: rights.   1025| 1840: By his sole agency. On   1863: "Let us
have Rome again! On   1026| 1840: up Rome again—me, first   1863: up Rome—on
me, the first   1027| 1840: Future <> Past!   1863: the Past!"   1868: future <>
past!"   1028| 1840: thus in <> twilight forth   1863: thus, in <> twilight,
forth   1030| 1840: The People's self, and let their truth avail   1863: The very
People—let their facts avail
§ 1-22| 1863: MANKIND TRIUMPH OF A SUDDEN? §   2| 1840: dawn? merely
1863: dawn?—merely   3| 1840: power like to   1863: power fit to   6| 1840: no

266

Drop arch by arch, Sordello! Art possessed
Of thy wish now, rewarded for thy quest
To-day among Ferrara's squalid sons?
10 Are this and this and this the shining ones
Meet for the Shining City? Sooth to say,
Your favoured tenantry pursue their way
After a fashion! This companion slips
On the smooth causey, t'other blinkard trips
15 At his mooned sandal. "Leave to lead the brawls
Here i' the atria?" No, friend! He that sprawls
On aught but a stibadium . . . what his dues
Who puts the lustral vase to such an use?
Oh, huddle up the day's disasters! March,
20 Ye runagates, and drop thou, arch by arch,
Rome!
        Yet before they quite disband—a whim—
Study mere shelter, now, for him, and him,
Nay, even the worst,—just house them! Any cave
Suffices: throw out earth! A loophole? Brave!
25 They ask to feel the sun shine, see the grass
Grow, hear the larks sing? Dead art thou, alas,
And I am dead! But here's our son excels
At hurdle-weaving any Scythian, fells
Oak and devises rafters, dreams and shapes
30 His dream into a door-post, just escapes
The mystery of hinges. Lie we both
Perdue another age. The goodly growth
Of brick and stone! Our building-pelt was rough,
But that descendant's garb suits well enough
35 A portico-contriver. Speed the years—

Palatine,   *1868:* no Palatine—   7| *1840:* possest   *1868:* possessed   8| *1840:*
now—rewarded   *1868:* now, rewarded   9| *1840:* sons—   *1868:* sons?
11| *1840:* say   *1863:* say,   12| *1840:* Our favoured   *1863:* Your favoured
15| *1840:* sandal. Leave   *1863:* sandal. "Leave   16| *1840:* atria? No, friend. He
1863: atria?" No, friend! He   17| *1840:* stibadium suffers . . . goose,   *1863:* stibadium
. . what his dues   *1888:* stibadium . . . what   18| *1840:* Puttest our lustral   *1863:* Who
puts the lustral   19| *1840:* disasters—march   *1863:* disasters! March,
22| *1840:* Study a shelter   *1863:* Study mere shelter   § 23–51| *1863:* WHY, THE WORK
SHOULD BE ONE OF AGES, §   23| *1840:* even him, to house them! any   *1863:* even
the worst,—just house them! Any   24| *1840:* Suffices—throw out earth. A   *1863:*
Suffices: throw out earth! A   30| *1840:* That dream   *1863:* His dream

What's time to us? At last, a city rears
Itself! nay, enter—what's the grave to us?
Lo, our forlorn acquaintance carry thus
The head! Successively sewer, forum, cirque—
40   Last age, an aqueduct was counted work,
But now they tire the artificer upon
Blank alabaster, black obsidion,
—Careful, Jove's face be duly fulgurant,
And mother Venus' kiss-creased nipples pant
45   Back into pristine pulpiness, ere fixed
Above the baths. What difference betwixt
This Rome and ours—resemblance what, between
That scurvy dumb-show and this pageant sheen—
These Romans and our rabble? Use thy wit!
50   The work marched: step by step,—a workman fit
Took each, nor too fit,—to one task, one time,—
No leaping o'er the petty to the prime,
When just the substituting osier lithe
For brittle bulrush, sound wood for soft withe,
55   To further loam-and-roughcast-work a stage,—
Exacts an architect, exacts an age:
No tables of the Mauritanian tree
For men whose maple log's their luxury!
That way was Rome built. "Better" (say you) "merge
60   At once all workmen in the demiurge,
All epochs in a lifetime, every task

36| *1840:* us? and lo, a   *1863:* us? at last, a   *1868:* At   38| *1840:* So our   *1863:* Lo,
our   39| *1840:* A head! successively   *1863:* The head! Successively   40| *1840:*
age that aqueduct   *1863:* age, an aqueduct   41| *1840:* And now   *1863:* But
now   42| *1863:* obsidian,   *1868:* obsidion,   43| *1840:*—Careful Jove's
1863:—Careful, Jove's   47| *1840:* ours? Resemblance what between   *1863:*
ours—resemblance what, between   48| *1840:* The scurvy <> and the pageant   *1863:*
That scurvy <> and this pageant   49| *1840:* rabble? Rest thy wit   *1863:* rabble? Use
thy wit!   50| *1840:* And listen: step by   *1863:* The work marched: step by
51| *1840:* With each <> to one's task, one's   *1863:* Took each <> to one task, one
§ 52–79| *1863:* IF PERFORMED EQUALLY AND THOROUGHLY;
52–80| *1868* §   54| *1840:* For bulrushes, and after, wood for withe   *1863:* For brittle
bulrush, sound wood for soft withe,   55| *1840:* loam and roughcast work a stage,
1863: loam-and-roughcast-work a stage,—   56| *1840:* age,—   *1863:* age:
57| *1840:* Nor tables   *1863:* No tables   58| *1840:* maple-log's their luxury,—   *1863:*
luxury!   *1888:* maple log's   59| *1840:* And Rome's accomplished! Better (say you)
merge   *1863:* That way was Rome built. "Better" (say you) "merge   61| *1840:*

In one!" So should the sudden city bask
I' the day—while those we'd feast there, want the knack
Of keeping fresh-chalked gowns from speck and brack,
65 Distinguish not rare peacock from vile swan,
Nor Mareotic juice from Cæcuban.
"Enough of Rome! 'Twas happy to conceive
Rome on a sudden, nor shall fate bereave
Me of that credit: for the rest, her spite
70 Is an old story—serves my folly right
By adding yet another to the dull
List of abortions—things proved beautiful
Could they be done, Sordello cannot do."
He sat upon the terrace, plucked and threw
75 The powdery aloe-cusps away, saw shift
Rome's walls, and drop arch after arch, and drift
Mist-like afar those pillars of all stripe,
Mounds of all majesty. "Thou archetype,
Last of my dreams and loveliest, depart!"
80 And then a low voice wound into his heart:
"Sordello!" (low as some old Pythoness
Conceding to a Lydian King's distress
The cause of his long error—one mistake
Of her past oracle) "Sordello, wake!
85 God has conceded two sights to a man—
One, of men's whole work, time's completed plan,
The other, of the minute's work, man's first
Step to the plan's completeness: what's dispersed
Save hope of that supreme step which, descried

---

life-time, and all tasks *1863:* lifetime, every task   ⁶²| *1840:* one: undoubtedly the city
basks   *1863:* one!" So should the sudden city bask   ⁶³| *1840:* those you'd feast there
want   *1863:* those we'd feast there, want   ⁶⁵| *1840:* not your peacock from your
swan,   *1863:* not rare peacock from vile swan,   ⁶⁶| *1840:* Or Mareotic <>
Cœcuban,   *1863:* Nor Mareotic <> Cœcuban.   *1888:* Cæcuban.   ⁶⁷| *1840:* Nay
sneer . . . enough! 'twas   *1863:* "Enough of Rome! 'Twas   ⁶⁹| *1840:* Us of   *1863:* Me
of   ⁷⁰| *1840:* serves us very right   *1863:* serves my folly right   ⁷¹| *1840:* For
adding   *1863:* By adding   ⁷²| *1840:* of devices—things   *1863:* of
abortions—things   ⁷³| *1840:* do.   *1863:* do."   ⁷⁴| *1840:* sate   *1863:* sat
⁷⁸| *1840:* majesty. Thou   *1863:* majesty. "Thou   ⁷⁹| *1840:* depart.   *1863:* depart!"
§ ^{80–108}| *1863:* AND A MAN CAN BUT DO A MAN'S PORTION.
^{81–109}| *1868* §   ⁸¹| *1840:* Sordello (lower than a Pythoness   *1863:* "Sordello!" (low as
some old Pythoness   ⁸⁴| *1840:* oracle) Sordello   *1863:* oracle) "Sordello

90   Earliest, was meant still to remain untried

Only to give you heart to take your own

Step, and there stay, leaving the rest alone?

Where is the vanity? Why count as one

The first step, with the last step? What is gone

95   Except Rome's aëry magnificence,

That last step you'd take first?—an evidence

You were God: be man now! Let those glances fall!

The basis, the beginning step of all,

Which proves you just a man—is that gone too?

100   Pity to disconcert one versed as you

In fate's ill-nature! but its full extent

Eludes Sordello, even: the veil rent,

Read the black writing—that collective man

Outstrips the individual. Who began

105   The acknowledged greatnesses? Ay, your own art

Shall serve us: put the poet's mimes apart—

Close with the poet's self, and lo, a dim

Yet too plain form divides itself from him!

Alcamo's song enmeshes the lulled Isle,

110   Woven into the echoes left erewhile

By Nina, one soft web of song: no more

Turning his name, then, flower-like o'er and o'er!

An elder poet in the younger's place;

Nina's the strength, but Alcamo's the grace:

84–93| *1840:* wake! / Where *1863:* § adds 85–92 §   92| *1863:* stay—leaving *1888:* stay, leaving   93| *1840:* count you, one *1863:* count as one   94| *1840:* step with *1863:* step, with   95| *1840:* Except that aëry magnificence— *1863:* Except Rome's aëry magnificence,   96| *1840:* you took first? an *1863:* you'd take first?—an   97| *1840:* You were . . . no matter. Let *1863:* You were God: be man now! Let   98| *1840:* This basis, this beginning *1863:* The basis, the beginning   99| *1840:* you one of us, is this gone *1863:* you just a man—is that gone   101| *1840:* ill-nature, but *1863:* ill-nature! but   102| *1840:* veil's *1863:* veil   104| *1840:* individual! Who *1888:* individual. Who   105| *1840:* The greatnesses you know?—ay *1863:* The acknowledged greatnesses? Ay   107| *1840:* poet—closer—what? a *1863:* poet's self, and lo, a   108| *1840:* Too plain form separates itself from him? *1863:* Yet too plain form divides itself from him! § 109–37| *1863:* THE LAST OF EACH SERIES OF WORKMEN 110–138| *1868* §   109| *1840:* Alcama's *1863:* Alcamo's   111| *1840:* Of Nina's *1863:* By Nina   112| *1840:* name, now, flower-like *1863:* name, then, flower-like   113| *1840:* poet's < > place— *1863:* poet · *1868:* place;   114| *1840:* Take Nina's strength—but lose Alcama's grace? *1863:* Nina's the strength—but Alcamo's the grace: *1868:* strength,

115 Each neutralizes each then! Search your fill;
    You get no whole and perfect Poet—still
    New Ninas, Alcamos, till time's mid-night
    Shrouds all—or better say, the shutting light
    Of a forgotten yesterday. Dissect
120 Every ideal workman—(to reject
    In favour of your fearful ignorance
    The thousand phantasms eager to advance,
    And point you but to those within your reach)—
    Were you the first who brought—(in modern speech)
125 The Multitude to be materialized?
    That loose eternal unrest—who devised
    An apparition i' the midst? The rout
    Was checked, a breathless ring was formed about
    That sudden flower: get round at any risk
130 The gold-rough pointel, silver-blazing disk
    O' the lily! Swords across it! Reign thy reign
    And serve thy frolic service, Charlemagne!
    —The very child of over-joyousness,
    Unfeeling thence, strong therefore: Strength by stress
135 Of Strength comes of that forehead confident,
    Those widened eyes expecting heart's content,
    A calm as out of just-quelled noise; nor swerves
    For doubt, the ample cheek in gracious curves
    Abutting on the upthrust nether lip:
140 He wills, how should he doubt then? Ages slip:

---

but   115| *1840:* then! gaze your   *1863:* then! Search your   116| *1840:* Search
further and the past presents you still   *1863:* You get no whole and perfect
Poet—still   117| *1840:* Alcamas   *1863:* Alcamos   118| *1840:*
Concluding,—better say its evenlight   *1863:* Shrouds all—or better say, the shutting
light   119| *1840:* Of yesterday. You, now, in this respect   *1863:* Of a forgotten
yesterday. Dissect   120| *1840:* Of benefitting people (to   *1863:* Every ideal
workman—(to   121| *1840:* The thousand   *1863:* In favour   122| *1840:* A
thousand   *1863:* The thousand   123| *1840:* Refer you <> reach)   *1863:* And point
you <> reach)—   124| *1840:* who got, to use plain speech,   *1863:* who brought—(in
modern speech)   127| *1840:* midst? the   *1863:* midst? The   128| *1840:* Who
checked, the breathless ring who formed   *1863:* Was checked, a breathless ring was
formed   129| *1840:* flower? Get   *1863:* flower: get   135| *1840:* of a forehead
1863: of that forehead   136| *1840:* Two widened   *1863:* Those widened
137| *1840:* noise, nor   *1863:* noise; nor   § 138–66| *1863:* SUMS UP IN HIMSELF ALL
PREDECESSORS.   139–67| *1868* §   138| *1840:* The ample check for doubt, in
1863: For doubt, the ample check in   139| *1840:* lip—   *1863:* lip: 140| *1840:*

Was it Sordello pried into the work
So far accomplished, and discovered lurk
A company amid the other clans,
Only distinct in priests for castellans
145 And popes for suzerains (their rule confessed
Its rule, their interest its interest,
Living for sake of living—there an end,—
Wrapt in itself, no energy to spend
In making adversaries or allies)—
150 Dived you into its capabilities
And dared create, out of that sect, a soul
Should turn a multitude, already whole,
Into its body? Speak plainer! Is't so sure
God's church lives by a King's investiture?
155 Look to last step! A staggering—a shock—
What's mere sand is demolished, while the rock
Endures: a column of black fiery dust
Blots heaven—that help was prematurely thrust
Aside, perchance!—but air clears, nought's erased
160 Of the true outline. Thus much being firm based,
The other was a scaffold. See him stand
Buttressed upon his mattock, Hildebrand
Of the huge brain-mask welded ply o'er ply
As in a forge; it buries either eye
165 White and extinct, that stupid brow; teeth clenched,
The neck tight-corded, too, the chin deep-trenched,
As if a cloud enveloped him while fought

slip—   *1863:* slip: 142| *1840:* discovering   *1863:* discovered   147| *1840:*
end,   *1863:* end,—   149| *1840:* allies);   *1863:* allies),—   *1888:* allies)—
150| *1840:* Dived he into   *1863:* Dived you into   151| *1840:* create out <> sect a
1863: create, out <> sect, a   152| *1840:* turn the multitude   *1863:* turn a
multitude   153| *1840:* To some account? Speak   *1863:* Into its body? Speak
155| *1840:* step: a staggering   *1863:* step! a staggering   *1868:* step! A staggering
156| *1840:* What's sand shall be demolished, but the   *1863:* What's mere sand is
demolished, while the   157| *1840:* Endures—a   *1863:* Endures: a   158| *1840:*
heaven—woe, woe, 'tis prematurely   *1863:* heaven—that help was prematurely
159| *1840:* Aside, that step!—the air clears—nought's   *1863:* Aside, perchance!—but air
clears, nought's   160| *1840:* outline? Thus much is firm based—   *1863:* outline. Thus
much being firm based,   161| *1840:* scaffold: see you stand   *1863:* scaffold. See him
stand   162| *1840:* mattock Hildebrand   *1863:* mattock, Hildebrand
166| *1840:* neck's   *1863:* neck   § 167–95| *1863:* WE JUST SEE CHARLEMAGNE,

Under its shade, grim prizers, thought with thought
At dead-lock, agonizing he, until
170 The victor thought leap radiant up, and Will,
The slave with folded arms and drooping lids
They fought for, lean forth flame-like as it bids.
Call him no flower—a mandrake of the earth,
Thwarted and dwarfed and blasted in its birth,
175 Rather,—a fruit of suffering's excess,
Thence feeling, therefore stronger: still by stress
Of Strength, work Knowledge! Full three hundred years
Have men to wear away in smiles and tears
Between the two that nearly seemed to touch,
180 Observe you! quit one workman and you clutch
Another, letting both their trains go by—
The actors-out of either's policy,
Heinrich, on this hand, Otho, Barbaross,
Carry the three Imperial crowns across,
185 Aix' Iron, Milan's Silver, and Rome's Gold—
While Alexander, Innocent uphold
On that, each Papal key—but, link on link,
Why is it neither chain betrays a chink?
How coalesce the small and great? Alack,
190 For one thrust forward, fifty such fall back!
Do the popes coupled there help Gregory
Alone? Hark—from the hermit Peter's cry
At Claremont, down to the first serf that says
Friedrich's no liege of his while he delays
195 Getting the Pope's curse off him! The Crusade—

HILDEBRAND, 168–95| _1868_ § 168| _1840:_ Under it all, grim _1863:_ Under
its shade, grim 173| _1840:_—A root, the crippled mandrake _1863:_ Call him no
flower—a mandrake 175| _1840:_ Be certain; fruit _1863:_ Rather, a fruit _1868:_
Rather,—a 176| _1840:_ Whence feeling _1863:_ Thence feeling 178| _1840:_ For
men _1863:_ Have men 179| _1840:_ seem _1868:_ seemed 180| _1840:_ you: quit
<> and we clutch _1863:_ you! quit <> and you clutch 184| _1840:_ May carry the
Imperial _1863:_ Carry the three Imperial 186| _1840:_ As Alexander _1863:_ While
Alexander 187| _1840:_ that the Papal keys—but _1863:_ that, each Papal
key—but 191| _1840:_ The couple there alone help Gregory? _1863:_ Do the popes
coupled there help Gregory 192| _1840:_ Hark <> Peter's thin sad cry _1863:_ Alone?
Hark <> Peter's cry 193| _1840:_ At Claremont, yonder to the serf _1863:_ At

Or trick of breeding Strength by other aid
Than Strength, is safe. Hark—from the wild harangue
Of Vimmercato, to the carroch's clang
Yonder! The League—or trick of turning Strength
200 Against Pernicious Strength, is safe at length.
Yet hark—from Mantuan Albert making cease
The fierce ones, to Saint Francis preaching peace
Yonder! God's Truce—or trick to supersede
The very Use of Strength, is safe. Indeed
205 We trench upon the future. Who is found
To take next step, next age—trail o'er the ground—
Shall I say, gourd-like?—not the flower's display
Nor the root's prowess, but the plenteous way
O' the plant—produced by joy and sorrow, whence
210 Unfeeling and yet feeling, strongest thence?
Knowledge by stress of merely Knowledge? No—
E'en were Sordello ready to forego
His life for this, 'twere overleaping work
Some one has first to do, howe'er it irk,
215 Nor stray a foot's breadth from the beaten road.
Who means to help must still support the load
Hildebrand lifted—'why hast Thou,' he groaned,
'Imposed on me a burthen, Paul had moaned,
And Moses dropped beneath?' Much done—and yet
220 Doubtless that grandest task God ever set

Claremont, down to the first serf § ¹⁹⁶⁻²²⁴| *1863:* IN COMPOSITE WORK THEY END
AND NAME. §   ¹⁹⁶| *1840:* strength *1868:* Strength   ¹⁹⁷| *1840:* strength, is
safe: hark *1863:* safe. Hark *1868:* Strength   ¹⁹⁹| *1840:* strength *1868:*
Strength   ²⁰⁰| *1840:* pernicious strength < > length: *1863:* length. *1868:*
Pernicious Strength   ²⁰¹| *1840:* Albert's *1863:* Albert   ²⁰²| *1840:* St. *1863:*
Saint   ²⁰⁴| *1840:* The use of strength at all, is *1863:* The very use of strength, is
1868: Use of Strength   ²⁰⁵| *1840:* future! Who shall *1863:* Future < > is *1868*
future. Who   ²⁰⁶| *1840:* Next step, next age—trail plenteous o'er the ground *1863:*
To take next step < > trail o'er the ground—   ²⁰⁶⁻⁰⁹| *1840:* ground / Vine-like,
produced   ²⁰⁹| *1840:* Vine-like, produced *1863:* O' the plant—produced
²¹⁰| *1840:* thence: *1863:* thence?   ²¹¹| *1840:* of Knowledge is it? No— *1863:* of
merely Knowledge? No—   ²¹³| *1840:* His work for *1863:* His life for
²¹⁴| *1840:* one must do before, howe'er it irk: *1863:* one has first to do, howe'er it
irk,   ²¹⁵| *1840:* No end's in sight yet of that second road: *1863:* Nor stray a foot's
breadth from the beaten road.   ²¹⁷| *1840:* lifted—why hast Thou, he *1863:*
lifted—'why hast Thou,' he   ²¹⁸| *1840:* Imposed, my God, a thing thy Paul *1863:*
'Imposed on me a burthen, Paul   ²¹⁹| *1840:* Thy Moses failed beneath, on me? and
1863: And Moses dropped beneath?' Much done—and   ²²⁰| *1840:* That grandest of

On man, left much to do: at his arm's wrench,
Charlemagne's scaffold fell; but pillars blench
Merely, start back again—perchance have been
Taken for buttresses: crash every screen,
225 Hammer the tenons better, and engage
A gang about your work, for the next age
Or two, of Knowledge, part by Strength and part
By Knowledge! Then, indeed, perchance may start
Sordello on his race—would time divulge
230 Such secrets! If one step's awry, one bulge
Calls for correction by a step we thought
Got over long since, why, till that is wrought,
No progress! And the scaffold in its turn
Becomes, its service o'er, a thing to spurn.
235 Meanwhile, if your half-dozen years of life
In store dispose you to forego the strife,
Who takes exception? Only bear in mind
Ferrara's reached, Goito's left behind:
As you then were, as half yourself, desist!
240 —The warrior-part of you may, an it list,
Finding real faulchions difficult to poise,
Fling them afar and taste the cream of joys
By wielding such in fancy,—what is bard
Of you may spurn the vehicle that marred
245 Elys so much, and in free fancy glut
His sense, yet write no verses—you have but

the tasks God   *1863:* Doubtless that grandest task God   **221|** *1840:* man left < > do: a
mighty wrench—   *1863:* man, left < > do: at his arm's wrench,   **222|** *1840:* The
scaffold falls—but half the pillars   *1863:* Charlemagne's scaffold fell; but pillars
225–53| *1863:* IF ASSOCIATES TROUBLE YOU, STAND OFF! §   **228|** *1840:* By
Knowledge! then—Ay, then perchance   *1863:* By Knowledge! Then, indeed,
perchance   **229|** *1840:* race—but who'll divulge   *1863:* race—would time
divulge   **230|** *1840:* Time's secrets? lo, a step's awry, a bulge   *1863:* Such secrets! If one
step's awry, one bulge   **231|** *1840:* To be corrected by   *1863:* Calls for correction
by   **232|** *1840:* long ago—till   *1863:* long since, why, till   **233|** *1840:* and that
scaffold   *1863:* and the scaffold   *1868:* And   **235|** *1840:* Meanwhile, your some
half-dozen   *1863:* Meanwhile, if your half-dozen   **236|** *1840:* Longer, dispose < >
strife—   *1863:* In store dispose < > strife,   **237|** *1840:* exception? 'Tis Ferrara,
mind,   *1863:* exception? Only bear in mind,   *1888:* mind   **238|** *1840:* Before us, and
Goito's   *1863:* Ferrara's reached, Goito's   **243|** *1840:* wielding one in   *1863:* wielding
such in   **244|** *1840:* you, may   *1868:* you may   **245|** *1840:* in mere fancy   *1863:*
in free fancy   **246|** *1840:* sense on her free beauties—we have   *1863:* sense, yet write no

To please yourself for law, and once could please
What once appeared yourself, by dreaming these
Rather than doing these, in days gone by.
250 But all is changed the moment you descry
Mankind as half yourself,—then, fancy's trade
Ends once and always: how may half evade
The other half? men are found half of you.
Out of a thousand helps, just one or two
255 Can be accomplished presently: but flinch
From these (as from the faulchion, raised an inch,
Elys, described a couplet) and make proof
Of fancy,—then, while one half lolls aloof
I' the vines, completing Rome to the tip-top—
260 See if, for that, your other half will stop
A tear, begin a smile! The rabble's woes,
Ludicrous in their patience as they chose
To sit about their town and quietly
Be slaughtered,—the poor reckless soldiery,
265 With their ignoble rhymes on Richard, how
'Polt-foot,' sang they, 'was in a pitfall now,'
Cheering each other from the engine-mounts,—
That crippled spawling idiot who recounts
How, lopped of limbs, he lay, stupid as stone,
270 Till the pains crept from out him one by one,
And wriggles round the archers on his head
To earn a morsel of their chestnut bread,—
And Cino, always in the self-same place
Weeping; beside that other wretch's case,

---

verses—you have   247| *1840:* please ourselves for <> and you could   *1863:* please
yourself for <> and once could   248| *1840:* What then appeared yourself by   *1863:*
What once appeared yourself, by   249–252| *1840:* These: now-fancy's trade / Is ended,
mind, nor one half may evade   *1863:* These, in days gone by / But all is changed the moment
you descry / Mankind as half yourself,—then, fancy's trade / Ends once and always: how may
half evade   253| *1840:* half: our friends are half of you: *1863:* half? men are found
half of you.   § 254–82| *1863:*—SHOULD THE NEW SYMPATHIES ALLOW YOU. §
255| *1840:* presently—but   *1863:* presently: but   256| *1840:* faulchion raised   *1863:*
faulchion, raised   257| *1840:* Elys described   *1863:* Elys, described   258| *1840:*
fancy,—and, while   *1863:* fancy,—then, while   259| *1840:* O' the grass completing
1863: I' the vines, completing   260| *1840:* that, the other   *1863:* that, your
other   261| *1840:* smile: that rabble's   *1863:* smile! The rabble's   266| *1840:*
Polt-foot, sang they, was <> now,   *1863:* 'Polt-foot,' sang they, 'was <> now,'
269| *1840:* lopt   *1863:* lopped   272| *1840:* chesnut   *1863:* chestnut
274| *1840:* wretches' case   *1863:* wretch's case,   275| *1840:* ear one   *1863:* ear,

Eyepits to ear, one gangrene since he plied
The engine in his coat of raw sheep's hide
A double watch in the noon sun; and see
Lucchino, beauty, with the favours free,
Trim hacqueton, spruce beard and scented hair,
Campaigning it for the first time—cut there
In two already, boy enough to crawl
For latter orpine round the southern wall,
Tomà, where Richard's kept, because that whore
Marfisa, the fool never saw before,
Sickened for flowers this wearisomest siege:
And Tiso's wife—men liked their pretty liege,
Cared for her least of whims once,—Berta, wed
A twelvemonth gone, and, now poor Tiso's dead,
Delivering herself of his first child
On that chance heap of wet filth, reconciled
To fifty gazers!"—(Here a wind below
Made moody music augural of woe
From the pine barrier)—"What if, now the scene
Draws to a close, yourself have really been
—You, plucking purples in Goito's moss
Like edges of a trabea (not to cross
Your consul-humour) or dry aloe-shafts
For fasces, at Ferrara—he, fate wafts,
This very age, her whole inheritance
Of opportunities? Yet you advance
Upon the last! Since talking is your trade,
There's Salinguerra left you to persuade:
Fail! then"—

        "No—no—which latest chance secure!"

one   **278|** *1840:* favors   *1863:* favours   **279|** *1840:* hacqueton and sprucely
scented   *1863:* hacqueton, spruce beard and scented   **282|** *1840:* Southern   *1863:*
southern   § **283–310|** *1863:* TIME HAVING BEEN LOST, CHOOSE QUICK! §
284| *1840:* Marfisa the <> before   *1863:* Marfisa, the <> before,   **286|** *1840:* Then
Tiso's   *1863:* And Tiso's   **287|** *1840:* once, Berta   *1863:* once,—Berta
291| *1840:* gazers. (Here   *1863:* gazers!"—(Here   **293|** *1840:* barrier)—What   *1863:*
barrier)—"What   **294|** *1840:* a shutting, if yourself have been   *1863:* a close, yourself
have really been   **297|** *1840:* Your consul-feeling) or   *1863:* Your consul-humour)
or   **298|** *1840:* Here at Ferrara—He whom fortune wafts   *1863:* For fasces, at
Ferrara—he, fate wafts,   **299|** *1840:* age her best inheritance   *1863:* age, her whole
inheritance   **300|** *1840:* opportunities? Yet we advance   *1863:* opportunities? Yet you
advance   **302|** *1840:* persuade,   *1863:* persuade: **303|** *1840:* And then— ¶ No
<> secure!   *1863:* Fail! then"— ¶ "No <> secure!"   **304|** *1840:* Leapt <>

Leaped up and cried Sordello: "this made sure,
305 The past were yet redeemable; its work
Was—help the Guelf's, whom I, howe'er it irk,
Thus help!" He shook the foolish aloe-haulm
Out of his doublet, paused, proceeded calm
To the appointed presence. The large head
310 Turned on its socket; "And your spokesman," said
The large voice, "is Elcorte's happy sprout?
Few such"—(so finishing a speech no doubt
Addressed to Palma, silent at his side)
"—My sober councils have diversified.
315 Elcorte's son! good: forward as you may,
Our lady's minstrel with so much to say!"
The hesitating sunset floated back,
Rosily traversed in the wonted track
The chamber, from the lattice o'er the girth
320 Of pines, to the huge eagle blacked in earth
Opposite,—outlined sudden, spur to crest,
That solid Salinguerra, and caressed
Palma's contour; 'twas day looped back night's pall;
Sordello had a chance left spite of all.
325 And much he made of the convincing speech
Meant to compensate for the past and reach
Through his youth's daybreak of unprofit, quite
To his noon's labour, so proceed till night
Leisurely! The great argument to bind
330 Taurello with the Guelf Cause, body and mind,
—Came the consummate rhetoric to that?

Sordello: this   *1863:* cried Sordello: "this   *1868:* Leaped   305| *1840:* The Past is yet redeemable whose work   *1863:* The Past were yet redeemable; its work   *1868:* past   306| *1840:* the Guelfs, and I   *1863:* the Guelfs, whom I   307| *1840:* help! He   *1863:* help!" He   310| *1840:* socket; And < > spokesman, said   *1863:* socket; "And < > spokesman," said   § 311-39| *1863:* HE TAKES HIS FIRST STEP AS A GUELF; §   311| *1840:* voice, is   *1863:* voice, "is   312| *1840:* such (so   *1863:* such"—(so   314| *1840:* Our sober < > diversified: *1863:*—"My sober < > diversified.   *1868:*"—My   315| *1840:* son!—but forward   *1863:* son! good: forward   316| *1840:* say!   *1863:* say!"   318| *1840:* in a single track   *1863:* in the wonted track   320| *1840:* pines to   *1863:* pines, to   321| *1840:* Opposite, outlined   *1863:* Opposite,—outlined   323| *1840:* Day < > Night's   *1863:* day < > night's   326| *1840:* He meant should compensate the Past   *1868:* Meant to compensate for the past   329| *1840:* At leisure! The contrivances to   *1863:* Leisurely! The great argument to   330| *1840:* Taurello body with the Cause and   *1863:* Taurello with the Guelf Cause, body and   331| *1840:*—Was the < > rhetoric just

Yet most Sordello's argument dropped flat
Through his accustomed fault of breaking yoke,
Disjoining him who felt from him who spoke.
335 Was't not a touching incident—so prompt
A rendering the world its just accompt,
Once proved its debtor? Who'd suppose, before
This proof, that he, Goito's god of yore,
At duty's instance could demean himself
340 So memorably, dwindle to a Guelf?
Be sure, in such delicious flattery steeped,
His inmost self at the out-portion peeped,
Thus occupied; then stole a glance at those
Appealed to, curious if her colour rose
345 Or his lip moved, while he discreetly urged
The need of Lombardy becoming purged
At soonest of her barons; the poor part
Abandoned thus, missing the blood at heart
And spirit in brain, unseasonably off
350 Elsewhere! But, though his speech was worthy scoff,
Good-humoured Salinguerra, famed for tact
And tongue, who, careless of his phrase, ne'er lacked
The right phrase, and harangued Honorius dumb
At his accession,—looked as all fell plumb
355 To purpose and himself found interest
In every point his new instructor pressed
—Left playing with the rescript's white wax seal
To scrutinize Sordello head and heel.
He means to yield assent sure? No, alas!
360 All he replied was, "What, it comes to pass
That poesy, sooner than politics,
Makes fade young hair?" To think such speech could fix

---

that? *1863:*—Came the <> rhetoric to that? ³³⁴| *1840:* spoke: *1863:*
spoke. ³³⁶| *1840:* accompt *1863:* accompt, ³³⁷| *1840:* suppose before *1863:*
suppose, before ³³⁸| *1840:* proof that <> God *1863:* proof, that <> god
§ ³⁴⁰⁻⁶⁷| *1863:* BUT TO WILL AND TO DO ARE DIFFERENT:
³⁴⁰⁻⁶⁶| *1868* § ³⁴²| *1840:* peeped *1863:* peeped, ³⁴⁶| *1840:* Lombardy's
1868: Lombardy ³⁴⁸| *1840:* thus missing <> heart, *1863:* thus, missing <>
heart ³⁴⁹| *1840:* Spirit in *1863:* And spirit in ³⁵²| *1840:* That way, who
1863: And tongue, who ³⁵⁴| *1840:* accession, looked *1863:* accession,—looked
³⁵⁵| *1840:* himself took interest *1863:* himself found interest ³⁵⁸| *1840:* heel:
1863: heel. ³⁵⁹| *1840:* Then means he . . . yes, assent sure? Well? Alas? *1863:* He
means to yield assent sure? No, alas! ³⁶⁰| *1840:* He said no more than, So it *1863:* All
he replied was, "What, it ³⁶²| *1840:* hair: to think his speech *1863:* hair?" To think

Taurello!
          Then a flash of bitter truth:
So fantasies could break and fritter youth
365 That he had long ago lost earnestness,
Lost will to work, lost power to even express
The need of working! Earth was turned a grave:
No more occasions now, though he should crave
Just one, in right of superhuman toil,
370 To do what was undone, repair such spoil,
Alter the past—nothing would give the chance!
Not that he was to die; he saw askance
Protract the ignominious years beyond
To dream in—time to hope and time despond,
375 Remember and forget, be sad, rejoice
As saved a trouble; he might, at his choice,
One way or other, idle life out, drop
No few smooth verses by the way—for prop,
A thyrsus, these sad people, all the same,
380 Should pick up, and set store by,—far from blame,
Plant o'er his hearse, convinced his better part
Survived him. "Rather tear men out the heart
O' the truth!"—Sordello muttered, and renewed
His propositions for the Multitude.
385   But Salinguerra, who at this attack
Had thrown great breast and ruffling corslet back
To hear the better, smilingly resumed
His task; beneath, the carroch's warning boomed;

---

such speech   ^{363|} *1840:* flash; he knew the truth: *1863:* flash of bitter truth:
^{364|} *1840:* fantasies shall break   *1863:* fantasies could break   ^{365|} *1840:* has   *1863:*
had   ^{366|} *1840:* power to express *1863:* power to even express   ^{367|} *1840:*
Even the need of working! Ere the grave   *1863:* The need of working! Earth was turned a
grave: § ^{368–96|} *1863:* HE MAY SLEEP ON THE BED HE HAS MADE.
^{367–95|} *1868* §   ^{369|} *1840:* One such in <> toil *1863:* Just one, in <> toil,
^{370|} *1840:* repair his spoil,   *1863:* repair such spoil,   ^{371|} *1840:* the Past—nought
brings again the   *1863:* the Past—nothing would give the   *1868:* past   ^{372|} *1840:*
die: he   *1868:* die; he   ^{376|} *1840:* trouble, suited to his   *1863:* trouble; he might, at
his   ^{377|} *1840:*—One <> other idle *1863:* other, idle   ^{378|} *1840:* prop
1863: prop,   ^{379|} *1840:* thyrsus these sad people should, the   *1863:* thyrsus, these sad
people, all the   ^{380|} *1840:* Pick up, set store by, and, so far   *1863:* Should pick up, and
set store by,—far   ^{381|} *1840:* hearse convinced *1863:* hearse, convinced
^{382|} *1840:* him. Rather   *1863:* him. "Rather   ^{383|} *1840:* Of the truth! Sordello
1863: truth!"—Sordello   *1868:* O'   ^{385|} *1840:* But Salinguerra who, the last attack,
1863: But Salinguerra, who at this attack   ^{386|} *1840:* Threw himself in his ruffling
1863: Had thrown great breast and ruffling   ^{388|} *1840:* Some task; beneath the   *1863:*

He must decide with Tito; courteously
390 He turned then, even seeming to agree
With his admonisher—"Assist the Pope,
Extend Guelf domination, fill the scope
O' the Church, thus based on All, by All, for All—
Change Secular to Evangelical"—
395 Echoing his very sentence: all seemed lost,
When suddenly he looked up, laughingly almost,
To Palma: "This opinion of your friend's—
For instance, would it answer Palma's ends?
Best, were it not, turn Guelf, submit our Strength"—
400 (Here he drew out his baldric to its length)
—"To the Pope's Knowledge—let our captive slip,
Wide to the walls throw ope our gates, equip
Azzo with . . . what I hold here! Who'll subscribe
To a trite censure of the minstrel tribe
405 Henceforward? or pronounce, as Heinrich used,
'Spear-heads for battle, burr-heads for the joust!'
—When Constance, for his couplets, would promote
Alcamo, from a parti-coloured coat,
To holding her lord's stirrup in the wars.
410 Not that I see where couplet-making jars
With common sense: at Mantua I had borne
This chanted, better than their most forlorn
Of bull-baits,—that's indisputable!"

                                   Brave!
Whom vanity nigh slew, contempt shall save!
415 All's at an end: a Troubadour suppose
Mankind will class him with their friends or foes?

His task; beneath, the   392| *1840:* Extend his domination   *1863:* Extend Guelf
domination   393| *1840:* Of the Church based   *1863:* the Church, thus based   *1868:*
O'   396| *1840:* sudden he looked, laughingly   *1863:* looked up, laughingly   *1868:*
suddenly   § 397–424| *1863:* **SCORN FLINGS COLD WATER IN HIS FACE,**
396–423| *1868* §   397| *1840:* To Palma: This <> friend's   *1863:* To Palma: "This
<> friend's—   399| *1840:* our Strength   *1863:* our Strength"—   401| *1840:* To
<> letting Richard slip,   *1863:*—"To <> let our captive slip,   402| *1840:* ope your
gates   *1863:* ope our gates   403| *1840:* with . . . but no matter! Who'll   *1863:* with . . .
what I hold here! Who'll   406| *1840:* "Spear-heads <> joust"   *1863:* 'Spear-heads
<> joust!'   408| *1840:* Alcama from <> coat   *1863:* Alcamo, from <> coat,
411| *1840:* at Mantua we had   *1863:* at Mantua I had   412| *1840:* chanted, easier
than   *1863:* chanted, better than   413| *1840:* bull-fights, that's indisputable! ¶
Brave!   *1863:* bull-baits,—that's indisputable!" ¶ Brave!   416| *1840:* Mankind's to

A puny uncouth ailing vassal think
The world and him bound in some special link?
Abrupt the visionary tether burst.
420 What were rewarded here, or what amerced
If a poor drudge, solicitous to dream
Deservingly, got tangled by his theme
So far as to conceit the knack or gift
Or whatsoe'er it be, of verse, might lift
425 The globe, a lever like the hand and head
Of—"Men of Action," as the Jongleurs said,
—"The Great Men," in the people's dialect?
    And not a moment did this scorn affect
Sordello: scorn the poet? They, for once,
430 Asking "what was," obtained a full response.
Bid Naddo think at Mantua—he had but
To look into his promptuary, put
Finger on a set thought in a set speech:
But was Sordello fitted thus for each
435 Conjecture? Nowise; since within his soul,
Perception brooded unexpressed and whole.
A healthy spirit like a healthy frame
Craves aliment in plenty—all the same,
Changes, assimilates its aliment.
440 Perceived Sordello, on a truth intent?
Next day no formularies more you saw
Than figs or olives in a sated maw.
    'Tis Knowledge, whither such perceptions tend;
They lose themselves in that, means to an end,

---

class   1863: Mankind will class   418| 1840: him in some especial link?   1863: him
bound in some special link?   419| 1840: tether's burst—   1863: tether   1868:
burst.   420| 1840: What's to reward or what to be amerced   1863: What were
rewarded here, or what amerced   422| 1840: gets   1863: got   423| 1840: conceit
his knack   1863: conceit the knack   424| 1840: be of verse might   1863: be, of verse,
might   § 425–53| 1863: AROUSES HIM AT LAST, TO SOME PURPOSE,
424–52| 1868 §   426| 1840: Of—Men of Action, as   1863: Of—"Men of Action,"
as   427| 1840:—The Great Men, in   1863:—"The Great Men," in   431| 1840:
at Mantua, he   1888: at Mantua—he   433| 1840: His hand on   1863: Finger
on   434| 1840: And was   1863: But was   435| 1840: Conjuncture? No wise < >
soul   1863: Conjecture? Nowise; since, within his soul,   1868: since
within   436| 1840: whole: 1863: whole.   438| 1840: plenty and, the   1863:
plenty—all the   439| 1840: aliment: 1863: aliment.   442| 1840: maw   1863:
maw.   443| 1840:—'Tis Knowledge whither < > tend,   1863: 'Tis Knowledge,

₄₄₅ The many old producing some one new,
A last unlike the first. If lies are true,
The Caliph's wheel-work man of brass receives
A meal, munched millet grains and lettuce leaves
Together in his stomach rattle loose;
₄₅₀ You find them perfect next day to produce:
But ne'er expect the man, on strength of that,
Can roll an iron camel-collar flat
Like Haroun's self! I tell you, what was stored
Bit by bit through Sordello's life, outpoured
₄₅₅ That eve, was, for that age, a novel thing:
And round those three the People formed a ring,
Of visionary judges whose award
He recognised in full—faces that barred
Henceforth return to the old careless life,
₄₆₀ In whose great presence, therefore, his first strife
For their sake must not be ignobly fought;
All these, for once, approved of him, he thought,
Suspended their own vengeance, chose await
The issue of this strife to reinstate
₄₆₅ Them in the right of taking it—in fact
He must be proved king ere they could exact
Vengeance for such king's defalcation. Last,
A reason why the phrases flowed so fast
Was in his quite forgetting for a time
₄₇₀ Himself in his amazement that the rhyme
Disguised the royalty so much: he there—
And Salinguerra yet all-unaware

whither <> tend;   ^{445|}   *1840:* Many Old <> One New,   *1863:* many old <> one
new,   ^{446|}   *1840:* Last <> First   *1863:* last <> first   ^{447|}   *1840:* The Caliph
Haroun's man   *1863:* The Caliph's wheel-work man   ^{448|}   *1840:* meal, ay, millet
1863: meal, munched millet   ^{449|}   *1840:* loose—   *1868:* loose;   ^{450|}   *1840:*
produce   *1863:* produce;   *1868:* produce: § ^{454–81|}   *1863:* AND THUS GETS THE
UTMOST OUT OF HIM.   ^{453–80|}   *1868* §   ^{454|}   *1840:* Parcel by parcel through
his life   *1863:* Bit by bit through Sordello's life   ^{456|}   *1840:*people   *1863:*
People   ^{456–63|}   *1840:* ring, / Suspended   *1863:* § added ^{457–62} §   ^{461|}   *1863:*
fought.   *1868:* fought,   *1888:* fought;   ^{466|}   *1840:* proved their lord ere they exact
1863: proved king ere they could exact   ^{467|}   *1840:* Amends for that lord's
defalcation   *1863:* Vengeance for such king's defalcation   ^{469|}   *1840:* for the time
1863: for a time   ^{470|}   *1840:* that his rhyme   *1863:* that the rhyme   ^{472|}   *1840:*
They full face to him—all yet unaware   *1863:* And Salinguerra—and yet   *1868:* And

Who was the lord, who liegeman!

                        "Thus I lay

On thine my spirit and compel obey

475 His lord,—my liegeman,—impotent to build

Another Rome, but hardly so unskilled

In what such builder should have been, as brook

One shame beyond the charge that I forsook

His function! Free me from that shame, I bend

480 A brow before, suppose new years to spend,—

Allow each chance, nor fruitlessly, recur—

Measure thee with the Minstrel, then, demur

At any crowd he claims! That I must cede

Shamed now, my right to my especial meed—

485 Confess thee fitter help the world than I

Ordained its champion from eternity,

Is much: but to behold thee scorn the post

I quit in thy behalf—to hear thee boast

What makes my own despair!" And while he rung

490 The changes on this theme, the roof up-sprung,

The sad walls of the presence-chamber died

Into the distance, or embowering vied

With far-away Goito's vine-frontier;

And crowds of faces—(only keeping clear

495 The rose-light in the midst, his vantage-ground

To fight their battle from)—deep clustered round

Sordello, with good wishes no mere breath,

Kind prayers for him no vapour, since, come death

Come life, he was fresh-sinewed every joint,

Salinguerra yet all unaware   *1888:* all-unaware   473| *1840:* the King and who . . . But
if I   *1863:* the lord, who liegeman! ¶ "Thus I   475| *1840:* lord—Taurello? Impotent
1863: lord,—my liegeman,—impotent   477| *1840:* been as   *1863:* been, as
478| *1840:* that he forsook   *1863:* that I forsook   479| *1840:* function! Set me free that
shame I   *1863:* function! Free me from that shame, I   480| *1840:* spend,   *1868:*
spend,—   § 482–510| *1863:* HE ASSERTS THE POET'S RANK AND RIGHT,
481–509| *1868* §   483| *1840:* any crown he   *1868:* any crowd he   484| *1840:* As
'tis my   *1863:* Shamed now, my   485| *1840:* Confess you fitter   *1863:* Confess thee
fitter   487| *1840:* behold you scorn   *1863:* behold thee scorn   489| *1840:* Unless
you help the world! And   *1863:* What makes my own despair!" And   492| *1840:* or,
embowering   *1863:* or embowering   494| *1840:* faces (only   *1863:* §
faces—(only   496| *1840:* from) deep   *1863:* from)—deep   498| *1840:* death,

500 Each bone new-marrowed as whom gods anoint
Though mortal to their rescue. Now let sprawl
The snaky volumes hither! Is Typhon all
For Hercules to trample—good report
From Salinguerra only to extort?
505 "So was I" (closed he his inculcating
A poet must be earth's essential king)
"So was I, royal so, and if I fail,
'Tis not the royalty, ye witness quail,
But one deposed who, caring not exert
510 Its proper essence, trifled malapert
With accidents instead—good things assigned
As heralds of a better thing behind—
And, worthy through display of these, put forth
Never the inmost all-surpassing worth
515 That constitutes him king precisely since
As yet no other spirit may evince
Its like: the power he took most pride to test,
Whereby all forms of life had been professed
At pleasure, forms already on the earth,
520 Was but a means to power beyond, whose birth
Should, in its novelty, be kingship's proof.
Now, whether he came near or kept aloof
The several forms he longed to imitate,
Not there the kingship lay, he sees too late.
525 Those forms, unalterable first as last,
Proved him her copier, not the protoplast
Of nature: what would come of being free,

1888: death   500| *1840:* Gods   *1868:* gods   501| *1840:* rescue: now   *1868:*
rescue. Now   502| *1840:* hither, Typhon's all   *1863:* hither! Is Typhon all
504| *1840:* Salinguerra's   *1863:* Salinguerra   505| *1840:* ¶ So was I (closed   *1863:* § ¶
omitted § "So was I" (closed <> inculcating,   *1868:* ¶ "So   *1888:* § ¶ omitted § "So
<> inculcating   507| *1840:* So was <> fail   *1863:* "So was <> fail,
508| *1840:* royalty ye <> quail   *1863:* royalty, ye <> quail,   § 511–39| *1863:* BASING
THESE ON THEIR PROPER GROUND,   510–38| *1868* §   512| *1840:* The
herald of   *1863:* As heralds of   515| *1840:* King   *1868:* king   516| *1840:* other
creature may   *1863:* other spirit may   520| *1840:* power whose novel birth   *1863:*
power beyond, whose birth   521| *1840:* proof—   *1863:* proof.   522| *1840:*
aloof,   *1863:* aloof   522–25| *1863:* aloof / The several forms he longed to imitate, / Not
there the kingship lay, he sees too late. / Those   525| *1840:* forms unalterable first to
last   *1863:* forms, unalterable first as last,   526| *1840:* her copy not   *1863:* her copier,
not   527| *1840:* Of Nature: <> could <> free   *1863:* nature   *1868:* would <>

By action to exhibit tree for tree,
Bird, beast, for beast and bird, or prove earth bore
530 One veritable man or woman more?
Means to an end, such proofs are: what the end?
Let essence, whatsoe'er it be, extend—
Never contract. Already you include
The multitude; then let the multitude
535 Include yourself; and the result were new:
Themselves before, the multitude turn you.
This were to live and move and have, in them,
Your being, and secure a diadem
You should transmit (because no cycle yearns
540 Beyond itself, but on itself returns)
When, the full sphere in wane, the world o'erlaid
Long since with you, shall have in turn obeyed
Some orb still prouder, some displayer, still
More potent than the last, of human will,
545 And some new king depose the old. Of such
Am I— whom pride of this elates too much?
Safe, rather say, 'mid troops of peers again;
I, with my words, hailed brother of the train
Deeds once sufficed: for, let the world roll back,
550 Who fails, through deeds howe'er diverse, retrack
My purpose still, my task? A teeming crust—
Air, flame, earth, wave at conflict! Then, needs must
Emerge some Calm embodied, these refer
The brawl to—yellow-bearded Jupiter?
555 No! Saturn; some existence like a pact

free,   529| 1840: beast for   1863: beast, for   530| 1840: A veritable   1863: One
veritable   531| 1840: proofs; and what   1863: proofs are: what   532| 1840: Your
essence   1863: Let essence   533| 1840: contract! Already   1868: contract.
Already   534| 1840: multitude; now let   1863: multitude; then let   535| 1840:
yourself, and <> is new;   1863: yourself; and <> were new: 536| 1840: you;
1863: you.   537| 1840: have (in them)   1863: have, in them,   539| 1840: That's
to transmit   1863: You should transmit   § 540–68| 1863: RECOGNIZING TRUE
DIGNITY IN SERVICE,   539–67| 1868: RECOGNISING §   541| 1840: When
the full   1863: When, the full   544| 1840: Will,   1863: will,   545| 1840:
King   1868: king   547| 1840: mid   1863: 'mid   549| 1840: Once deeds
sufficed   1863: Deeds once sufficed   550| 1840: deeds diverse so e'er, re-track   1863:
deeds howe'er diverse, re-track   1888: retrack   552| 1840: conflict—see! Needs   1863:
conflict! Then, needs   553| 1840: embodied these   1863: embodied, these
554| 1840: (Saturn—no yellow-bearded Jupiter!)   1863: The brawl to;—yellow-bearded
Jupiter?   1888: to—yellow-bearded   555| 1840: The brawl to; some   1863: No!

And protest against Chaos, some first fact
I' the faint of time. My deep of life, I know
Is unavailing e'en to poorly show" . . .
(For here the Chief immeasurably yawned)
560 . . . "Deeds in their due gradation till Song dawned—
The fullest effluence of the finest mind,
All in degree, no way diverse in kind
From minds about it, minds which, more or less,
Lofty or low, move seeking to impress
565 Themselves on somewhat; but one mind has climbed
Step after step, by just ascent sublimed.
Thought is the soul of act, and, stage by stage,
Soul is from body still to disengage
As tending to a freedom which rejects
570 Such help and incorporeally affects
The world, producing deeds but not by deeds,
Swaying, in others, frames itself exceeds,
Assigning them the simpler tasks it used
To patiently perform till Song produced
575 Acts, by thoughts only, for the mind: divest
Mind of e'en Thought, and, lo, God's unexpressed
Will draws above us! All then is to win
Save that. How much for me, then? where begin
My work? About me, faces! and they flock,
580 The earnest faces. What shall I unlock
By song? behold me prompt, whate'er it be,
To minister: how much can mortals see
Of Life? No more than so? I take the task
And marshal you Life's elemental masque,

Saturn; some   557| *1840:* of Time . . . my <> know,   *1863:* time. My   *1888:*
know   558| *1840:* show   *1863:* show" . . .   560| *1840:* Deeds   *1863:* . . .
"Deeds   561| *1840:* mind   *1863:* mind,   563| *1840:* From those about us,
minds   *1863:* From minds about it, minds <> less   *1888:* less,   564| *1840:* low, in
moving seek impress   *1863:* low, move seeking to impress   566| *1840:* sublimed:
1863: sublimed.   567| *1840:* and stage by   *1863:* and, stage by   568| *1840:* Is
soul from   *1863:* Soul is from   § 569–97| *1863:* WHETHER SUCCESSIVELY THAT OF
EPOIST,   568–96| *1868* §   574| *1840:* As patiently   *1863:* To
patiently   577| *1840:* Will dawns above us. But so much to   *1863:* us! All then is to
1868: Will draws above   578| *1840:* Ere that! A lesser round of steps within   *1868:*
Save that. How much for me, then? where begin   579| *1840:* The last. About   *1863:*
My work? About   580| *1840:* faces! What   *1868:* faces. What   583| *1840:* more?
I covet the first task   *1863:* more than so? I take the task   584| *1840:* elemental

287

585 Show Men, on evil or on good lay stress,
This light, this shade make prominent, suppress
All ordinary hues that softening blend
Such natures with the level. Apprehend
Which sinner is, which saint, if I allot
590 Hell, Purgatory, Heaven, a blaze or blot,
To those you doubt concerning! I enwomb
Some wretched Friedrich with his red-hot tomb;
Some dubious spirit, Lombard Agilulph
With the black chastening river I engulph!
595 Some unapproached Matilda I enshrine
With languors of the planet of decline—
These, fail to recognize, to arbitrate
Between henceforth, to rightly estimate
Thus marshalled in the masque! Myself, the while,
600 As one of you, am witness, shrink or smile
At my own showing! Next age—what's to do?
The men and women stationed hitherto
Will I unstation, good and bad, conduct
Each nature to its farthest, or obstruct
605 At soonest, in the world: light, thwarted, breaks
A limpid purity to rainbow flakes,
Or shadow, massed, freezes to gloom: behold
How such, with fit assistance to unfold,
Or obstacles to crush them, disengage
610 Their forms, love, hate, hope, fear, peace make, war wage,
In presence of you all! Myself, implied
Superior now, as, by the platform's side,
I bade them do and suffer,—would last content

Masque 1863: elemental masque,   585| 1840: Of Men   1863: Show Men
588| 1840: level: apprehend.   1863: level. Apprehend   589| 1840: Which evil is,
which good, if   1863: Which sinner is, which saint, if   590| 1840: Your Hell, the
Purgatory, Heaven ye wot,   1863: Hell, Purgatory, Heaven, a blaze or blot,
591| 1840: concerning: I   1863: concerning! I   592| 1840: tomb,   1863: tomb;
594| 1840: engulph;   1868: engulph!   597| 1840: These fail to recognise   1863:
These, fail   1888: recognize § 598–625| 1863: DRAMATIST, OR, SO TO CALL HIM,
ANALYST,   597–23| 1868 §   599| 1840: Masque   1863: masque
604| 1840: farthest or   1863: farthest, or   605| 1840: soonest in <> Light   1863:
soonest, in <> light   607| 1840: Or Shadow, helped, freezes   1863: Or shadow,
massed, freezes   611| 1840: all! Myself implied   1863: all! Myself, implied
613| 1840: Bidding them do and suffer to content   1863: I bade them do and suffer,—would

The world . . . no—that's too far! I circumvent
615 A few, my masque contented, and to these
Offer unveil the last of mysteries—
Man's inmost life shall have yet freer play:
Once more I cast external things away,
And natures composite, so decompose
620 That" . . . Why, he writes *Sordello!*

                      "How I rose,
And how have you advanced! since evermore
Yourselves effect what I was fain before
Effect, what I supplied yourselves suggest,
What I leave bare yourselves can now invest.
625 How we attain to talk as brothers talk,
In half-words, call things by half-names, no balk
From discontinuing old aids. To-day
Takes in account the work of Yesterday:
Has not the world a Past now, its adept
630 Consults ere he dispense with or accept
New aids? a single touch more may enhance,
A touch less turn to insignificance
Those structures' symmetry the past has strewed
The world with, once so bare. Leave the mere rude
635 Explicit details! 'tis but brother's speech
We need, speech where an accent's change gives each
The other's soul—no speech to understand
By former audience: need was then to expand,
Expatiate—hardly were we brothers! true—
640 Nor I lament my small remove from you,

---

last content   614| *1840:* that I wait not—circumvent   *1863:* that 's too far! I
circumvent   615| *1840:* few it has contented   *1863:* few, my masque contented
616| *1840:* mysteries   *1863:* mysteries—   617| *1840:* I boast! Man's life   *1863:* Man's
inmost life   618| *1840:* away   *1863:* away,   619| *1840:* And Natures, varied now,
so   *1863:* And natures composite, so   620| *1840:* That . . . but enough! Why fancy how
I   *1863:* That" . . . Why, he writes *Sordello!* ¶ "How I   621| *1840:* Or rather you
advanced since   *1863:* And how have you advanced! since   624| *1840:* invest?   *1863:*
invest.   625| *1840:* attained   *1863:* attain   § 626–54| *1863:* WHO TURNS IN DUE
COURSE SYNTHETIST.   624–52| *1868* §   627| *1840:* aids—To-day   *1863:*
aids. To-day   628| *1840:* of Yesterday—   *1863:* of Yesterday: 633| *1840:* Past
1868: past   634| *1840:* Your world <> bare: leave   *1863:* The world <> bare.
Leave   635| *1840:* details, 'tis   *1863:* details! 'tis   638| *1840:* audience—need
1863: audience: need   639| *1840:* were they brothers   *1863:* were we brothers
640| *1840:* my less remove   *1863:* my small remove   641| *1840:* already: ends   *1863:*

Nor reconstruct what stands already. Ends
Accomplished turn to means: my art intends
New structure from the ancient: as they changed
The spoils of every clime at Venice, ranged
645 The horned and snouted Libyan god, upright
As in his desert, by some simple bright
Clay cinerary pitcher—Thebes as Rome,
Athens as Byzant rifled, till their Dome
From earth's reputed consummations razed
650 A seal, the all-transmuting Triad blazed
Above. Ah, whose that fortune? Ne'ertheless
E'en he must stoop contented to express
No tithe of what's to say—the vehicle
Never sufficient: but his work is still
655 For faces like the faces that select
The single service I am bound effect,—
That bid me cast aside such fancies, bow
Taurello to the Guelf cause, disallow
The Kaiser's coming—which with heart, soul, strength,
660 I labour for, this eve, who feel at length
My past career's outrageous vanity,
And would, as its amends, die, even die
Now I first estimate the boon of life,
If death might win compliance—sure, this strife
665 Is right for once—the People my support."
      My poor Sordello! what may we extort
By this, I wonder? Palma's lighted eyes
Turned to Taurello who, long past surprise,
Began, "You love him—what you'd say at large
670 Let me say briefly. First, your father's charge

already. Ends   645| 1840: God   1863: god   649| 1840: Earth's   1863:
earth's   650| 1840: seal the   1863: seal, the   651| 1840: ne' etherless   1868:
Ne'ertheless   654| 1840: sufficient—but   1863: sufficient: but   § 655-83| 1863: THIS
FOR ONE DAY: NOW, SERVE AS GUELF!   653-81| 1868 §   656| 1840: A
single <> effect   1863: The single <> effect,   1868: effect,—   657| 1840: Nor
murmur, bid me, still as pact, bow   1863: And bid me cast aside such fancies, bow   1868:
That bid   661| 1840: vanity   1863: vanity,   662| 1840: would (as vain amends)
die, even   1863: would, as its amends, die, even   664| 1840: So death might bow
Taurello—sure this   1863: If death might win compliance—sure, this   665| 1840: Is
the last strife—the <> support.   1863: Is right for once—the <> support."
668| 1840: who, as past   1863: who, long past   669| 1840: Began, You   1863: Began,
"You
670| 1840: If I say briefly? First your   1863: Let me say briefly. First, your   672| 1840:

To me, his friend, peruse: I guessed indeed
You were no stranger to the course decreed.
He bids me leave his children to the saints:
As for a certain project, he acquaints
675 The Pope with that, and offers him the best
Of your possessions to permit the rest
Go peaceably—to Ecelin, a stripe
Of soil the cursed Vicentines will gripe,
—To Alberic, a patch the Trevisan
680 Clutches already; extricate, who can,
Treville, Villarazzi, Puissolo,
Loria and Cartiglione!—all must go,
And with them go my hopes. 'Tis lost, then! Lost
This eve, our crisis, and some pains it cost
685 Procuring; thirty years—as good I'd spent
Like our admonisher! But each his bent
Pursues: no question, one might live absurd
Oneself this while, by deed as he by word
Persisting to obtrude an influence where
690 'Tis made account of, much as . . . nay, you fare
With twice the fortune, youngster!—I submit,
Happy to parallel my waste of wit
With the renowned Sordello's: you decide
A course for me. Romano may abide
695 Romano,—Bacchus! After all, what dearth
Of Ecelins and Alberics on earth?
Say there's a prize in prospect, must disgrace
Betide competitors, unless they style
Themselves Romano? Were it worth my while
700 To try my own luck! But an obscure place

decreed   *1863:* decreed.   673| *1840:* Us bôth: I leave   *1863:* He bids me leave
680| *1840:* extricate who can   *1863:* extricate, who can,   682| *1840:* Cartiglione,
Loria—all go,   *1863:* Cartiglione, Loria!—all   *1888:* Loria and Cartiglione!—all must
go,   683| *1840:* hopes! 'Tis   *1863:* hopes. 'Tis   § 684–712| *1863:* SALINGUERRA,
DISLODGED FROM HIS POST,   682–709| *1868* §   687| *1840:* Pursues—no
1863: Pursues: no   688| *1840:* word,   *1888:* word   690| *1840:* of much   *1863:*
of, much   691| *1840:* youngster—I   *1863:* youngster!—I   693| *1840:* renowned
Sordello's—you   *1863:* renowned Sordello's: you   694| *1840:* me—Romano   *1863:*
me. Romano   695| *1840:* Romano,—Bacchus! Who'd suppose the dearth   *1863:*
Romano,—Bacchus! After all, what dearth   697| *1840:* a thing in   *1863:* a prize
in   698–701| *1840:* competitors? An obscure place / Suits   *1863:* competitors, unless

Suits me—there wants a youth to bustle, stalk
And attitudinize—some fight, more talk,
Most flaunting badges—how, I might make clear
Since Friedrich's very purposes lie here
705 —Here, pity they are like to lie! For me,
With station fixed unceremoniously
Long since, small use contesting; I am but
The liegeman—you are born the lieges: shut
That gentle mouth now! or resume your kin
710 In your sweet self; were Palma Ecelin
For me to work with! Could that neck endure
This bauble for a cumbrous garniture,
She should . . . or might one bear it for her? Stay—
I have not been so flattered many a day
715 As by your pale friend—Bacchus! The least help
Would lick the hind's fawn to a lion's whelp:
His neck is broad enough—a ready tongue
Beside: too writhled—but, the main thing, young—
I could . . . why, look ye!"
                                    And the badge was thrown
720 Across Sordello's neck: "This badge alone
Makes you Romano's Head—becomes superb
On your bare neck, which would, on mine, disturb
The pauldron," said Taurello. A mad act,
Nor even dreamed about before—in fact,
725 Not when his sportive arm rose for the nonce—

they style / Themselves Romano? Well it worth my while / To try my own luck! But an
obscure place / Suits   701| 1840: wants youth, bustle, one to stalk   1863: wants a youth
to bustle, stalk   703| 1840: badges—'twere not hard make   1863: badges—how, I
might make clear,   1868: clear   705| 1840:—Here—pity   1863:—Here, pity
706| 1840: Whose station's   1863: With station   708| 1840: liegeman, you <>
lieges—shut   1888: liegeman—you <> lieges: shut   709| 1840: now!—or   1863:
now! or   710| 1840: self; Palma were Ecelin   1863: self; were Palma Ecelin
711| 1840: me and welcome! Could   1863: me to work with! Could   712| 1840:
garniture   1863: garniture,   § 713–39| 1863: IN MOVING, OPENS A DOOR TO
SORDELLO,   710–37| 1868 §   713| 1840: You should <> for you? Stay—
1863: She should <> for her? Stay—   716| 1840: whelp—   1888: whelp:
718| 1840: Beside—too   1888: Beside: too   719| 1840: why look ye! ¶ And   1863:
why, look ye!" ¶ And   720| 1840: neck: this   1863: neck: "This   721| 1840: you
Romano's Head—the Lombard's Curb   1863: you Romano's Head—becomes superb
722| 1840: Turns on your neck which   1863: On your bare neck, which   723| 1840:
My pauldron, said   1863: The pauldron," said   724| 1840: Nor dreamed about a

But he had dallied overmuch, this once,
With power: the thing was done, and he, aware
The thing was done, proceeded to declare—
(So like a nature made to serve, excel
730 In serving, only feel by service well!)
—That he would make Sordello that and more.
"As good a scheme as any. What's to pore
At in my face?" he asked—"ponder instead
This piece of news; you are Romano's Head!
735 One cannot slacken pace so near the goal,
Suffer my Azzo to escape heart-whole
This time! For you there's Palma to espouse—
For me, one crowning trouble ere I house
Like my compeer."
                    On which ensued a strange
740 And solemn visitation; there came change
O'er every one of them; each looked on each:
Up in the midst a truth grew, without speech.
And when the giddiness sank and the haze
Subsided, they were sitting, no amaze,
745 Sordello with the baldric on, his sire
Silent, though his proportions seemed aspire
Momently; and, interpreting the thrill,—
Night at its ebb,—Palma was found there still
Relating somewhat Adelaide confessed
750 A year ago, while dying on her breast,—
Of a contrivance, that Vicenza night
When Ecelin had birth. "Their convoy's flight,

---

moment since—in fact   *1863:* Nor even dreamed about before—in fact,   728| *1840:*
declare   *1863:* declare—   730| *1840:* well)   *1863:* well!)   731| *1840:* That he
should make him all he said and more: *1863:*—That he would make Sordello that and
more.   732| *1840:* As good <> any: what's   *1863:* "As good <> any! What's
733| *1840:* face? he asked—ponder   *1863:* face?" he   *1868:* asked—"ponder
734| *1840:* are Romano's Head—   *1863:* are Romano's Head!   739| *1840:* compeer. ¶
On   *1863:* compeer." ¶ On   § 740–68| *1863:* WHO IS DECLARED SALINGUERRA'S
SON.   738–65| *1868:* SON, §   740| *1840:* visitation—mighty change   *1863:*
visitation; there came change   741| *1840:* them—each <> on each—   *1863:* them;
each <> on each: 742| *1840:* speech,   *1863:* speech.   746| *1840:* Silent
though   *1863:* Silent, though   747| *1840:* thrill   *1888:* thrill,—   748| *1840:*
ebb, Palma you found was still   *1863:* ebb, Palma was found there still   *1888:*
ebb,—Palma   750| *1840:* breast,   *1863:* breast,—   751| *1840:* contrivance that
<> night,   *1888:* contrivance, that <> night   752| *1840:* Her Ecelin had birth:

Cut off a moment, coiled inside the flame
That wallowed like a dragon at his game
755 The toppling city through—San Biagio rocks!
And wounded lies in her delicious locks
Retrude, the frail mother, on her face,
None of her wasted, just in one embrace
Covering her child: when, as they lifted her,
760 Cleaving the tumult, mighty, mightier
And mightiest Taurello's cry outbroke,
Leapt like a tongue of fire that cleaves the smoke,
Midmost to cheer his Mantuans onward—drown
His colleague Ecelin's clamour, up and down
765 The disarray: failed Adelaide see then
Who was the natural chief, the man of men?
Outstripping time, her infant there burst swathe,
Stood up with eyes haggard beyond the scathe
From wandering after his heritage
770 Lost once and lost for aye: and why that rage,
That deprecating glance? A new shape leant
On a familiar shape—gloatingly bent
O'er his discomfiture; 'mid wreaths it wore,
Still one outflamed the rest—her child's before
775 'Twas Salinguerra's for his child: scorn, hate,
Rage now might startle her when all too late!
Then was the moment!—rival's foot had spurned
Never that House to earth else! Sense returned—
The act conceived, adventured and complete,
780 They bore away to an obscure retreat

their <> flight   1863: When Ecelin had birth. "Their <> flight,   764| 1840:
colleague's clamour, Ecelin's up, down   1863: colleague Ecelin's clamour, up and
down   766| 1840: Chief, the Man of Men?   1863: chief, the man of men?
767| 1840: time her Ecelin burst   1863: time, her infant there burst   768| 1840: with
haggard eyes beyond   1863: with eyes haggard beyond   § 769–97| 1863: HIDDEN
HITHERTO BY ADELAIDE'S POLICY.   766–93| 1868 §   770| 1840:
aye—what could engage   1863: aye—and why that rage,   1888: aye: and   771| 1840:
Shape   1863: shape   772| 1840: Shape   1863: shape   775| 1840: hate   1868:
hate,   776| 1840: Rage, startled her from Ecelin—too   1868: Rage startled   1888:
Rage now might startle her when all too   777| 1840: A moment's work, and rival's
1863: Then was the moment! rival's   1868: moment!—rival's   778| 1840: that brow to
earth! Ere sense   1888: that House to earth else! Sense   779| 1840: adventured, and
1868: adventured and   780| 1840: They stole away towards an   1863: They bore away

Mother and child—Retrude's self not slain"
(Nor even here Taurello moved) "though pain
Was fled; and what assured them most 'twas fled,
All pain, was, if they raised the pale hushed head
785 'Twould turn this way and that, waver awhile,
And only settle into its old smile—
(Graceful as the disquieted water-flag
Steadying itself, remarked they, in the quag
On either side their path)—when suffered look
790 Down on her child. They marched: no sign once shook
The company's close litter of crossed spears
Till, as they reached Goito, a few tears
Slipped in the sunset from her long black lash,
And she was gone. So far the action rash;
795 No crime. They laid Retrude in the font,
Taurello's very gift, her child was wont
To sit beneath—constant as eve he came
To sit by its attendant girls the same
As one of them. For Palma, she would blend
800 With this magnific spirit to the end,
That ruled her first; but scarcely had she dared
To disobey the Adelaide who scared
Her into vowing never to disclose
A secret to her husband, which so froze
805 His blood at half-recital, she contrived
To hide from him Taurello's infant lived,
Lest, by revealing that, himself should mar
Romano's fortunes. And, a crime so far,
Palma received that action: she was told
810 Of Salinguerra's nature, of his cold

to an   781| *1840:* slain   *1863:* slain"   782| *1840:* moved) though   *1863:*
moved) "though   784| *1840:* if you raised   *1863:* if they raised   786| *1840:*
smile   *1863:* smile—   789| *1840:* path) when   *1863:* path)—when   790| *1840:*
Downward: they marched: no sign of life once   *1863:* Down on her child. They marched: no
sign once   793| *1840:* Slipt   *1868:* Slipped   794| *1840:* rash—   *1868:*
rash;   795| *1840:* font   *1863:* font   § 798–826| *1863:* HOW THE DISCOVERY
MOVES SALINGUERRA,   794–822| *1868* §   800| *1840:* magific <> end
1863: magnific <> end,   801| *1840:* first—but   *1868:* first; but   804| *1840:*
husband which   *1863:* husband, which   805| *1840:* half recital she   *1863:* recital,
she   *1868:* half-recital   806| *1840:* lived   *1863:* lived,   808| *1840:* fortunes:
and   *1863:* fortunes. And   810| *1840:* nature, and his   *1863:* nature, of his

Calm acquiescence in his lot! But free
To impart the secret to Romano, she
Engaged to repossess Sordello of
His heritage, and hers, and that way doff
815 The mask, but after years, long years: while now,
Was not Romano's sign-mark on that brow?"
    Across Taurello's heart his arms were locked:
And when he did speak 'twas as if he mocked
The minstrel, "who had not to move," he said,
820 "Nor stir—should fate defraud him of a shred
Of his son's infancy? much less his youth!"
(Laughingly all this)—"which to aid, in truth,
Himself, reserved on purpose, had not grown
Old, not too old—'twas best they kept alone
825 Till now, and never idly met till now;"
—Then, in the same breath, told Sordello how
All intimations of this eve's event
Were lies, for Friedrich must advance to Trent,
Thence to Verona, then to Rome, there stop,
830 Tumble the Church down, institute a-top
The Alps a Prefecture of Lombardy:
—"That's now!—no prophesying what may be
Anon, with a new monarch of the clime,
Native of Gesi, passing his youth's prime
835 At Naples. Tito bids my choice decide
On whom . . ."
            "Embrace him, madman!" Palma cried,

812| *1840:* Impart   *1863:* To impart   815| *1840:* long years!—while now   *1863:*
now,   *1868:* long years: while   816| *1840:* brow?   *1863:* brow?"   818| *1840:*
And 'twas, when speak he did, as   *1863:* And when he did speak 'twas as   819| *1840:*
minstrel, who < > move, he   *1863:* minstrel, "who < > move," he   820| *1840:* Not
stir < > Fate   *1863:* "Not   *1868:* "Nor stir < > fate   821| *1840:* Of this son's < >
youth   *1863:* Of his son's < > youth!"   822| *1840:* this) which   *1863:*
this)—"which   824| *1840:* 'twas better keep alone   *1863:* 'twas best they kept
alone   825| *1840:* meet till now: *1863:* met till now;"   § 827–53| *1863:* AND
SORDELLO THE FINALLY- DETERMINED,   823–49| *1868* §   827| *1840:*
The intimations   *1863:* All intimations   828| *1840:* Were futile—Friedrich means
advance   *1863:* Were lies, for Friedrich must advance   829| *1840:* then to
Rome—there stop—   *1863:* then to Rome, there stop,   832| *1840:*—That's
now—no   *1863:*—"That's now!—no   833| *1840:* Anon, beneath a monarch   *1863:*
Anon, with a new monarch   836| *1840:* whom . . . ¶ Embrace him, madman! Palma
cried   *1863:* whom . . ." ¶ "Embrace him, madman!" Palma cried,   837| *1840:*

Who through the laugh saw sweat-drops burst apace,
And his lips blanching: he did not embrace
Sordello, but he laid Sordello's hand
840 On his own eyes, mouth, forehead.

                                    Understand,
This while Sordello was becoming flushed
Out of his whiteness; thoughts rushed, fancies rushed;
He pressed his hand upon his head and signed
Both should forbear him. "Nay, the best's behind!"
845 Taurello laughed—not quite with the same laugh:
"The truth is, thus we scatter, ay, like chaff
These Guelfs, a despicable monk recoils
From: nor expect a fickle Kaiser spoils
Our triumph!—Friedrich? Think you, I intend
850 Friedrich shall reap the fruits of blood I spend
And brain I waste? Think you, the people clap
Their hands at my out-hewing this wild gap
For any Friedrich to fill up? 'Tis mine—
That's yours: I tell you, towards some such design
855 Have I worked blindly, yes, and idly, yes,
And for another, yes—but worked no less
With instinct at my heart; I else had swerved,
While now—look round! My cunning has preserved
Samminiato—that's a central place
860 Secures us Florence, boy,—in Pisa's case.
By land as she by sea; with Pisa ours,
And Florence, and Pistoia, one devours
The land at leisure! Gloriously dispersed—
Brescia, observe, Milan, Piacenza first
865 That flanked us (ah, you know not!) in the March;
On these we pile, as keystone of our arch,
Romagna and Bologna, whose first span
Covered the Trentine and the Valsugan;

sweatdrops burst apace   *1863:* apace,   *1868:* sweat-drops   838| *1840:* lips'   *1868:*
lips   844| *1840:* him. Nay <> behind!   *1863:* him. "Nay <> behind!"
846| *1840:* The <> thus you scatter   *1863:* "The <> thus we scatter   847| *1840:*
The Guelfs a   *1863:* These Guelfs, a   848| *1840:* From—nor   *1863:* From: nor
849| *1840:* you I   *1863:* you, I   851| *1840:* you the   *1863:* you, the
§ 854–82| *1863:*—THE DEVIL PUTTING FORTH HIS POTENCY:
850–78| *1868* §   854| *1840:* you towards   *1863:* you, towards   860| *1840:* boy, in

Sofia's Egna by Bolgiano's sure!" . . .
870 So he proceeded: half of all this, pure
Delusion, doubtless, nor the rest too true,
But what was undone he felt sure to do,
As ring by ring he wrung off, flung away
The pauldron-rings to give his sword-arm play—
875 Need of the sword now! That would soon adjust
Aught wrong at present; to the sword intrust
Sordello's whiteness, undersize: 'twas plain
He hardly rendered right to his own brain—
Like a brave hound, men educate to pride
880 Himself on speed or scent nor aught beside,
As though he could not, gift by gift, match men!
Palma had listened patiently: but when
'Twas time expostulate, attempt withdraw
Taurello from his child, she, without awe
885 Took off his iron arms from, one by one,
Sordello's shrinking shoulders, and, that done,
Made him avert his visage and relieve
Sordello (you might see his corslet heave
The while) who, loose, rose—tried to speak, then sank:
890 They left him in the chamber. All was blank.
And even reeling down the narrow stair
Taurello kept up, as though unaware
Palma was by to guide him, the old device
—Something of Milan—"how we muster thrice
895 The Torriani's strength there; all along
Our own Visconti cowed them"—thus the song
Continued even while she bade him stoop,
Thrid somehow, by some glimpse of arrow-loop,
The turnings to the gallery below,
900 Where he stopped short as Palma let him go.

<> case   *1863:* boy,—in <> case,   869| *1840:* sure . . .   *1863:* sure!" . . .
870| *1840:* proceeded. Half <> this pure   *1863:* proceeded: half <> this, pure
872| *1840:* do   *1863:* do,   877| *1840:* undersize; 'twas   *1863:* undersize: 'twas
879| *1840:* hound men   *1863:* hound, men   § *883–911*| *1863:* SINCE SORDELLO, WHO
BEGAN BY RHYMING,   *879–907*| *.1868* §   889| *1840:* speak—then   *1863:*
speak, then   890| *1840:* chamber—all   *1863:* chamber. All   891| *1840:* ¶ And
<> the castle-stair   *1863:* the narrow stair   *1888:* § ¶ omitted §   893| *1840:* was
guide to him   *1863:* was by to guide him   894| *1840:* of Milan—how   *1863:* of
Milan—"how   895| *1840:* there—all   *1863:* there; all   896| *1840:*

298

When he had sat in silence long enough
Splintering the stone bench, braving a rebuff
She stopped the truncheon; only to commence
One of Sordello's poems, a pretence
905 For speaking, some poor rhyme of "Elys' hair
And head that's sharp and perfect like a pear,
So smooth and close are laid the few fine locks
Stained like pale honey oozed from topmost rocks
Sun-blanched the livelong summer"—from his worst
910 Performance, the Goito, as his first:
And that at end, conceiving from the brow
And open mouth no silence would serve now,
Went on to say the whole world loved that man
And, for that matter, thought his face, tho' wan,
915 Eclipsed the Count's—he sucking in each phrase
As if an angel spoke. The foolish praise
Ended, he drew her on his mailed knees, made
Her face a framework with his hands, a shade,
A crown, an aureole: there must she remain
920 (Her little mouth compressed with smiling pain
As in his gloves she felt her tresses twitch)
To get the best look at, in fittest niche
Dispose his saint. That done, he kissed her brow,
—"Lauded her father for his treason now,"
925 He told her, "only, how could one suspect
The wit in him?—whose clansman, recollect,
Was ever Salinguerra—she, the same,
Romano and his lady—so, might claim
To know all, as she should"—and thus begun
930 Schemes with a vengeance, schemes on schemes, "not one

them—thus *1863:* them"—thus   ^{901|} *1840:* sate *1863:* sat   ^{903|} *1840:*
stopt *1868:* stopped   ^{905|} *1840:* of Elys' *1863:* of "Elys'   ^{909|} *1840:*
Summer—from *1863:* Summer"—from *1868:* summer § ^{912–39|} *1863:* MAY, EVEN
FROM THE DEPTHS OF FAILURE,   ^{908–34|} *1868* §   ^{916|} *1840:* spoke: the
1863: spoke. The   ^{918|} *1840:* frame-work *1863:* framework   ^{919|} *1840:*
aureole—there *1863:* aureole: there   ^{923|} *1840:* saint; that <> brow— *1863:*
saint. That <> brow,   ^{924|} *1840:* Lauded <> now, *1863:*—"Lauded <>
now,"   ^{925|} *1840:* her, only how *1863:* her, "only, how   ^{926|} *1840:* him?
whose *1863:* him?—whose   ^{928|} *1840:* so might *1863:* so, might   ^{929|} *1840:*
should—and *1863:* should"—and   ^{930|} *1840:* on schemes, not *1863:* on schemes,

Fit to be told that foolish boy," he said,
But only let Sordello Palma wed,
—Then!"
　　　　　　'Twas a dim long narrow place at best:
Midway a sole grate showed the fiery West,
935 As shows its corpse the world's end some split tomb—
A gloom, a rift of fire, another gloom,
Faced Palma—but at length Taurello set
Her free; the grating held one ragged jet
Of fierce gold fire: he lifted her within
940 The hollow underneath—how else begin
Fate's second marvellous cycle, else renew
The ages than with Palma plain in view?
Then paced the passage, hands clenched, head erect,
Pursuing his discourse; a grand unchecked
945 Monotony made out from his quick talk
And the recurring noises of his walk;
—Somewhat too much like the o'ercharged assent
Of two resolved friends in one danger blent,
Who hearten each the other against heart;
950 Boasting there's nought to care for, when, apart
The boaster, all's to care for. He, beside
Some shape not visible, in power and pride
Approached, out of the dark, ginglingly near,
Nearer, passed close in the broad light, his ear
955 Crimson, eyeballs suffused, temples full-fraught,
Just a snatch of the rapid speech you caught,
And on he strode into the opposite dark,
Till presently the harsh heel's turn, a spark
I' the stone, and whirl of some loose embossed thong
960 That crashed against the angle aye so long
After the last, punctual to an amount
Of mailed great paces you could not but count,—
Prepared you for the pacing back again.
And by the snatches you might ascertain

"not   931| 1840: boy, he   1863: boy," he   932| 1840: But   1863: "But
933| 1840:—Then! ¶ 'Twas   1863:—Then!" ¶ 'Twas   934| 1840: fiery West   1863:
fiery West,   936| 1840: another gloom   1863: another gloom,   § 940–68| 1863: YET
SPRING TO THE SUMMIT OF SUCCESS,   935–63| 1868 §   949| 1840:
heart—   1863: heart;   951| 1840: for: he   1863: for. He   957| 1840: dark
1868: dark,   962| 1840: count,   1863: count,—   963| 1840: again: 1863:
again.   964| 1840: snatches might you ascertain   1863: snatches you might ascertain

965 That, Friedrich's Prefecture surmounted, left
By this alone in Italy, they cleft
Asunder, crushed together, at command
Of none, were free to break up Hildebrand,
Rebuild, he and Sordello, Charlemagne—
970 But garnished, Strength with Knowledge, "if we deign
Accept that compromise and stoop to give
Rome law, the Cæsar's Representative."
Enough, that the illimitable flood
Of triumphs after triumphs, understood
975 In its faint reflux (you shall hear) sufficed
Young Ecelin for appanage, enticed
Him on till, these long quiet in their graves,
He found 'twas looked for that a whole life's braves
Should somehow be made good; so, weak and worn,
980 Must stagger up at Milan, one grey morn
Of the to-come, and fight his latest fight.
But, Salinguerra's prophecy at height—
He voluble with a raised arm and stiff,
A blaring voice, a blazing eye, as if
985 He had our very Italy to keep
Or cast away, or gather in a heap
To garrison the better—ay, his word
Was, "run the cucumber into a gourd,
Drive Trent upon Apulia"—at their pitch
990 Who spied the continents and islands which
Grew mulberry leaves and sickles, in the map—
(Strange that three such confessions so should hap
To Palma, Dante spoke with in the clear
Amorous silence of the Swooning-sphere,—
995 *Cunizza*, as he called her! Never ask
Of Palma more! She sat, knowing her task

---

§ 969–97| *1863:* IF HE CONSENT TO OPPRESS THE WORLD.
964–92| *1868* §   970| *1840:* with Knowledge, if   *1863:* with Knowledge, "if
972| *1840:* the Cæsars' Representative.   *1863:* the Cæsars' Representative."   *1868:*
Cæsar's   973| *1840:*—Enough   *1868:* Enough   977| *1840:* Him till, these long
since quiet   *1863:* Him on till, these long quiet   978| *1840:* a long life's   *1863:* a
whole life's   979| *1840:* good—so   *1868:* good; so   981| *1840:* the To-Come, to
fight   *1863:* the To-Come, and fight   *1868:* to-come   991| *1840:* Grew sickles,
mulberry leaflets in   *1863:* Grew mulberry leaves and sickles, in   993| *1840:* To
Palma Dante   *1863:* To Palma, Dante   994| *1840:* the Swooning-sphere.   *1863:* the
Swooning-sphere,—   995| *1840:* Cunizza   *1863:* *Cunizza*   996| *1840:* sate

301

Was done, the labour of it,—for, success
Concerned not Palma, passion's votaress.)
Triumph at height, and thus Sordello crowned—
1000 Above the passage suddenly a sound
Stops speech, stops walk: back shrinks Taurello, bids
With large involuntary asking lids,
Palma interpret. " 'Tis his own foot-stamp—
Your hand! His summons! Nay, this idle damp
1005 Befits not!" Out they two reeled dizzily.
"Visconti's strong at Milan," resumed he,
In the old, somewhat insignificant way—
(Was Palma wont, years afterward, to say)
As though the spirit's flight, sustained thus far,
1010 Dropped at that very instant.
                                        Gone they are—
Palma, Taurello; Eglamor anon,
Ecelin,—only Naddo's never gone!
—Labours, this moonrise, what the Master meant:
"Is Squarcialupo speckled?—purulent,
1015 I'd say, but when was Providence put out?
He carries somehow handily about
His spite nor fouls himself!" Goito's vines
Stand like a cheat detected—stark rough lines,
The moon breaks through, a grey mean scale against
1020 The vault where, this eve's Maiden, thou remain'st
Like some fresh martyr, eyes fixed—who can tell?
As Heaven, now all's at end, did not so well,
Spite of the faith and victory, to leave
Its virgin quite to death in the lone eve.

1863: sat   997| *1840:* it—for success   *1863:* for, success,   *1868:* it,—for   *1888:* success
§ 998–1026| *1863:* JUST THIS DECIDED, AND WE HAVE DONE.   993–1021| *1868:*
DECIDED, AS IT NOW MAY BE,   1022–26| *1868:* AND WE HAVE DONE. §
998| *1840:* votaress)   *1863:* votaress.)   999| *1840:* height, I say, Sordello   *1863:*
height, and thus Sordello   1003| *1840:* interpret. 'Tis   *1863:* interpret. " 'Tis
1005| *1840:* not! Out <> dizzily: *1863:* not!" Out <> dizzily.   1006| *1840:* he
1863: he,   1007| *1840:* old somewhat <> way   *1863:* old, somewhat <>
way—   1008| *1840:* wont years afterward to   *1863:* wont, years afterward, to
1009| *1840:* flight sustained <> far   *1863:* flight, sustained <> far,   1012| *1840:*
Ecelin, Alberic . . . ah, Naddo's gone!   *1863:* Ecelin,—only Naddo's never gone!
1013| *1840:*—Labours this moonrise what <> meant   *1863:*—Labours, this moonrise,
what   *1888:* meant: 1014| *1840:* purulent   *1863:* purulent,   1018| *1840:*
lines   *1863:* lines,   1022| *1840:* well   *1863:* well,   1024| *1840:* eve: *1863:*

₁₀₂₅ While the persisting hermit-bee . . . ha! wait
No longer: these in compass, forward fate!

BOOK THE SIXTH.

The thought of Eglamor's least like a thought,
And yet a false one, was, "Man shrinks to nought
If matched with symbols of immensity;
Must quail, forsooth, before a quiet sky
₅ Or sea, too little for their quietude:"
And, truly, somewhat in Sordello's mood
Confirmed its speciousness, while eve slow sank
Down the near terrace to the farther bank,
And only one spot left from out the night
₁₀ Glimmered upon the river opposite—
A breadth of watery heaven like a bay,
A sky-like space of water, ray for ray,
And star for star, one richness where they mixed
As this and that wing of an angel, fixed,
₁₅ Tumultuary splendours folded in
To die. Nor turned he till Ferrara's din
(Say, the monotonous speech from a man's lip
Who lets some first and eager purpose slip
In a new fancy's birth—the speech keeps on
₂₀ Though elsewhere its informing soul be gone)
—Aroused him, surely offered succour. Fate
Paused with this eve; ere she precipitate
Herself,—best put off new strange thoughts awhile,

eve.   ¹⁰²⁶| *1840:* longer—these   *1863:* longer: these
§ ^{1–24}| *1863:* AT THE CLOSE OF A DAY OR A LIFE, §   ²| *1840:* was, Man   *1863:*
was, "Man   ³| *1840:* immensity—   *1868:* immensity;   ⁵| *1840:* quietude:
1863: quietude:"   ⁷| *1840:* speciousness while evening sank   *1863:* speciousness,
while eve slow sank   ⁸| *1840:* further   *1863:* farther   ⁹| *1840:* left out of the
1888: left from out the   ¹²| *1840:* for ray   *1863:* for ray,   ¹⁵| *1840:* splendors
1863: splendours   ¹⁶| *1840:* die: nor   *1863:* die. Nor   ¹⁹| *1840:* birth; the
1888: birth—the   ²¹| *1840:* Aroused him,—surely <> succour; fate
1863:—Aroused <> succour. Fate   *1868:* him, surely   ²³| *1840:* Herself . . . put off
strange after-thoughts awhile,   *1863:* Herself,—put   *1888:* Herself,—best put off new

That voice, those large hands, that portentous smile,—
25 What help to pierce the future as the past
Lay in the plaining city?
                                    And at last
The main discovery and prime concern,
All that just now imported him to learn,
Truth's self, like yonder slow moon to complete
30 Heaven, rose again, and, naked at his feet,
Lighted his old life's every shift and change,
Effort with counter-effort; nor the range
Of each looked wrong except wherein it checked,
Some other—which of these could he suspect,
35 Prying into them by the sudden blaze?
The real way seemed made up of all the ways—
Mood after mood of the one mind in him;
Tokens of the existence, bright or dim,
Of a transcendent all-embracing sense
40 Demanding only outward influence,
A soul, in Palma's phrase, above his soul,
Power to uplift his power,—such moon's control
Over such sea-depths,—and their mass had swept
Onward from the beginning and still kept
45 Its course: but years and years the sky above
Held none, and so, untasked of any love,
His sensitiveness idled, now amort,
Alive now, and, to sullenness or sport
Given wholly up, disposed itself anew
50 At every passing instigation, grew
And dwindled at caprice, in foam-showers spilt,
Wedge-like insisting, quivered now a gilt
Shield in the sunshine, now a blinding race
Of whitest ripples o'er the reef—found place

strange thoughts awhile,   24| *1840:* smile . . .   *1863:* smile,—   § 25–52| *1863:* PAST
PROCEDURE IS FITLIEST REVIEWED, §   25| *1840:* Future <> Past   *1863:* as
the Past,   *1868:* future <> past,   *1888:* past   29| *1840:* His truth, like   *1888:*
Truth's self, like   30| *1840:* and naked   *1863:* and, naked   33| *1840:* checked
1863: checked,   34| *1840:* suspect   *1863:* suspect,   42| *1840:* his power, this
moon's control,   *1863:* his power,—this   *1868:* control   *1888:* his power,—such
moon's   43| *1840:* sea-depths, and   *1863:* sea-depths,—and   45| *1840:* course;
but   *1863:* course: but   48| *1840:* and to   *1863:* and, to   § 53–81| *1863:* AS MORE

55 For much display; not gathered up and, hurled
Right from its heart, encompassing the world.
So had Sordello been, by consequence,
Without a function: others made pretence
To strength not half his own, yet had some core
60 Within, submitted to some moon, before
Them still, superior still whate'er their force,—
Were able therefore to fulfil a course,
Nor missed life's crown, authentic attribute.
To each who lives must be a certain fruit
65 Of having lived in his degree,—a stage,
Earlier or later in men's pilgrimage,
To stop at; and to this the spirits tend
Who, still discovering beauty without end,
Amass the scintillations, make one star
70 —Something unlike them, self-sustained, afar,—
And meanwhile nurse the dream of being blest
By winning it to notice and invest
Their souls with alien glory, some one day
Whene'er the nucleus, gathering shape alway,
75 Round to the perfect circle—soon or late,
According as themselves are formed to wait;
Whether mere human beauty will suffice
—The yellow hair and the luxurious eyes,
Or human intellect seem best, or each
80 Combine in some ideal form past reach
On earth, or else some shade of these, some aim,
Some love, hate even, take their place, the same,
So to be served—all this they do not lose,
Waiting for death to live, nor idly choose
85 What must be Hell—a progress thus pursued

APPRECIABLE IN ITS ENTIRETY. §   55| *1840:* For myriad charms; not   *1863:*
For much display; not   59| *1840:* strengths   *1863:* strength   61| *1840:* It still,
superior still whate'er its force,   *1863:* Them still, superior still whate'er their
force,—   62| *1840:* course   *1863:* course,   63| *1840:* Life's <> attribute—
1863: life's <> attribute.   65| *1840:* degree, a stage   *1863:* degree,—a stage,
67| *1840:* and to which those spirits   *1863:* and to this the spirits   69| *1840:*
scintillations for one   *1863:* scintillations, make one   70| *1840:* afar,   *1863:*
afar,—   73| *1840:* glory some   *1863:* glory, some   75| *1840:* late   *1863:*
late,   77| *1840:* Whether 'tis human   *1863:* Whether mere human   § 82–109| *1863:*
STRONG, HE NEEDED EXTERNAL STRENGTH: §   82| *1840:* place the   *1863:*
place, the   83| *1840:* That may be   *1863:* And may   *1888:* So to be   85| *1840:*

305

Through all existence, still above the food
That's offered them, still fain to reach beyond
The widened range, in virtue of their bond
Of sovereignty. Not that a Palma's Love,
90 A Salinguerra's Hate, would equal prove
To swaying all Sordello: but why doubt
Some love meet for such strength, some moon without
Would match his sea?—or fear, Good manifest,
Only the Best breaks faith?—Ah but the Best
95 Somehow eludes us ever, still might be
And is not! Crave we gems? No penury
Of their material round us! Pliant earth
And plastic flame—what balks the mage his birth
—Jacinth in balls or lodestone by the block?
100 Flinders enrich the strand, veins swell the rock;
Nought more! Seek creatures? Life's i' the tempest, thought
Clothes the keen hill-top, mid-day woods are fraught
With fervours: human forms are well enough!
But we had hoped, encouraged by the stuff
105 Profuse at nature's pleasure, men beyond
These actual men!—and thus are over-fond
In arguing, from Good—the Best, from force
Divided—force combined, an ocean's course
From this our sea whose mere intestine pants
110 Might seem at times sufficient to our wants.

What Hell shall be—a *1863:* What must be Hell—a   87| *1840:* still towering
beyond *1863:* still fain to reach beyond   88| *1840:* range in *1863:* range, in
89| *1840:* sovereignty: not <> Love *1863:* sovereignty. Not <> Love,   90| *1840:*
A Salinguerra's Hate would *1863:* A Salinguerra's Hate, would   91| *1840:* all
Sordello: wherefore doubt, *1868:* doubt *1888:* all Sordello: but why doubt
92| *1840:* Love meet for such a Strength, some Moon's *1863:* That Love <> such Strength,
some moon *1868:* love <> strength *1888:* Some love   93| *1840:* To match his
Sea?—fear, Good so manifest, *1863:* Would match his sea?—or fear, Good manifest,
94| *1840:* faith?—but that the *1863:* faith?—Ah, but the *1868:* faith?—Ah but
96| *1840:* not: crave you gems? where's penury *1863:* not! crave we gems? no penury
1868: Crave <> No   97| *1840:* us? pliant earth, *1863:* us! pliant *1868:*
Pliant   98| *1840:* The plastic <> Mage *1863:* mage *1868:* And plastic
99| *1840:* Jacynth in balls, or *1863:*—Jacinth in balls or   100| *1840:* strand and veins
the rock— *1863:* strand, and *1868:* strand, veins swell the rock;   101| *1840:* No
more! Ask creatures? Life in tempest, Thought *1863:* Nought more! <> Life's i' the
tempest *1868:* more! Seek creatures <> thought   103| *1840:* fervours ... ah, these
forms <> enough— *1863:* fervours: ah <> enough! *1868:* fervours: human
forms   105| *1840:* Nature's <> Men *1863:* men *1868:* nature's   106| *1840:*
These Men! and thus, perchance, are *1863:* men *1868:* These actual men!—and thus
are   107| *1840:* from Good the *1888:* from Good—the § 110–38| *1863:* EVEN NOW,

External power! If none be adequate,
And he stand forth ordained (a prouder fate)
Himself a law to his own sphere? "Remove
All incompleteness!" for that law, that love?
115 Nay, if all other laws be feints,—truth veiled
Helpfully to weak vision that had failed
To grasp aught but its special want,—for lure,
Embodied? Stronger vision could endure
The unbodied want: no part—the whole of truth!
120 The People were himself; nor, by the ruth
At their condition, was he less impelled
To alter the discrepancy beheld,
Than if, from the sound whole, a sickly part
Subtracted were transformed, decked out with art,
125 Then palmed on him as alien woe—the Guelf
To succour, proud that he forsook himself.
All is himself; all service, therefore, rates
Alike, nor serving one part, immolates
The rest: but all in time! "That lance of yours
130 Makes havoc soon with Malek and his Moors,
That buckler's lined with many a giant's beard
Ere long, our champion, be the lance upreared,
The buckler wielded handsomely as now!
But view your escort, bear in mind your vow,
135 Count the pale tracts of sand to pass ere that,

WHERE CAN HE PERCEIVE SUCH? §   110| *1840:* Had seem   *1863:* Might
seem   111| *1840:*—External Power? If <> adequate   *1888:* ¶ External power! If <>
adequate,   112| *1840:* he have been ordained   *1863:* he stand forth ordained
113| *1840:* A law to his own sphere? the need remove   *1863:* sphere?—need to remove
1888: Himself a law to his own sphere? "Remove   114| *1840:* incompleteness be that
1863: incompleteness, for that   *1888:* incompleteness!" for   115| *1840:* Nay, really
such be other's laws, though veiled   *1863:* Nay, if all other laws be such, though veiled
1888: be feints,—truth veiled   116| *1840:* In mercy to each vision   *1888:* Helpfully to
weak vision   117| *1840:* If unassisted by its Want, for   *1863:* want,—for   *1888:* To
grasp aught but its special want   118| *1840:* stronger   *1863:* Stronger
119| *1840:* The simple want—no bauble for a truth!   *1863:* The unbodied want: no   *1888:*
no part—the whole of truth!   120| *1840:* himself; and by   *1863:* and, by   *1888:*
himself; nor, by   121| *1840:* condition was   *1863:* condition, was   122| *1840:*
Alter the discrepancy he beheld   *1863:* To alter the discrepancy beheld,   123| *1840:*
Whole <> Part   *1888:* whole <> part   126| *1840:* himself?   *1888:* himself.
127| *1840:* No: All's himself—all   *1863:* No! All's himself; all   *1888:* All is himself
129| *1840:* time! That   *1863:* time! "That   131| *1840:* Giant's   *1863:* giant's
132| *1840:* long, Porphyrio, be the lance but reared,   *1863:* long, O champion, be the lance
upreared,   *1868:* long, our champion   133| *1840:* now;   *1863:* now!

307

And, if you hope we struggle through the flat,
Put lance and buckler by! Next half-month lacks
Mere sturdy exercise of mace and axe
To cleave this dismal brake of prickly-pear
140 Which bristling holds Cydippe by the hair,
Lames barefoot Agathon: this felled, we'll try
The picturesque achievements by and by—
Next life!"
        Ay, rally, mock, O People, urge
Your claims!—for thus he ventured, to the verge,
145 Push a vain mummery which perchance distrust
Of his fast-slipping resolution thrust
Likewise: accordingly the Crowd—(as yet
He had unconsciously contrived forget
I' the whole, to dwell o' the points . . . one might assuage
150 The signal horrors easier than engage
With a dim vulgar vast unobvious grief
Not to be fancied off, nor gained relief
In brilliant fits, cured by a happy quirk,
But by dim vulgar vast unobvious work
155 To correspond . . .) this Crowd then, forth they stood.
"And now content thy stronger vision, brood
On thy bare want; uncovered, turf by turf,
Study the corpse-face thro' the taint-worms' scurf!"
      Down sank the People's Then; uprose their Now.
160 These sad ones render service to! And how

136| *1840:* through this flat, *1863:* through the flat,   137| *1840:* buckler up—next
1863: buckler by! Next   138| *1840:* A sturdy <> mace or axe   *1863:* Mere sturdy <>
mace and axe   § 139-65| *1863:* INTERNAL STRENGTH MUST SUFFICE THEN,
139-66| *1868* §   140| *1840:* That bristling   *1863:* Which bristling
141-43| *1840:* barefoot Agathon. ¶ Oh   *1863:* barefoot Agathon: this felled, we'll try / The
picturesque achievements by and by— / Next life!" ¶ Ay, rally, mock, oh   *1868:* O
144| *1840:* ventured to the verge   *1863:* ventured, to the verge,   147| *1840:* No less:
accordingly the Crowd—as   *1863:* Likewise: accordingly   *1868:* the Crowd—(as
148| *1840:* inconsciously   *1863:* unconsciously   149| *1840:* To dwell upon the
points   *1863:* 'I the whole, to dwell o' the points   *1868:* I' the   150| *1840:* horrors
sooner than   *1863:* horrors easier than   152| *1840:* off, obtained relief   *1863:* off, nor
gained relief   155| *1840:* correspond—however, forth they stood: *1863:* correspond
. . . this Crowd then, forth they stood.   *1868:* correspond . . .) this   156| *1840:* And
1863: "And   157| *1840:* want; the grave stript turf by   *1863:* want; uncovered, turf
by   158| *1840:* scurf!   *1863:* scurf!"   162| *1840:* for, move   *1863:* for

Piteously little must that service prove
—Had surely proved in any case! for, move
Each other obstacle away, let youth
Become aware it had surprised a truth
165 'Twere service to impart—can truth be seized,
Settled forthwith, and, of the captive eased,
Its captor find fresh prey, since this alit
So happily, no gesture luring it,
The earnest of a flock to follow? Vain,
170 Most vain! a life to spend ere this he chain
To the poor crowd's complacence: ere the crowd
Pronounce it captured, he descries a cloud
Its kin of twice the plume; which he, in turn,
If he shall live as many lives, may learn
175 How to secure: not else. Then Mantua called
Back to his mind how certain bards were thralled
—Buds blasted, but of breath more like perfume
Than Naddo's staring nosegay's carrion bloom;
Some insane rose that burnt heart out in sweets,
180 A spendthrift in the spring, no summer greets;
Some Dularete, drunk with truths and wine,
Grown bestial, dreaming how become divine.
Yet to surmount this obstacle, commence
With the commencement, merits crowning! Hence
185 Must truth be casual truth, elicited
In sparks so mean, at intervals dispread
So rarely, that 'tis like at no one time
Of the world's story has not truth, the prime

move   164| 1840: Have been aware <> Truth   1863: truth   1868: Become
aware   165| 1840: Truth   1863: truth   § 166–94| 1863: HIS SYMPATHY WITH
THE PEOPLE, TO WIT;   167–94| 1868 §   166| 1840: and of <> eased   1863:
and, of <> eased,   167| 1840: captor look around, since   1863: captor find fresh prey,
since   170| 1840: life's <> chain,   1868: life   1888: chain   171| 1840:
complacence; ere   1888: complacence: ere   172| 1840: captured   1863: captured,
he   173| 1840: the plumage—he   1863: the plume—which he   1868: plume;
which   175| 1840: Secure—not otherwise. Then   1863: How to secure—not else.
Then   1868: secure: not   177| 1840: breaths <> perfumes   1863: breath <>
perfume   178| 1840: bloom   1863: bloom: 1868: bloom;   179| 1840: Could
boast—some rose   1863: Some insane rose   180| 1840: the Spring, no Summer
greets—   1868: the spring, no summer greets;   182| 1840: bestial dreaming   1863:
bestial, dreaming   183| 1863: "Yet   1868: Yet   185| 1840: Truth <> Truth
1863: truth <> truth   188| 1840: Truth   1863: truth   189| 1840: Truth <>

Of truth, the very truth which, loosed, had hurled
190 The world's course right, been really in the world
—Content the while with some mean spark by dint
Of some chance-blow, the solitary hint
Of buried fire, which, rip earth's breast, would stream
Sky-ward!
        Sordello's miserable gleam
195 Was looked for at the moment: he would dash
This badge, and all it brought, to earth,—abash
Taurello thus, perhaps persuade him wrest
The Kaiser from his purpose,—would attest
His own belief, in any case. Before
200 He dashes it however, think once more!
For, were that little, truly service? "Ay,
I' the end, no doubt; but meantime? Plain you spy
Its ultimate effect, but many flaws
Of vision blur each intervening cause.
205 Were the day's fraction clear as the life's sum
Of service, Now as filled as teems To-come
With evidence of good—nor too minute
A share to vie with evil! No dispute,
'Twere fitliest maintain the Guelfs in rule:
210 That makes your life's work: but you have to school
Your day's work on these natures circumstanced
Thus variously, which yet, as each advanced
Or might impede the Guelf rule, must be moved

Truth which loosed had   *1863:* truth <> truth which, loosed, had   190| *1840:* Its
course aright, been   *1863:* The world's course right, been   191| *1840:* Content
1863:—Content   193| *1840:* rip its breast   *1888:* rip earth's breast   § 194–222| *1863:*
OF WHICH, TRY NOW THE INHERENT FORCE!   195–223| *1868* §
194| *1863:* Sky-ward!" ¶ Sordello's   *1868:* Sky-ward! ¶ Sordello's   196| *1840:* badge to
earth and all it brought, abash   *1863:* badge, and all it brought, to earth,—abash
198| *1840:* purpose; would   *1863:* purpose,—would   199| *1840:* His constancy in
1863: His own belief, in   200| *1840:* it, however   *1868:* it however   201| *1840:*
was that little truly service? Ay—   *1863:* were that little, truly service? "Ay—   *1868:*
service? "Ay,   203| *1840:* Effect   *1863:* effect   204| *1840:* intervening Cause;
1863: cause.   206| *1840:* filled as the To-come   *1888:* filled as teems To-come
208| *1840:* evil! How dispute   *1863:* evil! No dispute,   209| *1840:* The Guelfs were
fitliest maintained in rule?   *1863:* 'Twere fitliest maintain the Guelfs in rule:
210| *1840:* That made the life's work: not so easy school   *1863:* That makes your life's work:
but you have to school   211| *1840:* work—say, on natures   *1863:* work on these
natures   212| *1840:* So variously   *1863:* Thus variously   213| *1840:* impede

Now, for the Then's sake,—hating what you loved,
215 Loving old hatreds! Nor if one man bore
Brand upon temples while his fellow wore
The aureole, would it task you to decide:
But, portioned duly out, the future vied
Never with the unparcelled present! Smite
220 Or spare so much on warrant all so slight?
The present's complete sympathies to break,
Aversions bear with, for a future's sake
So feeble? Tito ruined through one speck,
The Legate saved by his sole lightish fleck?
225 This were work, true, but work performed at cost
Of other work; aught gained here, elsewhere lost.
For a new segment spoil an orb half-done?
Rise with the People one step, and sink—one?
Were it but one step, less than the whole face
230 Of things, your novel duty bids erase!
Harms to abolish! What, the prophet saith,
The minstrel singeth vainly then? Old faith,
Old courage, only born because of harms,
Were not, from highest to the lowest, charms?
235 Flame may persist; but is not glare as staunch?
Where the salt marshes stagnate, crystals branch;
Blood dries to crimson; Evil's beautified
In every shape. Thrust Beauty then aside
And banish Evil! Wherefore? After all,

---

that Guelf rule, it behoved   *1863:* impede the Guelf rule, must be moved   ^{214|}   *1840:*
You, for < > sake, hate what Now you   *1863:* Now, for < > sake,—hating what you
^{215|}   *1840:* Love what you hated; nor   *1863:* Loving old hatreds! nor   *1868:* Nor
^{217|}   *1840:* task us to decide—   *1863:* task you to   *1868:* decide: ^{218|}   *1840:* But
portioned < > Future   *1863:* But, portioned   *1868:* future   ^{219|}   *1840:* Present
1868: present   ^{221|}   *1840:* Present's   *1868:* present's   ^{222|}   *1840:* Future's
1868: future's   § ^{223–51|}   *1863:* HOW MUCH OF MAN'S ILL MAY BE REMOVED?
^{224–52|}   *1868* §   ^{225|}   *1840:* true—but   *1868:* true, but   ^{226|}   *1840:*
work—aught < > lost—   *1863:* lost.   *1868:* work; aught   ^{227|}   *1840:* half-done–
1863: half-done?   ^{228|}   *1840:* sink . . . one?   *1863:* sink—one?   ^{229|}   *1840:* Would
it were one step—less   *1863:* Were it but one   *1868:* step, less   ^{230|}   *1840:* things our
novel   *1863:* things, your novel   ^{231|}   *1840:* Harms are to vanquish; what? the
Prophet   *1863:* Harms to abolish! what? the prophet   *1868:* abolish! What, the
^{232|}   *1840:* Minstrel   *1863:* minstrel   ^{233|}   *1840:* courage, born of the surrounding
harms,   *1863:* courage, only born because of harms,   ^{235|}   *1840:* Oh, flame persists
but   *1863:* Flame may persist; but   ^{236|}   *1840:* branch—   *1868:* branch;
^{237|}   *1840:* crimson—Evil's   *1868:* crimson; Evil's   ^{238|}   *1840:* shape! But Beauty
thrust aside   *1863:* shape. Thrust Beauty then aside   ^{239|}   *1840:* You banish Evil:

240 Is Evil a result less natural
      Than Good? For overlook the seasons' strife
      With tree and flower,—the hideous animal life,
      (Of which who seeks shall find a grinning taunt
      For his solution, and endure the vaunt
245 Of nature's angel, as a child that knows
      Himself befooled, unable to propose
      Aught better than the fooling)—and but care
      For men, for the mere People then and there,—
      In these, could you but see that Good and Ill
250 Claimed you alike! Whence rose their claim but still
      From Ill, as fruit of Ill? What else could knit
      You theirs but Sorrow? Any free from it
      Were also free from you! Whose happiness
      Could be distinguished in this morning's press
255 Of miseries?—the fool's who passed a gibe
      'On thee,' jeered he, 'so wedded to thy tribe,
      Thou carriest green and yellow tokens in
      Thy very face that thou art Ghibellin!'
      Much hold on you that fool obtained! Nay mount
260 Yet higher—and upon men's own account
      Must Evil stay: for, what is joy?—to heave
      Up one obstruction more, and common leave
      What was peculiar, by such act destroy

---

wherefore <> all   *1863:* And banish Evil! wherefore <> all,   *1868:* Wherefore
²⁴⁰| *1840:* Is Evil our result   *1863:* Is Evil a result   ²⁴¹| *1840:* Seasons'   *1863:* Than
Good? For, overlook the seasons'   *1868:* Than Good? For overlook   ²⁴²| *1840:*
flower—the   *1863:* flower,—the   ²⁴³| *1840:* Of   *1863:* (Of   ²⁴⁴| *1840:*
solution, must endure   *1863:* solution, and endure   ²⁴⁵| *1840:* Nature's   *1863:*
nature's   ²⁴⁷| *1840:* fooling—and   *1863:* fooling)—and   ²⁴⁸| *1840:* For Men,
the varied People <> there,   *1863:* For Men, for the mere People <> there,—   *1868:*
men   ²⁴⁹| *1840:* Of which 'tis easy saying Good   *1863:* In these, could you but see that
Good   ²⁵⁰| *1840:* Claim him alike <> rose the claim   *1863:* Claimed you alike <>
rose their claim   ²⁵¹| *1840:* From Ill, the fruit of Ill—what   *1863:* From Ill, as fruit
1868: of Ill? What   § ²⁵²⁻⁸⁰| *1863:* HOW MUCH OF ILL OUGHT TO BE
REMOVED?   ²⁵³⁻⁸¹| *1868* §   ²⁵²| *1840:* Him theirs   *1863:* You theirs
²⁵³| *1840:* from him! A happiness   *1863:* from you! Whose happiness   ²⁵⁵| *1840:*
miseries—the   *1863:* miseries?—the   ²⁵⁶| *1840:* On one, said he, so <> to his tribe
1863: 'On thee,' jeered he, 'so <> to thy tribe,   ²⁵⁷| *1840:* He carries green   *1863:*
Thou carriest green   ²⁵⁸| *1840:* His very face that he's a Ghibellin—   *1863:* Thy very
face that thou art Ghibellin!—   *1868:* art Ghibellin!'   ²⁵⁹| *1840:* on him that   *1863:*
on you that   ²⁶⁰| *1840:* higher; and upon Men's   *1863:* higher—and upon
men's   ²⁶¹| *1840:* for what is Joy? To   *1863:* for, what is Joy?—to   *1868:* joy
²⁶³| *1840:* peculiar—by this act   *1863:* by such act   *1868:* peculiar, by   ²⁶⁹| *1840:*

Itself; a partial death is every joy;
265 The sensible escape, enfranchisement
Of a sphere's essence: once the vexed—content,
The cramped—at large, the growing circle—round,
All's to begin again—some novel bound
To break, some new enlargement to entreat;
270 The sphere though larger is not more complete.
Now for Mankind's experience: who alone
Might style the unobstructed world his own?
Whom palled Goito with its perfect things?
Sordello's self: whereas for Mankind springs
275 Salvation by each hindrance interposed.
They climb; life's view is not at once disclosed
To creatures caught up, on the summit left,
Heaven plain above them, yet of wings bereft:
But lower laid, as at the mountain's foot.
280 So, range on range, the girdling forests shoot
'Twixt your plain prospect and the throngs who scale
Height after height, and pierce mists, veil by veil,
Heartened with each discovery; in their soul,
The Whole they seek by Parts—but, found that Whole,
285 Could they revert, enjoy past gains? The space
Of time you judge so meagre to embrace
The Parts were more than plenty, once attained
The Whole, to quite exhaust it: nought were gained
But leave to look—not leave to do: Beneath

---

enlargement's to entreat, *1863:* enlargement *1868:* entreat; ^{274|} *1840:* self;
whereas *1863:* self! whereas for mankind *1868:* self: whereas for Mankind
^{275|} *1840:* Salvation—hindrances are interposed *1863:* Salvation by each hindrance
interposed; *1868:* interposed. ^{276|} *1840:* For them, not all Life's view at *1863:*
They climb, life's view is not at *1868:* climb; life's ^{277|} *1840:* creatures sudden on its
summit left *1863:* creatures caught up, on <> left, *1868:* on the summit
^{278|} *1840:* With Heaven above and yet <> bereft— *1863:* Heaven plain above them,
yet *1868:* bereft: ^{279|} *1840:* foot *1863:* foot, *1868:* foot. ^{280|} *1840:*
Where, range on *1863:* While, range on *1868:* So, range on § ^{281–308|} *1863:*—IF
REMOVED, AT WHAT COST TO SORDELLO? ^{282–309|} *1868* § ^{281|} *1840:*
Between the prospect *1863:* 'Twixt your plain prospect ^{282|} *1840:* Earnestly ever,
piercing veil by *1863:* Height after height, and pierce mists, veil by ^{283|} *1840:*
Confirmed with <> soul *1863:* Heartened with <> soul, ^{285|} *1840:* revert? Oh,
testify! The *1863:* revert, enjoy past gains? The ^{286|} *1840:* time we judge *1863:*
time you judge ^{287|} *1840:* The Parts, were *1868:* The Parts were ^{288|} *1840:* it:
for nought's gained *1863:* it: nought were gained
^{289|} *1840:* look—no leave *1863:* look—not leave ^{290|} *1840:* look Above, then!

290 Soon sates the looker—look Above, and Death
     Tempts ere a tithe of Life be tasted. Live
     First, and die soon enough, Sordello! Give
     Body and spirit the first right they claim,
     And pasture soul on a voluptuous shame
295 That you, a pageant-city's denizen,
     Are neither vilely lodged midst Lombard men—
     Can force joy out of sorrow, seem to truck
     Bright attributes away for sordid muck,
     Yet manage from that very muck educe
300 Gold; then subject, nor scruple, to your cruce
     The world's discardings! Though real ingots pay
     Your pains, the clods that yielded them are clay
     To all beside,—would clay remain, though quenched
     Your purging-fire; who's robbed then? Had you wrenched
305 An ampler treasure forth!—As 'tis, they crave
     A share that ruins you and will not save
     Them. Why should sympathy command you quit
     The course that makes your joy, nor will remit
     Their woe? Would all arrive at joy? Reverse
310 The order (time instructs you) nor coerce
     Each unit till, some predetermined mode,
     The total be emancipate; men's road
     Is one, men's times of travel many; thwart
     No enterprising soul's precocious start
315 Before the general march! If slow or fast
     All straggle up to the same point at last,

Death   *1863:* look Above, and Death   293| *1840:* claim   *1863:* claim,
294| *1840:* To pasture thee on   *1863:* And pasture   *1888:* pasture soul on
295| *1840:* That thou, a   *1888:* That you, a   296| *1840:* Art neither   *1888:* Are
neither   297| *1840:* Canst   *1888:* Can   298| *1840:* Thine attributes   *1888:*
Bright attributes   300| *1840:* to thy cruce   *1868:* subject nor   *1888:* subject, nor <>
to your cruce   301| *1840:* discardings; think, if ingots   *1863:* discardings! Though real
ingots   302| *1840:* Such pains   *1863:* Thy pains   *1888:* Your pains   303| *1840:*
all save thee, and clay remain though   *1863:* thee,—would clay remain, though   *1888:* all
beside,—would   304| *1840:* Thy purging-fire <> then? Would I wrenched   *1863:*
then? Had you wrenched   *1888:* Your purging-fire   305| *1840:* ample <> 'tis, why
crave   *1863:* ampler <> 'tis, they crave   306| *1840:* ruins me and   *1863:* ruins you
and   307| *1840:* Yourselves?—imperiously command I quit   *1863:* Them. Why
should sympathy command you quit   308| *1840:* makes my joy nor   *1863:* makes your
joy, nor   § 309–37| *1863:* MEN WIN LITTLE THEREBY; HE LOSES ALL
310–37| *1868* §   309| *1840:* Your woe   *1863:* Their woe   312| *1840:*
emancipate; our road   *1863:* emancipate; men's road   313| *1840:* one, our times
1863: one, men's times   315| *1840:* march; if   *1863:* march! if   *1868:* If   317| *1840:*

Why grudge your having gained, a month ago,
The brakes at balm-shed, asphodels in blow,
While they were landlocked? Speed their Then, but how
320 This badge would suffer you improve your Now!"
    His time of action for, against, or with
Our world (I labour to extract the pith
Of this his problem) grew, that even-tide,
Gigantic with its power of joy, beside
325 The world's eternity of impotence
To profit though at his whole joy's expense.
"Make nothing of my day because so brief?
Rather make more: instead of joy, use grief
Before its novelty have time subside!
330 Wait not for the late savour, leave untried
Virtue, the creaming honey-wine, quick squeeze
Vice like a biting spirit from the lees
Of life! Together let wrath, hatred, lust,
All tyrannies in every shape, be thrust
335 Upon this Now, which time may reason out
As mischiefs, far from benefits, no doubt;
But long ere then Sordello will have slipt
Away; you teach him at Goito's crypt,
There's a blank issue to that fiery thrill.
340 Stirring, the few cope with the many, still:
So much of sand as, quiet, makes a mass
Unable to produce three tufts of grass,
Shall, troubled by the whirlwind, render void

---

grudge my having gained a <> ago   1863: grudge your having gained, a <> ago,
319| 1840: While you were <> Speed your Then   1863: While they were <> Speed their
Then   320| 1840: suffer me improve my Now!   1863: suffer you improve your
Now!' "   1868: your Now!"   323| 1840: this and more) grew up, that   1863: this his
problem) grew, that   324| 1840: joy beside   1863: joy, beside   326| 1840: at all
his joy's   1863: at his whole joy's   327| 1840: Make <> of that time because   1863:
"Make <> of my day because   328| 1840: more—instead of joy take grief   1863: joy,
use grief   1868: more: instead   329| 1840: subside;   1863: subside!   330| 1840:
No time for <> savour—leave   1863: Wait not for   1868: savour, leave   331| 1840:
honey wine   1863: honey-wine   333| 1840: life—together   1863: life!—together
1868: life! Together   334| 1840: shape be   1863: shape, be   336| 1840:
doubt—   1868: doubt;   337| 1868: slipped   1888: slipt   § 338–66| 1863: FOR HE
CAN INFINITELY ENJOY HIMSELF, §   338| 1840: Away—You <> crypt   1863:
crypt,   1868: Away; you   339| 1840: thrill!   1868: thrill.   340| 1840: Few <>
Many   1863: few <> many   341| 1840: of dust as   1863: of sand as   345| 1840:

The whole calm glebe's endeavour: be employed!
345 And e'en though somewhat smart the Crowd for this,
Contribute each his pang to make your bliss,
'Tis but one pang—one blood-drop to the bowl
Which brimful tempts the sluggish asp uncowl
At last, stains ruddily the dull red cape,
350 And, kindling orbs grey as the unripe grape
Before, avails forthwith to disentrance
The portent, soon to lead a mystic dance
Among you! For, who sits alone in Rome?
Have those great hands indeed hewn out a home,
355 And set me there to live? Oh life, life-breath,
Life-blood,—ere sleep, come travail, life ere death!
This life stream on my soul, direct, oblique,
But always streaming! Hindrances? They pique:
Helps? such . . . but why repeat, my soul o'ertops
360 Each height, then every depth profoundlier drops?
Enough that I can live, and would live! Wait
For some transcendent life reserved by Fate
To follow this? Oh, never! Fate, I trust
The same, my soul to; for, as who flings dust,
365 Perchance (so facile was the deed) she chequed
The void with these materials to affect
My soul diversely: these consigned anew
To nought by death, what marvel if she threw
A second and superber spectacle
370 Before me? What may serve for sun, what still

---

smarts   *1863:* smart   ^{346|}   *1840:* Contributes <> make up bliss,   *1863:* Contribute
<> make your bliss,   ^{349|}   *1840:* So quick, stains   *1863:* At last, stains
^{350|}   *1840:* orbs dull as   *1863:* orbs grey as   ^{352|}   *1840:* The mischief—soon   *1863:*
The portent—soon   *1868:* portent, soon   ^{353|}   *1840:* you! Nay, who   *1863:* you! For,
who   ^{354|}   *1840:* home   *1863:* home,   ^{355|}   *1840:* For me—compelled to <>
Life   *1863:* And set me there to <> life   ^{356|}   *1840:* sleep be travail   *1863:* sleep,
come travail   ^{357|}   *1840:* life to feed my   *1863:* life stream on my   ^{358|}   *1840:*
always feeding! Hindrances <> pique—   *1863:* always streaming! Hindrances   *1868:*
pique: ^{359|}   *1840:* but wherefore say my   *1863:* but why repeat, my   ^{360|}   *1840:*
All height—than <> profounder   *1863:* Each height, than <> profoundlier   *1868:*
height, then every   ^{363|}   *1840:* never! Fate I   *1863:* never! Fate, I   ^{364|}   *1840:*
same my <> dust   *1863:* same, my <> dust,   ^{365|}   *1840:* Perchance—so <> deed,
she   *1868:* Perchance (so <> deed) she   § ^{367–95|}   *1863:* FREED FROM A
PROBLEMATIC OBLIGATION, §   ^{367|}   *1840:* That soul diversely—these   *1863:*
My soul   *1868:* diversely: these   ^{368|}   *1840:* death, why marvel   *1863:* death, what
marvel   ^{370|}   *1840:* Before it? What <> sun—what   *1868:* Before me? What <>

Wander a moon above me? What else wind
About me like the pleasures left behind,
And how shall some new flesh that is not flesh
Cling to me? What's new laughter? Soothes the fresh
375 Sleep like sleep? Fate's exhaustless for my sake
In brave resource: but whether bids she slake
My thirst at this first rivulet, or count
No draught worth lip save from some rocky fount
Above i' the clouds, while here she's provident
380 Of pure loquacious pearl, the soft tree-tent
Guards, with its face of reate and sedge, nor fail
The silver globules and gold-sparkling grail
At bottom? Oh, 'twere too absurd to slight
For the hereafter the to-day's delight!
385 Quench thirst at this, then seek next well-spring: wear
Home-lilies ere strange lotus in my hair!
Here is the Crowd, whom I with freest heart
Offer to serve, contented for my part
To give life up in service,—only grant
390 That I do serve; if otherwise, why want
Aught further of me? If men cannot choose
But set aside life, why should I refuse
The gift? I take it—I, for one, engage
Never to falter through my pilgrimage—
395 Nor end it howling that the stock or stone
Were enviable, truly: I, for one,
Will praise the world, you style mere anteroom
To palace—be it so! shall I assume

sun, what   371| 1840: me—what   1868: me? What   372| 1840: behind?   1863:
behind,   374| 1840: what's new laughter—soothes   1868: me? What's new laughter?
Soothes   376| 1840: resource, but   1868: resource: but   377| 1840:: rivulet or
1863: rivulet, or   378| 1840: from the rocky   1888: from some rocky   380| 1840:
Of (taste) loquacious pearl the   1863: Of pure loquacious pearl, the   383| 1840:
bottom—Oh   1863: bottom. Oh   1868: bottom? Oh   385| 1840:
well-spring—wear   1868: well-spring: wear   389| 1840: give this life up once for all,
but grant   1863: give life up in service,—only grant   390| 1840: I really serve   1863:
That I do serve   391| 1840: me? Life they cannot chuse   1863: me? If men cannot
choose   392| 1840: aside—wherefore should   1863: aside life, why should
394| 1840: through the pilgrimage—   1863: through my pilgrimage—   395| 1840:
Or end   1863: Nor end   § 396–424| 1863: AND ACCEPTING LIFE ON ITS OWN
TERMS, §   397| 1840: world you   1863: world, you   398| 1840: To the true

—My foot the courtly gait, my tongue the trope,
400 My mouth the smirk, before the doors fly ope
One moment? What? with guarders row on row,
Gay swarms of varletry that come and go,
Pages to dice with, waiting-girls unlace
The plackets of, pert claimants help displace,
405 Heart-heavy suitors get a rank for,—laugh
At yon sleek parasite, break his own staff
'Cross Beetle-brows the Usher's shoulder,—why
Admitted to the presence by and by,
Should thought of having lost these make me grieve
410 Among new joys I reach, for joys I leave?
Cool citrine-crystals, fierce pyropus-stone,
Are floor-work there! But do I let alone
That black-eyed peasant in the vestibule
Once and for ever?—Floor-work? No such fool!
415 Rather, were heaven to forestall earth, I'd say
I, is it, must be blest? Then, my own way
Bless me! Give firmer arm and fleeter foot,
I'll thank you: but to no mad wings transmute
These limbs of mine—our greensward was so soft!
420 Nor camp I on the thunder-cloud aloft:
We feel the bliss distinctlier, having thus
Engines subservient, not mixed up with us.
Better move palpably through heaven: nor, freed
Of flesh, forsooth, from space to space proceed
425 'Mid flying synods of worlds! No: in heaven's marge

palace—but shall   *1863:* To palace—be it so! shall   400| *1840:* My eye the glance,
before   *1863:* My mouth the smirk, before   401| *1840:* moment? What—with   *1868:*
moment? What? with   405| *1840:* for; laugh   *1863:* for,—laugh   407| *1840:*
shoulder; why—   *1863:* shoulder,—why,   *1888:* why   408| *1840:* and bye,   *1863:*
and by,   409| *1840:* of these recurring make   *1863:* of having lost these make
410| *1840:* new sights I reach, old sights I   *1863:* new joys I reach, for joys I
411| *1840:*—Cool <> pyropus-stone—   *1863:* pyropus-stone,   *1868:* Cool
412| *1840:* Bare floor-work too!—But did   *1863:* Are floor-work here!—But   *1868:*
floor-work there! But do   415| *1840:* Heaven to forestal Earth   *1863:* heaven <>
earth   *1868:* forestall   416| *1840:* Must I be blessed or you? Then my   *1863:* I, is it,
must be blessed? Then, my   *1888:* blest   417| *1840:* me—a firmer arm, a fleeter
1863: me! give firmer arm and fleeter   *1868:* Give   418| *1840:* you: but   *1863:* you,
but   419| *1840:* is too soft;   *1863:* was so soft!   420| *1840:* aloft—   *1863:*
aloft: 421| *1840:* distinctlier having   *1863:* distinctlier, having   422| *1840:*
us—   *1863:* us.   423| *1840:* through Heaven—nor   *1863:* heaven   *1868:* heaven:
nor   424| *1840:* flesh forsooth   *1863:* flesh, forsooth   § 425–53| *1863:* WHICH, YET,
OTHERS HAVE RENOUNCED: HOW? §   425| *1840:* worlds—but in Heaven's

Show Titan still, recumbent o'er his targe
Solid with stars—the Centaur at his game,
Made tremulously out in hoary flame!
   "Life! Yet the very cup whose extreme dull
430 Dregs, even, I would quaff, was dashed, at full,
Aside so oft; the death I fly, revealed
So oft a better life this life concealed,
And which sage, champion, martyr, through each path
Have hunted fearlessly—the horrid bath,
435 The crippling-irons and the fiery chair.
'Twas well for them; let me become aware
As they, and I relinquish life, too! Let
What masters life disclose itself! Forget
Vain ordinances, I have one appeal—
440 I feel, am what I feel, know what I feel;
So much is truth to me. What Is, then? Since
One object, viewed diversely, may evince
Beauty and ugliness—this way attract,
That way repel,—why gloze upon the fact?
445 Why must a single of the sides be right?
What bids choose this and leave the opposite?
Where's abstract Right for me?—in youth endued
With Right still present, still to be pursued,
Thro' all the interchange of circles, rife
450 Each with its proper law and mode of life,
Each to be dwelt at ease in: where, to sway
Absolute with the Kaiser, or obey
Implicit with his serf of fluttering heart,
Or, like a sudden thought of God's, to start

1863: worlds! No! In heaven's   *1868:* world's! No: in heaven's   427| *1840:* game
1863: game,   432| *1840:* concealed   *1863:* concealed,   433| *1840:* thro'   *1863:*
through   435| *1840:* chair: *1863:* chair.   437| *1840:* Life   *1863:* life
438| *1840:* Life's secret but disclose   *1863:* What masters life disclose   440| *1840:*
know what I feel   *1868:* know what I feel;   441| *1840:*—So <> Truth to me—What
Is then   *1863:* truth to me. What Is, then   *1868:* So   442| *1840:* object viewed
diversely may   *1863:* object, viewed diversely, may   444| *1840:* repel, why   *1868:*
repel,—why   446| *1840:* Who bids <> leave its opposite?   *1863:* What bids <>
leave the opposite?   447| *1840:* No abstract <> me—in   *1863:* Where's abstract <>
me?—in   451| *1840:* in: thus to   *1863:* in: where, to   452| *1840:* Regally with
1863: Absolute with   453| *1840:* Serf   *1863:* serf   § 454–80| *1863:* BECAUSE THERE
IS A LIFE BEYOND LIFE,   454–81| *1868* §   455| *1840:* Up in <> go forth and

Up, Brutus in the presence, then go shout
That some should pick the unstrung jewels out—
Each, well!"
                    And, as in moments when the past
Gave partially enfranchisement, he cast
Himself quite through mere secondary states
460 Of his soul's essence, little loves and hates,
Into the mid deep yearnings overlaid
By these; as who should pierce hill, plain, grove, glade,
And on into the very nucleus probe
That first determined there exist a globe.
465 As that were easiest, half the globe dissolved,
So seemed Sordello's closing-truth evolved
By his flesh-half's break-up; the sudden swell
Of his expanding soul showed Ill and Well,
Sorrow and Joy, Beauty and Ugliness,
470 Virtue and Vice, the Larger and the Less,
All qualities, in fine, recorded here,
Might be but modes of Time and this one sphere,
Urgent on these, but not of force to bind
Eternity, as Time—as Matter—Mind,
475 If Mind, Eternity, should choose assert
Their attributes within a Life: thus girt
With circumstance, next change beholds them cinct
Quite otherwise—with Good and Ill distinct,
Joys, sorrows, tending to a like result—
480 Contrived to render easy, difficult,
This or the other course of . . . what new bond
In place of flesh may stop their flight beyond
Its new sphere, as that course does harm or good

---

shout   *1863:* Up, Brutus in <> go shout   457| *1840:* Were well! ¶ And <> Past
1863: Each, well!" ¶ And   *1868:* past   459| *1840:* thro'   *1863:* through
461| *1840:* mid vague yearnings   *1863:* mid deep yearnings   463| *1840:* And so into
1863: And on into   464| *1840:* a Globe: *1863:* globe.   465| *1840:* And as that's
easiest half   *1863:* As that were easiest, half   467| *1840:* In his <> break-up—the
1863: By his   *1868:* break-up; the   469| *1840:* and Joy, Beauty and Ugliness   *1863:*
and Joy, Beauty and Ugliness,   472| *1840:* Modes <> Sphere,   *1863:* modes <>
sphere,   473| *1840:* these but   *1863:* these, but   474| *1840:* As Time—Eternity,
as Matter   *1863:* Eternity, as Time—as Matter   475| *1840:* If Mind, Eternity
should   *1863:* If Mind, Eternity, should   § 481–509| *1863:* AND WITH NEW
CONDITIONS OF SUCCESS,   482–510| *1868* §   486| *1840:* this World, all

To its arrangements. Once this understood,
485 As suddenly he felt himself alone,
Quite out of Time and this world: all was known.
What made the secret of his past despair?
—Most imminent when he seemed most aware
Of his own self-sufficiency: made mad
490 By craving to expand the power he had,
And not new power to be expanded?—just
This made it; Soul on Matter being thrust,
Joy comes when so much Soul is wreaked in Time
On Matter: let the Soul's attempt sublime
495 Matter beyond the scheme and so prevent
By more or less that deed's accomplishment,
And Sorrow follows: Sorrow how avoid?
Let the employer match the thing employed,
Fit to the finite his infinity,
500 And thus proceed for ever, in degree
Changed but in kind the same, still limited
To the appointed circumstance and dead
To all beyond. A sphere is but a sphere;
Small, Great, are merely terms we bandy here;
505 Since to the spirit's absoluteness all
Are like. Now, of the present sphere we call
Life, are conditions; take but this among
Many; the body was to be so long
Youthful, no longer: but, since no control
510 Tied to that body's purposes his soul,

1863: this world: all   487| *1840:* of the past   *1863:* of his past   488| *1840:* (Most imminent   *1863:*—Most imminent   489| *1840:* Of greatness in the Past—nought turned him mad   *1863:* Of his own self-sufficiency; made mad   *1888:* self-sufficiency: made   490| *1840:* Like craving   *1863:* By craving   491| *1840:* Not a new <> expanded)—just   *1863:* And not new <> expanded?—just   493| *1840:* 'Tis Joy when   *1863:* Joy comes when   494| *1840:* On Matter,—let the Soul   *1863:* Soul's   1888:* Or Matter: let   495| *1840:* beyond its scheme   *1863:* beyond the scheme   496| *1840:* Or more   *1863:* By more   497| *1840:* follows: Sorrow to avoid—   *1863:* follows: Sorrow how avoid?   498| *1840:* Employer <> Employed,   *1863:* employer <> employed,   503| *1840:* beyond: a sphere <> a sphere—   *1863:* beyond. A sphere   *1868:* but a sphere;   504| *1840:* here—   *1868:* here;   506| *1840:* like: now of   *1863:* now, of   *1868:* like. Now   507| *1840:* conditions—take   *1868:* conditions; take   508| *1840:* Body   *1863:* body   509| *1840:* longer—but   *1868:* longer: but   § 510–38| *1863:* NOR SUCH AS, IN THIS, PRODUCE FAILURE.   511–39| *1868* §   510| *1840:* Body's <> Soul,   *1863:* body's <> soul,

She chose to understand the body's trade
More than the body's self—had fain conveyed
Her boundless to the body's bounded lot.
Hence, the soul permanent, the body not,—
515 Scarcely its minute for enjoying here,—
The soul must needs instruct her weak compeer,
Run o'er its capabilities and wring
A joy thence, she held worth experiencing:
Which, far from half discovered even,—lo,
520 The minute gone, the body's power let go
Apportioned to that joy's acquirement! Broke
Morning o'er earth, he yearned for all it woke—
From the volcano's vapour-flag, winds hoist
Black o'er the spread of sea,—down to the moist
525 Dale's silken barley-spikes sullied with rain,
Swayed earthwards, heavily to rise again—
The Small, a sphere as perfect as the Great
To the soul's absoluteness. Meditate
Too long on such a morning's cluster-chord
530 And the whole music it was framed afford,—
The chord's might half discovered, what should pluck
One string, his finger, was found palsy-struck.
And then no marvel if the spirit, shown
A saddest sight—the body lost alone
535 Through her officious proffered help, deprived

511| *1840:* It chose <> Body's   *1863:* She chose <> body's   512| *1840:* Body's
1863: body's   513| *1840:* Its boundless, to <> lot—   *1863:* Her boundless <> lot:
1868: lot.   *1888:* boundless to   514| *1840:* So, the soul   *1863:* Hence, the soul
515| *1840:* Scarce the one minute <> here,   *1868:* here,—   *1888:* Scarcely its
minute   516| *1840:* instruct its weak   *1863:* instruct her weak   518| *1840:*
thence it holds worth experiencing—   *1863:* thence, the held worth   *1868:* thence, she held
worth experiencing: 520| *1840:* minute's <> power's   *1863:* minute <>
power   521| *1840:* acquirement! Broke,   *1863:* That's portioned to <> Broke
1868: Apportioned to   522| *1840:* Say, morning o'er the earth and all   *1863:* Morning
o'er earth, he yearned for all   523| *1840:* vapour-flag to hoist   *1863:* vapour-flag,
winds hoist   524| *1840:* sea, to the low moist   *1863:* sea,—down to the moist
526| *1840:* to raise again—   *1863:* to rise again—   527| *1840:* (The Small a   *1863:*
(The Small, a   *1868:* The   528| *1840:* absoluteness)—meditate   *1868:* absoluteness.
Meditate   529| *1840:* On such an Autumn-morning's   *1863:* Too long on such a
morning's   530| *1840:* afford,   *1863:* afford,—   531| *1840:* And, the cord's
might discovered   *1863:* The cord's might half discovered   *1868:* chord's   532| *1840:*
string, the finger   *1863:* string, his finger   533| *1840:* then what marvel <> Spirit
1863: then no marvel <> spirit   534| *1840:* Body   *1863:* body   535| *1840:*

Of this and that enjoyment Fate contrived,—
Virtue, Good, Beauty, each allowed slip hence,—
Vain-gloriously were fain, for recompense,
To stem the ruin even yet, protract
540 The body's term, supply the power it lacked
From her infinity, compel it learn
These qualities were only Time's concern,
And body may, with spirit helping, barred—
Advance the same, vanquished—obtain reward,
545 Reap joy where sorrow was intended grow,
Of Wrong make Right, and turn Ill Good below.
And the result is, the poor body soon
Sinks under what was meant a wondrous boon,
Leaving its bright accomplice all aghast.
550   So much was plain then, proper in the past;
To be complete for, satisfy the whole
Series of spheres—Eternity, his soul
Needs must exceed, prove incomplete for, each
Single sphere—Time. But does our knowledge reach
555 No farther? Is the cloud of hindrance broke
But by the failing of the fleshly yoke,
Its loves and hates, as now when death lets soar
Sordello, self-sufficient as before,
Though during the mere space that shall elapse
560 'Twixt his enthralment in new bonds perhaps?
Must life be ever just escaped, which should
Have been enjoyed?—nay, might have been and would,
Each purpose ordered right—the soul's no whit

Thro' its officious   *1863:* Through her officious   ⁵³⁶| *1840:* contrived,   *1868:*
contrived,—   ⁵³⁸| *1840:* Vain gloriously   *1863:* Vain-gloriously   § ⁵³⁹⁻⁶⁷| *1863:*
BUT, EVEN HERE, IS FAILURE INEVITABLE?   ⁵⁴⁰⁻⁶⁸| *1868* §   ⁵⁴⁰| *1840:*
Body's   *1863:* body's   ⁵⁴¹| *1840:* From its infinity   *1863:* From her infinity
⁵⁴³| *1840:* That Body may, with its assistance, barred—   *1863:* And body may, with spirit
helping, barred—   ⁵⁴⁶| *1840:* make Right and <> below—   *1863:* make Right, and
<> below.   ⁵⁴⁷| *1840:* Body   *1863:* body   ⁵⁵⁰| *1840:* Past;   *1868:*
past;   ⁵⁵³| *1840:* Exceeded, so was incomplete for   *1888:* Needs must exceed, prove
incomplete   ⁵⁵⁴| *1840:* One sphere—our Time   *1863:* Single sphere—Time
⁵⁵⁷| *1840:* when they let soar   *1863:* when death lets soar   ⁵⁵⁸| *1840:* The spirit,
self-sufficient   *1863:* Sordello, self-sufficient   ⁵⁵⁹| *1840:* Tho' but the single space
1863: Though during the mere space   ⁵⁶⁰| *1840:* 'Twixt its enthralment   *1863:*
'Twixt his enthralment <> bonds, perhaps?   *1888:* bonds perhaps?   ⁵⁶¹| *1840:*
Must Life be ever but escaped   *1863:* life be ever just escaped   ⁵⁶²| *1840:* enjoyed?
nay   *1863:* enjoyed?—nay   ⁵⁶³| *1840:* Once ordered rightly, and a Soul's   *1863:* Each

Beyond the body's purpose under it.

565 Like yonder breadth of watery heaven, a bay,
And that sky-space of water, ray for ray
And star for star, one richness where they mixed
As this and that wing of an angel, fixed,
Tumultuary splendours folded in

570 To die—would soul, proportioned thus, begin
Exciting discontent, or surelier quell
The body if, aspiring, it rebel?
But how so order life? Still brutalize
The soul, the sad world's way, with muffled eyes

575 To all that was before, all that shall be
After this sphere—all and each quality
Save some sole and immutable Great, Good
And Beauteous whither fate has loosed its hood
To follow? Never may some soul see All

580 —The Great Before and After, and the Small
Now, yet be saved by this the simplest lore,
And take the single course prescribed before,
As the king-bird with ages on his plumes
Travels to die in his ancestral glooms?

585 But where descry the Love that shall select
That course? Here is a soul whom, to affect,
Nature has plied with all her means, from trees
And flowers e'en to the Multitude!—and these,
Decides he save or no? One word to end!

---

purpose ordered right—the soul's   564| *1840:* More than the Body's <> it   *1863:*
Beyond the body's <> it—   *1888:* it.   565| *1840:* (A breadth <> heaven like a
1863: Like yonder breadth <> heaven, a   566| *1840:* A sky-like space of   *1863:* And
that sky-space of   § 568-96| *1863:* OR FAILURE HERE MAY BE SUCCESS ALSO
569-97| *1868:* OR MAY FAILURE HERE BE §   570| *1840:* die) and which thus, far
from first begin   *1863:* die—would soul, proportioned thus, begin   571| *1840:*
discontent, had surest quelled   *1863:* discontent, or surelier quell   572| *1840:* The
Body if aspiring it rebelled.   *1863:* body if, aspiring, it rebel?   573| *1840:* Life   *1863:*
life   574| *1840:* world's method—muffled   *1863:* world's way, with muffled
575| *1840:* before, shall after be   *1863:* before, all that shall be   576| *1840:* This
sphere—and every other quality   *1863:* After this sphere—and every quality   *1888:*
sphere—all and each quality   577| *1840:* immutable Great and Good   *1888:*
immutable Great, Good   580| *1840:*—before and after and   *1863:* Before and After,
and   586| *1840:* a Soul whom to affect   *1863:* soul whom, to affect,   587| *1840:*
means—from   *1868:* means, from   588| *1840:* flowers—e'en to the Multitude . . . and
these   *1863:* the Multitude!—and these,   *1868:* flowers e'en   589| *1863:* end!"

590 Ah my Sordello, I this once befriend
And speak for you. Of a Power above you still
Which, utterly incomprehensible,
Is out of rivalry, which thus you can
Love, tho' unloving all conceived by man—
595 What need! And of—none the minutest duct
To that out-nature, nought that would instruct
And so let rivalry begin to live—
But of a Power its representative
Who, being for authority the same,
600 Communication different, should claim
A course, the first chose but this last revealed—
This Human clear, as that Divine concealed—
What utter need!
          What has Sordello found?
Or can his spirit go the mighty round,
605 End where poor Eglamor begun? So, says
Old fable, the two eagles went two ways
About the world: where, in the midst, they met,
Though on a shifting waste of sand, men set
Jove's temple. Quick, what has Sordello found?
610 For they approach—approach—that foot's rebound
Palma? No, Salinguerra though in mail;
They mount, have reached the threshold, dash the veil
Aside—and you divine who sat there dead,
Under his foot the badge: still, Palma said,
615 A triumph lingering in the wide eyes,
Wider than some spent swimmer's if he spies

1868: end!   591| *1840:* you. A Power above him still   *1863:* you. Of a Power above you
still   593| *1840:* thus he can   *1863:* thus you can   594| *1840:* Man—   *1863:*
man—   596| *1840:* out-Nature   *1863:* out-nature   § 597–624| *1863:* WHEN
INDUCED BY LOVE? SORDELLO KNOWS: 598–624| *1868* §   601| *1840:*
course the   *1863:* course, the
603| *1840:* The utter   *1863:* What utter   604| *1840:* round   *1863:* round,
605| *1840:* At length, and where our souls begun? as says   *1863:* End where poor Eglamor
begun   *1868:* begun?—So, says   *1888:* begun? So   606| *1840:* the two doves were sent
two   *1863:* the two eagles went two   607| *1840:* world—where in the midst they met
1863: world: where, in the midst, they met,   608| *1840:* Tho'   *1863:* Though
609| *1840:* temple? Quick   *1863:* temple. Quick   610| *1840:* rebound . . .   *1888:*
rebound   611| *1840:* tho'   *1863:* though   613| *1840:* dead   *1863:* dead,
614| *1840:* badge; still   *1863:* badge: still   615| *1840:* eyes   *1863:* eyes,

Help from above in his extreme despair,
And, head far back on shoulder thrust, turns there
With short quick passionate cry. as Palma pressed
620 In one great kiss, her lips upon his breast,
It beat.
　　　　By this, the hermit-bee has stopped
His day's toil at Goito: the new-cropped
Dead vine-leaf answers, now 'tis eve, he bit,
Twirled so, and filed all day. the mansion's fit,
625 God counselled for. As easy guess the word
That passed betwixt them, and become the third
To the soft small unfrighted bee, as tax
Him with one fault—so, no remembrance racks
Of the stone maidens and the font of stone
630 He, creeping through the crevice, leaves alone.
Alas, my friend, alas Sordello, whom
Anon they laid within that old font-tomb,
And, yet again, alas!
　　　　　　　And now is't worth
Our while bring back to mind, much less set forth
635 How Salinguerra extricates himself
Without Sordello? Ghibellin and Guelf
May fight their fiercest out? If Richard sulked
In durance or the Marquis paid his mulct,
Who cares, Sordello gone? The upshot, sure,
640 Was peace; our chief made some frank overture
That prospered; compliment fell thick and fast
On its disposer, and Taurello passed
With foe and friend for an outstripping soul,

617| *1840:* despair　*1863:* despair,　　619| *1840:* short and passionate cry; as Palma prest　*1863:* short, quick, passionate cry: as　*1868:* pressed　*1888:* short quick passionate　620| *1840:* kiss her <> breast　*1868:* kiss, her <> breast,　621| *1840:* beat. ¶ By this the　*1863:* beat. By this, the　622| *1840:* at Goito—the new cropped　*1863:* at Goito: the new-cropped　624| *1840:* day—the <> fit　*1863:* day: the <> fit,　§ 625-52| *1863:* BUT TOO LATE: AN INSECT KNOWS SOONER. §　625| *1840:* for; as easy　*1863:* for. As easy　626| *1840:* them and　*1868:* them, and　628| *1840:* so no　*1863:* so, no　630| *1840:* thro' <> alone—　*1863:* through <> alone.　631| *1840:* friend—Alas Sordello! whom　*1863:* friend—alas Sordello, whom　*1868:* friend, alas　632| *1840:* Anon we laid <> that cold font-tomb—　*1863:* Anon they laid <> that old font-tomb—　*1868:* font-tomb,　633| *1840:* And yet again alas　*1863:* And, yet again, alas　637| *1840:* fiercest? If Count Richard　*1863:* fiercest out? If Richard　643| *1840:* soul　*1863:* soul,

Nine days at least. Then,—fairly reached the goal,—
645 He, by one effort, blotted the great hope
Out of his mind, nor further tried to cope
With Este, that mad evening's style, but sent
Away the Legate and the League, content
No blame at least the brothers had incurred,
650 —Dispatched a message to the Monk, he heard
Patiently first to last, scarce shivered at,
Then curled his limbs up on his wolfskin mat
And ne'er spoke more,—informed the Ferrarese
He but retained their rule so long as these
655 Lingered in pupilage,—and last, no mode
Apparent else of keeping safe the road
From Germany direct to Lombardy
For Friedrich,—none, that is, to guarantee
The faith and promptitude of who should next
660 Obtain Sofia's dowry,—sore perplexed—
(Sofia being youngest of the tribe
Of daughters, Ecelin was wont to bribe
The envious magnates with—nor, since he sent
Henry of Egna this fair child, had Trent
665 Once failed the Kaiser's purposes—"we lost
Egna last year, and who takes Egna's post—
Opens the Lombard gate if Friedrich knock?")
Himself espoused the Lady of the Rock
In pure necessity, and, so destroyed
670 His slender last of chances, quite made void
Old prophecy, and spite of all the schemes
Overt and covert, youth's deeds, age's dreams,
Was sucked into Romano. And so hushed
He up this evening's work that, when 'twas brushed

644| *1840:* least: then, fairly <> goal, *1863:* least. Then,—fairly <> goal,—
647| *1840:* With Este that *1863:* With Este, that 650| *1840:* the Monk he *1863:*
the Monk, he § 643–681| / ON HIS DISAPPEARANCE FROM THE STAGE, §
655| *1840:* pupilage—and *1863:* pupilage,—and 658| *1840:* For Friedrich, none
1863: For Friedrich,—none 660| *1840:* dowry, sore *1863:* dowry,—sore
662| *1840:* daughters Ecelin *1863:* daughters, Ecelin 663| *1840:* nor since *1863:*
nor, since 664| *1840:* Enrico Egna <> child had *1863:* Henry of Egna <> child,
had 665| *1840:* purposes—we *1863:* purposes—"we 667| *1840:* knock?)
1863: knock?") 669| *1840:* and so *1868:* and, so 673| *1840:* into Romano:
and *1863:* into Romano. And 674| *1840:* work, that when, 'twas *1863:* work that,

327

675 Somehow against by a blind chronicle
Which, chronicling whatever woe befell
Ferrara, noted this the obscure woe
Of "Salinguerra's sole son Giacomo
Deceased, fatuous and doting, ere his sire,"
680 The townsfolk rubbed their eyes, could but admire
Which of Sofia's five was meant.
                                    The chaps
Of earth's dead hope were tardy to collapse,
Obliterated not the beautiful
Distinctive features at a crash: but dull
685 And duller these, next year, as Guelfs withdrew
Each to his stronghold. Then (securely too
Ecelin at Campese slept; close by,
Who likes may see him in Solagna lie,
With cushioned head and gloved hand to denote
690 The cavalier he was)—then his heart smote
Young Ecelin at last; long since adult.
And, save Vicenza's business, what result
In blood and blaze? (So hard to intercept
Sordello till his plain withdrawal!) Stepped
695 Then its new lord on Lombardy. I' the nick
Of time when Ecelin and Alberic
Closed with Taurello, come precisely news
That in Verona half the souls refuse
Allegiance to the Marquis and the Count—

when 'twas   677| *1840:* Ferrara, scented this   *1863:* Ferrara, noted this
678| *1840:* And "Salinguerra's   *1863:* Of "Salinguerra's   679| *1840:* Sire,"   *1863:*
sire,"   § 681–709| *1863:* THE NEXT ASPIRANT CAN PRESS FORWARD. §
681| *1840:* five he meant. The   *1863:* five was meant. ¶ The   682| *1840:* Of his dead
1863: Of earth's dead   684| *1840:* crash—scarce dull   *1863:* crash—but dull   *1868:*
crash: but   685| *1840:* Next year, as Azzo, Boniface withdrew   *1863:* And duller, next
year, as Guelf chiefs withdrew   *1868:* duller these, next <> Guelfs withdrew
686| *1840:* stronghold; then (securely   *1863:* stronghold. Then (securely   687| *1840:*
slept—close by   *1863:* by,   *1868:* slept; close   688| *1840:* lie   *1868:* lie,
690| *1840:* Cavalier   *1863:* cavalier   691| *1840:* Young Ecelin, conceive! Long since
adult,   *1863:* Young Ecelin at last!—long   *1868:* last; long since adult.   693| *1840:*
blaze? so hard 'twas intercept   *1863:* blaze? ('twas hard to intercept   *1868:* blaze? (So
hard   694| *1840:* till Sordello's option! Stept   *1863:* till his plain withdrawal.)
Stept,   *1868:* withdrawal!) Stepped,   *1888:* withdrawal!) Stepped   695| *1840:* Its
lord on Lombardy—for in the   *1863:* Then, its new lord on Lombardy. I' the   *1868:* Then
its   696| *1840:* when he at last and   *1863:* when Ecelin and   697| *1840:* came

328

700 Have cast them from a throne they bid him mount,
 Their Podestà, thro' his ancestral worth.
 Ecelin flew there, and the town henceforth
 Was wholly his—Taurello sinking back
 From temporary station to a track
705 That suited. News received of this acquist,
 Friedrich did come to Lombardy: who missed
 Taurello then? Another year: they took
 Vicenza, left the Marquis scarce a nook
 For refuge, and, when hundreds two or three
710 Of Guelfs conspired to call themselves "The Free,"
 Opposing Alberic,—vile Bassanese,—
 (Without Sordello!)—Ecelin at ease
 Slaughtered them so observably, that oft
 A little Salinguerra looked with soft
715 Blue eyes up, asked his sire the proper age
 To get appointed his proud uncle's page.
 More years passed, and that sire had dwindled down
 To a mere showy turbulent soldier, grown
 Better through age, his parts still in repute,
720 Subtle—how else?—but hardly so astute
 As his contemporaneous friends professed;
 Undoubtedly a brawler: for the rest,
 Known by each neighbour, and allowed for, let
 Keep his incorrigible ways, nor fret
725 Men who would miss their boyhood's bugbear: "trap
 The ostrich, suffer our bald osprey flap
 A battered pinion!"—was the word. In fine,

1863: come   701| 1840: worth: 1863: worth.   705| 1840: suited: news   1863:
suited. News   706| 1840: to Lombardy—who   1863: to Lombardy: who
707| 1840: Taurello? Yet another year—they   1863: Taurello then? Another year: they
§ 710-38| 1863: SALINGUERRA'S PART LAPSING TO ECELIN, §   710| 1840:
After conspired <> "the   1863: Of Guelfs conspired   1868: "The   711| 1840:
Opposing Alberic, these Bassanese,   1863: Opposing Alberic,—vile Bassanese,—
713| 1840: observably that   1863: observably, that   716| 1840: page: 1863:
page.   717| 1840: sire was dwindled   1863: sire had dwindled   721| 1840:
professed—   1863: professed;   722| 1840: brawler—for   1863: brawler: for
723| 1840: neighbour, so allowed   1863: neighbour, and allowed   725| 1840: who
had missed <> bugbear—trap   1863: bugbear—"trap   1868: bugbear: "trap   1888: who
would miss   727| 1840: pinion—was   1863: pinion"—was   1868:

One flap too much and Venice's marine
Was meddled with; no overlooking that!
730 She captured him in his Ferrara, fat
And florid at a banquet, more by fraud
Than force, to speak the truth; there's slender laud
Ascribed you for assisting eighty years
To pull his death on such a man; fate shears
735 The life-cord prompt enough whose last fine thread
You fritter: so, presiding his board-head,
The old smile, your assurance all went well
With Friedrich (as if he were like to tell!)
In rushed (a plan contrived before) our friends,
740 Made some pretence at fighting, some amends
For the shame done his eighty years—(apart
The principle, none found it in his heart
To be much angry with Taurello)—gained
Their galleys with the prize, and what remained
745 But carry him to Venice for a show?
—Set him, as 'twere, down gently—free to go
His gait, inspect our square, pretend observe
The swallows soaring their eternal curve
'Twixt Theodore and Mark, if citizens
750 Gathered importunately, fives and tens,
To point their children the Magnifico,
All but a monarch once in firm-land, go
His gait among them now—"it took, indeed,
Fully this Ecelin to supersede
755 That man," remarked the seniors. Singular!
Sordello's inability to bar
Rivals the stage, that evening, mainly brought
About by his strange disbelief that aught
Was ever to be done,—this thrust the Twain

___

pinion!"—was   730| _1840:_ We captured   _1863:_ She captured   732| _1840:_
truth—there's   _1863:_ truth; there's   734| _1840:_ man—fate   _1868:_ man; fate
735| _1840:_ threads   737| _1840:_ A great smile your   _1863:_ The old
smile, your   § 739–67| _1863:_ WHO, WITH HIS BROTHER, PLAYED IT OUT. §
741| _1840:_ years—apart   _1863:_ years—(apart   743| _1840:_ with Taurello—gained
_1863:_ with Taurello)—gained   744| _1840:_ Our galleys   _1863:_ Their galleys
753| _1840:_ among us now—it   _1863:_ among them now—"it   755| _1840:_ man,
remarked <> Singular   _1863:_ man," remarked <> Singular!   759| _1840:_ Was to be

330

₇₆₀ Under Taurello's tutelage,—whom, brain
And heart and hand, he forthwith in one rod
Indissolubly bound to baffle God
Who loves the world—and thus allowed the thin
Grey wizened dwarfish devil Ecelin,
₇₆₅ And massy-muscled big-boned Alberic
(Mere man, alas!) to put his problem quick
To demonstration—prove wherever's will
To do, there's plenty to be done, or ill
Or good. Anointed, then, to rend and rip—
₇₇₀ Kings of the gag and flesh-hook, screw and whip,
They plagued the world: a touch of Hildebrand
(So far from obsolete!) made Lombards band
Together, cross their coats as for Christ's cause,
And saving Milan win the world's applause.
₇₇₅ Ecelin perished: and I think grass grew
Never so pleasant as in Valley Rù
By San Zenon where Alberic in turn
Saw his exasperated captors burn
Seven children and their mother; then, regaled
₇₈₀ So far, tied on to a wild horse, was trailed
To death through raunce and bramble-bush. I take
God's part and testify that 'mid the brake
Wild o'er his castle on the pleasant knoll,
You hear its one tower left, a belfry, toll—
₇₈₅ The earthquake spared it last year, laying flat
The modern church beneath,—no harm in that!
Chirrups the contumacious grasshopper,
Rustles the lizard and the cushats chirre
Above the ravage: there, at deep of day
₇₉₀ A week since, heard I the old Canon say

---

done, should fairly thrust   *1863:* Was ever to be done,—this thrust   ^{760|}   *1840:*
tutelage, that, brain   *1863:* tutelage,—whom, brain   ^{763|}   *1840:* world—should thus
allow the   *1863:* world—and thus allowed the   ^{766|}   *1840:* alas) to   *1863:* alas!) to
§ ^{768–96|}   *1863:* AND WENT HOME DULY TO THEIR REWARD. §   ^{769|}   *1840:*
good: anointed   *1863:* good. Anointed   ^{779|}   *1840:* mother, and, regaled   *1863:*
mother; then, regaled   ^{781|}   *1840:* bramble-bush: I   *1863:* bramble-bush. I
^{782|}   *1840:* mid   *1868:* 'mid   ^{783|}   *1840:* on Zenone's knoll   *1863:* on the pleasant
knoll,   ^{784–87|}   *1863:* toll— / The earthquake spared it last year, laying flat / The
modern church beneath,—no harm in that! / Cherups   ^{787|}   *1840:* Cherups   *1868:*

He saw with his own eyes a barrow burst
And Alberic's huge skeleton unhearsed
Only five years ago. He added, "June's
The month for carding off our first cocoons
795 The silkworms fabricate"—a double news,
Nor he nor I could tell the worthier. Choose!
    And Naddo gone, all's gone; not Eglamor!
Believe, I knew the face I waited for,
A guest my spirit of the golden courts!
800 Oh strange to see how, despite ill-reports,
Disuse, some wear of years, that face retained
Its joyous look of love! Suns waxed and waned,
And still my spirit held an upward flight,
Spiral on spiral, gyres of life and light
805 More and more gorgeous—ever that face there
The last admitted! crossed, too, with some care
As perfect triumph were not sure for all,
But, on a few, enduring damp must fall,
—A transient struggle, haply a painful sense
810 Of the inferior nature's clinging—whence
Slight starting tears easily wiped away,
Fine jealousies soon stifled in the play
Of irrepressible admiration—not
Aspiring, all considered, to their lot
815 Who ever, just as they prepared ascend
Spiral on spiral, wish thee well, impend
Thy frank delight at their exclusive track,
That upturned fervid face and hair put back!
    Is there no more to say? He of the rhymes—
820 Many a tale, of this retreat betimes,
Was born: Sordello die at once for men?
The Chroniclers of Mantua tired their pen
Telling how *Sordello Prince Visconti* saved

Chirrups   793| *1840:* Five years ago, no more: he added, June's   *1863:* Only five years
ago. He added, "June's   794| *1840:* A month   *1863:* The month   795| *1840:*
fabricate—a   *1863:* fabricate"—a   § 797–825| *1863:* GOOD WILL—ILL LUCK, GET
SECOND PRIZE.   *1868:* PRIZE: §   798| *1840:* Believe I   *1863:* Believe, I
799| *1840:* courts: *1863:* courts!   806| *1840:* crossed   808| *1840:* But on a few
enduring   *1863:* But, on a few, enduring   809| *1840:* A   *1863:*—A   820| *1840:*
tale of < > betimes   *1863:* tale, of < > betimes,   823| *1840:* Relating how a Prince

Mantua, and elsewhere notably behaved—
825 Who thus, by fortune ordering events,
Passed with posterity, to all intents,
For just the god he never could become.
As Knight, Bard, Gallant, men were never dumb
In praise of him: while what he should have been,
830 Could be, and was not—the one step too mean
For him to take,—we suffer at this day
Because of: Ecelin had pushed away
Its chance ere Dante could arrive and take
That step Sordello spurned, for the world's sake:
835 He did much—but Sordello's chance was gone.
Thus, had Sordello dared that step alone,
Apollo had been compassed: 'twas a fit
He wished should go to him, not he to it
—As one content to merely be supposed
840 Singing or fighting elsewhere, while he dozed
Really at home—one who was chiefly glad
To have achieved the few real deeds he had,
Because that way assured they were not worth
Doing, so spared from doing them henceforth—
845 A tree that covets fruitage and yet tastes
Never itself, itself. Had he embraced
Their cause then, men had plucked Hesperian fruit
And, praising that, just thrown him in to boot
All he was anxious to appear, but scarce
850 Solicitous to be. A sorry farce
Such life is, after all! Cannot I say

Visconti   *1863:* Telling how *Sordello Prince Visconti*   ⁸²⁴| *1840:* Mantua and
1863: Mantua, and   ⁸²⁵| *1840:* thus by fortune's <> events   *1863:* thus, by <>
events,   *1868:* fortune   § ⁸²⁶⁻⁵⁴| *1863:* WHAT LEAST ONE MAY I AWARD
SORDELLO? §   ⁸²⁶| *1840:* posterity to all intents   *1863:* posterity, to all
intents,   ⁸²⁷| *1840:* God <> become: *1863:* god <> become.   ⁸³¹| *1840:*
take, we   *1863:* take,—we   ⁸³²| *1840:* of; Ecelin   *1863:* of: Ecelin   ⁸³³| *1840:*
arrive to take   *1863:* arrive and take   ⁸³⁵| *1840:* but Sordello's step was   *1863:* but
Sordello's chance was   ⁸³⁶| *1840:* Thus had Sordello ta'en that   *1863:* Thus, had
Sordello dared that   ⁸³⁷| *1840:* compassed—'twas   *1888:* compassed: 'twas
⁸⁴¹| *1840:* home—and who   *1863:* home—one who   ⁸⁴²| *1840:* had   *1863:*
had,   ⁸⁴⁶| *1840:* itself—had   *1863:* itself: had   *1868:* itself. Had   ⁸⁴⁷| *1840:*
Our cause <> Men   *1863:* Their cause <> men   ⁸⁴⁹| *1840:* appear but   *1863:*
appear, but   ⁸⁵⁰| *1840:* be: a   *1863:* be. A   ⁸⁵¹| *1840:* is after all—cannot

He lived for some one better thing? this way.—
Lo, on a heathy brown and nameless hill
By sparkling Asolo, in mist and chill,
855 Morning just up, higher and higher runs
A child barefoot and rosy. See! the sun's
On the square castle's inner-court's low wall
Like the chine of some extinct animal
Half turned to earth and flowers; and through the haze
860 (Save where some slender patches of grey maize
Are to be overleaped) that boy has crossed
The whole hillside of dew and powder-frost
Matting the balm and mountain camomile.
Up and up goes he, singing all the while
865 Some unintelligible words to beat
The lark, God's poet, swooning at his feet,
So worsted is he at "the few fine locks
Stained like pale honey oozed from topmost rocks
Sun-blanched the livelong summer,"—all that's left
870 Of the Goito lay! And thus bereft,
Sleep and forget, Sordello! In effect
He sleeps, the feverish poet—I suspect
Not utterly companionless; but, friends,
Wake up! The ghost's gone, and the story ends
875 I'd fain hope, sweetly; seeing, peri or ghoul,
That spirits are conjectured fair or foul,
Evil or good, judicious authors think,
According as they vanish in a stink
Or in a perfume. Friends, be frank! ye snuff
880 Civet, I warrant. Really? Like enough!

1863: is, after all! cannot   *1868:* Cannot   852| *1840:* way—   *1863:* way.—
§ 855–82| *1863:* THIS—THAT MUST PERFORCE CONTENT HIM, §   856| *1840:*
rosy—See   *1863:* rosy. See   857| *1840:* inner-court's green wall   *1863:* inner-court's
low wall   858| *1840:*—Like <> some fossil animal   *1863:* Like <> some extinct
animal   859| *1840:* thro'   *1863:* through   860| *1840:* maize)   *1863:*
maize   861| *1840:* crost   *1868:* crossed   863| *1840:* camomile: *1863:*
camomile.   866| *1840:* feet   *1863:* feet,   867| *1840:* at the   *1863:* at "the
869| *1840:* Sunblanched <> summer.—All   *1863:* summer,"—all   *1888:*
Sun-blanched   871| *1840:* forget, Sordello . . . in   *1863:* forget, Sordello! In
874| *1840:* up; the   *1868:* up! The   875| *1840:* sweetly—seeing   *1868:* sweetly;
seeing   879| *1840:* perfume: friends be frank: ye   *1863:* perfume. Friends, be frank!
ye   880| *1840:* warrant: really? Like enough—   *1863:* warrant. Really? Like

334

Merely the savour's rareness; any nose
May ravage with impunity a rose:
Rifle a musk-pod and 'twill ache like yours!
I'd tell you that same pungency ensures
885 An after-gust, but that were overbold.
Who would has heard Sordello's story told.

enough!   881| *1840:* rareness—any *1863:* rareness; any   882| *1840:* rose—
1863: rose: § 883–86| *1863:* AS NO PRIZE AT ALL, HAS CONTENTED ME. §
883| *1840:* yours: *1863:* yours!   885| *1840:* after-gust—but < > overbold: *1863:*
overbold. *1868:* after-gust, but

By the same Author.

PARACELSUS

A Poem
Small 8vo, Price 6s.

STRAFFORD

An Historical Tragedy.
As acted at the Theatre Royal, Covent Garden.
8vo, Price 4s.

===

Nearly Ready.

PIPPA PASSES.

KING VICTOR AND KING CHARLES.

MANSOOR THE HIEROPHANT.

Dramas by R. B.

STRAFFORD

Publication and Production

There is no known MS of *Strafford*. The first edition was published by Longman, Rees, Orme, Brown, Green, and Longman, Paternoster Row, London, in 1837, in the form of a paper-covered volume 9″ × 6″ with the text of the play covering 131 pages. A label on the cover gives the title STRAFFORD / AN HISTORICAL TRAGEDY / BY / ROBERT BROWNING / *Price* 4s. The play was excluded from the collected edition of 1849 but was restored thereafter. The greatest changes occur between 1837 and 1863. From 1863 the text is altered only in minor ways, except that in Act V, scene ii, the 1863 text drops lines 331–342, 344–348 and 351.

B had settled on a subject for his play by August 3, 1836 (Hood, p. 296), and on March 30, 1837, Macready read it to Daniel Osbaldiston, manager of Covent Garden, who immediately accepted it for production, in spite of Macready's misgivings (Hood, pp. 296–297). *Strafford* had only four performances (May 1, 3, 5, and 9) partly because John Vandenhoff who played Pym withdrew. But its failure was undoubtedly due also to its esoteric subject and bad acting. In 1886 B wrote to F. J. Furnivall: "You see the judicious remarks of the Critic in this morning's *Daily News*: not a doubt as to whether the bankrupt management of that day did what was requisite for the success of the piece, whether the wretched acting of the inferior people might not have done harm (a stone-deaf Charles, a silly, simpering Carlisle, etc.), and whether the management 'that dressed the Scots Commissioners in kilts' might not refuse, as it did, 'one rag for the new piece' " (Hood, p. 259). B further notes: "He [Macready] acted very finely—as did Miss Faucit. Pym received tolerable treatment,—the rest,—for the sake of whose incompetence the play had to be reduced by at least one third of its dialogue,—*non ragionam di loro!*" (Hood, p. 297). The play was revived by the Browning Society at the Strand Theatre on December 21, 1886.

Sources

Unquestionably the direct inspiration of *Strafford* was Forster's *Life*, in which B had a hand. B was probably not only thoroughly familiar with Forster's biography, but he must have examined Forster's materials. The early nineteenth-century biographer of Strafford had a wealth of materials at his disposal. Primary sources included the numerous contemporary accounts of the trial of Strafford and the events surrounding it: *A briefe and perfect relation of the answeres and replies of Thomas, earl of Strafford, to the articles exhibited against him, by the House of commons on the thirteenth of Aprill An. Dom. 1641* (London, 1647); *The Conclusion of the Earle of Straffords defence. The twelfth of Aprill, 1641* (London, 1641); George Digby, *The Lord Digby: his last speech against the Earle of Strafford, occasioned upon reading the bill of attainder touching the point of treason* (London, 1641); *Depositions and articles of impeachment, against Thomas, Earl of Strafford. Feb. 16, 1640* (London, 1640); John Pym, *The Declaration of John Pym esquire upon the whole matter of the charge of high treason against Thomas, earle of Strafford* (London, 1641); *The atheistical politician; a brief discourse concerning Nicholas Machiavell* in *Harleian Miscellany* III (1809), 243–246 [an attack on Charles I, Strafford, and Laud]; *The Earl of Strafford characterized, in a letter sent to a friend in the country* in *Harleian Miscellany*, V (1810), 46–48; *A protestation against a foolish, ridiculous, and scandalous speech, pretended to be spoken by Thomas Wentworth, late earl of Strafford, to certaine lords before his coming out of the Tower* (London, 1641); John Glyn, *The Replication of Master Glyn ... to the general answer of Thomas earle of Strafford* (London, 1641); Sir John Maynard, *Mr Maynard's speech ... in answer to the Earle of Strafford's reply* (London, 1641); *The tryal of Thomas earl of Strafford* (London, 1680). From the evidence of his notes, however, Forster seems to have relied chiefly upon the following: *The Earl of Strafford's Letters and Dispatches, with an Essay towards his Life by Sir George Radcliffe* (London, 1739); *The History of the Troubles and Tryal of William Laud: Wrote by himself,* ed. H. Wharton (London, 1695–1700); Thomas Dunham Whitaker, *The Life and the Original Correspondence of Sir George Radcliffe* (London, 1810); *Biographia Britannica*; Collin's *Peerage of England*; Clarendon's *History of the Rebellion*; John Macdiarmid, *Lives of British Statesmen* (London, 1804); *Commons Journals*; and *Lords Journals*.

   References to Forster are to John Forster's "Life of Strafford" in *The Statesmen of the Commonwealth of England* (London, 1840) V. References to Radcliffe are to Thomas Dunham Whitaker, *The Life and the Original Corespondence of Sir George Radcliffe* (London, 1810). References to Clarendon are (by book and section) to Edward [Hyde], Earl of Clarendon, *The History of the Rebellion and Civil Wars in England,* ed. W. Dunn MacKay (Oxford, 1958), 6 vols. References to Hickey are to *Strafford: A tragedy by Robert Browning,* ed. Emily H. Hickey (London, 1884).

Preface] *Eliot* Sir John Eliot (1592–1632) was educated at Oxford and the Inns of Court, and first entered Parliament for St. Germans (Cornwall) in 1614. He was the chief instrument in the impeachment of Charles I's favorite, Buckingham (III, i, 41n), and was imprisoned in 1627 for refusing to pay the forced loan by which Charles was trying to raise money. In the Parliament of 1628–1629 he resisted Charles's efforts to raise Tonnage and Poundage (a tax of two shillings on every ton of wine and sixpence on each pound of merchandise). Finally, in 1629, Charles contrived to have him imprisoned for supposedly conspiring to prevent the dissolution of Parliament (III, i, 40n). Dying of consumption in the Tower of London, he wrote to the king humbly begging to be released for the sake of his health. Charles's reply was "Not humble enough." Eliot died in prison in 1633. He left several works in manuscript, including *The Monarchie of Man* and *An Apology for Socrates*, none of which was published until the nineteenth century (1879–1882). John Forster's *Life of Sir John Eliot* appeared in 1864.

Strafford] See note on *Wentworth* under *Persons*.

Lardner's Cyclopaedia] Dionysius Lardner (1793–1859), Professor of Natural Philosophy and Astronomy in London University, issued his *Cabinet Cyclopaedia* in 133 volumes between 1829 and 1849.

a writer whom I am proud to call my friend] John Forster (1812–1876), lawyer, historian, biographer of Swift, Landor, Dickens and others, and friend of many authors, edited the *Foreign Quarterly Review* (1842–1843), the *Daily News* (1846), and the *Examiner* (1847–1855), in the last of which he reviewed *Paracelsus* (September 6, 1835). Soon after, he met B at the house of Macready. Forster's interest in seventeenth-century English history probably first directed B's attention towards Strafford. While he was working on his "Lives of the Statesmen of the Commonwealth" for Lardner's *Cyclopaedia*, Forster became ill (February-March, 1836) and B helped him finish his life of Strafford. The contention of F. J. Furnivall, founder of the Browning Society, that B actually wrote most of the biography (first made in a letter in the *Pall Mall Gazette*, April, 1890) has never been substantiated. B's friendship with Forster ended in a quarrel over a trifle.

Hampden, Pym, and Vane] See notes under *Persons*.

Trial concerning Ship-Money] During the eleven years (1629–1640) he ruled without a parliament, Charles I was in constant need of revenue. In 1634 the Attorney-General, William Noye (1577–1634), hit upon the plan of reviving an old Plantagenet law requiring coastal towns to provide funds (ship-money) for naval vessels. This move was bitterly resented because it was originally a war tax and the country was at peace, it was used to fit out an army, not a navy, and it was imposed on inland counties as well as coastal areas without consent of a parliament. In February, 1637, twelve judges ruled in favor of Charles's right to levy it. See *Select Documents of English Constitutional History*, G. B. Adams and H. M. Stephens, eds. (New York, 1929), pp. 349–350.

Carlisle] See note on *Lucy Percy* under *Persons*.

Matthew] Sir Tobie Matthew (1577–1655), courtier and writer, was Strafford's secretary during his Irish regime. Matthew's character of Lady Carlisle was probably circulated in manuscript and was included in his *Letters*, which were published in 1660, and in a life of Matthew (1907) by A. H. Mathew and A. Calthrop.

Voiture] Vincent Voiture (1598–1648), French poet and letter-writer, noted for his wit and conversation, a member of the Académie and celebrated frequenter of the famous Hôtel de Rambouillet, the intellectual center of seventeenth-century Parisian society. His letters, essentially familiar essays, were published posthumously. His sketch of Lady Carlisle in which he describes her as enchanting, lovable, but at heart unscrupulous is given in a letter to M. Gourdon, December 4, 1633, and is printed in his *Oeuvres*.

Waller] Edmund Waller (1606–1687) a polished English lyrist, best remembered for his "Go, Lovely Rose." His chief works included *Poems* (1645) and *Divine Poems* (1685). He wrote several pieces relating to Lady Carlisle including "The Countess of Carlisle in Mourning," "To My Lady of Carlisle" and "Of Her Chamber." Waller was a member of Parliament and hatched "Waller's Plot," an attempt to seize London for Charles in May, 1643. The standard edition of his poems was edited by G. Thorn-Drury (1893 and 1905).

Redi] Francesco Redi (1626?–1697?) was physician to the Grand Duke of Tuscany, a minor poet, and a naturalist of some note, doing valuable pioneer work to disprove the old theory of spontaneous generation—that fly larvae, for example, were spontaneously generated by and in decaying matter. He wrote his *Bacco in Toscana (Bacchus in Tuscany)* (1685), a poem about the joys of wine, in dithyrambics.

Leigh Hunt] James Henry Leigh Hunt (1784–1859), English poet and journalist, best remembered for his "Abou Ben Adhem" and *The Story of Rimini* (1816), and for his friendship with Byron, Shelley, and Keats. In November, 1835, he reviewed *Paracelsus* favorably in his *Journal*. Much of his work deals with Italy and he translated a number of Italian poets, including Redi, whose *Bacchus in Tuscany* he published in 1825 (V, ii, 1–4n).

Dedication] *Macready* William Charles Macready (1793–1873), the son of a provincial actor-manager, was educated at Rugby but was soon forced by financial need to go on the provincial stage where he first appeared as Romeo in 1810. He rose to be one of the finest actors in theater history and quickly came to rival Edmund Kean (1787?–1833) as a tragedian, gaining acclaim especially in Shakespearean roles. His first appearance on the London stage came in 1816 at Covent Garden. He later visited America where his rivalry with the American actor Edwin Forrest precipitated the famous Astor Place Riot in New York in 1849. He was manager of Covent Garden from 1837 to 1839 and of Drury Lane from 1841 to 1843. He last appeared as Macbeth at Drury Lane in 1851. Macready first met B on November 27, 1835, at the home of W. J. Fox the Unitarian minister and social reformer whom B regarded as his literary father. See *The Diaries of William Charles Macready, 1833–1851*, ed. William Toynbee (London,

1912), I, 264. Later, on May 26, 1836, at the memorable supper at the house of the dramatist Thomas Noon Talfourd, where B met Wordsworth and Landor, Macready said to B "Will you not write me a tragedy and save me from going to America?" and by August 3 Forster told Macready that B had settled on Strafford as a subject (see Hood, pp. 296–297). Macready worked hard to stage *Strafford*. Later, he and B quarreled over the production of *A Blot in the 'Scutcheon* when B preferred Samuel Phelps to play the role of Lord Tresham.

Dramatis Personae § 1837 only §] *Theatre-Royal, Covent Garden* In Bow Street, near Covent Garden (originally a convent garden) Market, Holborn, London. The theater was originally built by John Rich in 1732 and was rebuilt after a fire in September, 1808. During the eighteenth and nineteenth centuries, many famous actors, including David Garrick, Peg Woffington, Mrs. Siddons, and Charles Kemble, appeared there. In April, 1847, it became the Royal Italian Opera House and has been the home of London opera ever since. Under the Licensing Act of 1737, only those theaters licensed by the Lord Chancellor (Theatres-Royal) could produce "legitimate" drama. Covent Garden though called Theatre-Royal is, with Drury Lane, a Patent Theatre, its original license going back to a Letter-Patent granted by Charles II in 1662 to Sir William Davenant, whence it ultimately descended to John Rich.

Persons] *Charles I* Charles Stuart (1600–1649) was the second son of James VI of Scotland, who became James I of England in 1603, and Anne of Denmark. His paternal grandmother was Mary Queen of Scots. He succeeded his father as King of Great Britain and Ireland on March 27, 1625, and was executed on January 30, 1649. Charles never really understood the forces which were at work in his kingdom and which brought him to the block. Though warm and charming in his personal and family relationships, politically he was obstinate, vacillating, fickle and obtuse. He believed even more firmly than had his father in the divine right of kings, and the story of his reign is that of a continuous struggle between the King and Parliament—in short, between absolute and constitutional monarchy. It was a struggle that Parliament eventually won.

Earl of Holland Sir Henry Rich (1590–1649), first Baron Kensington and first Earl of Holland, was the son of Robert Rich, first Earl of Warwick. Knighted in 1610, he rose rapidly in royal favor and negotiated the marriage of Charles and Henrietta Maria. He joined the parliamentarians in 1642, but fought for the King during the Civil War (1642–1648). He was captured and executed in 1649.

Lord Savile Thomas Savile (1590?–1658?), first Viscount Savile of Castlebar (Irish peerage), second Baron Savile of Pontefract and first Earl of Essex was the son of John Savile, whom Strafford replaced as *custos rotulorum* of the West Riding of Yorkshire (hence his hatred of Strafford). He had a stormy political career, plotting with the Scots and losing his seat in Parliament. He promised assistance to the Scotch invaders in a letter bearing the forged signatures of Bedford, Essex, Brooke, Warwick, Scrope and Mandeville. He became Lord President of the Council of the North and Lord-Lieutenant of Yorkshire in 1641. He was impeached on a charge of treason in 1645, but managed to join the parliamentarians and died in retirement.

Sir Henry Vane, the elder (1589–1655), held several high posts under Charles, including Comptroller (1629), Treasurer (1639–1641), and Secretary of State (1640–1641). He opposed the war with Scotland and clashed with Strafford. He was a member of the Long Parliament, supported the impeachment of Strafford and gave evidence against him on the question of the Scottish war. He lost his post in 1641 and joined the parliamentarians. He was owner of Raby Castle (County Durham) and was therefore embittered when Strafford was created Baron Raby in 1640.

Wentworth] Sir Thomas Wentworth, Baron Raby, first Earl of Strafford (1593–1641) was born in London, son of Sir William Wentworth of Wentworth-Woodhouse in Yorkshire. Educated at Cambridge and the Inner Temple, he entered Parliament in 1614 and was appointed *custos rotulorum* (virtually Lord-Lieutenant) of Yorkshire in 1615 after the forced resignation of Sir John Savile (see note under *Persons*), which resulted in a lifelong enmity between the two men. In 1622 he contracted the fever from which he suffered for the rest of his life and from which his first wife Margaret Clifford died. Active in Parliament for a number of years, Wentworth often supported the popular cause without abandoning his loyalty to the crown, and was a strong and influential proponent of the Bill of Rights in 1628 (see I, i, 56n). In 1629 he uncovered a plot to discredit Charles I and was rewarded by being made Privy Councillor. From this time, his growing dislike of the truculent puritanism that was developing in the government swung him more and more to the side of the King and Laud. In 1628 he was created Viscount Wentworth and appointed President of the Council of the North where he used the Star Chamber to suppress resistance to his desires. In 1632 he became Lord Deputy of Ireland where he put into effect the policy he frequently referred to in his letters as "Thorough," by which he meant complete disregard of private interests to establish the undisputed authority of the crown. In many ways his Irish policy was good bringing about as it did a number of much needed reforms, especially in the Irish branch of the Anglican church; but he tried to make the Irish people like the English and bring them completely under English control. By 1628 Wentworth had come completely round to a position of full support of the King against the puritan elements in government. In July, 1638, he took a stand against the Covenant (see I, i, 92n) and supported the view that Scotland should be conquered and Laud's policies maintained. After the attempt to invade Scotland failed (see II, i, 90n), Wentworth became Charles's chief advisor and on January 12, 1640, was created Baron Raby and Earl of Strafford. The events of B's play begin at this point, emphasizing the fear the Commons had of Wentworth, especially of the possibility that he might bring an Irish army to the support of the King's cause. Therefore led by Pym they attempted to impeach him (see III, ii, 3n) and when that attempt failed brought in the Bill of Attainder (see IV, ii, 120n) which Charles signed in fear of mob violence. Wentworth was executed on Tower Hill on May 11, 1641.

John Pym (1583–1643) was educated at Oxford and the Middle Temple, and first entered Parliament as member for Calne (Wiltshire) in 1614. He soon become a leading speaker, supporting the Petition of Right (1628) and the impeachment of Buckingham. He was always an active opponent of Charles's policies and staunchly fought against such measures as Tonnage and Poundage. On November 11, 1640, he was empowered to carry out the impeachment of Strafford—and of Laud a month later. The Court was probably more afraid of him than of any other parliamentarian and, as a bribe, Queen Henrietta offered him the post of Chancellor of the Exchequer, which he declined. He was among the Five Members, the others being Holles, Hazelrig, William Strode, and Hampden, accused of plotting to impeach the Queen, and escaped with the others, perhaps warned by Lady Carlisle, when Charles marched on Parliament to arrest them (January 4, 1642). He was buried in Westminster Abbey, but was disinterred after the Restoration. B's suggestion that he and Strafford had once been friends seems to have no historical basis.

John Hampden (1594–1643) was educated at Oxford and the Inner Temple and became a Member of Parliament for Grampound (Cornwall) in 1621, and later for Wendover (Buckinghamshire). As a member of Charles's third parliament (1629), he became a popular hero by refusing to pay Ship-Money, stimulating general resistance to the tax. He was powerful in the Short Parliament (1640) and had great influence over Pym. He was one of the managers of Strafford's impeachment, but opposed the change to Bill of Attainder and allowed Strafford's council to be heard. He served in the Civil War under Essex and was mortally wounded at Chalgrove Field.

The younger Vane Sir Henry Vane (1613–1662), eldest son of Sir Henry Vane, the elder. He became a puritan in 1628 and lived for a while in Boston, where he was Governor of Massachusetts (1635–1637). Returning to England, he entered Parliament as member for Hull (Yorkshire) in 1640. He may have helped to seal Strafford's fate by revealing to Parliament his copy of a memorandum in which Strafford suggested that Charles use the Irish army to subdue the kingdom—the kingdom being construed by his judges as England and by Strafford, in his defense, as Scotland. After 1643, Vane became extremely powerful in Parliament, and, now an ardent religionist, published a number of speeches and pamphlets. He was executed under Charles II. He is addressed in Milton's sonnet "To Sir Henry Vane the Younger" as "in sage counsel old."

Denzil Hollis (or Holles) (1599–1680), first Baron Holles of Ifield was the second son of John Holles, first Earl of Clare. He first entered Parliament as member for St. Michael (Cornwall) in 1624. He was an opponent of Buckingham and Laud (whom he helped impeach), but tried to save Strafford from the block. He was Strafford's brother-in-law (see I, i, 12), his sister Arabella being Strafford's second wife, and he vainly attempted to buy Strafford's life by negotiating an arrangement by which the King would consent to an abolition of episcopacy as the price. His *Memoirs* (1641–1648) were published in 1699.

Benjamin Rudyard Sir Benjamin Rudyard (1572–1658) was educated at Oxford and first entered Parliament as member for Portsmouth (Hampshire) in 1620. He became a mediator between the King and Parliament but later turned against Charles because of what he considered to be his wicked counselors.

Nathaniel Fiennes (1608?–1669), son of William Fiennes, first Viscount of Saye and Sele (III, ii, 167n), entered Parliament as member for Banbury (Oxfordshire) in 1640. He served in the Long Parliament and was on the Committee of Safety. He fought in the Civil War, but was excluded from the House of Commons by Pride's Purge (1648), by which the army, under Colonel Pride, forcefully excluded those members considered unfaithful to public interests because they wanted to treat with the King. He became a member of the House of Lords during Cromwell's regime.

Earl of Loudon John Campbell, (1598–1663) first Earl of Loudoun, became a member of the Scottish Parliament in 1622 by virtue of having married the heiress to the barony of Loudoun. He opposed episcopacy and took a leading part in organizing the Covenant (I, i, 92n). He was Scottish envoy to Charles in 1640 and joined the Scottish invasion forces the same year. He was a frequent envoy from his parliament to Charles between 1642 and 1647 and was Lord Chancellor of Scotland, 1641–1660. He was created Earl of Loudoun in 1641.

Maxwell James Maxwell, of whom little is known, is mentioned in the *Calendar of State Papers Domestic* (1638–1639) as appointed Gentleman Usher of the Black Rod and by Laud in his diary as treating him kindly during his imprisonment. He is probably not the same James Maxwell (1600–1640), noted as poet, historian, and genealogist.

Usher of the Black Rod The staff of office of the Usher to the House of Lords is a black rod surmounted by a golden lion.

Balfour Sir William Balfour (d. 1660) was a soldier in the Dutch service until 1627. He was made Constable of the Tower in 1630. He was a lieutenant-general during the Civil War.

A Puritan The Puritan party originated during the reign of Elizabeth. Its members objected to episcopacy and thus regarded the reformation of the English church as incomplete and in need of further "purification" of church ritual. In 1567 some members were imprisoned for engaging in private worship, the first instance of punishment of Protestant dissenters. By Stuart times, the designation had become semi-political and was generally applied to the Roundheads.

Queen Henrietta Henrietta Maria (1609–1666) Queen Consort of Charles I and daughter of Henry IV of France and Marie de Médici. She married Charles in 1625 and as a Roman Catholic was very influential in furthering the Catholic cause in England and thus alienating the Puritans. She was active in intrigues including attempts to save Strafford and urging the arrest of the Five Members. Charles, after the death of Buckingham, was completely under her sway. After the King's death, she fled to France and retired to a nunnery, but she continued her activities by such means as attempting to convert her younger son, the Duke of Gloucester, to Catholicism.

Lucy Percy Lucy Hay, Countess of Carlisle (1599–1660), was the daughter of Henry Percy, ninth Earl of Northumberland. She married James Hay, first Earl of Carlisle in 1617 and was widowed in 1636. She was a favorite of the Queen and an intimate of Strafford and later, of Pym. Her great beauty made her the subject of poems by Edmund Waller, Robert Herrick, Sir John Suckling, and others, as well as the subject of sketches by Matthew and Voiture. Strafford's own estimate of her is given in his *Letters* (II, 120): "I judge her ladyship very considerable, she is often in place and extremely well skilled how to speak with advantage and spirit for those friends she professeth unto, which will not be many. There is further in her disposition, she will not seem to be the person she is not, an ingenuity I have always observed and honoured her for."

Presbyterians By 1640, three parties could be discerned as far as advocacy for church reform was concerned—all ultimately stemming from Puritanism—Erastian (after Thomas Erastus, sixteenth-century German-Swiss theologian who advocated state supremacy in religious matters), represented by Pym and the Parliamentary majority, who wanted a Puritan State Church controlled by Parliamentary Lay Commissioners instead of bishops, not tolerating any dissent; Sectarian or Independent, who demanded a congregational system with liberty of worship and belief; Presbyterian, who wanted local democratic ecclesiastical rule under clerical synods, governed, however by the orthodoxy of Geneva. The last scheme, of course, was supported by the Scots. G. M. Trevelyan notes: "If, then, it be remembered that comparatively few persons were Erastian, Presbyterian, or Independent with any consistency, it is safe to distinguish the main features of the three rival schemes. They had, indeed, one common element, besides a sternly Protestant faith and worship: all three proposed to introduce democracy into the Church. The priest was to be subjected to some measure of election and control by the people. This change would require a high spiritual level throughout the country, and a democracy of intellect such as the Presbyterian system had found or fostered in Scotland" (*England under the Stuarts* [London, 1965], pp. 195–196).

Scots Commissioners Representatives of the Scottish Parliament. Scotland supported Parliament in its struggles with Charles, and the King made abortive invasions of that country in the two so-called Bishops' Wars (1639 and 1640). After the second of these, the Scots occupied Northumberland. As a result, negotiations took place between Charles and the Scots in 1640. Clarendon says that allowing the Scots Commissioners to reside in London while the treaty was being conducted was a great mistake (II, 127).

Two of Strafford's children Strafford had four children by his second wife, Arabella Holles (d. 1631) and one by his third, Elizabeth Rodes. The two eldest depicted in the play, William and Anne, would have been fourteen and thirteen respectively at the time of their father's death. William received his father's titles when the Attainder was reversed by Parliament in 1662. Although married twice, he left no issue on his death in 1695 and thus the direct male line of the Straffords ended. According to Miss Hickey, the roles of the two children were taken by a Master and Miss Walker (p. iv).

§Of the actors listed in the 1837 edition, only two, besides Macready, achieved any kind of distinction§

Vandenhoff John Vandenhoff (1790–1861), who played Pym, first went on the stage in 1808 playing the provinces and later London where at Drury Lane and Covent Garden he achieved some distinction in Shakespearean roles. His career declined after 1839.

Helen Faucit Helena Saville Faucit (1817–1898), who played Lady Carlisle, was a famous beauty who first appeared in *The Hunchback* at Drury Lane in 1836. She became one of the most celebrated actresses of her day, frequently playing opposite Macready, and was famous in such roles as Lady Macbeth, Juliet, Desdemona and others. She played Mildred Tresham in B's *Blot in the 'Scutcheon* and Colombe in *Colombe's Birthday*. She married Theodore (afterwards Sir Theodore) Martin in 1851 and became famous in society as Lady Martin. She published a book *On Some of Shakespeare's Female Characters* (1885).

ACT I, scene 1

§*Stage Directions*§] *Whitehall* is traditionally the political heart of London. In Stuart times, Whitehall Palace was the royal residence. The home of the archbishops of York from the late thirteenth century, it was seized in 1529 by Henry VIII, who changed the name from York House to Whitehall Palace. It occupied an area stretching from the present St. James's Park to Charing Cross and Westminster Bridge. It burned down in 1698, and today little remains of the original buildings though the name is perpetuated in that of the street that runs from Charing Cross, where King Charles's statue now stands, to the Houses of Parliament.

1] *here* Strafford arrived back in London in early November, 1640. In a letter to Sir George Radcliffe (November 5, 1640), he speaks of going to London the next day (Radcliffe, p. 218).

12] *his brother* his brother-in-law. Strafford's second wife was Holles' sister Arabella.

18–20] *The Philistine . . .* See I Samuel 17.

22] *ten years' disuse of Parliaments* Charles's third Parliament, which pressed the King into granting the Petition of Right, was dissolved in 1629 and none was called again until 1640 (the Short Parliament).

23] *Wentworth sat with us!* Strafford was a leader of the Parliament of 1628–1629 in its struggle to pass the Petition of Right (I, i, 56n).

24] *returns* from Yorkshire where he was with the army and whence he was summoned by the King with an assurance of safety (November, 1640).

34] *Exalting Dagon* . . . See I Samuel 5. Dagon was the chief god of the Philistines.

50] *one dear task* Strafford's policy of "Thorough."

56] The Bill of Rights or the Petition of Right was framed by Parliament in June, 1628. It stipulated that no one could be taxed without consent of Parliament, or imprisoned without cause; military could not be billetted without consent of the householder; and no one could be tried by martial law in peacetime. Charles, needing money for a war with France, signed it with his usual mental reservations.

57] *obscure small room* Probably in Pym's house, where some of the members met secretly.

62] *Hamilton* James Hamilton (1606–1649), third Marquis and first Duke of Hamilton (Scottish peerage) and second Earl of Cambridge (English peerage). He was Charles's advisor on Scottish affairs and persuaded him to revoke the prayer book and oppose the Covenant, and tried to prevent the Scots from supporting the English Parliament. He was captured during the Civil War and executed.

63] *Cottington* . . . *Laud* Francis Cottington (1578?–1652) Baron Cottington was in the service of Charles from 1622, when he became his secretary. He held a number of high offices and was noted as a political opportunist (hence "muckworm"). He was Chancellor of the Exchequer from 1629 to 1642, after having been a Commissioner both for Irish and Scottish Affairs. After the Civil War he joined Prince Charles abroad and died in retirement in Valladolid. *William Laud* (1573–1645) was educated at Oxford, ordained in 1601, and rose to become Archbishop of Canterbury in 1633. As Primate of England he maintained a policy, which amounted almost to an obsession (hence "maniac"), of suppressing any form of opposition to, and bringing all sects into uniformity with, the Anglican Church. He saw Puritanism as his special enemy and his policy had a disastrous effect on Charles's relations with Scotland. Laud used various methods to bring uniformity into the worship services, but his three chief weapons were the Court of High Commission, made up of clergy and laity, which had, by royal delegation, absolute authority in ecclesiastical matters; the Metro-political Visitation, the revival of an old custom of visiting and overseeing, either by the primate or by deputy, all parishes; and the Elizabethan law that required all books to be approved by the Archbishop of London. Laud was in religious matters of much the same temperament as Strafford was in military and political. Trevelyan calls him "this Richelieu of religion," though he admits that he was not cruel (*England under the Stuarts* [London, 1965], pp. 160, 162). His policies were responsible for much Puritan emigration to North America. Laud was impeached for high treason by the Long Parliament and executed in the Tower in 1645. From his cell, he blessed Strafford on his way to the block. Laud left a number of autobiographical and theological works, including sermons and a diary. The complete *Works* were published by the Library of Anglo-Catholic Theology, 1847–1860.

75] *The iron heel shall bruise her* See Genesis 3:15

80] *Runnymead* in Surrey, near Windsor, where King John signed the Magna Carta in 1215.

85] *On other service* As Captain-General of the army in Ireland, 1640.

90] *Haman* was the confidant of King Ahaseurus (probably Xerxes I of Persia, 485–465 B.C.) who plotted to have the Jews of the kingdom massacred. See Esther 3.

90] *Ahitophel* David's counselor who joined the revolt of Absalom. See II Samuel 15:12; 16:20–17:23. Cf. John Dryden's *Absalom and Achitophel* (1681).

91] *Gentlemen of the North* Scots

92] *League and Covenant* In 1633, Charles visited Scotland and was crowned at Holyrood. The warm reception he received encouraged him to allow Laud to proceed with his policy of restoring episcopacy to Scotland and abolishing Presbyterianism. The introduction of the Liturgy, July 16, 1637, was met with riots and violence. In 1638, the Privy Council of Scotland appointed a committee known as the four Tables, after the four classes represented, which renewed the League and Covenant (originally drafted in 1581 as a bond between Scottish Protestants against Catholicism). Most of the Scottish nation then signed the National Covenant (1638) vowing to defend the "true" religion. Soon after, the General Assembly of the Scottish Church excommunicated the bishops and abolished Prelacy. The Scots then made an alliance with France and invaded England, seizing some northern towns. This invasion forced Charles to call his fourth (Short) Parliament in 1640. In 1643, the English Parliamentary party joined the Scots in subscribing to the Covenant.

101] *war* with Scotland.

112] *Greenwich* Now a part of Greater London, Greenwich was rural in Stuart times. The Tudors had a palace there (now the Royal Naval College), and Queen Henrietta Maria had a house designed originally for Anne of Denmark by Inigo Jones.

131–134] *Seven long years . . .* See Judges 6–8. The *Midianites* were a nomadic people of the Gulf of Aqaba (Jordan), who carried Joseph to Egypt. See Genesis 37:28, 36. *Gideon* was a judge of Israel who defeated the Midianites with three hundred men. See Judges 6.

135] *ravaged body* Strafford contracted a serious fever in 1622, which seems to have recurred throughout his life. He was also subject to gout.

142] *just dissolved your Parliament* Hamilton was negotiating for Charles with the Scottish Parliament, but after they abolished episcopacy, Charles dissolved them (l. 92n).

181] *Joab* was the treacherous nephew of David who murdered David's son Absalom. He was executed by order of Solomon (about 1015 B.C.). See I Kings 2:5, 6, 28–34.

184] *Feltons* assassins. John Felton (1595–1628) was the army officer who stabbed Buckingham to death at Portsmouth in 1628 (III, i, 41n). He was captured and hanged. He is hailed as a national hero in some popular ballads of the day.

200] *Gracchus' death* Tiberius Sempronius Gracchus (d. 133 B.C.) and his brother, Gaius Sempronius Gracchus (d. 121 B.C.), sons of a Roman praetor, were brought up by their mother (daughter of Scipio Africanus), to whom the Romans erected a statue. The brothers are remembered for their struggles, as tribunes, to institute political reforms including repeal of land laws giving unfair advantage to the wealthy. After his brother's death, Gaius attempted to stabilize the price of wheat and enlarge the franchise. He committed suicide. Their lives are recounted by Plutarch.

201] *choicest clause* probably clause X, which summarized the main stipulations of the Bill (l. 56n).

203] *One month before* Wentworth had supported the Petition of Right, which was accepted by the King on June 7, 1628. On July 22, Wentworth was created Baron Wentworth and on December 10, Viscount Wentworth (the rank between Baron and Earl). On Christmas Day, he was made President of the Council (or Court) of the North ("Northern Presidency"). This council, originally instituted by Elizabeth I, with its center at York, was used to govern the northern counties. It could impose those injustices—martial law in peacetime and so forth—against which the Petition of Right had been framed.

213] *Aceldama* The field of blood. See Acts 1:16–19.

231] *travail of our souls* See Isaiah 53:11.

ACT I, scene 2

37] *Secretary* Secretary of State (1640–1641).

54] *Archbishop* Laud. See I, i, 63n.

58] *Customs* Historically, customs were dues on lands and goods paid by a tenant to his lord. Charles had various ways of extracting extra money from land-holders—a favorite one was to declare a fine or forfeiture on an estate by invalidating, on some pretext, an ancient letter patent granting the land from the crown. In Ireland, it was Strafford's duty, as Lord Deputy, to collect these customs. (See Elizabeth Cooper, *The Life of Thomas Wentworth, Earl of Strafford* [London, 1874], I, 321–324 and Radcliffe, p. 188).

96] *Weston* Sir Richard Weston (1577–1635), Baron Weston, first Earl of Portland, became Chancellor of the Exchequer in 1621, but was unpopular because he was a Roman Catholic. He incurred the Queen's enmity because he refused grants to her favorites. He was later Lord-Treasurer and an advisor to Charles.

157] *thirty silver pieces* See Matthew 26:15, 27:3,9.

158] *Earldom you expected* Strafford had requested an earldom in September, 1634, as a mark of the King's confidence in him, but was refused.

175] *obscene dream* See Ezekiel 8:10.

176] *Ezekiel chamber* See Ezekiel 8:12.

190–192] *Scots' League* . . . See I, i, 92n.

240] *this* The George of II, ii, 58 and III, iii, 94. Strafford was given the Order of the Garter in 1639.

241] *Earl* Strafford was created Baron Raby and Earl of Strafford in January, 1640. In showing him receiving the Garter and Earldom at the same time, B has compressed history.

247] *apple of my sight* See Deuteronomy 32:10; Psalms 17:8; Proverbs 7:2; Zechariah 2.8; Lamentations 2.18.

ACT II, scene 1

1] *subsidies* taxes on goods and land granted by Parliament to the King in time of need.

2] *Strafford called the Parliament* Strafford urged the King to call the Parliament (April to May, 1640) known as the Short Parliament. See Clarendon I, 167n.

3–4] *Out of the serpent's root* . . . See Isaiah 14:29.

9] *fiery flying serpent* See Isaiah 14:29.

34] *Star Chamber* The Court of the Star Chamber, founded by Henry VII, was a means of punishing offenses. The source of its name is not quite clear, but it originally met in a room in Westminster Palace which was used for storing starrs (bonds) of Jewish merchants and which supposedly had stars painted on the ceiling. In Charles I's day, the court was very unpopular because it was empowered to punish (by fine, mutilation, or imprisonment) anyone, without recourse to regular legal procedures.

54] *The lump till all is leaven* See Galatians 5:9.

54] *Glanville* Sir John Glanville the younger (1586–1661) was the speaker of the Short Parliament. He spoke in favor of the subsidies on the grounds that they were inconsiderable. See Clarendon, II, 73.

70–71] *like those/In Ireland* Sir Edward Poynings (1459–1521), deputy to the Governor of Ireland, had passed in 1494 an act known as Poynings' Law by which all acts of the Irish Parliament to be valid needed prior approval of the English Privy Council.

90] *Bishops' war* During Laud's campaign to impose episcopacy on the Scots, Charles had tried to raise an army to invade Scotland. This attempt known as the First Bishops' War (1639) was unsuccessful for various reasons. The King attempted a similar campaign in August, 1640, the Second Bishops' War, but many of his conscripted soldiers were Puritans and had no heart to fight the Scots, who, realizing this, seized Newcastle and occupied parts of Northumberland and County Durham. Parliament's fear of the military ability of Strafford and the aid he might now give the King was largely responsible for their attempt to impeach him.

105] *ancient path* See Jeremiah 18:15.

ACT II, scene 2

30] *Northumberland* Sir Algernon Percy (1602–1668), tenth Earl of Northumberland, became general of all the English forces south of the Trent in 1639. Clarendon says: "The progress of the King's advance for Scotland was exceedingly hindered by the great and dangerous sickness of the earl of Northumberland the general, whose recovery was either totally despaired of by the physician, or pronounced to be expected very slowly, so that there would be no possibility for him to perform the service of the north: whereupon he sent to the King, that he would make choice of another general. And though the lord Conway in all his letters sent advertisement that the Scots had not advanced their preparations to that degree that they would be able to march that year, yet the King had much better intelligence that they were in readiness to move, and so concluded that it was necessary to send another general; and designed the earl of Strafford for that command" (II, 88). Northumberland was Lady Carlisle's brother (IV, i, 101n). On his sickness, see Shakespeare's *I Henry IV*, IV. i. 16 for an interesting parallel.

42] *passes of the Tyne* The river Tyne separates Northumberland on the north from County Durham on the south. The passes would be strategic, of course, in any English-Scottish conflict.

90] *Wilmot* Henry Wilmot (1612?–1658), first Earl of Rochester, was Commissary-General of horse in Charles's army. He fought in the Civil War and was active in attempts to restore the monarchy during the Commonwealth.

91] *Conway* Edward Conway, second Viscount Conway, was appointed a General of horse by Strafford and was defeated by the Scots at Newburn in 1640, after which, Clarendon says "he never after turned his face towards the enemy" (II, 89).

92] *Ormond* James Butler (1610–1688), twelfth Earl and first Duke of Ormonde (Irish peerage). At first he had opposed Strafford in the Irish Parliament, but later switched and supported him, assembling, in 1640, the Irish army that was to invade Scotland. He later became Lord-Lieutenant of Ireland (1643) and commanded the royalist forces there during the Civil War.

93] *the City* The City of London, the area around St. Paul's, the Tower and the Guildhall, as distinct from Westminster, the seat of Parliament, about a mile to the SW.

94] *debase the coin* to issue adulterated coins for profit. Charles I's reign saw a number of new coins minted, including the gold three-pound piece and the silver one-pound.

95] *seize the bullion* the bullion, which belonged to merchants, was stored in the Tower, where the King could easily hold it for ransom or forced loan.

96] *Herbert* Sir Edward Herbert (1591?–1657), Solicitor-General (1640) and Attorney-General (1641).

258] *George* The medal of a member of the Order of the Garter. The medal depicts St. George and the Dragon, and hangs from a collar bearing broaches with the motto *Honi soit qui mal y pense* [Shame be to him who evil thinks of it]. Founded by Edward III about 1346, the Order is the highest in England.

275] *among the tombs* See Mark 5:5.

286] *whited sepulchre* See Matthew 23:27.

ACT III, scene 1

§ *Stage Directions* §] *Westminster Hall* is a part of the complex of buildings known as the Houses of Parliament. Built by William II in 1097, it was, from the thirteenth century until 1882, the chief seat of English law courts. Strafford and Charles I were both tried there.

3] *news from Scotland* With the Scots occupying parts of the N of England, the English army mutinous and for various reasons no Irish army forthcoming, Charles was forced to make peace with the Scots and grant their demands for a large sum of money to pay their soldiers. To get this payment Charles was forced to call a parliament, which became known as the Long Parliament because it met from 1640 to 1653 (see "new Parliament" III, i, 12).

8] *Lenthal* William Lenthall (1591–1662), appointed Speaker of the House of Commons in November, 1640.

36] *twinkling of an eye* See I Corinthians 15:52.

40] *Eliot's old method* When Charles attempted to dissolve Parliament in 1629, Eliot, who insisted on Parliament's right to self-adjournment, and others caused the doors to be locked against the King's officers until a resolution against Tonnage and Poundage could be passed.

41] *the great Duke* George Villiers (1592–1628), first Duke of Buckingham of the second creation, was a favorite of Charles as he had been of James I, who made him a duke in 1623. His war-like ways and peevish nature made him very unpopular with Parliament and the people. He quarreled with Richelieu and made an ill-fated expedition to La Rochelle where he was defeated by Richelieu, a blow which intensified the hatred of the English for him. While he was preparing a second expedition he was murdered by a discontented naval officer, John Felton. See I, i, 184.

ACT III, scene 2

3] *impeach* To bring a public official to trial for crimes against the state. In the English system, the House of Commons is the accuser and the House of Lords the tribunal. Strafford was impeached on a charge of treason, in this case construed as an "endeavour to overthrow the fundamental government of the kingdom, and to introduce arbitrary power" (Clarendon, III, 107). The main charges were that he seized the monopolies on flax and tobacco; illegally used martial law; furthered his private interests in the Government (all during his rule in Ireland); and attempted to gain absolute power of the northern counties as President of the Council of the North. The trial (March-April, 1641) was a fiasco as far as Pym and his party were concerned. Strafford defended himself brilliantly and adequate witnesses could not be brought against him. When it appeared that the Lords would not find him guilty, Pym and his party, determined to destroy him at all cost, brought in the Bill of Attainder (see IV, ii, 120), introduced by Haselrig on April 10, 1641.

28] *Theobald's* a manor in Hertfordshire built by Sir William Cecil, Lord Burghley, and acquired by James I who died there. Charles was proclaimed King at the gates and set out from there to conduct the Civil War. Like many other symbols of monarchy, it was demolished during the Commonwealth.

43] *Windebank* Sir Francis Windebank (1582–1646) was a member of both the Long and Short Parliaments who had been a negotiator with the papal representatives when Charles was exploring the possibilities of a union of the Anglican and Catholic churches. Accused of signing pro-Catholic documents by the House of Commons in 1640, he fled to Paris.

52] *York* In Yorkshire, an ancient city of great military, ecclesiastical, and cultural importance.

53] *In his own county* Strafford's family seat, Wentworth-Woodhouse, was in Yorkshire, though he was born in London.

97] *Durham* in County Durham, about 50m. S of Newcastle, was of great strategic importance in the Scotch wars.

158] *Ripon* Town in Yorkshire, where Charles negotiated for peace with the Scots (III, i, 3n).

165] *Bedford* Francis Russell (1593–1641), fourth Earl of Bedford, was a leader in the House of Lords and a Privy Councillor. He sympathized with Pym and his followers but opposed the Attainder of Strafford.

Essex Robert Devereux (1591–1646), third Earl of Essex, son of the famous favorite of Elizabeth I, held Puritan sympathies and as a member of the House of Lords opposed many of Charles's desires. He became a Parliamentary general in the Civil War. He harbored a grudge against Strafford (see Clarendon, II, 101).

166] *Brooke* Robert Greville (1608–1643), second Baron Brooke, represented the King at Ripon but was opposed to Laud's policies. He was one of the members of the Lords (Speaker, 1642) who, like Essex under whom he served, joined the Parliamentary cause during the Civil War. He was killed at Lichfield.

166] *Warwick* Sir Robert Rich (1587–1658), second Earl of Warwick. His mother was Penelope Devereux, Sir Philip Sidney's "Stella." In his early life, he was active in colonizing America. He gradually came to embrace the Parliamentary cause and in 1643 became Lord High Admiral of the Parliamentary naval forces.

167] *Saye* William Fiennes (1582–1662), first Viscount Saye and Sele, was the father of Nathaniel Fiennes and was an opponent of the Church. Clarendon says he was the only member of the Independent party in the House of Lords (VIII, 260). He was treacherous to the King's cause, promising to save Strafford's life in return for the Treasurership (Clarendon III, 193) and later, when appointed by Parliament in 1648 to treat for peace with the King was refused safe conduct by Charles.

167] *Mandeville* Edward Montagu (1602–1671), Baron Montagu, Viscount Mandeville, second Earl of Manchester, was a Commissioner to the Scots at Ripon, a Privy Councillor and member of the House of Lords, who went over to the Parliamentary side. In 1642 he was accused by the King of treason, along with the Five Members (see Clarendon IV, 149). The evidence (mentioned in lines 165–167) that Strafford may have had by which to impeach this group has never come to light, but that some of them eventually hurt the King's cause cannot be doubted. Trevelyan says: "These few Lords, by their social position and personal character, made rebellion respectable. When men stopped on the brink of treason to look round for company, Essex 'broke the ice', and 'by his very name commanded thousands' all over England into the service of Parliament" (*England under the Stuarts*, p. 225).

176] *Mainwaring* Sir Philip Mainwaring (1589–1661), member of Parliament (1624–1640) and Secretary for Ireland, became Strafford's secretary in 1634.

182] *Tower* The collection of buildings known as the Tower of London, founded by William I (the Conqueror) about 1078 as a fortress and enlarged by Henry I (1100–1135) as a royal residence, was still used as a prison and place of execution for political prisoners until the nineteenth century, and occasionally, during the two World Wars. Its famous prisoners have included Henry VI, Edward V, Sir Thomas More, and Anne Boleyn, as well as Strafford and Laud. Its buildings include the original White Tower, the Bloody Tower, the Wakefield Tower (which houses the Crown Jewels), and the Beauchamp Tower. Charles II, the night before his coronation (April 23, 1661), was the last monarch to sleep there.

183] *Brian* John Byron (d. 1652), first Baron Byron, who served under Strafford in the Scotch wars.

192] *Willis* Unidentified

203] *Goring* Colonel George Goring (1608–1657), Baron Goring, son of George Goring, Earl of Norwich, he rose to be a general in the Civil War. He was a leader in the "Army Plot," a plan by certain army officers in 1641 to support the King by force of arms and to rescue Strafford from the Tower (Clarendon III, 177).

ACT III, scene 3

4] *rufflers* bullies, swaggerers, ruffians.

8–9] *Where the carcass is* . . . See Matthew 24:28.

10] *Geneva* Switzerland, the city of John Calvin, hence the cradle of Presbyterianism.

13] *"King Pym"* Pym was nicknamed this by friend and enemy alike.

15] *St. John* Oliver St. John (1598?–1673), Solicitor-General (1641–1643), who drew up Strafford's Attainder and defended it before the Lords. Clarendon says he had, with Hampden, great influence on Pym (VII, 411).

29] *St. John's head* See Matthew 14:8.

41–42] *Pride before destruction* . . . See Proverbs 16:18.

43] *A word in season* See Proverbs 15:23.

44] *A golden apple in a silver picture* See Proverbs 25:11.

47–52] *How hath the oppressor ceased* . . . See Isaiah 14:4–6.

78] *Slingsby* Sir Robert Slingsby (1611–1661), naval officer and a secretary to Strafford. He became Comptroller of the Navy in 1660. His *Discourse upon the Past and Present State of His Majesty's Navy* was first published in 1801.

82] *Allerton* Northallerton, county town of the North Riding of Yorkshire.

ACT IV, scene 1

25] *close curtain* "There being a close box made at one end [of Westminster Hall], at a very convenient distance for hearing, in which the King and Queen sat, untaken notice of, his majesty, out of kindness and curiosity, desiring to hear all that could be alleged" (Clarendon, III, 105). Legally, a trial could not take place in the presence of the King, hence the curtain. Clarendon says "he afterwards repented himself, when his having been present at the trial was alleged and urged to him as an argument for the passing the bill of attainder" (III, 105).

42] *Floods come, winds beat,* . . . See Matthew 7:24–27.

65] *Those notes* See note on the *Younger Vane* under *Persons*.

95] *That paper* The petition from the army officers ("Army Plot") to support the King by force of arms (III, ii, 203n).

101] *your brother* Northumberland (see II, ii, 30n).

ACT IV, scene 2

5] *prophet's rod* See Exodus 4:20.

17] *Haselrig* Sir Arthur Hesilrige (or Haselrig) (d. 1661), an avid opponent of Charles and member of Parliament who opposed Laud's policies. He introduced the Bill of Attainder against Strafford and in 1641, promoted the famous "Root and Branch Bill," so named because it called for the abolition of episcopacy in all its "roots and branches." He was one of the Five Members. Clarendon called him "an absurd, bold man" (III, 127).

48 *Stage Directions*] *Lane* Sir Richard Lane (1584–1650), lawyer of the Middle Temple, who defended Strafford at his trial. In 1645 he became Lord Keeper.

54] *Radcliffe* Sir George Radcliffe (1593–1657), lawyer of Gray's Inn and member of Parliament, was Strafford's advisor on legal, financial, and private affairs for many years and his close friend. Pym's party had contrived

357

to have him imprisoned on a charge of treason in 1640 so that he would not be able to give evidence at Strafford's trial (see Clarendon III, 93). In 1643, Radcliffe became advisor to the Duke of York, afterwards James II. Radcliffe's *Life and Original Correspondence of Sir George Radcliffe* was published in 1810 and is an important source of information about Strafford.

120] *Bill of Attainder* a terrible instrument, as attested to by the "Horrible!" of l. 112, was a means of prosecuting dangerous enemies of state when legal technicalities (such as the lack of at least two witnesses for the prosecution which were required in cases of treason) precluded regular impeachment procedure. Attainder (from Latin *attinctus*—stained) can be introduced by either House and, after passing both, requires royal sanction. It carries an automatic death-sentence and forfeiture of titles, estates, privilege and so forth for all heirs and descendents. Attainder was last used against Sir John Fenwick in 1697. (See also note on *Strafford's children* under *Persons*.)

ACT IV, scene 3

27] *two Estates* the House of Lords and the House of Commons.

ACT V, scene 2

1–4] *O bell' andare* How beautiful to go in a little boat on the sea in a spring evening. Leigh Hunt's *Bacchus in Tuscany* (1825) translates it "O what a thing / "Tis for you and for me / On an evening in spring / To sail on the sea." Redi's poem was first published at Fiorenza (Florence) in 1685. The most recent edition to which B could have had access would have been one published at Florence in 1822. The poem had not been written at the time of Strafford's death when Redi would have been only fifteen. The song is to be found at lines 832–835.

18] *old quiet house* Wentworth-Woodhouse, the Wentworth family mansion, in the West Riding of Yorkshire near Sheffield. Another house now stands on the site but part of the original remains.

20] *Venice* (Venezia) capital of Venetia, in the extreme NW of Italy, and one of the ancient city-states, is on the Adriatic and is built on 118 islands. Venice reached its height as a maritime and commercial power in the fifteenth century, after which it declined until it was annexed by France in 1797. It did not become a part of modern Italy until 1866. It is noted for its canals, its beauty, and its rich antiquity.

42–43] *the ignoble Term, / And raise the Genius on his orb again* In the preface to her edition, Miss Hickey says she is indebted to B for most of the note on this passage (p. vii). The note is as follows: "The *Term* was a statue, representing the Roman *Term*, the god who presided over bounderies. The figure was an ignoble one, with ignoble attributes. The *Genius* was the image that represented the guardian spirit who was supposed to accompany every created being from the cradle to the grave. The Roman *Genius* corresponded to the Greek *daimon genethlios*. This spirit, as the instigator of man's actions, was representative of his main endeavour. The Genius of a male person was represented as a beautiful boy, with a chlamys [outdoor cloak] on his shoulders, and with the wings of a bird. The *Juno*, or Genius of a female, was represented as a maiden, draped, and with the wings of a bat or moth. In Mr. Browning's own words, 'Suppose the enemies of a man to have thrown down the image and replaced it by a mere *Term*, and you have what I put into Strafford's head.' 'Putting the Genius on the pedestal usurped by the Term means—or tries to mean—substituting eventually, the true notion of Strafford's endeavour and performance in the world, for what he conceives to be the ignoble and distorted conception of these by his contemporary judges' " (p. 91).

72] *Garrard* Forster refers to him as Strafford's "newsmonger" (p. 214). There are letters from him to Strafford, one of which refers to Prynne (l. 123 below): "Mr. Prynne, prisoner in the Tower, who hath got his ears sewed on that they grew again as before to his head, is relapsed into new errors" (Strafford *Letters*, I, 266).

74–75] *Saints / Reign* Possibly an anachronistic reference to a speech made by Oliver Cromwell in 1653 at the opening of Parliament (The Barebones Parliament) in which he hailed the coming rule of saints, i.e. non-conformist members of Parliament.

88] *Sejanus* Lucius Aelius Sejanus (d. A.D. 31) Prefect of Praetorians under the Roman Emperor Tiberius, became his confidant, plotted to seize the throne, was denounced by the Emperor and executed. Ben Jonson's play, *Sejanus: His Fall*, produced in 1603, deals with his life.

88] *Richelieu* Armand Jean du Plessis, Cardinal de Richelieu (1585–1642), a bishop who rose to become chief minister of Louis XIII of France. He wielded tremendous power, extending the boundaries of France and making Louis an absolute monarch. He founded the French Academy. Bulwer-Lytton's play *Richelieu* was produced only two years after *Strafford* with Macready in the title role.

123] *Prynne* William Prynne (1600–1669) was a Puritan lawyer and a voluminous writer of pamphlets. His *Histriomastix: The Players' Scourge, or Actors' Tragedy* (1633), an attack on the stage, was suspected of containing slanderous allusions to the Queen and Laud. Prynne was sentenced by the Star Chamber in 1634 to have his ears sliced and to be branded and pilloried. After a turbulent career he finally became Keeper of the Records in the Tower of London.

153–155] *Put not your trust / In princes . . .* See Psalms 146:3.

173] *Wandesford* Christopher Wandesford (1592–1640), a fellow Yorkshire-man and friend of Strafford, was a member of Parliament who had led the attacks on Buckingham. He later switched to the King's side and became Lord Justice of Ireland (1636 and 1639) and Lord-Deputy in 1640.

219] *St. Antholin's* A London church appropriated by the government for the use of the Scots Commissioners. The church probably goes back to the twelfth century, but was burned during the Great Fire of London, 1666, and rebuilt, according to John Stow's *Survey of London* (ed. J. Strype, 1720, I, iii, 17–18). It was demolished in 1874. It was in the parish of St. John Baptist, Walbrook. The present St. Mary Aldermary is near the site.

231] *Billingsley* Captain of the men who were to effect Strafford's escape from the Tower.

288] *David* The shepherd-boy who succeeded Saul as King of Israel (c. 1012–972 B.C.). His story is told in I and II Samuel and in I Chronicles.

289] *Jonathan* son of Saul, was David's beloved friend. He was killed at the battle of Mount Gilboa. See I Samuel 1–19.

319] *awful head* that of King Charles.

323] *word of fire* See Jeremiah 23:29.

SORDELLO

The Text

B apparently began *Sordello* shortly after he finished *Pauline* in 1833, but his first specific reference to it is in a letter to the Reverend William Fox in April, 1835. The poem was not published, however until early March, 1840. We know that B conceived his central purpose gradually and that the poem went through several revisions. Moreover, twice during the time he was writing, he interrupted his work to travel abroad, the second time (April 13–July 31, 1838) to visit spots in N Italy associated with the historical background of his poem. In the interval he also published *Paracelsus* (1835) and *Strafford* (1837).

The meaning of *Sordello* is intricately related to the complex, often confusing and contradictory, source material out of which it is fashioned. B's original information came largely from the article on Sordello in Volume XXXIX of *Biographie universelle* (Paris, 1825). By the time he had finished the poem, however, he had read numerous articles and books on the history of the period in addition to visiting the places where much of the action of his poem had occurred. B seems to have feared that his intense interest in the historical period was at odds with his stated poetic purpose to tell Sordello's story, or as he was later to describe it, to trace "the development of a soul." At any rate, the poem published in 1840 mystified many of his contemporaries because of both the novelty of its structure and the complexity of its subject matter. Some knowledge of B's sources is indispensable for the modern reader. We have not attempted here, however, to explore that subject fully. The notes which follow provide, instead, the basic information which we consider essential to an understanding of the poem. For a fuller treatment of the subject of B's indebtedness to his predecessors, we recommend Stewart Holmes's article, "The Sources of Browning's *Sordello*," (SP, xxxiv, 467–496) and his unpublished dissertation *Browning's Sordello: A Study of its Development and Sources* (Yale University, 1934).

Professor Holmes lists the following books which, he says, "contain those works which Browning probably used in writing *Sordello*." The books actually referred to in these notes are identified in the text by the short title

NORTH SEA

BALTIC SEA

K. OF DENMARK

FRIESLAND

DUCHY OF SAXONY

Elbe R.

DUCHY OF POMERANIA

M. OF BRANDENBURG

KINGDOM OF POL

Cologne

DUCHY OF LOWER LORRAINE

Aix-la-Chapelle ◉

L. OF THURINGIA

DUCHY OF SILESIA

Rhine R.

Frankfort

D. OF FRANCONIA

KINGDOM OF BOHEMIA

MARCH OF MORAVIA

Mayence

Würzburg

HAMPAGNE

KINGDOM OF FRANCE

DUCHY OF UPPER LORRAINE

Danube R.

D. OF AUSTRIA

DUCHY OF BAVARIA

Vienna

KING

BURGUNDY

DUCHY OF SWABIA

Munich

OF

Inn R.

HUNGA

KINGDOM OF ARLES

Rhine R.

Innsbruck

Brenner Pass

C. OF TYROL

Rhone R.

Tyrol

Meran

Trent

Como

Monza

Bergamo

Bassano

Treviso

M. Vicenza

OF VERONA

Rhone R.

Legnano

Brescia

Vercelli

Milan

Lodi

Verona

Padua

Venice

Mincio R.

LOMBARDY

Mantua

Este

Susa

Turin

Pavia

Po R.

Piacenza

Cremona

Po R.

Ferrara

DALMATIA

Alessandria

Roncaglia

Parma

Reggio

Canossa

Modena

Ravenna

Zara

Bologna

Faenza

COUNTY OF PROVENCE

Florence

Pisa

Arno R.

Ancona

ADRIATIC

Siena

Assisi

Spoleto

CORSICA

Rome ◉

SEA

APULIA

SARDINIA

TYRRHENIAN SEA

Naples

KINGDOM

OF THE

ION

S

THE HOLY ROMAN EMPIRE
UNDER THE HOHENSTAUFEN
1138-1254

Messina

0   100   200

Scale of Miles

Palermo

TWO SICILIES

Credit: Holt, Rinehart & Winston, Inc.

Cartography by Norman C. A

AUSTRIA

Adige R.

TRENTINO ALTO ADIGE

● BOLZANO

FRIULI
VENEZIA
GIULIA

◉ TRENTO

V E N E T O

● Possagno

Oliera
Bassano ●● Asolo
● Romano

*Lago
di
Garda*

Castelfranco ●
◉ TREVISO

● Campo San Pietro

SCIA

VICENZA ◉

Brenta R.

◉ VERONA

● St. Boniface

V E N E T O

PADUA ◉

◉ VENICE

Góito ●

● Isola

● Este

MANTUA ◉ Mincio R.

Adige R.

◉ ROVIGO

PROVINCE
OF
VENETO

Po R.

ADRIATIC SEA

● FERRARA

E M I L I A

Scale of Miles

0   10   20   30

GIO ◉

◉ MODENA

Norman Clark Adams, 1970 Credit: Touring Club of Italy

indicated in parenthesis immediately following the bibliographical information.

(1) *Biographie universelle* (Paris, 1811–1855). (*Biographie*)

(2) Frizzi, Antonio. *Memorie di Ferrara* (5 vols., Ferrara, 1791–1809), vols. II, III. (Frizzi)

(3) Muratori, Ludovico Antonio. *Rerus Italicarum Scriptores* (28 vols., Milan, 1723–1751). (Muratori, *Scriptores*)

    (a) Vol. VIII (1726):

    Rolandino. *De factis in Marchia Travisina*. (Rolandino)

    Anonymous. *Chronica Parva Ferrariensis*. (*Chro. Parva Ferr.*)

    Monachus Patavinus. *Chronicon de Rebus Gestis in Lombardia* . . .

    Uncertain. *Ricciardi Comitis Sancti Bonifacii Vita* (*Ricciardi*)

    Maurisius, G. *Historia de Rebus Gestis Eccelini de Romano*. (Maurisius)

    Anonymous. *Memoriale Potestatum Regiensium* . . .

    (b) Vol. XX (1732):

    Platina. *Historiae Mantuanae*. (Platina)

(4) Muratori, Ludovico Antonio. *Annali d'Italia* (12 vols., Milan, 1744–1749), vol. VII. (Muratori, *Annali*)

(5) Pigna, G. B. *Historia de Principi di Este* (Venice, 1572). (Pigna)

(6) Simonde de Sismondi, J. C. L. *Histoire de Republiques Italiennes du moyen âge* (16 vols., Paris, 1809–1818). (Sismondi)

(7) Ughi, L. *Dizionario Storico degli Uomini Illustri Ferraresi* (2 vols., Ferrara, 1804).

(8) Verci, G. *Storia degli Eccelini* (3 vols., Bassano, 1779) vols. I, II. (Verci)

For each of the above the first edition is indicated. It is not always clear, however, which of the editions B used. He drew largely upon his father's library and the British Museum for his information. That his father's library was large we know. Mrs. Orr says that it contained 6000 volumes (*Life and Letters of Robert Browning* [London, 1908] p. 73). It is equally clear that B read at the British Museum. Griffin and Minchin say that he read Muratori there (p. 102). William Sharp states, without citing authority, "For a brief period he went often to the British Museum, particularly the library, and to the National Gallery. At the British Museum Reading Room he perused with great industry and research those works in philosophy and medical history which are the bases of 'Paracelsus,' and those Italian Records bearing upon the story of Sordello" (*Life of Robert Browning* [London, 1890] p. 54).

What precisely B might have found in his father's library is not certain. It is at present impossible to reconstruct a list of more than a fraction of the books which the older B owned. What happened to the rest of his library is uncertain. The elder Browning, involved in a breach of promise suit in 1852 as a result of which he was ordered to pay damages of eight hundred pounds, left England abruptly and took up permanent residence in Paris. Details of his move are shrouded in secrecy and we find no specific information about what happened to his treasured books. His son came from Italy to assist him in the move, and remained behind for a few days to dispose of certain of those possessions which he could not take with him. Considering the haste with which his departure was conducted, it seems unlikely that the entire library was transplanted. It is certain, however, that at least a portion of it was preserved either in storage in England, or by transfer to Paris or to Florence where Robert and Elizabeth maintained Casi Guidi. In the introductory remarks to Bertram Dobell's catalogue, *Browning Memorials* (London, 1913), we find the following comment about the books in the great Sotheby sale of May of that year: "The collection generally represented the tastes of three generations of Brownings. By far the largest portion of the books was collected by the poet's father." The listing in the Sotheby, Wilkinson and Hodge's catalogue (*The Browning Collection* [London, 1913] is disappointing, however. The catalogue lists only 1334 items under the section "Books" (pp. 65–141). Although an item may consist of from one to thirty-one volumes and often several titles, the total undoubtedly falls short of the actual number of books accumulated by the father, the two poets, and their son. Not only does the sale represent less than the total of what the library must have been, but we do not know even the titles of all those items that were sold. Shortly after the great Sothby sale, catalogues from other dealers appeared (all London, 1913 unless otherwise noted), containing items apparently bought at that time for resale. The following, although listing a wealth of other material, make no reference to any of the works listed as sources for *Sordello*: Bertram Dobell Cat., *Browning Memorials: Books, Drawings, Autographs, Letters and Other Relics*; Bernard Quaritch Cat., *Rare and Valuable Books*; Henry Sotheran Cat. 42, *Beautiful Old Engravings and Browning Relics and Manuscripts*; Henry Sotheran Cat. 737, *Old Engravings and MSS, Books, and Relics of R. and E. B. Browning*; P. and A. Dobell Cat. 249 (London, 1915); R. H. Dodd, *An Important Collection of MSS and Authgraph Letters of R. and E. B. Browning, With Presentation Copies of Books* (New York, 1916). It is possible that some day a fairly accurate list of those titles offered at that time for sale may be compiled. It would be possible also to supplement such a list by reference to other sources, some perhaps not yet known to us. At present, however, there is no concrete evidence that any of the titles which Holmes lists were in the Browning library at the time of its disposal in 1913. It appears however that all were in the British Museum.

Griffin and Minchin do state, without citing the source of their information, that the family library contained copies of *Biographie universelle* and of Vasari's *Lives of the Painters* (p. 15). More details about these follow.

There are certain conjectures which we can make about editions available to the poet either in his own library or in the British Museum. In the following comments the numbers refer to those assigned to the titles listed above.

(1) *Biographie universelle* was published in Paris over a period of years

beginning in 1811. By 1840 the basic volumes (1–52) and the three volumes (53–55) entitled *Partie mythologique* had appeared. The volume containing the information on Sordello (xxxix) is dated 1825. The first of the supplementary volumes, designed to correct errors in the original and to provide new materials, appeared in 1834; the last, in 1856. It would seem that B's subject did not require use of any of the supplementary volumes. There was no new edition between the completion of volume 55 and the appearance of the first supplementary volume in 1834. There was no new edition of the complete set until long after B had published *Sordello*. It is clear, therefore, that he used the first edition, which according to Griffin and Minchin was in his father's library.

(2) The full title is: *Memorie per la storia de Ferrara racolte da* A. F. [tom. 5 ed., G. Frizzi], 5 vols. B obviously used this first edition since there was not another until 1847–1850.

(3) The British Museum lists no new printing of this work before 1900.

(4) There were certainly subsequent editions of the *Annali* in 1752–1754, 1762–1770, 1804, and 1838. In the absence of evidence, it may be assumed that B used any one of these. At the time the last edition mentioned appeared, B was reorganizing his poem and increasing his emphasis on its historical background.

(6) Simonde's history was published in a second edition in 1818 and in still another in 1826–1833, both in Paris.

(5, 7, 8) The British Museum lists only one edition of each of these works.

In addition to the sources listed by Holmes, B might also have used Simonde's *A History of the Italian Republics*, published as part of the *Cabinet Cyclopaedia* conducted by the Reverend Dionysius Lardner (London, 1832). Simonde refers to this one volume work as "not an abridgement of my great work, but an entirely new history, in which, with my eyes fixed solely on the free people of the several Italian states, I have studied to portray, within a compass which should be compatible with animations and interests, their first deliverance, their heroism, and their misfortunes."

For information on Italian artists and art of the period, B perhaps drew upon Giorgio Vasari's *Le Vite de Più Excellente Pittori, Sculptori e Architetti*. It is impossible, however, to determine which edition he used. *The Lives*, from the time of its publication in 1550, enjoyed considerable popularity and went through several editions. Griffin and Minchin report that the book was in the family library. The Sotheby catalogue lists (p. 137) a copy in 13 volumes published at Firenze, dated, however, 1846–1857. One would assume that the edition B used earlier had been left in England and that he purchased this one while he lived in Italy, probably at the time he was writing *Men and Women*. Griffin and Minchin also state that B gained "most of his early knowledge of art" from Matthew Pilkinton's *Dictionary of Painters* (rev., Henry Fuseli, London, 1805), a copy of which was in the B library (p. 15). A still further source is suggested by item 501 in the Sotheby catalogue: Berti, Giovani-Battista, *Nuova Guida per Vicenza* (Padua, 1830). On the paper cover B has written: "R. B. Vicenza, June 24, 1838." We have been unable to locate this book but have consulted an earlier edition, 1822, which has as its complete title: *Guida per Vicenza/ ossia/ memorie storico-critico-descriptive/ di questa regia citta/ e delle principali sue opere di belle arti.* It contains both text and illustrations.

The sale catalogue lists one other item associated with the period during which B was writing *Sordello*. It offers for sale a copy of Thomas Penrose's *A Sketch of the Lives and Writings of Dante and Petrarch with some account of Italian and Latin Literature in the Fourteenth Century* (London, 1790), in which B has written "Robert Browning, Nov. 16, 1838." The contents of this book suggest, however, that any information which B acquired from it had a general rather than specific relevance to *Sordello*.

Index to Often Used Names

Certain names, particularly of persons and places, appear so often in *Sordello* that to enter in each case a cross reference to the basic annotation on that item would appear cumbersome. We offer therefore the following index which indicates where the primary information on each item may be found.

BOOK THE FIRST

1] *Sordello* B's initial information about Sordello came from the thirty-ninth volume of the *Biographie universelle*. In fact, there is little in his poem about Sordello that B could not have obtained from that source. The article may be divided into three parts: (1) a chronological survey of the various accounts of Sordello's life; (2) an attempted evaluation of the historical accuracy of the various reports; (3) a description of Sordello's extant works.

Rolandino, the only historian of Sordello's time to write about the poet, says that the sister of Ecelin III, called Cunizza, wife of Count Richard of St. Boniface, was abducted by Sordello, who he says was *de ipsius familia*. The statement is unclear, however, because it does not indicate specifically whether it was to the house of Romano or of St. Boniface that Sordello belonged, and, moreover, whether the relation was one of blood or servitude. Rolandino continues by saying that after spending some time with Cunizza's family, the "abductor was finally driven out," presumably by the Ecelins themselves.

Dante adds a little more to our knowledge. He places Sordello at the entrance of Purgatory and in his sympathetic treatment of the poet implies: (1) that he was born in Mantua; (2) that he was perhaps of noble ancestry; and (3) that he met a violent death. In a Latin treatise (*Treatise de Vulgari Eloquentia*, lib. i, cap. 15), Dante says that Sordello excelled in poetry of all genres, and that he contributed to the development of the Italian language by the creation of a new dialect made up from the speech of Cremona, Brescia, and Verona.

In the fourteenth century, Benvenuto d'Imola annotated *The Divine Comedy*, and in one of his notes states that Sordello was born in Mantua, that he was a famous soldier, courtier, and poet. A man, "naturally virtuous, serious, and of very good manners," he was trapped into an affair with Cunizza, and eventually forced to flee from her brother's wrath. He was quickly overtaken, however, according to this source, by Ecelin's emissaries and assassinated. He is reported to have written one book *Thesaura Thesaurous*, says Benvenuto, although he has never seen it.

In certain Provençal chronicles, written at about the same time Benvenuto was composing his account, Sordello is reported to have been born in Mantua, son of a poor chevalier named El Cort. He achieved early fame as a poet and became attached to the Court of Richard of St. Boniface. Here he fell in love with the Count's wife, Cunizza, eventually eloping with her. He is said then to have passed into Provence where he gained great renown as a poet and received as reward for his skills a chateau and an honorable marriage.

In the fifteenth century, Aliprando wrote in Italian verse a fabulous chronicle of Mantua that became the source for Platina's *History of Mantua*. Both Aliprando and Platina deal at length with Sordello, and, according to them, Sordello was born in 1189, of the Visconti family, originally from Goito. While still a youth, he launched his literary career by producing the *Tresor*. By the time he was twenty-five, he had distinguished himself as a soldier and a gallant. At about this time he entered into an alliance with Ecelin, and established himself at Verona. There, Beatrice, Ecelin's sister, fell in love with him and pursued him in the disguise of a man to Mantua where he had fled to free himself from her. He did marry her but almost immediately left her and went to France where he achieved great acclaim and was richly rewarded by the king. He eventually returned to Italy where, his fame having preceded him, he was received in town after town with great honor. Between 1250 and 1253 he successfully defended Mantua against a siege by Ecelin III, and shortly afterwards performed a similar service for Milan. It was during the struggle for Milan that Ecelin received his death wound. What happened to Sordello after this great military victory, Platina does not record. His account has been proved unreliable by later historians (for example, Sordello was never married to Beatrice; Louis was not king of France at this time; the siege of Milan did not take place at the time specified by Platina).

Nostradamus, writing in the sixteenth century (*Lives of the Provençal Poets*) says, in contradiction to other reports, that Sordello entered the service of Berenger, Count of Provence, when he was fifteen years old, and that there he distinguished himself for his philosophical poems, not for his love poems (an obvious error according to the writer of the *Biographie* article). Nostradamus states that Sordello died around 1281 (a date rejected by later historians).

None of the other accounts provide significant new material. Tiraboschi, examining all historical sources, concludes in the summary words of the author of the *Biographie* article: ". . . the poet was born in Goito, a Mantuan village, sometime during the last twenty years of the twelfth century, that he carried off the wife of his protector, that at sometime, but not at the age of fifteen, he spent a rather long sojourn in Provence . . . that Sordello belongs to a noble family; that he had been a soldier without having occupied the position of Captain General or Podestà of Mantua, which were attributed to him by some authors; that finally he perished by a violent death, one does not know at what age: it is unlikely that it was in 1281, since he would have been between ninety and one hundred years old."

In the last section of the article, the author describes the extant works of Sordello. Twenty-four in number, they are all in the Provençal language. They include love songs, *tenzons* (dialogues or controversies), and *sirventes* or satires. Among the latter, there are several against the troubadour Pierre Vidal. "Four other *sirventes* of Sordello," we are told, "relate to the moral and political history of his century and merit in every respect more attention." The most famous of these is his complaint upon the death of Blacas in which the reigning sovereigns of Europe are invited to parcel out among them the heart of that brave man and to eat it with the hope that they may partake of his strength and courage.

These are essentially the materials upon which B based his character Sordello. The sparsity of real information, the contradictory nature of many of the reports, and the obvious historical errors and the fabulous creations of many of the writers (Tiraboschi suggests that sometimes the writers projected themselves into their works "making themselves the heroes of chivalric and gallant adventures which they imagined") perhaps seemed justification enough to B for refusing to be bound in his treatment of Sordello by any so-called historical account. He obviously drew upon them all, borrowing such information as suited his purpose, which was not to present an historically accurate character, but to "trace the development of a soul."

4] *friendless-people's friend* Don Quixote, hero of Cervante's novel of that name.

6] *Pentapolin* Watching the dust cloud of a flock of sheep in a valley, Don Quixote makes Sancho envision the army of Alifanfaron pursued by "the king of the Garomanteans, known by the name of Pentapolin of the naked arm, for he always goes to battle with the sleeve of his right arm pulled up" (*Don Quixote*, part 1, chapter 4).

11] *Verona* City in N Italy located on the Adige River. An ancient city, it was one of the chief residences of the Lombard kings in the early Middle Ages. Toward the end of the twelfth century it became the scene of bitter struggle between Guelf and Ghibelline (see I, 103n). It was a member of the Lombard League (see I, 110n). After years of rule by first one party and then another it fell in 1227 under the control of Ecelin III who ruled it savagely until 1259. At the beginning of *Sordello*, the scene is that of the turmoil caused by the capture of its "prince," Count Richard of St. Boniface (see I, 102n) during the siege of Ferrara (see IV, 1n).

60] *thou, spirit* Percy Bysshe Shelley, who had exerted a strong influence on B's earlier poems, *Pauline* and *Paracelsus*. See headnote which B prepared for the 1863 edition.

65–68] *The thunder-phrase of the Athenian, . . . Braying a Persian shield* Aeschylus, the Greek dramatist, who, as a young man, fought against the Persians at Marathon, Plataea, and Salamis. B is probably in mind of Shelley's lyrical drama, *Hellas* (1821), which, in the dominance of the lyric over the dramatic element and in the long narrative accounts, resembles Aeschylus' *Persae* (*The Persians*). In the "Prologue" to *Hellas*, Shelley says, "The *Persae* of Aeschylus afforded me the first model of my conception, although the decision of the glorious contest now waging [the last and successful Greek struggle for independence from the Turks in 1821] being yet suspended forbids a catastrophe parallel to the return of Xerxes and the desolation of the Persians." In a letter to John Gisborne (October 22, 1821), he describes *Hellas* as "a sort of immitation of *The Persae* of Aeschylus, full of lyrical poetry."

69] *Of Sidney's self* Sir Philip Sidney (1554–1586), poet and soldier, whose sonnet sequence to Stella (star) was written under the name Astrophel (lover of the star). He is sometimes credited with having developed English as a literary tongue. He influenced Shelley a great deal (especially obvious in *A Defense of Poetry*).

78] *The second Friedrich* Frederick II (1194–1250), King of Sicily from 1197; king of Germany from 1212; Holy Roman Emperor from 1220; king of Jerusalem from 1229. He was born in 1194, son of Emperor Henry VI and Constance, daughter of the Norman king Roger II (see IV, 510). Henry died in 1197 without having united the crowns of Sicily and the Empire. Constance abandoned her husband's imperial policy and before she died in 1198, she appointed Pope Innocent III suzerain of Sicily and guardian of her young son. In 1208 Innocent turned the government of Sicily over to Frederick. During the years of his minority the southern kingdom had been so neglected (intentionally the enemies of the Pope insisted) that the young ruler had a tremendous task of reconstruction before him. His election to the kingship of Germany came after Otto IV had been deposed by the Germans, an act approved by the Pope, since Otto had failed to keep his promises to support the Pope's territorial policies in Italy and to respect his claims over Sicily. Frederick became Holy Roman Emperor in 1220, after making compromising concessions to Pope Honorius (see I, 79n) by which he agreed to recognize the Pope's territorial as well as his spiritual supremacy in Italy; to turn over the kingdom of Sicily to his young son in order to avoid uniting the crowns of the two kingdoms; and to lead a crusade to the Holy Land in an effort to recapture Jerusalem for the Church. Perhaps Frederick never intended to keep his promises. At any rate, he remained throughout his life in constant warfare with the Pope and his Church Party for control of Italy and Sicily; he nominally surrendered the crown of Sicily but continued to rule the country vigorously and efficiently. He constantly delayed his crusade perhaps because he did not trust the Pope and his partisans and was unwilling to give them in his absence an opportunity to undermine his interests (see I, 194n; 195n; 195–197n). In 1227 he was excommunicated by Pope Gregory (see I, 200n). In 1228 he did undertake a crusade, although without the Pope's blessing, and in 1229 he victoriously entered Jerusalem and there crowned himself King of Jerusalem. Frederick spent most of his remaining years in bloody warfare with the Church party. The revival of the Lombard League in 1226 was largely in response to his imperial designs over N Italy (see I, 110n). In the early thirties he entered into league with Ecelin III and the two remained allies throughout the rest of their lives although neither ever really trusted the other. In 1239 Frederick was excommunicated a second time by Pope Gregory IX, and in 1245 he was deposed as Emperor by Innocent IV. This act by the Church only intensified Frederick's determination and he continued to wage war until his death in 1250. Although he had spent most of his life fighting against Church power he considered himself a good Catholic and requested the sacrament of communion before his death.

Frederick was a man of tremendous intellect and broad cultural interests (see I, 395–396n); his sensuous nature and high spirits led him into escapades which shocked Christendom (see I, 142n; III, 119–120n; III, 121–123n).

79] *the Third Honorius* Honorius III, member of an aristocratic Roman family, was pope from 1216 to 1227. During his reign the position of the Church was considerably strengthened. He continued the strong policies of his predecessor Innocent III. Under him were approved the Dominican and Franciscan Orders which were later to provide tremendous support for the Papal cause against Imperial encroachment. Honorius resisted the threats upon his authority by Frederick II but avoided an open break with him in hopes that the king would undertake his promised crusade to the Holy Land. By the time of his death in 1227, however, it was already clear that he had failed to curb the ambitions of the energetic Emperor.

102] *Count Richard of Saint Boniface* Richard was a Lombard noble, member of a distinguished Guelf family (see I, 113n), ruling over Verona under Azzo VII of the House of Este (see I, 103n). The historical Richard was married to Cunizza, sister of Ecelin III, who fell in love with Sordello and eloped with him (see I, 1n). Richard was Azzo's constant ally and Ecelin's continuing foe.

103] *Azzo, Este's Lord* Azzo VII (1205–1264) of the distinguished House of Este. The Este family were of Lombard descent, a branch of the Obertenghi dynasty of the tenth century. They took their name from the township castle located 17 mi. SW of Padua. During the latter part of the twelfth century the Este Family, already leaders of the Guelfs (see I, 113n) in Lombardy and Venetia, achieved political power in Ferrara through a marriage into the Adelardi family (see I, 104n).

104] *Taurello Salinguerra* Frizzi provides the following table of the House of Salinguerra:

> Piettro Torelli, alive in 1083 and dead in 1119
> Salinguerra, alive in 1120, dead in 1163
> (Ludovico?) Torello, alive in 1164, dead in 1195
> Salinguerra II, born about 1160, died in 1245
>> Married (1) Retrude
>>> (2) Sofia, a widow of Henry of Egna and sister of Ecelin III.
> Bartolommeo Ariverio Tommaso Salinguerra Rizzardo Giacommo

Salinguerra II, character of B's poem, was son of Torello, head of the Ghibelline faction (see I, 113n) in Ferrara. The family was embroiled in a continuing feud with the Este family, leader of the Guelfs (see I, 113n), a conflict that was intensified by the rape of Linguetta (daughter and heiress of the Adelardi family) by the Este family in the latter part of the twelfth century (see IV, 477–513n). That Salinguerra went to Sicily following that affair only Platina records, and that he was closely associated with Henry and returned to the north as his emissary is B's own invention. Apparently he was married to a Retrude, about whom, however, we know only her name. She was certainly not of royal blood as B asserts. Having Salinguerra participate in the expulsion of Ecelin II from Vicenza in 1194 is also imaginary. There is no record that Salinguerra and Sordello ever became acquainted; certainly there is no evidence that the two were related. Muratori (*Annali*) first mentions Salinguerra as an ally to Ecelin in relation to the struggle in 1207 in which Azzo drove Ecelin from Verona. Declaring himself Ecelin's friend, Salinguerra, in retaliation, drove the adherents of Azzo from Ferrara. Muratori, under the date of 1215, writes "This crafty fox in the present year insinuated himself so much, by fair words and promises, into the good graces of Pope Innocent (probably after the death of Marquis Aldrovandino), that he obtained from them the investiture of the lands which had belonged aforetime to Countess Matilda (see III, 492n) in the Bishoprics of Modena, Reggio, Parma, Bologna, and Imola, with the obligation of serving the Pontiff in the field with arms. This act, and his oath taken of 7 September, can be read in the Ecclesiastical Annals of Rinaldi.

As we proceed, we shall see his fidelity to the supreme Pontiffs." (Translated by William M. Rossetti, *Browning Society Papers*, III, 85). Indeed for most of the remaining years of his turbulent life Salinguerra devoted his full energies to the support of the imperial faction against the Church party. He was the dominant figure in the siege of Ferrara in 1224, the central episode in B's poem, at which Count Richard was taken prisoner (see IV, 1n). By this time, we learn from Muratori (*Annali*), Salinguerra was "in closest league" with Ecelin. The same source reports that in 1232, Frederick II had as his "intimate counsellors" Ecelin and Salinguerra in his efforts to control the Lombard cities. His career came to an end in 1240 when he was captured by trickery (see VI, 730) in Ferrara and carried off to Venice as a prisoner. He was around eighty years old at the time. He died five years later, ending his days, Muratori tells us, "in holy peace."

105] *Ecelin Romano* Verci provides a genealogical table of the House of Ecelin of which the following is a condensation:

Arpone
Ecelon
Ecelo
Alberico
Ecelin I (The Stammerer)
Ecelin II (The Monk)
    Married (1) Agnes Este
            (2) Speronella Dalesmannini
            (3) Cecilia da Baone
            (4) Adelaide da Mangone
    Palma Novella
    Emilia
    Sofia
    Ecelin III
    Alberico
    Cunizza (B's Palma)

The founder of the powerful Ghibelline family (see I, 113n) came from Germany with Conrad II in the early eleventh century. The Ecelins were enfeoffed by the Emperor with lands in N Italy including the castle of Romano near Vicenza. By the thirteenth century, the time of B's poem, the Ecelins were among the strongest and most feared leaders of the Imperial party in Italy. For B's condensed history of the family see I, 237ff and 457ff. For a more extended account of individual members of the family see: I, 138n (Ecelin II), II, 327n (Ecelin III), 461n (Adelaide), 941n (Palma-Cunizza).

106] *Ferrara* Located 30 mi. NNE of Bologna, Ferrara lies thirty feet above sea-level on a branch channel of the Po River. Its known history dates from 753. By the tenth century it enjoyed an independent government under the protection of the Pope. It was occupied successively by Tedaldo of Canossa, the great Countess Matilda (see III, 492n), and Frederick Barbarossa. During the early twelfth century it was the scene of conflict between the Adelardi (see I, 104n) and Torello families. In 1240, sixteen years after the siege which B describes, the city came with the capture of Salinguerra (see VI, 730n) under the undisputed rule of the House of Este.

110] *Lombard League* When Pope Leo III crowned Charlemagne as emperor and restorer of the Western Empire in 800, he unwittingly initiated a struggle between Pope and Emperor for supremacy that was to dominate Italian history for centuries. The theory of the division of sacred and secular interests and power was discovered to be unworkable in practice, and, depending upon the relative strength of the two, Pope or Emperor continually infringed upon the pretended rights of the other. For the masses of the people, the conflict was originally primarily one between two great powers, neither of which touched their lives intimately. During the eleventh and twelfth centuries, however, the contest took on a vastly different coloration. A new struggle had developed between the rising class of city dwellers and the Lombard, Frankish, and German nobility that possessed the countryside. In general the country nobility aligned themselves with the Emperor, and the city dwellers, with the Pope. The latter preferred the Pope because they thought under him Italian nationalism and local autonomy had a better chance of developing. Frederick Barbarossa agitated the situation when in his efforts to bring Italy under his control he appointed Imperial representatives, called *Podestàs* (see I, 150n), to rule over the cities. In reaction to the tyranny which they practiced and as a measure of resistance against the Emperor's allies, the urban nobility, representatives from Verona, Vicenza, Padua, and Treviso made a pact pledging mutual support as early as 1164. In 1167, this association was expanded to include many of the cities of Lombardy. Thus, the Lombard League, an association of Italian cities pledged to support each other against Imperial encroachment, came into existence. The fifteen cities to which B refers are: Milan, Bologna, Piacenza, Verona, Brescia, Faenza, Mantua, Vercelli, Lodi, Bergamo, Turin, Alessandria, Vicenza, Padua, and Treviso. In 1176 they demonstrated their strength and unity by defeating Frederick Barbarossa at Legnano, an important victory which destroyed for the time being the pretended authority of the Emperor over Italy. The League remained incipient in the years that followed and was formally called back into existence in 1226, two years after the siege of Ferrara, the central event in B's poem, in an effort to repulse the threat of Frederick II, who was soon to have one of his most dreaded allies in N Italy the brutal tyrant Ecelin III.

113] *Guelf* Long before 1200 the Italians were divided into warring factions representing the opposing interests of Pope and Emperor (see I, 110n). The terms *Guelf* and *Ghibelline* came into existence early in the thirteenth century. They derived from the German house of Welf and a town Waiblingen, seat of the Hohenstaufen in Swabia. Originally they designated the opposing parties of Otto IV and Frederick II (see I, 78n), rivals for the German kingship and the Empire after the death of Henry VI in 1197. They were quickly assumed by traditional factions in Italy, the Guelf being the Papal party and the Ghibellines, the Imperial. The appearance of common names tended to unify and give wide significance to a struggle that had more often than not been previously fragmented and local. In N Italy the Guelfs' leaders were the Adelardi and the Este families; the Ghibellines', the Ecelins and the Torellos.

115] *purple pavis* Buckler so-called because it was first made in Pavia. It was a convex shield large enough to cover the whole body, used as a defense against archery especially in sieges. The term was extended to denote any large shield. The pavis of a knight was usually carried by his attendant and was deep enough to shelter both him and his master. The emblem of the House of Este was a white eagle on a purple field.

119] *The patron* The Emperor.

121] *"Duke o' the Rood* Azzo VII, who as head of the Lombard League, was called Knight of the (Order of the) Holy Cross, or Rood.

121] *The hill-cat* Ecelin II. Since the hill-cat is not the coat-of-arms of Ecelin, he is perhaps so-called because of his extensive holdings in the hills and mountains.

126] *the lion* Azzo VII of Este. The lion is a symbol of Verona, chief city of the Este family, and also of Papal authority.

127–187] *"Taurello," quoth an envoy . . . Into the trap* The events to which B refers in these lines are part of the long struggle between the Torello and the Este families for control over Ferrara, this particular phase of the contest having begun in 1120 and culminated in 1224 with the capture of Count Richard of St. Boniface. B, drawing upon many historical sources, is more concerned to communicate a sense of the intrigue, treachery, and bloodshed that characterized the struggle than to detail specific historical events (see IV, 1n).

128] *osprey* The osprey, a long-winged eagle, was the coat-of-arms of Salinguerra.

131] *Kaiser's coming* Frederick II (see I, 78n). After his crowning in 1220, Frederick occupied himself for some time in reestablishing order in Sicily to the despair of the Ghibellines in N Italy.

138] *the Pontiff* Honorius III (see I, 79n).

138] *Ecelin* Ecelin II, husband of Adelaide the Tuscan and father of Ecelin III, Alberic, and Palma (Cunizza). In 1221 Adelaide died, and Ecelin, in a fit of remorse, divided his lands between his two sons, and according to B's story, betrothed his daughter Palma (Cunizza) to Richard of St. Boniface in hopes of creating peace between the Guelfs and Ghibellines. He then retired to the monastery at Oliero (see next note). Leadership of the Ghibellines fell to Ecelin III. Ecelin II, according to B's chronology, died in 1224–1225. Actually the date of his death is not known but it is supposed to have occurred around 1235, Simonde reports that the Pope entreated Ecelin III to deliver his father to the inquisitional tribunal on the grounds that he was a member of an heretical movement, the adherents of which were known as *paterino*. The *paterino* (or Paterines) are related to but distinguished from the Paulicians (see II, 617n and 860–861n). Their main thrust was against a corrupt clergy; their demands, that marriage of the clergy and simony (the purchase of clerical office) be discontinued. The latter demand had particularly far-reaching effects for the upper class laity since habitually they advanced their members into the higher ranks of the clergy by simoniac practices (see II, 860–861n).

139] *Oliero* A tiny village on the bank of the Brenta River some 5 mi. N of Bassano, site of the monastery to which Ecelin II retired. Between Bassano and Oliero lies Campese where Ecelin I founded a Benedictine monastery and where perhaps Ecelin II was buried (see VI, 687–688).

142] *Satan's Viceroy* Frederick II was variously known as the "Servant of Satan," the "Beast of the Apocalypse," and the "Prophet of the Antichrist." (See also III, 119–120n; 121–123n.)

145] *When Cino Bocchimpane . . . Buccio Virtu* Imaginary characters, citizens, that is, typical men on the street, here representing the two political factions. The *Parma Chronicle* lists the Bocchimpane family as residents of the San Vitale quarter of Ferrara and B may have borrowed the name for his representative character.

146] *God's wafer* "Ostia di Dio," or Host of God, an Italian oath. The host is the wafer of bread used in the Mass.

147] *Tutti Santi* "All saints," an oath.

148] *Ghibellines* See I, 113n.

150] *Padua* A city of N Italy located on the Bacchiglione River, 25 mi. W of Venice and 18 mi. SE of Vicenza. According to Verci it was the site of one of Ecelin's early palaces. During the eleventh century the city became scene of another of the struggles between Ecelin and Este. Toward the end of the twelfth century the city felt obliged to defend itself by electing a podestà (see I, 150n) and chose in favor of an Este. By the time of the events here recorded, however, Ecelin had again gained control of the city.

150] *Podestà* The office of Podestà was created by Frederick I at a diet held at Roncaglia in 1158 (see I, 257n). He took the administration of cities from local consuls and placed it in the hands of a single judge, a foreigner chosen initially by the Emperor. See also I, 110n. The podestà was not necessarily German but was required to be imported from another city in order to secure impartiality. He was allowed to bring neither wife nor relatives with him and was not permitted even to eat and drink with any citizen during his one year term of office. At first, the office was much hated by the Italians but came in time to be accepted as a necessity for maintaining political and social stability. In subsequent years the podestà was sometimes appointed by the ruling noble or ecclesiastical authority but more often at least nominally elected by the people. By the beginning of the twelfth century the strife between the Guelfs and the Ghibellines had become so intense that the presence of a strong podestà was frequently the only hope for maintaining order. It was perfectly natural that Ecelin should send Salinguerra to Padua as podestà. The fact that he was able to secure his election to the post illustrates the power which a strong leader could exert over the people.

166] *like lynx and ounce* Lynx is a name applied to any number of small to medium sized wild cats with tufted ears and comparatively short tails. Bold hunters, they often kill wantonly, sometimes slaughtering a dozen or more sheep in a single night. The young remain with the mother for some time after they are weaned and accompany her in hunting. The ounce, a term originally the equivalent of lynx, was subsequently applied to other spotted cats, including the common leopard, and, most often, the snow leopard. B is probably thinking of the leopard. The osprey is the natural enemy of both lynx and ounce (see III, 263).

167–172] *The burghers ground their teeth . . . Men fed on men.* The army within the city had the advantage of the protective walls, but, at the same time, were constantly faced with the danger of starvation since their crops, chief source of their food, were grown outside the city walls, and therefore, subject to ravage and destruction by the attacking enemy. It was a common stratagem of the Imperial army to gain control of the city's food supply and thus starve it into submission.

172] *At length Taurello calls* See IV, 1n.

193] *Hohenstauffen* Frederick II. See I, 78n.

194] *John of Brienne's favour* King of Jerusalem and Latin emperor of Constantinople (c. 1148–1237), his daughter Isabella or Yolande was married to Frederick II in 1225 (see I, 870n).

195 [*Foreswore crusading* In 1215 and again at the time of his coronation in 1220 Frederick agreed to undertake a crusade in an attempt to recover the Holy Land from the Saracens. He nevertheless delayed his departure year after year. His marriage in 1225 was in part manipulated by the Pope in order to encourage his long delayed campaign. Honorius III died in March, 1227, and was succeeded by Gregory IX who displayed less understanding and greater impatience with the vacillating Frederick. Finally in September of that year, Frederick set sail but within a few days was back again at Otranto, having been taken gravely ill according to his report.

195–196] *no mind to leave / Saint Peter's proxy* B explains Frederick's delay and his failure to complete the crusade once he had undertaken it as a result of fear that in his absence the Papal party would attempt to undermine his position in Italy.

197] *Otho and to Barbaross* Frederick's predecessors as Holy Roman Emperor who made significant gains against the Papal party.

198] *Or make the Alps less easy* Frederick feared that the Guelfs would seize the northern towns, gain control of the passes over the Alps, and thus make it difficult for him to cross into Germany.

199] *Pope Honorius' fear* That he would not keep his pledge to lead a crusade.

200] *Was excommunicated* After the death of Honorius III, Frederick's attitude toward the Church became more openly hostile. In 1227, he was excommunicated by Gregory IX after his failure to complete the crusade which he had undertaken (see I, 195n). Frederick responded to the excommunication in the following words: "The Roman Church is like a leech; she calls herself my mother and nurse; but she is a stepmother, and the root of all evils. Her legates go throughout all lands, binding, loosing, punishing; not to sow the seeds of the Word, but to subdue men and wring from them their money."

201] *"The triple-bearded Tuton* Frederick I, or Barbarossa ("Redbeard") (c. 1123–1190), Holy Roman Emperor from 1152 when he succeeded his uncle, the German king, Conrad III. His Italian surname, Barbarossa, derives from the fact that he had a reddish beard. These lines refer to a legend which says that he still sits with his knights in the Kyffhäuser mountain in Thuringia waiting until his flowing beard, grown through a rock-table, has twined around it three times. Then, so the story goes, he will wake up and answer the need of his country.

243–244] *a Saxon scout/ —Arpo or Yoland, is it* Founder of the House of Romano. According to Verci, Arpone, a Saxon and possessor of a single horse, came with Conrad II to Lombardy in 1036 (see I, 105n).

247] *Trevisan* Province of Treviso located in N Italy on the plain between the Gulf of Venice and the Alps.

248–249] *Conrad descries ... Than Ecelo* B can hardly mean Conrad II who died in 1039, three years after he had enfeoffed Arpone and obviously before the Ecelin family had so prospered. Ecelo, son of Arpone, died in 1091. By that time there was indeed no fitter house in the Trevisan than that of Ecelin. He obviously refers to Conrad III (1093–1151), German King, who was never crowned Emperor. Conrad III was the son of Frederick I, duke of Swabia, and Agnes, daughter of Emperor Henry IV. Conrad III was the first king of the Hohenstaufen family. He was crowned king of Italy at Monza in 1128 and in spite of the papal ban was generally recognized in N Italy, stronghold of the Imperialist party.

249–250] *as they enrolled/ That name* According to Simonde, during the first half of the eleventh century, the prelates in Lombardy organized the cities against the nobles, the result of which was almost continuous warfare. Conrad attempted to end the strife by establishing a constitution that became the basis of feudal law. Among other things, it provided protection for the inheritance of fiefs against the lords and prelates. Under such protection, the Ecelins advanced their fortunes rapidly. B has Arpo registering his fiefs, gifts from Conrad, at Milan.

250] *Milan* A city of Lombardy, on the Olona river, near the middle of the rich Lombard plain, 93 mi. ENE of Turin. Milan and Pavia were the most powerful and wealthy cities of Lombardy during the eleventh and twelfth centuries. Milan was consistently a stronghold for the Church party and Pavia, for the Imperialist party. The city, after having been starved into submission, was completely razed by Frederick Barbarossa in 1162. In 1167, however, it was rebuilt by the cities comprising the Lombard League (see I, 110n), and by 1176, the Milanese had so recovered that under the leadership of nine hundred young men comprising what was known as "the company of death" they were able to defeat Frederick at Legnano. Milan remained one of the staunchest anti-Imperialist centers in N Italy and among the strongest forces for nationalism and independence.

251–253] *Godego's lord. . . . And every sheep-cote* Hamlets enfeoffed to the Ecelins by Conrad II and his successors.

253] *Suabian's fief* Conrad III and his nephew Frederick I were Suabians.

254] *"the Lombard Chief"* Ecelin I, called the Stammerer. He was the grandson of Ecelo (see I, 105n), and son of Alberico (d. 1154), whom B does not mention. He was father of Ecelin II, The Monk (see I, 105n; 138n).

256] *Vale of Trent* The valley surrounding the city of Trent, located on the left bank of the Adige River where the Adige is joined by the Fersina River, 34 mi. S of Bolzano and 56 mi. N of Verona. It is the capital city of the province of Trent. It was a station on the road from Verona to Innsbruck over the Brenner Pass. It was ruled in turn by the Ostrogoths, the Lombards, and the Franks. After its capture by the Franks it became part of the kingdom of Italy, but in 1027, Conrad II transferred it to Germany. It was a strategic point throughout the struggle between Emperor and Pope for sovereignty over Italy since the party which controlled Trent controlled an important pass between Germany and Italy. Much of the early Ecelin power was concentrated in this area.

257] *Roncaglia* A camp located on a plain about 3 mi. from Piacenza between the Po and the Nura Rivers. It was the site where kings traditionally held out-of-doors parliaments, or diets. B refers to the diet held by Frederick I in 1154 to which he summoned the consuls of many cities and the greater feudatories, both ecclesiastical and lay. Ecelin II was among them. He demanded their homage and required the restitution to the Empire of all the prerogatives which had been infringed upon by the Italians during the reign of Lothair II.

258–260] *Tyrol's brow . . . and the Julian* Parts of the Alps which separated Germany from Italy. If the German Emperors were to exercise rule over Italy, they had to control the strategic mountain passes which served as thoroughfares from N to S. It was decidedly to their advantage, therefore, to turn these villages over to the loyal Ecelins and to encourage them to build castles and fortifications throughout the area.

271] *A Signory* Title of a town office carrying unlimited powers. Begun in 1237 and given temporary powers, the position soon became permanent and later hereditary.

274–275] *Of Otho . . . Your Este* Otto IV (1182?–1218) disputed the German crown with Philip Duke of Swabia after the death of Henry VI. After Philip was assassinated Otto became first king of the Germans and then Roman Emperor. He was distantly related to the house of Este through the marriage of the sister of Welf the Younger to Azzo III in 1055. Thus, if he or his representative Ecelin were to defeat Azzo VII, the Ghibelline branch of the Este family would have triumphed over the Guelf branch.

276–279] *A Son . . . Romano (so they styled him) throve* Ecelin II and Ecelin III (see I, 105n).

290] *While his lord* See I, 138n.

294–295] *(Atti . . . the Hun)* Pigna traces the Este family to one Caio Atio. He also relates the bravery of the Este family in repelling the Hunnish invasion led by Attila.

297] *Rovigo's Polesine* A city of Italy, Rovigo is about 30 mi. W of Mantua. From the eleventh to the fourteenth century the Estes were usually in authority. Originally subject to a bishop, the city was controlled by the Este family during the thirteenth century but became a bone of contention between Ferrara and Venice until the sixteenth century. The Polesine district is the area between the Adige and the Po River.

298] *Ancona's march* The frontier or boundary of Ancona, a city and Adriatic seaport on the E coast of central Italy. The city at this time was a semi-independent republic under Papal control. The march, or border region, was held by German vassals of the emperor until Innocent III granted it as a fief to Azzo IV of Este in 1280. The Pope's authority was disputed by the Hohenstaufen and by various local powers.

306] *Father Porphyry* An imaginary monk.

308] *Hildebrand* Pope Gregory VII from 1073–1085. One of the most powerful popes of the medieval period, he was known as the reformer, insisting on strict celebacy of clergy and on the absolute power of the Church to make all ecclesiastical appointments. He elevated the moral tone of the Church and strengthened the political powers of the pontiff. His firm stand against secular investiture of clergy/ laid the ground work for the Concordat of Worms in 1122 (see V, 154n). Due in no small measure to his influence on Church policy in the years following his death, Innocent III was able in 1198 to declare himself the Vicar of Christ on Earth (see V, 186n) and to proclaim in his consecration sermon "I have set thee this day over nations and over kingdoms" (see IV, 966n).

310] *Was vested in a certain Twenty-four* After 1196, Verona was ruled for many years by a Podestà. However, the ordinary jurisdiction remained in the hands of native judges, the Consuls. Twenty-four of the total thirty-two formed a tribunal for ordinary civil actions and were known as *Consules Rationis*.

317] *carroch* Simonde gives a colorful account of the carroch: "The militia of every city was divided into separate bodies, according to local partitions, each led by a *gonfaloniere*, or standard-bearer. They fought on foot, and assembled around the *carroccio*, a heavy car drawn by oxen, and covered with the flags and armorial bearings of the city. A high pole rose in the middle of this car, bearing the colors and a Christ, which seemed to bless the army, with both arms extended. A priest said daily mass at an altar placed in the front of the car. The trumpeters of the community, seated on the back part, sounded the charge and the retreat. It was Heribert archbishop of Milan, contemporary of Conrad the Salic, who invented this car in imitation of the ark of alliance, and caused it to be adopted at Milan. All the free cities of Italy followed the example; this sacred car, intrusted to the guardianship of the militia, gave them weight and confidence. The nobles who committed themselves in the civil wars, and were obliged to the protection of towns, where they had been admitted into the first order of citizens, formed the only cavalry" (*A History of the Italian Republics* [New York, 1966] pp. 21–22).

344–345] *Armenian bridegroom . . . wool wedding-robes* An Armenian custom in which a torch is half burned at a man's wedding and then wrapped in his wool wedding robe and saved to be burned at his funeral.

346] *Gate-vein* The portal or great abdominal vein (see III, 556n); the *Vena Portae*, or "moving soul." In the second use of this term, B clearly means "moving soul," but not necessarily here.

348] *thy forerunner, Florentine* Dante, native of Florence, pays tribute to Sordello in *De Vulgaria Eloquentia* for attempting to form the Italian language by fusing the dialects of Cremona, Brescia, and Verona. In *The Divine Comedy*, Dante places Sordello in Ante-Purgatory among the unshriven, that is, among those who died suddenly by battle, or murder, or some other calamity, thus giving credence to the legend that Sordello met a violent death. Sordello becomes Dante's and Vergil's guide through Ante-Purgatory. See especially *Purgatory*, VI-IX. Dante, incidentally places Cunizza, B's Palma, in the Third Heaven, Venus, among those whose ardent temperament led them to yield wantonly to love. He places her brother, Ecelin III, in the seventh circle of Hell among the violent tyrants.

365] *In John's transcendent vision* St. John's vision of the new heaven and earth recorded in the Book of Revelation in the *New Testament*.

366–372] *Dante, pacer of the shore . . . where his chosen lie* Dante by an act of divine grace was permitted to pass through Hell unharmed. He emerged from Hell into Purgatory and eventually entered Heaven. The "pluckers of amaranths" could refer to the participants in one of two episodes in *The Divine Comedy:* the garden in Ante-Purgatory into which Sordello led Vergil and Dante at evening on Easter Day; or to the Earthly Paradise in which Dante met Beatrice after he had passed through Purgatory.

374–376] *In Mantua . . . even Mincio . . .* Mantua is a fortified city, capital of the province of Mantua, 25 mi. SSW of Verona and 100 mi. ESE of Milan. It is situated on an almost insular site among the swampy lagoons of the Mincio River. It is famous as the birthplace of Vergil. During the twelfth and thirteenth centuries the city often enjoyed the favor of the Hohenstaufen emperors, perhaps because its isolation made it a strategic military center. Frederick I granted the city right to elect its own Consuls, pledged it his support against Verona, and released it from the obligations of the *foderum* and *spedizione*. Mantua, nevertheless, became a member of the Lombard League (see I, 110n). There are many legends which celebrate Sordello as a valiant defender and savior of the city. He is supposed to have delivered Mantua from a three year siege by Ecelin III (see I, 110n). Even today the central piazza of Mantua—once the forum—bears his name.

381] *Goito* Today Goito is a small, one-street village about 10 mi. from Mantua (see above note) on the road to Brescia. The castle which B describes no longer stands, but there are traces of a very old red brick wall which suggests that perhaps it once did. There is still standing a red brick tower called the "Torre Sordello."

395–396] *And in light-graven . . . The Arab's wisdom* Quotations from Arabic literature and philosophy. Italians were beginning to feel the influence of Arabic culture. Frederick II, himself, was able to converse with the Arab philosophers of Palermo in their own language, and he made his court a meeting place between scholars of the East and the West. He was widely regarded among Churchmen as a sinister free-thinker, perhaps an atheist. That B attributes to the Ecelins an interest in Arabic culture identifies them with the Emperor rather than with the Church, and, also, perhaps, surrounds them with an atmosphere of mystery and evil. Adelaide, the Tuscan, was learned in astrology, an art that reached Italy through the Mohammedans in Spain.

412] *Caryatides* Draped female figures employed instead of columns as architectural supports. The Roman architect, Vitruvius, in *De architectura* (Book I) relates that caryatides represent women of Caryae, doomed to hard labor because the town sided with the Persians in 480 b.c. (a historical impossibility). They are also called *canephoros* or *korai* (maidens).

422] *buried vestal* At Rome, the sacred fire of Vesta (goddess of hearth and fire) was tended by six chosen virgin-priestesses who took a vow of thirty years service. If found guilty of unchastity, they were buried alive in a vault in the Campus Sceleratus (situated just within the wall near the Porta Collina) with only a lamp and a small ration of bread, wine, and water and there left to starve to death.

434] *Gold seven times globed* A primitive method of refining gold was to place it in a globe with liquids and float off the impurities.

457–461] *—Ecelo, dismal father . . . Lady of the castle, Adelaide* B's condensed version of the genealogical table of the Romano family (see I, 105n).

461] *Adelaide* A Tuscan, one of the four wives of Ecelin II, mother of Ecelin III (see I, 105n). B depicts her as a very strong-willed woman with political ambitions to emulate her namesake Adelaide of Susa (see III, 488–491n; IV, 569n). All ancient authorities say that she was learned in astrology and possessed the power to foretell the future (see I, 395–396n). Verci suggests that she was also in league with the devil (see VI, 764n).

515–516] *So runs/ A legend* B might have had any one of several legends in mind. Hesiod in his *Theogony* writes. "Verily at first Chaos came to be. . . . From Chaos came forth Erebus and black Night; but of Night was born

Aether and Day, whom she conceived and bare from union in love with Erebus. And Earth first bare starry heaven . . ." (Tr. by H.G. Evelyn-White, 1914). The *Old Testament* account is as follows. "In the beginning God created heaven and earth. And the earth was without form, and void; and darkness was upon the face of the deep, . . . And God said, Let there be light; and there was light. . . . And God said, Let there be lights in the firmament of the heaven to divide the day from the night; . . . And God made two great lights; the greater light to rule the day, and the lesser light to rule the night; he made the stars also" (*Genesis* I).

559] *Emprize* Attempt of danger; undertaking of hazard; enterprise (Johnson's *Dictionary*).

570] *With the new century* The thirteenth. Sordello was born towards the end of the twelfth century. The thirteenth century might be considered new in several respects. It marked the demise of the Hohenstaufen dynasty and the rapid rise to power of the Italian cities. B in the lines which follow (570–583) suggests the great renaissance of the arts and the emergence of the Gothic, a style of painting and architecture which he admired and considered superior to that of classical Greece and Rome.

572] *Witness a Greek or two* The influence of Byzantine art was beginning to be felt in the West at this time. The Eastern Empire had entered its final struggle with the Turks. In 1204 the crusading armies of the West had sacked Constantinople. Vasari, from whose *Lives of Italian Painters* B drew so much information throughout his life, tells us that Nicolo "was originally associated with some Greek sculptors." He continues, "Among the many marble remains brought home by the Pisan fleets were some ancient sarcophagi, now in the Campo Santo of that city. . . . Nicola, considering the excellence of this work, which greatly delighted him, applied such diligence in imitating that style, and other excellent sculptures on the other antique sarcophagi, that before long he was considered the best sculptor of his time" (A. B. Hinds, trans. [New York, 1927] I, 40]).

574] *that Pisan pair* Pisa, located on the Arno River 7 mi. from the sea and 49 mi. W of Florence, was the center of the new sculpture in Italy. The pair refer to Nicolo Pisano (1220?–1278?) and his son and pupil Giovanni Pisano (1245–1314?). Nicolo, influenced strongly by Byzantine painting and sculpture, was a precursor of the Renaissance, and Giovanni is generally considered a link between the art of Pisa and that of Florence.

576] *Siena is Guidone set* Guido da Siena was the first really important painter of that city. He probably worked during the middle of the thirteenth century, although in B's time he was thought to be active around 1221.

578] *Saint Eufemia's sacristy* Many churches were built in Europe in honor of this early fourth-century martyr. There is one at Verona which B perhaps saw on his Italian journey in 1838 while he was writing *Sordello*. On one of its altars there is a painting of the Madonna and saints by Moretto (c. 1498–1554).

590] *pyx* A small wooden box, usually round and with a lid. In the Roman Catholic Church it is the box in which the consecrated host is kept. In ancient times, it was the box, or coffer, sacred to pagan religions.

593–603] *mad Lucius . . . choicest gifts of gold* Marcus Aurelius Antoninus (121–180), the Roman Emperor and philosopher (*Meditations*), and his weak and vicious colleague, Lucius Verus (Marcus' adopted brother and co-ruler). During the war with the Parthians (161–165) which was conducted by Verus, a Roman force led by Avidius Cassius stormed Seleucia (Babylon), burned the city, and carried off a statue of the Cumaean Apollo from the temple. According to legend, soldiers, after the sacking, found a narrow hole in the temple which they opened to search for treasures. Out of the hole came a terrible plague which ravaged the world from the borders of Persia to the Rhine. *Loxian* is the surname of Apollo.

693] *Naddo* Italian name for common man, the conventional critic of poets and poetry.

693] *Eat fern-seed* The "seed" of the fern. Before the mode of reproduction of ferns was understood, they were popularly supposed to produce an invisible seed, which was capable of communicating its invisibility to any person who possessed it.

768] *Lord, liegeman, valvassor and suzerain* All terms to designate social levels in the feudal society. A lord was one for whom a fee or estate was held in feudal tenure; a liegeman, a vassal bound to a lord for feudal service; a valvassor, a sub-vassal among whom vassals divided their fiefs; suzerain, a superior feudal lord to whom first fealty was due. Originally, each liegeman had only one lord, but, as time passed, the custom developed whereby one man might become vassal of more than one lord. It became necessary, therefore, to distinguish between the ordinary lords and one lord to whom the vassal owed allegiance above all others. The latter became known as liege lord.

813] *Imperial Vicar* Representative of the Emperor. Ecelin II was designated Imperial Vicar by Otto IV in 1207; Ecelin III, by Frederick II.

816] *Trentine-pass* Pass through the mountainous Trentino region of N Italy which the Ghibellines were bent on keeping open since it constituted their direct link with the Hohenstaufen.

820] *St. Mark's spectacle* In 1209, Ecelin II claimed before the court of Otto IV that while he and Azzo were strolling on St. Mark's Plazza in Venice the latter had him attacked by assassins and even pinioned his arms so he couldn't defend himself. Only by a violent effort did he pull away from Azzo and save himself. The story is related by Simonde, Verci, and others.

841] *Malek* A general name for a Saracen chief. The word is the same as the Hebrew for "King."

868] *Miramoline* A Saracen prince. From the title Emiral Maromenium, meaning Prince of the Faithful.

871–873] *Are dates plucked . . . of Canaan* (See I, 194n). Dates sent by John of Brienne, King of Jerusalem, to remind his son-in-law, Frederick II, of his promised crusade to Jerusalem. It is uncertain whether this incident is historical or simply an invention of B. Jerusalem is located in the Biblical province of Canaan.

887] *Eglamor* An imaginary troubadour whose singing Sordello surpasses at the Court of Love which Palma conducts (see II, 1–66).

928] *The Pythons* In Greek myth, Python, an enormous serpent, crept out of the slime which covered the earth after the flooding of the fount of Castalia and the stream Cephissus. This serpent lurked in the caves of Mt. Parnassus until Apollo slew him with arrows, weapons which he had not used before except on small game. In commemoration of this victory, he instituted the Pythian games in which the victor was to be crowned with beech leaves. Apollo was patron of music and poetry.

932] *his Delians* The maidens of Delos (central island of the Cyclades group in the Aegean where Apollo was born). Sordello is likening Apollo's Delian maidens to his own Caryatides on the font in the Castle at Goito.

938] *Daphne* Apollo (who, by Cupid, had been struck in the heart by a golden arrow which had the power to excite love) pursued the nymph, Daphne (who had been shot by a lead arrow which had the power to repel love). Daphne called on her father, the river god, Peneus, to save her from Apollo either by opening up the earth to swallow her or by changing her form. Immediately, she began to take on the appearance of a laurel tree. Hence, the laurel became consecrated to Apollo.

941] *Palma* Palma was the sole child of Agnes Este, but it was Cunizza, daughter of Adelaide the Tuscan, half-sister of Palma, that was consort of Count Richard. It was Cunizza who provided the basic materials out of which B created the character whom he called Palma. B himself certainly did not confuse the two figures and we can only speculate about his motive for fusing them into a single character. It is perhaps no more complex than his poetic preference for the name Palma. Cunizza, consort of Count Richard, fell madly in love with Sordello who was minstrel at her husband's court. In the disguise of a man she deserted the Count and eloped with Sordello. Their union, however, was not of long duration. In all, she had no less than two lovers and four husbands (see I, 457–461n). After the death of her brother Ecelin III and of her last husband, she went to live in Florence where in 1279 she freed her father's slaves and made herself widely known for other acts of mercy and compassion. She was past eighty years old when she died. That B departed radically from his historical source is obvious.

980] *the Isle* Sicily. An island off the southern coast of Italy, Sicily was the scene during the middle ages of cosmopolitan races, culture, and religions. In the division of the Roman Empire the island fell to the East; it was captured in 831 by the Saracens, and in 1061 it became the first permanent conquest of the Normans. In 1194 it fell to the Hohenstaufen under Henry VI who was married to the Sicilian Constance, daughter of Roger II.

Constance outlived her husband and upon her death in 1198 appointed the Pope suzerain of her kingdom and ward of her young son, Frederick (see I, 178n). B vividly conveys the shocked attitude of the provincial mainland Italians toward the place where Greek, Italians, Arabs, and Jews lived together in relative peace. Greek, Arabic, Latin, and French were all spoken on the island and religious toleration was widely practiced. The Arabs, students of Greek philosophy, initiated a renaissance of learning in Sicily long before the intellectual awakening of S Europe.

981] *Messina* A very ancient city in NE Sicily (see I, 980n). It was an important harbor town approached by the Messina straits which separate the island from mainland Italy.

984] *Provence* An area on the Mediterranean bounded on the W by the Rhone, and on the N by the Dauphiné, and on the E by the Alps. By the end of the eleventh century it had developed a distinguished native vernacular poetry that was to influence the literary development of all Europe (see I, 987–989n). At the time of which B is writing, Provence was still a part of the Empire. It became a part of France toward the end of the twelfth century.

987] *in their very tongue* The Troubadours sang not in Latin but in their native dialects.

987–989] *Troubadour . . . Trouveres* The name *troubadour* originally applied to the Provençal lyric poets of the twelfth and thirteenth centuries. A troubadour was one who invented new poems, discovering verse forms for his elaborate lyrics. He sang his songs to his own accompaniment on a guitar or similar instrument. Troubadours had a surprising amount of political and social influence owing to the freedom of speech generally allowed to them. Moreover, they provided artistic and intellectual sophistication and an atmosphere of cultivation for the courts that they attended. Many of them noblemen—Richard Cœur de Lion and Emperor Frederick II were poets in this tradition—the troubadours were accorded a position of high respect at the court. Early in the thirteenth century some Italians began to write similar poetry in Provençal dialect. At the same time troubadour lyrics were beginning to be written in Italian at the Court of Frederick in Sicily. The group of poets has been called the "Sicilian School," although many of them came from other parts of Italy and even outside of Italy, thus bringing to their poetry various influences. They gradually created literary Italian out of Sicilian with mixtures of Provençal, Latin, French, and, of course, a variety of local dialects. Perhaps the chief innovation of the Sicilian troubadours was in the development and sophistication of versification; they are, for instance, credited with inventing the sonnet. *Trouveres*, by origin, are connected with the courts of N France, the troubadours with those of S France. The former were certainly more limited than the troubadours, for they devoted themselves almost exclusively to the composition and recitation of a special kind of poetry, the subject of which was some refinement of love. The continual movement of trouveres throughout France, N Spain and

Italy at this time matched that of the troubadours and, with the added confusion and movement brought about by the successive crusades, the two groups became mixed and eventually indistinguishable in their poetry. This blurring of traditional distinctions may be seen in the case of John of Brienne (see I, 871–873n), also a poet, who has been labeled both "troubadour" and "trouvere." Though Italian court poets, particularly the influential Sicilian group, of this period are ordinarily called "troubadours," the very fact that B mentions "trouveres" suggests that some or all of the traditional distinctions are intended, though this matter is unclear.

BOOK THE SECOND

65] *Jongleurs* Provided a variety of entertainment for courts and castles during the Middle Ages. They were required, among other things, to juggle, pantomime, do bird imitations, perform acrobatics, play many instruments, and do magical tricks. As singers, they were quite inferior to the troubadours and trouveres, on whom they attended and whose songs and stories they usually either borrowed or imitated in their own compositions.

66] *Court of Love* B refers here not to the courts of love for example, of such women as Eleanor of England and Marie of France, the purpose of which was to settle love disputes and define the laws of courtly love, but to a poetry contest, similar to the Tournaments of Song of the German minnesingers, in which the lady of the court where the contest was held presided, judged the best song, and awarded laurels and other prizes to the winner. The poets in these tournaments composed songs around a common theme.

68] *Elys* El-lys, the lily. Refers to the subject of Eglamor's song, an ideal woman. Sordello appropriates Eglamor's theme in "Elys" for his own expression of ideal beauty.

89–93] *Than some Egyptian ... Insulted.* Apis (Hopi) was the bull-god of the ancient Egyptian pantheon. He was supposed to be the image of the soul of Osiris. One of his distinguishing marks was a knot under his tongue in the shape of a scarabaeus.

118–119] *Squarcialupe ... Tagliafer* Jongleurs, of the sort that Naddo would praise. There is some indication later (II, 783–788n) that Squarcialupe is a trouvere, that is, an original poet, as well. The names Tagliafer, Strojovocca, and Dularette appear in Verci but in connections which have nothing to do with the poet's use of them here.

152–155] *"Her head that's ... the livelong summer ..."* These verses are from Sordello's version of Eglamor's "Elys." They give a conventional description of the ideal of beauty in a woman of this time.

177–179] *"a Roman bride, ... in memory still* An ancient Roman custom of parting a bride's hair with a sabine dart commemorates the famous Sabine rape. Romulus, so the story goes, invited the Sabines from a neighboring village to attend a Roman religious spectacle. While the men were absorbed in the events, Roman soldiers seized the Sabine wives and spirited them away so that they might become brides of the Romans. This act of treachery initiated a bloody struggle between the Sabines and the Romans which was finally terminated when the women appeared on the field of battle, imposing their own bodies between the warring armies, and demanded that the two be reconciled.

211] *(Like Perseus . . . naked love)* Perseus was the son of Zeus and Danaë. Once in his wanderings he discovered a beautiful girl chained to a rock on a remote sea coast. It was Andromeda, daughter of King Cepheus and Queen Cassiopeia, who was being sacrificed to a sea monster which Poseidon had in anger sent to ravage the land. The god's anger could be appeased only by the sacrifice of Andromeda. Perseus fell in love with her, slew the monster, and in reward received her in marriage.

290] *A plant they have* A flower, Eglamor, the *anthericum liliastrum*, or day-lily, also called St. Bruno's lily.

296–297] *My own month . . . May* B was born May 7, 1812.

300–301] *Massic jars/ Dug up at Baiae* Baia, 10 mi. W of Naples, was a fashionable watering place during the latter years of the Roman republic and under the Empire. Both Julius Caesar and Nero built villas there. As a result of a rise in the sea level a part of the old city is now submerged. From out of the debris excavators have unearthed jars formerly containing Massic wines from the vineyards of Mons Massicus which still retained the odor of the wine.

322–341] *when at Vicenza . . . retreat where Adelaide* The expulsion of the Ghibellines from Vicenza occurred in 1194. B tells the story four times in his poem: II, 322–341; IV, 535–546; IV, 725–747; V, 751–799. It is told from three perspectives and for three purposes. It appears here in the form in which Adelaide wished it to be known. In Book IV it is related as Salinguerra recalls it and wants it to be remembered; in Book V Palma renders an apparently objective account of the event as it actually occurred. For his materials, B perhaps drew most heavily upon Verci, although his account differs in some important aspects from his source. Verci, for example, does not mention Azzo and Count Richard.

322] *Vicenza* The ancient Vicentia, a city of modern Veneto, 42 mi. W of Venice. The founder of the Ecelin family was enfeoffed by Conrad II in the early eleventh century with lands in N Italy (see I, 102–104n) and a castle at Romano near Vicenza. The Ecelins were from the beginning a powerful political force in the town, Ecelin I being elected according to B as its first podestà ("one of the first" according to Verci). Vicenza was a member of the Lombard League (see I, 110n), and like other Italian cities of the time, victim of intense internal strife and frequent change of administration. B in his poem refers to one such event in 1194 when the Ecelin family (Ecelin II was then podestà) was driven from the city by the Guelfs (see IV, 725–736n). During the first half of the thirteenth century, Vicenza was primarily under the control of the Ecelin family and their Ghibelline supporters.

322] ... *both her counts* It cannot be determined precisely whom B had in mind since there are more than two possibilities. He may very well have meant Count Uguccione (see II, 323–324n). Whyte (p. 104) suggests that he might refer to Pilio da Celsano or his son, Count Albert.

323–324] *the Vivaresi ... Those Maltraversi* The two political factions between which Vicenza was split. According to Verci, Count Uguccione was head of the first, and Ecelin, of the latter. These two parties were later identified with Guelf and Ghibelline.

326] *Ecelin was born* Verci does not mention the birth of Ecelin III as occurring at the time of this siege. In the article on the Romano family in *Biographie*, however, Ecelin is said to have been born April 4, 1194.

331–332] *Elcorte ... his child to thank* There is no historical basis for this account of Elcorte's bravery. In the Provençal chronicles of the lives of the poets, Sordello is reported to have been the son of a poor chevalier named El Cort (see I, 1n).

336] *Bishop Pistore* Bishop of Vicenza in 1194, a tool of Ecelin, who was expelled from the city along with Ecelin and (according to B) Salinguerra. He was found shortly afterward drowned in a castle moat.

345–346] *When Azzo ... That pledge of Agnes Este* Ecelin II was first married to Agnes Este (see I, 105n). Azzo would like in exchange to see Palma married to his ally Count Richard. Undoubtedly matters of dowry and political power were at stake.

474] *truchman* Interpreter.

516] *In rondel, tenzon, virlai or sirvent* Rondel is a poem of fourteen lines on two rhymes with a refrain, the first two lines of the opening quatrain recurring at the close of the second quatrain and that of the concluding sestet. The meter varies, as does the rhyme scheme, a frequent arrangement being ABBA, ABAB, ABBAAB. Occasionally the rondel is shortened to thirteen lines, one line of the refrain being omitted from the last stanza. The rondel is a French verse form, a variant of the rondeau, to which it is related. The *tenzon* or contention (from *tende*, to strive) was both a verse form and a poetic contest of troubadours held before a court of love. The form of the contest was a dialogue between two poets in which they alternately maintained different sides of some question of love or chivalry, using the same stanzas and rhymes. The *virlai* is a French form composed of stanzas of long lines rhyming with each other and short lines rhyming with each other, the short lines of each stanza furnishing the rhyme for the long lines of the next, except for the last stanza, in which the short lines take their rhyme from the short lines of the first, so that every rhyme occurs in two stanzas. The poem is of indefinite length, but the pattern may be exhibited in a structure of four quatrains, the first and third lines being long, the second and fourth short. ABAB, BCBC, CDCD, DADA. The *sirvent* was chiefly a war-song or satire on individuals or public matters; it was of no definite form. Often it was used to attack political and social injustices and was a means of bringing grievances to the attention of the public. Typical themes were the abuses of the Church and the follies of war.

518] *angelot* A musical instrument somewhat like a flute.

537–538] *Anafest . . . Lucio* Characters in Sordello's song.

541] *Bianca* A person in Sordello's song; the power and suggestiveness of the song have convinced the youth, who loves Bianca, that Sordello's love for her is more intense than his own.

574–575] *slow re-wrought/ That language* See I, 1n.

600] *Destroy* Here used in the etymological sense of "unbuilding" or "building down," the opposite of construction. The context rules out the usual negative connotation: to spoil, ruin, wreck.

600] *Muse* A means of expression. The muse is the particular genius inspiring poets.

615] *Of Hyacinth . . . luckless quoits* Apollo, in charge of the education of Hyacinth, was teaching the youth how to play quoits (throwing the stone discus) when Zephyrus, who loved the boy too and was jealous of Apollo, blew the discus that Apollo had thrown off the ground and into the face of Hyacinth who was running to pick it up. Hyacinth was killed by the blow.

617] *Of Montfort o'er the Mountaineers* In the early thirteenth century Simon de Montfort (c. 1160–1218) led the crusade of the Roman Church against the Albigenses (officially called Cathari and sometimes popularly called Paulicians) who professed an austere dualist belief that God existed in spirit alone and that all matter was the creation of the devil. In open rebellion against the official church, they gathered great strength in S France and N Italy, having at one time eleven bishops. Their presence only added to the complexities of the already turbid condition of the empire. In response to the threat which they offered, Pope Lucius III and Frederick Barbarossa met at Verona in 1184 and issued the decree *Ad abolendam* which, laying down procedures for ecclesiastical trials, in effect initiated the inquisition. The province of Languedoc was at the close of the twelfth century one of the wealthiest and most cultured portions of France. As a result of the austere crusade, however, led by Montfort, the area was utterly devastated. The rebellion within the Church had wide-spread political and religious effects. The Dominican Friars were founded partly to combat the Albigenses heresy. The Pope attempted to undermine the political power of the Ecelins by having Ecelin II tried for heresy (see I, 138n).

622] *ballad-rhyme* A short, simple narrative poem. The stories for these ballads were founded on dramatic incidents from the old romances or on some older legend. Such ballads present a simple romantic theme, impersonally treated, and are characterized by the simplicity of the language, the repetition of epithets and phrases, the casual handling of rhyme, and the liberties allowed by stress prosody.

646] *A fairy dust* A magical dust with the power to change the ordinary and mundane into its ideal form.

684] *Quiver and bow* The quiver and bow of Apollo, which he used to kill the Python, marked his bravery and heroism (I, 928n). In short, it is used to symbolize the active life and is here analogous to Sordello's conception of manhood, as opposed to bard-craft, or the passive life.

691] *John's cloud-girt angel* The Revelation of St. John the Divine 10.1–3. "And I saw another mighty angel come down from heaven, clothed with a cloud: and a rainbow was upon his head, and his face was as it were the sun, and his feet as pillars of fire. And he had in his hand a little book open: and he set his right foot upon the sea, and his left foot on the earth, And cried with a loud voice, as when a lion roareth; and when he had cried, even thunders uttered their voices."

714] *Let Vidal* Peire Vidal twelfth-century troubadour of Toulouse. His patron was Raymond V, Count of Toulouse (see I, 1n).

740] *twenty-cubit plectre* An eighteen-inch ivory wand for striking the strings of an antique lyre.

748] *retailed* "Told in broken parts, or at second hand" (Johnson's *Dictionary*).

768] *Bocafoli* Probably a fictitious poet (boca: braggart; fola: idle tale or nonsense). Suggests a type of poet, one dealing in bare abstractions and didacticism.

769] *Plara* Another imaginary poet, a sample of whose verse is given in the following lines (770–773). His work parodies a typical, decorous style. (See also III, 881–900.)

770] *"As knops* Allied to know. Probably a corruption of "knap," which Samuel Johnson defines as "a protuberance; a swelling of prominence."

770] *almug* Sandalwood. The tree was the source of "gum ammoniac" or "gum arabic." In the Bible it meant a tree, probably sandalwood, from which Solomon made the pillars of the Temple (I Kings 10.12). It is called *algum* in II Chronicles 2.8.

722] *river-horse* A hippopotamus.

773] *breese* "A stinging insect, a gad-fly" (Johnson's *Dictionary*).

776] *pompion-twine* Pumpkin vine.

825] *Pappacoda, Tagliafer* See II, 118–119n.

859] *Count Lori* The name B gives to the apparently fictitious gallant which he first chose as his hero.

860–861] *peasant-Paul,/ Like those old Ecelin* B perhaps has no historical character in mind, indicating rather any unlearned follower of the Paulician heresy. Obviously this heresy (see II, 617n) derived from Paul but it is not clear whether it was from the son of the legendary Manichaean woman,

Kallinike, who sent her sons John and Paul to Armenia to preach the heresy (thus Paul is sometimes falsely identified with the followers of the third century heretic Paul of Samosata) or whether it was from St. Paul, whom the heretics held in special reverence.

865] *Paulician* See II, 617n; 860–861n.

873] *"I am sick too* Ecelin II. Verci (I, 90n) records Ecelin's retirement to the monastery as occurring in 1221, actually three years before the siege of Ferrara which B describes (see I, 138n).

879] *Monk Hilary* Apparently the fictitious name of one of the monks at Oliero.

881–882] *for many things/ You know . . . never knew* His knowledge and complicity in Adelaide's scheme to conceal Sordello's real identity.

883–886] *Azzo's sister . . . my Palma* B found this information in Maurisius and altered it only by substituting the name of Palma for that of Cunizza.

889] *the Tuscan's death* Adelaide's death.

890–891] *With Friedrich sworn to sail . . . for Syria* According to B's imaginative account, Salinguerra was at the time of Adelaide's death with Frederick at Naples ready to sail for the crusade the Emperor had long promised to make (see I, 78n).

892] *Vesuvius* The only active volcano on the European mainland. It is located in S Italy near the E shore of the Bay of Naples. The most famous eruption was that of A.D. 79, which destroyed Pompeii and Herculaneum.

909] *The green and the yellow* The colors of the Ecelins which by extension became the colors of the Ghibelline party.

910] *Retrude's death* Frizzi records that Salinguerra was married to Retrude. No other historian of the period mentions this, however. There is no evidence whatever that she was "From Otho's house" or that she was of "Heinrich's very blood."

929] *Strojavacca* A rival troubadour. The name occurs in Verci but not in connection with a troubadour (see II, 118n).

932] *cobswan* Male swan; chief of the flock; head-swan.

966] *between cat's head and ibis' tail* Emblems of the small animals which the Egyptians worshiped set in mosaic in the pavement.

969] *Soldan* The Sultan, ruler of the Mohammedans. After a schism, the first seat of government, Damascus (set up in the seventh century), had the competition of Cairo, where the dissenting sect, the Fatamites, set up government in the tenth century. The Soldan alluded to here seems to reside in the latter city.

989] *smelling of the iris root* The iris root is extensively cultivated in N Italy. It is widely used in perfume sachets. For centuries it was considered an effective treatment for various kinds of "head ailments," including loss of memory and deterioration of rational faculties.

990] *The Tuscan* Adelaide.

993] *Carian group* An obvious reference to the sculptures described in I,

406–442. An ancient district of SW Asia Minor, forming the Cibyraeot theme of the Byzantine Empire until it was conquered by the Turks in the thirteenth century. It is located on the Aegean Sea and comprised what is now roughly the modern Turkish districts of S Aydin and W Mugla. After having fallen temporarily into the hands of the Moslems, it was recaptured and plundered by the Crusaders in 1097. B suggests that the marbles at Goito derived from this E area.

1016] *bull-bait* (bull-chase) The tormenting of bulls by dogs; formerly a popular sport, especially in England.

BOOK THE THIRD

2] *moonfern* Moonwort, hemionitis, having healing qualities. Along with trifoly, it belongs to the "sleeping" order of plants because its leaves close at night. In Culpepper's *Herbal* this description is given. "It is reported that whatever horse casually treads upon the herb will lose its shoes; it it also said to have the virtue of unlocking their fetters and causing them to fall off."

2] *mystic trifoly* Heart trefoil, trifolium, clover. "Mystic" has been applied to the trifolium because it was used (by, among others, St. Patrick) to demonstrate the doctrine of the Trinity, the three lobed leaves suggesting three persons in one god. Clover was the emblem of Ireland from which the shamrock was derived. Culpepper in his *Herbal* says. "It is under the dominion of the sun, and if it were used it would be found as great a strengthener of the heart and cherisher of the vital spirits as grows."

12] *painted byssus* A tuft of silky filaments used by shell-fish to attach themselves to objects, usually rocks.

13] *Tyrrhene whelk* The shell-fish from which the famous Tyrian purple was made. The latter was a purple or crimson dye used by the ancient Romans and Greeks.

14] *trireme* An ancient Greek or Roman galley, usually a warship with three tiers of oars on each side.

15] *satrap* The Persian title for the governor of a province; literally "protector of the land."

119–120] *The hot torchlit ... wickedest carouse* The Emperor's villa near Palermo, in Sicily, called La Favora. His sensuous indulgences were legendary throughout Italy. It is said that once St. Francis himself came to Bari, where Frederick was staying, with the express purpose of preaching a sermon denouncing the vices of the Court. On one occasion, before the open break between the Pope and the Emperor, the Pope wrote Frederick a letter in which he exhorted. "Take heed that you do not place your intellect, which you have in common with the angels, below your senses, which you have in common with beasts and plants."

121–123] *to the gay Palermitans ... Nuocera holds* Inhabitants of Palermo and Messina. In 1222, Frederick shocked the Christian world by transporting 20,000 Saracens from Sicily to the mainland and settling them at

Nuocera in the plain of Apulia. He deported Christians from the city and turned a cathedral into a Mosque. By this bold enterprise he ended the Saracen threat to Sicily and, moreover, provided himself a source of manpower for the wars he was to wage. The Saracens remained intensely loyal to him. He also established here a permanent harem composed primarily of infidel "little dears" guarded by black eunuchs. A number of these concubines accompanied him wherever he went, even into battle.

123–126] *grave dazzling Norse . . . through icy seas* A reference to the Normans, derived from the Northmen, who had settled in the two Sicilies and with whom Frederick was on friendly terms. We find no evidence, however, that Frederick himself imported them into his kingdom. Actually the Normans first appeared in S Italy in 1017 in response to an invitation from Melo of Bari who had since 1009 been leader of a rebellion in Apulia and adjoining areas against Byzantine rule. Although Melo's efforts failed, the Normans, once settled in S Italy, remained and became feared by the Italians for their fierce courage and audacious enterprise. Very possibly, Normans, Saracens, and Greeks were all associated in the minds of the more provincial N Italians with the forces of the devil.

124] *morse* A water-horse, or walrus.

129] *mollitious* Sensuous.

130] *Byzant domes* In the style to be found in Constantinople where Greek architecture had been modified by Saracenic influence. Because of its pagan derivation it would be widely regarded in N and central Italy, particularly among ardent Churchmen, as devil-built.

132] *Dandolo* The blind doge of Venice (c. 1108–1205) and one of the leaders of the fourth crusade. He first induced the crusading army to assist Venice in the capture and destruction of Zara, a town then held by the king of Hungary, on the coast of Dalmatia (1202). He next directed the crusaders against Constantinople with the result that the city was captured and pillaged in 1204. In addition to securing territorial and commercial advantages for Venice, Dandolo carried priceless art treasures back to the city, including the famous bronze horses on St. Mark's (see V, 648n).

220] *Of the bulb dormant* It was an Egyptian custom to bury hyacinth bulbs with embalmed bodies as a sign of the life to come. This was part of the ritual for preserving the body so the soul could return to it.

228] *marish* A marsh.

233] *Has played Taurello an astounding trick* See II, 883–886n.

235] *. . . goes into a convent* See I, 138n; II, 873n.

240–241] *made bold/ By Salinguerra's absence* See I, 155n.

245–248] *how the Count . . . Absorbing thus Romano* Richard's marriage to Palma would give him political advantages over the Romanos and the Ghibellines.

262] *osprey's swoop* See I, 128n.

263] *On lynx and ounce* See I, 166n.

271] *His barons from the burghers* See I, 110n.

272–273] *The rule of Charlemagne . . . By Hildebrand* See I, 308n.

297] *Is any beacon* A method of signaling commonly used at the time.

302] *Tiso Sampier* Tisolino di San Piero (Sampier) or Campo San Pierre or Pietro. One of a family with whom Ecelin had been involved in a vicious feud. Once friends, an outrage committed by Ecelin against Maria di Camposanpietro was said to be revenge for a similar outrage against his family. An elder Tiso of this house was killed in 1222 in Salinguerra's victorious assault on the Este faction in Verona. This Tiso is undoubtedly a descendant, eager for revenge.

350] *Richard's Love-court* See II, 66n.

361] *Cesano* A town located between Como and Milan. During the early thirteenth century it frequently changed loyalties, favoring first one and then another of the parties. Dante refers to it in the *Inferno* (XXVII, 52–54):

> The town where Savio bathes the city wall,
>
> Lying betwixt the mountains and the plain,
>
> Like as she lies, so lives 'twixt free and thall.
>
> (Dorothy Sayer, trans.)

370–378] *she at liberty to sit . . . Mine and Romano's* Adelaide is repeatedly said to have had magical powers. Verci (I, 88) writes that she possessed perfectly the science of astrology, knowing both the way of the stars and of other celestial motions, and that she could predict the future. See especially IV, 76n; IV, 600–604n.

382] *insuperable Tuscan* Adelaide. See I, 461n.

386–387] *Ecelin . . . With Alberic* The two brothers were often at odds. In 1229 Ecelin assisted Alberic in putting down the peasant revolt in Bassano (see VI, 710–714n). By 1240, however, Alberic had joined with the Guelf forces and engaged in the attack on Ferrara during which Salinguerra was taken prisoner (see VI, 730n). In 1256, the brothers met at Castelfranco and exchanged the kiss of peace. They were still united at the time of the battle of Cassano and of Ecelin's death in 1259.

422] *Gate Saint Blaise* There is now no gate Saint Blaise in Vicenza. Whyte (pp. 152–53) observes that Pagliarni in his *Storia di Vicenza* mentions a church Saint Biasio which lay outside the city wall, and asks: "Can it be S. Blasio, and was there a gate in the outer ramparts named after it?" No one as yet has answered the question.

429–430] *the orb I sought/ To serve* Dante places Cunizza (B's Palma) in the third heaven of the planet Venus. B here has his character early dedicating herself to the service of love.

430] *Fomalhaut* A star of the first magnitude in the Southern Fish which Dante associates with Venus, fish goddess:

> The lovely planet, love's own quickener,
>
> Now lit to laughter all the eastern sky,
>
> Veiling the Fishes that attended her.
>
> (*Purgatory*, I, 19–21. Dorothy Sayer, trans.)

434] *had else been Boniface's bride* See II, 914n.

447-448] *which late allied/ Our House with other Houses* See I, 138n.

447-451] *late allied ... in his one steed* See I, 243-244n.

460] *Saponian strength of Lombard grace* Earlier commentators have not agreed on the meaning of the word Saponian. P-C says "the strength of the Saponi family, the founders of the Ecelins." We know of no historian who gives Saponi as the family name of the Ecelins (see I, 105n). Whyte says: "Professor Sonnenschein, in his notes on *Sordello*, gives Saponian-Samponian Pass, probably Simplon. Dr. Berdoe suggests the derivation from Savona, of which Saponian would be the Latin form. . . . In the commentary on *Sordello* by K. M. Loudon is this note: 'Saponi, a branch of the Ecelin family, settled in Lombardy before Sordello's time,' but no authority is given for the statement." Stewart Holmes says: "for 'Saponian' Browning probably meant 'Saxonian.' Cape Sapone is in the extreme south of Italy, a place where the Ecelini, particularly their German progenitors, never lived" (p. 469). It is unlike B to make so obvious an error; we have not, however, been able to provide additional enlightenment. B possibly intended to contrast Saxonian strength with Lombardian grace.

466-471] *Old strength propped ... In Conrad's crew* Ecelin I. In these lines B follows Verci precisely (I, 65, 231). Remains of his palace bear the date 1150.

472] *Romano* See I, 106n.

488-491] *Adelaide of Susa...'Twixt France and Italy* Adelaide (1020-1091) was Marquise of Turin. She wielded tremendous political power, generally in support of the Imperial cause. Her daughter Bertha was married to Henry IV. Nevertheless, she remained for the most part on friendly terms with the Church, joining in 1077 with Countess Matilda and Abbot Hugh of Cluny to bring about a reconciliation between Gregory VII and Henry IV (see II, 492n). There is no record, however, that she gave her donative to Matilda or to the Pope.

492] *Matilda* Countess of Tuscany, staunch friend of Pope Gregory VII and Paschal III. It was before her castle in Canossa that Gregory kept the penitent King Henry IV standing for three days in the snow before he finally admitted him into his presence and granted him absolution (January 25-28, 1077). When Matilda died in 1115 she left her vast possessions (Mantua, Modena, Tuscany, Spoleto, and Ancona) to the Holy See, drawing no distinction between the feudal land she held from the Empire and the estates over which she held undisputed permanent rights. This action became a source of contention between Pope and Emperor for many years.

501] *Kaiser excommunicate* See I, 78n; 200n.

507-512] *The day I was betrothed ... Convicting Richard of the fault* That Sordello and Palma schemed thus to ensnare Richard is purely B's fiction (see I, 138n).

517-518] *A month since ... into a monk* See I, 138n.

537–538] *mating with/ Este* See I, 138n.

545–546] *we in some gay weed/ Like yours* According to some accounts (see I, 1n) Cunizza, dressed as a page, did flee from Richard's court with Sordello.

554] *Pollux* Pollux, son of Leda and Zeus, and his brother, Castor, son of Leda and King Tyndareus, took a small part in the quest for the Golden Fleece. During a raging storm, two globes of fire suddenly appeared and danced about the brothers' heads, after which the storm was calmed. Thus, the brothers are usually represented riding white horses with stars on top of their egg-shaped helmets.

587] *Verona's Lady* An ancient statue on a fountain in the Piazza del Erbe in Verona popularly known as the "Madonna Verona." Legend has it that the statue was originally found on the site of the old capitol, now occupied by the Castle di San Pietro. The association here is with Palma.

588] *Gaulish Brennus* A general of the Gauls who first invaded Italy in 387 or 390 B.C. His name, which first appears in the works of Livy, is not mentioned by Polybius or Diordorus Siculus. Much of his story is tangled in legend, but it is clear that he defeated the Roman army at the Allia River (about 12 mi. from Rome) and then went on to sack the capitol, besieging it for seven months. According to legend, his army scaled the Tarpeian Rock (on which the capitol was situated) by night and was about to storm the citadel when Manlius, awakened by the noise of the sacred geese in the Temple of Juno, gave the alarm and hurled down the first climber. It was Brennus who during the ransom of prisoners is said to have thrown his sword into the scales with the famous words *vae victus* (woe to the vanquished).

592] *Manlius* See III, 588n.

596] *platan* The oriental plane-tree. A handsome tree, it is a native of Greece and Western Asia. It was a favorite shade tree of the Greeks and Romans and was introduced by the latter to SW Europe. Its name derives from the fact that it is a large tree with widely spreading branches.

597] *archimage* A chief magician or enchanter, a great wizard. The word was used by Spenser in *The Faerie Queene* as the name of his personification of hypocrisy, "Archimago."

603] *Bloom-flinders* Fragments or pieces of flowers, that is, petals (see VI, 437n).

633–635] *Charlemagne . . . restive daughters* There is no record that Sordello wrote a poem on this subject (see I, 1n). Charlemagne is said to have refused his daughters permission to marry because he could not bear for them to leave him.

656] *colibri* Humming birds.

676] *I muse this on a ruined palace-step* From here to the end of Book III B himself is speaking, presumably recounting a personal experience which occurred on his trip to Italy in 1838. Discouraged by his failure to finish *Sordello*, he departed from England in April of that year, "intending," he wrote John Robinson in a letter dated Good Friday, 1838, "to finish my poem among the scenes it describes" (Orr, *Life*, 135). Later he summarized his visit in a letter to Miss Fanny Haworth. "I went to Trieste, then Venice—[here he spent the first part of June] then thro' Treviso to Bassano [Alberic's headquarters, his inheritance from his father Ecelin II upon his retirement to the monastery] to the mountains, delicious Asolo, all my palaces and castles, you will see. [Apparently to Possagno and Romano where the ancestral castles of the Ecelin family once stood. From Romano he could see San Zenone where Alberic, the last of the family, was finally hunted down, tortured, and killed. He went to the convent at Oliero to which Ecelin II retired and from there to Solagno where reputedly the monk was buried.] Then to Vicenza [early stronghold of the Ecelin family and part of the inheritance of Ecelin III from his father], Padua, and Venice again. Then to Verona, Trent, [both rich in associations with the Ecelin family] Innsbruck (the Tyrol) Munich, 'Werzburg in Franconia'! Frankfort and Mayence,—down the Rhine to Cologne, thence to Aix-la-Chappelle, Liege, the Antwerp—then home" (Hood, *Ltrs.*, 3). B's attributing a more humane position later as motivation for Sordello's desertion of the Ghibelline cause reflects Simonde's point of view.

693] *Guidecca* An island, really a part of Venice, for which a canal is named.

710] *sumpter-cloth* Cloth or covering, often of a rich material or embroidery, worn on the back of a beast-of-burden (pack-horse or mule).

727] *Piazza* The plazza of St. Mark's in Venice, which Napoleon called "*le plus beau salon de l'Europe*" is surrounded on three sides by a continuous row of artistic buildings which seem to form one vast marble palace. It is one of the most famous public squares in the world and since the Middle Ages the great gathering place of all of Venice. The plazza forms an oblong rectangle of 579 feet in length and 269 feet in its greatest width. On the east side it is bounded by the Basillica, one of the most celebrated churches in the Christian world.

738] *Fastuous* Proud, haughty.

746] *shent* Blamed, harshly rebuked.

761] *Venice* The state of Venice was originally composed of twelve townships, the chief of which was Rialto or Venice. Isolated as they were by their location in the shallows and mudbanks of the lagoons, they became the refuge of island inhabitants fleeing from invading Huns and Lombards. The Venetian Republic took something of its modern shape following the final Lombard invasion in the late sixth century. These island inhabitants, true to their heritage, remained fiercely independent. Because of their location they achieved quick maritime importance. They early formed ties with the Eastern Empire, and, after their victory over Pippen in 810, Venice was recognized as a subject of Byzantium with trading rights on the mainland of Italy. As a result of the sack of Constantinople in 1204 (the Fourth Crusade),

Venice advanced both its territorial and its material significance so that by the time of the opening of B's poem it was undisputed master of the seas, a center of wealth and culture, and a respected and feared independent European power. It sometimes participated in the factional wars between the various parties of Italy but nevertheless remained essentially aloof and independent.

765] *the Basilic* St. Mark's Church in Venice.

766] *Corpus Domini* (*Festum sanctissimi Corporis Christi*) Corpus Christi, a feast in honor of the Holy Eucharist. Celebrated the Thursday following Trinity Sunday, it is usually a feast of elaborate ceremony, often taking place out-of-doors.

789] *losel* Worthless fellow.

815] *mugwort* (*Artemisia vulgaris*) It was called "mugwort" because it gave a bitter flavor to drink. It has a red, rough stem and grows to a height of from two to four feet.

817–818] *Zin/ The Horrid* Alludes to Moses and the Children of Israel in the Wilderness of Zin (Numbers 20: 1–5): "Then came the children of Israel, even the whole congregation, into the desert of Zin. . . . And there was no water for the congregation: and they gathered themselves together against Moses and against Aaron. And the people chode with Moses, and spake, saying, Would God that we had died when our brethern died before the Lord! And why have ye brought up the congregation of the LORD into this wilderness, that we and our cattle should die there? And wherefore have ye made us to come up out of Egypt, to bring us into this evil place? It is no place of seed, or of figs, or of vines, or of pomegranates; neither is there any water to drink."

822] *Potiphar's mishap* (Genesis 39) Potiphar, an officer of Pharaoh, bought Joseph as a slave from the Ishmeelites who had brought the boy down from Egypt. Eventually Joseph was made overseer to the officer's house where the latter's wife persistently attempted to seduce him. Finally, she tore at his clothing and he, pulling himself out of them, escaped from the house. She retaliated by screaming that Joseph had tried to seduce her. When her husband returned, this was the story she told him. Enraged, Potiphar had Joseph put in prison. "Mishap" refers to the incident in general.

823] *the earliest ass that spoke* (Numbers 22) God, speaking through the mouth of Balaam's ass, reproached Balaam for beating the animal three times with his staff; for the latter had been blocked from passing along the road three times by an angel which, while visible to the ass, was invisible to Balaam.

825] *Potsherd him, Gibeonites* (Joshua 9) To throw fragments of pottery at him. The Gibeonites were self-appointed servants to Joshua and the people of Israel. Because of their treachery—they disguised as beggars, left their country, which was about to be seized by Joshua, and, offering themselves to the Israelites, gained a pledge of immunity—they were dropped even lower to the status of bondsmen—"Hewers of wood and drawers of water."

826–827] *Moses smites . . . Promised land* (Numbers 20: 9–13) "And Moses took the rod from before the Lord, as he commanded him. And Moses and Aaron gathered the congregation together before the rock, and he said unto them, Hear now, ye rebels; must we fetch you water out of this rock? And Moses lifted up his hand, and with his rod he smote the rock twice; and the water came out abundantly and the congregation drank, and their beasts also. And the Lord spake unto Moses and Aaron, because ye believed me not, to sanctify me in the eyes of the children of Israel, therefore ye shall not bring this congregation into the land which I have given them."

828] *have Satan claim his carcass* (Jude 9) "Michael the Archangel, when contending with the devil, he disputed about the body of Moses."

830] *Meribah* (Numbers 20: 13; Exodus 17: 7) The place where Moses struck water from the rock. The word means "strife."

851] *gin* General name for a war engine.

876] *Piombi* Prison of the Doge's Palace in Venice.

879] *Zanze* His mistress.

881] *Plara* See II, 769n.

895] *grey glass oriel-pane* An oriel-window (sometimes used for stained-glass window); a projecting window in an upper-story, of the same design as a bay-window (ground level).

900] *Tempe's dewy vale* The ancient name of the beautiful valley, sacred to Apollo, through which the Peneus River (modern Salambria) runs to the sea from the plain of Lower Thessaly. The name has come to represent any beautiful, unspoiled natural retreat, usually a valley.

939–941] *Hercules . . . pomp to suit* The incident centers around Busiris who, in Greek legend, was an Egyptian king. After Egypt had been afflicted with famine for nine years, Phrasius, a seer of Cyprus, arrived in Egypt and announced that the famine would not end until the yearly sacrifice of a foreigner to Jove was made. Busiris began the custom by sacrificing the prophet. Later, Hercules, who had arrived in Egypt from Libya in search of the Apples of Hesperides, was seized and bound over to be offered at the altar of Jove in Memphis. Hercules burst his bonds and, seizing his club, slew Bursiris, his son, Amphidamus, his herald, Chalbes, and, according to some authorities, all those attending. The exploit is often represented on vase paintings from the sixth century B.C. and on, and the legend is referred to by Herodotus and later writers.

948] *hecatomb* A great public sacrifice (properly of a hundred oxen) among the ancient Greeks and Romans. Commonly used in the looser sense of a great number or quantity, a "heap" of persons, animals, or things presented at a sacrifice.

950] *patron-friend* In a letter to Dr. Furnivall, December 16, 1881 (Hood, *Ltrs.*, 206–207), B identifies this person as Walter Savage Landor (1775–1864): "Yes, Landor was the friend, and his praise was prompt, both public and private." Landor's early appreciation and encouragement of B (in his poem "To R.B." November 19, 1845, he compares the young poet, on the basis of his energy, his "enquiring eye," and his "tongue/ So varied in discourse," to Chaucer) went contrary to the general low esteem of his work at the time. B always claimed that Landor had helped him more than any contemporary poet.

952–959] *Like your own trumpeter . . . ships at Salamis* Probably an allusion to Aeschylus whom Landor celebrated in his "Idyllia Heroica," printed in Latin at Pisa in 1820. Aeschylus served in the Greek army and fought in the battles of Marathon, Plataea, and Salamis, the experience serving as material and inspiration for his *Persae*. Later Aeschylus went to Sicily and gave his "Women of Aetna" under the patronage of King Hiero who is said to have been engaged in building the city of Aetna. There is probably a second reference in III, 553–554 and this to Landor's experience as the colonel of a regiment (which he supported) fighting with the Spanish patriots against Napoleon I. After the disillusionment of seeing the reinstated Ferdinand VII repudiate the constitution of 1812 (which he was bound to support) and all liberal reform, and after the dispersal of his own regiment, Landor left Spain to wander on the continent for several years before settling in Italy.

961] *Had I a flawless ruby* Polycrates, King of Samos, warned by his friend Amasis of Egypt that his long-standing prosperity would make the gods jealous, was advised to throw away his most precious possession. Thus, he had himself rowed out to sea where he flung into the water a treasured ring. Seven days later a fisherman made him a gift of an especially large fish, inside of which the king discovered the ring he had thrown away. Amasis broke off his friendship and later Polycrates was crucified. The story is related by Herodotus, Book III.

967] *My English Eyebright* Euphasia Fanny Haworth, a minor nineteenth century poetess. B met her in the early thirties at the home of the theater manager William Macready and they became fast friends. She was eleven years his senior. On July 24, 1838, B wrote to her: "I did not write six lines while absent (except a scene in a play, jotted down as we sailed thro' the Straits of Gibralter)—but I did hammer out some four, two of which are addressed to you, two to the Queen—the whole to go into book 3—perhaps. I called you 'Eyebright'—meaning a simple and sad sort of translation of 'Euphasia' (Hood, *Ltrs.*, 2)."

991–992] *John the Beloved, banished Antioch/ For Patmos* The beloved disciple, John, accepted unquestionably until recent times as author of The Book of Revelation. Of his life, we can say positively that he was pastor of at least seven Churches in Asia and that he was banished from Antioch to the penal colony of Patmos ("on account of the word of God and the testimony of Jesus," Revelation, 1: 9).

996] *Xanthus* An imaginary character, a disciple of St. John.

402

999] *Polycarp* Christian martyr of the second century, appointed Bishop of Smyrna, supposedly by John.

1000] *Charicle* Another imaginary character.

1011] *"Get thee behind me* St. Luke, 4:8.

1015–21] *I to thy roof beguiled . . . You're painted with* An image of John with his pastoral cross, symbol of his priestly office, obviously installed for magical purposes. It is mistaken by John for an image of the devil with his twy-prong, his pitchfork, or magical divining rod.

BOOK THE FOURTH

1] *Meantime Ferrara lay in rueful case* B took his primary information on the siege of Ferrara from Rolandino but used other sources as well. The events of 1224 were the culmination of a long struggle between Salinguerra and Azzo of Este. Muratori (*Annali*) says that in 1221 Azzo attacked Salinguerra and his followers and after a severe fight forced him to abandon the city. "On this occasion," Muratori writes, "the palace of Salinguerra himself was consigned to flames." Salinguerra's exile lasted only a few days, however, and he was soon back in the city reassembling his scattered forces. Throughout the year 1222, it would seem, Salinguerra held supremacy in Ferrara, and Azzo was forced to assemble a large army drawn from great distances in an effort to regain power. With the army encamped just outside the city walls, Salinguerra resorted to trickery. "The old fox," as Muratori calls him, "invited Azzo to enter the city on the pretense that he wished to reach an amicable settlement of differences with him. Once inside the walls, however, Azzo and his party were attacked and many of them were killed, including Azzo's dear friend Tisolino of Campo San Pietro." The Marquis himself managed to escape. About the 1223 episode Muratori writes: "The trick played in Ferrara in the year 1222, by Salinguerra upon Azzo VII, Marquis of Este, and the death of Tisolino of Campo San Pietro, who was among the dearest friends of the Marquis, had sunk deep into the Prince's heart. He therefore in the present year collecting a good army from his own states and from his friends in Mantua, Padua, and Verona, bent upon vengeance, returned to the siege of Ferrara. The astute Salinguerra exerted himself so much by affectionate letters and embassies that he induced Count Richard of San Bonifazio, with a certain number of horsemen, to enter Ferrara, under the pretext of concluding a friendly pact. But, on entering, he was at once made prisoner with all his company; and therefore the Marquis of Este, disappointed, returned from the siege. It is astonishing how sensible rulers, sufficiently warned by the preceding deception, could allow themselves to be again entrapped by so notorious a word-breaker" (*Browning Society Papers*, III, 86–87. William M. Rossetti, trans.).

28] *League* See I, 110n.

30–32] *snowy oxen … its white field* The Paduan carroch was drawn by white oxen and carried the standard of the city, a red cross on a white background.

33] *Legate Montelungo* Grigorio de Montelungo who according to B's account represented the Pope as Papal Legate in the strife that followed. He assisted also in the capture of Salinguerra in 1240 and was afterwards Archbishop of Aquileia. See also IV, 285–289.

34] *flock of steeples* The author of *Chronica Parva Ferrariensis* (which B undoubtedly read since it is found along with Rolandino's chronicle in the eighth volume of Muratori) recalls hearing his father tell of thirty-two towers in Ferrara that were pulled down and destroyed during the conflict.

41] *Tito, Friedrich's Pretor* Sodegerio de Tito was the Imperial Legate, Podestà in Trent. Verci refers to him as a "great friend and ally of Ecelin" (II, 312).

43] *Mainard Count of Tyrol* Tyrol is now a province of Austria, wholly alpine, consisting of the basin of the Inn River together with the upper Lechtal. In 1004 Henry II gave land in the Brenner area to the Bishop of Trent and in 1202 Conrad enlarged his fief (see I, 256n). The bishop held his lands directly from the Emperor but delegated secular rule mainly to the Counts of Tyrol near Merano, who gradually extended their rule over the whole Tyrol area.

45] *Tito* See IV, 41n.

47–49] *The lazy engines … manganel and catapult* See IV, 326n.

51] *gangs of mercenaries* It was customary for both Guelfs and Ghibellines to hire mercenary soldiers, often foreigners, to fight for them. Thus Milo of Bara first brought Normans into S Italy (see III, 123n) and Frederick II maintained his Saracen mercenaries at Nuocera (see III, 121–123n).

59] *osprey's nare* See I, 128n.

63] *White ostrich with a horse-shoe in her beak.* Ecelin's crest.

71] *Jubilate* Rejoice ye! ("Jubilate Deo,") Psalm 66.

82] *cautelous* Wary.

83] *Old Redbeard* Frederick I. He tried vainly to take Alexandria, the city which the League built and named after the then reigning Pope as a gesture of defiance to the Emperor.

84] *Saint George* Patron saint of Ferrara. Ferrara's Cathedral of St. George, the work of Guglielmo (Adelardi) and the sculptor Nicolo Pisano (see I, 574n), was consecrated in 1135. Ferrara was surrounded by marshes.

88] *Brenta and Bacchiglion* The Bacchiglion River which runs near Vicenza, breaks into numerous canals which empty into the Brenta River.

91] *Cino's cost* The incident appears to be imaginary.

95] *Concorezzo* According to Rolandino, Robertas de Concorezzo was podestà of Padua at this time. See also IV, 225.

96] *San Vitale* The SE section of Ferrara, next to the San Pietro Quarter where Salinguerra's palaces and gardens were located.

102] *za, za, Cavaler Ecelin* Ecelin's war cry. Rolandino is the source (Muratori, *Scriptores*, VIII, 188): "To arms, to arms, za, za, Cavaler Ecelin."

143–144] *Naples marbles/ . . . Messina marbles* Many of the marble statues in Naples, of Greek design, are ancient and crumbling excavations from Pompeii and Herculaneum. Messina marbles date from a much later period and are of a superior structural quality.

155] *the Isle* Sicily. See I, 980n.

157] *the Fighter* The "Fighter" and the "Slave" (IV, 166) were statues on the terraces of Salinguerra's palace.

165] *The pertinacious Gaul* Another statue, the imaginary foe of the "Fighter" who is represented as being in action.

166] *The Slave* See IV, 157n.

171] *San Pietro Palace* A castle situated in the SE corner of the city. Surrounded by walls and towers, it included within its grounds the churches of San Pietro, San Salvadore, and San Georgio. Thus, it was called the San Pietro Quarter. Salinguerra fortified this district which was centered around the old castle.

224] *Mainard* See IV, 43n.

225] *Concorezzi* See IV, 95n.

285] *"The Legate, look* See IV, 33n.

322] *Count Mainard* See IV, 43n.

324] *archers, slingers* Archers (bowmen) shot the longbow, as opposed to arbalisters or crossbowmen. By this time the crossbow or arbalist, because of its efficiency, had replaced the longbow. Slingers (slingmen) were often attached to Western armies even up to the sixteenth century. At this time the weapon was used to hurl "sling-stones." Archers and slingers were regular sections of Greek and Roman armies. "Caesar calmly sent back his cavalry and his archers and slingers" (James Anthony Froude, *Caesar: A Sketch* (New York: Charles Scribner's Sons, 1891) 1:240).

326] *Arbalist, catapult, brake, manganel* Arbalist, crossbow. Crossbows at this time were drawn by machinery. The chief kinds were the "hind's foot," the "lever," and the "rolling purchase"—the names indicating the various means employed for bending the bow and drawing back the bow-string. The crossbow had a reputation in the twelfth century as a weapon terrible beyond all others. When it was introduced it was considered so murderous that the Second Council of Lateran (1139) forbade its use among Christian armies engaged in warfare. *Catapult* was a medieval engine usually used for throwing stones, though the Romans used it for throwing darts and it was sometimes employed to hurl barrels of combustible material. Its construction at this time is nowhere explained with any fullness and it is uncertain whether its action was that of a crossbow or whether springs were the propelling power. *Brake* is a name often used interchangeably with catapult and manganel, the function of these weapons being much the same. Ballista is the general name often given for such medieval engines used for hurling missiles (usually stones). *Manganel* was the name of another stone-throwing machine. The mangonella is discriminated from a quite similar machine, the mangona, by the fact that it threw small stones, the latter, large ones.

354]   *With purple trappings* The carroch with the colors of the city.

376]   *Tito of Trent* See IV, 41n.

378]   *Montelungo* See IV, 33n.

387]   *The Kaiser's ominous sign-mark* Frederick's insignia.

390]   *Romano's green and yellow* Romano's colors (see II, 909n).

391]   *Tito* See IV, 41n.

397]   *nor asked what badge he wound* See IV, 466n.

410]   *Tito* See IV, 41n.

412]   *Friedrich's rescript* The Emperor's offer, through Tito, that Salinguerra become Vicar-General, leader of the Imperial party in N Italy. The incident is B's fiction.

436]   *basnet* A light basin-shaped helmet.

441]   *the mystic mark the Tuscan found* See I, 461n.

463]   *That eagle* Frederick's insignia (see IV, 387).

465]   *Rescript* See IV, 412n.

466]   *baldric* A belt to be worn over the shouder, in this case, the badge of the imperial office.

477–535]   *As after Salinguerra . . . to Mantua* This account as rendered by B is based upon but deviates in important ways from history. The head of the Adelardi family (not Marchasella as B says), leader of the Guelf party, died in 1184 without leaving a male heir. His express wish was that his daughter Marchasella (not Linguetta) be married to Taurello Salinguerra in order to restore peace between the Guelf and the Ghibelline factions in the city. Before this was accomplished, however, apparently (the historians are not agreed) a band of Ravennese Guelfs stormed the San Pietro Quarter where the Torellos lived and where Marchasella (B's Linguetta) was residing, and abducted the young lady. They carried her off to be the bride eventually of Azzo of Este. Actually, it is not certain that she married Azzo. Both Simonde and the *Chro. Parva Ferr.* say that she died before the marriage was consummated, but Frizzi, after considering all the evidence, concludes that she was married to Azzo. There seems to be no historical justification for B's involvement of the Count of St. Boniface in this affair. According to B the Ferrarese reacted to this event by inviting the House of Este to become ruler of Ferrara. Consequently, Salinguerra, in disgust, went to Sicily and there married Retrude, daughter of Henry and Constance (see I, 104n). Of all the historians only Pigna (p. 162) mentions this trip to Sicily. It is certainly B's fiction that Retrude was "of Heinrich's very blood." That Salinguerra reached an agreement with and returned to N Italy as an imperial emissary is apparently B's creation also. Actually, according to Pigna, Henry died shortly after Salinguerra arrived in Sicily (the chronology here is obviously confused: Henry died in 1197, four years after Salinguerra and the Ecelins were, according to B's poem, driven from Vicenza) and that he, failing to get support from his successor Philip, returned to the N and allied himself with Ecelin.

481] *Blacks and Whites* Ferrara's city shield is an equal division of black and white. It is clear that B is simply using this as an image of the two factions, Guelf and Ghibelline, and not referring to the two parties—the Blacks and the Whites—that grew out of a later division in the Florentine Guelf party in 1300.

492] *valvassors* See I, 768n.

504] *goshawk* A short-winged hawk. The European variety was used in falconry.

513] *Where Heinrich ruled in right of Constance* Constance was the daughter of Roger II and sole heiress to the southern kingdom. She also was the aunt of William II, King of Sicily. William, who had no son to succeed him, arranged for a marriage between Constance, then age thirty-one and Henry, son of Frederick Barbarossa, barely twenty. By this marriage Henry became heir to both the Empire and the southern kingdom, which meant the extension of Imperial authority over all Italy. Frederick II was son and heir of Henry and Constance.

525] *Celano* The Counts of Celano whose castle was near Ferrara. See IV, 477–535n.

528] *Heinrich's very blood* See IV, 477–535n.

528–529] *a band/ Of foreigners* B represents Salinguerra as building elaborate palaces and gardens for his new southern wife who was accustomed in Sicily to a life that the cruder, more rigorous N Italy did not afford. That he built these palaces and gardens is B's own creation.

534] *San Pietro with Tomà* Bastione di St. Tomaso in Ferrara where Count Richard was imprisoned. See also V, 283.

535] *To visit Mantua* Apparently an error. Salinguerra was in Mantua already (see l.523). Moreover, San Pietro, scene of his palace and of the new construction ordered for his bride, was in Ferrara.

542] *expelled/ Both plotters* Ecelin and Salinguerra.

559] *mortised* A mortise is a place hollowed out, as in a timber, to receive a tenon or the like. Here it is used in the sense of a graft.

569] *her namesake* Adelaide of Susa (see III, 488n).

570] *the great Matilda* See III, 492n.

579] *Philip* Duke Philip, brother of Henry VI, and Viceroy in Tuscany. When Henry died, in 1197, Frederick was only three years old. One year later Constance died, having entrusted her son to the guardianship of the Pope, whom she also appointed administrator of her kingdom. Immediately a struggle for the throne ensued. It was claimed, on the one hand, by Philip, a staunch Ghibelline, and, on the other, by Otto of Brunswick, nephew of Richard Cœur de Lion, and a Guelf. Otto was crowned king of the Romans at Aix-la-Chapelle in July, 1198, and, shortly thereafter, Philip was crowned at Mayence. The contest between the two was prolonged until 1208 when Philip was assassinated by a private enemy. In November, 1215, a council held at the Lateran deposed Otto and recognized Frederick, who had been crowned king of the Romans by the Ghibellines at Aix-la-Chapelle in 1212.

584] *Otho* See IV, 579n.

600–601] *since Arab-lore/ Holds the stars' secret* See III, 370n; 603n.

603] *Jove trined for her* When Jupiter assumed such a relation to a second planet that in conjuction with the earth they form a 120° angle, or a third of the Zodiac. Adelaide, learned in astrology, considered this a favorable sign.

604–605] *Friedrich . . . man puts aside* That Salinguerra was responsible for Frederick's decision not to continue the crusade is B's invention. See also II, 890–891n.

606] *John Brienne* See I, 194n.

607–611] *Come to Bassano . . . Ecelin's exploits* Verci says that according to ancient tradition the Church of St. Francis in Bassano was built by Ecelin I in fulfillment of a vow made to the Virgin Mary when his ship was about to sink on his return from the Holy Land (I, 111). By the time B visited Bassano in 1838 (see III, 676n) no trace remained of the frescoes. Obviously every evidence of the domination of the Ecelins was destroyed after the death of Alberic.

612] *angelot* See II, 518n.

614] *Tiso* See III, 302n.

633] *Old Azzo and Old Boniface* Azzo VI (1170–1212) who at his death left two sons, Aldobrandino and Azzo VII, surnamed Novello, the Guelf leader of the poem (see I, 103n). Boniface, father of Count Richard (see I, 102n).

634] *By Ponte Alto, both in one month's space* Ecelin defeated Azzo and Boniface at Ponte Alto in 1212. Both men died within a month's space, but not as a result of wounds received in this battle.

637] *Lost Guglielm and Aldobrand its heir* B is in error in saying that Guglielm was Boniface's heir. Richard was the older son. Aldobrand, it was believed, was poisoned by the Ghibelline Count of Celano (See IV, 525n).

681] *On Azzo's calm refusal* See I, 818n. Salinguerra's challenge of Azzo to combat, delivered before the court of Otto, was met with a "calm refusal" on the assumption by Azzo of certain defeat for the Ghibelline chief. An argument ensued, and, finally, German nobles attending had to draw swords to separate them. The incident is recorded by Maurisio and recounted by Verci, Simonde, and others.

684] *Pharoah* The hebraized title of the king of Egypt. Pharoahs of the Old and Middle Kingdoms were embalmed in huge stone block pyramids.

698–699] *old Boniface/ Old Azzo* See IV, 633n.

703] *Marquis* Azzo of Este.

716] *Lactance, brother Anaclet* Imaginary names of Monks at Oliero.

725–736] *we fire Vicenza . . . the reeking gate* Salinguerra recalls the expulsion from Vicenza in 1194. B follows fairly closely Verci's account (II,

111). The two factions in the city quarreled over the election of a podestà in 1194, and in order to settle the dispute peacefully agreed that each party would choose an elector and that they would be empowered to elect a podestà. The Ghibellines chose Sulimano and the Guelfs, Pilio da Celsano. Pilio, acting alone, promised the office to Giacomo de Bernardi providing he would throw his weight against Ecelin and the Ghibellines. His election was accomplished and he fulfilled his promise by banishing Ecelin. In retaliation, Ecelin took up arms, but was, nevertheless, driven from the city. In the battle about one half of Vicenza was burnt. There is no historical evidence that Salinguerra was present on this occasion.

736] *Slidder* To slide or slip.

737] *And then the vow* To give his life to God in thanksgiving for the safety of his wife and child—B's imaginative contribution.

740] *basnet* See IV, 436n.

753] *Ay, Heinrich . . . Otho* See IV, 579n.

780–781] *in Messina's . . . when Heinrich* See IV, 477–535n.

786] *Constance* See IV, 477–535n; 510n.

790] *Tito* See IV, 41n.

825] *Her Moorish lentisk* The mastic tree, *Pistacia lentiscus*, native to the African coast of the Mediterranean, obviously cultivated in Sicily.

870] *poison-wattles* Excrescent baggy flesh on the lizard's neck.

956] *Consul of Rome* See IV, 960n.

960] *Crescentius Nomentanus* Crescentius II, son of Crescentius de Theodora, was one of a powerful Italian family that ruled Rome late in the tenth century and was responsible for restoring Republican principles and institutions. The exploits of his brother, John, who had been named Patricius Romanorum by Boniface VII and who ruled before him, are often attributed to Crescentius, who did not rule Rome as Consul Romanorum until the death of his brother in c. 990. Both John and Crescentius helped Boniface VII to seize power in Rome after returning from exile in 984. John assisted the Pope in governing until the latter died in 985. He then chose his successor, Pope John XV, formerly cardinal of San Vitale. When Crescentius II became consul, he kept the Pope a virtual prisoner in the Lateran. Pope John appealed for help to Emperor Otto III in 995, but died before Otto could reach Rome. Crescentius then appointed as John's successor his own cousin, Bruno, who became Pope Gregory V in 996. At the latter's request, Otto pardoned Crescentius, but when the Emperor left Rome in the summer of 996, Crescentius drove Gregory from the city. He then appointed John Philagathos, the Greek-speaking Archbishop of Piacenza, as Antipope (with the title of John XVI), possibly hoping thus to secure Byzantine support. In 998 Otto III again took refuge in the Castle St. Angelo, but the fortress was taken by treachery and the rebel was probably beheaded on the battlements and buried in the church of San Pancrazio. Sources differ on the exact manner of his death, some claiming he was crucified (see IV, 994).

965] *brown-sleeve brother* The speaker is obviously a Franciscan friar. Originally, the Franciscans wore habits of natural wool and as a result were called grey friars. Very early, however, they exchanged their grey garb for brown.

966] *till Innocent* Pope Innocent III (1198–1216) who took for the text of his consecration sermon the Biblical quotation, "I have set thee this day over nations and over kingdoms." This established the tenor of his reign. He originally asserted the supremacy of the Papal office over the temporal rulers, first crowning and then deposing Otto. Before enthroning Frederick II, he extracted from him the most stringent terms (which Frederick apparently had no intention of keeping). He ruled his spiritual kingdom with severity and vigor. In 1208, he launched a crusade against the Albigensians (see II, 617n); he made important changes in canon law; and he instituted strict new rules governing celebacy among the clergy.

969] *Crescentius* See IV, 960n.

977] *Pope John, King Otho* John XV and Otto III. See IV, 960n.

978] *Crescentius, haply dressed* Crescentius wore the white robes of a Roman Consul.

981] *Brutus* Perhaps Lucius Junius Brutus who, according to tradition, led the Romans to expel from Rome the despotic King Lucius Tarquinius Superbus, founded the republic, and was elected one of its two consuls in 509 B.C.

989] *phanel* Beacon light.

991] *Otho, with John* See IV, 960n.

994–995] *"They crucified/ Their Consul* According to some accounts Crescentius met death by crucifixion (see IV, 960n).

997] *Was once a brown-sleeve brother* See IV, 965n; 966n.

1013] *Pandects* The digest or abridgment in fifty books of the decisions and opinions of the old Roman jurists, made in the sixth century by order of the Emperor Justinian and forming the first part of the body of the civil law.

1014] *Castle Angelo* See IV, 960n.

1020] *Theatre* Probably the coliseum. Duff quotes Lanciani as saying: "The Coliseum was bristling with churches. There was one at the foot of the Colossus of the Sun. . . . There were four dedicated to the Savior, a sixth to S. James, a seventh to S. Agatha, besides other chapels and oratories within the amphitheatre itself" (*Pagan and Christian Rome*, Chapter III).

BOOK THE FIFTH

6] *Palatine* Ruler, one invested with royal power.

15] *mooned sandal* The crescent-toed shoe worn by Romans and popular throughout the Middle Ages.

16] *atria* The entrance hall, consisting of a court open to the sky, which formed the central and common principal apartment of a Roman house, and into which the other rooms opened.

17] *stibadium* A semicircular reclining seat or couch used by the Romans in their baths.

18] *lustral vase* A vase holding lustral water, which was used in purification ceremonies such as funerals, sacrifices.

28] *hurdle-weaving any Scythian* A movable framework of split timbers, sticks, osiers, twigs, wattled together and used for making gates, fences, huts. Because of the uncertainties surrounding the origin and locale of the Scythians, classical literature has employed "Scythia" to mean all regions to the N and NE of the Black Sea, and "Scythian" to mean any barbarian coming from these parts. The Scyths were a primitive, nomadic people, constantly moving in search of fresh pastures, spending the spring and autumn on the open steppe, the winter and summer by the rivers for moisture and shelter. Naturally, their building materials were crude.

39] *cirque* Natural amphitheater.

53] *osier* Any species of willow, producing long, flexible shoots used in wickerwork.

57] *Mauritanian tree* The citrus tree, celebrated product of this ancient country of N Africa. The fragrant and costly citrus wood was prized by the Romans and used to make tables.

66] *Mareotic . . . Cæcuban* Wine from Lake Mareotis in Egypt which was of a better quality than wine from Caecubum, a town in the province of Latium. In classical times, the shores of Lake Mareotis were a region of great fertility, covered with gardens and vineyards. The Ager Caecubus was a marshy district near the coast in the lower part of Latium. Its wine gained the reputation as the finest in that part of the world until the reign of Nero, whose canals damaged its vineyards.

81–83] *some old Pythoness . . . his long error* Croesus, King of the Lydians, sent his messenger to the Pythian priestess at the shrine of Apollo to ask if he could win a war he was planning against the Persians. The reply came back that "a great empire would be destroyed." Encouraged, he proceeded with his plan. After he was defeated by Cyrus, the leader of the Persians, he asked the same oracle of Apollo for an explanation and was told that "he might have asked which kingdom was meant." See Herodotus, I, 92.

109] *Alcamo's song* Ciullo d'Alcamo, a poet of Palermo in Sicily. Next to nothing is known of this early Italian poet, though his one extant poem, "Lover and Land," has been dated between 1172 and 1178 by Dante G. Rossetti. The following is part of a prefatory note by the latter to his translation of Alcamo's poem: "Ciullo is a popular form of the name Vincenzo, and Alcamo an Arab fortress some miles from Palermo. The dialogue, which is the only known production of this poet, holds here the place generally accorded to it as the earliest Italian poem (exclusive of one or two dubious inscriptions) which has been preserved to our day. . . . At first

411

sight, any casual reader of the original would suppose that this poem must be unquestionably the earliest of all, as its language is far the most unformed and difficult; but much of this might, of course, be dependent on the inferior dialect of Sicily, mixed however in this instance (as far as I can judge) with mere nondescript patois" (*Dante and his Circle*, II, 233).

111] *Nina* A Sicilian poetess, predecessor of Alcamo, who for the love she bore Dante of Majano, a Florentine poet whom she had never seen, was called the Nina of Dante. Tiraboschi says that she is perhaps the oldest of Italian poetesses.

132] *Charlemagne* King of the Franks from 768 to 814. On Christmas day, 800, he was crowned Holy Roman Emperor by Leo III.

144–145] *priests for castellans / And popes for suzerains* In its normal development the Church assumed a structure paralleling that of the medieval state, priests serving as governors of castles and popes as feudal lords.

154] *God's church lives by a King's investiture* The war of investitures between the church and the empire occurred during the last half of the eleventh century and the first half of the twelfth century. It was, officially if not actually, settled by the Concordat of Worms in 1122. The rulers of the empire claimed authority not only over temporal property but also over ecclesiastical power to appoint bishops and to render decisions on spiritual as well as temporal matters. The weak papacy of the tenth century proved ineffectual against the rising authority of the Emperors, but by the beginning of the eleventh century the Church began to rebel against increasing secularization, realizing that simony and immorality within the Church were directly related to the practice of lay investiture. Archdeacon Hildebrand exerted tremendous influence upon Pope Nicholas II and was partly responsible for the Pope's decree in 1059 forbidding "any cleric to receive in any way a church from the hands of laymen." Becoming pope himself in 1073, Hildebrand, as Gregory VII, continued to press strongly for moral reform in the church, and in 1075 firmly condemned all forms of lay investiture, declaring the church totally free in this respect from lay interference. The struggle, often intense, came officially to an end with the agreement reached in 1122 by which the Emperor and the Pope recognized the distinction between temporal and ecclesiastical power, and the former renounced his claim to the power of investiture.

173] *mandrake* A plant with a forked root giving it the appearance of man's body. It was said to shriek with pain when pulled from the earth.

177] *Full three hundred years* Charlemagne was crowned Holy Roman Emperor on Christmas Day, 800, three hundred years before the action of this poem. His coronation began a long struggle between the two powers, the Church and the Empire, to discover a proper reconciliation of their functions.

184–185] *the three Imperial crowns across, / Aix' Iron, Milan's Silver, and Rome's Gold* The crown of Aix-la-Chapelle made the recipient "King of the

Romans, always Augustus"; the crown of Milan (Lombard), King of Italy or of the Lombards; and the double crown of Rome the Holy Roman Emperor. Historians disagree about the composition of the crowns. All say that the Roman crown was gold. B here follows those who say that the German crown was iron and the Lombard crown, silver. Others contend, however, that the German crown was silver and the Lombard crown, iron, containing a nail from the true cross.

186] *Alexander* Pope Alexander II (1061–1073). With the support of Hildebrand and Norman arms Alexander was elected pope without participation of the German king. Dissident bishops, aided by the Imperial party, in reaction, elected Antipope Honorius II who was proclaimed by the future emperor, Henry IV. Honorius was condemned and deposed at the Council of Mantua in 1064, leaving Alexander free to continue the strengthening of the Church against the Empire.

186] *Innocent* Innocent III was pope from 1198 to 1216. He was the first of the popes to proclaim himself the Vicar of Christ on Earth, a title which all popes have since assumed. Constance recognized his authority when upon her death she not only left her young son, the future Frederick II, in his charge but also made the kingdom of Sicily a fief of the papacy, and appointed the Pope regent of Sicily during her son's minority. His reign marks the culmination of papal authority and influence

187] *each Papal key* Matthew 16:19: "And I will give unto thee the keys of the kingdom of heaven: and whatsoever thou shalt bind on earth shall be bound in heaven: and whatsoever thou shalt loose on earth shall be loosed in heaven." The passage is interpreted by the Roman Catholic Church to mean that Christ conferred upon Peter, and, thus upon his successors in the Papal office, vicarious authority over his Church on earth. The Pope holds also the key of heaven in that his authoritative decisions are binding upon men's conscience and that those who accept his teaching of the gospel and his direction in the way of salvation gain eternal life.

191] *Gregory* See V, 154n.

192] *hermit Peter's cry* | *At Claremont* Peter enthusiastically preached the first crusade in N France, and in 1096 lead a considerable army of recruits through Hungary and the Byzantium's Balkin provinces to Constantinople.

194–195] *Friedrich's no liege . . . curse off him* See I, 78n.

198] *Vimmercato* A town near Milan. B probably refers to the call there for a league against Frederick I, an action related to the second call in 1226 for reformation of the Lombard League against Frederick II (see I, 110n).

201] *Mantuan Albert* In 1207, Fra Alberto da Mantua preached peace so effectively in Ferrara that forty-five warring families were reconciled.

202] *Saint Francis* St. Francis of Assisi (1182?–1226), founder of the Franciscan Order, gave up his wealth and dedicated his life to preaching love and peace and in doing good work among the poor.

218]. *Paul* St. Paul the Apostle, first century missionary to the Gentiles, and largely responsible for the rapid spread of Christianity through Asia Minor and S Europe.

219] *Moses* The leader who conducted the Children of Israel from bondage in Egypt to the Promised Land.

222] *Charlemagne* See V, 132n.

241] *faulchions* Swords which appeared in the thirteenth century. They were of two kinds: the first, a broad blade, widening toward the point, the edge convex, the back concave; the other, differing from it only in having the back straight.

266] *Polt-foot* Clubfoot.

273] *Cino* See I, 145n.

278] *Lucchino* Perhaps an imaginary character.

279] *hacqueton* A quilted jacket worn under armor.

283] *Tomà* See IV, 534n.

284] *Marfisa* Perhaps an imaginary character.

296] *trabea* A Roman toga decorated with horizontal purple stripes.

336] *accompt* Account.

353] *Honorius* See I, 79n.

379] *thyrsus* A staff or spear tipped with an ornament like a pinecone, and sometimes wreathed with ivy or vine branches; borne by Dionysius and his votaries.

389] *Tito* See IV, 41n.

406] *Spear-heads . . . burr-heads* The spear-head is the sharp, pointed head or blade forming the striking or piercing end of a spear; the burr-head is the broad iron ring on a tilting spear just behind the place for the hand. Hence, Heinrich's command involves pointing the piercing end of the spear at the enemy in battle, but the blunt end, the burr-head, of the spear at the challenger in a joust.

407] *Constance* See IV, 510n.

407–408] *would promote/ Alcamo, from a parti-coloured coat* See V, 109n. The "parti-coloured coat" was the habit of the court poet.

432] *promptuary* Book or sheath containing the skeletal outline of a play, names of principal characters, entrances and exits. It was used by a prompter.

447] *Caliph's wheel-work* The Abbasid caliph, Harun al-Rashid, who had, among his numerous mechanical contrivances, automatons, or robots.

502] *Typhon* (Typhoeus) A gigantic monster with a hundred snake heads, eyes of fire, and the voices of many animals, who was created by Gaea (Earth) to punish Jupiter for deposing the Titans, the previous rulers of the universe.

503] *Hercules* A great hero of Greek and Roman mythology, renowned for his strength, Hercules was a demigod, that is, half man, half god. Among his famous twelve labors, he killed the Nemean Lion and Lernean Hydra, both offspring of Typhon and Echidna.

526] *protoplast* B uses the word here to mean the creator or originator of something, though, in his time, it referred to the product of creation (the sense in which he used it in the 1863 edition). "That which is first formed, fashioned, or created; the original or archetype. . . . *Q. Rev.* April 30 'The Book [Wisdom of Solomon] has given to modern science the term *protoplast*, which it twice uses of Adam' " (N.E.D.).

552] *Air, flame, earth, wave* The ancients, beginning with the Ionian philosophers, believed that the world was composed of four basic elements: fire, air, earth, and water.

554–555] *Jupiter?/ No! Saturn* In Roman mythology, Saturn, one of the twelve Titans, or the children of Uranus (Heaven) and Gaea (Earth), after subduing his father at the instigation of his mother, became the ruler of the universe. By dividing up the world to be governed by his brothers and sisters, he established a crude order. Jupiter, Saturn's son, warred against his father, who had the aid of the Titans, and eventually dethroned him. His reign was one of comparative peace and justice.

556] *Chaos* It is unlikely that B is referring specifically to the vague Roman diety, Chaos, who ruled over the shapeless mass that later was formed into the earth. Rather he is probably referring to the state of the universe (opposed to "Calm") as it was understood before apotheosized:

> Before the sea was, and the lands, and the sky that hangs over all the face of nature showed alike in her whole round, which state have men called chaos: a rough, unordered mass of things, nothing at all save lifeless bulk and warring seeds of ill-matched elements heaped in one (Ovid, *Metamorphoses*, The Loeb Classical Library, I, 3.).

592] *Friedrich . . . red-hot tomb* Emperor Frederick II (see I, 78n). Supposedly a neo-Epicurean, he had a reputation as a sensualist and unbeliever (see I, 142; III, 119–120n; III, 121–123n). Dante assigns him (along with a thousand others) to a fiery open sepulcher in the city of fire (*Inferno*, X, 120; *Purgatorio*, IX, X).

593] *Some dubious spirit, Lombard Agiluph* Chosen in 590 by Queen Theodolinda to be her husband's successor as ruler of the Lombards. By exercising control over Pope Gregory I (Saint Gregory the Great) and the major cities of Rome and Ravenna, Agiluph reigned for twenty-five years. As P-C suggest, the fact that he left Arianism to become a Trinitarian may account for B's description of him as a "dubious spirit." Agiluph is not mentioned by Dante.

595] *Matilda* Most commentators identify Dante's Matilda with the Countess Matilda of Tuscany (see III, 492n), though some argue that she is one of the ladies of *La vita nuova*. Approaching the Terrestrial Paradise at the summit of Purgatory (where Dante hopes to find Beatrice), the poet and his guide, Vergil, encounter a lady (the glorified realization of the Leah, representing the active life of Eden and the virtuous use of earthly things, of Dante's dream, described in Canto XXVI) whose name is later given (Canto

XXXIII) as Matilda. As Vergil, who is not permitted to go on, must depart, Matilda takes Dante across the River Lethe, which separates the Earthly Paradise from the rest of Purgatory. Later, with other nymphs and Beatrice, she accompanies Dante to the Spring of God's Grace at the point where the Rivers Lethe and Eunoe separate. Here, as before, she instructs Dante and makes him drink the water for the remission of his sins. See *Purgatorio* XXVIII–XXXIII.

596] *With languors of the planet of decline* The "planet of decline" is Venus the morning and evening star, and Dante's third heaven. Later in this Book (l.994), B refers to Venus as the "Swooning-sphere," mentioning it in regard to Dante, who spoke with Palma there:

To Palma, Dante spoke with in the clear
Amorous silence of the Swooning-sphere,—
Cunizza, as he called her.

Thus, "Some unapproached Matilda" in the preceding line is probably a veiled allusion to Palma, for Cunizza, the former's historical counterpart, is the second person Dante meets in the planet Venus.

645] *horned and snouted Libyan god* Probably the Egyptian deity, Set, who is said to have reigned over the upper valley of the Nile from near Memphis to the first cataract. With the rise of the cult of Osiris, who was Set's brother, Set became the personification of evil, for he killed and mangled Osiris while the great god was asleep in the forest. Taking the form of a black pig, Set fought with Horus, the son of Osiris, for the right to rule the kingdom. Some authorities claim that the abomination, as well as the sacrifice, of pigs derives from this incident (see Sir James Frazer, *The Golden Bough*, abr. ed. [New York, 1963] pp. 550–551).

647] *Clay cinerary pitcher* A container for the ashes of the dead.

648] *Byzant rifled* Throughout the twelfth century, victorious Venetian mercenary forces ransacked Eastern cities for art treasures which were used to adorn St. Mark's Cathedral (the major construction and embellishment of which began in 1106 after several fires—the worst in 976—had practically destroyed the original building). Nearly every doge from 1106 till the fall of Venice added some rich decoration to the church, mainly from spoils from abroad. Among the monuments "rifled" were the Egyptian temple in Thebes, the Parthenon in Athens, and various temples in Rome and Constantinople. In 1205, the most famous loot, four bronze horses, was brought from Constantinople, these taken during the Fourth Crusade, begun in 1198 by Dandolo, the Blind Doge of Venice, and Baldwin of Flanders. The pillages also netted great amounts of marble, alabaster, gold, porphyry, jasmine, and other precious metals and stones.

The ship of war brought home more marble in triumph than the merchant vessel in speculation; and the front of St. Mark's became rather a shrine at which to dedicate the splendour of miscellaneous spoil, than the organized expression of any fixed architectural law, or religious emotion (John Ruskin, *Stones of Venice*, II, 4).

649] *reputed consummations* P-C take "reputed" only in the sense of "widely famed," but the more common meaning of the word—"generally accounted or supposed to be such"—seems more appropriate here: "those works supposed to be the consummation of art."

649–650] *razed/ A seal* Erased the distinguishing mark. The distinctive works of these civilizations lose their particular identity when mixed together in St. Mark's. The latter transmutes them into its own distinctive style, signified by the Triad.

650] *Triad* P-C explain Triad as the statues on St. Mark's of the three patron saints of Venice. We can find no reference to these statues or to three patron saints. It appears that Venice had only two patrons, though not at the same time. The current one, St. Mark, replaced St. Theodore as patron saint in 828. In regard to the statues, possibly P-C are confusing these with the well-known fourteenth century statue of three apostles in the interior of the church. B is probably referring to the domes of the cathedral. The plan of St. Mark's is a Greek cross; it is roofed with five low domes, one at the crossing and one over each arm of the cross. Thus, the front of the cathedral would present three domes to view.

681–682] *Treville, Villarazzi, Puissolo,/ Loria and Castiglione* Small towns and villages in the area of Treviso and Vicenza, over which Ecelin exercised control and which now would become the object of conflict between the rival factions.

718] *writhled* "Wrinkled; shriveled or withered" (N.E.D.).

723] *pauldron* A piece of plate armor to protect the shoulder. Sometimes it is used synonymously with "epaulet."

745] *baldric* See IV, 466n.

755] *San Biagio* A church within the city walls of Vicenza, located in the extreme N section of the city.

816] *sign-mark on that brown* See I, 461n.

864] *Brescia . . . Milan . . . Piacenza* The three cities mark a westward advance into Lombardy from the Veneto province, center of Ecelin's power.

867] *Romagna . . . Bologna . . . the Valsugan* An area stretching from the Trentine Pass along the Adige Valley where the Ecelins first gained power toward the Valsugan region along the Brenta road between Trento and Venice.

869] *Sofia's Egna by Bolgiano's* Sordello intimates that Sofia Ecelin, widow of Henry of Egna, controlled the strategic Bolgiano pass in 1224 (see VI, 660–667n).

895–896] *Torriani's strength . . . Our own Visconti* A faction of Valsassina struggling against Visconti, the Ghibelline family to which Otho Visconti, Archbishop of Milan belonged.

953] *ginglingly* Jinglingly.

994] *Swooning-sphere* See III, 429–430n; 596n.

998] *passion's votaress* See III, 429–430n; 596n; 994.

1006] *Visconti's strong at Milan* See V, 895–896n.
1014] *Squarcialupe* See II, 118–119.

BOOK THE SIXTH

130] *Malek and his Moors* See I, 841n.
140–141] *Cypidde . . . Agathon* Fictitious names having no classical refer-
ence.
181] *Dularete* See II, 118–119n.
258] *green and yellow* See II, 909n.
300] *cruce* Crucible.
318] *brakes at balm-shed* Brake ferns at seed time (that is, autumn).
348] *asp* Specifically, the Egyptian cobra, but asp or aspis is also the
well-known classical name for snake, any snake. "Uncowl" refers to the hood
or covering of the snake.
381] *reate* The water crowfoot. The name is often applied generally to
waterweeds and floating plants of a stream.
382] *grail* Contraction of gravel.
426] *Titan* A reference to Orion, the giant hunter or warrior, and perhaps
the most brilliant and best known constellation in the Northern Hemi-
sphere. He is said to wield a lion-skin shield as he advances in combat
toward Taurus the Bull. Orion is "recumbent" in the sense that he is
sometimes imagined to be kneeling.
427] *Centaur* A constellation in the Southern Hemisphere. It is very pos-
sible however, that B is referring to Sagittarius, the archer, a northern
constellation representing the famous centaur Chiron in the act of shooting
an arrow. Johnson defines "centaur" as "the archer in the Zodiac." Orion
and Sagittarius are linked mythically because of their opposition in the sky
and their mutual combat with both Taurus and the Scorpion.
583–584] *As the king-bird . . . ancestral glooms* According to ancient fable,
the phoenix was a large bird of bright plummage, always male, the only one
of its kind, who lived for a very long time—some say five hundred years. At
the end of that period, it was supposed in one way or another, to build a
nest, fertilize it, and then set fire to it. Out of the ashes a new bird was born.
According to some versions of the legend the young bird took the body of its
father to Heliopolis in Egypt and deposited it on the altar of the sun. B
follows the version which has the father bird go to Heliopolis and there
produce its offspring before he destroys himself.
606–609] *Old fable, the two eagles . . . Jove's temple* According to legend,
Zeus (Jupiter, Jove) released two eagles, one from the east and one from the
west, and caused them to fly until they met, which was at Delphi, a spot then
supposed to be the center of the world. Delphi became the seat of the most
important temple and the oracle of Apollo.
639–640] *The upshot, sure,/ Was peace* B again alters the facts of history.

Muratori in *Annali* (William M. Rossetti, trans., *Browning Society Papers*, III, 82–97) records what happens following Richard's capture: "Enraged at the results, Marquis Azzo proceeded to the siege of the Castle of La Fratta, one of the fortresses most cherished by Salinguerra: and he abode there so long that by stress of famine, he gained it, afterwards acting with barbarous severity against the defenders and inhabitants. Salinguerra wrote about this to Ecelino da Romano, his brother-in-law, with bitterness; and they both together began thereafter, more than ever, to study means for abasing the Guelfic faction, of which the Marquis of Este was chief. In the old Annals of Modena, we read that the Veronese, Mantuans, and Ferrarese, were at the siege of Il Boldeno, and departed from it with scant satisfaction or honor. These Ferrarese, united with the Veronese and Mantuans, must have been exiles, adhering to the Marquis of Este."

660–667] *Obtain Sofia's dowry . . . if Friedrich knock* Sofia was the third, not the last of Ecelin's daughters born of Adelaide. She was first married to Henry of Egna, whose castle, standing between Trent and Bolgiano, was in a strategic position to control passage over the Alps. Henry died young, and as B relates Sofia was then married to Salinguerra. B places the marriage after the siege of Ferrara but both Rolandino and Muratori place it before. B says that Salinguerra married Sofia in order to obtain her dowry and to control the pass over the Alps. This could hardly be right, however, since Henry left a son and heir to his properties.

675] *a blind chronicle* The anonymous *Chronica Parva Ferrariensis.*

678–679] *"Salinguerra's . . . ere his sire* An almost direct quotation from the *Chronica Parva Ferrariensis.*

681] *Which of Sofia's five was meant* Verci says that Salinguerra had one son, "di nome Jacobo" by Sofia. Frizzi says also that Salinguerra had five children by his first wife and only one by his last. B obviously altered the facts so as to make Sordello the single son born of Salinguerra's marriage to Retrude who died shortly after his birth.

687–688] *Ecelin at Campese . . . Solagna lie* Campese, two miles above Bassano, site of a Benedictine monastery founded by Ecelin I. At Solagna, half-a-mile farther up, a sculptured slab of a Benedictine monk, "With cushioned head and gloved hand" as B describes him, is built into the outside wall of the church. According to tradition, this is the tomb of Ecelin II. B, no doubt, saw the slab on his visit to Italy in 1838 (see III, 676n).

690–693] *Then his heart . . . In blood and blaze* Ecelin III took no part in the struggle between Ecelin II and Boniface and Azzo for the control of Verona in 1207, although he was at that time thirteen years old, an age at which Italian boys of that period would ordinarily enter combat. It was not until some ten years later that he fought his first engagement, defeating a troop of Vicentines outside Vincenza.

694] *Sordello . . . plain withdrawal* See VI, 669–673; 660–667n.

696–697] *Of the time when . . . Closed with Taurello* The alliance referred to by Muratori (see VI, 639–640n).

698–703] *That in Verona ... Was wholly his* In 1225 the lower classes, rigorously excluded from the government of the city, revolted in Verona, took Count Richard prisoner, and replaced the podestà, Guifredo da Pirovale, with one of their own choosing. Ecelin III was apparently in the city at the time but seems to have taken no part in the revolution. Afterwards, however, he took advantage of the opportunity afforded him, and rose rapidly to power, becoming podestà himself in 1126. The town, however, was not wholly his for at least six more years. In 1227, a second uprising occurred, and this time Ecelin was deposed in favor of a new podestà. The years following, 1227–1230, witness Ecelin's power at its lowest ebb in Verona.

703] *Taurello sinking back* In the struggle for Verona, Salinguerra played a secondary role. In 1230, after Ecelin had once again gained power in Verona, Salinguerra served for a period as nominal podestà, but lost the position when the League succeeded in wresting control of the city in 1231.

706] *Friedrich did come* In 1225 at the time of the uprising in Verona (see VI, 698–703n) Ecelin was not on friendly terms with Frederick. In that year he was both banned by the Emperor and excommunicated by the Pope. Frederick did come to N Italy in 1226 but his attempt to hold a great diet at Cremona was scornfully rejected by the Lombard cities and in his anger he pronounced the ban of the empire against all of them. In 1231 however Ecelin in desperate straits with the League, felt impelled to form a pact with Frederick, agreeing to win over Verona to the Imperial cause in exchange for the Emperor's help in taking the city from the League. As a result, the city was secured and it did take the oath of allegiance to the Empire. Frederick himself, however, did not come to Verona until 1236. B has telescoped historical events in order to serve his poetic purpose.

710–713] *Of Guelfs ... so observably* In 1227 the rustics of Bassano, who belonged to the half-free, half-servile class known as *masnodi*, rebelled against Alberic, and Ecelin joined his brother in crushing them. Ecelin suspected the Dominican and Franciscan friars of having instigated the rebellion; it is certain that they were sympathetic with the rebels. This episode marks the real beginning of Ecelin's violent hatred for the clergy in general and the friars in particular.

728–729] *Venice's marine/ Was meddled with* The Venetians reportedly joined the attack against Ferrara in 1240 (See VI, 730n) in retaliation for an assault upon the Venetian fleet by Ecelin.

730] *She captured him* Verci gives an account of Salinguerra's capture quoting Riccobaldi Ferrariensis (*De Obsidone Ferrariae*) as his source. B apparently read both Verci and Riccobaldi and drew upon them for his version of the event. In 1240, Azzo in alliance with Alberic da Romano and with assistance from the Bolognese, under the leadership of Legate Montelungo (see IV, 33n) and the Venetian fleet (see VI, 728n) attacked Salinguerra at Ferrara. After four months of failure, the leaders of the besieged army decided to achieve by trickery what they had not

420

accomplished by force. Under the pretense of seeking peace they first made terms with Salinguerra and then accepted the hospitality of a banquet at his palace in Ferrara. During the meal, Salinguerra's lieutenant, Ugo da Ramberti, having been bribed by the enemy, rose from the table and denounced his leader for having committed various serious crimes. Professing to take the charges seriously, the Guelfs seized Salinguerra and deported him, a prisoner, to Venice where after five years he died. Muratori in *Annali* (*Browning Society Papers* III, 89) describes the event as follows: "Pope Gregory IX incited, by means of Gregorio da Montelungo his Legate, the Lombards, Bolognese, Venetians, and the Marquis of Este, to form the siege of Ferrara. The Doge of Venice, Jacopo Tiepolo, attended in person, and the aforenamed Marquis, to whom such a conquest was of more moment than to the others. Moreover the Mantuans, who had already withdrawn from allegiance to Frederick, and Count Richard of San Bonifazio, concurred; also Alberico da Romano came with the Lords of Camino. The siege lasted from the beginning of February up to the close of May, or indeed until 3 June: nor did any likelihood appear of forcing the city to a surrender. Recourse was had to the device of gaining over by money Ugo de' Ramberti and other leading men of Ferrara, who declared their desire for peace. Fair terms were proposed, and Salinguerra came to the camp of the confederates to ratify them. None the less, as Ricobaldi narrates, he was entrapped by the Pontifical Legate, who was at that time simply a notary, a man of great activity but of lax conscience. By attestation of Ricobaldi, the Marquis of Este denounced this fraud, alleging honour and oath: '*cui Legatus persuasit ut, calcato honesto et juranmento, amplecteretur quod utile sibi foret—ut scilicet urbe potiretur, illo excluso.*' Thus Salinguerra, not an octogenarian, was transferred as a prisoner to Venice; where, treated courteously, he ended his days in holy peace: and the House of Este, after so many years, re-entered Ferrara."

749] '*Twixt Theodore and Mark* B is probably referring to two twelfth-century granite columns in St. Mark's Plazza between the Doge's Palace and the Library. On one of the pillars is the winged lion of St. Mark holding the Gospel in his paw, on the other St. Theodore (the old patron of Venice) standing with sword and shield on a crocodile.

759] *the Twain* Ecelin and Alberic.

764] *Grey wizened dwarfish devil Ecelin* Verci describes Ecelin as being dark and hairy (I, 154). He tells as a "ridiculous story" the report that one night as Adelaide was sleeping with her husband, a demon appeared and had intercourse with her and that of this union Ecelin III was born (I, 146).

776] *Valley Rù/ By San Zenon* After Ecelin's death, Alberic took refuge in the castle of San Zenon, located in the Valley Ru 3 mi. S of Bassano. Here he and his entire family were slaughtered by the enemy.

781] *raunce* A bramble.

785] *The earthquake* There is no record of a violent earthquake anywhere in or near this area in 1837, the year before B visited Italy, though it is possible that it was one of the many (about 50,000 each year) small earthquakes that occur regularly across the earth.

788] *the cushats chirre* Cushats are woodpigeons or ring doves, also called cushat doves. Chirre is probably a form of "chirp"—at any rate, a word describing the sound of the ring dove.

790] *heard I the old Canon say* B perhaps heard this story when he visited Italy in 1838 (see III, 676n).

822–823] *The Chroniclers of Mantua . . . Visconti* B obviously has Platina's *Historiae Mantuanae* in mind. Platina says that Sordello was of the Visconti family (see I, 1n).

847] *Hesperian fruit* Like the apples of the Garden of Hesperides which were guarded by the nymph daughters of Atlas. As one of his twelve labors, Hercules took the golden apples.

854] *Asolo* A favorite spot of B's about 10 mi. E of Bassano among the Italian Alps and on the E periphery of the Romano territory.

868–869] *Stained like . . . livelong summer* Words of Sordello's first poem imagined being sung by a modern child at Asolo.

875] *peri or ghoul* In Persian mythology, a peri is one of a race of superhuman beings, originally represented as of malevolent character. A ghoul is an evil spirit supposed (in Mohammedan countries) to rob graves and prey on human corpses.